The Stackhouses of Appalachia

Even to Our Own Times

By Jacqueline Burgin Painter

*In loving dedication to Juanita Caldwell Stackhouse –
An inspiration to all who knew her.*

Published by:
Grateful Steps, Inc
1091 Hendersonville Road
Asheville, North Carolina
www.gratefulsteps.com

Library of Congress Cataloging-in-publication Data   2006936608

Painter, Jacqueline
The Stackhouses of Appalachia: Even To our Times
Includes biographical references, photography and index

   ISBN 978-0-9789548-1-9 Paperback
   ISBN 978-0-9789548-0-2 Hard Cover

A few illustrations have previously appeared in *May We All Remember Well*, Vol. II, Robert Brunk editor, under *"Putman, Runion and Stackhouse"* by Jacqueline Painter, 2001.

Layout, design and printing by Biltmore Press, Inc. Asheville, NC.

INTRODUCTION

Even To Our Own Times is the story of Amos Stackhouse and his impact upon Western North Carolina's Madison County. In the Southern Appalachian mountain communities of the post Civil War period, where newcomers – especially Northerners – were regarded with suspicion and often avoided, Amos was accepted, respected, and even loved. He homesteaded, improved the area and died here, unlike many of the day who, after exploiting the resources and the vulnerable mountaineers, returned North.

Presently at Stackhouse, North Carolina, there is little to see, except in summer, when rafting companies provide color and activity through their bright buses and life jackets. For the rest of the year, one is left to imaginings of the bustling bygone settlement. Amos' cleared fields have grown over; his home, barns, water wheel, store and school are gone; and only a short stretch of foundation marks the barytes mill location. There is still a small community cemetery, railway siding, and twisted steel bars rising from the river where they reinforced the wooden power dam a century ago. The large house built by Amos' son is also visible, while the few other community dwellings are mostly hidden from Stackhouse Road (the residents being ordinary folk who value their privacy and discourage sightseers). Two miles below Stackhouse on Pisgah Forest land, however, the public is invited to the Putnam/Runion site containing old concrete ramps, foundations, chimneys, logging train bed, village road remnants and the concrete strong-house of the commissary. More rebar can be seen where the Big Laurel River was dammed to form the sawmill lake. One can also hike up the ridge to the water reservoir crater which supplied the logging company village.

Despite the fact that Amos Stackhouse was a Yankee and a stranger in Hot Springs in the early 1870's, he managed to build a profitable store and drover's business. He joined the local leaders in civic matters, and then bought a large farm four miles up the French Broad. Here, the North Carolina community of Stackhouse developed as Amos erected another general store with post office, a large home, lumber mill, school and church building, rail siding, and several tenant houses. Until 1882 he operated both stores before closing the one in Hot Springs. Amos farmed and also mined barite, becoming instrumental in its milling and shipping. All of these enterprises provided needed jobs for those highlanders who barely eked a living from their rocky steep acres.

Next, Amos sold part of his property to a lumbering corporation, which promised to bring long-term prosperity. Called "Putnam" and later, "Runion," it became the site of most employment in Madison County. Stackhouse fairly bustled at times, situated as it was so near both the railroad and the French Broad River.

Amos' general store stocked the needed staples of salt, flour, lamp oil and tobacco, as well as coffins, burial clothes, slates and more. For special clothing or hardware needs, Amos took orders for his purchasing trips North once or twice a year. When his mountain neighbors, who were bright but unschooled, had need of "readin' and writin'," Amos helped them. He served as banker, lending agent, and pharmacist, weighing out herbs from recipes in his book The Household Physician. (He used a similar book for the treatment of cattle illnesses.) To his customers Amos offered credit and barter, sometimes taking such produce as pelts and herbs on consignment. Amos Stackhouse became indispensable to the settlement, the wary mountaineers finding him to be friendly, cheerful, fair and accommodating, but most of all, trustworthy.

At his death in 1909, Amos' son – Amos, Jr. – followed in his father's footsteps, maintaining the store, post office and mills, offering jobs and serving community causes. Through both World Wars, the influenza epidemic, the closing of Runion, and the Great Depression, Amos, Jr. carried on his father's legacy. Although each of these events reduced the Stackhouse population slightly, due to deaths and lack of employment opportunities, the most jobs were lost in 1916 when the French Broad River ruined the barite plant, and again in the 1920's when the lumber town of Runion succumbed to depletions of both timber and funding. Additionally, the Stackhouse family lost portions of their large farm during the Depression. Diminishing the community even more, the Stackhouse store, post office and lumber yard closed in 1948 when Amos, Jr. died. However, his son Gilbert continued to live in the old home, preserving the Stackhouse community, although he became one of those forced to work away from home, returning to Stackhouse only on weekends. Even then, he provided several jobs by taking neighbors along as crewmen on his commercial building projects in other counties and states. Gilbert also ran the Stackhouse farm and periodic mining operations until his own death in 1989.

Two years later the U.S. Forest Service purchased the site of Runion and other tracts around the Stackhouse home place. So now, Stackhouse, North Carolina, only a ghost of its former self, is best known for its recreational value, enjoyed by hikers, campers and river enthusiasts. These visitors often ask questions about the lovely Victorian mansion rising mysteriously out of the green mountainside, the name STACKHOUSE emblazoned across the porch fascia. Unfortunately, few people are left who can provide answers.

As a Madison County native and a student of its history, I felt compelled to record the Stackhouse story before all vestiges of its past were gone. As I began the research, facts turned up, but so did myths, such as that the name "Stackhouse" had derived from the stacking of one house on top of another. People have driven there to see this "oddity!"

In the most-published histories of Western North Carolina, I found scant information about Stackhouse. Samuel Ashe's History of North Carolina (1908) had no mention, nor did Van Noppen's Western North Carolina Since the Civil War (1973), nor Wilma Dykeman's The French Broad (1955). John P. Arthur used the word "Stackhouse" once in a sentence about barite mining in Western North Carolina: A History (1914). Short references to the community appeared in Eller's Miners, Millhands and Mountaineers (1982), as well as in T.R. Dawley, Jr.'s The Child That Toileth Not (1912). But I found more about Stackhouse and Runion, as I expected, in the Madison County histories The Kingdom of Madison (1973) by Wellman, and This is Madison County (1974), by Jinsie Underwood. However, they devoted only four and two pages respectively to Stackhouse. In addition, Wellman's book contained critical errors despite his using Amos Stackhouse's grandson, Gilbert, as a source.

Consequently, most of the information for this book has come from Stackhouse family members and their private papers. While stressing that they did not want their homes or lives in the public eye, they have been gracious, candid and helpful in every way. They are a family who cherish and protect the legacy of their ancestors but have agreed to share it in this special publication in order that the facts not be lost to posterity.

I have also interviewed oldtimers and former residents of the area in person, by mail, and by telephone, cross-checking much of their oral material through

4

public records. For more details I visited the Stackhouse, Runion, and Hot Springs sites where Amos had lived and worked. Deeds, family Bibles, census reports, newspapers and periodicals, library books, maps, photographs, diaries and letters from both private and public records provided additional facts. Using all these sources I have pieced together the chain of events that will hopefully answer the "who, what, when, where, and why" queries about Stackhouse, North Carolina and its founder.

I have opened my first chapter with Amos Stackhouse at mid-life in Florida, discontent and searching for direction. I then use retrospective commentary to reveal his reflections of his early years in Pennsylvania and how he went to Florida, remembered as he goes to North Carolina. Subsequent chapters explain his life between Pennsylvania and Florida, the founding of the community named for him, and the generations following Amos to the present.

Ever since the discovery of the mineral springs in southern Madison County, the region has attracted tourists. Now, at the beginning of still another century, when the passenger train no longer runs and the highway traffic is routed mostly through Haywood County, river sportsmen make up the bulk of visitors to this county. (In 1999, 30,000 boaters passed Stackhouse.) Nonetheless, this history is not primarily for them, but for those of us born deep in the Southern Appalachian Mountains, that we can proudly preserve our heritage for the coming generations.

As a 2006 postscript, Harvey W. Stackhouse – Amos' great grandson – made the pilgrimage to the Dales of Yorkshire, observing that, "Stackhouse, England, is pretty much the same as Stackhouse, America." What was once a community of Stackhouse families is now one farm located on *Stackhouse Lane*, its buildings dating only to the 1800s. The current owner is John Helliwell, a professional jazz saxophonist who plays in the "sophisto-rock" band Super Tramp – well known throughout Europe.

Also in England, Harvey collected books and essays about the area, presenting much old research but some new details. One in particular is Cyril Stackhouse's derivation of the ancient surname:

> The Original name as entered in the Domesday Book is "Stachus," which is of Saxon origin, from Staca, a stake or pile, and Hus, a building – and so, a building surrounded with stakes, a fortress. This stockade had become necessary as protection for their livestock from the periodic raids by the Picts and the Scots from the North.*

*Taken from booklet *Stackhouse* by T. Ian Roberts; published by North Craven Heritage Trust, undated.

The Stackhouses of Appalachia

Even to Our Own Times

Chapter One

Phil., 6th mo., 27, 1870

Dear Father,

Thy letter was rec'd on the 20th. If I can get any money of Uncle P., will send it down. Am sorry thee still keeps sick. If thee can get anyone to look after things, perhaps thee can go up in Georgia or come here. I know thee is very lonely but must try and keep in as good spirits as possible. Thy loving son, Ellison.[1]

Amos Stackhouse, reading this in Duval County, Florida, was certain to be disappointed at his son's reply. For months, besides collecting debts due Amos from friends and relatives in Pennsylvania, Ellison Stackhouse had lent his father money out of his own pocket and had borrowed against his grandfather's estate.

Less than a decade before – sometime around 1863 – Amos had been in Piqua, Ohio, when his second wife Anna had moved back to her parents' in Philadelphia, leaving him to raise his daughters Elizabeth and Rebecca, thirteen and eleven respectively, and his son Thomas, age five. Another daughter, Anna Mary, seven years old, had gone East with Anna.[2]

During the unrest following the Civil War, Amos had become one of those seeking new direction and prosperity. In 1867, he bought a farm near Jacksonville, Florida, on the St. John's River, moving next door to Levi Myers, a former neighbor in Ohio.[3]

Now, Amos wanted to build a house so that he could make a home for Rebecca and Thomas, who were, by that time, living in Pennsylvania with their mother. Twenty-year-old Elizabeth was likely married or earning her own way, while twenty-five-year-old Ellison (by Amos' first wife Rebecca) worked in Philadelphia.[4]

Moreover, as Ellison's letter indicated, Amos' farm operation in Florida was not prospering, and living alone was not satisfying. Evidently the year-round sunshine, abundance of fresh fruit and fish, the saltwater air, all attracting him so strongly four years before, had by now grown dull and unappealing. In a subsequent letter, Ellison advised Amos to "not get discouraged or low-spirited," and to sell part of his farm to pay off his creditors. "There is nothing that worries one so much as being in debt," declared Ellison.[5]

Within eight months of reading his son's letter, fifty-two-year-old Amos had taken Ellison's advice. Lifting his own spirits, he married his third wife – yet another Anna – (sometimes called Nannie), age nineteen.[6]

Born in Piqua, Ohio, to Levi and Lucinda Scott Myers, Anna Myers was likely of the community of Friends who had migrated to the Midwest a half-century earlier. The 1870 census for Mandarin voting district of Duval County, Florida, listed Levi Myers' occupation as "farm laborer," owning real

Right: The Stackhouse Family Crest.
Below: Taken from old copy of An Historical Sketch of the First Ancestors of the
Stackhouse Family in America, a booklet by William Romig Stackhouse, publisher, 1907.
Photographer unknown. Courtesy, Neil Alford, Jr.

estate worth $200, while Amos Stackhouse was recorded as "farmer" with real estate worth $4000.[7] In all probability, Levi Myers and Amos were partners in the Florida farm, or else, Myers worked for Amos. Soon after his marriage, Amos sold his orange groves, ended his business in Florida, and prepared for his move to Warm Springs, North Carolina.

According to family tradition Amos had become acquainted with Warm Springs and its reputation for healing when he stopped there on his way to Florida four years previously. The Stackhouse stories also say that Amos sought the mineral springs to benefit his new wife, although neither census records nor family letters attribute any health problems to young Anna, who would bear several children and enjoy an average life span, dying at age 65.[8]

On the other hand, letters from Ellison Stackhouse make reference to his father's ill-health and despondency. In his June 27th letter when Ellison had suggested "going up in Georgia," he might have meant to the Warm Springs of Georgia which touted cure-all powers, as did the "health waters" of Warm Springs, North Carolina.[9]

Whether it was middle-aged Amos or his young bride who sought treatment, the couple obviously planned to find contentment along the French Broad River in Madison County, North Carolina.

The long trip from Florida to Western North Carolina gave Amos time

7

to reflect upon his peregrinations and those of his antecedents. Often, Amos had read how his first-known Stackhouse ancestor had likely come from Saxony into England during the first century, at the time of the conquests, settling what land he could defend in battle.[10]

From the approximated three hundred acres grew the village of Stackhouse in the West Riding of Yorkshire. Although the Stackhouses were there even earlier, the first record of the name appears in the Domesday Book of 1086 – that census required by William the Conqueror for taxation purposes and to satisfy his curiosity about what he now owned.[11] (The name "Domesday" meant "day of judgment" in the legal or economic sense.) Ordered and begun in 1085, the survey took only one year to complete and was highly accurate, making it not only extraordinary in medieval times, but unique in history.[12] The original

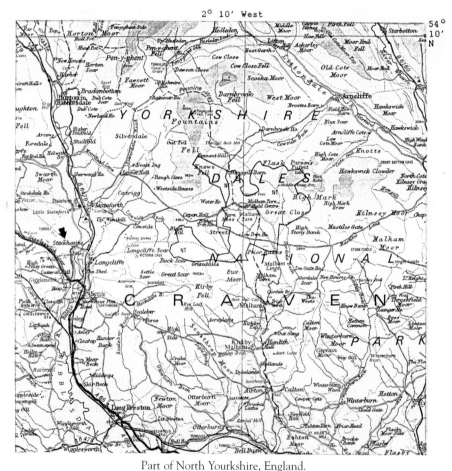

Part of North Yourkshire, England.
Bartholomew's National Map Series: West Yorkshire 1:100,000
John Bartholomew & Son LTD., Edinburgh, Scotland. Courtesy, Eugene G. Stackhouse.

volume – written in Latin on sheepskin – is kept on public record in London even today, and has actually been used on occasion to settle current disputes.[13] *Stacuse, Staykhus,* and Stackhouse are only a few spellings for the Anglo-Saxon name, but this last – the English form of the surname – has retained its original lettering through eleven centuries.

In 1870, Amos Stackhouse traveled by train where there were railroads and by stagecoach where there were not. As he watched the countryside go past, Amos could conjure up pictures of the ancient English countryside and the hamlet occupied by the early Stackhouse men. His nephew William Romig Stackhouse would actually visit old Yorkshire, and write:

> "In this ancient parish… and in and about this hamlet, have our Family had their home from time immemorial. It was evidently here at a period antedating authentic documentary history; still here during the long dark ages when Romanism spread its black pall of injustice, ignorance and superstition over the fair land; here when the Bastard Conqueror set his ruthless foot upon English shores and trampled out the rights of English men, and even to our own times has it dwelt here."[14]

William also noted that the Stackhouse coat-of-arms was granted by Emperor Maximillian on December 11, 1518, to Christopher Stackhouse, who may have been a hired mercenary in the service of the Holy Emperor. "The arms, with little variation, seem to have been borne by our family in all its branches ever since," states William.[14]

Over three centuries later, Amos Stackhouse would likely share some of his family background with young Anna, but most of his reflections remained with himself. Some were queries. "Was he making a wise change? Was God blessing this decision? Would Anna be content far from her family? Why did he need to move so often?" Perhaps it was in his blood, he reasoned to himself. After all, his father and his grandfather, in their genealogical research, had found that many Stackhouses, throughout the centuries, roamed far from England. One of Amos' Canadian relatives had written that his ancestors "were wanderers for religion's sake, actuated by no motives of commercial gain or of enriching themselves in this world's lucre."[15]

Indeed, a large number of the Stackhouses, though not all, were of the Society of Friends, or "Quakers." James Stackhouse of New Brunswick, Canada, wrote the following undated comments after his own study of the family history:

> "It seems that a religious feeling has been prevalent amongst the Stackhouse family from the first, with the name of Thomas Stackhouse, who was principal of St. Austins in 1502, then Trustee at Queens College. He was Vice Chancellor in 1521 and Chaplain to King Henry VIII, before his alleged death in 1533. From this date down, I find many of them collegious and of letters, many of them, father and son, ministers of the established church. Among them I will mention Thomas Stackhouse, Vicar of Birnham, the Bible historian."[16]

This Thomas Stackhouse was held in particular esteem by Amos' brother Powell, who owned one of the rare editions. Amos' nephew, William R. Stackhouse, wrote, "In my father's book closet, *History of the Bible* by Stackhouse occupied a distinguished station… It was published in two tomes, several of the editions containing an engraving of the author with the Arms of Stackhouse."[17]

Part of Holme's Map of Bucks County showing Thomas Stackhouse's Property, 1681.
Courtesy, Eugene G. Stackhouse.

During the years 1722-1775, numerous additional works by Thomas Stackhouse were published, some posthumously, including sermons, poems, devotions, essays, biographies and memoirs.[18]

Another scholar cousin much admired by Amos' family was John Stackhouse, the botanist, who devoted himself to the study of sea plants. Born in 1741, John, too, had numerous publications, his name having been perpetuated by Sir James Edward Smith in naming an Australian seaweed of the tere binthaceous genus *Stackhousia*.[19]

Research by Amos' nephew placed their direct ancestors in the little village of Stackhouse, located, as mentioned before, in the West Riding of Yorkshire, in the Deanery of Craven and the Parish of Giggleswick.[21] Here, in the early 1500s, was born one John Stackhouse from whom descended Amos' great, great, great grandfather, Thomas. Over a century later, between 1650 and 1680, Amos' relatives in Stackhouse responded to the preaching of George Fox, considered the founder of the Society of Friends. The Quaker explosion began in England and spread rapidly to other countries, including English colonies on the Eastern shore of North America.

At that time English law persecuted all who did not conform to the worship of the Church of England ("Anglicanism"). Friends believed that, in religious matters, each soul was illumined directly by the Holy Spirit and stood face to face with its Maker without the need of a priest, hence, they were considered traitors to the English crown. In addition, the Quakers made statements of reform, speaking openly in church services and stirring great interest. They stressed equality, treating all persons the same. Indomitable under persecution, they sang in prison and witnessed to their faith behind prison walls. In their ordinary lives, plain dress, sobriety, industry, thrift, shrewdness, even the use of "thee" and "thou," in place of the fashionable "you," were the Quakers' peculiarities. They declined to take oaths of any sort and refused to use the "heathen" names of the days of the week or of the month, speaking of "first day, second day, first month, second month," instead of "Sunday, Monday, January, February," etc. At their services they practiced group silence, broken only when a member felt moved by the Holy Spirit to contribute a profound thought.[22]

By 1656, there were over one thousand members of the Friends' Society, or Quakers, in English prisons.[23] At this point, they began to cross the Atlantic to the New World, where they would settle. In 1681, the Colony of Pennsylvania was secured by William Penn as a place of refuge for oppressed Friends.

The very next year, Stackhouse village's governing body of Quakers, called "Monthly Meeting" (instead of "church") met at the nearby town of Settle on the seventh day of the fourth month. A certificate was drawn for several Friends in the congregation to

> "Remove to Pennsylvania, and particularly our dear friend Cuthbert Hayhurst, his wife and family... for whose welfare and prosperity we are unanimously concerned. And also for our friends Thomas Wrightsworth and his wife; Thomas Croasdale, Agnes his wife and six children; Thomas Stackhouse and Marjory Hayhurst Stackhouse, his wife; Nicolas Waln... who we believe are single in their intentions to remove to the aforesaid Pennsylvania in America, there to inhabit, if the Lord permit, and we do certify unity with their said intentions."

The document was signed by eleven officials of the Settle Meeting.[24] Since Cuthbert Hayhurst had been jailed and fined, time after time, and Thomas Stackhouse had also been jailed for his beliefs, it seemed their only chance to worship as they chose was to leave their homeland.[25]

Thus it was that Thomas and Marjory Hayhurst Stackhouse, along with her family members and Thomas' two young nephews, John and Thomas Stackhouse, Jr., boarded the HMS *Lamb*, one of twenty – three ships coming to America with William Penn.[26]

It is thought that they arrived in October, 1682, settling on 312 acres previously bought and surveyed on Neshaminy Creek in Bucks County, Pennsylvania. Unfortunately, Marjory Stackhouse did not long enjoy this new freedom. She died in November and was one of the first to be buried at Middletowne. In 1702, Thomas married a widow, Margaret Atkinson, but then he died four years later at age 71.[27]

Thomas' nephew, Thomas Stackhouse, Jr., had wed Grace Heaton in 1688 and become a prominent leader in the new Quaker province. He seems to have been a man of means, for he owned 507 acres which joined the lands of his father-in-law Robert Heaton and of his uncle, Thomas Stackhouse, in Bucks County. Located in Middletowne Township, the settlement soon grew into a hamlet, and a Meeting was established there. In 1689, Thomas Stackhouse, Jr., erected a Meeting House at Middletowne, Bucks County's oldest structure.

On his plantation, Thomas raised cattle, grew grains, fruits, timber and other products. He became a successful and service-minded citizen, acquiring other tracts of land and serving in the Colonial Assembly of Pennsylvania Province in 1711, 1713, and 1715 (when reelected in 1716, he refused the seat). After his wife Grace died in 1708, Thomas married Ann Mayos, siring five children in addition to the nine Grace had borne him. One of Grace's sons was Robert Stackhouse, Amos' great great grandfather, born in 1692.[28]

Robert's marriage to Margaret Stone (c. 1724) produced eight children: Benjamin, Thomas, Joseph, James, Grace, Robert, Alice and William. Robert and Margaret removed their family to Berwick on the Susquehanna River, Pennsylvania, where Robert died in 1788.[29]

James Stackhouse, the third son of Robert and Margaret, was born in 1725 or 1726 (exact date unknown), moving to Philadelphia as a young man. Although his occupation was not recorded, we can be assured he would have found work and a chance at prosperity in the "city of rapid growth." In 1750, he married Martha Hastings, whose ancestor was *Hastings the First*, sea king or pirate Norman chieftain of 843 A.D.[30]

James Stackhouse and Martha had eight children before his death at age 34. Their fifth child, born in 1757 and named Amos (no middle name), grew along with Philadelphia.[31] From a few hundred inhabitants in 1683-the year after the Stackhouses had arrived in America-the city's population reached 2000 by 1700. The trading center for the Delaware Valley, Philadelphia soon became America's largest city for a time.[32]

However, by 1750 this growth had changed both the city and Quakerism from the days of George Fox. The Friends' community was transformed culturally as the Scot-Irish immigration of Presbyterians and other denominations began to compete in numbers. Moreover, increased material wealth resulted in the bending of many straight-laced Quakers. Their dwellings showed stylish touches and their "plain" clothing took on color. With Philadelphia's population and commerce increases, the Monthly Meeting decreased its participation in civic responsibilities, although it never shirked its aid to widows, orphans, and others in need.[33]

In 1779, amid the conflict between America and England, 22-year-old Amos courted and married Mary Powell, whose ancestors had been among the early Friends on the ship *Kent*.[34] As the American revolt fermented, Amos evidently followed the Society of Friends' urgings to keep its members from involvement in rebellious activities. According to the Philadelphia Yearly Meeting of 1774, the liberties that Quakers enjoyed in America were attributable to the King and he should not be opposed. As to the *Declaration of Independence*, Friends were absolutely forbidden to take part in any government or to support the war effort through their occupations.[35]

However, by 1777, Pennsylvania had required all males over age 18 to swear allegiance to the Colony and faithfulness to the Commonwealth of Pennsylvania, renouncing George III.[36] In order to remain in Philadelphia, Amos and many of his relatives must have taken the oath. Unfortunately, a rift developed in the Stackhouse family as several of Amos' uncles and cousins remained loyal to the Crown, even to the point of fighting under the

Union Jack. When America won its freedom, Robert Stackhouse, son of James' brother Joseph, went to New Brunswick, Canada, having been honorably discharged from the British army in 1783 after serving six and a half years. For having fought as Loyalists in the war, some Stackhouse men received land grants from Britain, thus beginning the large Canadian branch of the Stackhouse family.[37]

Amos' older brother, Hastings Stackhouse, a pronounced Loyalist, was discovered in a plot during the war to help General Howe bring the British Fleet up the Delaware River.[38] He fled behind British lines until after the war when his unpopularity in Philadelphia prompted him to move to Savannah, Georgia. There his descendants remained – not far from other Stackhouses who had come from Pennsylvania to South Carolina two decades before.

Back in Philadelphia, Amos and Mary Stackhouse stayed busy during these politically volatile years, raising their children – 13 in all. At some point they moved across the Delaware River to Mount Holly, New Jersey, not far from Philadelphia, where Amos taught school for a number of years. Considered a man of some literary attainment, he began the recording of the Stackhouse family history to be passed from generation to generation.[39]

In 1785 Amos' second son Powell married Edith Dilworth, also a Quaker, by whom he had eleven children. Powell named his fifth child Amos (again without a middle name), after his grandfather.[40] Powell Stackhouse operated a stove and machine foundry in Philadelphia, and owned a large home there. Edith came of a moderately well-to-do family whose American founder, the pioneer James Dilworth, a minister, had come from Lancaster, England, on Captain John Teach's ship *Lamle* in August, 1682.[41] Dilworth's property then joined the boundaries of Thomas Stackhouse in Bucks County. And while Powell was not rich, he made a comfortable living, able to hire a tailor on occasion to make coats with velvet collars and satinet sleeve linings, all in sober colors, of course.[42]

Five decades later, Amos Stackhouse thought back to his childhood with fondness. In addition to his many cousins, he had enjoyed the companionship of seven siblings – four older than he, and three younger. (Three others died in infancy.) They had all attended the School of the Society of Friends in Philadelphia, for Quakers always stressed education for girls as well as boys.[43] At a young age Amos developed learning skills and a love of reading which served him well for a lifetime. Besides having books in his home, Amos had access to Philadelphia's public library and museums. After finishing school, Amos joined his brother, Charles Dilworth, in their father's foundry business. With his sons in charge, Powell Stackhouse was able to retire in 1840.[44]

Now traveling northward to the Southern Appalachian Mountains, Amos vividly recalled his courtship of Rebecca Shaw (daughter of Alexander Shaw on Seventh Street) whose sister Sarah was the wife of Amos' older brother Joseph. Among their many Quaker relatives and friends, Amos and Rebecca had enjoyed the social life of the upper middle class in Philadelphia. After their marriage, on July 11, 1843, they had been blessed with a son, Ellison, in 1845, who would serve his father as close friend, advisor and life-long comfort. Most sadly, when Ellison was only a year old, his mother Rebecca died at the age of 27, leaving Amos lonely and depressed. He moved back into his father's home where his mother could provide for baby Ellison. Amos' life would never be quite the same again.

ENDNOTES FOR CHAPTER ONE

[1] Aumiller, Nancy Stackhouse. Interview, July 11, 1999. Private papers.
[2] Private papers.
[3] Ibid.
[4] Ibid.
[5] Duval County, Florida, marriage register. Book 2, p.821.
[6] Duval County, Florida, census record 1870, p.551.
[7] Family Bible, courtesy Carthene Stackhouse Cole, 1992.
[8] Private papers.
[9] Stackhouse, Wm.R., and Walter F. Stackhouse. *The Stackhouse Family.* 2nd edition. Morehead City, N.C.: Stackhouse Foundation, 1993, p.3.
[10] Hinde, Thomas. *The Domesday Book: England's Heritage, Then and Now.* New York: Crown Publishers, 1985, p.321.
[11] Wood, Michael. Domesday: *A Search for the Roots of England.* London: BBC Books, 1948.
[12] Ibid.
[13] Stackhouse and Stackhouse, p.17.
[14] Ibid, p.82.
Stackhouse, Eugene Glenn. *Stackhouse, An Original Pennsylvania Family.* Baltimore: Gateway Press. 1988, p.5.
[15] Private papers.
[16] Ibid.
[17] Stackhouse and Stackhouse, p.65.
[18] Ibid.
[19] Ibid, p.90
[20] Ibid, p.vii.
[21] Trueblood, D. Elton. *The People Called Quakers.* New York: Harper & Row, 1966, pp.2-4.
Standard Reference Work, Vol.III. Chicago: Standard Education Society, 1927.
[22] *Standard Reference*, Vol.III.
[23] Unpublished private papers.
[24] Stackhouse, Eugene Glenn, p.7.
[25] McCracken, George E. *The Welcome Claimants Proved, Disproved and Doubtful.* Philadelphia: Welcome Society of Penn. 1985.
[26] Stackhouse and Stackhouse, p.138.
[27] Ibid, p.142.
History of Chester and Delaware Counties, Pennsylvania, c. 1903. Author and publisher unknown.
[28] Stackhouse and Stackhouse, p.149.
[29] *History of Chester Co.*, p.15.
[30] Ibid.
[31] Weigley, Russell F. Philadelphia, A 300 Year History. New York: W.W.Norton & Co., 1982, pp.10, 20, 218.
[32] Ibid, p.43.
[33] *History of Chester Co.*, p.15.
[34] Weigley, p.131.
[35] Stackhouse, Eugene Glenn, pp. 13, 14.
[36] Private papers.
[37] Stackhouse and Stackhouse, p.151.
[38] Stackhouse, Wm. Romig, and Powell Stackhouse, Jr. A *Historical Sketch of the First Ancestors of the Stackhouse Family in America.* Moorestown, New Jersey: The Settle Press, 1907, p.4.
[39] Private papers.
[40] *History of Chester Co.*, p.16.
[41] Private papers.
[42] *History of Chester Co.*, p.16.
[43] Ibid.

Chapter Two

Three years later, in July, 1849, Amos Stackhouse married his second wife, Anna Williamson, a Quaker. She bore him a daughter Elizabeth (called Lizzie) the next year. Then, during the early spring of 1851, evidently afflicted by wanderlust, Amos made plans to buy a farm and embark upon a different life altogether.[1]

The exact reason for his decision to roam was known only to himself. But the 1840s in Philadelphia had been a decade of freezing winters, followed by spring floodings and the closing of the Bank of the United States. "Depression, psychic as well as economic," settled over Philadelphia, wrote one historian.[2] Nonetheless, throughout the decade the city's population increased 58 per cent, crowding its old sections and forcing development to the outskirts. Commercial buildings, and some residences, were being constructed with large-paned windows and marble steps. The municipality improved and extended its gas supply for lighting streets and homes. It replaced its wooden water pipes with iron ones, many newer homes installing bathtubs and water closets. (The poor, of course, continued to get water at the public hydrant and could rarely afford bathing.) Trade unions had organized in Philadelphia as in other major cities, demanding compliance of the ten-hour workday law. Ensuing strikes and unstable social conditions, on top of urban expansion and the changing character of the city, might have contributed to Amos' decision to leave his hometown for life in the country.[3]

On February 28, 1851, Amos signed a legal note borrowing $1600 from his brother Powell Stackhouse, Jr. Amos considered land in Tazewell, Virginia, owned by a Philadelphia friend, but then decided to go West where there was already a strong Friends colony. He and Anna stored their carpets and furniture with their families, rented their house and packed up the children and necessities for the trip.[4]

Traveling to Miami, Ohio, to the home of their cousins Tom and Hannah Darlington, the Stackhouses stopped temporarily, Anna and the children remaining there while Amos moved on to look at the land tracts. After deliberation, he finally purchased 162 acres in Chester, Indiana. Located in Wayne County, the little village was only a few miles from Richmond, Indiana, the area's Quaker stronghold. Amos built a log cabin, bought his needed seeds, tools, draft animals and milk cow.[5] Then he sent for his wife and children in Ohio.

Amos would soon understand how both the terrain and the weather of Indiana contrasted to Pennsylvania's. Indiana was subject to sudden change of temperature across the entire state because there were no mountains to break the sweep of north and south winds. While the soil was fertile and the climate good for temperate-growing crops, there were periodic droughts, dust storms and grassfires to plague the prairie farmer.

However, not having actually experienced the plains travails, Amos began his new way of life with excited anticipation. As he plowed and planted, spending long days in the fresh air, close to the earth, he put behind him the memories of the noisy, hot foundry and city.

Although living conditions in Wayne County, Indiana, were filled with deprivations compared to those in Philadelphia, the situation was considerably less primitive when compared to those endured by the first

Quaker settlers. Grist mills, saw mills, tanyards and small industries were operating. General stores, day schools, meeting houses, turnpikes and railroads had been built. Even a Friends' boarding school (later Earlham College) had opened in 1847. The Indians had not been hostile since the War of 1812, but before that, there had existed a special friendliness between the "redmen" and the Quakers, who were against all warring and did not build blockhouses. It was said that the Friends' garb gave security to the wearer, evoking respect from the natives. They recognized the "plain people."[6]

Wayne County had been first settled by whites in 1805, and North Carolinian Quaker David Hoover moved there the next year. He was searching for a place for his father Andrew Hoover, minister in the Friends Society. When he reported that he had found "the promised land," the great wave of immigration from North Carolina flooded Wayne County, Indiana. The Quakers, who did not believe in slavery, were fleeing the intrusion of that institution.[7]

These Quaker immigrants felt that it was also wrong to use anything produced by slave labor.[8] North Carolina-born Levi Coffin, who lived a few miles from Richmond, began to buy *free-labor* goods to sell to his Quaker community. The Friends Society raised $3000 in 1847 to start a large wholesale store of non-slave-made merchandise to be operated by Coffin. He and his wife Catherine moved to Cincinnati to run it just four years before Amos and Anna arrived in Wayne County.[9]

While still living in Indiana, however, Levi and Catherine Coffin were credited with having protected hundreds of slaves escaping from the South. (The couple appeared in Harriett Beecher Stowe's *Uncle Tom's Cabin* as "the Holidays.") Journalists of the day gave Coffin the name of "President of the Underground Railroad." Of course, there was no actual travel by train, just by foot, horseback or wagon. The runaways moved almost always by night, hiding during the daytime. Coffin's former Wayne County home-now a state monument-was on three major escape routes and only a few miles from Amos Stackhouse's new farm at Chester.[10]

Slaves continued to be hidden and forwarded to Coffin in Cincinnati until after the Civil War. If Amos and Anna Stackhouse had become involved with the Underground Railroad, they might have hidden passing slaves behind secret doors, or contributed clothing, food, and shoes, or turned a deaf ear when owners came questioning. At the very least, they would have been sympathetic to the fugitives' cause. (Anna's brother, Passmore Williamson, serving on Philadelphia's Vigilance Committee, was jailed in 1855 for his part in the attempted freeing of three slaves traveling through the city.[11])

From Wayne County Amos wrote relatives and friends left behind about his satisfaction in the Midwest location, even though he considered it temporary. Amos still searched for his dream place in the new country, among members of his faith, not unlike his ancestors Thomas and John in their migration from Yorkshire over two centuries earlier.

In May, 1851, Amos and Anna received a letter from their cousins, the Darlingtons, with whom they had stayed in Miami, Ohio: "We received thy letter and were pleased to hear little Lizzy and Ellison are getting fleshy. I am pleased to hear you have not perched yet and hoping you will settle in our neighborhood yet. Will try to send thy trunk tomorrow."[12]

One week later, on May 17, Amos' brother Powell Stackhouse, Jr., wrote Amos about affairs at home in the city: "I am glad to hear that you have come to a halting place, at least, for a time… Father thinks that the neighborhood of Richmond will be a good place for thee… He has missed Ellison very much." Powell reported that he had collected Amos' house rent and had subscribed to the *Daily Ledger* for him. "Let me know whether they come punctually, if not I will have it corrected." After giving news of the family, Powell concluded, in a postscript: "Thinking you would like to see a 3-cent piece, I send it enclosed. They are just out." This first U.S. subsidiary coin, authorized by Congress on March 3, 1851, was the result of the new three-cent postage rate. It was minted in New Orleans as well as Philadelphia and would be the smallest of our country's silver coins. Of course it pleased Amos to get this novelty from Powell.[13] Powell's pale blue letter paper was folded into a small rectangle and sealed on the back with brick-red wax, the front addressed in his beautiful calligraphic script to Amos Stackhouse, Chester Post Office, Wayne County, Indiana. (Envelopes were expensive at this time and rarely used for common mail.)[14]

However, by September, Powell was addressing his letters to "Amos Stackhouse, *Postmaster*, Chester, Indiana." Amos had either rented a store or built his own, wherein he kept a United States Post Office. He sold groceries and other items, saving the small settlement the trip to Richmond for such purchases. Amos also continued his long physical hours as farmer – plowing, harrowing, planting, then hoeing, treating pests and diseases, and finally, reaping, raking, binding and storing.

Anna had the helpmate's never-ending responsibilities for the cooking, milking, churning, butter making, poultry tending, and kitchen gardening, in addition to the caring of her children and household. In February of 1852, a second daughter, Rebecca, was born, giving Anna even more to do. Breaking the monotony, however, were cherished letters from her parents and sisters, telling of family and happenings back in Philadelphia.

Amos, too, wrote to relatives and friends, evidently expressing satisfaction in his Midwest situation. His brother-in-law, Dan Morrell, wrote from Philadelphia in April, 1852 that their cousin Charles Dilworth, evidently encouraged by Amos, was leaving in a few days. "The Friends and others have raised funds to send Charles and children to Indiana." The next month, Amos' first cousin, Abram Lower, asked Amos to send rates of wage for carpenter or millwright, cost of living and the probability of locating a small home and garden in Indiana. "Finding it difficult to make anything here more than a living, I have had my mind turned toward the West for some time… I should like to get in a neighborhood of Friends on account of the Society for my children who are growing up… I have understood from Powell that thee's much pleased with the change of thy own abode and I presume there's still room for me."[15]

Abram hoped to earn for his old age, as did all Quakers. "To provide for one's family and one's own future was part of the Gospel the Quakers practiced," declared Francis C. Anscombe in his 1959 book *I Have Called You Friends*. "The present practice of living on the installment plan and then retiring upon pensions provided by the government would have been abhorrent to early Quakers," writes Anscombe.[16]

Amos Stackhouse was also concerned with his future in the same manner.

Pleased as he might be with his Chester farm, he still considered it to be temporary. He searched for a better place, announcing his intention to visit locations in Minnesota, near St. Paul. In the summer of 1852 he made the trip, mostly by riverboat, but also on foot in some sections to better see the lay of the land, accompanied by a traveling companion or servant identified only as "Joe."[17]

Writing to Anna from Galena, Illinois, September 8, Amos began: "My dear Anna, We arrived at this place last evening. Before going to our hotel, I went to the post office and was glad to receive thy letter. I am right glad to think you get along so well." He cautioned her to "watch the milk" from a certain cow, and to notice the pig having the "sore eye." "I wish thee and Caroline [a neighbor's daughter hired to help Anna] would see that the young chickens are not eaten up by her [this pig] or the other hogs running the road." Amos then told her a little about his trip up the Mississippi to Rock Island and from there to Galena where he and Joe visited lead mines. "We were let down by ropes about 100 feet and then, with candles, walked all about the mine and got some pretty specimens of lead ore which I intend bringing home… Expect to leave tonight for St. Paul. Thee will send thy letters now to Chicago and I will be there in two weeks from this date." Amos also told Anna he would stop next in Dubuque, Iowa, and would write her from there. "Galena lies in between hills which are 500 feet high, giving us a beautiful view of the country. The dwellings are very pretty situated on the hills… It is very dry here and I'm afraid we will not get up the Minnesota, Mississippi, or Wisconsin Rivers from St. Pauls unless there is rain." As he traveled, Amos also collected souvenir flower seeds. He wrote, "I have been trying to get ripe seeds from one which is most beautiful. Joe and I named it the 'Quaker Prairie' flower. It is white and full of bloom at this time." In closing his three-page letter to his wife, Amos said, "Kiss Lizzie for me and let her kiss thee for me, as I should like to do it myself. Thy affectionate husband, Amos."[18]

Anna Stackhouse's family back East did not agree, however, that she "was getting along so well." They thought that Anna should give up the harsh pioneer life and return to civilization as she had known it. Her father even offered land in Delaware. A letter from her sister Mercie in Philadelphia admonished Anna, saying: "We had expected a visit from thee this fall-why was it not arranged for thee to come on while Amos was away? It would have been much better than remaining there in the woods by thyself."[19]

Reinforcing these thoughts, perhaps, was another letter to Anna from a friend, Mary Haines, in nearby Richmond, Indiana. Mary, who was in similar circumstances, pleaded that Ada (sister to Caroline, Anna's helper) might spend "a few weeks with us this winter if her father can spare her and she is willing to come." Mary Haines was desperate to find both a nurse and a domestic helper for her upcoming confinement. "Anna, it is rather a trying situation to be in without a mother or sister or any of one's own people to help one thro'. Tho' I feel very thankful that I have two or three kind friends here who will do what they can to make me comfortable. I would like to have a good talk with thee, for I sometimes feel almost discouraged, then again I endeavor to be resigned to whatever may be my lot." She thanked Anna for the loan of sewing patterns for the layette, closing her letter with another plea for Anna to send on the stagecoach either Caroline to help, or Caroline's sister, Ada, within the next two weeks.[20]

The following day, a letter came to Anna from her sister Mary Coggins in Philadelphia. "Oh Anna, how earnestly I wish I could see thee… If all things work as I hope, I will in the Spring, even should Amos move thee to Minnesota … Western life has wrought its changes in thy appearance, I hear, but I will not feel surprised, as I know how it was with the women I visited in Indiana, and from accounts, there is still a fair proportion of work allotted them…" Mary wrote news of family members and mutual friends in the East, closing with, "I'm sorry Amos is again unsettled, as I thought when he was here he bragged on Indiana as the right spot to live, and his indifference to wealth."[21]

The letters from Amos' family were somewhat more supportive, containing, also, the warm trivia of relatives. Amos' brother, Charles Dilworth, wrote, "There is some prospect of sister Sarah getting married to a man living on Long Island. How do you like the West by this time?" Charles' wife Alice added: "As Charles has not filled up his extra sheet, I concluded I would write a few lines… Amos, Charles likes cigars better than ever. He is a match for thee – buys them by the hundred. I expect Lizzy grows and can talk, and Ellison must ride that horse he talked so much about."[22]

And from Amos' cousin Brinton Dilworth in Harrisburg, Pennsylvania, came queries about the possibility of "making a comfortable living" in Indiana, near Amos. "How are the corn and potatoes likely to yield in your part of the country?" he wrote. "It would be good to live near Richmond where there are several large Societies of Friends, to hear the plain language used nearly constant." (Although Brinton never moved West, he often wrote to Amos, who kept and re-read his letters for years to come.)[23]

On April 21, 1853, Anna Stackhouse gave birth to a daughter, Mary Williamson, who died the same day.[24] In her sorrow, Anna surely wondered if the event could have resulted from her dread of moving farther west, or of the lack of city medical care, or of the manual work required of the pioneer wife. Whether or not these concerns were voiced to Amos, he began looking also at land near Cincinnati, where his uncle, James Stackhouse, lived, and at land near Bremen, Ohio. Finally he made his decision after receiving a note from Joseph Pipher in Colerain, Ohio. Pipher, who owned land at Fort Recovery, Ohio, just across the state line, northeast of Chester, wrote: "I received your letter saying that you wished to buy my land. I have concluded to take $700 providing you will pay the taxes on the year 1852. But you must come down to make the writings."[25]

Subsequently, Amos' records were audited by the United States Postal Department in May for his official last day as postmaster of Chester, Indiana- June 21, 1853.[26]

In a letter to Anna's father, Thomas Williamson in Philadelphia, Amos declared:

> "I have purchased land in Mercer County, Ohio, and expect to leave this place tomorrow to go and build my house, leaving Anna and the children here until that is accomplished. The place I have bought, I paid $700 for 120 acres cleared and 40 acres nearly cleared of timber. The neighbors say I can easily get in my fall wheat and 20 acres of corn next spring with the help of a man for about 2 months… I intend building a frame house, Anna thinking

it will be more comfortable than log. It will be small as my means are too limited to build it all at one time, but I can add to it as our means warrant. I hope thee and Mother will come see us as soon as convenient. We will do all we can to make you comfortable. I want to return some kindness for the many presents Mother gave the children and Anna, and also for the kind offer thee made to my Father in regards to our moving back to Delaware, which under some circumstances should have been glad to accept. But after moving out here, and land equally cheap, and so much better quality and requiring less means to make it productive, it would give me more pleasure to see the results than to receive so much help... The place is just two miles from Recovery and quite well settled, being 14 houses or farms within less than a mile."[27]

Amos would find Fort Recovery's climate much like that of Chester. The fertile Miami River Valley was eminently productive of corn and wheat and other grains. On the main route of the westward movement, the fifty-year-old state had settled rapidly, taking its place as one of the Union's principal agriculture producers.

However, this positive-appearing future for Amos and Anna was suddenly invaded by deep sorrow. Writing to her sister Mercie on September 1, 1853, Anna Stackhouse sadly related:

> "We followed the remains of our darling Rebecca to the grave yesterday. The day after we arrived she was fretful, but on the 27th and 28th she had a high fever and slept most of the time. During the night of the 28th she had severe spasms but was better the next morning, sitting up to play with the cat for some time. About four in the afternoon the spasms returned and by 11 o'clock that night she was unconscious of any further suffering, in which state she remained until near five o'clock the afternoon of the 30th when she breathed her last. I wish Mary or Passmore [Anna's siblings] would see Mother Stackhouse and let her know of our loss. Amos will write soon but does not feel able at the present. I remain thy sister, Anna."[28]

The deaths of two daughters within four months was especially difficult for Anna. How she must have longed for home and family in the East!

After a few weeks Anna wrote to her father about Rebecca's death, requesting, at the same time, a loan, perhaps to buy a grave stone or finishing materials for the house. Thomas Williamson's reply from Philadelphia on October 22, 1853, enclosed a bank draft for two hundred dollars and stated:

> "Thy letter advised the loss of little R. in which we truly sympathized with thee and thy family. But that is a dispensation to which it is especially your duty to bow with submission and look to Him, who in his inscrutable wisdom has seen meet to inflict the wound, to heal it. In conformity with thy wish, I enclose a draft, endorsed payable to thy order, for two hundred dollars... I look forward to visiting you next summer, and until then, the matter of my lending on mortgage, as proposed in thy letter, must be deferred. Affectionately, thy father."[29]

[1] Author's private papers.

[2] Weigley, Russell F. Philadelphia, *A 300 Year History*. New York: W.W.Norton & Co., 1982, p.308.

[3] Ibid, pp.316, 317, 338.

[4] Private papers.

[5] Ibid.

[6] Fox, Henry Clay. *Memoirs of Wayne County and the City of Richmond*, Indiana. Madison, Wisconsin: Western Historical Association, 1912, pp. 41, 42.
Trueblood, D. Elton. *The People Called Quakers*. New York: Harper & Row, 1966, p.183.

[7] Fox, p.27.
Trueblood, p.163.

[8] Fox, p.154.

[9] Fox, p.164.

[10] Ibid, p.165.

[11] Weigley, p.388.

[12] Private papers.

[13] Private papers.
Yeoman, R.S. *Guide Book of U.S. Coins*. New York: Golden Books, 1998, p.11.

[14] Private papers.

[15] Ibid.

[16] Anscombe, Francis C. *I Have Called You Friends*. Boston: The Christopher Publishing House, 1959, p.40.

[17] Private papers.

[18] Anscombe, p.40.

[19] Private papers.

[20] Ibid.

[21] Ibid.

[22] Ibid.

[23] Ibid.

[24] Family Bible record.

[25] Private papers.

[26] Ibid.

[27] Ibid.

[28] Ibid.

[29] Ibid.

Shown with a modern dime, one of these 3¢ coins minted March, 1851, was sent to Amos Stackhouse in May, 1851, by his brother Powell in Philadelphia. Photo by L. Eddington.

Chapter Three

During Amos' remaining years in Fort Recovery, Ohio, Anna bore him three more children – a daughter in 1854, named Rebecca for her dead sister (as was the custom), and two years later, another daughter, Anna Mary, while the long-awaited boy's arrival came in May of 1856.[1] Amos' second son, Thomas W., was born in Philadelphia where Anna was visiting her father, the baby's namesake.

Amos' elder son, Ellison, often visited his grandparents, too, in the City of Brotherly Love. He probably attended school there during the winter, paid for, in part, by his mother's inheritance. Upon the death of his Grandmother Shaw he was to receive his mother's share of the estate – "the interest and income from such share to be from time to time applied towards the support, maintenance and education of my said grandson."[2] Any remainder would come to Ellison in full when he turned twenty-one.

The June 18th, 1860, census record of Fort Recovery, Gibson Township, Mercer County, Ohio, lists Amos Stackhouse as a forty-one-year-old farmer with $3500 of real estate, and personal property worth $500. Living with the Stackhouse family was twelve-year-old Ann Hockins, helper for Anna. (There were forty-one other household heads named Stackhouse in the state of Ohio that year, who were, no doubt, related to Amos, but he was the only one in Mercer County.)[3]

As far as we know, Amos and his family were enjoying the good life of the rural midwest, when, as historian Bruce Catton puts it, "for the last time in American history, the nation's farms were worth more than the output of its factories."[4] The Stackhouses had no premonition that over 600,000 of their fellow citizens would perish during the next four years, or that the pastoral scenes and town views, alike, would be spattered with bloody complications and changed forever.

While Amos, at age forty-two, might not have been subject to the draft, many of his cousins, nephews and friends were called to fight. Pennell Stackhouse, son of Amos' brother, Charles Dilworth, enlisted at age twenty-three in the Pennsylvania Volunteers.[5] He would survive the war despite his participation at Antietam–termed "the bloodiest day of the Rebellion." Strangely enough, that same day, unbeknownst to Amos, on the opposite side of the battle, was his first cousin twice removed, Eli Thomas Stackhouse, with South Carolina's 8th Company Volunteers. Though wounded seriously in the battle, Eli would also live through the conflict.[6]

Strife was not only a national concern – it was present in Amos' personal life, too. Sometime during the war, Anna Williamson Stackhouse ended her marriage with Amos. We rely on conjecture as to the reason. Perhaps she grew lonely and tired of the rigorous farm life, missing her family and the culture she had left in Philadelphia – museums, theaters, cathedrals, large libraries, paved streets, gas lighting, running water – life that was not at the mercy of the elements.[7]

Either before or after Anna's leaving, Amos changed his abode once again, moving Southeast, this time, to Piqua, Ohio, a small town north of Dayton on the Great Miami River. Family tradition declares that Amos was postmaster there, also, but official records do not list his name. It is entirely possible that he worked in the Piqua post office as assistant, bearing most of the job responsibility.[8]

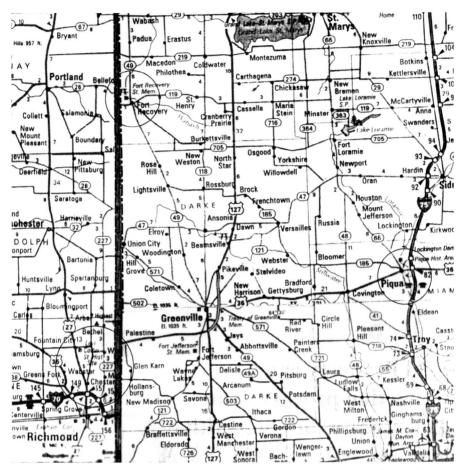

Indiana & Ohio towns where Amos lived, 1850s & 60s. By permission, Rand McNally Co.

Three of Amos' children – Elizabeth, Rebecca, and Thomas – lived with him. Anna Mary was with her mother in Pennsylvania. Teenaged Elizabeth (Lizzie) became proficient at bread baking and other domestic duties, but Amos also hired a housekeeper.[9]

On December 26, 1863, Amos and his family suffered another loss when his father, at seventy-eight years old, died. Powell Stackhouse left everything to his widow, Edith Dilworth Stackhouse, but provided for bequests after her death to each of his children. The three daughters were to receive small sums of money, but the four sons would get shares of stock "to be used for the education of their children, or in making permanent improvements on the several farms on which they live, especially bringing, by pipe and hydraulics or other suitable means, water to their dwellings." What a boon this would have been to Amos' wife Anna, had she stayed on the prairie! Powell Stackhouse left other stock to "the Pennsylvania Society for the Abolition of Slavery and for the relief of free negroes unlawfully held in bondage and for the improvement of The African race to be expended… for teaching young colored females the various branches of dressmaking and needlework. I have yet a hope, justice will be done for this disgraceful act."[10]

To the Friends Library on Arch Street, Powell gave his *Eusebius History Folio*, an old Bible quarto, printed about the year 1578; also, an old Welsh Bible Octavo printed in the year 1630. "My other books to be divided among my children," he had written.[11]

Amos' father was buried in the Friends Southwestern Burial Ground near Cardington, Delaware County, Pennsylvania. He had directed that three of his children who lived nearby be his administrators – Charles Dilworth; Powell, Jr.; and Anna D., a spinster who lived with her mother. After payment of all debts and burial expenses, the estate was to go to their mother for her lifetime. Then Powell's possessions were to be sold by public or private sale and the proceeds divided among his children, "except such articles of household furniture she may wish to give to our children or grandchildren," stated Powell's will.[12]

Powell, Jr., was the youngest of the will administrators and was an accountant by occupation, and since he was the only son living in the city, he managed his father's estate, sending reports to the others by mail. On January 27, 1864, he wrote to his brother in Piqua, Ohio: "Thy letter was received, and now I have to inform thee of another misfortune – the destruction by fire of the old factory building and the roof of our old mansion house." Evidently, in 1851 when Amos and Charles Dilworth had closed their foundry business, their parents moved into a smaller house, fairly close to the original home, since Powell, Jr., says, "Fortunately, I was at Mother's at the time and was soon upon the ground after the alarm. The fire originated in the old factory and had gained such a head-way, that was impossible to save it. The Western & Eastern walls now alone remain, the cupola, no doubt, saved by the latter & prevented it from falling on the new addition made by thee. That part is little damaged. The roof of the office is partially burned. The old mansion will require a new roof and rafters and plastering throughout. The foundry men want us to repair the factory by roofing over one story high. The expense probably would be 3 or 4 hundred dollars. I am at a loss what to do. If we should repair it, it will exhaust one year's rent. If we leave it remain, we lose the income from that part of the Estate."[13]

Powell's long letter continued to present the advantages and disadvantages of repairing the buildings or selling them, adding, "I had forgotten to say that there is no insurance upon the foundry. The policy expired about a year ago, and the Co. refused to renew the risk. The Mansion House is insured to cover the loss. The Co., I suppose, will put that in repair. The estate can hardly bear the loss of rents, etc." Their father had good assets, but evidently, indebtedness, too. After two more pages of detailing their few options to Amos, Powell, Jr., lamented, "It was only a day or two ago that I was congratulating myself that we had now got the tenants in order, and that rents would flow in sufficient to keep things afloat, and with little management, there would be sufficient for Mother, Aunt Sarah and Anna's comfort. Now this loss will throw us back… The responsibility upon me, I feel greatly. You are all absent, and Anna is the only one I have to consult with. Charles, to all purposes, is as far away as thee."[14]

In July there were more problems for Powell, Jr., as he dealt with his mother's rental properties. One in particular he called "the Court property," which was fraught with title discrepancies. At last Powell sold it, telling Amos, "I am right glad the matter is settled." Powell also responded, at the same writing, to a previous letter from Amos requesting that Powell ship him some fish. "I had to pay $11.00 a barrel, No 3, forwarded to thy address via Pa. R.R. Please let me know if they arrive."

Two months later, in September if 1864, Powell rode the train to visit Amos. On his way home he stopped at Dayton, Columbus, and Cincinnati, checking the cities' economic pulses and reporting their growth potential to Amos. During his visit, Amos had evidently discussed the prospect of changing his business once again. In this letter Powell advised him, saying, "A business like what we were talking about – one of household articles, etc… I believe would pay, but, now I do not think is the time. When the war is over, an impetus will be given to trade by the demand from the South, that, now, is almost bare of these articles."[15]

Unlike their Southern cousins, the Stackhouses in the North suffered only inconvenience and mild deprivations from the war that was devastating the Confederacy. Powell wrote to Amos, "Little business is doing, everything is dull, and I had hoped the end of the last peace *humbug* would brighten up matters, as yet no change for the better. No one wants to buy when they believe Peace will lower prices, so we have all been waiting for events. I hope now that we will have that 'short, quick and decisive War,' the *Tribune* has been laboring to induce the government to adopt and the government has so often promised."[16]

Within three months, on April 9, 1865, Powell's wish came true as the Confederate surrender brought the formal end to the Great Rebellion. About three weeks later, Powell Stackhouse, and possibly Ellison, along with many other of Amos Stackhouse's relatives, likely joined the crowd of 85,000 people who paid their respects and viewed their slain idol Abraham Lincoln at Independence Hall in Philadelphia.[17]

Death soon struck closer home for the Stackhouse family. On November 1, 1865, Amos' mother, Edith Dilworth, died, also at age seventy-eight, and was buried beside her husband. Though filled with the deep sorrow that a mother's death brings, Amos had not been surprised at the news. Back in February, his brother Powell had predicted in a letter: "Mother's health is not promising since her fall. I see that she is very feeble and though I would like to hope that we might have her with us a long time yet, it appears to me, it would be against all chances."[18]

Losing both parents in two years left Amos in low spirits and vulnerable to his loneliness. Anna had apparently obtained a divorce and custody of their minor children. (It is probable that their oldest daughter, Elizabeth, had married by this time.) On February 1, 1866, Amos Stackhouse received more bad news by telegraph from Thomas Williamson, Anna's father, followed three days later by Powell Stackhouse's detailed letter:

> "Thos. Williamson called on me this morning, informing me of the sickness of thy son Thomas and wishing me to write thee more fully than he had telegraphed. Anna and the children are at Excildown, all of them attending school. Thos, about ten days ago, complained of being unwell. He alternated between better and worse till yesterday. Thos. Williamson rec'd a telegram from the attending doctor, requesting him to come up immediately and bring with him Dr. Wilson as a consulting physician… They found Thomas very ill in critical condition… The doctors

pronounce it inflammation of the walls of the stomach."

The next day Powell wrote to Amos that the physician's dispatch had declared Thomas no better, although the pain had abated some and his suffering was less. "Thos. Williamson is doing everything possible. He sent up to him the best stimulants that could be had... Doctor says there is no immediate danger." But on the third day Powell's letter to Amos reported on a morning telegram to Williamson from the attending doctor: "Thy grandson no better. Do not see any prospect of his improving."[19]

We can imagine Amos' despair at not being able to see his seven-year-old son. Despite assurances from Thomas Williamson and from Powell that the best of care was being administered, Amos still wanted to judge for himself. As he made preparations for travel to his son's deathbed, an evening telegram brought great relief, stating that the pain and swelling had reduced and little Thomas would eventually be healed. The whole episode reinforced Amos' despondency. He missed seeing his children and having them daily in his household. Once again, he began planning and searching for a fresh place with a different way to make a living, putting such separation behind him.

The means to make this change might possibly come from a portion of his mother's estate if it could ever be closed. On June 15, 1867, Powell Stackhouse wrote to Amos:

> Dear Brother, Yesterday I enclosed to Joseph [their older brother] a statement of my account as acting executor of Father's estate with a request to forward it to thee after signing it, and have it here before the 27th instant as that is the last day this term, the court will consider it, otherwise it will have to layover till September. I urge immediate action and after thee signs it, mail it to Daniel J. Morrell, and I will write to him. Thine, affectionately, Powell.[20]

The exact fate of the old Stackhouse mansion in Philadelphia is unclear, but Amos and each of his siblings eventually received a handsome humidor or desk box made from the walnut mantles of their childhood home. After their mother's death, as directed by their father's will, the house was likely sold and demolished, some millwork items having been salvaged by Powell for mementos.

As it turned out, the estate would not be settled even three years later. In the meantime, Amos Stackhouse joined the many other Americans striving for prosperity and stability during the post-war upheaval and economic reconstruction. He sold his home and business in Piqua, Ohio, purchasing an orange grove on the outskirts of Jacksonville, Florida, along the St. John's River. And yet one more time, Amos pulled up stakes to begin a new life.

ENDNOTES FOR CHAPTER THREE

[1] Family Bible.
[2] Will of Eliz. P. Shaw, dated May 30, 1845, amended June 6, 1846, Author's private papers.
[3] Ohio census, 1860, p.366.
[4] Catton, Bruce. *The Civil War*. New York: Fairfax Press, 1980, p.1.
[5] *History of Chester and Delaware Counties*, Pennsylvania, c. 1903. Author and publisher unknown, p.17.
[6] *Stackhouse*, Wm.R., and Walter F. Stackhouse. The Stackhouse Family. 2nd edition. Morehead City, N.C.: Stackhouse Foundation, 1993, p.186.
[7] Weigley, Russell F. *Philadelphia, A 300 Year History*. New York: W.W.Norton & Co., 1982, pp. 281-345.
[8] Private papers.
[9] Ibid.
[10] Ibid.
[11] Ibid.
[12] Ibid.
[13] Ibid.
[14] Ibid.
[15] Ibid.
[16] Ibid.
[17] Weigley, p.417.
[18] Private papers.
[19] Ibid.
[20] Ibid.

Chapter Four

The fertile setting of the St. John's in Florida did not improve Amos Stackhouse's situation right away. Perhaps he had counted on the estate settlement or on the recovery of pre-war stock investments, or on better citrus market profits. Nevertheless, he clearly resorted to borrowing from his elder son. On December 8, 1867, Ellison Stackhouse wrote his father from Philadelphia saying that "the enclosed $40" was all he could spare now. Ellison described his work at "Truman and Shaw Hardware and Tools" on Market Street (co-owned by one of his mother's relatives) where "business has been quite dull and very poor prospects ahead." He probably worked on a sales commission. "I average $6.50 per week," he said, adding optimistically, "It is quite cold today and there will be skating tomorrow; then the skates will sell." He gave his father news of marriages and changes of address and health conditions of family members and friends, remarking on something novel concerning the cousin with whom he boarded: "Julia is quite well, the boy six months old. She feeds him with a bottle!"

Then Ellison told his father about a party he would be attending during the holiday season and about further aspirations: "If I can raise the money I am going to Dancing School next year." Ellison was still unmarried at twenty-two, but apparently hoping to find a wife.

Another letter from Ellison to Amos in October of the next year stated: "Thy letter rec'd last third day, and I had only $10 that I could send. I do not like to borrow money for myself but have for thee… That will be all I can spare this year, having to get winter clothes yet. Uncle Powell has to advance money for Aunt Anna [Amos' unmarried sister] to live on. Business is dull and money is hard to find." Ellison again reported news of their Philadelphia family and asked about selling a carpet Amos had left there in storage. He answered Amos' question from a previous letter as to Philadelphia prices for products: "Flour is $12 to $13 per barrel for good, and apples are high – 5 & 6 per bbl." Next, Ellison asked his father, "Will thee vote this fall? I think we are sure of Grant this time since Pennsylvania, Ohio, Indiana and Nebraska have gone Republican. This city polled a majority for the Democratic mayor. They imported New York and Baltimore roughs in large quantities and issued fraudulent naturalization papers. We are going to contest the election." Ellison closed his letter saying, "I am 23 years old tomorrow – time slips away fast."[1]

Amos wrote and received other letters from his brothers and cousins, even from a lady friend back in Ohio. He invited them to visit him in Florida, although few made the long journey. Amos had always taken one or two trips yearly to his home in Philadelphia, seeing his children and friends, and buying supplies not available where he lived, but it is not known if he continued to afford these annual highlights.

In August, 1869, yet another letter came from Ellison – the subject, familiar: "Dear Father, I have succeeded in getting one hundred dollars for six or eight weeks of Aunt Sally Phipps and thee must send me an order on Uncle Powell for that amount." Evidently Amos had also requested farm supplies from Ellison's store. Ellison discussed the bill of lading and agreed to send more of any needed items. Then, back to money, he wrote, "If I can let thee have any more I will do so but don't go into debt with that expectation… There is no use getting discouraged or low spirited. I think it will be best to sell part and get out of debt. There is nothing that worries one so much as being in debt. Then thee can go to work and make a nice little home and take Rebecca and Thomas to live with thee."[2] Under the obvious pressures of financial disappointments, Amos may not have been much cheered by the next letter he received.

Amos' daughter Rebecca wrote four days after Christmas voicing her disappointment at not having him visit her in Philadelphia: "Santa Claus brought me a new dress – 2 yds – from Brother [Ellison], a writing desk, and so much candy that I am sick. I was in hopes he would bring Father, but he did not." She also reminded him that he had forgotten to send her some promised oranges. Rebecca mentioned that she hoped to come to Florida to see him soon.

The new decade brought little change to the financial theme of Ellison Stackhouse's letters. On April 4, 1870, he stated: "Dear Father, I expect thee has been looking for a letter from me quite anxiously. I have been disappointed about getting money as I wished, but through the kindness of Uncle John have just got this today – two hundred and twenty-five dollars." Ellison told Amos that his cousin Julia would pay $25 for the sewing machine Amos had in storage. Moving from money to family news, Ellison also reported that his sisters, Rebecca and Anna Mary, were well.

In Florida Amos continued to feel lonely, having the company only of James Cook, the twenty-one-year-old Black helper who lived with him. Soon he began to pay court to young Anna Myers, the daughter of Levi and Lucinda who lived next door. Early in the year 1871, just fifty-six days short of his fifty-second birthday, Amos Stackhouse began his third marriage.[3] The bride Anna would soon be twenty.

Whether before his wedding or soon afterwards, Amos made plans to relocate, this time to Warm Springs, North Carolina. He was likely lured by announcements in the Jacksonville newspaper or in one of the Philadelphia papers to which he subscribed. There is even a good chance that one of his siblings had sent him copies of the *New York Tribune*. As an attempt to encourage business in the poverty-stricken South, Northerners were trying "colonization," generally a plan to make money for Yankee investors. One of these groups, calling themselves *The Western North Carolina Cooperative Manufacturing and Agricultural Association*, purchased in December of 1870 almost 500 acres in Madison County, including the small but well-known hundred-acre resort of Warm Springs. This corporation was backed by the *New York Tribune* Company, whose president was Horace Greeley, a farmer's son from New Hampshire. Greeley and his *Tribune* newspaper carried tremendous public influence. Active in the Republican party, he would have been much read and admired by Amos Stackhouse and his relatives. Greeley's famous slogan, "Go West young man," might even have influenced Amos to leave Philadelphia in the first place. Greeley was no doubt familiar with the famous Warm Springs health resort, having visited there with his North Carolina-born wife. He delighted in agricultural concerns such as the promised productivity of rich alluvial river bottoms. The stockholders felt that the Warm Springs would be an excellent site for a town, and that they could make it a success.[4]

They began planning, among other things, to dam Spring Creek – a good-sized stream converging with the French Broad River at the rear of the Warm Springs hotel. On December 21, 1870, ten days after signing the lease mortgage and paying the down payment to James H. Rumbough of Warm Springs, the Association began publishing an eight-page newspaper called *The Colonist*. The dateline read "New York City and Warm Springs, N.C." In other large city newspapers, too, the WNC Cooperative Association advertised for people to buy shares and come to the new "colony." Needed, especially, were those skilled in wood, iron, and stonework, as well as farmers. Each shareholder was promised a building lot and accommodations in the large hotel until his home could be built. It was expected that with the abundance of wood on the mountains, wagon and furniture-making could become profitable businesses. "Western North Carolina and Eastern Tennessee must, and will, soon become the New England of the South," predicted *The Colonist*.[5]

Amos Stackhouse had been farming for twenty years, and before that, had had experience in his family's iron foundry. He would fit well into the Association's plans, and probably bought stock in the new endeavor.

Approaching Madison County, Amos had to travel the last miles of his journey by stagecoach on the Buncombe Turnpike. Officially opened in 1828, this became a fine road the full length of Buncombe County, connecting Greeneville, Tennessee to Greenville, South Carolina. Even after Madison County was created from the Western parts of Buncombe and Yancey Counties, the Buncombe Turnpike continued to be the main thoroughfare to Warm Springs.

Besides the many tourists headed for the mineral springs, at certain times of the year, the turnpike was filled with livestock being driven to market by farmers from Tennessee, Kentucky, and other points. These *drovers*, as they were called, walked along or rode a horse in the lead of hundreds of hogs, sheep, cattle, horses, mules, turkeys, or ducks, stopping at nightfall where they could find water and feed for the animals, and, hopefully, bed space and a hot meal for themselves. (Drovers often worked in pairs, the second one in the rear, making sure the stragglers didn't get lost.) Drover "stands" had sprung up every few miles to provide these needs, earning a fair living for the host.

The road had been a major trade route for years, but in anticipation of having rail connection through Buncombe and Madison, the Buncombe Turnpike Company in 1869 sold all its stock to the Western North Carolina Railroad Company. Some of the toll gates were removed, and the future of Warm Springs showed nothing but promise.

Traveling along the French Broad, Amos Stackhouse was struck with the natural beauty alongside, which had recently been described in the article "Picturesque America, On the French Broad River, North Carolina," in *Appleton's Journal*, November 1870. This weekly magazine of general literature, published in Massachusetts, lavishly described the French Broad's "wild and romantic course" from Asheville to the Tennessee line: "It cuts its way through mountain gorges of fearful height, runs dimpling among green hills, winds itself around mountain islands, whose heavy and tangled undergrowth, with their clinging vines and glowing flowers, are of a tropical luxuriance, slips sullen and dark between huge cliffs, rushes down rocky

Buncome Turnpike at Lovers Leap,
Warm Springs

declivities with a deafening roar, ever changeful in its wild beauty… A fine highway follows the banks of the river, often trespassing upon its waters as it is crowded by the overhanging cliffs."[6] Another writer, James Buckingham, from England, observed on his trip down this same road: "While on the left we could almost drop a stone into the water from the carriage window on that side, we could put out our hands and touch the rock of the perpendicular cliff on the other."[7]

Amos had always lived near a riverfront, but had never been so enclosed by mountains. He was now in the *Blue Ridge*, called the "unending mountains" by the Cherokee, while European settlers said, "You have to lie down and look up to see out."[8] A part of that great and ancient Appalachian system (named from the Appalaches, a local Indian tribe), the Blue Ridge mountain range extends from northern Georgia to Harrisburg, Pennsylvania. Furthermore, the western portion of the southern Blue Ridge network, called the Unaka Mountains, includes a number of mountain ranges, the best known being the Great Smoky Mountains. Warm Springs, N.C., nestled in the French Broad Valley basin, is surrounded by the Unakas and almost touches the Great Smokies.

These mountains, developed long before the Rockies, are among the world's oldest – 600 to 800 million years old – going back to what scientists have labeled the Precambrian period. Heat and pressure through the centuries have made the Blue Ridge rocks tougher and more resistant to erosion. "This and their great thicknesses, especially the Unakas, account for their high elevation even after many millions of years of erosion," writes one geographer.[9] (Amos would learn that Max Patch Mountain in southwestern Madison County was 4,629 feet high and was one of the most beautiful balds in the Appalachian chain.)

In fact, the entire Warm Springs area captured Amos' heart at once. Springtime here, so different from that of the prairie, displayed a lush variety of ferns and wildflowers, showy rhododendron and laurel, silverbell and dogwood, flame azalea and serviceberry. The many shades of green and the changing play of light and shadow on the rounded contours was as lovely as any painting Amos had seen in the museums of Philadelphia.

Photo by Edward Anthony, noted photographer, engineer and founder of Ansco Co.

Now, in sight of their destination, Amos and Anna, preparing to leave the turnpike, enjoyed the experience described by writer Constance Fennimore Woolson, niece of James Fennimore Cooper: "The approach to Warm Springs is very lovely. Crossing the river on a long bridge, we drove up to the large hotel which stands here alone, maintained in the heart of the wilderness by the maimed and the halt and the blind who come here to bathe in the magical waters. The springs bubble up from the ground in a large pool near the river's edge…"[10]

Verandahs wrapped three sides of the hotel's first floor and portions of the second, while the front one, facing the river, was two stories high, supported by thirteen round white columns over two feet through, and representing the thirteen original colonies. Several of the third-floor rooms had large individual balconies. There were also a few separate guest cottages on the grounds. Even to the well-traveled Amos Stackhouse, the old "White House," as it was often called, was impressive.

In the previous November, a journalist writing for *Appleton's Journal* had declared: "A more beautiful spot could scarcely be found. The pleasant hotel and cottages in the midst of the grounds and under the shelter of the noblest old trees; the Warm Springs itself, in whose limpid waters it is almost impossible to sink, and whose temperature stands at eighty degrees the year around; the French Broad in its varied course almost encircling the plateau on which the hotel is built, and filling the air with its rushing music; the everlasting hills rising around; the lofty mountains majestic and fatherly,

By Rufus Morgan, leading Civil War photographer; husband of Mary Devereux Clarke, poet; and father of Bayard Wooten, renowned female North Carolina photographer.

standing with a saintly presence like a benediction over the gentle valley, give one the impression irresistibly of security and protection."[11]

Whether or not Amos had bought stock in the new Warm Springs enterprise, he would likely have stayed at the famous hotel, there being no other accommodations except, possibly, a home or two with spare rooms to let. There was no village, no school, no church. The resort on the river consisted of widely scattered log cabins, a few framed dwellings, the large hotel and the new four-story Victorian mansion (called "Rutland") built by James Henry Holcombe Rumbough on the river's west bank, overlooking the springs.

Born in Virginia, Rumbough had come from Greeneville, Tennessee, as the war heated up, operating the hotel and living there until 1868 or 1869 when he built his handsome frame and clapboard house. A small one-story brick building toward the rear of the hotel was said to be the oldest structure on the premises. Called Hampton Cottage, it had been built – reliable sources stated – for General Wade Hampton's own use. Shortly after the mineral springs were discovered by white men in 1778, tourists began coming from South Carolina to escape the summer heat and mosquitoes of their Low Country. The bricks for Hampton Cottage had come from England as ship's ballast, then hauled to the mountains from South Carolina's coast by wagons.[12] James Rumbough, his wife Carrie, and their six children lived in the brick cottage when they first came from Tennessee. Although his younger brother Thomas had been a Captain in the Confederacy (and killed in battle),[13] James Rumbough had served more behind the lines by procuring horses and supplies. He was not a military officer, but his friends came to title him "Colonel."[14] Although large estate owners were often called "Squire," the designation "Colonel" took precedence over "Squire" for any important man who had served in the War. Rumbough did own the nearly six hundred acres that would become the town of Hot Springs. He was a literate man and civic-minded, owned a large fancy home, wore suits and ties and earned his living without "sweat of brow" – all befitting the Southern "Colonel" description. Besides operating the Warm Springs hotel, he ran the stage coach line for a few years.[15] "Colonel" Rumbough would become acquainted with Amos Stackhouse soon after his arrival to the springs and they would become lifelong friends.

On May 29, 1871, Amos applied for the position of Warm Springs Postmaster, as had the WNC Cooperative president, Dwight S. Elliott, three weeks earlier.[16] Both, evidently, were turned down in favor of William A. Morgan, who took over June 22, 1871.[17] According to Stackhouse family tradition, Amos served as Warm Springs postmaster, suggesting that, with his background experience, he could have, in the beginning, worked at the hotel as clerk, handling postmaster duties, all but signing government reports.

Oath signed by Amos Stackhouse, May 29, 1871, Warm Springs, N.C.

Amos eventually took over Rumbough's drovers' stand and stagecoach stop on the turnpike opposite the Warm Springs hotel where the wooden bridge crossed the French Broad.[18] He planted crops to meet the needs of the various driven stock and horse teams. The small riverside store was probably the only one in the area of the springs, having grown out of the stand operated by James E. Patton, Warm Springs owner from 1831 to 1862.[19] The nearest stock stand to the north of Amos was C.T. Garrett's, two miles down the river, and the closest one in the other direction was Farnsworth's, about three miles upriver where the Big Laurel drained into the French Broad. These stock stands were needed every two or three miles – the distance most stock could travel in a day's time. If dusk fell before reaching a "stand," turkeys would go to roost in the trees, forcing the drover to bed down on the spot, no matter how damp or rocky the ground.

Stackhouse store location of 1870s circled in this 1960s photo of Hot Springs bridge
(by Linda Eddington).

The stock-drive seasons posed long busy work days for Amos and Anna Stackhouse – building and repairing the pens (Amos had three), planting, harvesting and storing enormous quantities of corn and other grains, procuring food and merchandise for the drovers and their helpers.[20] However, the droves were exciting and colorful with the noisy cries, grunts, squawks and bleats of the various animals, accompanied by the pounding of hooves, flapping of wings and snapping of the drover's whip, usually a piece of bright red flannel tied to its lash end.[21]

Still, the most active period along the life of the Buncombe Turnpike had been before the Civil War. Because of the economy during the late sixties, trade of all kinds in the South was diminished, but the turnpike traffic had lessened for another reason: many farmers now shipped by train. Railroads had been built in some states, making possible the alternate route to Augusta, Charleston and other points. In 1869 a railroad line had reached Wolf Creek, Tennessee, only a few miles below Warm Springs. Merchants in Asheville,

Marshall (Madison's county seat), and places in between bought their manufactured goods in northern cities, had them sent by rail to Morristown, Tennessee, then to Wolf Creek after the railroad reached that point. The merchants then hauled their orders in wagons the rest of the way along the turnpike.[22] Two years before Amos arrived, the WNC Railroad had reached Old Fort in McDowell County, adjoining Buncombe on the East.

As the source of his living, the Buncombe Turnpike became important to Amos Stackhouse, who enjoyed learning its history. Closely following the French Broad, it had been built on the bed of the old Catawba Trail, a major Indian route of the Southern Appalachians.[23] Farmers up and down the river regularly plowed up flintstones, spearheads and other Indian relics. According to tradition, the area around Warm Springs had, before the white people moved in, never been used for dwellings, but only hunting grounds, or as a sacred place for powwows and healing. In the late 19th century, Cherokee would walk from their reservation two counties away, dragging their sick on litters to drink and bathe again in the spring's curative waters. Some historians believe that Hernando DeSoto, on his western North Carolina exploration in 1540, had also come down this Indian trail searching for valuable minerals.

During the Great Rebellion, the Buncombe Turnpike served troops of both sides and would be the center of many events described to Amos as a newcomer. One such was the killing of Major John W. Woodfin during the autumn of 1863 by Union forces holding the Warm Springs hotel. As the Major led his men across the French Broad bridge, he was easily picked off by riflemen lining the upstairs verandah. "His body lay on the hotel porch all night with but one to watch over it, a Mrs. Rumbough," stated the *Asheville Citizen-Times* years later.[24] Under a truce flag the next day, an escort was sent to bring Woodfin to Asheville for burial.

Moreover, toward the war's end, the Warm Springs bridge was again the site of strife for Rumbough's wife, Carrie. Learning that the Yankees were coming up the pike, Mrs. Rumbough and a Negro servant, "Uncle Goen," slipped out after dark and burned the river bridge to keep the soldiers from crossing to the hotel. On the other side was the stagecoach stop (where Amos now lived). When the next stage came along, the Yankees took the doors off the coach and used it to paddle across the river anyway.[25]

Either on this occasion or an earlier one, Mrs. Rumbough was "required" by the Union officers to play her square rosewood piano for their dancing entertainment. Then, yet another day, Carrie heard that raiders were in the neighborhood, so she had floor boards taken up and her fine saddle horse hidden underneath, along with the good silver, crystal, and china. The mare was saved, but in the confined space, she had stepped on some of the dishes, providing grim reminders of the war to future family diners.[26]

For some time after the war, hostilities continued in Madison County, where, as in most of the rest of the country, allegiance had been divided between the North and the South. Because of its mountainous isolation, Madison County was home to many settlers who exhibited traces of Elizabethan language and feelings of loyalty to the united government for which it had fought only two generations back. There was no quarrel with the North from highland farmers, only a few of whom owned slaves, and who were seldom bothered by the federal officials. Consequently, when word of the draft reached Madison, many men walked or rode their horses over the ridges to Greeneville, Tennessee, to enlist for the Union. An equal number, or more, signed up with the Confederate companies, pitting cousin against cousin, and sometimes, brother against brother. Throughout the war and for several years afterwards, small outlaw bands along the Tennessee-North Carolina borders, usually Union sympathizers, raided homes of Confederate supporters, taking animals, food, and anything else of worth. When news came that these renegades were approaching, people tried to hide their valuables, but their livestock was either confiscated or scattered far up into the mountains. At one point the marauders tried to take away the beloved riding horse of Bessie, the Rumbough's young daughter, but the girl threw herself around the animal's neck, begging tearfully to keep her pet. Finally, the thieves gave in to her pleadings and left the horse there.[27]

In fact, during the first decade, at least, following the Great Rebellion, the highlanders were beset with "just plain rogueing," as they described it, calling up an old term from their British roots. Even Ku Klux Klan activities crept toward the mountains from the Piedmont. Dense growth and rough terrain of the ridges and hollows had provided natural cover for bushwhackers, renegades and deserters from all over, fleeing to the hills to hide. "Often it meant a dual plague descending on the countryside, the deserters and their pursuers, and it was difficult to tell which stripped the farms down the most," wrote Glen Tucker in his book about Zeb Vance.[28] Still another historian observed that in Western North Carolina, "The Civil War ended, but bitterness between opposing factions lasted for years."[29]

Less than a decade old in 1871, these stories would be heard by Amos, perhaps stirring cautiousness in his mind. Older tales, told now more for entertainment than warning, were grisly hair-raisers about trickery, robbery and murder of many unfortunate travelers in the Buncombe Turnpike's early history.

Nonetheless, the Stackhouses surely felt safe in this place on the Turnpike, despite the fact that it was primitive and sparsely settled. There had been no recorded threat of Indian hostility since the late 1700s when blockhouses were built along the French Broad at four stations, beginning at the Warm Springs and moving north. Historian Ramsey wrote that on September 27, 1793, Indians had been seen at Warm Springs and at another location, "Probably watching the guards who were stationed for the protection of the frontier on the French Broad."[30]

Although he would find many differences between the French Broad and the St. Johns' basins, peace-loving Amos looked forward to his new situation.

1 Author's private papers.
2 Ibid.
3 Duval County, Florida, Register of Deeds, Bk.2, p.821.
4 *Asheville Citizen-Times*, Nov. 30, 1983.
5 Ibid.
6 *Appletons' Journal of Literature, Science and Art*, Vol. IV, p.644.
7 Wellman, Manly Wade. *The Kingdom of Madison*. Chapel Hill: UNC Press, 1973, p.49.
8 Robinson, Cecilia C., Ed. *The Land of the South*, Birmingham, Ala.: Oxmoor House, 1989, p.144.
9 Ibid., p.147.
10 Woolson, Constance Fennimore. "The French Broad." *Harper's New Monthly Magazine*. Apr., 1875, p.635.
11 *Appletons'*, Vol. LV., p.644.
12 Dotterer, Elizabeth R.B.; Izlar, S.O.; Smith, Mary L.I., Interviews.
13 Doughty, Richard H. *Greeneville: One Hundred Year Portrait*. Kingsport, Tenn.: Kingsport Press, 1974, pp. 218, 222.
14 Dotterer, E. and Izlar, S. Interviews.
15 Arthur, John Preston. *Western North Carolina, A History*. Raleigh: Edwards & Broughton Printing Co., 1914, p.242.
16 Private papers.
17 Stroupe, Vernon S. *Postoffices and Postmasters of N.C., Vol.II*. Charlotte: N.C. Postal History Society. 1996, p.2-274.
18 Private papers.
Dotterer, Elizabeth R.B.. Interview, 1989;
Aumiller, Nancy Stackhouse. Interview, 1997.
19 Arthur, p.286.
20 Aumiller, 1997.
21 Sondley, F.A. *A History of Buncombe County*. Asheville, N.C.: The Advocate Printing Co., 1930, p.665.
22 Ibid.
23 Myer, Wm. E. *Indian Trails of the Southeast*. Nashville, TN: Blue and Gray Press, 1971, reprint.
Allen, Martha Norburn. *Asheville and Land of the Sky*. Charlotte, N.C.: Heritage House, 1960, p.48.
24 *Asheville Times*, Dec. 11, 1927, Sect. B, p.1.
25 Izlar, Mildred Hill. Interview, 5-16-1960.
Baker, Martha Rumbough. *Memories of Another Day*. Baltimore: Gateway Press, 1986, p.112.
26 Izlar, Sydney O. Letter, Dec. 11, 1989.
27 Dotterer, interview, 1987.
28 Tucker, Glen. *Zeb Vance, Champion of Personal Freedom*. New York; Bobbs-Merrill Co., 1963, p.313.
29 Van Noppen, Ina W. and John J. *Western North Carolina Since the Civil War*. Boone, N.C.: Appalachian Consortium Press, 1973, p.17.
30 Ramsey, J.G.M. *Annals of Tennessee*. Kingsport, Tenn., Kingsport Press, 1926 reprint, p.569.

Chapter Five

Amos Stackhouse had been content in his new situation less than a year when, to his surprise, the Warm Springs hotel and grounds were back in the hands of J.H. and Carrie Rumbough. The Western North Carolina Cooperative Manufacturing and Agricultural Association evidently had failed to pay the agreed money. One reason might have been linked to Horace Greeley's preoccupation with his presidential nomination and his wife's fatal illness.[1] The corporation had, however, built the promised dam (thereafter known as "Colony Dam") across Spring Creek about a mile above the hotel, providing a lasting benefit to the resort settlement. WNC Co-Op had also brought a few more settlers besides Amos who would remain in the beautiful, health-giving place. There were the Turners and McFalls from South Carolina, and the Garenflos, French Huguenots – all skilled woodworkers, destined to use their craft in the village's development. The DeForrest family would also contribute, as would the Sowers family.* However, the most valuable asset left by the Co-Op might have been its publicity. While long frequented by Southerners, Warm Springs had finally caught the attention of New Yorkers.

The agreement between the Rumboughs and the WNC Co-Op, made in December, 1870, had called for a down payment of $500 with another $4,500 on the 15th of January, 1871, and followed by another payment of $16,666.67, due one year later, and a final amount of $16,666.67 more to be paid on January 1, 1874, bringing the total to $70,000.[2] Perhaps there were too few persons answering the call to colonization, making it impossible to establish the expected manufacturing and agricultural operations. Possibly, not enough stock was sold to meet the needed investment. Moreover, the promised railroad connection down the French Broad had stopped at the same time in McDowell County, when the Western North Carolina Railroad officials, Swepson and Littlefield, absconded with the project funds.[3] It could be that Warm Springs Co-Op had stock in the railroad, too, since it would have greatly affected their plans for the resort. Whatever the reason for the Springs mortgage failure, it prompted the Rumboughs to sell the repossessed 150 acres including the hotel to W.W. Rollins and Charles Sowers on June 5, 1872. In a subsequent transaction on June 6th, Rollins and Sowers sold Rumbough a third interest in the same property.[4] (Rumbough still controlled the "three or four hundred" outlying acres of the small valley surrounding Warm Springs.)

One of Rumbough's partners was William Wallace Rollins, a lawyer who owned a large tobacco farm near Marshall. He had served on the five-man commission to investigate the Western North Carolina Railroad scandal in 1870 and would continue to work for the completion of the rail connection to Tennessee through Warm Springs.[5] Rollins, Sowers and Rumbough began planning for remodeling to receive tourists who would arrive eventually by rail.

The next year, on June 12, the Asheville paper reported from Warm Springs: "This celebrated watering place in Madison County, on the line of Clemmons' Great Western Stage route, within 8 miles of…railroad

* A DeForrest daughter married N.J. Lance, prominent Hot Springs leader. Sowers, too, was a community and church leader. (From unpublished family papers.)

connection, is being put out in readiness for the usually large number of guests who gather to spend the summer. The scenery and grounds are unsurpassed for beauty."[6] Elsewhere in the same issue, an advertisement explained that the Clemmons Stage line left Old Fort railroad terminal at two p.m. every day but Sunday, reaching Asheville at 8 p.m. The next day it connected with the Cumberland Gap, Cincinnati and Charleston railroad at Wolf Creek, Tennessee, by way of Warm Springs at 8 p.m.

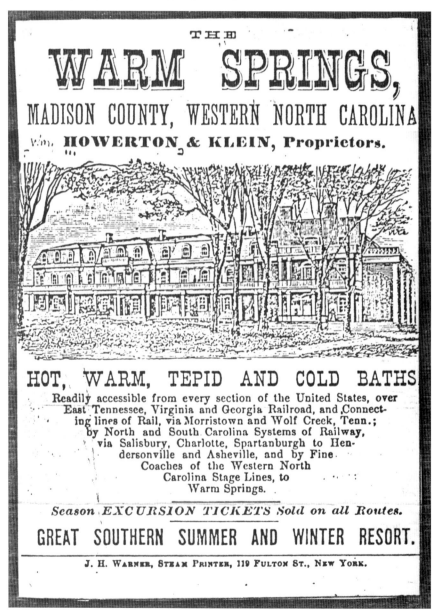

Newspaper advertisement describing stage coach connections.

Back Cover from 1876 almanac advertising Amos' store on the Buncombe Turnpike.

We cannot know how deeply involved Amos Stackhouse had been with the Western North Carolina Railroad or the Colony Co-Op. He might have lost money from investments in either or both, or he might have been an interested, independent onlooker. Nonetheless, Amos did not pull up stakes, but stayed on at Warm Springs and participated in its further development.

Even though there was little community life beyond the hotel grounds, it is doubtful that Amos and Anna took part in the hotel's dining and dancing. Occasionally, however, a visiting minister or priest held worship services for hotel guests and owners, and to these services the Stackhouses would have been invited. As to his own denomination of Friends, Amos missed his lifelong participation, but the nearest Meeting was in the Piedmont or over in Tennessee; Asheville did not acquire one for almost another century.[7]

The sparsely populated Warm Springs settlement did not present a lonely life, however, for Amos and Anna, living as they did on a public highway. The store had people coming and going daily and would have been a clearinghouse for news from far and near. Besides the drovers who still preferred the familiar method of walking their wares through, there were the stagecoach travelers, plus the few people living around the springs and the settlers on the surrounding mountains who trudged to Amos' store with their "barter" on their backs.

Amos stocked salt, sugar, coffee, meal and flour staples; shoes, boots and clothing; farming tools and harness; tobacco, snuff and candy; even a pint of bitters for the thirsty traveler. As an additional convenience, he kept a credit ledger for those who needed to pay at a later date.[8] To meet his own needs and those of his customers, Amos studied books about diagnosing and treating diseases, as well as those about veterinary medicine. A thick volume, *The Household Physician*, was his favorite reference, being well-indexed and illustrated, with proper methods and equipment detailed for preparing prescriptions and formulas. Many potions were derived from plants found in the area, such as black cohosh, goldenseal, bloodroot and boneset, to name a few.[9] Amos soon became an indispensable fixture on the Turnpike, serving the settlement as merchant, grocer, ticket agent, and pharmacist.

Two of Stackhouse's turnpike neighbors were the Garretts and the Oettingers, both of whom owned large farms and operated drovers' stands. Two miles down the river below Warm Springs, Charles Thomas "Tom" Garrett and his brother William Neilson "Bill" Garrett, Confederate officers, had returned from Johnston Island prison in Ohio to find the plantation responsibilities on their young shoulders. Their father, James Garrett, had been "murdered at his own door by bushwhackers, presumably Unionists, and had fallen back into the arms of his wife and daughters."[10] (The attack obviously came without warning, for the Garretts had a secret tunnel leading from house to river.) James had come from South Carolina to marry Jane Neilson, daughter of Scottish-born William Neilson, Warm Springs founder and first postmaster. At low cost from grants and purchases, Neilson acquired lands on both sides of the French Broad. One of his sons received the west bank property, including the mineral springs and tavern, while his daughters, Jane and Sarah, inherited some of the east bank acres. A sister of Tom and Bill Garrett – Mary Neilson Garrett – also lived on the large Garrett farm and was married to Edward Sevier, grandnephew of Tennessee's famous governor, John Sevier, also of French Huguenot lineage.[11]

About the time of the war, or just after, Henry Oettinger and his wife Catherine from Tennessee had built a large brick home on their six hundred-plus acres. Located three miles north of Warm Springs, the Oettingers' place was on the French Broad's west bank, reached by boat from the turnpike. After receiving a state ferry charter in 1869, Henry became known up and down the turnpike as "the ferryman," as well as drover host.

"These drovers… were our most outstanding citizens; men who owned the best farms," wrote a Tennessee historian, many years later.[12] Besides this particular class of mountaineers who had used slaves to work their large plantings before the war, and who could afford to send their children away to school, there were two others, at least, whom Amos would soon distinguish. A few Western North Carolinians were able to "get by" on their small farms with the help of their children or with one or two hired hands, while the third class of local people owned no land, but managed by renting or sharecropping. Amos learned to get along with all three groups and to learn from each. As a missionary at Warm Springs would later state, "There are as many different grades or classes of mountain people as there are… in a large village in the North. When we think of all mountain people as ignorant and poor we make a great mistake."[13]

Amos also had to learn his new neighbors' dialect, which was distinct due to their isolation. Their speech and ways reflected their Scot-Irish and Old English ancestry, much as Amos' "plain language" pointed to his Quaker heritage. "It is true that mountain speech is developed from Elizabethan English, in which an unusually large number of the old words have survived," declared writer James Watt Raine fifty years later. Words like *clum* for climbed, *drug* for dragged, *wropt* for wrapped, and *holp* for helped came straight from Chaucer, Shakespeare, and the King James Bible. Explaining further, Raine says: "They go back to Chaucer and form plurals by adding *es*, especially in words ending with *st*; as post*es*, beast*es*, frost*es*, nest*es*, in which cases the es forms a second syllable… The habit transfers occasionally to verbs; 'Hit cost*es* a lot,' or 'The rope twist*es* all up.' And they still *gorm* their shoes with sticky mud."[14]

In addition to his new friends and acquaintances, Amos kept up with old friends and relatives by mail and through Philadelphia newspaper subscriptions. His spinster sister Anna wrote on March 24, 1873: "Thy kind letter was received last seventh day evening and thy present very timely… Daniel [a nephew] sent $100 at New Year's with which I paid 6 months' rent and have only $10 left… I am glad to hear thee is doing so well in thy business." After four pages of news about family members, friends and weather, Anna chastised Amos:

> "I was so sorry to hear of thy marrying again. I know the law sanctions divorces, but I do not think it was right while Anna was living. You married until death should part you. Besides I thought thee wanted to have a home for Rebecca and Thomas. Aunt Sarah does not know – we never speak to anyone about it. It is unpleasant to us."

His sister did not hide her disappointment in Amos, but she closed her letter saying, "Thee must give my love to thy wife and accept a large share thyself, from thy affectionate sister, Anna."[15]

Since she did not discuss Amos' situation, she evidently had not heard that the month before, his wife had delivered a son, Amos, Jr., on their second wedding anniversary. Nor did his sister comment on another family event upcoming and important to Amos – the marriage in April of his son Ellison to Ella Walton, daughter of Lewis Love Walton and Elizabeth Stockton Walton, Philadelphia Quakers. Ella's father, a hardware merchant, had died at age sixty-six in 1867.[16]

Also in April, 1874, Amos received a letter from his brother Charles Dilworth in Edgemont, near Philadelphia. He was pleased because he rarely heard from Charles, with whom he had worked in the foundry business. Charles asked, "How is my little nephew coming on, called Amos? Tell him to be a good boy and… his Uncle Charley will come see him by and by." On the fourth and last page, Charles reflected, "After reading my letter over, I was quite at a loss to find how such nonsense will creep in anybody's head, such as penned in this letter. However, time changes man, and hope we will grow wise hereafter, even if thee is postmaster and I, a farmer. I could not dare write to any other of my brothers in such a manner, but I know thee was fond of talk and told many long yarns to amuse thy hearers." This reference to postmaster further supports the Stackhouse tradition that "Amos was postmaster at Warm Springs."[17]

In September a second son was born to Amos and Anna, named Frank Myers Stackhouse, but sadly he lived only five weeks and three days. As the autumn led to year's end, Amos would think back on 1874: It had taken away another child, but had given him a daughter-in-law. From his early upbringing, Amos was taught not to question the Maker's plan – all was ordered for the best. Putting aside his grieving, Amos found himself in position to observe firsthand, even to share in, the interesting and sometimes history-shaping events of Warm Springs.

BUNCOMBE TURNPIKE

"COMPLETED IN 1827 FROM SALUDA GAP TO BUNCOMBE COUNTY COURT HOUSE AND ALONG THE FRENCH BROAD RIVER BY WAY OF BARNARD'S AND WARM SPRINGS TO TENNESSEE LINE SERVED AS THE MAJOR TRADE ROUTE THROUGH MOUNTAINS OF WESTERN NORTH CAROLINA UNTIL 1882."

[1] The Standard Reference Work, Vol. IV, Chicago, 1927.

[2] Madison County Register of Deeds, Book E, p.481.

[3] Van Noppen, Ina W. and John J. *Western North Carolina Since the Civil War*. Boone, N.C.: Appalachian Consortium Press, 1973, p.256.
Sondley, F.A. *A History of Buncombe County*. Asheville, N.C.: The Advocate Printing Co., 1930, p.630.

[4] Madison County Register of Deeds. Book F pp.113, 147.

[5] Arthur, John Preston. *Western North Carolina, A History*. Raleigh: Edwards & Broughton Printing Co., 1914, p.462.

[6] *N.C. Citizen*, Asheville, June 12, 1873, p.2.

[7] Neal, Dale. *Asheville Citizen-Times*, June 7, 2000, p. A4.

[8] Author's private papers.

[9] Warren, Ira, A.M., M.D. *The Household Physician*. Boston: Ira Bradley & Co., 1872.

[10] Tucker, Glen. *Zeb Vance, Champion of Personal Freedom*. New York; Bobbs-Merrill Co., 1963, p.307.

[11] Buncombe County Land Records, Will Records; Madison Co. Census.

[12] O'Dell, Ruth Webb. *Over the Misty Blue Hills*. Easley, S.C.: Southern Historical Press, 1982 reprint, p.78.

[13] Painter, J.B. *Season of Dorland-Bell*, Boone, N.C.: Appalachian Consortium Press, 1996, p.66.

[14] Raine, James Watt. *The Land of Saddle-bags*. New York: Council of Women for Home Missions, 1924, pp. 96, 97.

[15] Private papers.

[16] Swayne, Norman Walton. *Byberry Waltons, An Account of Four English Brothers*. Decorah, Iowa: Anundsen Pub. Co., 1989, reprint, pp. 280, 489.

[17] Private papers.

Amos Stackhouse's medical books and box of dried Buchu leaves used in his pharmacist role.

Chapter Six

Whether by the owners' design or by happenstance, 1875 would carry several instances of advantage and advertisement for Warm Springs. As hotel patronage increased, so did the need for employees, which, in turn, brought more people to the settlement and more customers to Amos.

It began in April when *Harper's New Monthly Magazine* in New York featured "The French Broad" by Constance Fennimore Woolson. The twenty-page travel story was illustrated with eight accurately detailed engravings of the French Broad and Warm Springs, plus seven more of the surrounding mountain area. Moreover, the author's word pictures were true to fact:

> "The road but one inch wider than our wheels, and ponderous mountain wagons, drawn by oxen, thinking nothing of coming crashing and creaking around every corner... meeting the three-horse Tennessee stage on its way to Asheville... The river grew more wildly beautiful with every western mile, the cliffs on each side towering above us almost perpendicularly hundreds of feet... Passing Laurel Creek with the Walnut mountain behind us, we came in sight of Mountain Island."[1]

Woolson also alluded to the abandoned Western North Carolina Railroad project, writing:

> "I have noticed a phantom pursuing us all the way from the other side of the Blue Ridge... ruined culverts, half-excavated tunnels, shadowy grading and lines of levels. I have even fancied that I heard a spirit whistle." Whereupon the reply came: 'The ghost of the mountain railroad. Swindlers made off with all the money, the robbed mountaineers gloomily make fences of the ties – all that is left to them.'"[2]

Oddly enough that ghost became less of an apparition on June 22, 1875, when the Western North Carolina Railroad was auctioned by federal court order at Salisbury, and purchased by the State for $850,000. The governor named Warm Springs partner W.W. Rollins to a three-man commission in charge.[3] Having no idea that it would still take nearly a decade for trains to reach Warm Springs, Amos and his neighbors thrilled at this renewed start. The state agreed, also, to furnish convict labor, a fact mentioned in an Asheville newspaper five months later: "The Striped Boys have gone to work in earnest on our W.N.C. Road."[4]

In the meantime, during the summer of '75, the Warm Springs resort manager placed a long advertisement on the front page of the newspaper in Asheville and likely other cities, stating:

> "These Springs are... easy of access from all Southern cities by all the lines of railroad converging in East Tennessee at Morristown... And from the Eastern Cities by railroad to Old Fort, thence by coach to Asheville and down the banks of the French Broad... All the accessories to pleasant amusement are at the command of the guests; croquet grounds, ball room, band of music, bar, billiards, bowling alley, livery stable, trout fishing – not 20 miles distant – but at the very doors. Rates of board – $40.00

per month, $12.00 per week; $2.00 per day; children and servants, half-price. As references – Gen'l Braxton Bragg, John S. Holmes, Esq., and others."[5]

Rufus Morgan photo titled: "Paint Rock on the French Broad Near Warm Springs." Gen'rl Braxton Bragg (for whom Fort Bragg is named) in foreground. N.C. Dept. Archives & History

Calling further attention to the French Broad, Warm Springs, and western North Carolina was the book *The Land of the Sky, Adventures* in

Mountain By-Ways, written by Frances Fisher, a native of Salisbury (using her pen name, Christian Reid). Like *Harper's* April publication by Woolson, and just as factual, Miss Fisher's novel resulted from years of first-hand trip experiences she had had when she vacationed in the mountains with her family.[6] Of the forty-six works published during her lifetime – many having appeared in the widely-read *Lippincott's* and *Appletons'* – *Land of the Sky*, her tenth book, and her best known, gave the region of western North Carolina its lasting title, first appearing in the September 4, 1875, *Appleton's Journal*. The New York magazine featured one chapter each week (a few issues excepted), ending on February 19, 1876.[7]

Since quite a portion of this book was set in and around Warm Springs, Miss Fisher no doubt did much of her writing at the hotel during 1873 and '74, and might have met Amos Stackhouse at the river crossroad. An avid reader, Amos would follow with interest Miss Fisher's "travelogue" about his new area. "No summer resort in the country possesses greater advantages," she wrote, as she described both its strong points and weak ones. Her fictional characters enjoyed the mineral baths, shaded lawns, hiking trails and other entertainments of the hotel, thus providing the hotel further advertisement.[8]

Later the same month, a journalist from the Vicksburg, Mississippi *Monitor* visited Warm Springs and wrote yet another article luring guests with details about the "beautiful scenery" and the "literary celebrities" staying there. Her three-column composition appeared in the *Asheville Citizen* paper as well as the *Monitor*.[9] Besides authors from Memphis, Baltimore, and Atlanta, Frances Fisher was there again. Other Warm Springs visitors noted in this article included Winnie Davis, Jefferson Davis' youngest daughter, and both the daughter and the wife of Stonewall Jackson, Julia and Mary Anna Morris Jackson. "The company at Warm Springs hotel was, almost without exception, composed of the elite of Southern society, the majority being from Georgia and Tennessee, though, I believe that each Southern state had some representative," wrote the lady who identified herself simply as "a Vicksburgeress." "In natural beauty, the resort far surpasses that famous resort of the Northern fashionables, and railroad facilities are all that is needed to make it the most popular resort South of Mason and Dixon's line," she concluded.[10]

Indeed, the promised railroad was the speculation of many conversations and newspaper articles. One Asheville merchant advertised his wares as "the best to be had, RAILROAD OR NOT."[11]

On November 25, 1875, another significant Warm Springs item in the Asheville daily declared: "Today is the winter of discontent made glorious summer at Warm Springs. Four hearts are made to beat as two, and so on. Capt. Rumbough of the Warm Springs company loses two accomplished daughters and gains two charming sons-in-law."[12] In a double wedding at Rumbough's home "Rutland," his daughter Mary Lee ("Bonnie") married Beverly W. Hill from Virginia, while his daughter Elizabeth Kate Mae ("Bessie") took Andrew ("Frank") Johnson, Jr., as her husband. B.W. Hill would work for development in the Warm Springs village, becoming its first mayor, and Frank Johnson, youngest son of the 17th president, would bring a certain amount of fame to the resort. Both men soon built large imposing dwellings, broadening the settlement's boundaries.

It is doubtful that Amos and Anna Stackhouse, though friends of the

Rumboughs, would have been invited to the wedding, since the deaths of both President Johnson and Jacob Rumbough (grandfather of Bonnie and Bessie) the last week of July would likely have made the affair a quiet one for the family.[13]

Amos' family, too, increased early in the next year. His granddaughter, Laura, was born in Philadelphia to Ellison and Ella on January 24, 1876. Then his own wife gave birth, three weeks later, to her first daughter, Edith, named for Amos' mother. Once again, however, the infant lived only eleven days, even Amos' *Household Physician* failing to save her.[14]

On his spring buying trip North, Amos took along three-year-old Amos, Jr., both to lessen Anna's responsibilities during Amos' absence and to answer the many relatives' requests to "see the baby." Their journey began by crossing the river at their door, continuing past the hotel and on down the Shut-In road to Frank Lawson's stock stand, to Wolf Creek just across the Tennessee line. Here Amos would catch the train to Morristown and on to Pennsylvania – surely exciting for young Amos.

Anna had exacted a promise from her husband to write daily, as she was anxious about her only child. But in his letter from Morristown, Amos explained, "The train for Wolf Creek left at one o'clock instead of two, so I will put this in the office to go tomorrow. I will give you an account of our journey so far. After I left you the boy was very quiet. Broke a spring or bolt off the wagon and stopped at Lawson's $1/2$ hour to get it fixed. Amos fell asleep on the road but at Wolf Creek was delighted with everything – went in the kitchen and made himself at home and talked to all the men very familiarly." Unfortunately, the next four pages of this six-page letter have been lost through the years. On page six, Amos advises Anna about store business, mentioning some freight evidently being held at the depot for Amos to pick up on his way back home. He says:

> "If you run out of soda, there's a $1/2$ keg at Wolf Creek, also 2 casks coffee. Do not sell flour for less than $4 1/2$ cts. I forgot to fix those two room doors in the manner spoken of. So you must fix them and I hope you will do just as I wish about them. Never allow that front door to stand open. Perhaps you had better nail a block on the floor or pay attention to my wishes in this particular, for I think you will try to, but others will not think of it. Write me at Ellison's next Sunday or perhaps Saturday would be best. I will write first chance. With a great deal of love, I will close. Affectionately, Amos."[15]

Possibly his reference to securing the doors was to prevent thievery while he was not there to watch the front, or it might have been a matter of Amos' concern about Anna's personal safety. According to family tradition, the trip to Philadelphia was a milestone for Amos, Jr.: "He left home in skirts and came back in britches." The train rides, the large boats on the Delaware, the city buildings and the meeting of cousins and half-brothers, would all stay in young Amos' memory for the rest of his life.[16]

Amos' family continued to expand. In June, 1877, Ellison's wife gave birth to a son, Ellison Dilworth, in Phildelphia, and this was followed in September at Warm Springs by the birth of another son, Charles Dilworth, to Anna and Amos. This brought the total of living children to seven for the fifty-eight-year-old father.[17]

MAHAN & KELLER,
PHOTOGRAPHERS,
No. 1427 Ridge Avenue,   Philadelphia, Pa.

Amos Stackhouse, age 3

[1] Woolson, Constance Fennimore. "The French Broad." *Harper's New Monthly Magazine*. April, 1875, p.621.

[2] Ibid., p.634.

[3] Ibid.

[4] *N.C. Citizen*. Asheville, November 25, 1875, p.1.

[5] Ibid., August 28, 1875, p.1.

[6] Powell, Wm. S., *Dictionary of N.C. Biography*, Vol. 6, Chapel Hill: UNC Press, 1979.

[7] Reid, Christian. "The Land of the Sky," *Appletons' Journal*, Vol. 14 (Sept., 1875), p.644.

[8] IIbid.

[9] *N.C. Citizen*, Asheville, December 2, 1875, p.1.

[10] Ibid.

[11] Ibid.

[12] Ibid., November 25, 1875.

[13] Baker, Martha Rumbough. *Memories of Another Day*. Baltimore: Gateway Press, 1986, p.242.

[14] Author's private papers.

[15] Ibid.

[16] Aumiller, Nancy. Interview, 1998.

[17] Swayne, Norman Walton. *Byberry Waltons, An Account of Four English Brothers*. Decorah, Iowa: Anundsen Pub. Co., 1989, reprint, p.489.

Rear view of famous Warm Springs Hotel, located on French Broad River opposite Stackhouse store.

Chapter Seven

Now in his midlife, Amos Stackhouse still searched for a place "to light." His rented store at Warm Springs was profitable but located in the narrow hollow of Cascade Branch with no space to expand. The long-promised railroad would cross the river before it reached his store, leaving the turnpike rarely used. Amos hoped now to find farm land in the captivating southern Appalachians.

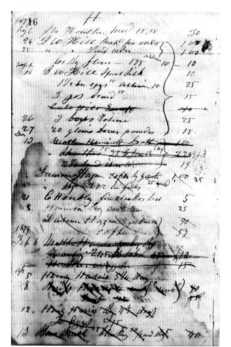 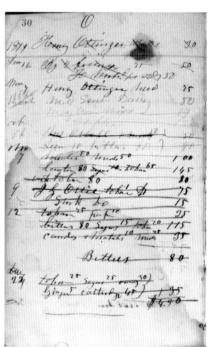

Sample Pages from Amos' Warm Springs store ledger

Meanwhile, he talked and listened to the customers of all classes who crossed his threshold. His ledger showed "medicines" charged to Henry Oettinger, as well as sugar, corn meal, coffee, tobacco, cartridges, matches and "bitters." Moreover, appearing in Amos' charge book were names of other large farmers along the river – John Bartley, J.H. Rumbough and his son Edd Rumbough, Charles "Tom" Garrett, George W. Gahagan and Ed Sevier. Mrs. Bonnie Hill bought silk thread at ten cents, two yards braid at fifteen cents, and 1 1/2 dozen eggs at 15 cents, among other items. Amos sold merchandise to Thomas Bailey, the official post master of Warm Springs, as well as to Dr. Howerton and Dr. Weir, the Warm Springs Hotel's physicians. Dave Robinson, carpenter, charged medicine several times. From the Spring Creek community ten miles away, and from the upriver settlements between Warm Springs and Marshall, came farmers Rob and Adolph Worley; George Bullman; Thomas Sawyer; Nathan Davis; Barney, John and Jim Landis; Miles Goforth; Robert Sams; James Dockery; Enoch Hensley; Malley Reeves; and Jesse Harrison. Other frequent customers were the Codys, Robertses, Goslins (Gosnells), Rectors, Cooks, Riddles, Hagans, Baldwins, Waldrups,

Andersons, Bakers, and Gunters – all Madison County pioneers whose descendants would be there a century and a quarter later.[1]

Since Warm Springs was the township voting and tax-listing center, people came in, at times, from a broad surrounding area. Amos' customers also included a few blacks, identified in his ledger as "col'd," one of whom was Prince Stokely, former slave of prominent East Tennessee produce farmers. Having little or no cash, many mountaineers traded corn, fodder, or their labor for his medicine and other essential items. They also brought him items on consignment which Amos sold to "A. David & Co." For instance:

19 $\frac{1}{2}$ lbs. hides at 9 cts. = 1.76
40 lbs. hides at 10 cts. = 4.00
91 lbs. goose feathers at 36 cts. = 32.76.

Amos paid fifty cents to have the hides and feathers hauled by wagon to the railroad at Wolf Creek. A hogshead of tobacco earned its grower $2.35.

A sense of Amos' stock can be gained from the following inventory: horse collar – 15 cts., a pair of ham strings – 25 cts., a lamp chimney – 10 cts, a lamp – 65 cts., a garden hoe – 80 cts., a bucket – 50 cts., Bradburn file – 75 cts., water dipper – 20 cts., bottle of laudanum – 15 cts., two bottles nitro – 25 cts., imported Buchu leaves – 20 cts., 8 yards of calico – 80 cts., a pair of brogans – $1.85. A farmer who brought his mare to Amos' horse paid $4.00. Other often-purchased wares were coffin tacks, rope, sole leather, curry combs, rifles, pistols, knives, indigo, gingham, hats, soap and bacon.[2]

Meanwhile, in addition to learning about his neighbors, Amos was interested in his natural surroundings, in the wide variety of trees, plants and wildflowers, many so unlike those he had known in Florida and on the prairie. At every free chance, especially on Sundays, Amos took long walks up and down the French Broad and its byways. One hike took him southwest past the Colony Dam along Spring Creek, so named because it flowed into the French Broad at the mineral spring.[3] He also became familiar with the Painted Rock five miles north down the turnpike at the Tennessee line (passing on the way Garretts, Seviers, and Oettinger's ferry landing). On top of the colored Painted Rock cliff, Amos likely admired piratebush, one of the rarest plants in the world, discovered at Painted Rock by botanist Samuel Buckley in the 1840's.[4]

As Amos walked upstream to the south, he would marvel that a road had been built between water's edge and the close, overhanging rock formations. One historian wrote: "It is probable that buffaloes made the first road over these mountains and that Indians, following where they led, made their trading paths by pursuing these highways."[5] Having no means of blasting and only crude hand tools for construction across the rocky, steep, thickly wooded mountains, each successive generation of users simply improved the route already begun. Since the ground alongside creeks and rivers had been leveled and cleared to a degree by frequent flooding, it offered the least resistance to the earliest travelers. Next, men pulled litters and sleds along the trail, then narrow two-wheeled carts, but it was 1795 before the French Broad route between Asheville and Warm Springs was navigated by a four-wheeled vehicle. Job Barnard, who owned a large farm between Marshall and Warm Springs, became widely known as the first man to bring a wagon through from Asheville to Knoxville. He managed the feat by placing the two large wheels on the lower side of the wagon and the two smaller ones on the upper side.

Then by drawing, pushing and even carrying the wagon at times, Barnard would get the cargo to Tennessee, at a charge of five dollars.[6]

In addition to his respect and appreciation at having the good road along the river, Amos would agree with travel writer Charles Lanman, who in 1848 had described the north-flowing French Broad as "one of the most beautiful rivers in this beautiful land… With regard to its botanical curiosities, it can safely be said that a more fruitful and interesting valley can nowhere be found in the Union."[7] Before Lanman's praises there had come those of Rev. Henry Boehm, friend and traveling companion of the famous Methodist bishop

Appletons' Journal, No. 87.]

PICTURESQUE AMERICA.

ON THE FRENCH BROAD RIVER, NORTH CAROLINA.

"THE LOVERS' LEAP"—AT EARLY SUNRISE.

Francis Asbury in the early 1800s: "This is an astonishing river in its meanderings through beautiful valleys and mountain gorges, with overhanging rocks. Here nature is seen in her beauty and grandeur."[8]

Less than a mile upstream from his home, Amos could see over the Warm Springs vale by climbing the renowned Lovers Leap point. This ancient rock cliff had been immortalized by the artist Harry Fenn, notable for his illustrations of Tennyson's "In Memoriam," Whittier's "Snowbound," and many others. In 1871, shortly before his travels to Warm Springs, he had helped found the American Water Color Society. Fenn's accurate and

"The Lover's Leap – Approach By Night" From Appleton's Journal, No, 87

effective representation of details was characteristic in his two depictions of Lovers Leap – one, "At Early Sunrise," the other "Approach by Night."[9] For an *Appleton's Journal* article, Fenn's drawings were further enhanced by two expert engravers – Joseph Harley and Henry Linton. In fact, the French Broad story joined several others in *Appleton's* "Picturesque America" series (edited by William Cullen Bryant), to be called "one of the greatest books of American illustration… containing the best landscapes engraved in the country."[10] These classic renderings of Lovers Leap in Warm Springs have commanded attention well over a century after their first publication.

Continuing past Lovers Leap, Amos' hiking brought him to Peters Rock, another imposing promontory that hugged the road and drew the interest of tourists and travel writers. The next landmark admired by visitors – Mountain Island – could be reached by hiring a boat and rowing oneself across. In 1850, *The Asheville Messenger* had declared:

> "Mountain Island is perhaps half a mile in length, and is really a little mountain, carpeted and decorated with all that rich variety of evergreens, forest trees, shrubbery, flowers, etc., which nature… bestows on our mountains generally. The river below is smooth, deep, narrow and polished as a mirror for some distance… "[11]

It was probably near this section of the French Broad, Amos mused, that a famous author's work had perpetuated one of the old tales told at Amos' store. In September, 1842, popular Southern historical novelist and poet James Gilmore Simms had composed at Warm Springs a long rhyming piece titled "Tselica, An Indian Legend," later published as "The Syren of Tselica."[12] Simms' introduction explained:

> "The following is a tradition of the Cherokees. The substance of the story, stripped of its poetry, is simply this: A young white man, heated with travel after descending the mountain, came to a river where cool waters delighted his eye, and tempted him to bathe. Lingering too long in the water he became chilled and died in consequence. The stream indicated is the French Broad in North Carolina. Its primitive name, or one of its names, seems to have been Tselica; hence its application to the nereid by whom, according to legend, the youth was beguiled into the stream…"[13]

Furthermore, during this same period, the same stretch of river inspired North Carolina-born editor and author Mary Bayard Devereaux Clarke to publish a poem, shorter than Simms', but again, using one of the legendary Indian names for the river – Tahkeeostee." From an old and prominent family, the widely-read Clarke, suffering from tuberculosis, often visited Warm Springs for "the cure." One critic declared: "Her poetry in the parlor was what Daniel Webster's speeches were in the Senate."[14]

> "Miss Marie Bowen, of Atlanta, who is making a tour in North Carolina and Virginia, giving recitations at the principal watering places, read on Monday, 31st of July to a Large audience at Warm Springs, N.C., the following poem, written for her by Mrs. Mary Bayard Clarke, descriptive of the scenery around the springs. As it has never before been published we give our readers a copy of it. There are over seven hundred visitors now at the springs."

French Broad. (Tahkeeostee.)

"Racing Waters," who can paint thee,
 With thy scenery wild and grand?
It would take a magic pencil,
 Guided by a master hand.

Here are towering rugged mountains,
 Granite rocks all scarred and gray,
Nature's alter, whence her incense
 Floats in wreaths of mist away.

At their feet thy murmuring waters
 Now are singing songs of praise,
Or in sonorous notes triumphant
 A majestic pean raise.

Down the canyon's rocky gorges,
 Now they wildly, madly sweep,
As, with laughing shout triumphant
 O'er the rocks they joyous leap.

Then in calm and limpid beauty
 Still and deep they silent flow,
With the verdant banks o'erhanging
 Pictured in the depths below.

"Tahkeeostee"—Racing Waters—
 Was thy sonorous Indian name,
But as "French Broad" thou art written
 On the white man's role of fame.

Perish that! but live the other!
 For on every dancing wave
Evermore is shown the beauty
 Of the name the red man gave.

Poem "Racing Water" from F.A. Sondley's History of Buncombe County.

Yet another tribute to the French Broad, albeit one which Amos Stackhouse probably had not seen, was a shaped-note hymn published in *The Southern Harmony*, written by William "Singin' Billy" Walker of South Carolina. Walker became popular all over the South and Southwest, and his books were used in rural singing schools and conventions for at least a century after his death. His song "The French Broad" was written in the fall of 1831 while Walker was traveling through the Western North Carolina mountains.[15]

FRENCH BROAD. L. M.   Wm. Walker.   265

1. *High o'er the hills the mountains rise, Their summits tower toward the skies; But far above them I must dwell.

2. Oh, God! forbid that I should fall And lose my ever-lasting all; But may I rise on wings of love,

Or sink beneath the flames of hell.

And soar to the blest world above.

3. Although I walk the mountains high,
 Ere long my body low must lie,
 And in some lonesome place must rot,
 And by the living be forgot.

4. There it must lie till that great day,
 When Gabriel's awful trump shall say,
 Arise, the judgment day is come,
 When all must hear their final doom.

5. If not prepared, then I must go
 Down to eternal pain and wo,
 With devils there I must remain,
 And never more return again.

6. But if prepared, oh, blessed thought!
 I'll rise above the mountain's top,
 And there remain for evermore
 On Canaan's peaceful, happy shore.

7. Oh! when I think of that blest world,
 Where all God's people dwell in love,
 I oft-times long with them to be
 And dwell in heaven eternally.

8. Then will I sing God's praises there,
 Who brought me through my troubles here
 I'll sing, and be forever blest,
 Find sweet and everlasting rest.

* This song was composed by the Author, in the fall of 1831, while travelling over the mountains, on French Broad River, in North Carolina and Tennessee.

If these many professionals could be believed, then it is no wonder Amos Stackhouse would have been equally enchanted by these spectacular sights and have sought to make his final home in the midst of the French Broad Valley. As he continued his search, his turnpike walks brought him to the mouth of Big Laurel Creek, one of the French Broad's important tributaries. Here, since the small bridge was often washed out, Amos hired Wash Farnsworth, a former slave, to pole him to the other side.

The large farm joining N.A. Farnsworth's (Wash's former owner) intrigued Amos from the beginning. Obviously abandoned, it held acres of virgin timber, was flanked by both the French Broad and the Buncombe Turnpike, and was crossed by the old Hopewell Road from Paint Rock. Bold and babbling Woolsey Branch added the final charm, prompting Amos to inquire into the farm's status and to make an offer.

Amos learned that the "old Woolsey place" contained about 600 acres, and had been a drovers' stand during the Turnpike's early days. All the buildings were burned during the Civil War and the fields had all grown up.[16] Nonetheless, if the state kept its promise, the railroad would be built through the farm on the turnpike bed, adding great potential to the rundown property.

Thus, on January 26, 1878, a deed of transfer was written to Amos Stackhouse from the surviving children of James Robert Love of Haywood County, who had died in 1863. Love, prominent owner of hundreds of thousands of acres in Western North Carolina, had lent Thomas Woolsey $1500 on April 19, 1841, for a period of two years. In the mortgage Woolsey agreed to give Love:

> "All my equitable and legal interest in and to all lands adjoining and including my plantation and stand whereon I now live and all my household furniture, my waggon and ox team and all my farming tools, three cows, three calves, and six other head of cattle, 30 head of hogs, and 15 head of sheep, and one brown horse, all of which land and property the said J.R. Love is to have and to hold. But if Woolsey can pay the $1500 with lawful interest thereon within two years, then the above obligation is to be void."

After a year Woolsey must have seen that he could not repay the loan, so he made a deed to J.R. Love on April 10, 1842, for his "six hundred acres, more or less," with no mention of animals, tools or furnishings. According to the new document, Love paid Woolsey $200, bringing the farm's total worth to $1700. (This deed was not recorded in Madison County until June 1877, possibly spurred by Amos' inquiring about its purchase.) The sum paid in 1878 by Amos Stackhouse to Love's heirs was $685, reflecting the property's condition after thirty-six years of disuse; a new survey defined the boundaries at "605 1/2 acres." The deed also carried an exception – one undivided half-interest in all mines and minerals formerly owned by "the Hon. Thos. L. Clingman."[17] It is confusing that, in 1846 – four years after the property had been sold to Love – another document from Woolsey had given Clingman (for whom the Great Smokies' highest peak is named) these mineral rights: "On and of the land owned by said Woolsey."[18] Perhaps Woolsey had retained the mining privileges by oral agreement when the 1841 and 1842 deals were transacted. However it occurred, Clingman activated his half interest shortly after Amos' purchase, adding another dimension to his farmstead.

According to family tradition, the property had come to Thomas Woolsey from James Doan either by inheritance or by purchase, and the Woolsey Branch flowing through to the French Broad was then called Doan's Creek. In the early 1800s when Madison County was still a part of Buncombe,

Doan bought some of his property, if not all, from John Strother, land agent and state surveyor.[19] (Strother had acquired over 4,440 acres for speculation in Buncombe County, "including the ferry and adjoining lands at Warm Springs." Here Strother laid out the town of Spaightville, incorporated in 1802,[20] but for some reason the ratification was never acknowledged.)

Now Amos Stackhouse, having bought the land, worked on his new farm whenever he could leave his Warm Springs business, clearing fields for planting and grazing, erecting a barn and miles of fencing, locating springs and a site for his new store.[21] Close to the turnpike's edge, he constructed a good-sized frame building having two side rooms for living quarters. Finally, one year from the date of purchase, Amos, Anna, and the two boys – Amos, Jr. and Charles Dilworth – moved from Warm Springs four miles upriver to what they would call "the upper store," still maintaining their "lower store."[22]

For sawing the logs Amos planned to cut on his land, he constructed an undershot water wheel and wheel house at the edge of the French Broad, two hundred yards above his store. In his ledger, May 3, 1879, Amos noted that Miles Goforth, who lived near Woolseys, paid for store merchandise by making Amos "2000 shingles in 2 months." The hand-riven shakes of thick white oak were ready to be nailed, one at a time, onto the roof of his building.

But, strangely enough, on May 12, 1879, Amos moved his family back to the lower store at Warm Springs for a time. We can only conjecture as to the reason. Perhaps his trusted employee became ill or moved away, or the water spring at the upper store dried up, or Anna or one of the boys became ill. Besides the availability of the healing mineral water at Warm Springs, there was always a doctor on the hotel staff.

The move back might also have been connected to Amos' part in the newly-formed Warm Springs Toll Bridge Company. Applied for, no doubt, in 1878, but ratified on March 5, 1879, by the N.C. General Assembly, the act read:

> Sect.1. – That James H. Rumbough, William H. Howerton, Charles Thomas Garrett, Amos Stackhouse, Beverly W. Hill, W.A. Wedden, Thomas H. Bailey, W.W. Rollins… are hereby created a body corporate for the purpose of acquiring or erecting and keeping in repair a bridge across the French Broad river at or near the Warm Springs in Madison County.

Sections two through four dealt with the usual powers, stock, bylaws, etc. assigned a corporation. The state also set standard rates of toll in Section 5:

> "The Company shall be entitled to receive the following toll, to wit: Six-horse wagons seventy-five cents, three-horse wagons forty cents, two-horse wagons twenty-five cents, one horse wagon fifteen cents each, cattle, sheep and hogs two and one-half cents each, pleasure carriages four horse one dollar, two horse fifty cents, horse and buggy twenty-five cents."[23]

Hopefully, by charging a toll, Amos and the other associates could build a bridge strong enough and high enough to thwart the rampaging French Broad in her flood seasons. Access to the hotel and the train connection affected business for all who lived along the river and turnpike. Even characters in *Land of the Sky* five years earlier had been subject to the ferry, the Warm Springs bridge having been washed away once again.[24]

This new bridge would provide a dependable way for stagecoaches, private carriages and farmers' wagons to reach the Wolf Creek railroad for at least two more years. Western North Carolina Railway had come to the edge of Buncombe County in March, exciting the populace, but it was still far from Warm Springs.

Meanwhile, in early July, the Asheville newspaper announced that "late prominent arrivals at Warm Springs" included numerous doctors, judges, and former military officers from each of the southern states, including Texas and Arkansas, as well as Illinois, Maryland, and New York. The Russian envoy from Washington, the ex-assistant Secretary of the Navy from Boston, plus the Secretary of State from Raleigh also attended. The July-fourth ball and subsequent summer festivities were reported, even including descriptions of the ball gowns of many of the ladies. "The music rendered by the Charleston, South Carolina, brass band was fine, the dance hall and corridors crowded, and 'all went merry as a marriage bell.'"[25] A week later the *Citizen* declared that "The last few days have added hundreds of guests to the Warm Springs Hotel, and Dr. Howerton is winning golden opinions as a genial landlord."[26] Perhaps the new bridge encouraged more tourists after all.

Stackhouse general store where Amos lived in connected 'siderooms' at right. c. 1879.

On September 18th, the same newspaper noted that the Asheville to Warm Springs road was being put in better condition under the leadership of Mr. D.F. Davis of Marshall to "Thus remedy an evil that has prevented much traveling this summer between here and the Warm Springs."[27]

Nevertheless, enough patrons had made it to the resort to require added rooms. "The right wing of the building, now single-story cottages, will be carried up two more stories, making it the handsomest and most complete hotel in the South," stated the *Asheville Citizen*. Dr. Howerton, the proprietor, seeing that the railroad was so near, had renewed his lease for another year, and the hotel owners were adding seventy-five new rooms.[28]

Even back in 1850 the Warm Springs hotel operated by the Patton brothers had been described as large and lavish:

> The present building is… 230 feet long, two stories high… studded with thirteen massive columns, 20 feet in height. The dining room is 40 by 80 feet; the bar, ball and dancing rooms are all airy, spacious and comfortable… Two hundred fifty persons can be accommodated and two hundred forty can be seated at one time."[29]

Now, thirty years later, the resort expected to accommodate *one thousand* guests.[30]

Moreover, the hotel had been a place for the well-to-do and well-known of Southern society in its earlier years. A biographer of North Carolina's revered Zebulon Vance wrote that, when he was a needy college student, Zeb had worked "for a time as clerk at the Warm Springs. Here he was thrown in social contact with the first men of Western Carolina, South Carolina and Tennessee," influencing his great career.[31]

Presently, however, high society and its activities had no appeal to Amos, who, once again, near the end of the tourist season, left Warm Springs to return to his new farm. "We moved back to upper store, Sunday, October 12, 1879," he noted in the back of his ledger.[32] Here Amos would remain, ending his peregrinations at last.

ENDNOTES FOR CHAPTER SEVEN

[1] Author's private papers.

[2] Ibid.

[3] Sondley, F.A. *A History of Buncombe County*. Asheville, N.C.: The Advocate Printing Co., 1930, p. 426.

[4] Mohlenbrock, Robert H. "Paint Rock, N.C.," *Natural History*, August, 1989, pp. 64-66.

[5] Arthur, John Preston. *Western North Carolina, A History*. Raleigh: Edwards & Broughton Printing Co., 1914, p. 229.

[6] Bennett, Daniel K. *Chronology of North Carolina*. New York: J.M. Edney, 1858, p.102.

[7] Lanman, Charles. *Letters From the Alleghany Mountains*. New York: G.P. Putnam, 1849, pp.127-128.

[8] Boehm, Rev. Henry. *Reminiscences*. New York: Carlton & Porter, 1865, p.211.

[9] *Appletons' Journal of Literature, Science and Art*, Vol. IV, No. 87, 1870.
National Cyclopedia of American Biography, Vol. VI. New York: James T. White & Co., 1929, p.368.

[10] *Early American Book Illustrators and Wood Engravers 1670-1870*, Vol.I. Princeton, N.J.: Princeton Univ. Press, 1968, pp.125-126.

[11] Bennett, p.84.

[12] Calhoun, Richard J. *A Tricentennial Anthology of South Carolina Literature, 1670-1970*. Columbia, S.C.: U. of S.C. P., 1971, pp. 206-207.

[13] Unpublished ms. In Simms' hand, dateline, "Warm Springs, N.C., September, 1842." Beinecke Rare Book and Manuscript Library, Yale University, New Haven, Conn., 1990.

[14] Powell, Wm. S., *Dictionary of N.C. Biography*, Vol. 1, Chapel Hill: UNC Press, 1979, p.380.
McFarland, J.F. *A Greeting from the Mountains and Valleys of Western North Carolina*, circa 1903.

[15] Walker, William. *The Southern Harmony*. Los Angeles: Pro Musicamericana, 1966 rpt., p. 265. Jackson,
George Pullen. *White Spirituals in the Southern Uplands*. Chapel Hill: UNC Press, 1933, pp. 55-57.

[16] Private papers.

[17] Madison County Deeds Register, Bk. 8, p. 11.
Buncombe County Deeds Register, Bk. 22, p. 234.
Ibid, Bk. G, p. 312.

[18] Ibid., Bk. G, p. 164.

[19] Ibid., Bk. 14, p. 351.

[20] Powell, Vol. 5, p. 467.

[21] Private papers.

[22] Ibid.

[23] Public and Private Laws of North Carolina, 1879 session. Raleigh: Observer, State Printer, 1979, pp. 632-634.

[24] Reid, Christian. "The Land of the Sky," *Appletons' Journal*, Vol. 14 (Sept., 1975), p.644.

[25] *N.C. Citizen*, Asheville: July 3, 10, 1879, p.1.

[26] Ibid., July 17, 1879, p.1.

[27] Ibid., Sept. 18, 1879, p.1.

[28] Ibid., Oct. 16, Nov. 27, 1879, p.1.

[29] Bennett, p. 83.

[30] *N.C. Citizen*, Nov. 27, 1879, p.1.

[31] Wheeler, John A. *Reminiscences and Memories of North Carolina*. Baltimore: Genealogical Publishing Co., 1966, p.65.

[32] Private papers.

Chapter Eight

After living eight years in the doorway of luxury and high society, Amos and Anna Stackhouse were entering the primitive, remote setting of rural Madison County and preparing to carve their own niche into the old hills. It would not be easy to leave behind the friends made at the crossroads settlement or the graves of their two babies, but they looked forward to being on their own property and answering only to themselves. The upriver location was even less populated than Amos' prairie home at Fort Recovery had been, where there were "fourteen houses within less than a mile."[1] The new farm, Woolsey Field, "'was' just a big beautiful woodland, with the old Hopewell Road running through it," recalled Susan Hunnicutt Harrison years later. "There were no homes between Jewel Hill and Woolsey Field [about five miles] except one or two shacks which were scarcely noticeable in the Woolsey Field."[2] Eventually, though, Amos' site on the French Broad would become a thriving community.

Meanwhile, the upper-store customers were not all strangers, many having formerly walked or ridden wagons to Warm Springs. Glad for the new store nearer their homes, they came from Doe Branch, Big Pine Creek, Little Pine Creek, Worley, Walnut Creek, Jewel Hill*, Sandy Bottom and other areas. One small farm owner two miles away, Jesse Harrison, had lived on the river's west bank for over twenty years. He traded at Amos' Warm Springs store and now came to the upper store.[3] His son James, another patron, had married Susan Hunnicutt, who would remember in her old age, "My parents traded at the Stackhouse's Warm Springs store, and seven or eight years later, we traded at the new store."[4]

Other customers from the lower store who patronized the new were George W. Gahagan and his brothers – grandchildren of Lawrence and Sarah Pringle from Ireland. They owned large tracts (about 10,000 acres) in Madison County's Laurel and Walnut Creek sections, adjoining Amos' land at one boundary. George's father, the well-respected George Robert Gahagan, had represented Madison County in the State Legislature several terms until his death in 1870.[5] The Gahagans would become not only Amos' largest-volume store customers, but also his lifelong friends.[6]

Besides his store, barn, and waterwheel, a house for Anna was in Amos' plans – and all this construction required more money than Amos netted from his store sales. He again asked his Philadelphia son's help in financing. Ellison's letter of November 25, 1879, stated:

> "My Dear Father, Thy letter was rec'd yesterday, and I went to Fidelity Trust Co. Paid thy interest on the note for $150 and gave them a note for $500 at 6 percent payable in 3 mos., making it due Feb. 25th, 1880, or payable sooner if you want to sell stock. Stock is 49 today. I mailed thee check to thy order for $350 this afternoon. My cold is not any better..."[7]

Productivity and profit would eventually come from Amos' timber and farm ventures. In the beginning, along with his cattle, Amos raised sheep, useful for their wool, skins, tallow and mutton. But after watching his flock

---

*Later named Walnut.

dwindle, he gave up keeping the animals that frequently broke their limbs by catching their hooves between rocks, fell off the steep cliffs, ate poisonous plants, or were attacked by wolves, wild dogs, and other predators. Amos hoped that if he planted the mountain cash crop – bright leaf tobacco – on some of his cleared land, he would be able to produce a better yield. It was in this way that Amos' Warm Springs associate, W.W. Rollins, had profited; at this time Rollins had sixty tenants growing the "gold leaf."[8] One historian wrote: "Uncleared land could be purchased for three dollars per acre, and a tract of one and one-half acres, when cleared, could be planted, cultivated, and harvested by a man and two small boys for a harvest worth $900."[9]

It was not that simple, of course. Most tobacco farmers said that tobacco raising was a job "requiring thirteen months of the year." From the bedding, sowing, tilling, transplanting, fertilizing, hoeing, thinning, suckering, and topping, to the chopping, sticking, hanging, curing, stripping and packing into hogsheads, then loading onto wagons for the journey to market – it was arduous work. Prior to Amos' arrival in Madison County, the tobacco markets were at the coastal cities, but later warehouses were established at Knoxville, Tennessee; at Danville, Virginia; and at Hickory, North Carolina.[10] By 1878, Asheville had four markets and could handle 7,000,000 pounds.[11] Finally, on October 2, 1878, a Marshall correspondent to the *North Carolina Citizen* announced: "We are to have a warehouse for the sale of tobacco, to be erected by a joint stock company."[12] Rollins, no doubt, was involved, and possibly so was Amos, who was no stranger to stock investing.

Late in 1880, Amos and Rollins and the other stockholders of Warm Springs Toll Bridge Company asked the State Assembly to amend their charter of 1879. Although it would not be ratified until January 31, 1881, changes were few: in Section Six, the word "state" would read "county," and the word "company" would read "county," pertaining to the collection of penalties for failure to pay tolls. Until the railroad finally arrived, and even afterwards, it was necessary to maintain a bridge at the hotel for tourists and others crossing the French Broad. Published in 1881, a small book by a Miss Chunn mentioned that on the left bank of the river at Warm Springs "a long bridge leads across to the handsome, spacious hotel rising imposingly near, with cottages and bath houses dotting thickly around."[13]

Another project taking not a little of his time was Amos' selected dwelling site, centered in the Hopewell Road as it crossed his land, requiring him to move the road up the hill eastward about fifty feet.[14] Stackhouse tradition says that Amos hired twenty black men to prepare the hillside, using hand picks, shovels, flatbed wheelbarrows, ropes and draft animals in shaping the ground for the foundation of his eight-room house. (In years to come, he would enlarge it by three rooms.) From Amos' river-powered saw mill came the joists, rafters and other framing members, while the moldings, finish lumber, windows and hardware were likely ordered from up North.

One peculiarity of Amos' new house was a secret passage or hideaway, "in case of Indian attack," so stated family tradition through the years.[15] Whether this reason had been given in jest to his children by Amos, we cannot know. There is no record of Indian trouble in Madison County after 1795, although there were stories handed down by word of mouth as to later Indian problems around the Stackhouse area.[16] Community tradition, also, placed an old Indian camp ground not far from Amos' store. Arrowheads, flints, grinding stones and pottery had been collected as farmers tilled. In the future, former Stackhouse resident Clyde Dockery noted: "It would have been a good camp site for Indians – close to water and game, and good corn-growing fields."[17] In light of the many turnpike tales about bandits, bushwhackers, and "rogues," in a time when mountaineers far from law enforcement frequently had to provide their own protection, Amos might have felt the need for such a safeguard. It could have served, if nothing more, as a place to hide valuables, or perhaps he remembered his days of living along the Underground Railroad. From whatever influence, the trap door was cut into the concrete-floored outbuilding, just off the back porch.[18] Fitted with a water spigot, the room served as a spring house to keep milk and butter cold in summer.

When finished, Amos' house could be compared to the few large houses in Warm Springs and Marshall, with its white-painted two stories, twin front porches flanking a large bay section, and dark green shutters at all the curved-top windows. Broad wooden steps led to the entrance from the curving driveway, and a long flight of concrete steps was terraced into the slope of his side yard for Amos' daily walks to store and mill. (Each room had its own fireplace, while one room served as a library – unusual in mountain homes.) Amos and Anna now had a comfortable and attractive place to raise their two sons and to receive visiting relatives and friends. (The side rooms at the store were available for travelers or employees.)

Home of Amos Stackhouse, built c. 1880. His grandson, Ernest, in foreground.

Ernest & Amos III in front of their grandfather's home with background steps leading to new Hopewell Road

From their front porch, the Stackhouses looked down not only upon the mill, store and turnpike, but also upon the "wild and beautiful" French Broad as it tumbled over rapids, stretched past small islands, then swept around the bend to meet Big Laurel. Capping this scene were blue mountaintops, covered in forest, and changing hues with the seasons. Amos would be reminded of his visit, over twenty-five years earlier, to Galena, Illinois, where he had described that city as "lying on the river between the hills, giving a beautiful view of the country."[19]

Soon to be included in the panorama were train tracks, according to the State's March 29, 1880, act selling its Western North Carolina Railroad interest to William J. Best and three associates, who pledged themselves to bring the railroad to its western terminus at Paint Rock on or before the first day of July 1881.[20] In October 1880, it had reached the area near Asheville known in the future as Biltmore, filling Madison County residents with fresh hope. By virtue of an operating lease, the Richmond & Danville Railroad now controlled the Western North Carolina line assigned to William Best.[21] Since Asheville was the R & D western terminus, Danville businessmen suddenly developed interest in Asheville's tobacco warehouses and the tobacco business grew. Bright leaf offered the poverty-stricken postwar mountain farmers a cash crop lifeline, and for those along the Buncombe Turnpike, it took the place of the stock-feeding industry lost to the approaching rails.[22]

Meanwhile, Amos Stackhouse continued to make improvements to his farm. On the hillside toward the east he planted an apple orchard, then cherry trees and plums; he built wooden arbors to support both white grapes and Concords. To the west, a hundred yards or less from his home, Amos built a gazebo called "the summer house" by family members. It sat at the end of a rock cliff point offering a grand upriver view of the rapids called "Stackhouse Palisades," while collecting breezes from the water – a wonderful place for picnics. As the number of Amos' projects increased, more workers were hired, offering much-needed employment to the local people. Some came from other communities, prompting Amos to build tenant cabins on his farm. "Stackhouse's" place was taking on the look of a lasting settlement.

Amos Stackhouse's family, too, was growing. On the day after his tenth anniversary of marriage to Anna Myers – February 3, 1881 – Amos was pleased to add the name of another grandchild to his family Bible record: Mary Shaw Stackhouse, born in Philadelphia to Ellison and Ella.[23] During his annual Spring trip North, he would meet her firsthand, as he usually stayed with Ellison for a week or more.

It was probably during this visit that young Amos, Jr., left at home in Madison County, wrote his father, evidently, in receipt of clothing Amos had already shipped:

> "Dear Papa, I want you to come home and bring sister Becka with you and bring me some oranges and some picture books and toys and a gun and a little Ellaphint one that wont scratch and bite. I have got on my pants and like them pretty well. Send me some blocks and a little iron and board. I send Papa six kisses. I love you a wagon full, Amos Stackhouse."[24]

These stagecoach trips would end for Amos and his neighbors in a matter of months, as the railroad inched closer to Warm Springs and the Wolf Creek/Paint Rock connection. By July 4th it had reached Alexander, then miles below Asheville, with depot buildings almost finished at Marshall and Warm Springs, as well as trestles over Big Laurel mouth and Spring Creek in Warm Springs.[25] "On September 5th, the old Buncombe Turnpike Company surrendered, and the commissioners accepted its charter," stated John P. Arthur in his Western North Carolina history in 1912.[26] The steel-truss trestle, 263 feet long, was completed December 12, 1881, across the French

Broad at Deep Water, only two miles below "Stackhouse's."[27]

At the end of December, a writer traveling from Tennessee to Asheville, Edmund Kirke, described the Buncombe Turnpike condition as told to him by a fellow at Henry Oettinger's inn: "Thar hain't no road; it's all torned up by the cussed railroad. It's a reg'lar dog in the manger; it don't travil itself, nor let no one else travil.'[28] Kirke noted that, in their hurry to meet their new deadline of February 1, 1882, the builders had skipped every other crosstie, planning to fill in after completion, but, for now, leaving them four feet apart and difficult to traverse by foot. Continuing along the French Broad, Edmund Kirke encountered several working groups of stripe-suited convicts, state appointed for construction of the Western North Carolina Railroad, and without whose labor, little progress would have been made. (After leaving the stagecoach at Wolf Creek, Kirke had been forced to walk the route taken over by the track laying.) As Kirke followed the old turnpike now covered with fresh snow, he headed where Oettinger had advised – "Stockhouse's" (spelled as it was pronounced by the local residents). When he came to the Big Laurel Creek, Kirke crossed, not by way of the turnpike bridge, which was half washed away, but over the newly-constructed railway trestle, "encrusted as the stringers and sleepers now were with ice, taking half an hour," he wrote.[29] Here Kirke tried to rent a mule for his journey on to Asheville, but was told, "by the deaf landlord" (this was surely Amos Stackhouse), that he could not trust his critter with a stranger on the treacherous, icy road.[30] Amos suggested "a pore man half a mile up the road," who would likely let his animal go. Kirke called the next stretch of road, "probably the worst road ever invented in this country – where it was not slush and railroad ties, it was broken stones and ice-covered rocks."[31]

Amos Stackhouse patiently endured this track-laying period although it restricted his store trade to those on foot or horseback, denying stagecoach, drover-team and pleasure-buggy customers. He did, however, make some profit by selling nails and other items to the WNC Railroad crew foremen. Furthermore, as the railroad took the highway, it promised to build another road to replace the turnpike.[32] Also in Amos' interest was the deal he made with the railway officials who bought rights-of-way up and down the turnpike; Amos agreed to give them whatever land they needed, if, in return, they would build him a siding at his mill.[33] (This would prove more astute than any other of Amos' decisions.)

While watching and waiting for the track completion, Amos had time to reflect on his decade with the Buncombe Turnpike – that important highway connecting Southern Appalachian points to Charleston and Augusta for almost sixty years. This way of life faced great change and near extinction, but should follow with a prosperity Amos knew to be possible as in other parts of the country. He would be trading yellow swirls of dust for cinders and soot; the loud cries of animals for the low thunder of wheels; the blare of the stage trumpet for the blast of the steam whistle; the familiar teamsters and drovers for waving engineers and conductors. Amos Stackhouse, along with his adopted Western North Carolina, stood at the threshold of a new sixty-year era – exciting, history-making, and map-changing.

[1] Author's private papers. (See also p.25 of this book.)

[2] Ibid.

[3] Ibid.

[4] Ibid.

[5] Painter, J.B. *The Season of Dorland-Bell.* 2nd ed. Boone, N.C.: Appalachian Consortium Press, 1996, p.274. (Originally from Nita Gahagan letter to author, 1985)

[6] Private papers.

[7] Ibid.

[8] Wellman, Manly Wade. *The Kingdom of Madison.* p. 110.

[9] Van Noppen, Ina W. and John J. *Western North Carolina Since the Civil War.* Boone, N.C.: Appalachian Consortium Press, 1973, p.276.

[10] Ibid.

[11] Ibid.

[12] *N.C. Citizen,* Oct. 2,1878, p.1.

[13] Chunn, Miss. *Descriptive Illustrated Guide – Book to North Carolina Mountains, Their Principal Resorts.* New York: E.J. Hale & son, 1881, p.76.

[14] Private papers.

[15] Aumiller, Nancy Stackhouse. Interview by author, 1997.

[16] Dockery, Clyde. Interview, 2005.

[17] Ibid.

[18] Ibid.

[19] Private papers.

[20] Arthur, John Preston. *Western North Carolina, A History.* Raleigh: Edwards & Broughton Printing Co., 1914, p.476.

[21] Ibid, p 477.

[22] Allen, Martha Norburn. *Asheville and Land of the Sky.* Charlotte: Heritage House, 1960, p.50.

[23] Swayne, Norman Walton. *Byberry Waltons, An Account of Four English Brothers.* Decorah, Iowa: Anundsen Pub. Co., 1989, reprint, p. 489.

[24] Private papers.

[25] Wellman, p.108.

[26] Arthur, p.245.

[27] Cundiff, H.B. (Chief Engineer Bridges, Southern Railway System), letter to author, May 2, 1984.

[28] Kirke, Edmund. "On the French Broad." *Lippincott's Magazine,* Nov., 1884, p.426.

[29] Ibid, p. 436.

[30] Ibid. (Amos' early deafness described to author by great granddaughter, Nancy Aumiller, 1997.)

[31] Ibid, p.438.

[32] Wolcott, Mary Ellen. *Asheville Citizen-Times.* Sept. 24, 1978, p. 1-C.

[33] Aumiller, Nancy Stackhouse. Interview by author, 1998.

Chapter Nine

Scarcely a month into winter – January 25, 1882 – the event took place that Amos Stackhouse and his family would remember forevermore.[1] Puffing down the widely-supported steel tracks came the huge black iron horse, pulling a few cars behind. (More than likely, the engine was a Baldwin, manufactured on Philadelphia's Broad and Spring Street, near Amos' childhood home.[2]) His sons – Amos, Jr., almost nine, and Charles, age four and a half – had ridden trains before, but having one pass within touch of their Papa's store, and knowing that it would come again every day, that they would not have to go all the way to Wolf Creek to board it, created a different excitement.

New railroad and loading platform at Stackhouse general store.

Many of their mountain neighbors had never been any farther than Warm Springs or Marshall, and would observe the powerful pistons chugging behind the cow-catcher nose, and hear the shrill whistle for the first time. Watching the train go by, or better, seeing it flagged to a stop, would add incentive for trading at Amos' store. Nor would the newness wear off quickly – many, for months to come, stopping their day's work to watch the marvel's passing.[3] Despite their fascination, however, they could not foresee how greatly this large inanimate object would change their lives and their culture.

The finished route followed the ancient Indian pathway down the Buncombe Turnpike bed, past Amos Stackhouse's, to the Deep Water narrows of the French Broad, where it crossed to the west bank and continued through Warm Springs to Paint Rock at the Tennessee border. Here it connected to the Morristown, Tennessee, line and the Mid- and Southwestern states. With this new accessibility, the oft-touted turnpike scenery would become even more popular among travel writers, novelists, photographers and artists.

Given the long wait, it was nothing short of miraculous that the WNC Railroad had come to fruition, overcoming poverty, war, politics, carpet baggers, even tragic loss of lives – a process described by eastern North Carolinians as a "costly, unproductive boondoggle."[4] It would be considered a monumental feat of engineering, and written about far into the future.[5] Nearly three decades had passed since the first meetings to secure a railroad for western North Carolina. In July, 1854, at Jewel Hill, site of Madison County's first courthouse, a resolution was adopted, and delegates appointed "to attend the Railroad Convention to be held at Asheville on August 25th, in the interest of extending the Central Railroad to the Tennessee line, as the best means of improving our county."[6]

Now, in 1882, that foresight would pay off, not only in convenience, but through taxation on twenty-nine miles of road length, valued at $252 per mile, adding to county coffers seventy-one and one-third cents "on every $100 of said valuation."[7] Moreover, Amos and the other western North Carolina merchants could receive goods practically at their doorsteps rather than at the end of a two-way wagon trip over roads and bridges often rendered impassable by the weather.

Distance.	STATIONS.	1st Class.	2d Class.	
177	Salisbury..........	7 90	6 90	
164	Third Creek	7 35	6 45	
159	Elmwood...........	7 15	6 25	
152	Statesville	6 80	5 90	
139	Catawba............	6 25	5 45	
126	Newton..............	5 65	4 90	
123	Conover.............	5 50	4 80	
116	Hickory.......	5 25	4 55	
106	Icard.........	4 75	4 20	
96	Morganton..	4 35	3 75	
90	Glen Alpine	4 00	3 55	
86	Bridgewater	3 85	3 40	
75	Marion......	3 40	2 95	
63	Old Fort...	2 85	2 50	
60	Henry's..........	2 70	2 40	
48	Black Mount...	2 25	1 90	
45	Cooper's.............	2 00	1 80	
37	Asheville Junction.......	1 70	1 50	
32	Asheville.............	1 50	1 30	
22	Alexander's..........	1 00	85	
12	Marshall......	60	50	
5	Barnard's Stand............	35	35	
0	Stack House	00	00	
5	Warm Springs............	35	35	
12	Paint Rock	60	50	

DUCKTOWN LINE.

| 42 | Hominy.............. | 1 90 | 1 65 | |
| 52 | Pigeon River......... ...... | 2 40 | 2 00 | |

WNC Railway Cost Tariff book page

Mountain ways of daily existence would change, too, though slowly, as packaged dyes and cheap cotton cloth came by rail, taking the place of the picking, carding, retting, spinning, coloring and weaving. (Indigo rarely appears in Amos' ledger.) Barrels of molasses, flour, lamp oil; slabs of cured pork; casks of nails; and even ready-made shoes, would be available without the weeks, or sometimes months, of toil and uncertainty involved in the growing or crafting of their own. Not all the people could afford to take advantage of the convenience, but, as time passed, the speedy accessibility of life's necessities replaced, for many mountaineers, the slow hand methods that had been brought from the old world to Appalachia.

Unfortunately, without the turnpike, and with the railroad on the other side of the river, Amos' Warm Springs store had little trade. Furthermore, B.W. Hill had opened another general store near Spring Creek, adjacent to the hotel's westside boundary, and facing the railroad.[8] This, along with a livery stable, depot and saloon, formed the nucleus for an emerging village at Warm Springs. Thus, one month to the day of the first train's passing, February 25th, 1882, Amos Stackhouse closed his "lower store," channeling all his resources to the upriver location.[9]

Amos had recorded sales at this Warm Springs store for January and February of 1882, to be $432.15, while he sold, in the same period at the upper store, $994.96. During the next six months, Amos' new store's ledger showed a profit of nearly $2200.[10] He would hardly notice the absence of turnpike trade.

Another boost came when the little settlement called "Stackhouse's place" suddenly was listed by WNC Railroad as a "flag station" with the lasting name of "Stackhouse, North Carolina." Passenger trains regularly stopped at the depots of Marshall and Warm Springs, but, when flagged, would stop at the smaller stations. To determine ticket prices for each station from Salisbury to Paint Rock, Amos Stackhouse used the WNC Railroad "Tariff Cost Book," effective April 15, 1882.[11] Between Asheville and Warm Springs, there were only four stops, located at former turnpike stock stands: Alexander's, Marshall, Barnard's Stand, Stackhouse, and Warm Springs. The fare from Stackhouse to Asheville, second class, was $1.30, and to Warm Springs – 35 cents.

To facilitate the loading and unloading of freight, Amos added a broad wooden dock in front of his store siderooms. He also greatly improved a road from Walnut Gap, at the old State road, down to Woolsey Branch, past his home, and on to the railroad, midway between his store and his water wheel.[12] To be called the "Walnut Gap Road," or sometimes "Lonesome Mountain Road," it made a shorter route for those coming from other parts of the county, now that the turnpike was gone. It led directly to Amos' rail siding, providing accessibility for years to come to farmers bringing their wagonloads of tobacco, logs, or other products.

Old sign from Stackhouse post office.

With the train's offering a ready way to market, tobacco turned even more of a profit for Amos and his neighbors. Travel writers Wilbur Zeigler and Ben Crosscup observed in 1883: "The tobacco interests of Madison County are extensive, and… the county seat is reaping wealth from this source."[13] An anecdote often told visitors was that, when Jonah had been imprisoned in the whale's belly, he had "smoked away like a house afire, smoked away to kill, smoked away till the whale, not being used to 'baccer, took sick at the stummack and throwed Jonah right up on the coast of North Ca'lina, and that's how this kentry come to be discivered."[14]

Another boon for Stackhouse at Amos' store occurred one year after the railroad completion to Tennessee. On January 25, 1883, in the back section, a United States Post Office was established, with Amos as the first postmaster.[15] Here, Amos sold stamps and envelopes, sent a few packages, deciphered letters for those who could not read, and made detailed monthly reports to the Postal Department in Raleigh – all for which he had trained well in his previous postmaster jobs. A canvas sack was provided for the outgoing mail and hung on a tall hook beside the track to await the train. Without slowing down, the trainman grabbed the mail bag from the hook, drawing it into the train, and dropping a matching sack of incoming mail. Stackhouse, North Carolina, was now a recognized place *on the map*.

Railway steam engine approaching Stackhouse where flagman will grab mail bag.

During the spring of 1883, Amos Stackhouse began yet another venture that made use of his resources and employed a few more people – a fish trap in the French Broad.[16] Gigging by torchlight from canoes was profitable and a favorite sport. In a single night a good fish trap could sometimes produce a barrelful.[17] Amos had always liked fish, even to having it shipped from Philadelphia when he lived on the prairie. Many years before, a short distance upriver, toward Sandy Bottom, a successful fish trap had been operated by Zacariah Candler, who was a member of the prominent Buncombe County Candler family, inventors of Coca Cola.[18]

Through Amos' new positions as postmaster and station master, and through the jobs he was creating, he was making more friends and earning the trust of those who had lived in Madison County far longer than he. In May, 1883, a former '70s customer at the lower store, Malachi "Malley" Reeves, even named his baby son "Amos Stackhouse Reeves," to be known as "Stack" throughout his life.[19]

Other farmers sometimes asked Amos to hold sums of cash "for safekeeping," there being no banks closer than Asheville. But more often he was asked to lend cash to his customers. Those who grew tobacco mortgaged their crops at fifteen percent to Amos – he, in turn, furnishing seed, fertilizer, and other merchandise until the harvest, when the farmer could expect some cash. This arrangement gave the mountaineers a chance to participate in the profit venture, at the same time bringing Amos store sales plus interest on his loans. Amos' own "bank" was a trunk at his home where he kept his uninvested money. Each week he tallied his expenditures and receipts, adding and subtracting from "amount in trunk" to determine his profit, then recording the total number of silver pieces, gold pieces and paper dollars.[20]

Included in his ledger were occasional entries for "cash account, wife took in," evidently received by Anna from boarders or from travelers who had no other place to eat. If a mountaineer could spare any food at all, it was customary for strangers to be fed when they appeared in his dooryard, the traveler then paying by cash or work "in kind." Several other charges in Amos' books were for "board," likely to tenants renting from Amos and for workers who ate their meals at Anna's. Amos hired one, for instance, "at $9.00 per month, and board."[21]

Although Amos' new store was larger than his Warm Springs store, and this allowed him to keep more inventory, the most commonly purchased items, just as ten years earlier, were tobacco, snuff, medicine, lamp oil, flour, bacon, corn meal, salt, soda and sugar. Not as common, but frequently bought, were cartridges, matches, powder, lead and caps; clothing and leather; tools and nails; lamp wicks and chimneys; candy, nutmeg, pepper and coffee. Customers who traveled a distance often ate their lunches at the store, charging the "cheese and crackers" or "sardines and crackers." Once in a while Amos sold coffins and burial clothes; silver watches and pistols; trace chains and singletrees; spelling books, readers, and copy books; stockings and corsets. (Most mountain people made their own clothes and filled their own cartridges, even late in the nineteenth century.) Rarely, someone bought a "suit of clothes" at $10.25, or a stove for $12.00, sheep shears at $1.25, a hay fork at $1.00, or a satchel for 75 cents. The account of Thomas Sawyer, shoe cobbler, showed charges for shoe thread, 55 cents; mucilage, 10 cents; leather, 25 cents; eyelets, 10 cents; account book, 40 cents; and shoe brush, 35 cents, but also for a harmonica at 35 cents and banjo strings at 45 cents, reflecting the family's after-work interests. In November, 1883, one man surely had an important matter requiring that he make a trip. He purchased from Amos a coat at $6.00, a pair of pants at $6.00, two shirts for $3.40, socks at 60 cents, a valise at $1.00, boots at $4.50, soap at 10 cents, neck bow at 50 cents and gloves at $1.20.[22]

When Amos himself went to New York to visit his sister Sarah Vandervoort, he also kept expense records carefully: the ticket to Roanoke, Virginia, cost $9.95, and that from Roanoke to New York was $16.30, with an added two dollars for a sleeping car. He spent twenty-five cents at Morristown for watch repair, another seventy-five cents for one supper, and fifty cents on other meals.

In making these trips, Amos sometimes took Anna and the boys, but he always carried a pocket notebook listing items to be purchased for store stock, as well as special items for his neighbors: "Rigsby pants – 40x36; coat – 36x34x40; shoes – No.11 for Lemly." Another of Amos' lists, titled "Buy in Philadelphia," contained the following: "brass nails, coffin screws, field glass, eye glasses, odd door keys, lace for wife, glass cutter, veiling blue and brown, castile soap, claw hammers, curtains, bow and arrow for Amos." One more, dated 1883, included: "ploughs, window sashes, oil lamps, 2 – inch augers, steel horse shoes, sewing needles, 44 cartridges, scale for drugs, and photo for Rebecca – don't forget."[23]

Scale for weighing medicinal herbs at Stackhouse general store. Photo by John Newman.

His daughter Rebecca had probably asked him several times to sit for a photographer in Philadelphia, so that she would have a likeness of her father, whom she saw only a few times a year. And the drug scale was needed for Amos' role as pharmacist, which continued to be an important part of his service at Stackhouse. Hanging by delicate chains from the hook-balance point, the small weighing device had two shallow brass saucers, less than two inches in diameter, upon which Amos placed leaves and powders to determine doses. Furthermore, from Dr. David Jaynes and Son Company, Amos stocked bottles of patent medicines, such as expectorants, alteratives, ague mixtures, liniment, tonic of vermifuge, balsams and plain "pills."[24] The more he studied his *Household Physician*, the more practiced he became, until the mountaineers learned to depend upon him for almost all non-life threatening illnesses, thus saving a physician's fee.

However, not all the mountain men's means went for essentials. They especially liked their music, purchasing harmonicas for 40 cents, and violin strings – both singly and in sets – at 25 cents each, or one treble banjo string for 15 cents. Occasionally, they bought decks of playing cards as well.[25]

Having a dearth of schools and churches, the people in this area were reduced to such celebrations as barn raisings, molasses boilings and corn shuckings. Even though his literate customers had the dates on advertising calendars Amos gave away at his store, Christmas was little more than an ordinary day in most mountain cabins. And when observed, it might be on January 6th, called "old Christmas."[26] Not that the mountaineers did not know and revere the Biblical birth; it was simply that their years of poverty and isolation had prohibited the sorts of celebrations held in other places. Most of Amos' neighbors would never have seen a Christmas tree or tinsel, for instance.

One exception was Dr. George W. Reynolds of the Pine Creek section, who traveled on his horse, "Charley," over the hills and hollows, treating the sick, receiving payment sometimes in cash, but mostly in produce.[27] Having several children of his own, Dr. Reynold's charges at Amos' store on December 19, 1883, included four pounds of candy, $1.00; four pounds of nuts, $1.00; four toy horses, 60 cents; one other "toy," 25 cents; three yards linsey, 30 cents; one wool skirt, $1.65; and finished off with a dollar's worth of coffee beans.[28] Clearly, his household could expect a special holiday. The Stackhouse family, another southern Appalachian exception, would also enjoy a celebration of the privileged, the sons accustomed to receiving toys, books, and warm clothing, as well as oranges, nuts, candy and a well-laden dinner table. In his 1883 ledger, Amos Stackhouse noted that, "Christmas was a fine, beautiful day."

Amos continued to have good fortune, allowing him more expansion. On December 31, 1883, he added to his large farm the purchase of fifty-six acres from George W. Gahagan, at a cost of $336.[29] This property, too, would prove a valuable asset through the years, bringing prosperity and recognition to the Stackhouse community.

As long as there were job opportunities, people were lured to the Stackhouse area and, quite often, onto Amos' charge accounts ledger. To pay for their necessities, the customers bartered in a variety of ways, since very few had cash. Besides the mortgaging of their tobacco crop, many worked on the Stackhouse farm at forty cents per ten-hour day; in addition, a few, having skills such as blacksmithing, providing their own tools, earned sixty or sixty-five cents a day. Also appearing on the credit side of Amos' charge accounts were sometimes the following: 10 bushels apples, $4.00; mutton, 87 cents; 26 lbs. tallow, $1.30; 4 ½ days ploughing, $2.93; 14 lbs. hides, $1.40; and "1300 clapboards and putting on," for $6.29.

The consignment method was another form of payment, and prices had not changed since Amos opened his lower store. Sold by Amos, and bringing the producer only $11.45, was an assortment of items: 18 ½ lbs. beeswax, 4 ½ lbs. ginseng, 3 lbs. snake root, 11 'coon skins, 3 Red fox and 7 muskrat skins. At another time, Amos was paid for his customer's consignment, a total of $1.47 for one bear skin, 3 Gray foxes, 7 'coons, 6 'possums, 3 ¼ lbs. beeswax and 15 ½ lbs. beef hides.[30]

In the winter some workers paid their bills "by cutting ice," the river blocks then packed in sawdust under a northerly tree bank for use in summer. Other workers paid by "work at fire," likely in the barns to cure tobacco, or at the kilns to slowly dry the fresh-cut lumber. Yet more workers' accounts were paid by "cutting firewood," or "making rails" and building the miles of rail fences needed around Amos' farm to prevent his livestock from wandering away or grazing on a neighbor's property.

However, not all Amos' charge customers paid their accounts. One of these Amos identified with the note, "Ran away." Another account was finally paid but Amos was required to "give half for collecting to Mr. Curry," the railroad section boss, who possibly took the owed sum of $29.44 from the worker's wages. In addition, a few customers died before they could pay their on-running charges, a loss Amos had to absorb at this time before life insurance.

By late January, 1884, these ledger entries were made in a different, more legible handwriting.[31] Ellison Stackhouse was working at his father's store, either because Amos was sick, or, possibly because Ellison needed the mountain air for his own persistent colds and cough. He could even have come for the curative waters at nearby Warm Springs. With the expanding tobacco business and other projects, Amos might have enticed his son to come to western North Carolina and participate in the prosperity. Now sixty-five years old, Amos surely had dreams of retiring and turning his business over to his son. For whatever reasons, Ellison spent the spring at Stackhouse, either with or without his wife and children, then returned to Philadelphia to ponder a permanent move the next year.[32]

During the summer of 1884, Amos became involved in yet another field of endeavor through Thomas Lanier Clingman, or "General Clingman," as people still called him. In dire financial straits and suffering from his Civil War leg wound, Clingman grasped at the straw of prospecting, reviving his mineral half-interest on Amos' farm.[33]

A former lawyer and statesman, Clingman had spent much of his money on electric light experiments and in dealing with Thomas Edison, who ended up using a different type filament, refusing Clingman's offerings. (Clingman's zirconia lamp, however, did illuminate for a long period of time, earning him a patent on April 17, 1883.[34]) His funds exhausted, and unqualified for a bank loan, Clingman was rendered unable to compete with Edison. Thus he turned, in his seventy-second year, to the hope of profit through barite mining.

Like ore samples showing barite (on right) to be almost double the weight of feldspar (on left). Courtesy Geological Survey, Asheville, N.C.

Clingman was prompted, no doubt, by another result of the railroad completion, the new barytes processing plant operating about two miles below the Warm Springs hotel. The ore was dug from the mountain above and hauled by wagon or tram to the mill at the railroad for crushing, bagging and shipping. "Barytes" is the commercial name for barite or sulphate of barium – a heavy mineral, commonly white, opaque to translucent, and crystalline – often called "heavy spar."[35] It was used in the manufacturing of paint, paper, pottery glazes, rubber and chemicals. As early as 1818, geologist William McClure had reported barite in the area of Warm Springs. In 1875, W.C. *Kerr's Report of the Geological Survey of North Carolina*, Vol. I, under "Barite," stated: "A vein of eight feet in width of the white granular variety exists at Chandler's [Candler], nine miles below Marshall in Madison County." Thus, Clingman, who also studied the geology of western North Carolina, knew that Madison County harbored valuable minerals and stones.[36] Moreover, Clingman surely knew that the baritic zone discovered by McClure likely extended across the mountain and river to the Stackhouse area. Hoping to bring a profitable amount of ore to the surface, the old general likely rode the train from Asheville to discuss it with Amos. Even though Amos Stackhouse might lack the knowledge of geology, he was not ignorant of the operation, having gone underground to observe the lead mining in Galena, Illinois, years back. He had few reservations, if any, about joining Clingman, who was highly respected in western North Carolina. (This regard can be seen by the number of children given the first name "Clingman.")[37]

Decades later the esteem for Clingman was shown in a note attached to two letters found among the personal effects of Amos Stackhouse, Jr.: "General Clingman was a Gen. in the Confederate Army and a Senator from

N.C. and a partner in the Barytes... on the Stackhouse property... I knew Clingman when I was a boy of 12 years old. Amos Stackhouse, Jr."[38] The first of the two cherished letters had come to Amos from Asheville, dated September 13, 1884:

> "Dear Sir, I have engaged Richard Bostick to go down with another man on Monday morning. I have given him $3.00 to pay their passage down and they are willing to work for one dollar per day and find themselves. I think it probable they may be satisfied with less if you keep them sometime employed. I paid eighty cents for the picks which they carry down. I will probably come down in a few days. Yours truly, T.L. Clingman."[39]

Nine days later, Clingman again wrote to Amos:

> "I wish the men to blast at least six feet from the bottom across the vein in the direction of the river toward the west. I have advanced
> as follows to you $10.00
> for drill and fuse 2.45
> for picks .80
> to Bostick 3.00
> to Conner 1.80
> 18.05
>
> T.L. Clingman."[40]

The former congressman was careful in his accounting to Amos, who owned the other half of the mining interest. Amos, in turn, also kept a record of the prospecting expenditures and payroll from his store. Under *Baratta Mine*, Amos charged blasting powder, fuses and dynamite; flour and bacon; sharpening drills; days of work by Daniel Conner, Richard Bostick, and Hoppes; and to Mrs. Potter, board. For the months of September and October, the drilling, blasting, picking and shoveling continued, but with little profit, apparently.[41] There is no mention of resulting ore finds or of shipping to a crusher. However, old Mr. Clingman's suspicions were well founded, and the future would prove how close to success he had come.

Besides the barytes plant at Warm Springs, the new railroad was responsible for the addition of a section of rooms at the Warm Springs Hotel, bringing the total to 350, with other improvements throughout, including the refurbishment of its grand ballroom – second largest in the state.[42] J.H. Rumbough and W.W. Rollins had exchanged their partner, C.H. Sowers, for Mr. L.B. Pettyjohn, and hired the competent and respected Hezekiah Gudger as manager.[43] A Madison County native, Gudger's mother was Emmeline Barnard, descendent of Job Barnard, founder of Barnard's Stand community, five miles upriver from Stackhouse. After his admission to the bar, Gudger had been instrumental in establishing Buncombe County's school system, then headed the State School for the Deaf from 1877 to 1883.[44] During his first summer at Warm Springs, Gudger hosted as many as six hundred hotel guests at one time, heralding in a bright and promising future for the resort.[45]

Unfortunately, this hopeful future was short-lived. The shocking news came to Stackhouse on December 27, 1884, that the Warm Springs hotel was destroyed by fire, origin unknown. "There was a gale blowing from the east, and it required the greatest efforts to save Col. Rumbough's residence which

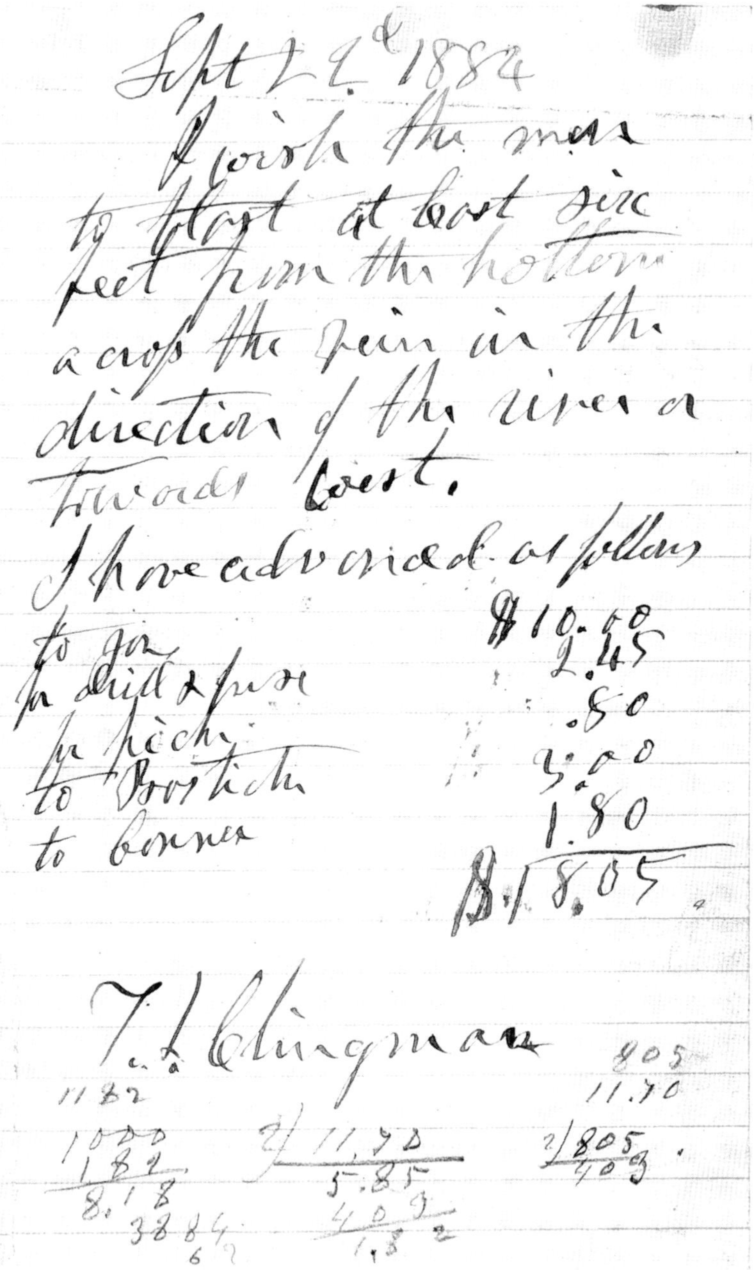

Sept. 2.d 1882

I wish the man
to start at least six
feet from the bottom
across the vein in the
direction of the river a
~~towards~~ West.

I have advanced as follows

to you $10.50
to drill & fuse   2.45
to pick   .80
~~to Bostick~~   2.00
to Conner   1.80
                    Bal. $8.05

T. L. Clingman

805
11.70

1182
1000
182
8.18
38.84
6?

2/11.70
5.85
4.0?
1?2

2/805
40?

The letter from Th. L. Clingman to Amos Stackhouse who jotted his
computations at bottom.

is a quarter mile from the hotel," stated the Philadelphia *Enquirer*.[46] Nor could the $150,000 building be replaced with the $50,000 insurance policy. The economic loss of one of the South's largest and best-known resorts would radiate throughout Madison County, affecting Stackhouse indirectly, but Amos' tollbridge company directly. He must have sympathized deeply with his colleagues, Rumbough and Rollins, for their misfortune, and with the hotel employees who were now forced to leave the area.

Nevertheless, Amos' projects at Stackhouse continued to grow, his most recent one being the new "cow stable" under construction toward the southern end of his side yard.[47] With the expected addition of Ellison's three children to the household, more cows were needed. The new barn was an imposing two-story structure, built over the Walnut Gap road that came by Woolsey's Branch to the railroad. The wagon road actually went under the stable's second floor, which was strongly built, as were all Amos' buildings, there being no shortage of large timbers or other materials.[48] With each such project, the Stackhouse farm increasingly resembled a village.

Finally, Ellison decided to add his home to the settlement. On January 20, 1885, though still in Montgomery County, Pennsylvania, Ellison paid $300 for sixty-five acres (adjoining Amos' farm on the south) from Robert Farnsworth, who had paid David Farnsworth $200 for the same tract over thirty years earlier.[49] Ellison also bought on the same day another 100 acres of the original David Farnsworth land from N.A. Farnsworth, who now lived in Washington County, Tennessee. Purchased from Peter Davis in 1828, this tract, as had been Amos' "Woolsey farm," was part of the 320,640 acres bought by John Strother in 1798 at cents per acre from the John Gray Blount auctioned holdings.[50]

The new deed, likely paid for by Amos, named Ellison Stackhouse *trustee* for his father's minor sons, Amos, Jr., and Charles Dilworth. As was the Quaker custom, Amos wanted to provide for his children's future before he retired. Called "the laurel farm" by Amos and Ellison, this 100-acre property was really a small, well-shaped mountain, including at its base the mouth of the Big Laurel where it converged with the French Broad – the point described by Christian Reid in Land of the Sky, as her characters were "poled across" the Laurel by the mulatto Wash Farnsworth, son of former Farnsworth slaves. (The 1860 Madison County census listed nine slaves held by Jane B. Farnsworth, widow of David Farnsworth.) Here, too, other artists invariably illustrated their articles with engravings of the picturesque "Laurel run." On this same French Broad River site, David Farnsworth, father of Robert and N.A. (Alexander) Farnsworth, had operated a stock stand during the prosperous days of the Buncombe Turnpike.[51] The "farm" of ten to twenty arable acres rested on a slight plateau midway up the mountain. Evidently, Washington Farnsworth, a frequent charge customer and employee of Amos', had been a tenant caretaker of the property. Coming into the hands of Amos, Jr., and Charles Dilworth on their respective twenty-first birthdays, this hundred acres would also become profitable and historic to the Stackhouse family and Madison County. Meanwhile, it presented a scenic view from Amos' front porch, centered, as it were, against the panoramic skyline.

[1] Arthur, John Preston. *Western North Carolina, A History*. Raleigh: Edwards & Broughton Printing Co., 1914, p.478.

[2] Weigley, Russell F. *Philadelphia, A 300 Year History*. New York: W.W.Norton & Co., 1982, p.429.

[3] Zeigler, Wilbur G., and Ben S. Crosscup. *The Heart of the Alleghenies*. Raleigh: A. Williams & Co., 1883, p.366.

[4] Powell, Wm. S., *Dictionary of N.C. Biography*, Vol. 1, p.35.

[5] Van Noppen, Ina W. and John J. *Western North Carolina Since the Civil War*. Boone, N.C.: Appalachian Consortium Press, 1973, p.214

[6] *Asheville News*, July, 1854.

[7] Private Laws of North Carolina, September 5, 1882.

[8] Madison County census records, 1880.

[9] Author's private papers.

[10] Ibid.

[11] Ibid.

[12] Ibid.

[13] Zeigler, p. 367.

[14] Kirke, Edmund. "On the French Broad." *Lippincott's Magazine*, Nov., 1884, p.432.

[15] Stroupe, Vernon S. *Postoffices and Postmasters of N.C.*, Vol.II. Charlotte: N.C. Postal History Society. 1996, p.2 – 273.

[16] Private papers.

[17] Arthur, p.282. Sondley, F.A. *A History of Buncombe County*. Asheville, N.C.: The Advocate Printing Co., 1930, p.   427.

[18] Madison County Deed Registry, Bk.1, p.138.

[19] Private papers.
Plemmons, Ernestine R. and Aumiller, Nancy S. Interviews, 1998.

[20] Private papers.

[21] Ibid.

[22] Ibid.

[23] Ibid.

[24] Ibid.

[25] Ibid.

[26] Burgin, Ora Henderson. Interview, 1985.

[27] Olson, Rebecca Reynolds, letters to author, 1988, 1989.

[28] Private papers.

[29] Madison County Deeds Registry, Bk. 3, p. 548.

[30] Private papers.

[31] Ibid.

[32] Ibid.

[33] Brumfield, L.S. *Thomas Lanier Clingman and the Shallow Ford Families*. Yadkinville, N.C.: Self-published, 1992, p. 142.

[34] Ibid.

[35] Oriel, Steven S. *Geology and Mineral Resources of the Hot Springs Window*. Raleigh, N.C.: Dept. of Conservation and Development, 1950, p. 48.

[36] Powell, Vol. 1, p. 388.
Van Noppen, p. 351.
Arthur, p. 546.
Sondley, pp. 132, 512. Oriel, p. 48.

37 Heritage Books of Madison, Haywood, Jackson, Buncombe Counties.
38 Private papers.
39 Ibid.
40 Ibid.
41 Ibid.
42 Zeigler, p. 369
43 Ibid.
44 Powell, Vol. II, p. 382.
45 Zeigler, p. 369.
46 Private papers.
47 Ibid.
48 Aumiller, Nancy S. Interview, 1998.
49 Madison County Deeds Registry., Bk. S, pp. 155, 161.
50 Buncombe County Deeds Registry, Bk. 15, p. 200
    Powell, Vol. I, p. 469.
51 Arthur, p. 196.

WESTERN NORTH CAROLINA RAILROAD

— VIA —

SALISBURY !

NOW COMPLETED TO THE

Famous Mountain Country !

"THE LAND OF THE SKY."

NO STAGING !

ALL RAIL LINE TO

ASHEVILLE,
WARM SPRINGS,
and PAINT ROCK.

PULLMAN SLEEPING CARS ON ALL NIGHT TRAINS DURING THE SEASON.
OBSERVATION CARS ON ALL TRAINS CROSSING THE MOUNTAINS.

A. B. ANDREWS,   V. E. McBEE,   J. R. MACMURDO,
    President.   Superintendent.   Gen. Pass. Agent.

Chapter Ten

During the winter and early spring of 1885, as Ellison Stackhouse in Pennsylvania prepared his move to western North Carolina, he received a letter from his father's sister, Sarah Vandervort of Brooklyn, New York, who seemed familiar with Madison Countians, no doubt, from having visited Amos. Dated "3rd month, 28th/85," her letter began:

> "My Dear Nephew – Thine was received and I was quite pleased to receive it...I feel quite sorry you are going so far away from us all, but no doubt thee will have better opportunities for getting along and I think the genial climate will greatly improve thy health, and Ella's, too. But you will find different society; less congenial, but may be equally kind and worthy, though not so refined and educated. Ella and Amos' wife will have, in turn, to be teachers... I am sorry Ella is not well. Moving is hard, exposing work, and you must both be careful. Does thee continue to have chills?
>
> Affectionately, Thy Aunt,
> Sarah D. Vandervort."[1]

Indeed, Ellison likely boarded the train shortly after his Aunt Sarah wrote, since a notation in Amos' business ledger by Ellison states: "Arrived at Stackhouse – 4th, 4, '85." Ellison had his own charge account, now, at the Stackhouse store, entering the first item on May 9th: "April 4th to May 9th – 5 weeks board for self, wife and 3 children."[2] Evidently, his agreement with his father was to pay for meals until they could move into their own quarters, or, possibly into one of Amos' rental houses. A letter from his father's unmarried sister, Anna, at the end of May, remarked: "I suppose you have got to housekeeping and feel more at home by yourselves... Did you ever get your trunk and clothing?" After giving news of the other relatives, Anna closed with the prediction, "Ella will be a great deal of company to Anna, and the two families can visit back and forth." More reaction to his new situation came a month later when Ellison received a letter from his half sister, Rebecca, who lived in Camden, Jersey, married to Harry Halderman:

> "I can never think of you and see anything familiar. Have you a creek or woods, or is it anything like we had in Ohio? I can imagine Ellison in a store behind the counter or on a porch on the hind legs of a chair with some men around him, if sales are slow... But I can never think of Ella or the children in any homelike position. Do tell me just how you are situated, where you sit to sew and talk, how the children play, and all about yourselves, so things will seem more natural and you won't seem so far away."[3]

However, Ellison was almost too busy to answer any of the letters since the spring plowing and planting were at hand on the Stackhouse farm in Madison County, and the store customers needed seeds, fertilizer and implements. Moreover, a new account in Amos' ledger was headed, "Tobacco Company, Ellison and myself."[4] It appeared to be a cooperative venture with neighbors, Mitchell Landers, Isham Fender, and others. In April, 1885, Amos has six men working at preparing seed beds, which were sown, then covered with loosely-woven fabrics lengths (8 $\frac{1}{2}$ cents per yard at Amos' store) tacked to frames. Workers also cleared land for new fields, and made rails for fences to keep out free-roaming cattle. Once the seedlings were transplanted to the fields, all hands, and several of their wives, concentrated on the hoeing.

After the initial push of getting the tobacco, corn and other crops growing, Amos and Ellison began preparing for the harvest and curing season. In August they cut trees, dragged them by ox, mule or horse teams to Amos' woodyard where the logs were trimmed and sized for building barns. A man earned fifty cents for his day's work, and extra for his draft animal, but the women were paid only twenty-five cents for their day's labor. On August 20, 1885, Ellison's ledger entry recorded: "Cutting logs – Harris, 1 day; Charley, 1 day, and ox; Lucy, 1 day in tob. field." On August 25th, two other men were credited with one day each on "foundation of Barn #2, Stackhouse Barn." Mitchell Landers' barn was listed as "#1." On September 3rd, Ellison noted at the side of the ledger page, "10 men raising." Lark Stanton, probably a stone mason, was paid one day to "build flues," and another day, to "chink," or fill with clay mud, the cracks between the field stones of the chimneys. On September 29th, Ellison, Mitch Landers, and eight other men, with one ox, spent the day "cutting and filling barn #1." On October 4th, "Mitch and Charley were entered as "curing tobacco – 4 days and nights." Others made the wooden sticks used in the fields for the initial drying period of the tobacco plants. On October 6th, Ellison, John, Jacob, George and Willis, spent one day each on barn #2, "chinking and daubing," which was the method used to spread clay mud into the openings left between the logs when they were stacked into walls. Ellison wrote, three days later, "Our team hauling three loads cured tobacco, $\frac{1}{2}$ day at Barn #1."[5]

While work done at "Barns #1 and #2" seemed to be a swap of labor, the ledger account of Isham Fender carried actual debit amounts. On the same page and mixed in with the charges of flour, sugar, shoes and coffee, were the following:

"John with team & wagon, hauling barn logs, 1$\frac{1}{2}$ days = $3.23.
Mule hauling wood to cure tobacco, 1 day = .75.
Ellison, Geo., Willis, 1 day ea.; John $\frac{1}{2}$ day raising barn = $2.28.
Ellison, John, Willis, Geo. & mule, filling tob. barn, 1 day ea. = $3.35"

For the privilege of buying groceries, merchandise, and his neighbors' labor before his crop was sold, Isham mortgaged his house to Amos at thirty dollars, and his tobacco crop at eighty dollars, with fifteen percent added to each.[6]

Because tobacco brought more cash than any other product, the farmers took many risks in growing it. If the season brought too little rain, the seedlings dried up in the fields or else produced stunted plants, affecting both quantity and flavor. If too much rain fell, mold and fungus might ruin the crop. Rain could also prevent the several steps of harvest in the fields from being carried out at the critical times – before the tobacco was even ready for the barn. Once the product was in the barn, the risks were lessened, but not by any means over.

The barns were equipped with crude stoves or fireplaces and thermometers to monitor the correct curing temperature; the fire was maintained night and day. Cutting, splitting and hauling load upon load of dry firewood made another job for the workers. The tobacco leaves were hung in the barns from horizontally-placed poles called "tierces," an old English word meaning "three parts," shortened to "tiers" in later years. The standard tobacco barn held three tierces. By heating the air in the barn at gradually increasing temperatures, the cured tobacco first became brittle, then pliable, as it absorbed just enough moisture for handling. At this stage – called "in case" – the leaves were finally packed into large casks of 63-gallon capacity, called hogsheads, which were easily rolled on their sides, or, when fitted with a pair of shafts, could be pulled to market by mule. During these early years of the Western North Carolina Railroad, the freight station was at Barnard, five miles up the railroad from Stackhouse, but better traveling than the four-mile trip to Warm Springs, now that the turnpike was blocked. Account page number 478 in Amos' ledger was titled, "E.B. Atkinson, Barnard freight agt."[7]

The destination of the Stackhouse tobacco was not recorded for the early eighties, but could have been Marshall, Asheville, Knoxville, or some other rail transport town. Amos might have sold to his friend J.H. Rumbough, who operated a tobacco-buying business in Knoxville after the Warm Springs hotel burned.[8] Three entries in Amos' store ledger on January 8, 1889, however, showed "tierces to Lynchburg."[9] Wherever the market, at long last the cash would come to the growers, Amos receiving what he had lent, plus his percentage.

Historians could speak of this time in western North Caroline as the tobacco craze – "The country roads were filled with tobacco wagons and the farms were dotted with curing barns and everybody thought and talked of tobacco," said one.[10]

A Raleigh *News and Observer* correspondent wrote from Marshall in February, 1886:

> "This place is the heart of the tobacco producing section of the mountains… It is remarkable what changes have appeared in this county since the culture of tobacco has been receiving the attention of the planters. It has put the county on a boon of prosperity… Some of the finest specimens of the weed ever grown in the State have come from Madison County."[11]

However, Amos Stackhouse could not give his fields solely to the cash "weed" – corn was still necessary for feeding his animals and for his own family's table. One especially productive location was the newly-purchased Laurel farm, an ideal place for both corn and tobacco growing. Immediately after purchasing the 100 acres from Farnsworth, Amos had begun "repairs to Laurel house," recording the expenditures and rent received in his store ledger. It helped Amos to have a tenant looking out for the place, an arrangement that provided badly needed housing for the settlement. It was likely an old house, the rent being only two dollars per month.[12]

Ellison's new house was also underway on his Farnsworth tract, according to his brother in Philadelphia, Thomas Stackhouse, who had recently returned with his wife, Eva, from Chicago:

> "Dear Brother, Eva's health has not been very good and I do not think the west agrees with her. I thought I would come back and give it another trial, but things do not look very encouraging so

far… I am awfully glad thee is getting along so well and likes it so much down there. I wish I could come down and help thee build thy house, for I am somewhat of a carpenter now that I have been working at it, and have become quite handy with tools… I think I shall write to Father and ask him if he will write a letter for me to Hood & Bombright & Co., or some other firm he has some influence with. If thee would do me the favor of speaking to him perhaps he would do it more willingly."[13]

In order to supply the variety of goods Amos sold in his general store, he did business with many Philadelphia firms besides Hood & Bombright. His ledger listed the houses of John Wanamaker's, Landreth's Seed Company, and A.D. Garden & Company, to name a few, plus dealers in New York, Boston, Chicago and Baltimore. Having spent the first twenty-five years of his life in Philadelphia, followed by forty years of merchandise-buying trips to the city, Amos had established numerous connections and a reputation for promptly paying his bills. No doubt he would be a big help in Thomas' job search; and Ellison, in his constant role of "big brother," would naturally "speak to Father" on Thomas' behalf.

Albeit, as Thomas' letter intimated, Ellison was well satisfied at Stackhouse, and his health improved, his wife, apparently, was not satisfied. The mountains' salubrious climate had not, it seemed, provided the panacea Ella needed. Compared to Philadelphia, Stackhouse was indeed primitive, and "not as refined," as Aunt Sarah had written. Even though her parents were dead, Ella surely missed her brothers and sisters and the support of a Meeting group of Friends. Perhaps she had not recovered well from the birth of her third daughter, Rebecca Stockton, at Stackhouse on February 9, 1886. Whatever the reason, on July 16, 1887, Ellison Stackhouse, placing, as Thomas had done, his wife's happiness before his own, moved Ella and their four children back to Pennsylvania.[14]

Three days before he left Madison County – July 13 – Ellison deeded his sixty-five acres, purchased from Robert Farnsworth two-and-a-half years before, to his father, as trustee for Amos, Jr., and Charles Dilworth, until their respective twenty-first birthdays.[15] In case of Amos' death, the boys' mother, Anna Myers Stackhouse, was designated to take trustee responsibilities. The amount paid by Amos for this property was $250, whereas Ellison had paid Farnsworth $300 at purchase. It is unclear whether Ellison's new house had been finished, but he had planted apple trees, built fences and made other improvements to the land. The fifty dollars difference, plus cost of improvements, must have been money Ellison owed Amos for store merchandise and cash loans noted in the ledger. Afterwards, Amos sold Ellison's ox for $25.00 and his heifer for $7.00, sending him the proceeds in Pennsylvania.[16]

Ever since the death of Ellison's mother, Rebecca Shaw, he and Amos had been close – confiding in each other, supporting each other through lean times and good. Being strongly family-oriented, Ellison took firm responsibility in the welfare of his siblings and family members – visiting, writing, and acting as mediator at times. Amos Stackhouse, now over sixty – eight years old, would miss Ellison's companionship and his help in the store and farm. He would miss Ellison's children as well, along with the prospect of retirement.

However, rolling up his sleeves, Amos began installing new water lines to his house, and he documented this fresh project for his memory and posterity:

"In laying pipes, August 15, 1887, from spring at top of hill south of store, I placed unions as follows:
1st – 9 ft. from box on spring.
2nd – 100 ft. from spring 4 ft. below burnt chestnut stump.
3rd – on bed of rocks 30 or 40 ft. west of road near east end of stone wall.
4th – union about 40 ft. from Hopewell road above fence near a rock.
5th – union 3 ft. south of holly tree in a box north side of creek."[17]

Besides aiding Amos in forgetting about Ellison's leaving, this well-laid system would provide the Stackhouse family with cold clear spring water for generations.

Oddly enough, a different kind of spring water, discovered the year before, probably affected Amos' business and that of others in Madison County. *The Raleigh News and Observer* of April 25, 1886, had carried a brief item from the *Asheville Citizen*, stating, "In excavating for the pool baths, fifteen feet below the surface was discovered… a cavity of unknown depth… Water boiled up… from 110 to 115 degrees. This makes known the source of the warm, or rather, hereafter, *hot* springs." Immediately the owners began to capitalize on the phenomenon, prompting the official name change of Warm Springs post office to Hot Springs on June 21, 1886, with Beverly Hill, the postmaster.[18] (Since the advent of the railroad, the post office had been located at Hill's store instead of the hotel.)

Back in October, 1885, the Raleigh paper had announced: "The celebrated Warm Springs hotel property in western North Carolina was sold… A new and elegant hotel… will be erected at once." The buyers were a syndicate of business men chiefly composed of Richmond & Danville Railroad stockholders, calling themselves The Southern Improvement Company. Besides the original one hundred acres of the mineral springs, Rumbough sold them the surrounding acreage, including his large home, Rutland. Adding to the settlement nucleus of train depot, livery stable, general store, saloon, and the few dwellings, the new owners began speculative building, laying out streets for a promising resort town. In June the Asheville newspaper reported "The Mountain Park Hotel at Hot Springs is now open." With four stories and over 1000 feet of piazzas, it was a handsome structure, "In every room of which the sun shone," wrote historian Van Noppen.[19] The mineral water was piped into the hotel bath rooms and into the separate bath house of sixteen marble-lined private pools, replacing the old three-compartment communal facility. Later, an outdoor swimming pool, 100 by 50 feet, also lined with marble slabs, was filled with the hot water. (This pool was near the location of the old toll bridge and almost directly across the river from Amos Stackhouse's former store and stock stand.) Inside the hotel there were two dining rooms, a ball room, gas lighting, and "an elevator for baggage and persons," declared the *Carolina Watchman* paper of Salisbury, North Carolina.[20] "The outlook for the western part of the state was never brighter, as this and other enterprises, not yet given to the public, will show," concluded the *Watchman*. Two passenger trains daily between Asheville and Louisville provided Amos the convenience to visit its grand new attraction whenever he had business in Hot Springs.

Tourists began, again, to frequent the mineral resort, a few buying lots, opening businesses and building homes. Mr. Harry T. Rumbough, son of J.H. Rumbough, opened a law office and did a good business processing deeds and other papers. Three churches – Roman Catholic, Episcopalian, and Southern Baptist – erected houses of worship, contributing to the makeup of a town. On the way to completing the picture was the arrival of Rev. Luke Dorland, retired missionary educator, who, with his wife, came for the rejuvenating spring water. Soon his neighbors persuaded him to teach their children in his home, leading to more youngsters walking from distances, eager to learn. By 1888, Dorland had started a schoolhouse on the hill above his home, next to the Baptist Church.[21]

Despite the fact that Luke Dorland and his wife earned the mountaineers' highest respect as teachers, their coming to Madison County was a little too late for Amos Stackhouse. Amos' sons – Amos, Jr., and Charles Dilworth – had received their elementary schooling at home with their mother and a hired tutor, as did most of the mountain pupils whose fathers could pay. When Amos, Jr., turned fifteen, he entered Parrotsville High School, a Tennessee boarding school, located, according to its brochure, "Twenty miles from Warm Springs, N.C., and seven miles from Newport." Mr. J.W. Lucas was the principal, and the school was "strictly non-sectarian, non-partisan, with trustees from the various religious denominations and both political parties… Students of good moral character only are wanted."[22] The term was eight-and-a-half months long, as opposed to the two-month sessions of most mountain schools. Amos bought flour from Parrotsville millers and knew that the old

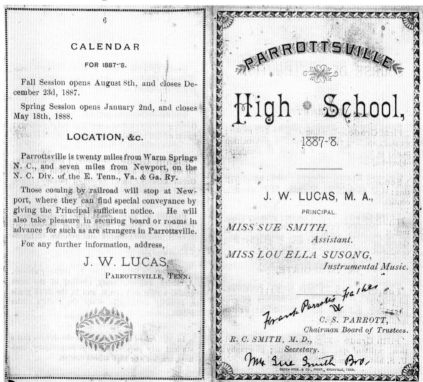

Parrotsville High School brochure.

east-Tennessee town had had private schools for at least fifty years. John E. Patton, former owner of the Warm Springs, had sent his sons there to school.[23] The Garretts, who had been Amos' turnpike neighbors and customers in Warm Springs, were also schooled in eastern Tennessee.[24] Besides tuition, Amos had to pay his son's room and board in Parrotsville. Several ledger entries noted, "Sent Amos $11.50," or "Sent Amos $10.00," probably to cover his lodging and incidental fees. Amos, Jr., made many friends in Cocke County and would often return to visit.

His brother Charles did not follow at the same school, but attended Weaver College, a Methodist institution – high school and junior college – near Asheville. "He was a sickly child, caught cold so easily, and had pneumonia several times," recalled Charles' daughter years later. "His mother taught him at home, mostly."[25]

The Stackhouses could partly blame the severe weather for Charles' illnesses. Winters, then, were harsh and long-lasting. At the end of his store sales account for the first week in December, 1886, Amos added this note: "Snow fell for 3 days, 3 feet deep, still on ground January 1st, 1887." He also wrote at the end of the month: "Sat., Jan 1st, 1887, New Years cold, rainy and snow." Twenty-six years later, historian J.P. Arthur affirmed Amos' report, saying, "On the 2d and 3d of December, 1886, a snow three feet deep fell in Buncombe and adjoining counties."[26] Other historians told how the French Broad froze bank to bank, supporting the crossing of a team of horses with wagon. A former Hot Springs resident recalled to a Knoxville *Sentinel* reporter:

> "The French Broad froze solid every winter, so one could walk across two to six weeks at a time. Mountain Park Hotel had an ice house and would chop big blocks of ice from the mill pond on Spring Creek in the heart of town, and store it until the middle of summer. Some of the more prosperous families did the same."[27]

Charles Dilworth Stackhouse, age 12.

When an old man, Amos Stackhouse, Jr., would enjoy telling how, as a teenager, he had ice skated all the way to Hot Springs on the French Broad.[28]

Weather was not the only problem the Stackhouses had to endure in the late 1880s. Ellison's wife, Ella, gave birth to a second son, Jesse Walton, in Altoona, Pennsylvania, on March tenth, 1888, but one month later she died, likely from childbed fever. Within the year, on March 4, 1889, the baby Jesse also died.[29] Ellison Stackhouse, widowed at age forty-three, faced a lonely life of responsibilities, raising his three daughters – Laura, Mary, and Rebecca Stockton, ages thirteen, eight, and three – plus son, Ellison, age twelve. Had the elder Ellison stayed in western North Carolina, his father and stepmother could have been a tremendous help to him.

More bad luck came to Amos in April, 1888, when one of his new barns burned to the ground. Then, on August 5th, 1889, a letter from his second oldest daughter, Rebecca Halderman, brought sadness, because he would rarely get to see her or her children again:

> "Dear Father, I did not know whether thee would hear it through others or not, so I write to tell thee that we have changed our home from Camden, N.J., to Kansas City, Mo. Harry had an offer here… and as thee knows, business is much better and more driving here than in Philadelphia. We have been in Kansas City a few days over a week, and I am delighted with the place… The business part of the city is well built – handsome, expensive buildings five and six stories high, comparing well with the best of Chestnut and Market Sts. in Phila… The city has parks which are beautifully laid out with lakes for rowing, and all well cared for and cultivated. It has over ten different lines of Cable Car… Our house will be 918 E. 16th St. in a good neighborhood and two squares from a good school for Anna. Will be glad to hear from thee. With love, Rebecca S. Halderman."[30]

While Amos enjoyed hearing that Rebecca was happy and in a good situation, he would sorely miss visiting her on his annual trips to Philadelphia.

Sitting at his desk, reflecting on another passing decade, Amos summarized his ledger entries of "store sales" for the eight years since closing the Warm Springs store, writing the total of $33,308.28 – a respectable income for western North Carolina.[31] When all was said and done, the coming of the railroad had indeed made a positive impact on the mountaineers' lives.

Mountain Park Hotel, Hot Springs, N. C.

New hotel at Hot Springs faced railroad, while old one had faced river and turnpike.

[1] Author's private papers.

[2] Ibid.

[3] Ibid.

[4] Ibid.

[5] Ibid.

[6] Ibid.

[7] Ibid.

[8] Rumbough, Martha Baker. *Memories of Another Day.* Baltimore: Gateway Press, 1986, p.104.

[9] Private papers.

[10] Sondley, F.A. *A History of Buncombe County.* Asheville, N.C.: The Advocate Printing Co., 1930, p.733.

[11] *News and Observer*, Raleigh, February 26, 1886, p.2.

[12] Private papers.

[13] Ibid.

[14] Ibid.

[15] Madison County Deed Registry, Book 1, p.138.

[16] Private papers.

[17] Ibid.

[18] Stroupe, Vernon S. *Postoffices and Postmasters of N.C.*, Vol.II. Charlotte: N.C. Postal History Society. 1996, p.2-267.

[19] Van Noppen, Ina W. and John J. *Western North Carolina Since the Civil War.* Boone, N.C.: Appalachian Consortium Press, 1973, p.388.

[20] *Carolina Watchman*, Salisbury, N.C., May 27, 1886, p.4.

[21] Painter, J.B. *The Season of Dorland-Bell.* 2nd ed. Boone, N.C.: Appalachian Consortium Press, 1996, p.17.

[22] Private papers.

[23] O'Dell, Ruth Webb. *Over the Misty Blue Hills.* Easley, S.C.: Southern Historical Press, 1982 reprint, p. 250.

[24] Doughty, Richard H. *Greeneville: One Hundred Year Portrait.* Kingsport, Tenn.: Kingsport Press, 1974, p. 323.

[25] Meek, Anna Stackhouse. Interview, 1998.

[26] Arthur, John Preston. *Western North Carolina, A History.* Raleigh: Edwards & Broughton Printing Co., 1914, p.296.

[27] Undated clipping, author's collection, Carson Brewer byline.

[28] Aumiller, Nancy Stackhouse. Interview, 1997.

[29] Swayne, Norman Walton. *Byberry Waltons, An Account of Four English Brothers.* Decorah, Iowa: Anundsen Pub. Co., 1989, reprint, p. 489.

[30] Private papers.

[31] Ibid.

Chapter Eleven

Although Ellison's tobacco "co-op" seems to have ended when he left Madison County, Amos entered the new decade continuing to grow the crop and to foster its cultivation by his neighbors, knowing that Madison tobacco always brought top dollar. The editor of the *Asheville Daily Citizen*, on a train trip to Hot Springs, observed: "I spent a night at Sandy Bottom [two miles above Stackhouse]... where I found all mountains and no valleys, yet the finest tobacco lands in western Carolina. The corn was also good, the mountain sides producing it like bottom land."[1] One farmer, Pinkney Smith, worked for Amos at seventy-five cents a day, charging his household needs from Amos' store, and pledging "$^1/_2$ of corn crop at $10" credit, plus "$^1/_3$ of tobacco crop – $10."[2] These products offered hope to the mountaineers who had no other industry at hand.

Springtime, however, brought a renewal of the barite mining to Stackhouse, as reflected in Amos' ledger accounts for "J. Turner Morehead," entrepreneur and son of John Motley Morehead, North Carolina's governor from 1841-1845. Amos kept a list of workers' hours, supplies and materials used in drilling and constructing underground tunnels. To Morehead, he sold lumber, nails, bolts, copper rivets, windlasses, oil, axle grease, mattocks, picks, buckets and wheelbarrows; plus oats, corn and hay for the animals; bacon, flour and coffee for the men, all paid by checks drawn on the Bank of Leaksville in Rockingham County. In April, 1890, Amos and Anna had deeded to Morehead their half-interest in the minerals on the "605-acre Woolsey tract," as well as their whole interest in the "56-acre Gahagan tract." They received $625 for the first two years, with $312.50 due at each successive year.[3] Turner Morehead also rented houses from Amos for employees and possibly one for himself. During the summer of 1890, Mrs. Morehead boarded with the Stackhouses for a short time, no doubt enjoying a respite from the Piedmont heat of their Leaksville home.[4]

Amos had probably become acquainted with Turner Morehead from Morehead's involvement in the building of the Western North Carolina Railroad, one of three constructed for Morehead's various business interests.[5] Thomas L. Clingman might also have directed Morehead to use Clingman's half interest on Amos' 605 acres, either to split the profit with Clingman or to keep as a token of friendship – Turner Morehead was married to Mary Elizabeth Connally, whose family were long-time next door neighbors of Clingman's family.[6] Morehead further shared with Clingman an interest in geological resources of the state, as well as experimental work with metals.

The Morehead mine adit (surface opening) was conveniently located about three-quarters of a mile from Amos' store and the railroad, with the tunnel burrowing hundreds of feet into the mountain. Thick lumps of white ore were hauled out to the adit, loaded onto wagons, and carried down the mountain to Amos' rail siding. Here, a different crew filled box cars with ore, listed by Amos in his ledger according to weight, individual car number and its railroad owner. Some cars were loaded at fifty cents per ton and some at seventy-five cents, then shipped, more than likely to Hot Springs, where a barytes mill had operated since 1884.[7] Situated alongside the railroad, two miles below the village, near Henry Oettinger's former drovers' inn, the Hot Springs Barytes Company crushed the ore into powder, packed it into barrels and shipped it to distributors.

In 1891 another barite-processing company, "Dingee & Weineman," began operating in the Sandy Hook section of Lynchburg, Virginia, and appearing, by October of that year, in Amos Stackhouse's store ledger. Simultaneously, Turner Morehead's account was settled and closed. Following in the footsteps of his friend Thomas Clingman, Morehead was bankrupt within two years, but his mark was left on Madison County, as the "Morehead mine" continued to be known at Stackhouse. (Later he regained his wealth through industrial developments that led, after his death, to the formation of Union Carbide Corporation.)[8]

Dingee & Weineman brought employment and profit to the Stackhouse community. Listed in Amos' ledger were the names and hours worked of forty-eight men, their respective wages running from ten cents a day to one dollar per day. Most of the names are recognizable as native to Madison County, but a few had probably come with Morehead from the Piedmont. Dingee & Weineman also rented houses for the laborers from Amos, in addition to buying necessities at his store for the draft animals – salt, hay, shoes, collarpads, liniment and "horse medicine."[9]

Amos continued to record in his ledger the boxcar loading of barytes at his railroad siding, at least through 1898. Thereafter, the Dingee-Weineman account did not appear, indicating either depletion of the Morehead vein or of necessary funding.[10] It seems improbable that the long illness of General Clingman had any bearing on the Stackhouse operation, but his death in 1899 would certainly have been felt deeply by his old friends, Amos Stackhouse and Turner Morehead. Another possible factor in the cessation of the Dingee-Weineman connection was the burning of the barytes mill at Hot Springs in September, 1899. According to the *Asheville Daily Citizen*, the plant was owned by Dingee & Weineman of Lynchburg, Virginia, who had only nominal insurance, but who pledged to rebuild.[11]

If barytes mining at Stackhouse was dwindling at this time, the lumber business was accelerating, as Amos, Jr., began taking more responsibility in his father's enterprises. Amos, Jr., encouraged his father to get business cards with his name across the top, his address at the bottom, and a description of his services filling the rest of the space: "Wholesale Dealer and Manufacturer of Flooring, Sash, Blinds, Doors, Mouldings and Finished Lumber; poplar, pine, oak and walnut lumber by the carload lots; Bridge and Building Timber Cut to Order." A small engraving at the card's corner pictured two styles of doors, louvers, a curving staircase, dentil-edged baseboard, and a fancy carved corbel.[12] Rough framing lumber could be sawn, sized and dried at Stackhouse, while the doors, windows, mantels, and other finishing items could be ordered by Amos from his numerous suppliers.

A further milestone of manhood for Amos' son was marked on April 6, 1891, with the notarized signing of the following oath:

"I, Amos Stackhouse, Jr., assistant postmaster, do solemnly swear that I will support and defend the constitution of the United States against all enemies, foreign and domestic… and that I will faithfully discharge the duties of the office of which I am about to enter… I will truly account for and pay over any money belonging to the United States which may come into my possession or contact… So help me God."[13]

Amos, Jr., could now perform in an official capacity the duties he had already learned by helping Amos at the store, allowing his father to take longer absences from the post office. (Incidentally, incoming mail was hand-stamped with date and time of arrival at Stackhouse, as was outgoing mail – each piece bearing two postmarks.)

In addition, Amos, Jr., ran the sawmill with the help of employee W. Joseph Balding. During one of Amos, Sr.'s, trips North in May, 1891, he received a letter from his wife, Anna, saying: "Balding and Amos are sawing; George Eakin and Charly are hauling logs." Two days later, Amos, Jr., also wrote his father: "Dear Papa, I am busy today at the saw mill and I am going to count stamps, as you requested… George is hoeing the corn. Mama and Uncle Frank [Myers] went to Jewel Hill to church yesterday… Your most affectionate son, Amos."[14]

Walnut Methodist Church, Walnut, N.C., (Formerly, Jewel Hill). Photo by author.

There is no record of the exact time the Stackhouse family had begun attending the Methodist Church at Jewel Hill, but having no Quaker Meeting within reasonable distance, it was better to worship "out of unity" than not at all. There were also societal rewards, as proven by Amos, Jr., who was paying court to one of this church's devout members – Miss Hester Ann Honeycutt, age fourteen. On June 4, 1891, he wrote what was to be the first of many letters to her:

"Dear Friend, I was at Jewell Hill on Sunday, but Davis told me that your mother and brother were sick, so I knew why you were not there. You may be surprised to hear from me, but I wanted to hear how your mother was getting along, and you, too. Hope you can be at Sunday School. Answer this as soon as possible by mail or by hand. If you send it by hand, tell the one you give it to, to give it to me, not my father, and if by mail, put, 'Jr.' at my name."[15]

The smitten Amos would grow even more faithful in his church attendance, joining the Jewell Hill Methodists by baptism a few months later. This action surely demonstrated to Hester and her family his sincere Christian character and worthiness as a suitor. It would also set him on a path of lifelong service to that particular institution, whose original structure had been built as a community meeting house.

In 1838, before the formation of Madison County, Joseph Barnard (descendant of Job Barnard), donated "an acre lying in the County of Buncombe on the west edge of the old Warm Springs road, including the Jewel Hill Meeting House," to a set of trustees. Privileges of firewood and water from the surrounding Barnard tract were granted with the land, which was designated, "for the use of school and meetings in said house, for all kinds of professions to preach in and schools, whatsoever."[16] Consequently, when the new Madison County in 1851 needed a place to conduct its business, centrally-located Jewell Hill Meeting House served as its first court house, complete with whipping post out front for those who broke the law.[17]

After the county seat was moved to Marshall in the fall of 1859, the Methodists – one of the earliest denominations established in Madison County – began using the Jewel Hill Meeting House on a regular basis.[18] In 1889, a corrective deed for the same property named the sole owner as "Methodist Church South."[19] As practically the only center for socializing in the community, the church would play an important part in the three-year courtship of Hester Honeycutt and Amos Stackhouse, Jr.

Meanwhile, the love letters continued to travel between the post offices of Stackhouse and Barnard (nearest to Jewel Hill), Hester's greetings progressing from "Dear Friend," to "Kind Friend," to "My Dearest Friend," while Amos moved quicker from "Dear Friend," to "My Dearest Darling." When he went to Newport, Tennessee, to visit his school friends, Amos even wrote her from there. Another time Amos penned a plea for Hester to come to mid-week prayer services, saying,

"Of course you can't go every Wednesday night, but I hope you will go at least twice a month. You know we ought to cultivate our love for God as well as for one another, and in whatsoever we do we ought not to forget God. And by our going, it may be that we could have a good Prayer Meeting by encouraging others to go. But be sure to go Wednesday night next, as I want to see you so bad."[20]

In November, 1892, Amos, Jr., wrote to a friend in Morganton, who had worked at the Stackhouse barytes mine, "I have one sweet being that I think is true to me as ever a girl could be, and you know who that is – Hester."[21]

Perhaps thoughts of matrimony inspired Amos, Jr., to work harder at his father's saw mill and dry kiln. Handling lumber daily, he was learning about its many grades and properties, gleaning information from older, more experienced co-workers, and honing a lifetime skill.

All over western North Carolina and eastern Tennessee there were lumber companies from the North seeking timber to replace their exhausted supply. Where roads did not exist they bought great stands of virgin forests, called "boundaries," sent down saw mill managers, who started up lumber camps and cutting operations, then shipped the product back North.[22] First-hand stories were frequently told of tall poplars and pines five feet in diameter being felled and floated by streams to the nearest railroad. These logs were usually cut at small "circle-saw" mills, although one band saw mill, belonging to a man from New Hampshire, operated in nearby Jackson County from 1888 until 1896. "Big virgin timber seemed inexhaustible, with easy logging into the river. Yellow poplar logs, six feet in diameter at the butt were not uncommon, also the finest of oak, chestnut and other species in abundance," wrote Fred Buffum about his father's Dillsboro operation, Blue Ridge Lumber Company. Unfortunately, the flooding rains of 1896 destroyed Buffum's dam, distributing their logs through the Smokies and well into Tennessee, ruining their business.[23]

In the southeastern part of Madison County, the Scottish Carolina Timber and Land Company, Limited, from Glasgow, Scotland, had bought tracts of land, cutting the timber for shipping from Newport, just over the ridge.[24]

Yet another, the New England Southern Timber and Land Company, purchased in the northern section of Madison, closer to Stackhouse, 38,500 acres, "more or less," along the Laurel River to the Tennessee line.[25] This corporation, too, was chartered in East Tennessee and owned other land tracts on the Tennessee side of the Madison boundaries. Moreover, the company president, James Wyman, planned a narrow gauge railroad to bring the logs from the Laurel country down to Hot Springs for rail shipping. The organized "Laurel River and Hot Springs Railroad Company" bought from landowners such as Benjamin F. Gahagan, "a right of way sufficient for the proper construction and maintenance of the said railroad, through and over... the tract of land... estimated at about 12 acres... including 15 feet each side of the center line of said railroad."[26] In Hot Springs the route left the Mountain Park Hotel property at the east bank of the French Broad about one half mile from Amos' former store, crossed the old Buncombe Turnpike and ascended the steep mountain (between the sites of the future Sanders and Bruce homes), toward Laurel River.[27]

Rail transportation brought a profitable factor to logging in the mountains. Without it, there were two methods: hauling logs by sled or wagon, a few at a time, or floating them in number downstream to the nearest railroad. While the latter moved more logs, it was less than efficient, having to be done when the water was at its highest, sometimes in the rain. Furthermore, the temporary dams or "booms" built to stop the logs did not always do the job, allowing the hard-earned product to be carried downstream, out of sight. Log jams presented another common hazard, requiring men in hobnail boots and armed with pike poles to break up the jams by walking the logs in the water. These jams frequently caused flooding of cropland along the way and the depositing of logs onto fresh-plowed fields, angering the neighboring farmers. When the timbers overshot the booms, or washed out of banks, retrieval was expensive and almost impossible, since, unless the logs were marked, it was "finders, keepers."[28]

Despite its advantages however, railroading through the rugged Appalachian terrain was difficult and expensive, as had been proven. It was not surprising that, coupled with the nationwide "panic of 1893," the high costs of the project forced the shutdown of "Hot Springs and Laurel River Railroad." "All hands were paid off yesterday and work on the road will stop for some time, pending reorganization of the company," stated the *Asheville Daily Citizen* on July 19, 1893. The tracks had been finished and operating for two and a half miles, with four miles of grading completed. Two weeks later, the *Citizen* announced that the railway had suspended operations entirely until financial matters assumed a more hopeful condition. "In the meantime," concluded the article, "that little 24-inch gauge road is getting a new crop of grass on its miniature track."[29] The New England Southern Land and Timber Company's short life was over. (It did, however, leave a bed for future highway building.)

Although disappointed at losing this source of income, Amos and his neighbor, W. Wade Gahagan, another son of George Robert, found a lumber market in Hickory, North Carolina – J. Gibson McIlvainey and Company.[30] The Catawba County business may have been a contact of Amos', since its parent company was in Philadelphia, and Joseph McIlvainey, brother to Gibson, attended the same Meeting as Ellison Stackhouse.[31] For several years during the 1890's, Amos Stackhouse loaded and shipped box cars at his siding, keeping records for himself and for Wade, who lived in the Laurel River section and owned a saw mill with large timber resources. White pine, yellow pine, ash, walnut, poplar, chestnut and oak in standard sizes were sent, plus large dimensions, such as 8/4 x 16'; 12/4 x 12' and 14' lengths; white pine and poplar in "seven, eight, and ten-inch squares" and a small amount of curly poplar, bright sap, and black sap poplar. The grades of the lumber ranged from "culls," to "common," to "common & better," to "good."[32]

More and more of Amos' projects were being conducted by Amos, Jr., whose after-hours relationship with Hester Honeycutt of Jewel Hill had grown steadily. At Christmas, 1893, he gave her the proper gift of a fine, brown, leather-covered Bible, followed by a Springtime proposal. On May 6, 1894, the marriage ceremony was performed in Greeneville, Tennessee, by Rev. W.C. Nelson, who also married another couple the same day, likely in a double wedding.[33] Mary Nelson might have been Rev. Nelson's daughter, acquainted with Amos when he was in school at nearby Parrotsville, while her bridegroom, Aaron Tweed, had been born in Madison County and later moved to Greeneville.

There is no evidence that members of Amos' family or of Hester's were present at the marriage, Hester being within two weeks of her eighteenth birthday. Nor do we know how the two families received the elopement news – though the marriage was certainly no surprise to anyone in the community. (Shortly afterwards, Hester learned that her older sister, Bonnie, had also secretly married four days before Hester and Amos.)[34] While proud and hardworking, Hester's mother had been poor since her husband died in 1888. Becoming proficient at sewing when young, Hester earned money as a seamstress, having often been called upon to sew burial clothes. Ancestry of Hester's father, James Matthew Honeycutt, is not available, but her mother,

Rachel Angelina Gilbert Honeycutt, mother of Hester Honeycutt Stackhouse, date unknown.

Rachel Angeline Gilbert, descended from Daniel Gilbert, who had come from Yorkshire, England, during the seventeenth century, as had the Stackhouses.[35] Hester's family were known and established in Madison County, her sister, Carrie, having married Van Buren Davis, Register of Deeds, while her cousin, Julina Gilbert, had married Malachi "Mallie" Reeves, old friend of Amos Stackhouse. In addition to Carrie and Bonnie, Hester Honeycutt had another sister, Mae, plus three brothers – Arthur, Lloyd and Frank.

While Hester had not had education beyond the basic home tutoring of her childhood, she possessed an inherent intelligence and was an avid reader. Throughout their courtship, Amos, Jr., had lent her books from his parents' library and from his own collection. In fact, Hester had told Amos, Jr., that she planned to go on to school, working her way, but there was usually a reason to keep her from enrolling. In one letter she mentioned to Amos that Dr. Atkins had been down, and, "I know you get tired of hearing me say it, but I am going to school as soon as Grandma is better." Associated with the Methodist Church, Daniel Atkins, D.D., lived in Weaverville, was a former president of Weaverville College, and likely preached at Jewel Hill Church from time to time.[36] Although Hester Anna Honeycutt did not bring to the union a large dowry, nor a line of nobility, she would be a faithful and fitting helpmate to Amos, Jr., as well as a credit to the community.

1 *Asheville Daily Citizen*, August 11, 1894, p.2.
2 Author's private papers.
3 Madison County Deed Registry, Book 3, p.105.
4 Private papers.
5 Powell, Wm. S., *Dictionary of N.C. Biography*, Vol. 4, p.320.
6 Brumfield, L.S. *Thomas Lanier Clingman and the Shallow Ford Families*. Yadkinville, N.C.: Self-published, 1992, p. 65.
7 Wellman, Manly Wade. *The Kingdom of Madison*. p. 111.
8 Powell, Vol. 4, p.321.
9 Private papers
10 Ibid.
11 *Asheville Daily Citizen*, September 9, 1899, p.1.
12 Private papers.
13 Ibid.
14 Ibid.
15 Ibid.
16 Buncombe County Register of Deeds, Book 21, p.313.
17 Stackhouse, Juanita. Interview, 1997.
18 Henry, Homer. *The Development of Public Education in Madison County,* Thesis, University of North Carolina, Chapel Hill, 1927, p.8.
19 Plemmons, Ernestine R., letter to author, August 13, 1998.
20 Private papers.
21 Ibid.
22 Van Noppen, Ina W. and John J. *Western North Carolina Since the Civil War*. Boone, N.C.: Appalachian Consortium Press, 1973, pp. 294, 296-7.
23 Parris, John. "Roaming the Mountains," *Asheville Citizen-Times,* July 27, 1978.
24 Madison County Register of Deeds, Book 20, p. 229. Dykeman, Wilma. *The French Broad*. Knoxville: University of Tennessee Press. 1965, p. 166.
25 Madison County Register of Deeds, Book 9, p.434.
26 Ibid, Book 5, p.399.
27 Ibid, Book 27, p.10; Book 28, p.198.
28 *Standard Reference Work*, Vol.V. Chicago: Standard Education Society, 1927.
29 *Asheville Daily Citizen*, August 3, 1893, p.1.
30 Baker, Elizabeth Gahagan. Interview, January, 2001.
31 Private papers.
32 Ibid.
33 Greene County Court Records, Book 5, p. 267, Greeneville, Tennessee.
34 Private papers.
35 Ibid.
36 Pickens, Nell. *Dry Ridge, Some of its History*, 2nd ed. Weaverville, N.C.: Friends of Weaverville Library, 1996, p.43.

Chapter Twelve

The newlyweds began their married life in the large home with Amos, Anna and Charles Dilworth (Charly). At the store Amos headed a new ledger page, "Amos Stackhouse, Jr.," but more than the typical household account, it included men's names and amounts paid to them by Amos. These would be workers at the sawmill and kiln, suggesting that Amos, Jr., was his father's foreman.[1]

Now that his father had placed him in management position, Amos, Jr., convinced Amos to deposit the cash money from his trunk, at home, into the National Bank of Asheville, located at the public square of the city. Now he often paid his bills by check instead of by cash in a registered letter, as before. It was not difficult to make a quick trip to Asheville with the convenience of the four daily passenger trains through Stackhouse – nos. 11, 12, 27 and 28.[2]

Amos could also make train trips to Hot Springs for meetings of Madison County's Republican Party, which he ardently supported. At one such gathering, Amos presided in the absence of Richard Gahagan (brother of Wade), and was chosen to represent the organization at an upcoming convention in Marshall, along with some of the county's prominent leaders: N.J. Lance, Hot Springs postmaster, entrepreneur, and brother to P.L. Lance, the "Lance Crackers" founder; H.T. Rumbough – attorney and son of "Col." J.H. Rumbough; Thomas and Joe Lawson – merchants and grandsons of Henry Oettinger, large landowner and ferry operator; and Van B. Davis – Madison County Register of Deeds.[3]

Although just old enough to vote, Amos, Jr., shared his father's enthusiasm, writing to his friend Lowdermilk: "Things are very lively here about the election. How is your county going this year? Madison will go Republican."

The Stackhouses had always taken interest in elections and politics, even the women, who read and kept abreast of current affairs. Sarah Vandervoort, Amos' older sister, wrote him from Brooklyn in April, 1898:

> "What does thee think of this war? I was in hopes the matter could be settled. I think much of McKinley, who showed good judgment and principle, doing all he could to prevent it. Our former war was warrantable, but this is cruel and unreasonable. I fear much for the result. The Spanish are so wicked – great fighters on the water where they do have the advantage. I can read only the large print headings, now, my eyes not permitting. What is thy opinion?"[4]

In a letter the year before, his cousin Tacie Gillingham had expressed her interest in efforts to bring a trolley line through her village of Fallsington, Pennsylvania, and, "the obstacle of crossing the Pennsylvania Rail Road, which will not allow them the right-of-way, nor to come within a certain distance of their property – I am afraid they will not come to terms." Commenting more broadly, Tacie said, "I suppose thee rejoiced in McKinley's victory – I hope business will improve after his inauguration. Does thee still read the newspapers in bed?"

Amos did read newspapers, avidly as always, having just renewed his subscription to the *Philadelphia Press*, for one, in addition to several local papers. Besides keeping up with community and national matters, Amos pursued his love of other reading, both prose and poetry – Thomas Hood, the humorous English poet, being a favorite.[5] He also admired the Quaker author John Greenleaf Whittier, and probably knew him personally between 1838 and 1840, when Whittier edited an anti-slavery paper, the *Pennsylvania Freeman*, at Philadelphia. The words of Whittier's well-known hymn "Dear Lord and Father of Mankind" would be sung and admired by succeeding Stackhouse generations. Another book in Amos' library, no doubt, would have been *Some Fruits of Solitude*, by William Penn, possibly an original old-colony printing passed down from Amos' grandfather. We can imagine that Amos gained comfort from this book in his old age, as had Robert Louis Stevenson when he read it fifteen years earlier.[6]

Furthermore, Amos himself occasionally composed verse for his own amusement. "Papa wrote this about January 14, 1890," was scribbled by Amos, Jr., on the page beside the following:

"'Tis pleasant to sit by a warm winter fire
When the night draws the curtain round
With wife and with children to make home complete
And peace and contentment abound."[7]

In the back pages of a Stackhouse store ledger, undated, was found a longer, more ambitious reminiscence, titled, "The Days of Long Ago." While the poem was not signed by Amos, it was written in his longhand with several words overstruck by new choices, as might be done in an original composition. The transcript follows:

In pensive mood I often sit through evening hours aglow
And think of all the happy days that passed in years ago

I love to fancy to recall these joyous dreams of yore
To visit past remembered scenes and live them ore and ore [sic]

My eyes are growing dimmer with the years that roll away
My step is slow and feeble and my locks are turning gray

But when in pensiveness I sit I feel again the glow
Of youth that thrilled my happy heart in days of long ago.

In days of long ago, alas how joyous was my lot
Those dear old scenes and happy dreams shall never be forgot

The world was filled with music with blossoms ever fair
And beamed a loving welcome ever courteous and rare
A happy song of cheer rang forth from every tree
Till every mountain every dell was echoing with glee
One blest sweet melody divine charmed all this earth below
And rose afar to skies above in days of long ago.

The days of long ago alas how distant now they seam [sic]
The past is but a memory a dear remembered dream
The future brings us palsied age and many sorrow tears
All hopes and joys how long since passed through dim receding years

And yet it does a mortal good to muse o'er youthful days
And tread in fancy once again life's unforgotten ways

And that is why I often sit through evening hours aglow
And dream again of happy days of long time ago.[8]

Leaving Amos Jr., in charge gave Amos the opportunity to travel North when family needs arose. On one particular trip he wrote Anna from Glen Mills, Pennsylvania, saying: "The people have not begun to come in for the funeral. Joseph's Rebecca is here – also, Emlen's Anna… Amos, keep the men's time correctly, and Charly must not forget to cut the weeds and clean up yard." Joseph and Emlen were Amos' brothers; Rebecca and Anna, their respective daughters, but we do not know whose funeral they were attending.[9]

Later that year, on November 23, 1890, Amos received a letter from his brother Powell in Philadelphia, telling of his wife's death:

"My Dear Brother, Emily passed away last evening about twenty minutes to six… We propose to have the funeral from Fair Hill Meeting House on fourth day afternoon. As thee has been called away from home frequently of late, and the expense is considerable, we will not look for thee on.

Thine affectionately, Powell Stackhouse, Jr."[10]

Amos and his younger brother, Powell, Jr., had always been close, visiting and corresponding regularly, but now that his wife was dead, Powell would appreciate Amos' attention even more.

Perhaps to assuage his loneliness, Powell turned to completing the Stackhouse family history begun by his grandfather, Amos, and expanded by his father, Powell, Sr. During the past few years, Powell had sent queries for genealogical information to Stackhouses in America, Canada and England, but now he attacked the project with zeal, possibly sensing that he had this decade, only, left to him. He wrote hundreds of letters in his unhurried, faultless calligraphy, and spent years examining records of all kinds that might provide related facts.

South Carolinian Eli Thomas Stackhouse, distant cousin of Powell and Amos, died in 1892 while serving in the 52nd Congress of the United States. About 1889, Powell, Jr., had contacted Eli who knew little family history, but opened the route of exchange with the South Carolina branch of Stackhouses. Photo from *Memorial Adresses on the Life and Character of Eli T. Stackhouse*, published 1893 by Government Printing Office, Washington, D.C.

Around 1892, his twenty-year-old son, William Romig Stackhouse, grew interested in tracing some of the branches not yet studied by his father, especially overseas.[11] He even installed a small printing press in his basement, setting the type by hand and producing form letters, saving Powell much time and hand work. The following is a facsimile:

OAK LANE, STATION A.

Philadelphia, ... *mo.* .... *189* ....

RESPECTED FRIEND:

The undersigned is collecting information relating to the genealogy and record of the descendants of THOMAS and JOHN STACKHOUSE, from Yorkshire, England, who settled in Middletown Township, Bucks County, Penna., about the year 1682, and respectfully requests information of the following nature:

1st. Copies of family records, giving names in full of members of thy own family, children, parents and grand parents, brothers and sisters, uncles and aunts, with Post-office address, and dates of births, marriages and deaths, and the place where, when known. If married, give full name of wife or husband of each, with names of her or his parents.

2d. Names of ancestors as far back as known with places of residence, whence they came, etc.; in all cases giving as full information of the first of the Stackhouse family in thy neighborhood, as possible.

3d. Miscellaneous facts such as occupation or profession, offices held, incidents, reminiscences, traditions and any facts thought worthy of mention.

4th. The names and Post-office address of persons of the name of Stackhouse and of such other persons as may be known, who are descendants of the family or connected with it by marriage.

It is not expected that all who receive this circular will be able to give information on all these points, but each is requested to send whatever he or she possesses, no matter how little it may be. Sometimes a very small item is an important clue to fuller details, or it may be a valuable link in connecting or verifying history already collected.

These inquiries are not made through idle curiosity or in any hope of pecuniary profit; but simply as a matter of history, that the records of the Stackhouse Family may be collected and put into intelligent form for permanent preservation.

As a possible assistance to some in tracing their families, I annex hereto a list of the children of Thomas and John Stackhouse, so far as I have a record of them.

Address communications to

POWELL STACKHOUSE, Jr.,

Oak Lane, Station A, Philadelphia.

Upon receipt of his copy, Amos was reminded of a similar work he received years before from their father, Powell, Sr., who seems to have written by hand a copy for each of his ten children. At the top of the first page, titled, "Memorandum," there was a quotation from "Dr. [Samuel] Johnson," stating, "Whatever makes the past distant or the future predominate over the present advances us in the dignity of thinking beings." There were also three scripture selections – the most pertinent from the first chapter of Joel, verse three: "Tell ye your children of it, and let your children tell their children, and their children, another generation." Obviously, Powell Stackhouse, Sr., had felt a Divine calling to make this record for posterity. In his long introduction to the several pages of genealogy, he explained his purpose with admonitions to his progeny, outlining a doctrine of sorts by which they should live, and hoping they would pass it down. A condensed version follows:

> "It is not because any of my ancestors were distinguished among men for any extraordinary endowments that I am induced to make this record,… but when in my youth I was inquisitive with regard to my family connections and descent, and also having obtained from my parents and grandparents some information relating to family concerns that I think will be gratifying to my children to know: I have endeavored as opportunity offered to record them for their satisfaction, my own honoured father (Amos Stackhouse) having made some essays in the same way; And as I am not conscious that any of my ancestors bore a character that would be esteemed men or degraded, but have generally… filled the stations in society they occupied with respectability, I am the more induced to offer… to my descendants, and do enjoin it on them, to let their conduct be so far in accordance with their forefathers as that no stigma may be justly attached to them… And with holy Job exclaim, 'All the while the breath is in me… my lips shall not speak wickedness, nor my tongue utter deceit, my righteousness I hold fast and my heart shall not reproach me so long as I live.'"[13]

Though he cherished his father's rendition of the Stackhouse annals, Amos looked forward to his brother's more complete version. As word of Powell, Jr.'s, genealogical search spread through Stackhouse kinsmen, its character changed from person to person until reports ran rife that money was available for the inheriting. In a letter to James O. Stackhouse in Canada on October 15, 1891, Powell explained that "rumours of estates, moneys, etc., in my hands waiting heirs have been prevalent for some time." Powell denied having ever intimated that the result of his family history would lead to a fortune of any sort. "I have understood," he continued, "that an advertisement appeared in an English newspaper several years back, calling upon heirs of a Thomas Stackhouse to make themselves known… It is possible the rumour originated from it." Powell acknowledged that the false assumption had, at least, helped his cause, explaining: "This rumour of money has stirred up many to whom I had written a long time back for their family records, and for the last month, they have come in quite lively."[14]

As Powell persevered in his research, Amos, Sr., maintained interest, lending help whenever he could. He wrote to several relatives – his cousin Tacie Lippincott Gillingham answering that she could not supply information of her antecedents, but thought that her brother, Matlack, could. She added, "I enjoyed my visit so much to your locality last summer… I thank thee for thy kind invitation to accompany Matlack and Ella on their visit to you, but I cannot make it this year."[15] In Amos' correspondence with his kinfolk, he urged them, one and all, to visit him in North Carolina.

On January 13, 1896, the senior Amos was pleased to have a special bit of news to share in his many letters – the birth of Hester's first baby, Amos Stackhouse III. With his other grandchildren living so far away, this grandson would be a daily pleasure for Amos in his old age. Cousin Tacie responded to the announcement, saying: "I recall hearing thee say thee would like to see a child running around, so thee will soon be gratified." In another letter, two years later, Tacie wrote, "I was much pleased to hear how your little boy adds to your happiness. It keeps old people young in heart to have children about them."[16]

Amos' granddaughter, Rebecca Stockton (Ellison's daughter who had been born at Stackhouse nearly twelve years before), was another with whom Amos corresponded. In a November letter she described the Philadelphia department store windows, particularly the Gimbel's one: "The elves and Santa rolled their eyes and moved their mouths and looked very funny," she said. "Wanamaker's has not fixed for Christmas yet. It is lovely when it is done – I should like thee to see it."

In a subsequent letter, Rebecca thanked Amos for money he had sent her:

"Dear Grandfather, I am very much obliged for the dollar. I had a very nice Christmas, and hope all at thy house did too. I have been on the ice twice this winter, but I cannot skate very well. Did thee skate when thee was a boy? I guess Papa did, didn't he?"

Rebecca also wrote concerning the weather, her upcoming twelfth birthday, and a play she was going to be in, "About the Lady Clare from a Tennyson poem." Through these letters, Amos could feel a small involvement in his grandchildren's lives.

Amos Stackhouse's widowed sister, Sarah Vandervoort in Brooklyn, despite poor health, often wrote him, too. One time she declared, "I would like to see that baby of yours, but, it is not likely." Her letters continued to Amos every few months, always mentioning her failing physical condition, until news came of her death on December 4, 1898, at age eighty-two. Only three years older than Amos, she had maintained a close relationship with him and with Ellison through the years. Amos mourned her passing and was glad that he and Anna had visited Sarah in Brooklyn two summers before. Having represented Amos' family at the funeral, Ellison dutifully wrote his father details on December 7th:

"She was in bed only two days before her death, and son Abram and grandson, Abram, Jr., were with her at the end. She looked very well and nice, had a coffin covered with black and lined with white sateen with her name on it… Had a Methodist minister who spoke very appropriately and it pleased Abram and his folks… Frank Vandervoort told me he stopped to see thee last summer and walked up from Hot Springs. Was pleased with the country and his visit to thee."[17]

Ellison also gave his father news of several other relatives in attendance, and of his trip home, filling a four-page letter, and, once again reminding Amos of Ellison's warm, caring qualities and his attentiveness to his family.

Nearly a year earlier, in response to Amos' letter telling that the National Bank of Asheville had closed (in 1897), Ellison showed typical concern:

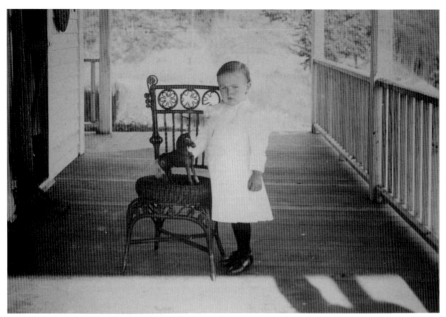

Baby (Amos III) on his grandparents' porch at Stackhouse.

"How does thee manage so as not to keep too much money about thee?" Ellison, too, had warned Amos about putting his cash "in the trunk" for safekeeping. However, Amos could assure Ellison, now, that he had switched to another Asheville institution – the Battery Park Bank – which had opened in 1891 and would operate for years before selling to equally-stable Wachovia Bank and Trust Company.[18]

Ellison's twenty-three-year-old son, Ellison, Jr., also visited his grandfather at Stackhouse from time to time. Following one such trip in the summer of 1899, Ellison wrote to Amos: "Ellison [Jr.] arrived today, is well sunburnt and seems to have had a good time. He had to wait two hours at Salisbury and ten minutes at Washington." From the same letter, Amos learned that Ellison's daughter Laura was getting ready for her college commencement – "She has passed the State Board with a very good average of 93." He added that Mary (his second daughter) had just finished high school.[19]

On one of Amos' trips to see Ellison, during which his wife, Anna, accompanied him, Amos wrote to his sons, Amos and Charles Dilworth, from Philadelphia, dated August 3, 1897: "My Dear Sons – We have just returned from a nice time visiting in Delaware County. Will go to the seashore tomorrow or next day." He reported that both he and Anna missed "the baby" (Amos III) and wished they had brought him along. Four days later, Amos wrote the boys from Ocean City, New Jersey, describing a steamboat excursion they had taken. "My cough is well and Mamma is better and getting fat," he stated. After expounding on his vacation plans and the weather, Amos asked, "What has become of Mr. Putnam? His option of 90 days expires on the 12th of August."[20]

Amos was referring to an option to lease part of his farm along the Big Laurel River to Charles W. Putnam, representing a Northern firm named "the

North Carolina Land and Timber Company." Its president, from Lynn, Massachusetts, Aaron F. Smith, had bought, back in March, nearly 40,000 acres of Madison County timberland from James Wyman and the bankrupt New England Southern Timer and Land Company.[21] Evidently, soon after Amos' return home from his vacation, he was contacted by Mr. Putnam, who had executed an agreement on August 10th, 1897, between his corporation and Ellison Stackhouse (trustee for the underage Charles Dilworth) and Amos, Jr. (over twenty-one). By paying in advance the yearly rent of $150, the timber company could use for ten years the eastern half – fifty acres – of Amos' hundred-acre Laurel farm, which he had purchased for his two sons back in 1885. Putnam, Smith, and the other stockholders received "the right to purchase [this land] at any time during the continuance of this lease for the sum of $1500."[22] The document further stated that the land would be used for the purpose of placing a large saw mill and lumber manufacturing plant thereon, and for damming the Big Laurel River at any point, for cutting roadway and tramways, for cutting and using all timber on the land, and "may construct mills, cribs, buildings or other works."

This transaction by the Stackhouse family would prove to be historic for the community and the county, opening opportunity to some of the most isolated coves and hollows.

ENDNOTES FOR CHAPTER TWELVE

1 Author's private papers.
2 *Asheville Daily Citizen*, "Richmond & Danville R Road Co. schedule," August 21, 1893, p.3.
3 Undated newspaper article from scrapbook of Elizabeth R.B. Dotterer.
4 Private papers.
5 Ibid.
6 Trueblood, D. Elton. *The People Called Quakers*. New York: Harper & Row, 1966, pp.208-09.
7 Private papers.
8 Ibid.
9 Ibid.
10 Ibid.
11 Stackhouse, Wm.R., and Walter F. Stackhouse. *The Stackhouse Family*. 2nd edition. Morehead City, N.C.: Stackhouse Foundation, 1993, p.5.
12 Private papers.
13 Ibid.
14 Ibid.
15 Ibid.
16 Ibid.
17 Ibid.
18 Sondley, F.A. *A History of Buncombe County*. Asheville, N.C.: The Advocate Printing Co., 1930, p.725.
19 Private papers.
21 Ibid.
22 Madison County Register of Deeds, Book 9, p. 434.
23 Ibid, Bk 9, p. 558.

Chapter Thirteen

North Carolina Land & Timber Company had also purchased in August, 1897, land along Big Foster's Creek, farther north of Stackhouse, for "the privilege of backing and ponding the water in the Big Laurel River from any dams for sluicing or 'pond-freshing' logs, timber, and lumber down said River."[1] Moreover, the company had bought from R.M. Gahagan the standing timber on his Mill Ridge property (joining Amos' Big Laurel farm) of a given size: "all timber on the 'Roberts tract,' fourteen inches and less in diameter and fit to be used in making railroad crossties."[2] (These crossties produced by most small sawmills in the mountains had found a ready market since the coming of the railroad, providing a 'bread and butter' commodity for the sawyers.)

N.C. Land & Timber immediately began building its dam, millhouse, kiln, commissary and other necessary structures, buying some materials from Amos, and opening a charge account, as had Dingee & Weineman.[3] On August 26, 1897, Amos, Jr., entered charges of $1.12 for 224 feet of "cull pine," at five cents per thousand feet, from his mill, plus $1.75 for "wagon, team and driver to deliver to the Big Laurel." In September the corporation paid Amos to haul roofing shingles, a stove, and 4,719 feet of dressed lumber, one inch thick, in widths of nine and twelve inches – all for $10.51. Through October and November, Amos, Jr., continued to sell them pine and poplar, both rough and dressed, as well as bolts, nails, stove pipe, carriage track for their mill, corn for their animals, and even the rent of Amos' horse to go to Foster Creek. Accounts were opened for the foremen who sent in orders for merchandise, as the logging camps and tree-cutting operations were set up. They bought mule shoes, leather back bands and steel trace chains for the draft animals.[4]

From the remote fastness of the Laurel River region tall virgin timber was cut to be stacked on the riverbank and released after a hard rain, or freshet, had swollen the creeks enough to float logs. All along the smaller feeder creeks, wooden dams were built by "cribbing" or stacking logs on mud sills fastened to rocks underneath. At a synchronized time, the temporary dams were dynamited (upper ones first), the created freshet, then, ideally, carrying the logs all the way to the sawmill at Putnam's, as it was called.

Philip Franklin, of the Laurel River area, recalled many years later, that his father (born around 1880)

N.C. Land & Timber employees in Laurel River working to prevent a log jam. Courtesy, Judy Shelton Hager.

had told him about watching the freshing, or splashing, of logs at Laurel. He said that men "in hobnail boots rode the logs to keep them from jamming up."[5] Another early resident, Roscoe Briggs, from his home on Foster's Creek, where a splash dam had been built, remembered how a similar dam on Spillcorn Creek would be blown at the same time as the one on Foster's Creek, heading all the logs to the Big Laurel.[6]

Although the logging operation brought much-needed jobs to the area, when parts of the procedure did not follow the ideal plan, flooding damaged farmers' fields, left logs and debris, or took out the simple bridges over creeks and branches. In fact, Miss Frances Goodrich, Presbyterian missionary on Laurel, made mindful her concerns to the Putnam manager, a Mr. Morrow.[7] She told him that the families who lived along the streams suffered danger, and without the footlogs and bridges, the children could not get to school, nor their mothers to meetings and study groups held at the several mission stations. Hopefully, her pleas would not fall on deaf ears.

The N.C. Land & Timber Company received its mail at Stackhouse post office, but the Stackhouse railway "flag station" was too distant for shipping and passenger service. With permission from the railway, the Putnam corporation constructed, close to the tracks, a depot building 16 ½ feet wide by 32 feet long, with a loading platform over 9 feet long, then deeded it to the Southern Railway Company, who had bought the Western North Carolina Railroad from the auction block in August, 1894.[8] This new station became another boon to the Stackhouse community.

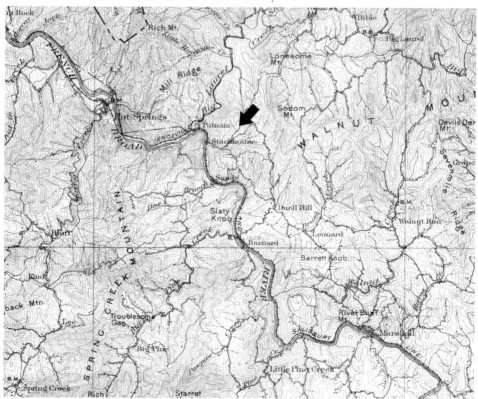

U.S. Geological Survey Map Series 1898 Courtesy, S.O. Izlar.

As Madison County's timber industry accelerated, its tobacco selling waned. Several theories have been offered by historians. One states that "The rank flavor of the mountain tobacco was unsuited to cigarettes, which had become very popular," the coastal product being milder.[9] Others thought the fault lay in the fertilizer, so it was recommended to try planting without it.[10] Yet another notion was simply that the market had been flooded with tobacco products. For whatever reason, the last tobacco warehouse to be operated in Asheville closed in 1897. "Like the stock-feeding days of the drivers, the business of tobacco came suddenly; rapidly grew to enormous proportions; engaged the entire activities and attention of everybody; and then, all at once, disappeared completely," explained historian Foster A. Sondley.[11] Madison farmers, however, did not give up their tobacco crop altogether, some markets for their product remaining in Greeneville, Tennessee, and other places. They would hold on for decades until their luck changed. After all, a small cash crop was better than none.

Meanwhile, Amos and his sons leased a portion (100 square feet) of the western half of the Laurel farm – where he had planted tobacco – to N.C. Land & Timber Company, "For the purpose of erecting buildings thereon… and the right to cut any timber on the devised land."[12] The lease, dated May 29, 1899, called for rent of $75 per year, with privilege to purchase at $800, and was signed by Amos, Jr., Hester and Charles Dilworth Stackhouse, who had turned twenty-one the year before.

With the Putnam expansion, even more families moved to the area, prompting Amos to build more rental houses. To help the children, N.C. Land & Timber built a one-room school, for which the county provided a teacher, beginning August 21, 1898. During the next five years, the Putnam school had an average daily attendance of twenty-four pupils, ages six through seventeen.[13]

Madison County people had become more mindful of education since the Presbyterian mission schools had begun to influence many communities. The aging Dr. Dorland in Hot Springs turned over his Dorland Institute to the Presbyterian Mission Board of New York City in 1893, resulting in expansion of the physical plant and the curriculum, as well as the production of trained teachers for the other mountain schools. In January, 1897, the Cumberland Presbyterians of Tennessee also opened a boarding school, nearer to Stackhouse – Jewel Hill Academy (name changed in 1899 to Bell Institute).[14] By late summer, a missionary working under the New York Presbyterians, Frances L. Goodrich, had built her home in the Laurel River section at Allen's old stand (Allanstand), followed by a church and school, the beginning of great change and benefit for the "Laurel Country," as she named it, and for western North Carolina.[15] In an 1897 article titled, "The Laurel," Miss Goodrich described for a mission magazine her trip to the area being logged by N.C. Land & Timber:

"From Asheville by train down the valley of the French Broad to Stackhouse, a flag station, where friends from Laurel were waiting with mules and horses to take us over the Walnut Mountains. I had heard the road from Stackhouse evil spoken of, but the steepness and roughness surpassed anything I had met with before. I wondered no longer at the price charged for hauling from there. It cannot pay to haul at any price, and yet over this apology for a road must come all the brick, lime, nails and dressed lumber for the house, in fact everything except rough lumber that can be sawed at Allenstand… The next day… was spent doing business and learning some of my future neighbors. My mule was not to be hurried… and I had more leisure to survey the glen and wonder at the enormous thickets of rhododendron (the mountain laurel), and to take delight in the rushing stream and the exquisite beauty of the forest with the changing color and the falling leaf."[16]

Thus began the mutual love affair between Miss Frances L. Goodrich and her "Laurel Country," the upper reaches of Amos' Big Laurel River.

Coincidentally, the same year, Mrs. R.F. Johnston, wife of the Jewel Hill Academy principal, wrote a similar description to her superiors, the Cumberland Presbyterian Board of Missions:

"These (the smoky mounts), unlike the Cumberland, have no table lands, but rise, hill on hill, till they become a bewildering mass. We have only narrow strips for valleys, could well say, none. These hills then are the farms… In addition to this, the soil is very poor and rocky. Then again the modern cultivators cannot be used to advantage here. If they could, the people are too poor to buy them, and you know the day is past when a man can make a living behind an ox… Add the fact that very few own their land, and rent must be paid from their already too meager living… We must take them by the hand…"[17]

These two women and their schools did "take by the hand" the neighboring communities of Stackhouse, making a tremendous difference over time. Besides the two boarding schools in Hot Springs and Jewel Hill, day schools would soon be built at over twenty other Madison County locations by the Presbyterians, who required cash tuition payment, or barter of produce, or work by the pupils for scholarships.[18] A few enrollees paid portions of all three.

On the other hand, small county-run schools, such as the one at Putnam, however inferior to the mission schools, were called "free school" by the people, and were financed through meager state funds, plus additional local taxes voted in at county polls. Unlike the mission schools that operated for eight months, the "free school" term in Madison County was ten weeks per year and the teacher's pay was twenty dollars per month.[19] Even with Madison County's share of state funding and the revenue derived from poll taxes, fines, liquor licenses, and property valuation percentages, there were simply not sufficient funds to maintain public schools longer than the mandatory two and a half months.

Using the Putnam school house, Amos, Jr., apparently organized a Sunday School for the sprouting mill village, then searched for study materials he would provide out of pocket. On December 29, 1898, Ellison Stackhouse wrote his father, "I send First Day School lessons to Amos to look over."[20] The supplies were surely a gift or, possibly, surplus from the affluent Philadelphia Quaker Society; otherwise Amos, Jr., would have used Methodist publications. His Putnam Sunday School most likely met on Sunday afternoons after Amos, Jr., had attended his regular morning worship and Sunday School at Jewel Hill Methodist Church, which was thriving.

Old Methodist minutes, dated June 3, 1899, declared: "Most all of the appointments where we preach need revival work, except Jewel Hill, where we had a most glorious outpouring of the Holy Spirit." Although there was no women's organization ("because our good sisters are so widely separated and so few in number"), there was a vigorous Sunday School, "with an average attendance of 128."[21]

Besides the Putnam developments, the Rumboughs had bought, in September, 1897, 3,300 acres adjoining Amos' Laurel farm and reaching all the way to Hot Springs.[22] In addition, the Southern Improvement Company, after laying out streets and building homes, went bankrupt, and so returned the Mountain Park Hotel, also, to the Rumboughs. The syndicate left behind, however, the large modern tourist facility and bath house, swimming pool, landscaping and the state's first golf course. When the 1896 flood had damaged the train trestle and station in Hot Springs, Southern Improvement worked with Southern Railway Company to build a long berm above flood level, installing new tracks, trestle, depot and waiting shed in the heart of Hot Springs. Broad wooden steps up to the depot from the Mountain Park completed the transition.

Improvements were also taking place upriver at Stackhouse – Amos, Jr., having built himself a buggy house (to protect his new buggy) on a rise in back of the store. Moreover, on the hill to the northeast, one hundred yards or more from their home, the Stackhouses constructed a long, narrow building of rough lumber, called a "ten-pin alley."[23] They had likely played the game on trips North, or observed it at the Hot Springs hotel, or, maybe even on a tour of George Vanderbilt's castle at Biltmore, recognizing its recreational merits for young and old. Amos' respected book, *The Household Physician*, advised for good health: "Exercise *must* be had every day, and, if possible… engaging the mind in the exercise; and for this purpose, some contested game is very useful, as playing billiards, nine-pins, pitching quoits, or, where strength will permit, playing ball."[24]

Old wooden bowling pins and balls with wood and steel ice skates used at Stackhouse.

Regular maintenance and repairs at Stackhouse were ongoing, as well, to prevent neglect from taking its toll on Amos' large property. One of his employees, William Capps – probably a blacksmith – received credit on his store account in a variety of ways at fifty cents per day: "Driving cattle, clearing land, mining and hauling ore, hauling crossties, work on wagon and yoke, shoeing horse and mare, work on mill dam, work on tramway, and filing wagon wheels." Another worker, James Capps, also paid his store bill for work done (at forty-five cents a day) on "ten-pin alley, fence, fish trap, stable, garden, hauling firewood, and mowing grass," plus "two days at buggy house for Amos, Jr.," and "work in mill for A & CD" (Amos, Jr., and Charles Dilworth).[25]

In his 80s, Amos Stackhouse rented his sawmill to his sons. This is their letterhead.

In July, 1897, Amos' store ledger showed for the first time an account headed, "A & C.D. Stackhouse," with a margin note, "Rented mill from July 1, 1897-July 1, 1898." Amos' two sons were running their own sawmill operation, working four regular employees. Besides McIlvaine, another Hickory customer was added – Hutton & Bourbonnais Lumber Company (Michigan-owned originally), who also bought lumber "squares" in the "box" grade.[26] Since this was before the advent of lightweight cardboard cartons, all packaging for shipping was made of fairly heavy wooden boxes, the main product of Hutton & Bourbonnais.[27] For a freight car of dressed white pine box lumber, Amos, Jr., received $107.61, including the usual two percent discount to the customer. His price was $7.25 per thousand board feet for 5/4-inch thick and $7.00 per thousand for 4/4-inch. Hutton & Bourbonnais relied upon the small mountain sawmills and the Southern Railway to supply its needs. Established in 1896, the Hutton & Bourbonnais Company of Hickory was still in operation well over a century later.[28]

Hauling logs for Amos, Jr., and Charles Dilworth provided jobs for men in the vicinity, one of whom was the miner John Harrison of Doe Branch community. (His father Jesse had traded with Amos at Warm Springs.) Probably in charge of the Stackhouse barytes operation, Harrison also secured mineral rights to land tracts for his own prospecting, signing at least one agreement with Hot Springs Barytes Company for "first quality white barytes ores, free from all impurities received by train at the rate of $2.00 per long ton" (2,200 pounds).[29] Harrison's store account with Amos was credited, at times, for hauling wagon-loads of barite, and also for hauling logs for "A & C.D. Stackhouse, Co." In May, 1898, Harrison rented Amos' "house and stable on Gap road," at $1.50 per month, and a "house in the bottom," at $2.00 per month, suggesting that he might be housing a crew, as foreman, possibly, either with Dingee & Weineman or with N.C. Land & Timber Company. His children were enrolled in the Putnam school.[30]

With the barytes operation, the Stackhouse store and post office, rental houses, sawmill and farm may have become more than Amos, Jr., and his brother could manage. On June 27, 1899, at the end of his sons' lease, Amos rented his sawmill to W. Joseph Balding, the sawyer who had been helping at the mill.[31] However, it is also possible that Amos, Jr., and Charles Dilworth went to work for N.C. Land & Timber, as lumber graders – a position always in demand at a saw mill – leaving their father to mind the store. Or Charles may have been left in charge while Amos, Jr., went to Putnam, since he was older and more experienced. Certainly at this time Amos, Jr., especially, would have been in need of extra money for the house he was planning to build for his growing family.

Back on December 29, 1898, a son, James Edmond, had been born to Hester, prompting Ellison, a week later, to write his father: "The baby came near to being a Christmas present for thee. What does Amos #3 think of the baby? He will have to be Grandmother's boy, now." Alas, little Amos had a short time only to share his special position, as noted by Hester years later: "James Edmond

James Edmond Stackhouse,
March 5, 1899, ready for burial.

was taken sick, February 26th, 1899, Sunday – Died, Sunday, March 5, 1899."[32] At two months old, he had contracted whooping cough when Hester took him to visit a neighbor. An obituary appearing in a Methodist publication stated: "His illness was of short duration and then his little spirit was kissed away by the Spirit of Christ and carried home to the bosom of God."[33] He was buried just below their house on Summer House Point, where Amos had leveled the ground by building a rock retaining wall on the bluff overlooking the French Broad.

Although still mourning, Hester agreed to go with Amos and Anna to Philadelphia for the high school graduation of Ellison's second daughter, Mary, from Friends Central School on "Sixth Day, Sixth month, Sixteenth, eighteen hundred and ninety-nine," according to the formal invitation. Hoping to get Hester's mind off her sorrow, they visited the seashore where her photograph was snapped and printed on an Atlantic City post card.[34]

During that summer, three-year-old Amos, III, also sat with his grandmother, Anna, for a photographer from Asheville – Ignatius Watsworth Brock – who

Hester Honeycutt Stackhouse, c. 1899.

114

would, under the name of "N. Brock," quickly earn the title of "photographic artist," winning awards in this country and abroad.[35] As Brock's camera portrayed, little Amos, though still in skirts, was growing tall and could hardly be called a baby anymore.

Anna Myers Stackhouse and Amos, Jr., Oct. 25, 1897. Photo By N. Brock.

It seemed to Amos that the years were passing quickly, even with retirement time on his hands. At the end of another decade he reflected on his many blessings and few sorrows. The "cruel and unreasonable" Spanish-American war, as described by Amos' sister, had ended, returning the sons of his neighbors to their respective communities: Sandy Bottom, Pine Creek, Barnard, Walnut Run, Leonard, Big Laurel, Hot Springs, Spring Creek, and

Marshall. Ephraim W. Reeves from Walnut, son of Amos' friend and former customer, Malley Reeves, was one in particular.[36] Amos was thankful that this war, unlike the Great Rebellion, had been short, and carried a minimum of casualties for western North Carolina. Of a cheerful nature, the octogenarian looked forward to a new century – surely war-free – but was hardly prepared for the changes coming to Stackhouse.

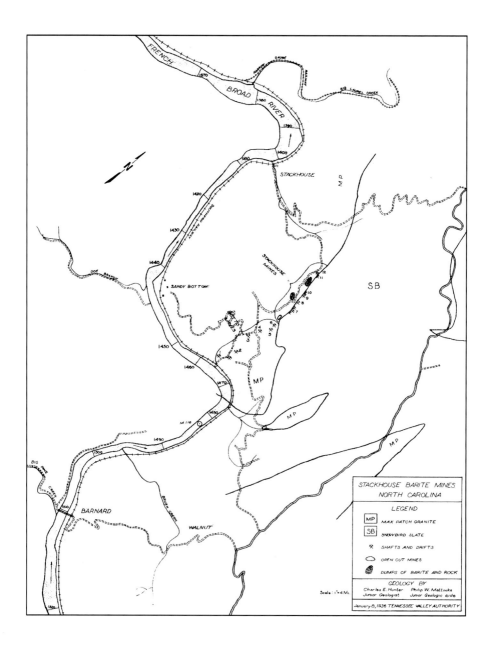

[1] Madison County Register of Deeds, Book 9, p. 529.

[2] Ibid., Bk. 10, p.1.

[3] Author's private papers.

[4] Ibid.

[5] Franklin, Philip. Telephone interview, October, 1999.

[6] Slagle, Dan. Telephone interview, February, 1999.

[7] Davidson, Jan. Introduction, p.8, to *Mountain Homespun* by Frances L. Goodrich, Knoxville, Univ. of Tenn. Press, 1989.

[8] Madison County Register of Deeds, Bk. 11, p.418.

[9] Van Noppen, Ina W. and John J. *Western North Carolina Since the Civil War*. Boone, N.C.: Appalachian Consortium Press, 1973, p.277.

[10] *Carolina Watchman*, Salisbury, N.C., April 29, 1886, p.2.

[11] Sondley, F.A. *A History of Buncombe County*. Asheville, N.C.: The Advocate Printing Co., 1930, p.733.

[12] Madison County Register of Deeds, Bk. 11, p.406.

[13] Private papers.

[14] Painter, J.B. *The Season of Dorland-Bell*. 2nd ed. Boone, N.C.: Appalachian Consortium Press, 1996, p.285.

[15] Ibid, pps. 144, 197.

[16] *Home Mission Monthly*, December, 1897, p.33. (Presbyterian Board of Home Missions, NYC.)

[17] Johnston, Mrs. R.F. "Mountain Missions," minutes of Cumberland Presbyterian Women's Board of Missions, 1897.

[18] Painter, *Season of Dorland-Bell*, p.278.

[19] Henry, Homer. "The Development of Public Education in Madison County," Diss. Univ. of N.C., 1927, p.35.

[20] Private papers.

[21] "A History of the Methodist Church in Madison County," undated, unsigned paper. Records of United Methodist Church, Asheville. Conference minutes. Records, United Methodist Church, Asheville.

[22] Madison County Register of Deeds, Bk.10, p.164.

[23] Private papers.

[24] Warren, Ira. *The Household Physician*, Boston, Ira Bradley & Co., 1872, p.276.

[25] Private papers.

[26] Ibid.

[27] *Hickory News. Hickory Daily Record*. Assorted undated clippings, Elbert Ivey Memorial Library, Hickory, N.C.

[28] Ibid.

[29] Madison County Register of Deeds, Bk.11, p.602.

[30] Private papers.

[31] Ibid.

[32] Ibid.

[33] Ibid.

[34] Ibid.

[35] *Asheville Citizen-Times*, May 10, 1942, n.pag.

[36] Adjutant General of N.C. *Roster of the N.C. Volunteers Spanish-American War*. Raleigh, Edwards & Broughton Presses, 1900, pps. 73-75.

Chapter Fourteen

The new century at Stackhouse was further made memorable on January thirtieth by the birth to Hester and Amos, Jr., of another son, Ernest Matlack. He was named for two of Amos' favorite cousins – Ernest Robert Stackhouse and his father, Dr. A. Matlack Stackhouse – who had just visited, as they did each year. Ernest greatly disliked his middle name as he grew older, but there was good reason for him to be proud of it.

Timothy Matlack portrait by Charles Willson Peale, c.1826. Doris Devine Fanelli and Karie Diethorn, The Portrait Collection at Independence National Historic Park (Philadelphia: America Philosophic Society, 2002).

Through the marriage in 1841 of Ann Matlack to Amos' uncle, Robert Stackhouse, came the connection to Timothy Matlack (1735-1829), Revolutionary patriot and Pennsylvania state official whose portrait by Charles Willson Peale hangs in Independence Hall. Timothy had found Quaker disciplines too restraining for his interests in horse racing, cock fighting and other convivialities of the day, not to mention his involvement in the military, and so he was disowned by the Quakers. During the war with England, he served in the field as militia colonel of a battalion, devoting himself after the war to civil service. Trustee of the University of Pennsylvania, officer of a bank, and member of the Continental Congress, Matlack also served as a Philadelphia alderman. Although he was imprisoned for a short time in 1782 due to debts resulting from his work as secretary of the Supreme Executive Council, he was subsequently appointed to other government jobs, both state and local, until his retirement from public life in

1818. He is best remembered by Quakers, perhaps, as having been active in forming the Society of Free Quakers, composed of those who, like himself, had left the Society of Friends by choice or by disownment because of military involvements.[1]

Charles Willson Peale, at age 85, asked permission to paint his old political friend Timothy Matlack – then age 90. The resulting oil on canvas, about two feet square, was signed and dated by Peale, and described by critics as a remarkably cohesive work, especially considering the artist's age and impaired eyesight. Another portrait of Matlack, now owned by the National Gallery of Art, was painted in 1805 by Rembrandt Peale, a son of Charles Willson Peale.[2]

More than likely, young Ernest, growing up in Stackhouse, North Carolina, knew little of the Matlack fame – only that the name was foreign-sounding here in Appalachia, eliciting sniggers from classmates and neighbors.

Clockwise from top: Amos Stackhouse, his wife, Anna, Hester H. Stackhouse, Amos III, Ernest Matlack, and Teeny Thomas, houskeeper, 1903.

Meanwhile Amos' dream of having grandchildren about the place was coming true as little Ernest and little Amos made good company for Amos in his old age. (With two Amoses already in the household, little Amos III would be called Junior to lessen confusion.) Alas, "the Lord giveth and the Lord taketh away." On April 2, 1900 a telegram from Oak Lane, Philadelphia, was sent by way of the railway agent at Putnam to Amos Stackhouse from his nephew, son of Powell: "Father died this a.m. suddenly."[3] Amos' beloved brother Powell was gone at age seventy-three. He and Amos had always been close – Powell, ever ready with advice, financial aid, and friendship, further endearing himself through his intense genealogical interest.

As a memorial of sorts, Powell's history work would be continued by his cousin William Romig Stackhouse, printing on the hand press in his basement at Moorestown, New Jersey, a small book of limited edition- *Stackhouse, an Old English Family Sometime of Yorkshire*.[4] In his foreword he explained how the Stackhouse data had been gathered and passed from generation to generation until reaching Powell,

> "Who was far and away the ablest genealogist our family produced... Unfortunately, before he could complete the work, he died suddenly, his pen dropping from his hand as he was writing that cherished name... Knowing the uncertainty of life and the certainty of death, which may come to me as quickly as it did to my revered cousin, I have thought to put in order the records of, at least, a portion of our family, in the interest of those who come after me."

Calling his publishing operation Settle Press, William Romig began his 110-page book with the Domesday Book entry of Stackhouse in Latin, continuing with records of Stackhouse branches in numerous Yorkshire villages, as well as lists of Stackhouse births, deaths and marriages extracted from parish registers.

In 1906, William Romig Stackhouse published *The Book of the Descendants of John Stackhouse and Elizabeth Buckingham, His Wife*, and also, *A Retrospect of Colonial Times in Burlington County*, by his father, the physician A. Matlack Stackhouse. William Romig expanded his first book the next year in a revised edition called *A Historical Sketch of the First Ancestors of the Stackhouse Family in America*, and included Powell's research in this country. Dr. A. Matlack Stackhouse wrote the introduction, stating:

> "The name of Stackhouse is a somewhat uncommon one and wherever it appears as the cognomen of a white person, we have every reason to believe that, were records extant, we could in all instances trace it back to the family, who, in remote times, gave the name, to, or received it from, the little hamlet of Stackhouse... in England."

At the end of his five-and-a-half-page introduction, Dr. Stackhouse lamented the fact that in the accumulated collection of data – "genealogical, biographical, and historical" – so little interest had been taken "by those who bear the name or carry the blood."[5] Nevertheless, this factual volume held its own with modern historical research, except in one respect. Knowing that their ancestors had crossed the Atlantic in 1682 with the William Penn party, the four generations of researchers – Amos, Powell, Powell, Jr., and William

Romig – assumed that the Stackhouses were on the ship *Welcome* with Penn himself. In 1985, an organization called the *Welcome* Society of Pennsylvania published a book entitled, *The Welcome Claimants Proved, Disproved and Doubtful*, listing Amos Stackhouse's ancestors as "disproved" through ships' records, diaries, publications, letters, journals, and passenger lists. Here, perhaps, could be built yet one more argument; but, having only tradition to bear up the *Welcome* story, we must accept the organization's well-supported finding: "It therefore seems inescapable that the Settle Friends crossed the Atlantic on the *Lamb*, a ship from a northern port, and not, as long suspected… on the *Welcome*."[6]

Amos Stackhouse in western North Carolina, at the threshold of the 20th century, certainly was not one of those "bearing the name but having so little interest." He must have felt sadness, however, that his brother Powell did not live to see the fruition of his labors preserved for posterity. Likely prompted by Powell's death, Amos also began to get his own affairs in order so as to save his wife and sons legal problems at his death, and to save himself some property taxes until then. He discussed his wishes for the division and distribution of his property with the family, sent his requests to his attorney, and, finally, on October 8th, 1900, the documents were ready for signing and registration.[7]

To his wife, Amos deeded the 56-acre tract he had purchased in 1883 from George W. Gahagan, reserving life estate privileges for himself. The original 605 acres purchased in 1878 Amos split between his sons, using Woolsey Branch, basically, as the dividing line. Amos, Jr., received 355 acres on the south side, including the sawmill, lumber yard and rail siding; while Charles Dilworth received the home, store, barn and buggy house, on 250 acres. Each deed carried the same life interest for Amos as long as he or Anna lived, reverting to the boys only after the parents were gone. But the Stackhouse heirs did not have their legacies on a silver platter. Amos also required from each son annual payments of $100 during his lifetime, and continuing to Anna after he died; in addition, Amos, Jr., and Charles made down payments of $400 and $550, respectively. Ownership of the land did not affect the brothers' business partnership in sawmill and store; they remained best of friends in all dealings.

It is possible that Amos deeded the 56-acre Gahagan tract, on which he owned all the mineral rights, to his wife for a special reason. An exciting discovery had been made by Amos, Jr., one day as he slipped on a rock, his shoe skinning away moss and dirt to reveal that hard whiteness they all recognized – barite.[8] Upon examination, the outcrop ran across the ground's surface, hardly covered, for a long distance – the lode J. Turner Morehead had hoped to discover in his diggings.

We do not know whether the Stackhouses contacted the Dingee & Weineman Company in Hot Springs, or whether a mining engineer, Henry J. Moore, just came prospecting. Nevertheless, Moore, a Northerner and MIT graduate, secured New York City financial backing from one Albert G. Stillwell. Then, in the spring of 1903, a rough draft was presented to Amos for leasing the property, followed by a binding agreement on May 9th.[9] Running from June 1, 1903, through May 31, 1913, with privilege of renewal, the lease granted Moore rights to use the fifty-six acres to "dig, quarry, obtain and remove barytes," and to build roads over the land, taking any timber under twelve inches in diameter for mining construction, with one exception: no hickory or oak wood. "If Moore should fail to find barytes ore on said lands in paying quantities or if said ore shall at anytime become exhausted, then in that event Moore may terminate lease upon giving sixty days notice," stated the contract paper. Moore agreed to pay $1,250 annually to Amos as rent – one third to be paid to Amos and two-thirds to he held in trust for Anna. Furthermore, the document required Moore to give "employees and others under his control, orders for merchandise on A & C.D. Stackhouse and that settlement shall be made on or before the fifteenth day of every month for the same." Amos retained full ingress and egress for removing timber from his land.

Four months later, Henry J. Moore of Stackhouse, Albert G. Stillwell of New York City, and P.A. McElroy of Marshall formed the Carolina Barytes Company, a corporation located at Stackhouse, North Carolina, whose object was to buy and sell minerals, mine and manufacture barytes, talc and any other minerals, and build mills and tramways.[10] Amos Stackhouse was doing well in his retirement.

Amos, Jr., and Charles Dilworth also became involved December ninth when they signed an agreement with Carolina Barytes to lease one and a quarter acres alongside the railroad and river, less than a quarter mile southeast of the Stackhouse store and just above their sawmill.[11] The strip fell on both sides of the dividing line between the boys' newly-acquired lands. Rights to build a mill for the manufacture of barytes, to build an access road and to pipe water to their mill from Woolsey Branch, came to the corporation, but not the right to use any buildings for the sale of liquor or merchandise. Moreover, Carolina Barytes agreed to pay taxes on the buildings and improvements made to the leased Stackhouse lands, and "to erect a dam in, and one half way of the way across, the French Broad River," with free discharge of water from dam and tailrace over the lands of Amos Stackhouse, Jr. Instead of rent paid on this lease, the manufacturer agreed to construct for A & C.D., after April, 1904, "a dam and wheelpit sufficient to generate 100 horsepower daily by using a turbine wheel, the head of water in said dam shall not be less than five feet."

This dam would serve both the large water wheel of the barytes mill and the smaller wheel of Amos' saw mill. The year before – on February 28, 1902 – the French Broad had flooded its full length, washing out Amos' water wheel and raceway and heavily damaging his sawmill. The bridge at Hot Springs was taken out and the train tracks damaged before the river crested at twenty-five feet – two feet higher than the injurious 1876 flood when Amos lived at Warm Springs.[12]

The Carolina Barytes package negotiated by the Stackhouses would prove beneficial to the family and to the community, earning a place of geological fame in the state and the region. For, indeed, Carolina Barytes had hit the mother lode, naming the rich vein "The Klondyke" and embarking upon years of profitable mining.

Early in 1904, as agreed, the French Broad was dammed (producing 165 to 250 horsepower depending upon the season), with water wheel, wheel house, grinding plant, roads and tramways. The beginning capital of $30,000 was increased in 1907 to $40,000, with new stockholders and officers added from New York, but leaving the manager, Henry Moore, in charge at

Barite crushing plant at Stackhouse, North Carolina, c.1910.

Stackhouse.[13] On April 13, 1904, Moore had transferred to Carolina Barytes Corporation the titles and interest in lands previously acquired by him, including his original lease from Amos and Anna in 1903.[14]

The Klondyke, according to geologists, was part of the "Hot Springs area," one of only two in North Carolina containing barite ore of economic value; the other was the "Kings Mountain area" in Gaston County. (A minor vein was located near Hillsborough.)[15] After years of mining, it would be seen that the Hot Springs overthrust is one of the major faults in the Appalachians. It extends from Bluff, four miles south of Hot Springs, in a northeast direction, down Doe Branch, across the French Broad River at Sandy Bottom, and to the northeast of Walnut Gap on the road to Marshall and Hot Springs. The N.C. Mining Industry's published report from 1906 stated in particular that the total barytes production of 3,340 tons in the state was obtained from Madison County. "For a number of years there has been a small production from Gaston County, but it did not report any in 1906," declared the report.[16]

At Stackhouse the Carolina Barytes mill house was a large three-story frame structure, painted white, with concrete supports and retaining walls built close to the railroad. After it began operating, a coat of fine white dust covered the surrounding landscape, but no one at Stackhouse objected. The home of Amos and Anna was distant enough to miss the drift except on very windy days, and the other people in the community considered it small sacrifice for the jobs it provided, especially since the North Carolina Land & Timber Company at Putnam had declared bankruptcy on January 7, 1904.[17] Soon there were two ten-hour shifts a day with six to eight men per shift (more at times), receiving wages of about one dollar per day. Men walked in from Doe Branch, (crossing the river in a boat), Mill Ridge, and other communities to get the steady paycheck farming could never provide.[18] A local man, William Ramsey, was mill superintendent, while his brother, Marion, served as mine captain – both former employees of the Putnam sawmill.

Although some of the barite ore ran along the surface, the vein was thick, requiring tunneling into the earth deeper and deeper as time went by. From the mine adit, a central shaft extended, the tunnel supported overhead by timbers called stulls, cut from the property and likely sawed at the Stackhouse mill. Passages, called levels, branched in various directions and at different depths from the main air shaft. Another shaft was dug for hoisting the ore to the surface where it was dumped on a "grizzly screen" that allowed all ore smaller than an egg to pass through. The remaining rocks were loaded into tram cars which traveled by gravity on wooden tracks down the mountainside one mile to the grinding mill.[19]

By today's standards the methods were primitive and slow. All drilling was done by hand-hammering for nearly ten years before an air drill was brought in. Having no carbide lamps, the men underground worked by crude "coonshine" lamps which burned a smoky, thick grease. Still, the plant produced thirty to fifty tons every twenty-four hours.[20]

At the plant the barite was crushed to the size of corn, then placed in large tanks of steaming water where a small amount of sulphuric acid was added to dissolve the mine stains, resulting in a clean white material. Next the acid was flushed out, the coarse-ground ore dried and ground in a series of three burrstone mills before being packed into 750-lb. barrels made in the plant's cooper shop of low-grade oak cut on the place. The barrels were loaded onto freight cars and connected to the trains, but the shipping tickets were handled at the Putnam depot – still operating although the North Carolina Land & Timber sawmill had closed.

The raw mineral was sent mainly to paint manufacturers such as Sherwin-Williams and John F. Lucas in Ohio. Flour and sugar processors also bought the harmless white powder as an adulterant to add weight to their bagged products. Many years later, Amos Stackhouse, Jr., would relate to his grandchildren how a certain flour mill in East Tennessee had ordered at least one car load a month.[21] (Even after enactment of the Pure Food law in 1907, the law was not strictly enforced for some years.)

Hardly giving Amos Stackhouse time to mourn the failing promise of the North Carolina Land & Timber Company at Putnam, his deal with Carolina Barytes Corporation brought fresh opportunity for community jobs and growth, and much satisfaction to the old man.

ENDNOTES FOR CHAPTER FOURTEEN

[1] "Matlack," *Dictionary of American Biography*, Vol. VI, 1933.

[2] Unsigned draft from unpublished catalog, Independence National Park, Philadelphia: 2001.

[3] Author's private papers.

[4] Stackhouse, William Romig. *Stackhouse, an old English Family, Sometime of Yorkshire*. Moorestown, New Jersey: Settle Press, 1905, pp.1,2.

[5] Stackhouse, William Romig and Powell Stackhouse, Jr. A *Historical Sketch of the First Ancestors of the Stackhouse Family in America*. Moorestown, New Jersey: Settle Press, 1907, pp. 2, 5, 6.

[6] McCracken, George E. *The Welcome Claimants, Proved, Disproved and Doubtful*, Publication Number 2. Philadelphia: Welcome Society of Pennsylvania, 1985, pp. 29, 32, 488-491.

[7] Madison County Register of Deeds, Book 13, pp. 57-59.

[8] Aumiller, Nancy Stackhouse. Interview 1999.

[9] Madison County Register of Deeds, Book 17, p.144.

[10] Madison County Record of Corporations, p.67.

[11] Madison County Register of Deeds, Book 29, p.56.

[12] "Floods on French Broad River & Spring Creek, Vicinity of Hot Springs, North Carolina," Tennessee Valley Authority report to N.C. Dept. of Water Resources, Raleigh, 1960, p.19.

[13] Madison County Record of Corporations, p.141.

[14] Madison County Register of Deeds, Bk. 19, p.87.

[15] Stuckey, Jasper L. *North Carolina: Its Geology and Mineral Resources*, Raleigh: Dept. of Conservation & Development, 1965, p.365.

[16] Pratt, Joseph H. "The Mining Industry," N.C. Geological and Economic Survey, Paper No. 14. Raleigh: Uzzell State Printer, 1907, p.108.

[17] Madison County Register of Deeds, Bk. 19, p.530.

[18] Private papers.

[19] Ibid.

[20] Ibid.

[21] Ibid.

Chapter Fifteen

Other barite mining, besides Stackhouse, had taken place for some time, too, on the Candler property in the adjoining community of Sandy Bottom, where there was also a rail siding, and at Bluff, near Hot Springs.[1] The miner John Harrison from Doe Branch surely became involved with both projects at some time or another. On April first, 1905, at Hot Springs, Harrison and a partner, Hugh W. Dougherty, leased the old Colony Mill dam property on Spring Creek from Newton J. Lance.[2] This site was likely that of the former Hot Springs Barytes Company which had closed, probably due to flooding on February 28, 1902.[3]

The lease agreement gave the two men the right to use land and water power to erect a barytes mill and mill dam, and "the use and control of any or all the buildings on the aforesaid lands... during the continuance of this lease and to keep the same in as good condition as when received." Harrison and Dougherty would rebuild the old dam, and use the power house, offices or other former facilities not ruined by flooding.

The day after leasing the property, Harrison and Dougherty brought in a third partner, Frank Roberts, forming the Hot Springs Manufacturing Company, for the purpose of: "Mining barytes and other minerals, manufacturing gas for lighting streets, houses, public buildings..., buying and selling real estate, manufacturing electric lights... and to sell electric lights to any person, firm or corporation."[4] The opening capital for the business was $7000, borrowed from a Frank Liebrock in sums of $200 at a time, "as needed," according to the deed of trust.[5] Harrison and Dougherty owned one hundred shares each, with Roberts having eighty shares. The next year, Amos Stackhouse's old Turnpike friend, Tom Garrett, leased 700 acres for barite prospecting to Harrison's company in return for twenty-five cents per "long" ton (2240 pounds), "weighed at the mill of the parties of the second part [Harrison, Dougherty and Roberts] in the city of Hot Springs, N.C."[6]

Hot Springs electric plant, dam and lake. Date unknown. Courtesy, Talitha Price.

Whether the plant ever manufactured "water" gas for lighting is unclear; certainly the piping would have been difficult and expensive. However, according to records of Carolina Power and Light Company of Raleigh, a forty-horsepower steam electric plant and distribution system were constructed in 1906 by Hot Springs Manufacturing Company. There is no record of how long the barytes mill operated but the electric plant was sold to J.W. Fisher of Marshall in 1908 and produced Hot Springs' electricity for many years.[7]

Either for personal reasons or because of financial difficulties, Dougherty left Hot Springs, but Harrison continued to prospect for minerals in the Hot Springs area, likely sending his ore to the Stackhouse plant for grinding. Eventually, in addition to lump ore from local mines, the Carolina Barytes Company was processing barite from several Tennessee mines, including Sweetwater.[8]

In the store ledger of A & C.D. Stackhouse, the account of Carolina Barytes Company showed that Amos, Jr., sometimes paid its workers and foremen, as well as its lawyer, James E. Rector (a local boy who had graduated down in Hot Springs at Dorland Institute before studying law).[9] From the Stackhouse store, the barytes corporation also bought axes, ax handles, nails, stoves and pipe, dynamite, coal, a few barrels and other merchandise. Still more store business came from Amos' sons' rental-house tenants who were employed at the mill.

With the increase in store trade, rents, mining royalties, and sawmill business, the Stackhouses were making a good profit – so much so that Amos, Jr., and Hester began planning their own home. Charles Dilworth sold to his brother, for fifty dollars, a building site of one and an eighth acres to the northeast and below the Amos Stackhouse residence.[10] Amos, Jr.'s, house would be about a hundred yards away and would not block the view from his father's dwelling. In fact, each home would command its own lovely panorama of river and mountaintops, with the little Laurel Farm (Putnam) mountain almost centered in the shared skyline.

Hester and Amos, Jr., might have hired an Asheville architect to draw their house plan, but they probably selected their blueprint from one of the popular mail order catalogs of the day. (Hester frequently ordered sewing material and clothing items from Philadelphia, Boston and New York.)[11] Wherever purchased, the house design was ambitious, requiring skilled craftsmen for its construction. Amos, Jr., hired Mr. J. Napolean Bonaparte Campbell (called "Boney" for short) of Asheville, member of the local carpenter's union, who had come from Virginia in 1892 to work on the Presbyterian school at Victoria (later, Biltmore), the Asheville Normal.[12]

Thus began the arduous task of creating on the steep hillside a level place large enough to receive the foundation, excavating even farther for a cellar under half the structure.

Larger and grander than his parents', the new dwelling would have two full stories, plus large attic and two future bedrooms on a third floor. Amos, Jr., would cut large hemlocks to provide the long hand-hewn sills, twenty-four inches thick, that would rest on masonry piers alongside the huge chimney base. Even at this stage the structure took on complications, as the footings for two round towers were begun, and from seven feet below, cellar walls rose, two-feet thick, to ensure a cool steady temperature for keeping fruits and vegetables through the winters.[14]

After some time, the first floor framing stood ten feet tall for dining room,

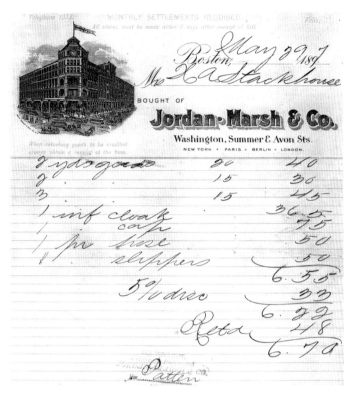

1897 invoice from Hester's order for clothing items, including infant cloak and cap for baby Amos.

parlor, bedroom and reception hall, and nine feet tall for kitchen and pantry. The round tower on the north side carried the stairwell to the second floor, while the tower to the south contained living room windows, the dining room and reception hall being accented with angled bay windows. The second story framework created four more bed chambers, plus a large bathroom and a small den or office for Amos, Jr., all with nine-foot ceilings. Another large angle-bay was added to the front bedroom, and clothes closets framed into each room for convenience. Topping the second floor, the steep roof provided attic space for storage as well as three more bedrooms – one with four windows in the full-circle tower on the southern front side, its roof joists laid in a circle to a center peak. The entire roof frame was a series of complicated hips, gables, dormers, and cones. Tying into the main structure at the first and second levels were the large kitchen porch at back, plus the front porch running the full width of the house and swelling wider at the north end to follow the angles of the foyer's bay window. Six fireplace flues in parlor, dining room and upstairs bedrooms gradually reduced to one corbeled brick stack penetrating the main roof, with another chimney coming from the kitchen end of the house.

All the rough lumber would have been cut on Stackhouse land and sawn in their sawmill. It is possible the basswood weatherboard siding also had grown there and been prepared at Amos' mill. For a decorative effect, the third story of the south tower was sheathed in cedar shingles instead of weatherboarding – the top and bottom thirds being diamond-shaped, while the center third were scalloped (called "round fishscale").

A broad flight of wooden steps with fancy, turned ball-topped newel posts led to the main porch and its supporting ten Tuscan columns. Above the porch, an attic gable featured four-foot long carved brackets at the sides, as well as horseshoe-shaped collar bracing and king post. Matching wooden balustrades, each connecting post thickly carved and topped by eight-inch balls, decorated this short section of the third story inside the gable horseshoe. Oak window sashes were large, modern, single-panes that admitted light and air to the rooms, while the front door was paneled oak with curved moldings and patterned oval glass insert.

As soon as the house had its roof, siding, doors and windows, electric wires were pulled into the frame cavities for ceiling lights-a rare feature in a mountain home. The Carolina Barytes Company generated power for its own use, as well as enough to furnish lights at the homes of Amos, Jr., and his father. Water and drain pipes were also connected behind the walls to kitchen and bathroom, with one dining room wall concealing hot and cold lines for a small marble sink. Lathwork topped by plaster then finished the inside walls and ceilings in all rooms except the kitchen and pantry, which were paneled in narrow beaded-edge pine. Glazed ceramic tiles in rich mosaic faced the small-grated fireplaces to be fed from coal stored in the cellar. (By way of a large trap door on the back porch floor, Amos, Jr., could fill the coal scuttles and carry them inside, protected by the wide roof cover.) Hardwood floors, oak moldings and quartersawn oak mantles finished the downstairs rooms with the exception of the parlor, which had a two-tiered cherry mantle enclosing a large mirror. Wide oak pocket-doors separated the dining room and parlor, the parlor sides stained to match cherry. Upstairs, the two front bedrooms were trimmed in Georgia red heart pine, clear-varnished, while two more had enameled woodwork.[15]

Needless to say, the many angles and circles were as tedious and slow in the finish trim-out as they were in the foundation and framing stages, requiring kerfing of the wood and soaking and drying in forms to obtain the desired shapes. During the construction, Hester Stackhouse, a perfectionist, often called for changes which further hindered progress.[16] "It took Boney Campbell, with his brother, helping, four years to build the house, and it cost my daddy $4000," declared a son of Amos, Jr., many years later.[17] When the exterior materials were finally in place, the siding was painted a cream color, except for the top floor of the main turret, which was stained dark green. Snow white fascia, banisters and other wood trim stylishly accented the whole. An exact date of occupancy is not recorded, but Amos, Jr., Hester and the boys moved in before the house interior was completed, some details being left for the future, such as the finishing of the bathroom. The family would continue the use of chamber pots and outdoor toilet for awhile. In fact, the third floor bedrooms were never finished; although business was good, funds were not unlimited.[18]

Nonetheless, over the years, as money allowed, Hester Stackhouse's home would be tastefully appointed with furnishings she selected in northern cities while visiting Amos' relatives, or from mail order catalogs of John P. Wanamaker – Philadelphia's finest store and one of the greatest in the nation – and from the respectable Quaker-founded Strawbridge & Clothier.[19] In her kitchen Hester would have a large Majestic-brand stove, complete with warming oven and connecting tank for hot water piped to the kitchen and

Newly-built home of Hester and Amos Stackhouse, c. 1904.

dining room sinks, and, in the future, to the upstairs bath (although water stayed hot only when there was a fire in the cook stove). Ending the need for trips outside to a spring house, an oak icebox conveniently kept milk and butter from spoiling. During the winter, ice chopped out of the river was stored inside the family's icehouse, insulated with piles of sawdust from their mill. In summer, blocks of the ice placed in the tin-lined bottom compartment of the icebox cooled the upper section, which held the perishables.

As mercantile dealers, Amos, Jr., and Charles Dilworth received a retail discount on most purchases. For instance, in 1903, Wing & Son Company of New York paid A & C.D. Stackhouse a commission on the sale of each organ or piano manufactured by Wing. Wing also offered an installment pay plan with $35 down. There were Wing pianos at both Stackhouse homes, Hester's being catalog style #29, listed at $1,200 (a small fortune to most Madison Countians). Her upright concert grand stood nearly five feet tall and was over five feet long, cased in figured mahogany with an instrumental attachment enabling the piano player to imitate perfectly the tones of mandolin, harp, guitar, zither and banjo, "as though played by the parlor orchestra."[20] The new Wing piano took its prominent place along the inside wall of Hester's living room.

At the tall windows, there were pull-down shades with lace curtains from Switzerland (costing $35 per pair), and heavy brocade draperies with deep fringed valance framing the doorway between parlor and dining room. The parlor furniture was mahogany, while quartersawn oak pieces were chosen for the other rooms – one fancy bedroom suite costing $500![21] Expensive light fixtures in the ceilings and Oriental rugs on the floors laid the background for the tasteful accessories Hester would collect and protect for the rest of her life.

Typical Madison County Cabin.

Even though it would be years before the landscaping and other details were done, the house was built to last – for one hundred years, at least – and was a showplace for Madison County. There were numerous other Queen Anne designs with polygonal towers, but the full-circle types, like Stackhouses', were extremely unusual in rural western North Carolina.[22] To many of the Stackhouse neighbors, living in one- or two-room log cabins, heated and lighted by single fieldstone fireplaces, and lacking even a small glass window, the new home of Amos, Jr., was a castle, evoking mixed feelings of respect, pride, repugnance and envy. Amos, Jr., would soon find that his place of privilege in the community carried responsibilities and restitutions which he would execute honorably in accordance with his grandfather's admonition "That no stigma may be justly attached to them [his descendants]."[23]

ENDNOTES FOR CHAPTER FIFTEEN

[1] Hunter, Charles E. "Report on Barite in the Vicinity of Stackhouse, Madison County, N.C." TVA Division of Chemical Engineering, January 3, 1949.

[2] Madison County Register of Deeds, Book 20, p.164.

[3] "Floods on French Broad River & Spring Creek, Vicinity of Hot Springs, N.C.," TVA report, p.27.

[4] Madison County Register of Deeds, Book 19, p.99.

[5] Madison County Register of Deeds, Book 22, p.42.

[6] Madison County Register of Deeds, Book 22, p.39.

[7] Letter to author from Library Director, Carolina Power & Light Company, Raleigh, January 24, 1986.

[8] Hunter, 1949 report.

[9] Author's private papers.

[10] Madison County Register of Deeds, Book 18, p.426.

[11] Private papers.

[12] Asheville Sunday Citizen, obituary article, Nov. 8, 1923.
Private papers.

[13] Wolcott, Mary Ellen. "Stackhouse and Runion Community," Asheville Citizen-Times, Sept. 24, 1978, Section C, p.1.

[14] Private papers.

[15] Meek, Anna Stackhouse. Interview, 1997.

[16] Aumiller, Nancy Stackhouse. Interview, 1998.

[17] Wolcott, 1978.

[18] Aumiller, Nancy S. Interview, 2001.

[19] Weigley, Russell F. Philadelphia, A 300 Year History. New York: W.W.Norton & Co., 1982, p.486.

[20] Private papers (Wing & Son catalog, New York, 1900).

[21] Aumiller, Nancy S. Interview, 2000.

[22] Griffith, Clay. Interview, Western Office of N.C. Dept. of Cultural Resources, Asheville, N.C., May, 2001.

[23] Stackhouse, Powell, Sr. Private papers.

Chapter Sixteen

In 1904 Amos Stackhouse's younger son Charles Dilworth used part of his new-found wealth to take a long trip out West to the Grand Canyon and other places.[1] Before he left home, perhaps at his father's urging, twenty-seven-year-old Charles wrote his "Last Will and Testament," in which he gave to his "honored mother," all his household furniture, and "all the real estate which I bought from my father containing about 250 acres," for her to hold during the term of her natural life.[2] At his mother's death, continued the will, that land and Charles' half of the Putnam farm, plus the 65-acre tract where Ellison had built a home, would go to Amos, Jr. Since Charles had no heirs, his father was possibly concerned that, without a will, the ownership of Stackhouse could become entangled in legalities if an accident befell Charles during his extended absence. Witnessing Charles' signature on the handwritten document were Hester's brother, Lloyd Honeycutt, and Henry J. Moore of the barytes corporation. Fortunately, Charles Dilworth Stackhouse enjoyed his vacation in good health, returning home to continue his quiet life, and to postpone his father's fears for nearly three decades.

Charles Dilworth Stackhouse and friends in the Grand Canyon, c. 1904.
Courtesy, Sandra M. Beaudry.

The next year Charles' parents also traveled, taking Hester, June and Ernest with them to visit Ellison and other relatives in Philadelphia, leaving Amos, Jr., and Charles in charge of business at Stackhouse. During the two-week absence, the family members wrote home regularly, and were answered by Amos, Jr., and Charles. After ten days, Amos, Jr., complained of loneliness in a letter to Hester, saying, "It has been so long since I've seen you. Tell Jr. to be a good boy, and kiss Ernest for me. Have your throat examined while you are there, and have it well when you get here, for I may court you over again."[3]

Just before leaving on her Philadelphia trip – July 27, 1905 – Hester had signed a deed, along with Amos, Jr., and Charles, to transfer nearly an acre of land to the Madison County Board of Education for thirty-five dollars.[4]

Located off the Walnut Gap Road, three or four hundred yards from Amos' house, the site held the old log cabin school built by Amos and used periodically at Stackhouse, but at this time probably owned by the county in order to receive state funds. Amos, Jr., as a school committeeman, was responsible for hiring the teacher (at $25 per month pay) for the school's four-month term, as well as providing a suitable building.

The county began a substantial new frame building, weather-boarded, with a porch. Its one large room had a stage at back, a cloakroom vestibule at front, plaster walls, heart pine floor, and several tall glass windows.[5] It is most likely that Amos, Jr., donated the lumber and some of the other materials in order to have a nice school for his sons, as well as his neighbors' children. With no hotel near Stackhouse, the school teachers always boarded with Amos & Anna, going home on weekends. (One particular teacher, Miss Robbie Bryan, however, stayed over one Saturday – September 12, 1907 – to marry Mr. Sanky Brigman in Amos' gazebo on Summer House Point.[6])

All around Madison County, interest was stirring to build "free" schools within walking distance of the pupils' homes, since most communities were now dependent upon the Presbyterian mission schools to educate their children. By July 5th, funds were allocated for a public school building – the first in Hot Springs – and a movement was underway in Marshall to do the same.[7] It is unclear whether the school at Putnam was still operating now that the N.C. Land & Timber Company had declared bankruptcy, even though the county newspaper, on June 7, 1905, had listed Amos Stackhouse, Jr., as school committeeman at Putnam.[8] By virtue of the train station's being there, people referred to the area (including Stackhouse) as Putnam. But, in February 1907, the schools listed by the Madison County Board of Education as being in the Hot Springs district were Hot Springs, Antioch, Bluff, Doe Branch, Stackhouse, Highland, and Hot Springs Colored. In June, 1908, the Board added a branch school "to be run at Paint Rock near Hot Springs for a three months term."[9]

Amos, Jr., accepted further community responsibilities on December 26, 1905, when he received the Postmaster appointment of Stackhouse, North Carolina, executing a bond and taking the oath of office on January 19, 1906.[10] No longer would he need his father's signature on postal reports; now old Amos was fully retired. Likewise, on January 26th, Charles Dilworth took Amos, Jr.'s, place as Assistant Postmaster, with Frank Honeycutt, Hester's brother, being sworn in on August 13th as Principal Clerk of the Stackhouse Post Office. (Frank and his brother Arthur had decided for some reason to change the spelling of their name from Honeycutt to Hunycutt.) Yet another postal form – No.6834 – signed by Amos, Jr., in December, 1906, authorized Charles Dilworth

> "To act in my place, in case of my sickness or absence, to discharge all the duties required of me by law, as Postmaster, subject to all provisions of the said section, and to the approval of the Postmaster General. And, in case of the sickness or unavoidable absence of the Assistant Postmaster above named, I authorize Frank L. Hunycutt, a clerk employed in this office, to discharge in like manner… all the official duties required of me by law."

Perhaps, now, Amos, Jr., could more freely take trips with his family.[11]

That family had expanded by this time. Back in August, when Hester had returned home, Amos, Jr., evidently made good his threat to "court you over again." On May 25, 1906, she gave birth to a fourth son, named Ellison Dilworth Gilbert Stackhouse, who would be called Gilbert. (It seems likely this birth involved severe complications, because, although longing for a daughter, Hester would have no more babies.)

Sadly, four days after Gilbert's birth, Amos received word of the death of his twenty-eight-year-old grandson in Philadelphia (Landsdowne), Ellison Dilworth Stackhouse, who, ironically, bore the same name as the newborn baby.[12] This son of Ellison, in addition to having lived at Stackhouse as a child, had often visited his grandfather there, and had even made a friend in the community, with whom Ellison, Jr., had corresponded occasionally. The cause of young Ellison's death was not recorded, but his passing brought great sorrow to the Stackhouses in North Carolina.

Day-to-day work and activities, however, continued, and by September, Amos, Jr., and Charles Dilworth had decided to open a second general store at Jewel Hill, about five miles away on the Asheville road. They rented the building from J.J. Drumheller for six dollars per month, hauling their beginning stock (1,480 dollars' worth) from the Stackhouse store and from the freight depot at Putnam.[13] Even though Amos and most of the local folk still called it Jewel Hill, the community's name had been officially changed to "Walnut" in 1902, when a U.S. Post Office was established.[14] Prior to the Civil War, Jewel Hill had had its own post office, but, afterwards, the nearest one was at Barnard, several miles away, down on the railroad.

Walnut had grown since the coming of the Presbyterian boarding school and the barytes plant at Stackhouse. In 1903, the N.C. Legislature gave permission for a ferry to be built on the French Broad at Barnard, further connecting other communities to Walnut.[15] Now the settlement had a couple of stores, churches, post office, county school and Bell Institute's large classroom building, plus girls' dormitory. (The boys stayed in private homes or boarding houses.) Rev. R.M. Johnston, Bell's headmaster, even printed a small newspaper for the community, largely supported by ads from Asheville and Marshall businesses, but also by small businessmen such as Amos & C.D. Stackhouse.

The Presbyterians had great influence on the Walnut area in setting standards, providing charity, and educating the youth. Besides the children of Amos' good friend and neighbor George W. Gahagan, the younger siblings of Hester Stackhouse had attended Bell Institute – Arthur, Lloyd, May and Frank.[16] (Hester and her older sisters would probably have taken advantage of the mission school had it been there during their youth.) In 1907, the school's sponsor, Cumberland Presbyterian Church, merged with the Presbyterian Church, U.S.A., bringing Bell Institute and three neighboring day schools under the same governing board as the other Presbyterian schools in Madison County, including Dorland at Hot Springs.[17]

Bell's principal, Rev. R.M. Johnston, had also worked to achieve civic improvements in his village. On February 20, 1905, the year before the Stackhouses opened their Walnut Store, the State Assembly ratified the incorporation of "the town of Walnut," with the Presbyterian principal, Johnston, as mayor, and Amos' old friend, Mallie Reeves, as treasurer.[18] Corporate limits and tax rates were set, but the sale of liquors was forbidden.

By an even earlier act of the Legislature (in 1903), the county roads leading from Stackhouse to Walnut had been improved, establishing a "public road system for Madison County." Every able-bodied male citizen between the ages of eighteen and forty-five years was required to work on roads three days each April and September–"six days per annum."[19] Those who could afford it, especially men with businesses to run (like the Stackhouses), were allowed to pay others to work in their stead. Moreover, the same act levied a special road tax of five cents on every hundred dollars worth of taxable property, and fifteen cents on each poll, yearly, for purchasing tools and materials necessary to build and repair roads and bridges. Lumber men, like the Stackhouses, were held responsible "for the unusual injury done to the roads in hauling lumber over them."[20] Although it meant extra expense to the Stackhouse brothers, the road improvements were beneficial to their businesses in both Stackhouse and Walnut communities.

For example, charge customers included Rev. Johnston, Henry Moore, J.J. Drumheller, and the International Order of Oddfellows fraternity.[21] Listed on the store's expense account were amounts paid to charity cases and to Johnston, for advertising in his little newspaper *Good Times*, as well as rent to Drumheller. Another frequent cost was the "teaming" of goods from Putnam depot and from Stackhouse to Walnut. However, despite this evidence of a thriving business, one year and two months after opening, Amos, Jr., and Charles D. closed their Walnut store, moving the stock of goods back to Stackhouse.[22] Furthermore, about that time, Walnut village lost its "town" status, for unknown reasons (only to be re-ratified in 1915).[23]

Another 1907 event to carry lasting impact – in the eyes of outsiders, at least – was the arrival in Madison County of a visitor who would publish a book about his trip, *The Child That Toileth Not*.[24] Appointed and paid by the U.S. Department of Commerce and Labor, Thomas Robinson Dawley, Jr., was directed to investigate and report upon the industrial, moral, educational and physical condition of female and child workers in the United States southern mountain section. The writer traveled by foot and horseback through remote parts of the county such as Laurel, later relating stories of his meetings with ignorant, poverty-stricken, backwoods families, whose children would be better off, in his opinion, working in factories.

Having stepped off the train at Putnam, heading for "the Sodom district" on Laurel, Dawley climbed the bluff above, hoping to hire transport, but "found only three or four rough-board deserted houses."[25] Returning to the railroad he asked a local fellow about getting a horse. "'Stackhouse up ter the store, 'as got the onlyest hoss round hyar'," replied the man. "'Tha's a store about half a mile up there, an' a barytes mill wha' they grind up the stuff to send off an' put inter flour an' we git it back agin ter eat,'" he added.[26] Walking on to Stackhouse, the Northern stranger did visit Amos' old store, about which he wrote the following:

> "As I entered the store two loungers on the porch followed me in
> with a shuffling gait, where they joined another idler or two
> lounging 'midst a confusion of boxes and barrels, and suspended
> horse collars, buckets, blankets and chains. A partition at one end
> of the counter enclosed a post-office with the usual number of
> official announcements tacked on the outside. A rather handsome
> girl with a very white face, and wearing a steeple-crowned straw

hat, stepped to the door, and pressing two fingers to her lips, shot through them with deadly accuracy a quantity of tobacco juice killing a bug on the post opposite.

The boss in the store informed me that he did not have any horse, or at least he did not have one that was available, and so I consoled myself with the knowledge that the only way to obtain an intimate knowledge of the people in the mountains is to travel on foot."[27]

The road to Sodom (its name changed to "Revere" in 1901 by the Presbyterian missionaries[28]) rose between the hills in back of the Stackhouse store, soon bringing Dawley to the little cabin of a widow and three children, who told him of their destitution, living on what berries they could pick and sell, until the son got a job at the barytes mine. "Now they were doing very well and the mother was happy in their prosperity,"[29] gloated Dawley, as he tried to prove that industrial employment for mountain people, even children, was the solution to their woes. Through his several pages devoted to Madison County, Dawley portrayed, as most outsiders did, the worst cases, rarely interviewing the farmer whose well-fed children were learning to read and write. Moreover, it was impossible to walk past Stackhouse store without seeing Amos, Jr.'s, brand new home towering above, or the older, but well-maintained, large house of Amos, close by; Dawley failed to mention either of the grand structures in his book. Incidentally, the Stackhouse store "boss" was not likely Amos, Jr., or Charles Dilworth, since they were operating their Walnut store, and, possibly the sawmill at this time. It might have been Frank Hunycutt, postal clerk, or someone else hired to manage in the owners' absence.

Nevertheless, while Dawley traveled along the French Broad, the Stackhouses traveled along the James River in Virginia where it meets the Chesapeake Bay, with the Atlantic Ocean in the distance.[30] They were there for the "Jamestown Exposition" at Sewell's Point, celebrating the three-hundredth anniversary of the first permanent settlement in America. The comprehensive exhibition ran from April 26th to November 26, 1907, in a small city with streets and permanent structures built on 340 acres. Although the exhibition was not financially successful, many enthusiastic visitors attended, especially after reading the *North American Review* in March:

"The Jamestown Exposition offers an opportunity for a historical, educational and uplifting exhibit such as no other has ever presented… The nation's growth as a moral force, as a leader in the new sense of the unity of mankind, as a higher development in the racial history of the sense of brotherly responsibility, of justice and education and enlightenment, and equal opportunities for all men, these are the points to be emphasized by the Exposition."[31]

What Quaker could resist such an invitation? Accompanying Amos and Anna, Hester and the three boys, was probably Amos, Jr., and, possibly, Charles Dilworth, leaving Frank Hunycutt in charge of business.

The trip would have been educational for June and Ernest, and entertaining to all. Of particular interest to the Stackhouses were the North

Carolina "State Building," the Post Office Department building, the Palace of Mines and Metallurgy, and the Arts and Crafts Village," where artisans worked by hand with textiles, iron, wood, copper, silver, rushes and felt.[32] They produced, on the spot, seventeenth-century household goods and wearing materials just as they had been made by the earliest colonists when the Stackhouse family first settled in America. The gardens along the streets and around the buildings were beautifully landscaped with trees, shrubs, perennials and annuals, displaying lush greenery and brilliant colors throughout the seasons. Of interest, too, to the young sons, would be the 500-foot-long Palace of Machinery and Transportation, with its showing of historical and modern methods; the Army and Navy exhibits featuring military parades and flags; the Marine Exhibits Building, displaying all classes of boats and nautical appliances, for "all who love the rivers, lakes, and oceans," stated the written guides.[33] Lying at anchor just off the point, were three or four great United States battleships, while naval fleets sailed at Hampton Roads – especially exciting to the men in the Stackhouse party. (Amos would remember 1849, when he lived in Philadelphia, and his shipbuilding cousins, Mark and Stephan Stackhouse, had built the U.S.S. Michigan, first iron ship of the U.S. Navy, right there in the city.[34]) Camels and other exotic animals of the international exhibits pleased the young boys, while the Stackhouse adults likely were curious about the Food and Products Building, "because of the great agitation of the subject of pure foods at the present time," declared the catalog.

The sights and wonders of this experience would remain with June and Ernest Stackhouse for a lifetime. Amos, Jr., and Hester brought home a handsome souvenir set of large beer steins – white porcelain with gold edging, matching Hester's Haviland china.[35] Even though beer was never served in that household, the accessories added a distinctive flair to the dining room.

Soon after returning from their Virginia vacation, the Stackhouses turned another profit for themselves and the community in the selling of the "eastern half" of their Laurel farm at Putnam to Joseph B. O'Brien of Albany County, New York.[36] He had been the "last and highest bidder" on the North Carolina Land and Timber's acres and leaseholdings in January, 1905. According to the original agreement, the Stackhouse brothers agreed to sell "the land and premises" at the price of $1500 cash "at anytime within ten years after said 10th day of August, 1897."[37] Mere days before the option's expiration – August 5, 1907 – the property was signed over by Amos, Jr., his wife, and Charles Dilworth, who were, no doubt, satisfied that O'Brien's plans to develop Putnam would benefit the Stackhouse community.

With their share of the sale money, Hester and Amos, Jr., continued to make improvements by digging out more of the mountainside behind their house for a stone retaining wall nearly a hundred feet long, and ten feet high, in places. (This project would take several years to complete, according to a 1978 *Asheville Citizen* reporter who quoted Gilbert Stackhouse as saying, "My father had eight or ten men all during my young days digging, putting down pipe, getting ready to build the brick building back of the house."[38]) In front of the wall they built a brick two-story multi-purpose building, 14 x 60 feet, which would be called "the annex" by the family.[39] A short driveway led up to the second floor level, then passed under a shed roof where the horses were unhitched and taken to the stable, and the buggies were pulled inside the two-stall buggy room. Also on this level there were adjoining storage rooms and a guest chamber with fireplace. Below, handy to Hester's kitchen porch, was a laundry room containing a sink with running water, plus two large tubs (one for washing, the other for rinsing) made from smooth slate pieces, mortared at the seams, and mounted on a table-high steel frame. The tub fronts were slanted to receive the wash boards. There was also an extractor with wooden rollers, saving Hester the hand-wringing of heavy wet garments and linens. Completing the laundry was a small stove for heating water. An adjoining bathroom held a water closet, with additional plumbing for a future bathtub and lavatory.

Retaining wall construction at Amos' and Hester's home, c. 1905.

At the end of the building, Hester's pride and joy was a small glass-roofed, angled-wall hot-house where she could over-winter house plants and start garden seeds early in the spring, as well as store her tools, buckets and flower pots neatly away from the back porch. Between the hot-house and laundry, a coal bin could be filled from above by wagons that drove to the upper level and dumped their loads down a chute. With its Cortwright tin roof and foot-thick brick walls, the annex building needed little maintenance. It was also resistant to fire – a constant threat from the flying hot cinders of passing trains.[40]

Besides providing a place for travelers and employees to stay, the annex offered Hester Stackhouse even more convenience and luxury compared to that of most mountain women. She used her saved time wisely by growing more vegetables and fruits; tending to her chickens and eggs; separating and churning the milk for butter and buttermilk; and sewing quilts and clothing for herself and the children. For all her fine surroundings and station in life, Hester Stackhouse was thrifty and hard-working, never wasting a minute, and never forgetting her lean days of growing up.

It was during the construction of this brick building that little Gilbert Stackhouse uttered his first sentence. To keep the baby entertained as she conducted her own kitchen chores, Hester had a play pen strapped to the kitchen window where Gilbert could watch the activities of excavation, brick laying, framing, etc. Old Amos spent his days, too, at the project, keeping an eye on things while Amos, Jr., worked at store and mill. One day, mimicking his grandfather's word to their faithful black employee, Gilbert said, to everyone's surprise, "Dig thy ditch, John."[41]

Another alteration was made to the house about 1908, when Hester decided to make a library of the dining room and move the dining room next door to the former downstairs guest room. Both Amos, Jr., and Hester enjoyed reading and placed great value on education, buying full sets of volumes by Shakespeare, Kipling, O. Henry, Dickens and many other authors from salesmen at the door or from catalogs. To furnish the room, Hester ordered a "Golden Quartered Oak" library case, 62" high by 53" wide, cross veneered, with full-length leaded glass doors, framed by half-round carved columns on short claw foot legs. In the center of the floor, an oak table held a green lamp and dictionary, with a set of encyclopedia on the bottom shelf. A green velvet and oak sofa near the open fireplace completed the invitation to read or study. As June and Ernest grew older, the library's contents expanded, since both sons were avid readers (June more so; when an adult, he would boast that he had read every book in the room at least once, and had some favorites that he had read several times).[42]

Eighty-eight-year-old Amos observed all these changes to his farm with interest, as he remembered its condition when he had purchased it thirty years before. He had few regrets, if any, and was proud of the little community that had grown up around him. He continued to spend his days writing to relatives and old friends and receiving many replies. His cousin Robert Stackhouse wrote from New Jersey, asking in particular, "Do you not think it would be a source of rare pleasure to you and your children to know that you are among those who have kept alive the interest and use of the Coat of Arms granted to us three hundred eighty-nine years ago?" Robert explained how he had hired an artist "with a knowledge of heraldry" to make a cut, and to print envelopes and writing papers carrying the Stackhouse emblem. He also offered framed copies, eleven by twelve inches, at a reasonable cost, which Amos ordered to hang in his own library.[43] (If he bought stationery, it did not survive the years.)

Besides correspondence, visiting gave Amos enjoyment, as he and Anna traveled North to his relatives, and to Florida to her parents and friends, receiving them all in return at Stackhouse. A memorable visit about 1906 was recorded by camera, as Amos and Anna posed in their front yard with sons Amos, Jr., Charles Dilworth, Thomas and Ellison.[44]

Amos Stackhouse with his wife and four sons in their yard at Stackhouse, c.1906.
Front Row, left to right: Amos and Ellison Stackhouse. Back row, left to right: Charles Dilworth, Amos, Jr., Anna M. and Thomas Stackhouse.

Amos' closest relationship away from the immediate family at Stackhouse was with his son Ellison, who, even at long distance, remained active in the care of his father's health and welfare, and keeping him informed, too, about their family in the North. Through letters and visits, Ellison and Amos exchanged confidences about their health, their aspirations, and their finances, frequently lending money to each other.

In one letter Ellison reported that he was sending Amos' eyeglasses which he had had repaired for him. "I hope they will be all right – but I think the trouble with them is they are too small for thee. Better give them to Anna." In another letter Ellison told his father, "I have been taking several roasted onions just before going to bed for several nights and it seems to help my cough." At yet a different time, Ellison remarked, "I am glad to hear Anna's cough is better. Does she want any more of the medicine? If so, let me know."[45]

Still later, Ellison acknowledged twenty-five dollars his father had sent him to buy headstones for the graves of Powell and Edith Stackhouse, Amos' parents, at the Friends Southwestern Burial Ground near Cardington, Delaware. Soon afterwards, a receipt came to Amos from Ellison for "eight dollars interest on Amos' note of $200 to date." Next time it was Ellison who asked for the loan, writing that he had rented a house in Lansdowne (a small town about ten miles west of Philadelphia) and needed fifty dollars to help with moving expenses. His new home was located on the West Chester Railroad, "quite near the station," he wrote. Ellison also promised to bring his father, on his upcoming trip to Stackhouse, "the cigarros mild," which Amos had requested.

On March 29, 1906, Ellison began a letter to Amos that read, "I sent thee by registered mail, one doz. pkgs. of those small cigars for a birthday present, hoping thee will be able to enjoy them on thy 87th birthday." Nine months later – December 23rd – Amos received a long newsy Christmas greeting which read, in part:

> "Thy letter of the 12th duly rec'd. W. is cold & windy tonight – 15 degrees above. I was very busy all last week. We worked at nights until 10 o'clock and after. Did not get home until near 12 and up at 5 a.m… Mr. Flake gave all the men $5 each for Christmas present. Wilmot never gave anything in the 17 years I worked for him."[46]

Ellison also described the chicken house he had just built for his thirty-five hens. "They commenced laying about 2 weeks ago and have laid 4 doz. eggs. It has cost about $3 per month for feed for the last 6 mos." He told Amos, furthermore, that in a letter from "Cousin Sarah Gerken" of Brooklyn, "she said to tell thee she often thinks of thee and the fun you had at Coney Island." About his change of employment, Ellison confided,

> "I like my work putting up orders of groceries. I am on my feet all day but have had rheumatism in heel of my right foot for 6 wks. Has been quite painful at times, hurts to walk on hard pavements."

In his closing paragraph, Ellison stated,

> "We are going to have a turkey for Christmas and would like to have thee & Anna here to help us eat it, but I don't think thee would like our cold weather. It is now 11 o'clock and I have to get

up at 5 a.m., so will say Good Night. Wishing you all a Happy Christmas. Write when thee can. With love, thy son, Ellison Stackhouse."[47]

Filled with small talk of weather and relatives, pains and victories, Ellison's letter, dutifully written at the expense of needed rest, was the comfortable, familiar conversation between father and son. His last extant letter, it would also be the next to last opportunity to wish his father "Merry Christmas." Amos Stackhouse died early in 1909, on February twenty-seventh, a month short of his ninetieth birthday. Only three years after burying his son, Ellison Stackhouse would, once again, grieve long and deeply in the loss of this lifelong mentor, friend and confidante.

Amos' death was surely peaceful, as had been his life. He had no worries about his wife's future welfare; Amos, Jr., and Charles Dilworth had comfortable livings; there were Stackhouse sons growing up to continue the name; Amos' children by his other two wives were settled in life; and the little community of his creation was flourishing. He would meet his Maker gratefully, in open-armed joy. Since he had prepared ahead of time his brick-lined grave out on Summer House point, in his adopted homeland of Western North Carolina, there was nothing for Anna and her sons to do except set up the small headstone, simply inscribed – "Amos Stackhouse, Mar. 31, 1819 – Feb. 27, 1909."

A few years before, in a history of Delaware County, Pennsylvania, Amos Stackhouse had been described as having

"Served the village of Stackhouse, North Carolina, in the capacity of school director and postmaster for the long period of thirty years. Throughout his long and useful life, Mr. Stackhouse has been upright and honorable in all his transactions, active and zealous in advancing the welfare and material growth of the community in which he resides, and a firm adherent of the doctrines of the Society of Friends."[48]

Because of Amos' legacies, life at Stackhouse would continue in the hands of his namesake, Amos, Jr., who would carry the torch for the rest of his own life. Except, from now on, he would be the one called "Amos," as was the custom, while his son, Amos, III, would be referred to as Amos, Jr.," and called "June" by family and friends.

Tombstone of Amos Stackhouse.

Amos Stackhouse, 1903. Founder of Stackhouse, North Carolina.

ENDNOTES FOR CHAPTER SIXTEEN

1 Meek, Anna Stackhouse. Interview, 1997.
2 Author's private papers.
3 Ibid.
4 Madison County Register of Deeds, Book 20, p.327.
5 Stackhouse, Juanita C. Interview, 1998.
6 Shupe, Dorothy Brigman. Interview, 1999.
7 Madison County School Board minutes, 1905.
  Marshall *News-Record*, June 7, 1905.
8 Ibid.
9 Ibid.
10 Private papers.
  Stroupe, Vernon. *Postoffices & Postmasters of N.C.*, Vol.II. Charlotte, N.C. Postal History
11 Society, 1996, p.2-273.

[12] Private papers.

[13] Swayne, Norman Walton. *Byberry Waltons, An Account of Four English Brothers*. Decorah, Iowa: Anundsen Pub. Co., 1989, reprint, p. 489.

[1] Private papers.

[14] Stroupe, Vernon S. *Postoffices and Postmasters of N.C.*, Vol.II. Charlotte: N.C. Postal History Society. 1996, pps. 2-268, 2-273.

[15] *Private Laws of N.C.*, 1903 Session, p. 264, Raleigh: State published.

[16] Painter, J.B. *Season of Dorland-Bell*. Boone, N.C.: Appalachian Consortium Press, 1996, pps. 302, 303.
The School Itemizer, school newspaper of Jewel Hill Academy, 1898.

[17] Painter, p.121.

[18] *Private Laws of N.C.*, 1905 Session, p.305.

[19] Ibid., 1903, p.242.

[20] Ibid., p.246.

[21] Private papers.

[22] *French Broad News*, Marshall, N.C., Dec. 07, 1907.

[23] *Private Laws of N.C.*, 1915 Session, p.356.

[24] Dawley, Thomas Robinson, Jr. *The Child That Toileth Not*. New York: Gracia Publishing Company, 1912, p.7.

[25] Ibid, p.357.

[26] Ibid.

[27] Ibid.

[28] Ibid, p.374.

[29] Ibid., p.359.

[30] Aumiller, Nancy Stackhouse. Interview, 1997.

[31] Harvey, George, "Singularity of the Jamestown Exposition," *North American Review*, 15 Mar. 1907.

[32] "Illustrated Souvenir of the Jamestown Ter-Centennial Exposition," p.36.

[33] Ibid., p.8.

[34] *Dictionary of American Naval Fighting Ships*, Vol. 3, p.710.

[35] Aumiller, Nancy Stackhouse. Interview, 1997.

[36] Madison County Register of Deeds, Bk.22, p.244.

[37] Ibid.

[38] Wolcott, Mary Ellen. "Stackhouse and Runion," *Asheville Citizen-Times*, Sept. 24, 1978, Section C, p.1.

[39] Private papers.

[40] Aumiller, Nancy Stackhouse. Interview, 1998.

[41] Ibid.

[42] Private papers.

[43] Ibid.

[44] Ibid.

[45] Ibid.

[46] Ibid.

[47] Ibid.

[48] *History of Chester and Delaware Counties*, Pennsylvania, c.1903. Author and publisher, unknown, p.16.

Chapter Seventeen

Within three months of their father's death – on May 24, 1909 – Amos and Charles Stackhouse acted upon another opportunity to improve the economy of their community by selling the western half of the Laurel Farm, or Putnam, to Harriett L. Betts of Troy, New York.[1] Mrs. Betts had bought the eastern half three weeks earlier from Joseph O'Brien, and, also, the 38,500 acres of timberland located farther up Laurel River, previously owned by N.C. Land & Timber Company.[2] These two purchases completed the hundred-acre tract "including the mouth of the Big Laurel," which had been obtained by old Amos for his sons in 1885.

In October, 1909, at Putnam, the Laurel River Logging Company was chartered, its objects: "cutting, logging, buying and selling timber; erecting and operating sawmills, telephone lines and systems…, delivering logs, timber and lumber by means of flumes, tramways or logging roads, and by floating and splashing the same in non-navigable streams."[3] Anson Gardner Betts, son of Harriett Betts, was the corporate executive, holding ninety-eight percent of the stock. It was hoped in the Stackhouse community that the Laurel River Logging Company, or the "LRLC," as it would be referred to, might pick up where the North Carolina Land & Timber Company had left off.

One significant change, however, occurred when it was discovered there was already a North Carolina railway station called Putnam, in Moore County, making a new name necessary for the LRLC depot. "Runion" was quickly chosen, after the man who had lived there many years, and carried the mail on his back twice daily from Stackhouse post office – Marion "Paddlefoot" Runion.[4] (Runion's slightly crippled right foot flapped when he walked.)

Southern Railway Depot at Runion. In foreground, plank road from Stackhouse parallel to train tracks.

The first timber cutting took place up in Laurel where a second small sawmill was built on Pounding Mill Branch – the old name common among pioneers before community grist mills came, and even afterwards, when it was a two-day journey down the steep mountainsides.[5] (At the side of a fast-running branch, a "pounding mill" would be set up, worked by a water-powered hammer to pulverize the dry corn kernels in a mortar, producing corn meal, a western North Carolina staple. However, in 2005, Blanche Trimble Chandler, niece of Frank Hunycutt, remembered growing up on Laurel and seeing the large rock on Pounding Mill Creek. Her mother always told her the Indians had hollowed it out – chiseled it in some way – for grinding corn.[6]) Logs cut at Pounding Mill came from trees felled by hand axe and crosscut saw, while the sawyers waited for the building of a standard-gauge railroad from Runion. This description of the project appeared in the February, 1911, issue of *Manufacturers' Record*, headed, "Laurel River Logging Company":

> "Two hundred men are employed on constructing 10 miles of railroad from Runion, near Hot Springs, N.C., up the Laurel River to the Tennessee line, and with a probability of ultimately extending through a section of Tennessee to connect with the C.C. & D. Railroad, making 35 miles in all. This is being built for the increased development of the Laurel River Logging Co.'s lumber interests. The company has a lumber mill at Runion and another at Pounding Mill, and it is the intention to begin operations in April. It has about 40,000 acres in Madison County and over 6000 acres across the Tennessee line (formerly owned by the N.C. Land & Timber Co.) is virgin forest, and will cut about 75,000,000 feet of white pine and 45,000,000 feet of poplar, large quantities of hemlock and other timbers.

> "The president of this company is Anson Betts of Troy, N.Y., who is quoted as saying that he expects to rush the construction through this almost inaccessible region, which will be greatly benefited. Hot Springs will also profit by this enterprise as the banking business of the company will be conducted there."[7]

Meanwhile, at Runion, renovation of the structures left behind by N.C. Land & Timber, plus construction of new buildings, trestles, and a dam, were soon finished. The dam on Big Laurel was built by cribbing large hemlock logs that were pinned to the underlying rocks with steel rods, creating the mill pond needed to clean the logs of debris as they came off the train from Pounding Mill and other logging camps.

Like many more springing up in the mountains, LRLC was a bandmill operation, using a very narrow toothed steel band that ran on two pulleys, sawing with the vertical edge of the teeth. The finely-tempered ribbon was so thin that it wasted far less of the log into saw dust than the circular blades employed by local sawmills such as the Stackhouses'. An efficient circle mill could produce five to ten thousand board feet per day, whereas bandmills turned out four to five times that amount.

When interviewed in 1997, Nealie Price, who had been a former Runion worker, recalled that daily, 25 to 30,000 feet of lumber – mostly virgin timber

Laurel River Logging Company at Runion on Big Laurel Creek.

– were sawn at Runion bandmill. "Poplars were four to five feet across, and we sawed them into seventeen-inch wide boards called 'paneling,'" he said. Price related that other species were also cut – wild cherry, oak, basswood, walnut, and "lots of white pine."[8]

Four great dynamos furnished electricity for LRLC's cutting and planing mills and the rest of the plant. A cabled incline carried the fresh-cut lumber up the hill to the two dry kilns, or to the large stacking yards for air drying, then down to the Southern Railway siding for shipping. One blacksmith shop served the draft animals and machinery, while a second one kept the train operating.[9]

LRLC's railroad was a separate entity called Madison County Railway, but was also owned and controlled by the Betts family. Used daily to carry workers from Runion to their logging stations, it sometimes brought injured woodsmen down to the Southern depot and Asheville's hospitals. Although splashing, flooding, and fluming would still be necessary in areas where no tracks had been laid, the train greatly reduced this crude method of getting logs to mill. Much danger, however, remained in the Laurel woods from falling trees and limbs, runaway logs, glancing saws and axes, snapping chains and slick mud and ice.

Since the LRLC operated in the same hollows as the Presbyterians, the missionaries – possessing at least basic first-aid knowledge and supplies – were accustomed to having serious logging wounds brought to their doorsteps. Occasionally a trained medical person from the North would donate a year at a time to the Laurel Mission field, but it wasn't until 1914 that the efforts of Miss Frances Goodrich finally paid off, bringing Dr. George Packard to live at White Rock, near Allanstand.[10] Coupled with the mission's service, the LRLC's railway was a great boon to the area (even though the patients sometimes died during the long train trip to Asheville).[11]

In the beginning there was only one small steam engine for the logging train, but later, two larger ones were added. Horses, mules or steers pulled the cut logs from deep within the mountain fastnesses to the temporary rails which had been laid into the Laurel communities of Spillcorn, Foster's Creek, Little Laurel, Shelton Laurel and others. When the timber was removed from one cove, the tracks and useable crossties were taken up and rebuilt in the next place. At the main station of Allanstand, a steam-powered loader machine with tongs lifted the logs to the train cars bound for Runion. An employee called the "tong-hooker" clamped the tongs over the logs on the ground before they were swung onto the car by the "loaderman." A fireman was also assigned to the loader, whose responsibility was fueling to keep up the steam. This loader was transported each day from Runion and back for loading and unloading, and "was the last piece to go on the train," stated Carrie Landers Johnson in 1999, a former Runion resident.[12] After riding the train down to Runion, the crew walked to their homes while the night shift rolled the logs into the mill pond, serviced the engine and prepared the train to go back North the next morning.[13]

From the water, the cleaned logs went to the millhouse sawing carriage, "A fast-sawing rig, taking three men to operate it," remembered Clyde Dockery, Runion native.[14] The first boards cut from the log were rounded on one side, often barked, and considered waste or "slabs." Ground into chips by a machine called a "hog," the slabs went into the steam boilers to operate the bandsaw and planer.[15] When the boards began coming off the carriage, an experienced lumberman, called a grader, quickly judged the quality or "grade" of the board before it was placed on the incline bound for drying, planing and shipping.

The Runion lumber plant was constructed on the steep hillsides of the Laurel River ravine in order to use the stream, as well as the Southern Railroad. On the north side, or the "eastern half," however, the hill flattened somewhat where the good farming land began. Here LRLC laid out its small mill village for the workers. The two rows of houses, numbering between twenty-five and fifty, were the typical rough-lumber structures of other WNC lumber towns, built to last only as long as it took to cut out the timber of the area. "Each one had four rooms, but large rooms," recalled Nealie Price. "And rent was three dollars a month."[16] In each room a pair of fiber-covered electric wires, fastened with white ceramic "knob and tube" insulators, ran up the wall and across the ceiling from a switch to a single light bulb. In some cases, the light was controlled by a pull-chain hanging from the bulb, thereby saving costs.[17]

"Every house had a water spigot outside, packed in sawdust to keep from freezing," said John Herbert Waldrup, former lumber grader at Runion.[18] The piped water came from the reservoir at the top of little Runion mountain, where a large oval crater had been created, probably by blasting and hand digging. Oldtimers said that nearby Pump Gap and Pump Branch received their names because, during dry weather, water was pumped at night to fill the reservoir. A few larger permanent houses for company officials had indoor plumbing, but the mill homes had privies.[19]

One of the large permanent painted homes, in particular, had two brick fireplaces, back to back, with second-story bedroom balconies overlooking the living room. "It was beautiful inside – had wallpaper, polished wooden floors, and a great view of the French Broad," described Nancy Stackhouse Aumiller, decades later.[20]

Plank sidewalks connected the dwellings to a non-denominational church and school building, commissary, club house for officials, and boarding houses for workers and visitors. Horses could be rented from the livery stable located right behind the school house. There was even an LRLC volunteer fire department and an LRLC baseball team, although, for lack of level ground, the games took place on a large island in the French Broad. To inform Runion village of work hours, the mill whistle blew loud and shrill three times a day – at six in the morning, at noon, and at six in the evening. In 1912 an average worker earned $1.50 for each ten-hour work day.[21]

Down at the foot of Runion mountain, near the Southern Railway trestle over Big Laurel, was the LRLC loading platform, called Shipping & Receiving, where the lumber was at last placed in freight cars and connected to the Southern trains. LRLC supplies came by train to this point, too, and were hauled by wagon team up the steep road to Runion.[22]

Another feature, new to the Stackhouse and Laurel communities, was the telephone line installed by LRLC from its Allanstand headquarters to Runion. Bearing little resemblance to modern-day systems, it was strictly a company line, but one or two farmers along the way were allowed to connect a telephone in their homes in exchange for right-of-way to cross their land.[23] (As early as 1902, there had been crude "farmer-line" telephones at Spring Creek, Hot Springs and Marshall, but not at Stackhouse and Laurel.)[24]

Jeter Edward Wardrep uses telephone in Laurel River Logging Company commissary. .

Laurel River Logging Company scrip coin, worth one dollar at the commissary. Courtesy Duckett House Inn.

One of the Runion telephone sites, the commissary, was also the payroll center and contained the thick-walled concrete strong-house.[25] However, to reduce the amount of cash kept on hand, LRLC issued company employees the typical paper "trade scrip" for commissary spending between paychecks. Besides extending LRLC's payroll period, scrip provided workers with food and other needs during the wait, but must be torn from the coupon books only at the commissary. Thin round tokens, stamped "Laurel River Mercantile Co." with "Good in Trade," on the obverse, represented the single dollar and coins of lesser amounts, respectively. These tokens were nicknamed "lightweights," remembered Clyde Dockery. "Everything over a dollar was paper scrip," he explained.[26]

The LRLC operation brought job-seekers from Hot Springs, Spring Creek, Walnut and other parts of Madison County into the Laurel River and Stackhouse areas, where they rented all available houses. Some walked miles from their homes, daily, to get the steady work; still others moved in with relatives near the sites or stayed at the Runion village boarding houses. From Hot Springs two children of Thomas Garrett (the Stackhouse's former Turnpike neighbor) came to Runion: Will Garrett and his sister Jean – both graduates of Dorland Institute – as operations manager and school teacher, respectively.[27]

Twenty feet or more above the mill dam, a swinging bridge was mounted on thick steel cables for those workers walking to Runion from Mill Ridge, Walnut Creek and other sections to the North. "The walkway was about four feet wide and one hundred feet long, floored with boards," recalled Clyde Dockery many years later.[28]

W.E. Finley, the editor of the Marshall News-Record, wrote, "Everything pointed to a care for the people on the part of the owners," after he had toured Runion in June, 1912. "This company is Madison County's largest enterprise and the thousands of dollars spent has meant money in the pockets of the persons working there, and money scattered far and wide over the county."[29]

Even though the northern lumber companies had arrived in Southern

Appalachia almost on the heels of the railroads, "The advance guard of the timber industry had been able to reach only a fraction of the vast timber reserves," wrote historian Ronald Eller forty years later.[30] In the remote Laurel Country of Madison County, the virgin forest seemed dense and endless to its inhabitants, who could not guess the rapidity of the bandmills' onslaught. In fact, not a county in western North Carolina was to be spared. By 1915, logging camps and temporary villages dotted the landscape where vast expanses of mountain land had been purchased or leased for timber cutting by lumbermen from New York, Illinois, Ohio, Maryland and Pennsylvania – the largest operator being William W. Ritter, a Philadelphian.

However, these efforts would eventually be at least slightly thwarted by one species, as described by Editor Finley in the *News-Record* on July fourth, two weeks after his first Runion trip: "Mr. J.A. Shelton… was sent by Laurel River Logging Company to Pennsylvania to study this blight and he now is ready to give us the benefit of his study… The Company desires to save the chestnut and stands ready to help others save theirs also. Examine the trees to see if there is anything wrong!"[31] Unfortunately, it would not take many years for this disease to devastate the great stands of chestnut in Appalachia.

Another deterrent to the ravaging of Madison County timber was the passage of the Weeks Act in 1911 by Congress, marking the beginning of the buying up of acres for Pisgah National Forest and woodland preservation. (It would also have significant impact upon the Stackhouse family and community, as well as the future development of Madison County.)

Showing tremendous foresight in another *News-Record* editorial on September 6, 1912, W.E. Finley reported that:

"A man who has spent much capital in the county, says that he will take ten years to cut off the timber which his company owns, but when that is done, what are the people of the county going to do? We ought to think ahead a little… Cut off the timber and you have left mountain land that is not the best for farming and so our population will diminish… It behooves the men with money invested here to lay plans for the future so as to conserve that which we have… In short, we must do something to keep the people here and not see the census of 1920 with less inhabitants than 1910. In 1900 we had more than in 1910; was this but a beginning of the outflow?"

Typical chestnut tree growth in 1910 in Western North Carolina. Courtesy National Park Service.

In her new prosperity, Hester sat for her photograph in 1910 at a Knoxville studio.

Meanwhile, the LRLC development, especially the railroad construction, had been costly, evidently exhausting Anson Betts' funds. On May 17, 1911, the LRLC charter was amended to increase capital stock from $10,000 to $350,000, with Harriett Betts, Anson's mother, holding over 10,000 shares, and Anson, though president, holding only three.[32] ("Sometimes Mr. Betts would run out of money and have to make a trip to New York to get more from his mother, a part owner in Arrow Shirt Company," recalled former Runion worker, Charlie Treadway, much later.[33]) Mrs. Betts also transferred to LRLC all the former N.C. Land & Timber lands bought by her in 1909, including the one hundred acres of Runion.[34] It is not clear whether she retained control of the stock, since the LRLC had moved its charter to Delaware where organization fees and annual taxes were lower and incorporation laws more liberal than North Carolina's.

With the Betts' LRLC development added to the Carolina Barytes plant, the Stackhouse sawmill and general store, business suddenly boomed along this section of the French Broad. In the 1912 annual edition of Southern Railway Company's *Western North Carolina Section at a Glance*, the combined population of Runion and Stackhouse was given at 500.[35] (Oldtimers in the area said that the number was much higher, perhaps counting those who walked in to work.) "While Runion is the name of the railroad station, the post office of this enterprising little town is called Stackhouse," stated the travel booklet, "from this office a large territory to the Northward is served with mail six days in each week by rural carriers." Indeed, just the year before, the neighboring Sandy Bottom and Lonesome post offices were discontinued and their mail sent to Amos Stackhouse's office for distribution.[36]

Moreover, the Carolina Barytes stockholders had also planned for expansion, albeit, mostly underground. On April 30, 1910, they renewed their lease to use the land of Amos, Charles and Hester for transporting ore from the Klondyke to the grinding mill.[37] A second lease, the same day, gave additional rights-of-way "for widening or changing their tramway gauge, switches or turnouts," as well as permission "to construct and operate one spur track and one bunker near the public or wagon road."[38] The Stackhouses would receive in advance an annual rent of ten dollars per single road and fifteen dollars for a double track, while an overhead tramway would bring twenty-five dollars per year. The lease renewal also granted the corporation permission to remove any Stackhouse rental house in the way of the tracks, to be later rebuilt at an adjacent location in "as good a condition as before removal."

Six months later, Carolina Barytes renewed, for fifty years, its lease with Anna Stackhouse on the fifty-six acres of the Klondyke.[39] Besides extending the privilege and power of the former lease at $1250 per year, it gave the option to buy the tract at any time for $5000, "the low rental and purchase price fixed on account of this consideration: that no liquors or merchandise be sold on the premises and that Carolina Barytes give its store trade to the firm of A & C.D. Stackhouse."

Evidently before renewing these leases, the New York stockholders had required Henry Moore, president of Carolina Barytes, to give an estimate of expected returns from their investments. Moore had begun mapping the underground network of tunnels, ore blocks and pillars for a large to-scale draft. These "pillars and blocks" were the columns of natural earth left as supports, holding up the tunnel ceilings when the blasting and digging took place. After the ore in a particular level had been removed, the robbing of the pillars began – as much ore from the supporting members as could be safely done without the tunnel's collapsing.

One "Plan of Stackhouse Mine," completed a week after the first lease renewal, was a view "perpendicular to Dip" with each supporting pillar bearing a number.[40] The corresponding legend gave dimensions, estimated ore tonnages and class of purity of each numbered block. From the total of sixty-two, there were 3,753 tons of "good ore," 350 tons of "low grade," 1,457 tons carrying lime, and 2,332 tons carrying galena. (As they followed the barite vein, the miners discovered lead in the deeper levels, rendering the ore worthless, because at this time, there was no easy method of separating the impurities of lead, lime or other minerals from the barite.) A findings summary at the map's corner stated:

Estimate of good ore to expect as extractable with safety from pillars and blocks above 3rd level:

Assured good ore   =2500 tons
Additional possible ore = 500 tons
             Total   =3000 tons.

On September 10, 1910, a second Klondyke map showed the vein thicknesses, as well as the four levels of the mines – the fourth level, close to 400 feet underground, and below water level. The map's legend explained that particular symbols indicated the approximate area of pillars already robbed, with a note: "Work of robbing began May 13, 1910."[41]

Having signed the long-term leases, Henry Moore looked forward to productive years at Stackhouse. The N.C. Geological and Economic Survey, in its 1910 report on the state's mining industry, described the varied uses for barite, "but by far the greater part of the mineral produced is used in the manufacture of mixed paints... It has a permanently pure white color." Furthermore, the paper declared, "The production the past three years (1908, 1909, 1910) has been made by but one producer [meaning Carolina Barytes Co.]."[42]

Unfortunately, in the early Spring of 1912, a fire destroyed the processing plant, reducing operations to the mining and shipping of crude barite until new structures could be erected. On March 11, 1913, Amos Stackhouse wrote his half-brother Ellison in Pennsylvania:

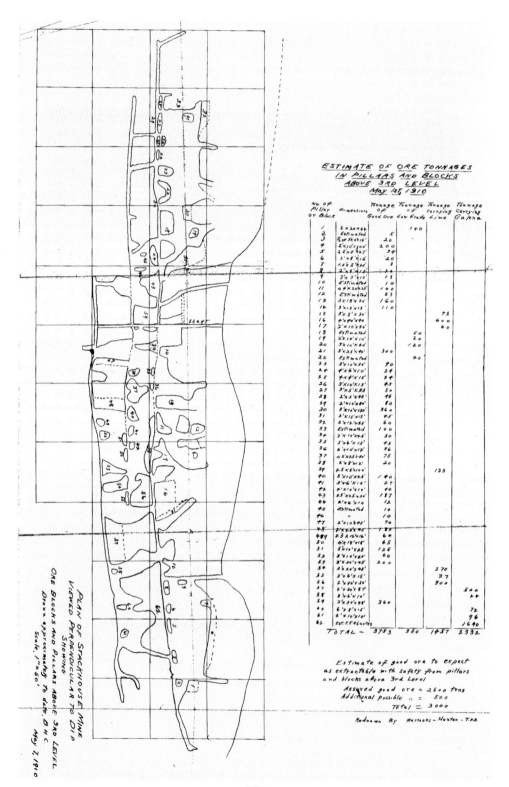

ESTIMATE OF ORE TONNAGES
IN PILLARS AND BLOCKS
ABOVE 3RD LEVEL
May 1st, 1910

No. of Pillar or Block	Dimensions	Tonnage of Good Ore	Tonnage of Low Grade	Tonnage Carrying Lime	Tonnage Carrying Galena
1	2x20x54			140	
2	Estimated	5			
3	2 or 3x6x16	20			
4	2'x10'x100'	200			
5	2.5x5x27	34			
6	2'x8'x12	20			
7	1.5x5x20	3			
8	2'x4'x11	11			
9	3'x5'x13	11			
10	Estimated	10			
11	2.4x20x25	100			
12	Estimated	25			
13	3x18x30	160			
14	3'x13'x13	110			
15	3'x5'x50			75	
16	4'x5'x50			600	
17	3'x10'x30'			60	
18	Estimated		50		
19	2'x10'x10		20		
20	3'x10'x40'		120		
21	3'x25'x40'	300			
22	Estimated		20		
23	3'x10'x30'	90			
24	4'x6'x10'	24			
25	4x4'x15'	34			
26	3'x10'x15'	45			
27	3'x5'x33	50			
28	2'x3'x30	75			
29	2'x10'x40'	70			
30	3'x10'x30	360			
31	3'x15'x15'	45			
32	2'x12'x55	60			
33	Estimated	100			
34	3'x10'x45	50			
35	5'x6'x15'	45			
36	6'x10'x17'	86			
37	2'x25'x40'	75			
38	2'x8'x3'	20			
39	2.5x5x100'			125	
40	5'x10'x33'	140			
41	3'x6'x16'	27			
42	4'x10'x10'	40			
43	5.5x25x30'	177			
44	2'x6'x10	12			
45	Estimated	10			
46	"	10			
47	2'x10x8'	70			
48	2'x25x45	180			
49	2.5x10x16	64			
50	4x15'x15'	65			
51	5x10'x35	126			
52	3'x15'x30'	60			
53	3'x40'x45'	200			
54	2'x30'x45'			170	
55	3'x6'x15'			27	
56	1'x30'x30'			300	
57	2'x30'x27				500
58	2'x6'x10'				24
59	3'x30'x45	360			
60	3'x8'x15'				72
61	6'x10'x10'				96
62	ext. F.K sulphur				1640
TOTAL –		3753	360	1457	2332

Estimate of good ore to expect
as extractable with safety from pillars
and blocks above 3rd Level

Assured good ore = 2500 tons
Additional possible " = 500
Total = 3000

Redrawn By Mattocks–Hoxton–T.K.R.

PLAN OF STACKHOUSE MINE
VIEWED PERPENDICULAR TO DIP
SHOWING
ORE BLOCKS AND PILLARS ABOVE 3RD LEVEL
Drawn approximately to date, B H C
Scale, 1"=50' May 7, 1910

Carolina Barytes Co. mill at Stackhouse, newly-built c. 1913 after fire. Couresy Am. Institute of Mining, Metallurgical and Petroleum Engineers.

"Dear Brother, I am sending you some new leases with Carolina Barytes Company which is of great importance to us that they be executed at once... You may wonder why we are sending you these, knowing that we made leases two years ago. The fact is that the entire plant burned down and we were anxious that they should remain here. They have built a nice mill with a greater capacity than they had before. We feel under obligation to these people and want to help them along, therefore, we trust you will see your way clear to attend to this immediately."[43]

Either these new leases were never signed, or were registered in New York, because copies are not among family records. The barytes company did stay on at Stackhouse, and, again, the *N.C. Geological and Economic Survey*, in its 1914 publication, stated that during 1911 and 1912, "All the barytes produced in North Carolina was from the mines near Stackhouse, Madison County, principal producer, Carolina Barytes."[44]

A photograph captioned, "Barite Mill of the Carolina Barytes Co., Stackhouse, N.C.," illustrated a paper by Thomas Watson and J. Sharshall Grasty of the University of Virginia, titled, "Barite of the Appalachian States." Presented at the New York meeting of the American Institute of Mining Engineers in February, 1915 (and later published by same), the paper's introduction explained the reason behind Watson & Grasty's research:

"Following the outbreak of war in Europe many users of foreign barite in the United States have been forced to seek their supplies at home. It seems opportune at this time, therefore, that a general review be given of the barite industry in the Appalachian States, one of the two areas from which the domestic supply of the mineral is derived, and that attention be directed to the undeveloped deposits in the region."

Deeper into their article, the authors declared:

"Deposits of barite are known in California, Idaho, Nevada and Alaska, but most of them are undeveloped... The domestic production is derived from Missouri and the Appalachian States, the greater part being obtained from Missouri... North Carolina is one of the important barite-producing states in the Appalachian Region... In Madison County in western North Carolina, the barite deposits occupy an area about 5 miles long, extending... from Bluff across the French Broad. Within this area, barite has been worked chiefly in the vicinity of Marshall, Stackhouse, Sandy Bottom and Hot Springs... At Stackhouse outcroppings have been observed on the surface for a distance of 2,200 ft."

The article also included a geological map showing the mines at Bluff and Stackhouse.[45]

Then an unforeseen problem arose. Caroline Barytes' costly new crusher – called a Raymond mill – ground the ore to dust at first crushing, instead of corn-kernel size, as the old burrstones had done. When this finer ore reached the bleaching vat with sulphuric acid, gypsum crystals formed, producing a partly fine, partly coarse product, not usable in most applications. Silk flour bolters were experimented with to remove the crystals, but the cost was too high. Furthermore, the Raymond mill introduced rust-forming iron particles, resulting in an off-color powder instead of the snow-white product the old mill had turned out.[46]

As it became necessary to follow the barite vein deeper and deeper, the proportion of galena increased and Carolina Barytes also lost its mill superintendent, William Ramsey, to the Laurel River Logging Company (perhaps during the fire shut-down). But the final blow came on July 16, 1916, as rains drove the French Broad out of its banks, taking down the company's wooden power dam as well as their large water wheel, wheel house, and the smaller water wheel of the Stackhouse's sawmill.[47]

Quickly named "The Great Flood," it caused devastation in numerous counties of western North Carolina and eastern Tennessee. The ferry at Sandy Bottom was destroyed; train tracks between Asheville and Knoxville were washed out in places; county bridges at Hot Springs, Little Pine Creek,

Marshall, N.C., July 1916.

Unidentified persons watch flooded Woolsey Branch converging with the French Broad, July, 1916. Amos' buggy house and Stackhouse General Store in background.

Charles Dilworth Stackhouse, July, 1916, with barytes mill and dam remnants in background.

Barnard and Redmon were taken downstream;[48] and sawmills located along the river were ruined, never to recover, including the one at Paint Rock. According to the U.S. Weather Bureau, the river crested at 28.6 feet – three feet higher than the 1902 flood, five feet higher than the 1876 flood (when Amos lived at Warm Springs), and the highest in 135 years of recording.[49] "It was doubtless the greatest flood in that and neighboring rivers since the Ice Age when the melting glaciers filled the valleys," wrote the N.C. Chief Justice Walter Clark, whom the flood had marooned in Morganton.[50]

These losses at Stackhouse, combined with the international war uncertainty, the lead-blackening of the barite ore, and the problems with the new mill, discouraged the stockholders from rebuilding, even though Henry Moore, the engineer and president of the Klondyke, felt that the mine had not played out and could still show profit. Had Carolina Barytes' stockholders known that the United States, in less than a year, would also be in the Great War, accelerating production of barite, they might have reacted differently. In fact, the N.C. Geological Survey's report of 1917 stated: "Since the beginning of the war, a barium chemical industry has been established in the United States to supply barium carbonate, nitrate, chloride, chlorate hydrate, and binoxide, which were formerly imported largely from Germany."[51] The chemicals were used in preparing hydrogen peroxide, water softener and optical glass-all vital to the war effort.

Unfortunately, despite Moore's urgings, the decision to reopen the mill was never made, nor would the Stackhouse community ever be quite the same. The tramways covering the mountain lay idle, the numerous adits sat gaping in darkness, and a powder-free silence settled over the area. Some people moved to other places of industry, a few went to work at Runion sawmill, a few were given jobs in Georgia barytes mines operated by the same New York stockholders who had owned the now-closed one, and a few went to work at Sandy Bottom for Anson Betts, who had, in 1914, bought the Candler barytes mine that Harrison and Dougherty had operated.

Gone, too, were the electric lights at the homes of Amos and Charles Stackhouse. Their kerosene lamps were brought out from storage, necessitating once again the messy jobs of pouring oil, trimming wicks, and cleaning smoked glass chimneys for years to come. The transition would not be easy for the Stackhouse families, having experienced over a decade of prosperity through receipts from the Klondyke, the tramways, tenant rents, and extra store trade. Nevertheless they would cut back, adjust, and endure – even to our own times.

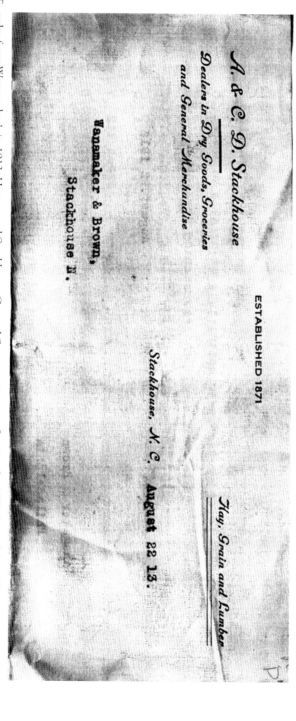

A. & C. D. Stackhouse

Dealers in Dry Goods, Groceries and General Merchandise

ESTABLISHED 1871

Hay, Grain and Lumber

Wanamaker & Brown,
Stackhouse N.

Stackhouse, N. C. August 22 13.

To order from Wanamaker's in 1913, Hester used Stackhouse General Store stationery reflecting the 1871 date of Amos' beginning at Warm Springs.

159

[1] Madison County Register of Deeds, Book 24, p.474.

[2] Ibid., p.571.

[3] Madison County Book of Corporations, p.46.

[4] Meek, Anna Stackhouse. Interview, 1996.
Price, Nealie. Interview, 1997.

[5] Underwood, Jinsie, *This is Madison County*. American Revolution Bicentennial Committee of Madison County, 1974, p.44.

[6] Chandler, Blanche Trimble. Interview, February 24, 2005.

[7] *Manufacturers' Record*, Vol.59. Baltimore: 1911, p.55.

[8] Price, Nealie. Interview, 1997.

[9] *News Record*, Marshall, June 21, 1912.

[10] Painter, J.B., *Season of Dorland-Bell*. Boone, N.C.: ASU Press, 1996, p.144.

[11] *Madison County Heritage, Vol.I*. Marshall: Madison County Heritage Book Committee, 1994, p.16.

[12] Johnson, Carrie Landers. Interview, 1999.

[13] Dockery, Clyde. Interview, 1999.

[14] Ibid.

[15] Underwood, p.45.

[16] Price, Nealie. Interview, 1997.

[17] Meek, Anna Stackhouse. Interview, 1996.

[18] Waldrup, John Herbert. Interview, 1991.

[19] Meek, Anna Stackhouse. Interview, 1996.

[20] Aumiller, Nancy Stackhouse. Interview, 1997.

[21] Price, Nealie. Interview, 1997

[22] Fowler, Randy. Interview, 1998.
Dockery, Clyde. Interview, 1999.

[23] Baker, Elizabeth Gahagan. Interview, 1999.

[24] Painter, p.71.

[25] Baker, Elizabeth Gahagan. Interview, 1999..

[26] Dockery, Clyde. Interview, 1999.

[27] *News-Record*, Marshall, June 21, 1912.

[28] Dockery, Clyde. Interview, 1999.

[29] *News-Record*, Marshall, June 21, 1912.

[30] Eller, Ronald. *Miners, Millhands and Mountaineers*. Knoxville: U.T. Press, 1982, p.104.

[31] *News-Record*, Marshall: July 4, 1912.

[32] Madison County Book of Corporations, p.64.

[33] Treadway, Kenneth. Interview, 1998.

[34] Madison County Register of Deeds, Book 29, p.224.

[35] *The Western North Carolina Section at a Glance*, Washington, D.C.: Southern Railway Company, 1912, p.32. (The same publication gave Hot Springs' population as 700 – about a third larger.)

[36] Stroupe, Vernon. *Post Offices and Postmasters of N.C.*, Vol.II. Charlotte, N.C.: Postal History Society, 1996, pps.270, 272.

[37] Madison County Register of Deeds, Bk. 27, p.274.

[38] Ibid., p.289.

[39] Ibid., p.296.

[40] N.C. Geological & Economic Survey map redrawn in 1936 by Mattocks and Hunter from original dated May 7, 1910.

[41] Ibid.

[42] *The Mining Industry in North Carolina During 1908, 1909 & 1910*, North Carolina Geological & Economic Survey, Paper No. 23, Raleigh: State Printer, 1911.

[43] Author's private papers.

[44] *The Mining Industry in N.C. During 1911 & 1912*, Economic Paper No. 34, North Carolina Geological & Economic Survey, Raleigh: State Printer, 1914.

[45] Watson, T.L., and J.S. Grasty. "Barite of the Appalachian States," *Transactions of the American Institute of Mining, Metallurgical and Petroleum Engineers, Vol. 51*. Denver: 1915, pp. 514-559.

[46] Private papers.
Oriel, Steven S., "Geology and Mineral Resources of the Hot Springs Window, Madison County, N.C.," *Bulletin No.60*, N.C. Dept. of Conservation & Development. Raleigh: 1950, p.48.

[47] Ibid.

[48] Madison County Minutes Docket, Book 4, pps. 500-513.

[49] *Floods on the French Broad River & Spring Creek, Vicinity of Hot Springs, N.C.*, Tennessee Valley Authority, Knoxville: 1960, p.19.

[50] Riley, Jack. *Carolina Power & Light Company, 1908-1953*. 50th Anniversary publication, Carolina Power & Light Co., Raleigh: 1958, pps. 112, 113.

[51] *The Mining Industry in N.C. During 1913-1917, Inclusive, Paper No. 49*, N.C. Geological & Economic Survey, Raleigh: State Printer, 1919, p.101.

Asheville train station often used by Stackhouse family. July, 1916.

Chapter Eighteen

By the time of his death in February, 1909, Amos, the founder of Stackhouse, North Carolina, had already begun to fade as the community's guiding light, his son, Amos, Jr., having gradually gained their trust and confidence. Even with the well-stocked commissary at Runion, neighbors still came to the Stackhouse store for many items, for special orders, and to get medical advice for themselves and their domestic animals.

Amos not only inherited his father's dependable reference books and pharmacy tools, but had also benefited from years of listening to and observing old Amos' practical applications.

As a mechanic is important to the modern trucker's vehicle, so was Amos valuable to his mountain neighbors' mules, steers and horses. When his customers came to the store describing their draft animals' symptoms, Amos could diagnose, and often treat, the illnesses. Likely due to the high volume of logging taking place in Madison County, pages 432 and 433 of Amos' copy of the book *Cattle* were dog-eared. This section addressed sprains, injuries and foot diseases – the following paragraph is a sample:

> Extensive wounds are never cured without suppuration; this is generally set up five or six days after the injury... If the pus be turbid and have a bad smell, *asafaetida* and *mercurius virus* should be employed; if it is thick with a bad color, *silica*; if proud flesh make its appearance, *chamomilla*, *sepia*, and *arsenicum*.[1]

For his customers themselves, Amos often prescribed, and weighed on his father's scales, doses of herbs and medicines from the old-time *Household Physician*. Numerous pages appeared well-thumbed, while a quick-reference index, jotted on the fly-leaf by either Amos or his father, included "Asthma & Typhoid – 243; wounds & cuts – 441; ulcers – 431; Tetter (Eczema) and Scabies – 139; Old Age – 710; Roseola – 51; Vomiting – 237." Moreover, the chapter titled, "Venereal or Sexual Diseases, Cure and Prevention," barely hung in the book, so frequent had been its usage. Amos Stackhouse, even as a child, had not been a talkative person, and now, his reticence and discretion were most appreciated by his customers. Indeed, the author of *Household Physician* empathized with his fellow prescribers, declaring:

> "Of all the diseases to which flesh is heir, none bring so much misery, moral and physical, as these. To the physician, they are the source of the greatest anxiety and perplexity. They bring him into possession... of delicate secrets, which his honor as a man, compel him to hold sacredly apart even from his nearest companions... These secrets are often a burden to him."[2]

A community anchor, Amos Stackhouse, like his father, kept his neighbors' confidences, helped them through weddings, births and funerals, through crop plantings and harvests, offering advice, medicine and credit. For the honest man who could not pay his store account, there was always work in kind around the Stackhouse farm.

Amos also made trips to Pennsylvania, as his father had – albeit not as often – to buy store merchandise and to visit relatives. Ellison and his daughters, in turn, visited Stackhouse annually and corresponded fairly regularly. One particular postcard to Amos from Ellison in 1910 related: "Laura and I are attending a Meeting to celebrate 225th anniversary of the Establishment of Concord Meeting in Delaware County, Pa." It was signed, "Thy Brother, Ellison S." Amos would find that, gradually, since his father's death, the ties with the northern Stackhouse cousins grew weaker each year, leaving only faithful Ellison as connecting link.

Through the broader Stackhouse community, Amos continued his leadership role at Walnut Methodist Church where he was Sunday School superintendent and church trustee. Since there were few places for assembly in the rural area, the Methodists shared their house of worship with other groups in an interdenominational Union Sunday School, which was "flourishing," according to the 1910 minutes.[3] However, the building could not accommodate the average one hundred members, prompting the trustees, with Amos in the lead, to let a contract for "enlarging and remodeling."[4] (Within two years after the expansion, oddly enough, attendance was down to forty, the Southern Baptists and the Freewill Baptists having obtained their own meeting places.) More widely, Amos Stackhouse also served on the Board of Directors of Marshall's oldest lending institution, the Bank of French Broad,[5] traveling at least once a month to meetings at the county seat. The camaraderie with other businessmen provided a pleasant change from Amos' daily routine.

Likewise, at Stackhouse, Amos enjoyed the new trade and new people brought in by the boom associated with Carolina Barytes and Laurel River Logging Companies. In fact, for a time, he left the sidelines to be an active participant, according to the jotting in his small pocket notebook: "Commenced work with Laurel River Logging Company, Nov. 7th, 1910." Amos' northern business associations proved valuable in this new job, as he wrote: "Went up to Pounding Mill Camp, Dec. 27th, 1910; made a trip North for Mr. Betts, July 1st, 1911, returned in 2 weeks." Names and addresses of lumber buyers and their orders filled several pages of Amos' pocket journal, for example:

W.M. Lloyd, Co., 29th Ridge and Susquhanna Ave.
quarter oak 1" x 10", 1&2 barn boards – $\frac{1}{2}$ car each.
> Larking Bros., North Phil., Pa.
> McIlvaine & Co., 502 Crozier Blvd., Phil. – want
> 6x6 & 6x8 poplar squares.
> Cooper Company, Camden, N.J. – moulding chestnut.
> Crane & Clark Lumber Co., 616 West 30th St., N.Y.
> Fulton & Walker, Coach & Wagon Builders, Filbert St., Phil.
> New Farson Furniture (China Closets, book cases), use plain
> oak, #1 common & quarter oak & sound wormy chestnut.[6]

During his selling trip for Betts, as a pleasant bonus, Amos took the July Fourth holiday to visit Ellison, writing to Hester from Lansdowne on July 5, 1911:

> Dear Sweetheart, Arrived in Phil. At 4:23 a.m. after a very hot ride. Spent the day getting cleaned up and walking around the city. (Street cars too slow for me.) Down at the wharves I saw some nice boats, but the water front is very little better than Norfolk. Saw boys the size of Ernest, naked and jumping off the wharf into the river…

Came through the Polish and Jewish section of the city which was something awful. Boys & girls 6 to 8 or perhaps 10, playing in the streets naked and lots of them with only short shirts on. There is no place in the South, I am sure, that is so low… Kiss the kids for me and take care of yourself. Your affectionate H., Amos.[7]

Other notes about Amos' employment at Runion showed that he traveled at times to Belva (at Laurel), to Biltmore, and to Asheville, grading lumber as it was loaded onto freight cars: "Loaded maple – 10 hrs; paid hands – see Tally Book."[8]

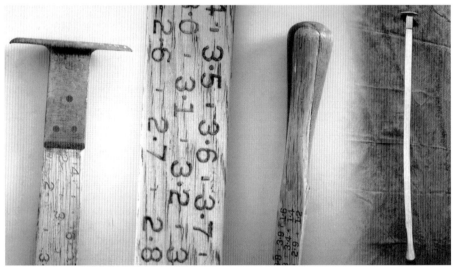

Four different sections of one of several lumber rules belonging to Amos Stackhouse during his years as respected grader. L to R: "foot" for flipping boards; closeup of numerals stamped along sides of rule; oak handle with walnut insert; Lumber rule, full length.

Many years earlier, the lumber industry had designed, especially for the grader, a TALLY notebook with thumb hole at top and pencil holder at the side, enabling the grader to have his record at the ready, while freeing his hands to measure the boards. The lumber rule – another standard tool particular to the industry – was made of strong oak or chestnut, three feet long, 7/8" wide and 3/8" thick, riveted into a two-inch-long brass ferrule which was flattened and broadened to an oval point. This formed a "foot" for flipping the board to reveal its other face. The opposite end of the wooden strip was split to receive a wedge (usually made of walnut), then glued together for a comfortable handle. Stamped into one side of the brass were markings – 8", 10" & 18", the reverse side showing 12", 14" & 16" – indicating board widths. Three lines of numerals ran horizontally along the full length of the rule, showing the square feet of lumber in each board measured, as the rule was laid across the width of the board. All the grader needed to know for quick computation was the length of the board to start with.[9]

Governing the lumber grader's decisions for each species of wood were standard specifications set by the American Lumber Standards Committee, used universally. For instance, *Standard Grading Rules for Eastern Spruce and Balsam Fir* showed how complex lumber grading could be, requiring each piece of wood to be judged for measurement; moisture content; knots, blemishes and other imperfections; manufactured condition – rough or dressed; uniformity to rest of cargo; and intended use – structural or other.[10] One of eleven rules under "Measurements and Tally" stated:

> In material measured with a board rule on actual widths, pieces measuring to the even half foot shall be alternately counted as of the next higher and lower foot count; fractions below the one-half foot shall be dropped and fractions above the one-half foot shall be counted as of the next higher foot.

There were sixty-one different definitions of "Defects," often including several types of each of the following: checks, decay, worm holes, pitch, shake, pith, split, stain, wane,* warp, bow, crook, cup, skip and knot. For example, a "tight knot" was one "so fixed by growth or position that it will firmly retain its place in the piece," whereas, a "firm or unsound knot is solid across its face but contains incipient decay." A "medium knot," as defined, "measures over $3/4$" but not more than $1 \, 1/2$" in diameter." Instructing the grader on the measuring of knots, the book dictated:

> To determine the average diameter of a knot hole, add the maximum width in inches and fractions thereof to the maximum length in inches and fractions thereof and divide the result by 2.

Nor was the classification of the lumber grades any less complicated. "B & BTR" should be judged according to the following paragraph:

> B and Better is the highest grade of Eastern Spruce. Shall be practically straight grained and shall be clear on both faces and both edges except that not more than five tight sound pin knots, or wane not exceeding one-half the thickness nor one-fourth the length are admitted on the reverse face of not over 15 percent of the pieces; will admit occasional small surface checks; also splits not longer than one-half the width of the piece. Decay, shake, worm and knot holes, gum seams or equivalent defects are not admitted.

The manual concluded that the grading of lumber cannot be considered an exact science because it is based on visual inspection and the judgment of the grader. Hence, a lumber grader's trust and character carried great weight with the customer. Amos and his brother Charles Dilworth had the reputation of being skilled, fair and honest lumber graders with years of experience from operating their own lumber business; plus, they had the education necessary for reading and interpreting the standards.

Amos Stackhouse was on his way to earning the title of the "best grader around." Nevertheless, for unknown reasons, he jotted in his little notebook, "Runion – Quit work about Aug.12th, 1911."[11] Perhaps he had agreed to help Betts get started in the new bandmill operation for a temporary period, or maybe Betts had a larger volume in the beginning, or else, Amos might have been too busy with his farm crops.

The end of summer and approaching harvest season brought the cutting and stacking of hay; stripping and tying fodder; picking grapes and apples, sowing the winter wheat; digging and storing of all root crops – sweet potatoes, Irish potatoes, turnips and rutabagas. Besides providing the winter's

---

* Defective bark or lack of wood at a corner or edge.

food for the family and livestock, these produce items were sold at the Stackhouse store. Fodder, bundled at fifty cents each,[12] was in demand by any who owned animals but had no farm. Moreover, as soon as the nights turned cold, it would be hog-butchering time, followed immediately by the detailed processing of the pork, an important staple.

Even though the Stackhouse farm was well-managed and productive, and the Carolina Barytes leases guaranteed certain income, Amos' expenses increased as his sons grew. Not only were the boys always needing shoes and clothing, they were ready for schooling not found in the little two-month community schools. Both were bright, inquisitive, and avid readers – June, at fourteen, was in fact ready for high school. At times, Hester had taken them to stay with her sister, Carrie Davis, in Marshall where they attended public school. While she was there, Amos would write to her, a sample being a letter dated April 8, 1910:

> "Dear Kid, I am sending you the pins and stamps, did not have the shoe strings. Old hen in Ten Pin Alley hatched 8 or 9 chickens… Take good care of yourself and the boys, Your loving husband, Amos."[13]

Finally, the next summer, Amos and Hester decided to enroll June at the Methodist-operated, co – educational boarding school in the Buncombe County town of Weaverville, while Ernest and Gilbert would attend the four-month public school at the same place. Weaverville College – June's high school – had also been attended by Amos' brother, Charles Dilworth, and was otherwise familiar to the Stackhouse family through their long membership in the Methodist Church. Its introductory pamphlet described Weaverville as a village of 500, "free from the forms of vice and coarse living, the noise and temptations of extravagance, characteristic of most towns and cities."[14] Begun in the 1830's, the institution was placed under supervision of the Methodist Church Conference in 1883. Historian John Preston Arthur would write in 1912, "It has done excellent work in the past and continues to do the same now."[15]

Despite all this, Hester felt she needed to go with the boys for their adjustment to being away from home, to start little Gilbert in first grade, and to help eleven-year-old Ernest, who suffered from the common childhood ailment, enuresis. Having written to the college president, Amos received this reply on August 2nd, 1911:

> "My Dear Mr. Stackhouse, We would be delighted to have your boys and their mother in our community. I am afraid, however, that the matters of board in such a place as you indicate, for all four, would be difficult to find, since the town is filled with summer boarders… The boys may be able to get room in our dormitory, should their mother not come… They can also secure board at some private house… Yours very cordially, Olin S. Dean, President."[16]

Hester did find rooms in the home of the church's pastor, Rev. Lyda, whose daughter, Mrs. Brown, lived there, as well as her daughter, "Miss Margaret." Settled in, but homesick, Hester wrote to Amos every few days, imploring him to answer soon. In one of her first letters she set the tone for the semester:

"Just one week ago today, Love, since I left home. I wonder if ten long months will ever pass by. It seems ages since I saw you… Gilbert wished he could see Grandmother and Teeny, but he walks to school with the teacher, Miss Gash, and likes her… Our expenses, so far, have been more than I expected. Paid 3 weeks' board, $31, and the boys' tuition and books have been $25, but more books to buy. Will have to pay for washing, too.

"We have not had a drop of milk since we've been here. Mrs. Brown thinks she will have a fresh cow soon… Has my cow gone dry yet? Ernest has wet the bed every night since we've been here, except one… Gilbert seems to like school, but I certainly had trouble with him at first – said he'd rather take castor oil than to go to school."[17]

Hester spent her days sewing, darning the boys' stockings, cleaning her rooms, mending, reading, and walking at evening time. "I don't think I shall start through town with the boys again," she wrote to Amos, "because Gilbert and Ernest are as wild as deer – I'm going to the woods this evening." Indeed, much of Hester's time would also be spent disciplining, as her boys would be boys. One day she wrote Amos that June had taken her iron all apart and could not get it back together, exactly, "Completely spoiling it." At another time her letter reflected panic as she told how Gilbert had run away from school, and it had taken an hour and a half of searching to find him. "I was worried to death," she said. Still later she wrote that Gilbert had been bad all week, until, "This afternoon I was compelled to give him the worst whipping he ever had, and he has behaved much better since."[18]

But Hester's middle son caused her the most anxiety, as she complained to Amos:

"On the way from Dr. Brigg's office in Asheville, Gilbert spied a large red ball, and I could not get him along the street until I bought it for him. It was such a fine ball and he had such a nice time with it, but last night, as usual, Ernest spoiled it, entirely, by throwing it against the electric light fixture and the sharp point made a hole in it."

Her next letter held more disturbing news about Ernest:

"After school I can't get him home until 6 every evening, and I find he tells me stories about where he goes. I went to hunt him at 4 this afternoon, came back at half past five and found him here. Hugh Byrd had him pinned down flat of his back with his head and heels tucked under his arm. Ernest was screaming and nobody paying any attention. Hugh had thrown a shovel-ful of manure into his face and water all over him. It is a wonder he did not break his back.

"I want you to write and tell Ernest just what he has to do. I'm afraid Hugh will kill him. You know he promised me to come straight home everyday if I would take him to the Fair, and he has never come the first time."[19]

Before long Hester wrote Amos about a similar incident involving June:

"I was really worried yesterday. The school janitor had oiled the study hall floor with Linseed Oil and one of the boys rolled Jr. over & over in the oil until his suit is most ruined. One whole pants leg is perfectly brown with it. It is the $26.50 suit, happened during study hours and just after dinner. There were two dreadful fights in the study hall – Hugh Byrd and a boy named Brittain had the first. Hugh cut Brittain's arm right bad, cut his coat, broke up a desk, upset a large stove – the red hot pipe and all in the floor. Then he cursed a boy named Rhinehart, who broke up a chair over Hugh's head… A pretty example, I think, in a church school. If Prof. Dean doesn't expel them, I guess we had better go some other place next year."[20]

Evidently, the matter resolved itself to Hester's satisfaction, for the boys remained in school.

Besides discipline, Hester had to deal with her sons' illnesses, which seemed almost constant. June had headaches (probably migraine) that lasted three and four days, and often had colds, making Hester fear pneumonia. "Jr. went to school today, his chest and side, a little better," stated Hester in a letter to Amos, "since I burned it red hot with a mustard poultice." In another letter, Hester told her husband, "Ernest has a fearful cold, as well as Jr. and myself… I have doctored them with hot poultices on the chest, plenty of purgatives, quinine, tea and cough syrups." She added that the college dormitory matron's daughter had serious pneumonia, requiring a nurse from Asheville, night and day.

Within her family, Hester was considered knowledgeable about home remedies and treatments which had been handed down for generations.[21] Her next letter to Amos explained that Gilbert's badly-cut finger was healing at last, but he still complained during the night that it hurt. "I think it must have healed outside first," she wrote.

About her own health, Hester reported that Dr. Briggs said the throat problem she had had for several years would only be cured by removing her tonsils, and the sooner the better. In another letter, a different affliction was called to Amos' attention, regarding Hester's eyes: "The lids are covered with little boils, just inside – must be granulated eyelids," she supposed. For this, Amos mailed salve from the store for her to try.

Hester complained more and more in her letters about being short of money, about the cold boarding house, and about the food served: "Mrs. Brown has churned 12 pounds of butter this week – no wonder our milk is blue!" Hoping to cut expenses, and improve comfort, Hester began looking at houses to buy or rent, scrutinizing the features important to home owners of the day. With her good business head and experienced eye, she wrote her findings to Amos on October 17th, 1911, after a visit to a nearby property for sale:

"The cow is short-horn Durham, not yet three years old, weighing 1000 lbs., with milk as rich as a Jersey's, the man says, but she is only giving a gal. a day, now – won't be fresh until February. They have 50 chickens, most, frying size; three pigs, the largest, he says, will weigh 200 lbs., but, I think, not more than 150, and it is a small-boned Berkshire in good condition. He has one white Chester which would be worth, I judge, about $8, and 1 small black pig worth $8 or $10.

"The closet [outdoor privy] is nice-looking from the outside, and has a door hinged from the back side to fit nicely down to the ground & can be raised to clean out same. They have outbuilding, rather small, but with three rooms or parts; first, a chicken yard in good condition, but rather small, and a door to open into the chicken house from the yard. The next room is the cow stall, very nice & warm, not floored, but has lumber enough to floor it. The next room is the feed room, has clover hay enough for about a week, and just outside, has two pig pens adjoining…

"They also have a new basement, and a little place fixed under house for tools. Have 3 rhododendrons, 2 gooseberry plants, 1 plum, and 3 small maples. They would like to know your decision this week, if possible…

"The Weaverville Cemetery is on the next knoll, just in front of this little house. Would this lessen the property value? It seems a bargain, but could you raise the money? And would it pay to borrow, and do you expect to send the children here to school until they finish? All this must be considered. I would estimate the house furnishings worth, close to $300. Everything, nearly, seems bright and new. Please write these parties soon."[22]

For whatever reason, Amos and Hester did not buy the little house, nor rent a different one under consideration, as she wrote near the end of November:

"I had better not undertake to keep house – would have to move at once, and don't feel able right now to do the work necessary, and don't want to expose Jr. in his weak condition. He is afraid as death of the consumptive in the house just across the street. I find that house rent and firewood would cost about $14.00 per month. I guess I will send them word tomorrow that I will not take the house."

On the positive side of their life in Buncombe County, Hester occasionally reported to Amos of the boys' development and progress. Soon after coming to Weaverville, Hester had taken Gilbert – age 5 $\frac{1}{2}$ – on the street car (which ran from Asheville to Weaverville) to an Asheville barber, who cut his long brown curls close to the head. His school mates called him "Beauty," according to Hester's letters, but he did not seem to mind. (Young Thomas Wolfe, living in Asheville at the same time, but three years older than Gilbert, would also keep his shoulder-length curls until he was nine.) "You would not know Gilbert," Hester wrote to Amos. "I never saw a child so changed in my life, and he is delighted with it – stands in front of the glass most of the time. I wish I could do as Mr. Agathe's mother did and pin the curls back on." She also told Amos that Gilbert was so very pleased with the latest letter from his father, and that he kept them all tied together in the trunk. "Today I told Gilbert there were seven days in a week," she continued, "and he says, 'As Toby [his pet sow] has seven piglets, why not name them the days of the week, and I should like Teeny to call her pig, Friday, after Robinson Crusoe's man'."[23]

In letters from his older sons, Amos learned that Ernest was doing, "alright with my lessons – made 99 on my last history examination." June gave his father similar news in October, 1911, "I'm getting along fine in my algebra, now – am sending you the problem that only one boy got besides myself." At a different time, June wrote, "I did an example in arithmetic the other day that had not been worked by any of the other boys & girls."[24]

Gilbert Stackhouse, c. 1911.

Around December 1st, Hester's letter informed her husband that Ernest's school had closed the day before and "he entered the College today." Overall, the older boys' report cards for that first quarter of the 1911-1912 school year reflected good standings. Ernest's teacher marked Excellent (90 to 100) in Spelling, Arithmetic, Grammar and Deportment, but Very Good (85-90) for North Carolina History. On the college level, June's grades were all A's and B's for the quarter, except one C (70) in English Grammar. He, too, received a 99 in General Conduct.[25]

Seventh Grade Report card of Ernest Stackhouse, 1911.

Report Card

REPORT OF

Ernest Stackhouse

a pupil in the 7 Grade of

Alearile School

State of N. C. County of
Buncombe District Number 2

for the school term beginning Aug. 16
1911 and ending 19

Promoted to _____ Grade.

Retained in _____ Grade.

Retained for special examination in _____

L. H. Blackmore Teacher

MONTHS	1st	2nd	3rd	4th	5th	6th	7th	8th	9th	Yr. Av.	COMMENTS
SUBJECTS											
Reading											1st Mo.
Writing											
Spelling	E	E	VG	E							2nd Mo.
Arithmetic	E	E	E	E							
Geography	E	E	E	E							3rd Mo.
Grammar	E	E	E	E							
History											4th Mo.
Physiology											
Civil Government											5th Mo.
Literature											
Physical Geography											6th Mo.
Algebra											
N. C. History	E	VG	VG	VG							7th Mo.
ATTENDANCE											
Days present	20	20	20	18							8th Mo.
Days absent											
Times tardy											9th Mo.
SUMMARY											
Average Scholarship											
Department	E	100	100	E							
Punctuality											
General Average											
Rank in Class											

EXPLANATIONS

1. Written examinations are reported in figures. 2. Class record are reported in words. 3. Results of special examination are entered in red ink. 4. Deportment and punctuality are important items and affect the General Average of a pupil. The General Average is not more than ... subjects may receive ... in ... by special examination. ... This report, if properly filled out and signed, is a certificate of promotion to be presented to the next teacher.

STANDARDS

1. 94 to 100 is Excellent (Ex)
2. 85 to 94 is Very Good (V. G.)
3. 77 to 85 is Good (G)
4. 70 to 77 is Medium (M)
5. 70 to 77 is Poor (P)
6. Below 70 is a Failure.
7. A general average of ... and not below ... in any subject is required for promotion.

June's letters to his father, however, were sometimes arrogant, due partly perhaps to the typical parental reminders that he was the oldest and should behave more responsibly and maturely. On September 13, 1911, June had written:

> "Dear Father, I wish you would hunt up my black ox and see what he looks like. Mamma says beef selling at 2 cts. a lb. there. If you had sold him when I wanted to, you could have got 6 cts. a lb. It would cost a lot to feed him over winter; at the same time, I don't want to sell him for less than $30."

On December 6th, June wrote to Amos:

> "Dear Father, I want you to order Moore to get that railroad out of that bottom you said I could plant next year… I want you to give the sixty days' notice right away… I'm going to plant it in cow peas and corn – peas, in the richest part, and corn in the poorest… Mama said for you to feed the pigs good, for she was going to give

Report of Amos "June" Stackhouse from Weaverville College, 1911.

us each one."

Amos also received orders from his wife during her stay in Weaverville. On September 10th, in planning a visit to Stackhouse, Hester told Amos (who was taking his meals with his mother while his wife was away) to clean the kitchen sink, turn on all the water and let it run all over the house, as often as he could, and "gather all the eggs for me." An October letter from Hester asked:

"Did you hang the boys' overcoats in Westervelt's† room? Be sure to air the house Sunday if it is clear, and fasten up everything again. Also, order moth balls to put under carpets in parlor and library and sun the new rug next fine day when you can be around. Roll it up with mothballs inside, but sweep it first, real clean. Put broom back in house and DO NOT SCRUB PORCH with my NEW broom. Be sure and clean up your bathroom, and by all means, sweep hall and stairway – the carpets will be ruined!"[26]

From the store, Amos was requested to send Hester "a 12-inch wide piece of black Sateen, darning cotton, 27 inches of Bleached Muslin, but not Cambric, and some more eye salve."

As had been his father's custom, Amos allowed his wife to receive moneys from tenant houses, garden produce, milk, butter and eggs. In several letters to Amos, she reminded him, "Be sure to get up all accounts for vegetables and house rent and collect – will need it to pay board Tuesday, next." Since one of the setting hens had built her nest in the old bowling alley building, Hester's advice to Amos was, "Turn your eggs each day."

Near the end of November, still further requests to Amos came from Hester's letters:

"Don't get me anything for Christmas. Remember, we must not spend money foolishly. Jr. wants a Remington 12-gauge shotgun (34 in. barrel, semi-hammerless) and 1 box Nublack Winchester cartridges, and the *Outing* magazine, 1 box of Rim-fire 32-caliber U.M.C. cartridges, and not a single piece of candy, not even a firecracker.

"For Ernest, one pair of gloves and some books by the same author as *Freckles*. Ernest wants you to get a peck of onions and 1 gal. of nice thick homemade molasses for him to eat Christmas. Gilbert wants a pair of gloves, and a little table large enough for him to sit by for his meals, and would like his own father to make it. He says he wants to help Teeny stuff the turkey.

"Jr. says for you to send $^1/_2$ doz. fountain pens, none smaller than 12 and not larger than 14 – price, $2.50 each. He says send at once before boys go home. Gilbert says to tell you to have cocoanuts for him, also plenty of cream nuts. You better get your seed potatoes into the cellar as fast as you can."

With the approaching holiday vacation and Hester's coming to Stackhouse, she included in her weekly letter a separate piece of paper, headed "Things to Do at Once":

"Put up 3 chickens to fatten – young roosters if you have them. Put up diningroom stove and polish – also polish top of range. Mend Ernest's shoes I sent home by you. You will find leather in

† Westervelt was an out-of-town mine official.

attic. He must have them the day he gets home to play in. Don't forget this – get your overcoat from your Mama's, also books and coats from Gahagans. The boys will need their old coats while at home. Write me by return mail if you want pants or suit, also color, size & price, then I will order at once, Shoe size 8 or 8¹/₂? Don't forget to write by return mail!"[27]

Even from a distance, Hester conducted the management of her home and her family's wardrobe needs. Unlike modern times, suits, dress shirts, and ties were worn daily by boarding school boys and store clerks; and ladies did not go out in public without hat and gloves, no matter the season. A portion of Hester's letters to Amos almost always dealt with clothing of some sort which she either sewed herself or ordered by mail from Strawbridge and Clothier in Philadelphia. Upon receipt of one particular mail order, Hester's letter to her husband declared:

"Jr.'s suit coat is the best fit yet, and he is much pleased with it. His hat looks funny – one of those hairy things – but I think it will be serviceable. I bought him two suits of underwear yesterday at $5.00. This rigs him out for a year, I think, except for underwear next summer."

As for her own apparel, she wrote to Amos that she had finished making a "beautiful red dress," pressed it and hung it away. She had also ordered a hat, "but I'm afraid you won't like it, it looks so odd – all black, with but one long feather," she added.[28]

In letter after letter, Hester urged Amos to send the information she needed for ordering his clothes:

"Do you want to take your best suit for everyday and get a new suit, or have it cleaned for best-wear and order separate pants for everyday? Write me by return mail, and send size desired. Also send your shoe preference. Did you order boys' shirts in the neck size I gave you?"

Despite Hester's claims that she had no money to spare, she occasionally ordered, from Philadelphia, house furnishings such as a settee at $22.50 and a Webster's unabridged dictionary at $12.00 – both, no doubt, for the new library – plus smaller accessories for other rooms: "comb and brush tray," and a "lace centerpiece" for her dining table.[29]

Part of the reason for the financial bind might have come from Hester's having finished, the year before, the bathroom which had been left incomplete when the house was built. She selected W.H. Westall & Co. of Asheville to lay small white ceramic hexagons on the floor, with larger white square tiles forming a wainscot five feet high, capped by a row of white and gold. Narrow tiles of pale gray, peach and white bordered the door and window, bringing the invoice total to $77.12 for all labor and materials of the 10' x 10' room.[30] Long white footed bath tub, matching water closet and pedestal lavatory made the room functional at last.

Moreover, Hester hired Piedmont Electric Company of Asheville to install a pair of bracket lights on the new bathroom walls, at a cost of $5.90, including fixtures, materials, labor and travel expenses. Then R.E. Bowles & Co. came from Asheville to paint the bathroom walls and ceilings a cream color, to enamel the woodwork glossy white, and to varnish the adjoining hallway and steps, at a cost of $116.32. The painting took ninety hours, for which the workmen received 35 cents an hour.[31] Even though the water would have to be turned off and the pipes drained on cold winter nights, the beautiful indoor bathroom was a luxury to be envied by most mountain dwellers.

To Hester's siblings and childhood friends, it probably seemed that she was "putting on airs," and "climbin' above her raisin'," but she had been influenced by her exposure to houses in the North on numerous visits to Amos' relatives. She had also visited in the manorial homes of the Rumbough family, longtime friends of the Stackhouses at Hot Springs, notwithstanding that the first Stackhouse home built by old Amos and Anna had been one of the few grand structures in Madison County when Hester joined the family. Consequently, Hester was extremely proud of her home, almost to the point of enshrinement, according to family members.[32]

While providing a generous and pleasant Christmas celebration for her family, she would not allow a tree in her house. Her descendants have conjectured that she resisted the mess and disruption which would have happened to her parlor. She might, also, have simply had no desire for what was not a Southern mountain tradition. Some Madison County old timers have said that they saw their first Christmas trees when the Presbyterian missionaries introduced them in the 1890's.[33] Not having been exposed to the Presbyterians, Hester perhaps thought it a strange custom. One tradition in which she did participate was the family Christmas dinner under her mother-in-law's direction at the old Stackhouse home. As Gilbert had noted in his letter, there would be turkey and oranges, cocoanut and other victuals not found on the typical mountaineer's table.

After Christmas when school resumed in the new year of 1912, Hester and the boys returned to Weaverville and the home of Rev. Lyda. Onset of winter's harsh weather prompted letters to Amos, typically:

> "Last night January 14, 1912 was by far the coldest night we have had this year. All yesterday afternoon ice froze in my washstand pitcher, with the stove red hot and everything closed up tight. We really did suffer… Jr. and Ernest slept with their dutch caps on; both were quite willing to wear their overcoats to school today."

Sleeping with open windows year round and breathing fresh air was thought to prevent the dreaded, incurable disease tuberculosis, or "consumption," responsible for one out of every six deaths worldwide. "Sleeping porches" were popular – protected from rain, but allowing plenty of fresh air. Nonetheless, Hester warned Amos in one letter:

> "I would not leave windows open in the north side this cold weather – but I imagine you did not, last night. Give your calves and pigs and chickens a little extra feed this kind of weather. I hope you drained pipes in house… Close the cellar doors and windows these cold nights."

In the same letter Hester included a paragraph dictated by Gilbert for Anna Stackhouse's housekeeper and companion:

> "Dear Teeny, Did you and Grandmother sleep on the porch last night? If so, I hope your nose got real cold. Take care of the sheep, cows and calves until I come home so we can go to Runion and peddle milk and butter together. I think it great fun. Did Papa tell you that I can read a little now? I will read for you and

Grandmother when I come."

The boys' school progress through the new year provided subject matter for Hester's letters. "Gilbert enjoys our reading of Uncle Remus this week more than usual," she commented. However, June was giving her considerable trouble, as she complained in her next letter:

"He just will not study, and when I compel him to get down to his lessons, he cries like a baby and declares he can't remember where his lessons are from the time school closes until night. Also, write him and Ernest about wasting tablets."[34]

Hester's dissatisfaction with the boarding house fare remained a point of contention, too, but she reserved her sharpest criticism for her husband in a nine-paged letter, January 29, 1912, which her family members say revealed her true character more than any other document.[35] Excerpts follow:

"Last night... sleep would not come, all night... As I lay there wide awake, I lived my life over from the cradle to the present, and as I weighed my life – you might say-on the scales of time, I'm afraid the hardships and worries over-balanced the real pleasures. I try to be appreciative and look at the bright side. I do not covet the baby girl mentioned, but it has been my hope and prayer for years that we should have one or more daughters, but we do not know what is for the best. Perhaps I have been only hoping for trouble.

"There are a great many questions we should ask ourselves. Are we worthy and competent of such a trust? Are we both setting the best examples before those given to us? Would you have your boys follow in your footsteps for the past twenty years? Let us each try – Oh, so hard – to make our lives just what they should be, setting, at all times, the best examples; try to make the world happier and brighter for us having lived in it. Then, perhaps, the one desire of our hearts will be granted...

"It breaks my heart when I hear you say our housekeeping has been a failure. I do not believe you weighed these words when you spoke. Many be the time they have... caused my pillow wet with tears – last night, for one.

"Speaking of the home life, I can truthfully say I have left nothing undone that I could do. I have tried so hard to be faithful and to crown your efforts with success, but my life has been hard. I do not say that it is through any fault of yours, but I would ask you to go carefully back at the beginning of our life as one, and see if you can find a mistake. I know you would not have a daughter do as I have had to do, and yet if you are ever so fortunate as to have one, your daughter will be treated as you have treated other men's daughters...

"I hope to be with you on your 39th birthday, but if I am, or am not, I want you to make some good resolutions... Am I asking too much when I ask you to try to cultivate a good memory; please do not be careless and put things off; and, by all means, get up, come to meals and go to bed at a certain time. By so doing, you will not only feel better, but save yourself time, money, confusion, worry and embarrassment. And... you will save me many an unpleasant hour, not counting the worry, hard work and inconvenience that it has caused me.

"I hope you will not be offended at this letter, but some how it came before me every hour last night, that I must write... I hope it will not cause any unpleasant feelings on your part, for I love you more than all the world..."[36]

We cannot be sure of Amos' reaction to Hester's sermon, whether he might have considered leaving her, or, whether he paid little attention, since she often preached at him. Alas, until his dying day, Hester would try to reform him, but Amos Stackhouse, according to his grandchildren, remained unhurried, unorganized, kind, lovable, always late for meals, and often caught running to catch the train with his outgoing mail bag.

Other ongoing complaints in Hester's letters were about the expense of her living in Weaverville, the inconvenience, and her difficulty in getting along with her boarding-house hosts. By mid-January Hester's regard for Mrs. Lyda had worsened to such a degree that she spent five pages railing to Amos about "a scene at the supper table last night," and her thoughts on the matter. "When she sees I've taken all I'll take, then she usually tries to see how nice she can be for awhile," wrote Hester. She further vented her ire to Amos, saying:

"This family takes the cake for hypocrisy. At first I thought it would be so nice to have the religious influence over the boys, that it might be a help to them in after years... But knowing how good Mr. L. pretends to be, and watching his everyday life, would ... come nearer to making one an infidel than a Christian..."

Finally, in late January, 1912, Hester made plans to move back to Stackhouse with Gilbert, leaving Ernest and June to live in the college dormitory. She wrote to Amos:

"I hope to be with you tomorrow night. Gilbert has not been well for several days – think he has the grippe... Just this minute has been vomiting, and I don't believe he will be able to get up today. Will doctor him well by tomorrow."

However, Gilbert did not mend quickly; he surely did have the grippe (influenza). Ten days later, Hester was still in Weaverville writing to Amos that Gilbert was sitting up most of the day, had a severe cold, and no appetite, but was a great deal better than before. "I asked Mrs. L. for an egg for him this morning, and her highness took the pains to tell me that eggs were 30 cents a dozen," Hester informed Amos. Gilbert needed nourishment in his weakened condition, so Hester declared, "I have decided to leave as soon as Monday week – he *has* to have something he can eat." She told Amos not to come see them on the weekend, because, "As much as we like to have you, we will have to count the expense – every trip costs $2.00, while every week I stay, means $5 more and your board on top of that." At the end of her

February 9th letter, she asked Amos to "Write me just what you think of me coming home Feb. 19th, if the boys are well of their colds."[37]

Evidently Amos agreed to his wife's plans, as usual, for there was no more correspondence between Hester and Amos – only dormitory bills from the college, and letters from June and Ernest to their parents at Stackhouse. One, in particular, signed by June on November 13, 1913, became a family keepsake:

> "Dear Mother, I've got some of the best news in the world to tell you. At the big revival meeting, Ernest and I were converted and I've already given my name to join the church, and Ernest says he is going to do the same, right away. And, Mama, I feel a thousand

Weaver College				**Weaver College**			
Weaverville, N. C.				Weaverville, N. C.			
REPORT FOR TERM ENDING *Dec. 18,* 1914				REPORT FOR TERM ENDING *Dec. 18,* 1914			
Mr. *Amos Stackhouse,*				Mr. *Ernest Stackhouse,*			
English Grammar		Chemistry		English Grammar	70	Chemistry	
Rhetoric		Physics		Rhetoric		Physics	
Literature	70	Biology		Literature		Biology	
Composition		Physical Geography		Composition		Physical Geography	
Expression		Education		Expression		Education	
Latin		Physiology		Latin	75	Physiology	
Greek		History	75	Greek		History	65
French		Civil Government		French		Civil Government	
German		Bible	*McErary*	German		Bible	89
		Spelling				Spelling	
Arithmetic		Literary Society		Arithmetic		Literary Society	
Algebra		Athletics		Algebra		Athletics	
Geometry	80			Geometry	60		
Trigonometry		Attendance	80	Trigonometry		Attendance	84
Analytical Geometry		General Conduct	90	Analytical Geometry		General Conduct	95

Weaver College reports for Amos "June" and Ernest Stackhouse, 1914.

times happier than I ever felt before. And, Mama, I want you and Papa to pray for Ernest and me, for we certainly need it."

At the end of the 1911-12 school year, Weaverville College had changed its name to Weaver College, adjusting the curriculum to Junior College level in the fall of 1912.[38] Without Hester's being there to monitor their studying, the boys' report cards carried barely average grades, but, June and Ernest would stay the course and graduate, at last, in the Spring of 1915.

Young Gilbert, in the meantime, enrolled at the one-room Stackhouse school which ran eight or ten weeks, then at the Runion school for a like session, since the two schools did not operate simultaneously.[39] When a bit older, he would live with his Grandmother Honeycutt so that he could attend the county school at Walnut.

Stackhouse School, Stackhouse, N.C. Gilbert Stackhouse, 2nd from left at front, in shoes.

Stackhouse was a wonderful place to spend a childhood – there in the mountains, along the railroad, and on the river. Gilbert hiked and rambled, played around the tramways, mines, and swimming holes of the several creeks, exploring every inch of his grandfather's original 600 acres. The French Broad, in good weather, became a community playground for fishing, picnicking, swimming, and boating – every family owning a boat built by their own hands. Gilbert's family often took their boat out to the islands or across to the opposite bank as part of their Sunday afternoon walks, a tradition stemming back to old Amos. One particularly enjoyable outing inspired Gilbert's father to record in his pocket notebook: "July 20th, Sunday, 1913-Hester, Gilbert, Mama [Anna], Amos, Jr., and Ernest went across the river and [I] am now, at this writing, sitting on a rock."

Summertime also brought baseball games across the river in a large field, and Fourth of July celebrations with "log jumping contests on the river and tub races on the creek," recalled Gilbert when an old man.[40] In the fall there was hunting, and trapping, and the excitement of hog-killing, which required a small gathering of neighbor men to handle the carcasses and water barrels. The Stackhouse boys could then reap the monetary rewards of their year's pig-raising efforts. Winter time provided snow play and excellent sledding. Once, riding down his steep front yard, Gilbert gathered so much speed, he went right under a standing train:

> "The old steam engines were so slow you could walk and catch them, depending on how heavy they were loaded. They didn't have but 30 or 40 cars. We'd ride up to Marshall, but coming back down empty, they'd be going so fast we couldn't get off, so we would stop at Hot Springs or Newport and ride back. Sometimes we would be told to get off, and we did, but as soon as the train man turned his back, we'd get back on."[41]

Needless to say, Gilbert's mother knew nothing of this dangerous amusement.

Further entertainment came from the various farm animals, some of which the boys petted and named, and watched their antics. One horse, Bugler Boy, usually pulled the buggy to the train station to meet June and Ernest when they came from college. However, the family's most treasured pet was a small white dog named Ring, who had probably escaped from one of the circus trains passing through.[42] Ring could climb a ladder, jump through a hoop, sit up and perform tricks.

The Stackhouse store and post office, too, could be counted on for happenings of interest. As in the old days, people in the community and surrounding hills came with news of sicknesses and deaths, marriages and births, hard times and good. Young Gilbert often watched the unloading of whole freight cars containing merchandise, which Amos would sell to smaller store owners deeper in the Madison County fastness. "It was nothing to have flour or tobacco and snuff fill an entire car," Gilbert would recall in 1978.[43] The Stackhouse private rail siding – capacity, eight cars – stayed full most of the time. "When I was a kid," Gilbert added, "everybody wanted freight cars; it was nothing to see them fighting over one."

In bad weather, Gilbert could sit in the store with his father or his uncles, observing checker games and listening to old timers' fascinating tales, and often sampling the cracker barrel contents. At times an inebriated customer would refuse to leave, prompting Amos, who was slender but strong, to pick up the drunk and throw him out the door, thrilling young Gilbert and impressing upon him Amos' views of drinking.[44]

During comfortable temperatures, the store's front porch would find old or unemployed neighbors tipped back on a few straight chairs.

The idlers on the store's porch were entertained by the passing trains, occasionally carrying notable persons on their way to Asheville, or circus troupes traveling South for the winter, or the beloved Irish engineer from Knoxville – Mike O'Connor – who would blow his engine's special melodic whistle for children up and down the line. In 1911 Southern Railway added the fast new Carolina Special, known as Numbers 27 and 28, from Charleston to Cincinnati, twice daily. Although it did not regularly stop at Stackhouse, it could be flagged if needed.

The large wheels and cylinders, gears and cogs, belts and pulleys, boilers and smokestacks which ran the railway, bandmill, the barite crusher, and the family sawmill, not only intrigued Gilbert, but also influenced his choice of life-work. Moreover, during his formative years, there were always construction projects and workmen around his home – digging ditches, laying pipes, excavating for out buildings, improving and adding conveniences.[45]

Unfortunately, injuries and accidents played their parts in the childhood scenes. Usually barefoot in warm weather, Gilbert, when seven or eight years old, cut off his little toe while trying to use a crosscut saw. Hester replaced the severed appendage, sewed the skin back, and wrapped it tightly so that the toe healed and became functional again.[46] A much worse incident prompted Hester to record in a small notebook:

> "Ellison Dilworth Gilbert Stackhouse had his left eye put out February 6th, 1918, about 6:45 p.m. Went to Dr. Briggs for operation on 7th. Piece of cartridge shell went through the sight…"[47]

A playmate, perhaps attempting to make a firecracker, had pounded on a cartridge that exploded, blinding Gilbert's eye. Following the surgery, eleven-year-old Gilbert was fitted with a glass eye which would need replacing often through the years as he grew. Dr. Briggs had left all muscles intact so that

Gilbert was able to turn the prosthesis normally, giving no clue to strangers that he had only one eye. However, this glass eye severely limited the spontaneity of his childhood, due to the sobering daily rituals of carefully removing the artificial orb at bedtime, storing it safe from scratches and breakages until morning, when he had to clean it meticulously before reinserting it in the dead socket. Beyond this, Gilbert adjusted well to his disability, not allowing it to interfere further with his enjoyment of life. It is worth noting that Gilbert never revealed the name of the boy responsible for the terrible injury.[48]

A few years prior to the accident, Gilbert's little world had begun expanding, to a degree, when his uncle, Charles Dilworth, prepared to take a wife. On April 26, 1912, the thirty-four-year-old bachelor applied for the license at the Marshall courthouse. While there, he signed a deed to his brother Amos, who paid him eighty dollars for an acre-strip of land running up between the two Stackhouse homes from the railroad,[49] widening the yard of Amos and Hester. Simultaneously, Charles deeded to Amos another acre across Woolsey Creek and along the Walnut Gap Road.[50]

Charles' bride-to-be, Clara Phipps, had lived in Walnut all her nineteen years, attending Bell Institute, the Presbyterian mission school. Descended from the pioneer James Reeves, Clara's mother Mollie was the daughter of Mallie Reeves, long time friend of Amos, while Clara's father, Joseph Phipps, an orphan, had come from Tennessee.[51] Rev. E.B. Stabler, Walnut Methodist Church pastor, performed the ceremony on May first, with Clara's brother, George Phipps, signing the certificate as witness.[52] The newlyweds took the train to Key West, then a ship to Cuba for a honeymoon, returning to make their home at Stackhouse with Anna and Teeny.

Just eight months later, on January 30, 1913, another of Gilbert's uncles, Frank Hunycutt, age twenty-eight, married Alyce Gahagan, age nineteen, in a ceremony at Hot Springs officiated by Rev. E.C. Gibbs.[53] Clara Stackhouse and Hester Stackhouse signed as two of the witnesses. Alyce Gahagan was a cousin of the Stackhouse's close friend and neighbor, Ben Wade Gahagan, and her grandfather had also traded at the general store of old Amos, decades earlier. Frank and Alyce would remain a close part of the Stackhouse family as long as they lived.

Since Frank was an official clerk of the Stackhouse post office and helped in the general store, he and his bride lived behind Amos' home in the apartment of the brick annex building, which had been undergoing more improvements. Amos and Hester had accepted a bid for repainting the exterior wood trim of the annex, using "two coats of pure lead and linseed oil paint," plus "all woodwork on inside of annex bathroom," as stated by R.E. Bowles from Asheville. He also

Charles Dilworth Stackhouse, c. 1911.

181

agreed to paint the exterior of Amos' home, furnishing all materials and labor on both buildings for $230. At the same time, Bowles would prepare and paint two coats on the exterior of Charles Dilworth's house, next door, for $110.54

Besides new paint, Charles' house was teeming with new life after the births of two daughters, Anna Elizabeth (for Charles' mother and Clara's grandmother) in October 1913 and Clara Helen in August, 1915. The two little girls filled the family void left by June and Ernest, who had graduated that Spring from Weaver College and were rarely at home except in summer.[55]

The boys had enrolled at the Methodist-supported Trinity (later Duke) University, a natural progression for Weaver alumni, who even had a Weaver Club on the Durham campus.[56] According to his family, Ernest was the youngest freshman ever enrolled at Trinity at that time. He would do well in the large setting, despite his youth, as would his brother.

Regrettably, changes in the Stackhouse idyll loomed ahead – some quite drastic for the family and for the community.

ENDNOTES FOR CHAPTER EIGHTEEN

[1] Youatt, W. *Cattle*, Columbus, Ohio: Ohio State Library, 1859, p.432.

[2] Warren, Ira, A.M., M.D. *The Household Physician*. Boston: Ira Bradley & Co., 1872, p.320.

[3] Methodist Conference quarterly minutes. April, 1910.
Plemmons, Cloice. "Historical Reflections," unpublished paper presented at Homecoming celebration, Walnut Methodist Church, August 9, 1998.

[4] Ibid.

[5] Author's private papers.

[6] Ibid.

[7] Ibid.

[8] Ibid.

[9] Aumiller, Nancy S. Interview, 2000.
Morgan, Ralph Siler III. Interview, 2000.

[10] *Standard Grading Rules For Eastern Spruce and Balsam Fir*, published by Northeastern Lumber Manufacturers Association, New York, 1938 edition.

[11] Private papers.

[12] Ibid.

[13] Ibid.

[14] Ibid.

[15] Pickens, Nell. *Dry Ridge, Some of its History*, 2nd ed. Weaverville, N.C.: Friends of Weaverville Library, 1996, p.20.
Arthur, John Preston. *Western North Carolina, A History*, Asheville, N.C.: Daughters of the American Revolution of Asheville, 1914, pp.428, 429.

[16] Private papers.

[17] Ibid.

[18] Ibid.

[19] Ibid.

[20] Ibid.

[21] Aumiller, Nancy S. Interview, 1998.

[22] Private papers.

[23] Ibid.

[24] Ibid.

[25] Ibid.

[26] Ibid.

[27] Ibid.

[28] Ibid.

[29] Ibid.

[30] Ibid.

[31] Ibid.

[32] Aumiller, Nancy S. Interview, 2001.
Meek, Anna S. Interview, 2001.

[33] Painter, Jacqueline. *An Appalachian Medley: Hot Springs and the Gentry Family*, Vol.1, Asheville, N.C.: Biltmore Press, 1994, p.55.
Clark, Lillie McDevitt. *Appalachian Memories*, Weaverville, N.C.: Reems Creek Valley Homemakers Club, 1984, p.22.

[34] Private papers.

[35] Aumiller, Nancy S. Interview, 1999.
Stackhouse, Juanita C. Interview,1999.

[36] Private papers.

[37] Ibid.

[38] Pickens, p.45.

[39] Wolcott, Mary Ellen. "Stackhouse and Runion Community," *Asheville Citizen-Times*, September 24, 1978, Sect. C, p.1.

[40] Ibid.

[41] Ibid.

[42] Aumiller, Nancy S. Interview, 2002.
Private papers.

[43] Wolcott, p.1.

[44] Aumiller, Nancy S. Interview.

[45] Wolcott, p.1.

[46] Aumiller, Nancy S. Interview, 2002.

[47] Private papers.

[48] Aumiller, Nancy S. Interview.

[49] Madison County Register of Deeds, Book 56, p.120.

[50] Ibid., p.121.

[51] Meek, Anna Stackhouse. Interview.

[52] Madison County Marriage Register.

[53] Ibid.

[54] Private papers.

[55] Ibid.

[56] Ibid.

Chapter Nineteen

The Stackhouse waterfront would show the impact of the 1916 flood for years, until weeds, vines and willows covered the riverbanks. Even then, twisted steel reinforcing rods protruded from rocks at the edge and from others out in the water, marking the former dam's path across the French Broad. The heavy headwall timbers, along with lumber from the Stackhouse sawmill, had washed downstream to Tennessee. (Patterson Lumber Company's operation at Paint Rock suffered complete destruction, leaving a ghost town.)[1] Not only did Amos Stackhouse lose his log piles, lumber stacks, sawmill and water wheel, he lost his investment in the Carolina Barytes operation and the monthly income it generated. Thus, physical scarring was not the only disfigurement from the 1916 inundation: the Stackhouse economic boom, which had been slowing for a couple of years, had been seriously undercut.

Train track washout at Runion. Photo from *The Floods of July, 1916* by Southern Railway Co., courtesy Overmountain Press.

Flooding along the gorge of the Big Laurel had also caused damage to Laurel River Logging Company, an important feature of the Stackhouse economy. Furthermore, rail shipping and receiving were stopped when a long section of track near Runion slid off its foundation and down the river bank, not to be restored to use until August third, nearly a month later.

Prior to 1916, however, Betts had suffered from a nationwide business panic brought on by the war in Europe. "In 1914, I had a half-million feet of Number Three common oak, dry, on sticks, and could not get eight dollars a thousand, and it was sold in 1915 for $5 a thousand," recalled Anson Betts many years later.[2] Looking elsewhere for profit, Betts purchased the former Dougherty and Harrison barite operation at Sandy Bottom from the J.M. Candler heirs and began shipping at the "old Dougherty switch," as local people called the siding.[3] The Sandy Bottom mine was on the same fault zone as the Klondyke and Gahagan veins, the property sharing a southern boundary with Amos' farm. Betts' 1914 agreement with Mary Candler Lusk for two tracts – 600 acres and 112 acres – was a deed of trust for $10,000, plus six percent interest, to be paid at the rate of ten dollars per day, monthly.[4] On November 27, 1916, Betts received his clear deed from Virgil S. Lusk, prominent Spring Creek-born attorney and husband of Mary Candler Lusk, who had died six months earlier.

Betts hired local men familiar to the occupation, many of whom had worked in the Carolina Barytes operation at Stackhouse.[5] Henry Moore, however, had moved to Tennessee, where he was developing the Mooneyham mine between Del Rio and Wolf Creek, just below Hot Springs – the mine was a part of the Cocke County overthrust which joins the Stackhouse, Sandy Bottom and Hot Springs fault, and was treated by geologists as one long deposit.[6] During 1915 and 1916, Betts sold his ore to N.J. Zinc Company at $4.25 per long ton.[7] He bought the mineral rights on at least one other tract (thirty-nine acres) in Buncombe County, but apparently it contained too little ore to develop.[8] Soon after, Betts quit his Sandy Bottom operation, stating later on that he could not get any orders and the price of labor had doubled.

Betts then leased to Biltmore Saw Mill Company timber rights to the 600-acre tract, as well as to 300 adjoining acres leased by Betts from Lawrence Hagan in 1915.[9] A year later Anson Betts sold the second tract of the Lusk purchase – 112 acres – to Charles B. Mashburn, a Marshall attorney and nephew of Hester Stackhouse.[10] In 1918 Anson Betts, age 42, married Hattie Ramsey, age 23, who worked at the Runion commissary and was the daughter of Will Ramsey, former Carolina Barytes mill superintendent.[11] Despite poor profits, Betts continued to operate the bandsaw mill at Runion for at least a few more years.

Meanwhile Amos Stackhouse and his family dealt with their own misfortune and sorrow. On June 13, 1916, six weeks after her sixty-fifth birthday, Anna Myers Stackhouse died rather unexpectedly at her home, during the early morning, with Dr. Frank Roberts of Marshall attending.[12]Though diagnosed with "arterio sclerosis" over two years earlier, she had not been seriously ill until the day of her death. In fact, Amos would place a short length of cotton lace insertion among his keepsakes, noting that it was crocheted by his mother on the day she died. He also wrote in his pocket notebook:

> Mama was buried June 14th, along with Papa on Summer House Point. There were a lot of people present. The Presbyterian minister officiated and Rev. Hensley from Marshall assisted. Mrs.

Safford [daughter of J.H. Rumbough] and Mr. N.J. Lance of Hot Springs attended.[13]

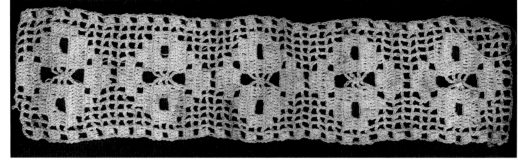

Lace crocheted by Anna Myers Stackhouse on the day she died.

Amos, no doubt, sought solace in his favorite collection of poems by Thomas Hood, one in particular, titled, "The Death Bed":

> We watched her breathing through the night,
>   Her breathing soft and low,
> As in her breast the wave of life
>   Kept heaving to and fro... .
> For when the morn came dim and sad,
>   And chill with early showers,
> Her quiet eyelids closed – she had
>   Another morn than ours.[14]

Buried with Anna Stackhouse were the last vestiges of Quaker customs and "plain language" at Stackhouse, except, perhaps, when Ellison came to visit. Amos sent a telegram to Ellison, but there was not time for him to get to the funeral from Pennsylvania. Afterward, Hester mailed details of Anna's sickness, death and burial in a letter to Ellison's family, receiving a reply from Laura, his oldest daughter: "We appreciated... your letter about Grandmother; I can imagine how you will miss her."[15] Laura reported that her father and sisters were well, and she, herself, having finished her university degree, would be teaching in the fall at Royersford, Pennsylvania, "So I will be home only once a week." Laura wrote, furthermore, that she had read in the newspaper about the terrible flood and miles of track destroyed. "I have been wondering if you suffered any," she asked. Laura would have been shocked at the damage to the Stackhouse community, coming just one month after Anna's death, seeming to add insult to injury for the family. However, the Stackhouse store was not flooded, nor, of course, the two homes situated high on their hillsides above, giving reason for thanksgiving.

Continuing her letter, Laura requested a picture of Charles Dilworth's newest baby daughter, Helen. "Little Anna was so cute when she was here," Laura wrote. "I'm afraid I wouldn't recognize Junior, Ernest and Curly (do you call him [Gilbert] that now?)," she concluded.

Indeed, her cousin, Gilbert, had no long curls and was growing tall, while June and Ernest had each reached over six feet. Keeping the three in school presented a challenge to Amos and Hester after the losses from the flood. The national economic woes caused by war in Europe had also trickled down to Madison County, affecting sales of such products as lumber, minerals, tobacco and grain. But having the importance of education in his Quaker blood,

Amos would mortgage, borrow, sell or do whatever was necessary to ensure his sons' training. Although the profit did not equal that of saw logs, pulpwood was being purchased by the Champion Fiber Company in Canton, and tanbark, by the Junaluska Leather Company of Hazelwood. Therefore, from the timber selling, truck farming, tobacco raising, and the borrowing against his home, Amos was able to keep the boys in school.

At Trinity, June and Ernest, in their second year, had begun to enjoy themselves, fitting well into campus life. Some of the former Weaver College baseball players, including June, tried out for the Trinity team, and while he did not make the first string, June was a serious contender. *The Trinity Chronicle*, on March eighth, 1916, listed Trinity's returning baseball lettermen, as well as freshman tryouts, according to the following excerpt:

Amos' sons request money in a clever mockup engineering company form.

The pitching staff promises to be a strong one. The candidates are Earnhardt, Lambe, Mason, Powell, Minshaw, Ellis, Bennett and Stackhouse, the first four, perhaps, holding the preference, although Minshaw and Ellis are likewise doing well.[16]

The next week, June wrote to Hester, saying, "I went to Raleigh with the ball team to play the Baltimore Orioles of the International League, and we got beat fifteen to eight, although we got more hits than they did." *The Trinity Chronicle*, on March 29th, covered the "practice game with the Orioles," but made no mention of "Stackhouse." Since he traveled to Raleigh with Trinity's team, June might have been a "bench warmer," or else the coach's final cut might not have been made until after the practice games. However, June enjoyed himself later as a member of the class baseball team, stating to his mother in a September 17th letter: "The class baseball season starts here Monday and I think sophomores will win the cup as we won it last year and if we win it three years in succession, it belongs to the class."[17]

In other ways the Stackhouse brothers found pleasant times at Trinity, as June described in one of his letters home: "Ernest and I went to 'Birth of a Nation' because our English teacher wanted us to, and we certainly had a grand time – it was well worth seeing." He also told about the freshman banquet he and Ernest attended at the Malbourne Hotel, where "everybody wore dress suits." Evidently the mountain boys from Madison County blended into the campus life with popularity. "You should have been here to see Ernest," June wrote his mother. "He had that McNutt girl there and she had on an evening dress and she's just five feet two inches tall." Over six-foot-tall Ernest and his short date "kept everybody in stitches," according to his brother, "because she's just as silly as he is." At another time, Ernest wrote Hester that he had joined the YMCA, June had joined the Literary Society, and that they both needed her written permission to attend the upcoming State Fair at Raleigh.

Still, Amos cautioned June about the dangers of too much socializing and too little studying, to which June replied, "I go with girls occasionally around here, usually about twice a week, but don't let them interfere with my school work." In a September 1916 letter to Amos, June had, though, mentioned that, "Ernest has been to see one of his girls every night since he has been here." Then, in November, June wrote his father: "Ernest is well and having a big time as usual, but I do wish you would write him about going out so much at night – I can't tell him anything because he thinks he knows more than I do about the ways of the world."[18]

Of course, most of the correspondence between Durham and Stackhouse concerned expense. The boys were in constant need of clothing, supplies, or board money. A letter from June to Hester in March 1916 pleaded:

> Mama, I've got to get a suit this Spring, for the seats are worn out of every one of my trousers. I just paid $2.23 yesterday to have entirely new seats put in them… Ernest's pants are all worn out, too. He just had two pairs patched.[19]

On September 28, 1916, Ernest sent his mother a statement and breakdown of his book costs, fees, supplies, room and board, laundry, pressing, and miscellaneous expenses. "I still have $28.75 in the bank but have to pay the college $37.50 Monday and board will be due again October 11th," he added. "Has Papa got Jr.'s drawing set yet-he will have to have it soon, also a pen for my set," continued Ernest. Two weeks later, Ernest implored his mother again, "I need $14.00 for board, now due, also my pressing and laundry for October." He listed his needs, summarizing with, "Board and everything except the slide rule, including the Fair, will be $23.00 – of course, this is a lot, but it won't be every month like this, and I must pay my board at once, as it was due the 11th."

Towards the end of October, June was examined for eyeglasses at a cost of $22, which was billed to Amos by mail. Amos also was compelled to chastise June for unauthorized check writing. He evidently had access to his father's bank account, either as an emergency solution or by virtue of having the same name. In a November 1916 letter, June assured Amos, "I haven't written any more checks since you wrote and told me to stop the last time and I'm not going to." June further explained that he was saving to buy Christmas presents by working a job that paid four dollars a month for six hours work every Saturday afternoon and night. "We are getting rather large now, you know, and both of us are trying to act like men," he added. Moreover, June made a suggestion of economy to his mother just before Thanksgiving. "If you will send me fifteen dollars to come home on, instead of ten, I can get a round trip ticket and save a couple of dollars."[20]

Both Ernest and June, at each writing, assured their parents that they were "studying hard," although there is only one extant report card for each. June's grades for the term ending January 1915 had shown barely passing, except for "Drawing – (85) Good." Ernest's "Report of Grades" for the same period was similar – 72 in German, 70 in mathematics, 75 in chemistry, 65 in drawing, and 80 in Bible. It is possible that after that first term, the boys did buckle down, study harder, and improve their grades.

Trinity report cards for Amos III "June" and Ernest Stackhouse, 1915.

189

During this second year, Ernest kept reminding his parents that he was carrying a twenty-hour course load and that "the sophomore year is always the hardest." He wrote fewer letters home than his brother, perhaps because of his full social life on top of the "twenty hours." June, however, often complained that his homefolk did not write enough, as evidenced to his father on November 12, 1916:

> Please write soon and tell all about what you are doing, how Mama is, and everything else that's going on. Please remember that whatever interests you, interests me, and I'm making every effort to be as careful as possible with spending and am trying to co-operate with you instead of pulling against you.[21]

In his next letter June told Amos, "I'm going to write Gilbert today and I want you to tell him he MUST answer me."

One change in June's next letter reflected his exposure to the city campus, as he greeted Amos with, "Dear 'Daddy'," instead of his usual, 'Dear Father." He also signed his letter "'June'," instead of the usual "Amos." On November 17th, June reminded his father:

> I turned twenty last Monday, Papa, and I'll bet this is the first time you have thought about it... Mama never writes like she used to and I miss her letters so much. I never found out how much you and Mama meant to me until this year and I'm loving you more and more everyday.

Hester received the prod, obvious in June's next writing to her: "I was so glad to get your letter... I think I'm beginning to see how much you dear home folks mean to me."[22]

By voicing these sentiments, June seemed to almost have a premonition of dangers forthcoming. Only five months later, President Woodrow Wilson declared war on Germany and requested volunteers. After a month, when an insufficient number had joined the military, Congress passed the Selective Conscription bill, requiring young men to register. September 12, 1917, June Stackhouse received his Registration Certificate from Mr. A.J. Runnion, assistant at the Hot Springs post office.

Immediately following Wilson's April address, Trinity College had offered its students military drilling for regular college credits,[23] but June and Ernest did not participate. As the war progressed, waves of patriotism flowed through all North Carolina campuses – students and professors volunteering in groups, leaving large gaps in graduating classes. On December 3, 1917, June Stackhouse sent a telegram to his father: "Have enlisted in the Army-will be home in the morning."

Hester and Amos were surely shocked, even though they knew their son's being drafted was possible. By enlisting, June was able to enter his field of choice – the Signal Corps Aero Squadron. Perhaps it was good that Anna Stackhouse was not alive to feel the disappointment that many other Friends families were experiencing in their conscientious conflict between devotion to peace and devotion to freedom. Coincidentally, one of Amos' Quaker cousins up North, Asa Matlack Stackhouse, had enlisted in the Army the same week as June.[24] Closer to home, Stackhouse neighbors were also joining, for instance, Nealie Price from Doe Branch, Monroe Sawyer of Mill Ridge,

Bob Dockery of Runion (he would lose a leg in the war), and numerous others of the Hot Springs and Walnut townships. A large number of Dorland Institute's boys had gone, too.

Mountain Park Hotel and grounds leased by the U.S. Government in 1917 for an internment camp in Hot Springs.

Moreover, the war had come to Hot Springs' doorstep earlier in the year when the Rumbough's hotel was closed to the public and turned into a prison camp for enemy aliens! All through the summer of 1917, the community of 500 received over 2000 German detainees, including the captain and crew of the world's largest ship – the luxurious 54,000-ton, seven-deck superstructure *Vaterland*, from Hamburg. Some of the officers' wives and children lived in Hot Springs, bringing the German language to the village streets. From the surrounding areas, practically every able-bodied male over draft age applied for the guard jobs being offered at the lucrative wage of seventy dollars per month, plus subsistence.[25]

Despite the many guards, one German prisoner escaped – a nineteen-year-old cabin boy from the *Vaterland* – only to be captured two days later near Sandy Bottom. He had likely followed the river and railroad, passing right through Stackhouse on his way.[26]

Wartime also came to the Stackhouse general store as Amos and Charles Dilworth dealt with shortages, merchandise rationing, erratic train schedules, and the selling of war savings stamps at the post office. The American people were urged to lend money to the government through stamps and bonds, and to sacrifice for the needs of the soldiers by doing without meat, wheat, sugar and other goods, by growing their own food, and by preserving through canning and drying. Vinegar making was recommended by the North Carolina Department of Agriculture, since ascetic acid was needed by military aeroplanes. "Let no apple rot on the ground" and "Let no acre be idle" were phrases often seen in local newspapers. As food production became paramount, an agricultural boom spread nationwide. Amos and Charles Dilworth would at least get better prices for their farm truck.

191

Hester Stackhouse and other North Carolina women were asked to knit socks, sweaters and neck scarves for the service men, as well as to work in Red Cross and YWCA organizations.[27] Hester was constantly worried that June might be sent overseas and subjected to reported German atrocities.

After his enlistment, June most likely was sent to San Antonio, Texas, since others from Trinity who had joined the Aero Squadron had gone there- for instance, Edwin Burge of the Weaver College Club. The *Trinity Alumni Register* in January, 1918, printed June's name only, with no location following it, while many others had rank and address.[28] Nevertheless, in April, 1918, Hester began receiving letters on a regular basis; June had been moved and was now settled for a while.

His first letter (on YMCA stationery) from Camp Benbrook, Carruthers Field at Fort Worth, Texas, began: "Dear 'Dad,' I got your letter today after it had been mailed to all the different fields within a 100-mile radius." June enclosed his new address and reported that he had already received a promotion for proficiency in his work, entitling him to wear the propeller on his sleeve-sign of first-class mechanic. The address confusion, perhaps, came from the fact that Benbrook was known initially as Taliaferro, Number Two, part of a three-field complex near Fort Worth. When the Army took it over, it was renamed Camp Benbrook and used as an aerial gunnery school for Americans and Canadians. It was also called Carruthers Field.[29]

Continuing with his letter, June explained something of the work he was doing:

> I have one thing that I feel proud in telling you about and you may tell Ben Wade Gahagan if you want. The U.S. took charge of this field last Friday and I've rebuilt three motors since then – every one turning better than 1400 RPM on the block... The last one was tagged for Capt. Harvey's machine – he is in charge of flying and always draws the best engines for himself. Because of their light construction, the engines must be rebuilt after 60 to 100 hours flying and are scrapped after 400 hours flight, as all the parts are so worn, they are not worth rebuilding.

In his letter of May 26, 1918, to his mother, June said that he was getting along nicely and liked his work, especially the studying of several new engines besides the Curtiss. He enjoyed writing the details about the different models, their gas consumption, magnetoes, crank shaft speeds, and efficiency comparisons, concluding with:

> Of course you won't be interested in this, but maybe Papa and Ernest will. I want you to send my baseball shoes and glove, as we are playing two games each week, and some more cake, if you can spare it, as the last was excellent.[30]

Since the war brought more homefront responsibilities, Hester, Amos and Ernest barely found enough hours in the day to take care of their chores. Time went fast without dragging, as it did, unfortunately, for June, far from home. In each letter he begged his family for mail and home news, for instance:

> How is Boss getting along, and how are Mama and Ernest doing?
> Be sure and sit down and write me a nice long encouraging letter,

Papa, for I have my trials and temptations, and it's very hard for a person to lead a good life, but I'm trying for your and Mama's sakes, so that I'll return a better man than I was when I went away.

I know you thought that it was easy for me to leave home but the reason I didn't cry and whimper was because I know that it doesn't help one to take a pessimistic view of everything. I joined the Army because for the first time in my life, I seemed to have a clear vision of what it was my duty to go do, and… it was the best step I ever made.

On June 2, 1918, June Stackhouse wrote: "Dear Parents, Can't understand what's the trouble you haven't written in a long time; I'm fine but get mighty lonesome for want of a letter." Later, he again implored his parents to write often, "for your letters are the only things that act as a connecting link between my life before… and my life at present."

Hester Stackhouse, understandably, continued to have apprehensions about June's going overseas. In response, June wrote her:

Please, never ask me not to go to France again, for I'm no better than thousands of other men that are going, and I would give my life any day to help whip the Germans. Of course, it is hard for you, but I don't think you should worry at all, for there is very little danger in my work.[31]

Once more, June tried to allay his parents' fears for his safety, as he described the advantages if his enlisted-man position in the aero group:

A squadron left this field this morning for France, and you never saw a happier or more cheerful bunch of men. It only shows, to a marked degree, the difference between being drafted men and enlisted. When the 36th division left Camp Bowie four or five days ago, several of them deserted, while others cried and tried to shoot themselves. Some even had to be chained in the cars, others went so far as to shoot themselves in the feet and legs and take a ten-year… sentence in Leavenworth.

Sometimes June included in his letters bits about his own social life, limited by the confined existence of a soldier. Besides playing baseball, June had been attending Sunday School, "here in the yard, and have taken considerable part in the discussion, so I was appointed Vice President." In another letter, he related:

We have lots of fun here at times. The fellows got together and passed an order that everyone should wear a mustache. Some are the most peculiar humans you ever saw – three whiskers on one side and 6 or 7 on the other. Mine doesn't look bad as the warm weather has made my beard heavy and black.[32]

Later, June described another incident. "Several of us caught a milch cow that had strayed into camp yesterday afternoon, and proceeded to get something to drink besides condensed milk." Moreover, he added that the fresh watermelons they had been enjoying were about gone from around there, "so we won't have many more." June was pleased to tell his parents that his squadron would give a dance the next Saturday evening for the enlisted men. "I think I'll go… as I've associated with women so little since I joined the Army," he wrote. In one particular letter, instead of the usual YMCA emblem at the top of his stationery, there was an engraving of the Metropolitan Hotel, about which he explained: "I came into Forth Worth to go to church and get a good supper, and, believe me, I enjoyed both."

At left, Amos "June" Stackhouse III, 1918, with unidentified Army pal.
Courtesy Clara Stackhouse Radin.

At Camp Benbrook, June also had opportunity to pursue a woodworking hobby, as he boasted a bit to Amos:

> I'm proud of something I want to tell you about. I've been doing wonders in the cabinet line here of late. The Lieut. wanted a desk some what like the one in your office and I told him I could do it… I made the whole thing, top and all, by hand, and mortised and glued the joints tight as wax, so maybe you'll think I'm improving on carpenter work… and I'm going to be recommended for sergeant again.[33]

Even through the hot Texas summer, June's enthusiasm for his work did not wither: "I got to study a Liberty aeroplane engine and a De Haviland plane yesterday, thoroughly – makes 140 m.p.h. and engine weighs 830# with 450 h.p." He also urged Ernest to join him by enlisting as a draftsman and specifying the aero squadron:

> Ernest, if you knew what it is to be drafted and treated like the infantry at Bowie, you would enlist at once. If you would come to Fort Worth, I could get you in my squadron, as we are short two men, and I know the recruiting officer. It might hurt Mama and Papa pretty badly to see you leave, but they don't understand conditions as I do. I'm sure you would like the aviation section… You could easily get in as a draftsman, as they are very short at present… Another thing you would like about this place is that the adjutant is a Trinity man.

It is unclear, incidentally, why Ernest had left Trinity when June did. Perhaps he did not want to continue by himself, or did not want to add to the family's indebtedness during wartime, or, most likely, his parents wanted to keep him home until the day of his impending conscription.

June now also sent financial advice to Ernest, who was farming, making himself exempt from the draft until the military grew more desperate for personnel. June wrote Ernest to try to save money by not dressing very nicely, "as it isn't any longer expected of a patriotic citizen." Later, he said, "We must both try and get some money ahead and get the place out of debt, so Mama and Papa won't have so much to worry about."[34] Writing again to Ernest, June recommended building a corn mill using some machinery left by the barytes operation. (The tram cars, rails and mine pump had been removed by the mill owners, but an engine of some sort was left for Amos, perhaps in lieu of rent or other debt.) "If it was run properly," June advised, "It ought to pay good dividends, besides bringing additional trade to the store."

Early in the summer of 1918, one of June's letters to his mother stated that when he became an officer he would send home more money, "and it won't take long to pay the debts off the place if Ernest and Papa will pitch in and help." He told her to, "Get rid of those chickens and Fred [a horse], for they are costing at least $1.50 a day and you get next to no benefit from either." Out of June's monthly pay of $38.00, the treasury department sent an allotment for $15 to Hester. In addition, June sent money orders at times, "to go towards the notes," which were evidently the results of bank loans for the Trinity College costs, and possible loans going back to Amos' having invested in the Carolina Barytes Corporation's rebuilding after its fire. "Tell Boss to be a good boy," June had written in a May 10th letter, "and I'll try and help educate him later."

Answering a letter from Hester in early summer, June demanded, "What in the world are you raising chickens again for – they must cost you $4 or $5 apiece by the time they are grown?" On July 10th June warned Amos:

> Whatever you do, keep enough wheat on hand to last the family all winter and don't buy flour as there is quite a shortage already. Forbid Mama from feeding wheat to the chickens. Don't you think that it would be a good idea to get rid of Frank [Hunycutt], as the business must be so small that his wages run the overhead way up? You know there is no such thing as sentiment in business.[35]

A month later, June again ordered Amos, "Get rid of Fred before fall." Then his patriotism prompted the following proposal to his father:

> Another thing that is being done elsewhere to win the war – farmers are banding together and raising a big crop of something that is well-adapted to the country, and, instead of selling locally, are shipping. There is no reason you couldn't do this with… pigs, sheep or broom corn, as nearly all the broom corn in the world comes from Germany, but you would have to get the entire county in the same business. If you would write the state board of agriculture, they would… probably send an expert to assist you… Personally, I think pigs would be the best, as you don't have to keep so many over the winter, and a pig can be made to weigh 150 or 200 lbs. from March to November by scientific feeding, then you don't have to carry so much over winter.

As the war intensified, so did shortages, spurring June to further advise his mother, "You had better get a lot of molasses this winter… because the government is stopping the sale of syrup so it can be refined into sugar, and there is to be a terrible shortage of both."

Moreover, as American soldiers were killed overseas or sent to hospitals, replacements were being drafted, superseding previous exemptions. Obviously replying to Amos' voiced concerns, June wrote: "In regard to Ernest being drafted, tell him to do exactly as I told him and the draft board will put us together." Consoling his mother, he added, "Tell Mama not to worry about either of us, not that I want to put in a 'I told you so,' but I foresaw this at Trinity and enlisted, and I've never regretted it."[36]

June's next letter to Hester is reminiscent of his haughty tone from grade school days, although his business ideas carried certain merit on the surface, at least:

> Dear Mother, I'm almost shocked to death because you got that Hupmobile. Altho' it has certain advantages not found in other cars of its price, it is not nearly as economical as a Buick light six, neither is it so well balanced, making it hard on tires.
>
> Besides, what in the world did you get a car for, just now, when automobiles are much higher than they were a year ago? The place is badly in debt, yet Papa's creditors seeing you riding around in a car will simply think that he is trying to deliberately beat them.
>
> And, another thing, Papa hasn't any business to speak of, why doesn't he start something instead of spending money foolishly. Tell him to move the engine and put up a corn mill, as cornbread is going to be the fashion this year. Get in touch with the municipal wood yard in Asheville and if he can get a decent contract, to build him a saw table, buy a 500-lb. splitter for $125, and put saw table, splitter and corn mill under same roof and run them with the engine. Wood is bringing $6 to $8 per cord in Asheville, I guess. This will give the mules something to do this winter, besides pulling a little trade to the store… .

Don't worry about Ernest, he probably won't have to join the Army before February [Ernest would be eighteen January 30] so you can get a lot done in that time.[37]

Amos and Hester Stackhouse with their automobile at the Methodist Assembly, Lake Junaluska, N.C.

We cannot be sure how much of June's advice Amos took, if any, but the automobile purchase, no doubt, had been done at the urging of Ernest, who would do all the driving. (Neither Hester nor Amos ever learned to operate an automobile.) Since Henry Ford's assembly line initiated the affordability of autos for the middle class, car owners were showing up even in Madison County. The year before, Charles Dilworth Stackhouse had bought a Dodge coupe with curtains at the windows.[38] Chappel Norton, who worked for LRLC and lived in its village, was said to have owned the first car at Runion.[39] The Stackhouse's friends, the Rumboughs, had owned autos early on-a grandson, John B. Rumbough, earning the title in 1905 of first man to drive a car from Asheville to New York City.[40] In 1911, he was the first to drive over the Appalachian Mountains. Still, it is surprising that Hester would allow the noisy newfangled horseless carriage on her place. Having no driveway large enough to accommodate the auto, the passengers and the driver were forced to walk up the steep hill to the house because she would not permit the building of a road through her landscape. (The Stackhouse cars would park at the old lumber yard one thousand feet away, for years to come.[41])

Western North Carolina's twisting narrow wagon roads were inadequate and became quagmires in rainy weather, often sinking automobiles to the axles. Anna Stackhouse Meek, daughter of Charles Dilworth, recalled that her family usually took the train when they needed to go to Marshall or Asheville: "because the roads were so bad, the car was unreliable."[42] However, as automobile ownership grew more common, so did the demand for improved roads, spurring interest for Western North Carolinians and East Tennesseans in the National Highway Plan. By 1913, there had been at least one stretch completed in Madison County, between Marshall and Walnut, described in the county paper as a "beautiful wide highway, smooth and almost level."[43] The hard-packed gravel surface, hand-graded by convict labor, caused "the horses to take on new life and strike up a livelier gait," according to the journalist.

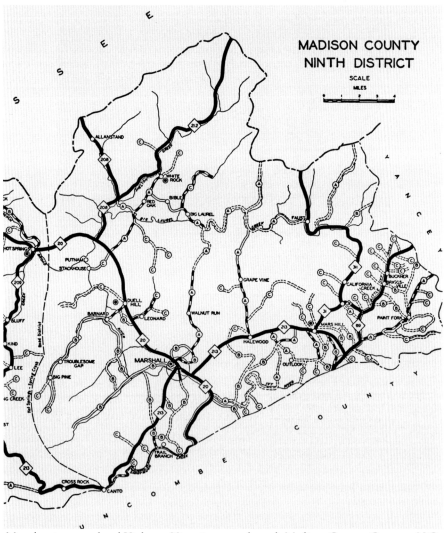

Map showing completed Highway 20, main artery through Madison County. Courtesy, N.C. Division of Transportation, c. 1930.

For those fortunate enough to both own an automobile and to live near a railroad, the need for horse and buggy seemed to have passed. At least, June

198

Stackhouse in Texas thought so when he again instructed Hester: "Fatten Fred and kill him, if you can't sell him, give him away for beef – horse meat is good as any, and, also sell his hide and the buggies."[44]

It is possible that Amos and Hester had bought the Hupmobile after receiving seven hundred and fifty dollars on August 16, 1918, when LRLC purchased the balance of the Laurel farm acres – a portion of the western half, which had been excepted in previous deeds to LRLC and N.C. Land and Timber Company.[45] The Betts family actually paid $1500 for this portion, but half went to Charles Dilworth and Clara, since the original 100 acres had been in the names of both Stackhouse sons. With no description or dimension for this tract portion appearing in the deed, we do not know its size or why the section had been kept by Amos' father, whether it was a particularly productive part of the farm, or whether it had a geographical separation from the rest, rendering it undesirable by LRLC at the time.

Earlier in the year, the LRLC (like many other large bandmills) had been hit by extreme weather, temporarily closing its operation, according to the *Asheville Times* of January 30, 1918.[46] First, the snow and cold shut down the logging and the portable mills in the woods, then flooding took out the private railway along the Laurel River, requiring several weeks to repair. "Water and ice concentrated in the gorge, washing away many trestles and considerable damage was done to the roadway," stated the paper.

Other stories of that winter's cold would be told for years to come. Mrs. Horace (Suella F.) Kimbrough had been in Hot Springs December 30, 1917, to bury her mother, and she recalled years later: "With deep snow and zero weather, none of the women could go to the grave." Returning home to Tennessee, it was no better, as she explained, "When we reached Morristown, Train 41 from Washington and Bristol, was frozen on the track and could not be moved for 36 hours."[47] Furthermore, the electric power plant in Hot Springs had shut down when Spring Creek froze over, leaving the German detention camp with no lights. Nor did the camp have any water, because the large supply line leading from the reservoir across to town froze too. John Sanders, who maintained the water systems of the Mountain Park Hotel and the town, finally wrapped the cast iron pipe in tar paper and set it afire to thaw the water.[48]

LAUREL RIVER LOGGING CO. SUFFERS FROM FLOOD

High Water and Ice Sweep Away Trestle of Lumber Road

Information received from Stackhouse, in Madison county, is to the effect that the logging railway of the Laurel River Logging company was placed out of commission by flood waters and ice early this week. From Runion, on the Southern railway, the lumber road runs through a gorge for ten or twelve miles into the heart of the timber which is being logged by the company. Water and ice concentrated in this gorge and as a result many trestles were washed away and considerable damage was done to the road-bed.

Officials of the company stated yesterday that it would require several weeks to repair the damage. The company had not been able to run its band mill at Runion lately on account of the impossibility of carrying on logging operations durng the severe weather of the past month, and the mill was preparing to start again yesterday.

All large sawmills in this territory have been handicapped lately by cold, snow and ice. The portable mills have not attempted to operate and there is said to be only a small supply of dry lumber at the railway sidings ready for shipment.

Article from *Asheville Times*, 1-30-1918

In the meantime, having the LRLC logging railway out of commission meant that anyone on Laurel needing to get to a hospital could not count on the train for transport. Although only at the foundation stage, a Laurel hospital had at last been started by the Presbyterian missionaries, and would soon save the lives of loggers and others.

Presbyterian changes were also taking place at Walnut during the spring and summer of 1918, as Bell Institute prepared to move to Hot Springs. There, enlarged buildings would be ready by fall to receive Bell students, completing the Board of National Missions' plan to consolidate Dorland Institute and Bell Institute. A matter of general economy was given as the reason, brought no doubt by conditions of the world-wide war. The New York board named the consolidated school "Dorland-Bell School."[49]

Another change in the Walnut community, although of lesser impact, and not mission-related, had occurred the year before when the North Carolina General Assembly abolished the municipal corporation, repealing the 1915 act to create the town of Walnut for the second time.[50] Here, again, the reason was likely lack of funds brought on by the 1916 closing of Carolina Barytes and the onset of war.

It was in Walnut, on November 11, 1918, that Dorland-Bell student Dan Gold Long was helping move a piano by wagon from the near-empty Bell school building to Hot Springs, when he had to pull out of the road to let pass another wagon loaded with tobacco. "The piano fell over in our wagon, making a terrible noise, and disturbed an armistice celebration service taking place in front of the Walnut post office," he recalled years later.[51]

Yes, it was true! The Great War had at last ended and jubilation reigned in western North Carolina. The *Asheville Citizen* put out an EXTRA edition of its paper, people danced, sang and shouted in the streets. This had been "the war to end all wars" forevermore, worldwide. At Stackhouse, Amos and Hester were surely on their knees in thanksgiving. Ernest was still safe at home, and June would be there by Christmas, having never been sent abroad into battle, after all.[52]

Armistice Day parade, Hot Springs, 1918. Courtesy Patrick Gentry.

Alas, on the heels of the Great War came the epidemic of Spanish influenza, or La Grippe, which was responsible for at least 367,000 American deaths, and six million, worldwide, between September and December of 1918. In western North Carolina schools were closed, quarantines imposed, and public gatherings prohibited. The entire Stackhouse family fell ill and were cared for by the school teacher from Johnston County who was boarding with them.[53] At Runion, Mrs. Ada Wardrep, wife of Jeter Wardrep, left black iron pots full of her chicken soup at sick neighbors' doorsteps, too afraid of the contagion to go inside. Twelve-year-old Gilbert Stackhouse, after recovering himself, was pressed into duty to help bury the corpses. "In households where all were stricken, they just laid their dead out on the porches," Gilbert remembered years later.[54]

As 1918 came to an end, few mourned its passing: it had been a difficult year.

ENDNOTES FOR CHAPTER NINETEEN

[1] Underwood, Jinsie. *This is Madison County.* American Revolution Bicentennial Committee of Madison County, 1974, p.48.

[2] Author's private papers.

[3] Madison County Register of Deeds, Book 34, p.584.

[4] Ibid.

[5] Treadway, Kenneth. Interview, November 1998. Private papers.

[6] Rankin, H.S., Head, Division of Chemical Engineering, Tennessee Valley Authority, letter to H.H. Sutherland. January 3, 1949.

[7] Private papers.

[8] Buncombe County Register of Deeds, Book 208, p.342.

[9] Madison County Register of Deeds, Book 34, p.41. Ibid., Book 34, p.310.

[10] Ibid., Book 35, p.315.

[11] Buncombe County Marriage Register, Vol. 10.

[12] Madison County Death Records, Book 3, p.143.

[13] Private papers.

[14] Hood, Thomas. *Poetical Works of Thomas Hood.* Boston: Phillips, Sampson and Company, 1857, pp.169, 170.

[15] Private papers.

[16] *The Trinity Chronicle*, Durham: Trinity College, March 8, 1916, p.1.

[17] Private papers.

[18] Ibid.

[19] Ibid.

[20] Ibid.

[21] Ibid.

[22] Ibid.

[23] *Trinity Alumni Register*, Vol. III. Durham: Trinity College Alumni Association, July, 1917, p.111.

[24] *Manual of the Legislature of New Jersey.* Trenton: State of New Jersey, 1940, p.272.

[25] Painter, Jacqueline. *The German Invasion of Western North Carolina.* Johnson City,

Tennessee: Overmountain Press, 1997, p.25.

[26] *Asheville-Citizen*, June 18, 1918, p.5.

[27] Lefler, Hugh T., *North Carolina History, Geography and Government*. Yonkers-on-Hudson, New York: World Book Company, 1959, p.435.

[28] Trinity Alumni Register, Vol. III, January, 1918, p.296.

[29] Hays, Robert. "Military Aviation in Texas," *Texas Military History, Vol.3*. Austin, Texas: National Guard Association of Texas, 1963.

[30] Private papers.

[31] Ibid.

[32] Ibid.

[33] Ibid.

[34] Ibid.

[35] Ibid.

[36] Ibid.

[37] Ibid.

[38] Meek, Anna Stackhouse. Interview, August, 1999.

[39] Bailey, Jean Norton. Interview, August, 1999.

[40] Ireland, Robert E. *Entering the Auto Age*. Raleigh: N.C. Div. of Archives and History, 1990, p.36.

[41] Stackhouse, Juanita C. Interview, 1997.

[42] Meek, Anna Stackhouse. Interview, 1999.

[43] *News-Record*, Marshall, Dec. 5, 1913, p.1.

[44] Private papers.

[45] Madison County Register of Deeds, Book 36, p.257.

[46] *Asheville-Times*, January 30, 1918, p.3.

[47] Brewer, Carson. "This is Your Community, There Was a Time." Undated article from unidentified Knoxville newspaper.

[48] Burgin, Kenneth S. Interview, 1973.

[49] Painter, Jacqueline. *Season of Dorland-Bell*. Boone, N.C.: Appalachian Consortium Press, 1996, pp.121-124.

[50] *Public and Private Laws of N.C., Session of 1917*. Raleigh: Edwards and Broughton Printing Co., p.310.

[51] Painter, *Season of Dorland-Bell*. p.124.

[52] Painter, *German Invasion of WNC*, p.74.
Terrell, Bob. "Asheville Marked Ends to Wars." *Asheville Citizen-Times*, February 4, 2001, p. C2.

[53] Meek, Anna Stackhouse. Interview, 2000.

[54] Stackhouse, Juanita C. Interview, 2000.

Chapter Twenty

Following the Great War, life at Stackhouse carried on much as it had before. Amos continued to serve on the Bank of French Broad directors' board and was elected its Vice President in 1919.[1] He also remained active in the Madison County Republican executive committee. August 27, 1920, the county coroner appointed him to an inquest jury in the sensational murder of a neighbor woman, Mrs. Frank Henderson, mother of five small children. "After being duly empaneled by Dr. Moore, and after gathering all the evidence obtainable, they rendered their verdict that the deceased came to her death by having been choked to death," stated the *News-Record*.[2] (Frank Henderson would be sentenced for the crime.)

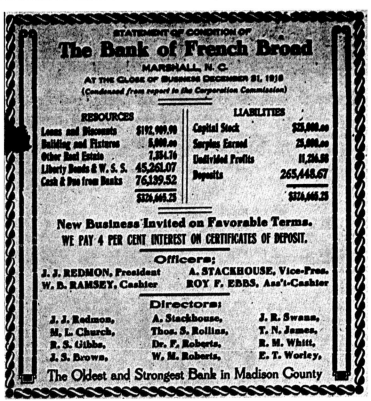

Bank of French Broad annual statement listing Amos Stackhouse, director and Vice President, *The News Record*, 1-17-1919.

Amos' brother, Charles Dilworth, was appointed to the school committee for the Stackhouse district,[3] his main job that of securing teachers and maintaining the school house. Charles had particular interest in the school system now that his two daughters approached six and four, and a son had been born in April, 1919 – Charles Dilworth, Jr., called Dilworth.[4]

"The county paid the Stackhouse teacher for five months only, and the parents chipped in to pay for two or three months longer," recalled Anna Stackhouse Meek, the elder daughter, many years later.[5] Young Gilbert lived

Wife of Charles Dilworth Stackhouse, Clara Phipps Stackhouse, holds son, Charles Dilsworth II, with daughter Anna at left and Helen at right. 1920.
Courtesy, Sandra Meek Beaudry.

at Walnut with Hester's mother while he attended the Walnut school in its large new building, with its longer term and academic advantages. One time (at least) in October, 1920, his name appeared in the Marshall *News-Record* under the heading "Walnut Honor Roll" for "being neither tardy or absent for the month."[6]

Amos' son Ernest finally settled on one girlfriend – Ruth Vandervort – whom he married on October 20, 1919.[7] He had met her while working at the Runion lumber mill where her father, Hiram E. Vandervort, was a bandsaw filer for Laurel River Logging Company. The Vandervorts had come to North Carolina from South Carolina, but were originally from Brookville, Pennsylvania. "Papa Van," as family members called him, had a dapper goatee and always wore a white shirt and tie to work. A year later Ruth and Ernest presented the first grandchild to Hester and Amos – a girl, Anna Carthene, to be known as Carthene.[8]

Amos and his sons benefited from the fact that food and tobacco products maintained a demand with American servicemen still in Europe or convalescing in hospitals. June Stackhouse could now put into practice his methods for "scientific farming," and for operating Amos' business, listing himself and Ernest as "farm managers" when the federal census taker came in January 1920. The tobacco market, especially, had steadily climbed since 1914, prices peaking in 1919. While June was in the Army, Ernest had grown the new type – burley – just catching on in the mountains. It hung in the barns to air-dry, requiring no flues or round-the-clock firing, enabling fewer workers to produce more leaf. When prices began dropping in 1920 and 1921, growers banded to form the Burley Tobacco Growers Cooperative, the beginning of the cooperative approach to agricultural production.[9] It is not known whether Madison County farmers organized at that time, but they soon became number one in North Carolina burley production.

Amos "June" Stackhouse at wheel; passenger, unidentified. Hauling logs down Stackhouse road in early 1920s.

Side view of June's "Truck" as he and crew brought logs to Stackhouse rail siding.

June Stackhouse also began cutting and buying logs which he sold for telephone poles. Phillip Franklin on Laurel explained, many years later, how his father, Thomas Franklin, used a cross-cut saw to cut standing blighted chestnut trees, thirty to forty feet tall, then hauled them by wagon to Stackhouse.[10] Before loading his wagon bed, however, Thomas Franklin cut a tall strong oak from which he made a long "coupling pole" two inches thick and eight inches wide to be placed in the wagon for support of the chestnuts to keep them from dragging on the ground behind. Still, he could haul only two at a time, but it was one of the few ways besides growing tobacco that mountain people had of earning cash.

When old enough, young Phillip was allowed to accompany his father on the day-long trip to Stackhouse and back, where he might see a long passenger train, visit the general store, view the wide French Broad and the large Stackhouse home with its fancy turrets – all exciting changes from his day-to-day routine.

The backless board seat of the wagon could be hard and bruising as it jolted along the rough mountain road from Laurel River to Stackhouse, crossing only a brief segment of the "fine new highway" being built from Marshall. To make the ride more comfortable, Phillip's father "took a tow sack and stuffed it with straw for a cushion," recalled Phillip, decades later. Coming up Laurel River road from Belva, they had to stop every fifty yards or so to let the mules rest. "It was hard climbing," related Phillip, "but once we started down Stackhouse Road, it was easy going – all down hill." His father told him one day that he could be the brakeman, quite a responsibility, he learned. Attached to the wagon near the back wheels was a wooden brake pole about two inches square and six to eight feet high. A rope tied to the brake pole would, when pulled, slow or stop the wagon. As they began rolling fast down the steep places, Thomas would call, "Pull," requiring young Phillip to use all his strength on the rope to prevent the wagon's running away. At journey's end, Franklin used a peavey to roll the logs off the wagon onto a platform where June Stackhouse paid him five dollars for each log.[11]

Next, June loaded the logs onto a freight car bound for Hot Springs and John Heilman's creosoting operation at Southern Railway's west yard. The trimmed tree trunks were unloaded from the freight car and stockpiled until a mechanical crane placed them into two steel vats about ten or twelve feet square, filled with hot creosote.[12] (Only one end of the pole was treated – the ground-contact portion.) After a week of saturation the poles were plucked out by the crane, drained, and loaded onto another car for shipment to the next buyer.

Even though the post-war years saw few changes at Stackhouse, there were several at Laurel River Logging Company in Runion. Will Garrett, former superintendent, had taken charge of a large lumber plant in Murphy,[13] while Anson Gardner Betts, former president, had moved to Hot Springs where he prospected in barite and worked as a chemist for Buquo Lime Company.[14] Anson owed $112 for his delinquent 1919 county taxes, LRLC owed $7,751 for theirs, plus $408 on the Madison County Railway, not to mention a compromise court settlement in May, charging LRLC $1300.[15] Anson's brother, Edgar, took over at Runion, leasing the Madison Railway to French Broad Railway Company, operated by Broad River Lumber Company of Huntington, West Virginia.[16] On May 25, 1920, Edgar sold the LRLC's land lying along the northern Madison County and eastern Tennessee border, about 38,000 acres, less exceptions, to Grove Land and Timber Company of Asheville, though he reserved "a right of way over 'first tract' of sufficient width for standard gauge railroad along boundaries of LRLC's logging railroad."[17]

The Grove Land and Timber Company was just one of several interests of Asheville entrepreneur Edwin W. Grove. In Hot Springs, his agent, William Ellerson (whose wife was Jean Garrett, a former Runion school teacher), managed a cattle business with corrals at Southern Railway's west yard for shipping. Located next to the telephone pole creosote vats, four separate pens sometimes held as many as one hundred wild horses brought from out West for auctioning. "Once Number Twelve came along, blowing its whistle, and scared the horses so, that they broke down the corrals and scattered," recalled Sydney Izlar, many years later.[18]

In a *News-Record* full-page advertisement on July 16, 1920, Grove announced that he had purchased the Laurel River Logging Company lands, comprising about 40,000 acres in western North Carolina and eastern Tennessee. "Twenty thousand acres of these lands have been reserved for a ranch for grazing, feeding, and raising of live stock of all kinds… ," he wrote. The remaining twenty thousand acres would be sold in small tracts on long terms at six percent per annum, after a cash down payment of ten to twenty percent of the price. At the bottom of the ad, a paragraph by Grove attorney James E. Rector stated: "I expect to be on Laurel about three days each week to close up with all persons who have contracts or who have filed application for land…"[19]

The following October 4th, a certificate of dissolution for Laurel River Logging Company was issued by North Carolina's Department of State, but the corporation was still chartered in the state of Delaware.[20] Five days later, LRLC transferred all its holdings to Harriet Betts (mother of Anson and Edgar) in Troy, New York, *excepting* the lands already conveyed to Grove, the standing timber "on any of said lands," the 100-acre bandmill operation at Runion, and all railroad lands along Shelton Laurel Creek.[21]

About the same time, Luther O. Griffith, also of Huntington, West Virginia, and probably connected with Broad River Lumber Company, began buying timber boundaries near Stackhouse from Wade Gahagan and William C. Cook.[22] On January 21, 1923, Luther chartered the Griffith Lumber Company, with its principal office in Asheville and authorized capital of $50,000. When Luther took over the bandsaw mill at Runion, Oscar J. Griffith (possibly his son) became mill superintendent. The next year Griffith Lumber changed its principal office to "Runion station and Stackhouse post office," increasing its capital to $100,000.[23]

Orville Cooper, experienced lumberman from the flooded Paint Rock sawmill operation, was placed over the lumber yard; Hilliard Rice became a lumber inspector; J. Bewley Tweed from Marshall ran the commissary;[24] and nineteen-year-old J. Herbert Waldrop from Bluff began a lifetime career in lumber manufacturing at Runion with Griffith.[25] From close around came Stackhouse neighbors George, Walter, and Curtis Dockery; Billy Anderson; Denver Capps; Charlie Wright; Nealie Price; Will Clubb; Charlie and Gordon Treadway; Bob and George Phipps; Ed Davis; Robert Norton; Stuart Reid; Joe, Earl and Edgar Fortner; and Andrew Plemmons – to name a few.[26] Some worked as mechanics, blacksmiths, and firemen; others stacked lumber and loaded cars. Charlie Warner and Manasses Hensley were train engineers. Young boys like Gordon Treadway carried bucketsful of drinking water.[27] Thomas Griffith from Virginia served as bookkeeper; Henry Guigou from New York was a stenographer; and Donald French of West Virginia, a foreman – all living at the large boarding house operated by Mrs. Kate Pittillo.[28] Another bandsaw filer was John Craigmile from Hot Springs. His neighbor, Henry T. Garenflo, loaded freight cars on the night shift. The job of handling the large steam-powered log loader fell to James "Buck" Landers, whose brothers Hobart, John, Bob and McKinley also worked at Runion.

The Landers family had moved to Runion from Allenstand, where Buck had done logging with mules, high on the head of Shelton Laurel, and his wife, Melvina Payne, had learned rug-making from Miss Frances Goodrich.[29] At Runion, Melvina ran a small boarding house, "mostly for family members who worked at the mill," recalled Melvina's daughter, Carrie Landers Johnson, many years later. In the little Runion school house Carrie learned her letters from teacher Robbie Meadows and also attended prayer meetings on Wednesday evenings. "Sometimes we had a preacher on Sundays," Carrie added. She remembered stacks of drying lumber all around the school. Another building, the "club house," was "like a café" and run by Miss Carrie Ramsey, or by Walter Lieb, at times, but Melvina Landers did not allow her children to go there because of the frequent card-playing, drinking, and weekend fighting.

Nevertheless, Carrie and her family had good times and social occasions in their own way. One was summertime swimming in the French Broad with other young people. "Mama made our bathing suits," stated Carrie, "although she didn't approve, wholeheartedly, because the toilets drained into the river." The women and girls at Runion met for quilting, bringing the quilt tops they had pieced at home to be finished by the group. Carrie remembered feeling special and grown-up when one woman allowed her to tie the thread knots of the "tacked" quilts which did not require a quilting frame. On weekends, the Landers family members gathered to make music – playing banjo, guitar, French harp and fiddle. Aunts and uncles came from Greeneville, Tennessee, and from "back home" on Shelton Laurel.[30]

Unfortunately, Carrie's family experienced one horribly sad loss when Carrie's uncle, McKinley Landers, was killed at Runion in July, 1923. "About ten o'clock at night, he was doing some work about the train and fell beneath the car," stated the *News-Record*,[31] his arm and a leg cut off by the train. Down through the years, some of the oldtimers' memories differed from the newspaper description, saying instead that Landers was "cut in two by the train."

Train wrecks occurred often along the Laurel River railway, but did not always cause human injury. A year later, the same logging train, carrying thirteen cars, wrecked, killing two cows.[32] At times the tracks were undermined when the creeks rose, causing more wrecks, one in particular being recorded *before* 1923, curiously enough by the popular award-winning photographer, Herbert W. Pelton, and portraying a few Runion employees, among whom was a smiling McKinley Landers.

Amos Stackhouse also did a fair amount of work at Runion for Broad River Lumber Company and for Griffith, grading lumber for fifty cents an hour – five times the wage of the average worker.[33] On a regular day with no bad weather, Amos worked the usual ten hours, receiving five dollars. He sold his Stackhouse general store interest to his brother around 1921, but the post office remained in the back of the store with Amos as postmaster.[34]

In 1923, however, Amos' son, Ernest, and Hiram Vandervort left their Runion jobs, taking their family to Buncombe County, first to Swannanoa, then to Biltmore, where both men took jobs with Biltmore Lumber Company, Ernest as superintendent.[35] Amos' youngest, Gilbert, also went to Buncombe County, entering Weaver Junior College and working part time in the maintenance of the school's heating and plumbing systems. He had stayed

In the early 1920s, Herbert W. Pelton photographed this train wreck in Spillcorn, Madison County. Tom Burns stands at forground left with his brother-in-law, James "Buck" Landers. Atop cars, one man is identified – James' brother, Mckinley Landers, seated over word "Chicago." The two men in over-coats are officials of Griffith Lumber Co., LRLC successor at Runion. Box cars were often added to the logging train to haul tools and repair supplies, according to Carrie Landers Johnson, James' daughter. "The men also ate their lunches inside them when the weather was bad," she added. Courtesy Carrie L. Johnson.

with Hester's sister, Carrie Davis, while he attended Marshall High School.[36] Now he would be taking the two-year business course sponsored at Weaver College by the 20th Century Bookkeeping Company.

Left to right – Ernest Matlack Stackhouse, Carthene Stackhouse and Ruth Vandervort Stackhouse, c. 1924.

Just as Amos did, this grader uses a lumber rule on wide poplar boards, plentiful in Madison and other mountain counties in the 1920s. Photo, National Park Service.

Amos' lumber grading job at Runion sometimes took him up Laurel to Revere, Belva, Spillcorn or Hurricane Communities where he would stay in lumber camps or board in private homes. Occasionally, he would be called by Ernest to Biltmore to settle a lumber grade dispute between buyer and seller. Using a small crew to help with the tallying and stacking, or loading onto freight cars, Amos kept their hours and his expenses, as well as other information in a small notebook, for instance: "loaded 1875 ft. of door boards at Belva with Collette's crew," and, "loaded a car of white walnut."[37] Sometimes he grade at the Runion bandmill "off the chains," as the newly-sawn boards came along the conveyors; at others, he graded "at the kilns." One entry described his day's work as "sawing lath." On July 30, 1924, Amos traveled to the Paint Fork of Ivy River (near Mars Hill) where he took Mr. Griffith's bookkeeper to tally for him during several days of grading oak, poplar and chestnut.

The work was not always steady, however. When it snowed, the sawmill and logging shut down, but there were always tasks to be done on the farm. Amos' notes showed that some days he thawed the pipes, milked the cow, hoed the late corn, sprayed the beans, picked apples, and, on occasion, "Took beans and apples to commissary at Runion." He commented in the summer of 1924 that he had an unusually fine apple crop that year. Some days Amos "weighed bark for Junior," referring to the selling of tanbark. Once, he "stayed in the store so that Charlie and Jr. could go to Hot Springs to vote." On Sundays Amos "worked the mails" at the Stackhouse post office, noting one Sunday that "mail on Number 11 was exceptionally heavy today." (Besides the mail for Stackhouse and Runion communities, that of the Laurel River communities was still distributed from Amos' post office.) He also mentioned that most Sundays Gilbert was home from Weaver College and sometimes Ernest brought his family from Biltmore for a visit.[38]

Other jottings, not work-related, appeared in his notebook at times, such as: "Today is my birthday – 51 years old"; on May 6, 1924, "Married 30 yrs. yesterday;" and on May 10, "Mr. Rumbough died today – Harry & Edd's father."

Amos' pocket journal entry for September 13, 1924, stated briefly, but significantly, "Not working at Runion anymore – laid off by being out of work." The fact that Griffith was "out of work" seemed doubtful to Amos at the time, but, in retrospect, it was the beginning of the final slow down. Back in June, Amos had noted that "Broad River Lumber Company is closing out, and it is said that L.O. Griffith will rent the mill to saw the balance of his lumber on the Gahagan estate." This reference, no doubt, was to the smaller mill which had been set up originally at Pounding Mill. Although the large-acreage stands were gone, there was still high quality timber in Madison County but it required going deeper into the mountains at more cost. Circular-saw, low-volume mills continued to operate at many Madison County locations. Gennett Lumber Company from Asheville had its mill on Spillcorn Creek; Frisbee and Wyatt had one on Paint Creek; and G.C. Myers was sawing at the Paint Rock-Wolf Creek area.[39] In conjunction with the electric power plant Hugh Lance operated at the edge of Hot Springs, he had installed a sawmill which was cutting 10,000 feet of lumber daily.[40]

Nonetheless, Amos Stackhouse, having no job to augment his farming income except the nominal position of postmaster, went to Biltmore Lumber Company where Ernest worked, "to help them out," he wrote in October, 1924. While there, Mr. Granville Taylor (probably the owner) asked him to go to South Carolina to grade lumber for him, requiring Amos to face the question of whether to travel away from Hester and his family. The offer must have been a worthwhile one, however, because within two weeks he was living in Monck's Corner, near Charleston, and working at a sawmill two miles away. He would journey over South Carolina as an arbitrator and lumber grader for Taylor to Abbeville, Allendale, Cayce, Fairfax, Greenville, Greenwood, Lugoff, Sycamore and many others. He referred to Kingstree as "a nice little town."

Amos came home only twice a month, as a rule, but June drove his mother in their automobile to visit at times.[41] Once again, through letter writing, Hester and Amos managed the farm, rentals and post office. When Amos spent his Sundays in South Carolina, he usually visited a Methodist Church, noting in May, 1925, that he had been to the Washington Street M.E. Church of Columbia, took the sacrament and met several people. "Mr. T.B. Stackhouse attends this church, but did not see him," wrote Amos, likely referring to a descendant of his Revolutionary War ancestor who had fled from Philadelphia to settle in South Carolina. Moreover, these distant cousins of Amos were assembling annually for a Stackhouse reunion which would result in a large organization over time.[42] (It is unknown whether Amos ever heard about the meetings during his stay in South Carolina.) Thus, Amos Stackhouse had joined the on-going exodus of Madison Countians who were forced to leave home to make a living, his case, albeit, a little different, in that he did not move household and family.

By now there was talk that Runion bandmill would be closing soon. An ad in the *News-Record*, for instance, listed for sale, Hot Springs real estate belonging to Chappell Norton of Runion, stating, "Owner leaving for West

Virginia."[43] (Norton, a good mechanic, had likely been offered a job by Griffith at his Huntington plant.) Herbert Waldrop found employment at Black Mountain in Buncombe County, moving his family from Runion in December, 1924;[44] Mr. R.F. Mull and family left Runion and rented a house in Marshall;[45] Miss Carrie Ramsey and Mr. Walter Lieb, operators of the Runion club house, married and went to Detroit for jobs in auto manufacturing.[46] The father-in-law of Charles Dilworth, Joe Phipps, who had worked at Runion in winter when he was not farming, also moved to Buncombe County's Woodfin community.[47]

Runion Mountain would never again be populated as shown at left in the 1920s. Stackhouse store at lower right corner.

Nearly every week in the *News-Record*, alongside items from local communities of Bluff, Pine Creek, Walnut, Antioch and numerous others, there were short articles titled: "From Detroit; From Crewe, Virginia; From Spartanburg; From Flag Pond, Tennessee; From Jenkins, Kentucky; and from Marion, North Carolina, giving news about small colonies of homesick Madison Countians dwelling in places of industry. A more recent one, headed "Grovestone (Near Black Mountain)," reported that the families of Herbert Waldrop and Robert Phipps – both from Runion – were adjusting to their new homes, at last.[48] Whole families often left for the cotton-mill towns in the North and South Carolina Piedmonts. At Marion, for example, Dock Hicks and all his sons and sons-in-law from Meadow Fork worked at Clinchfield Mills, as did the Fowlers, Allisons, Parkers, Rowlands, Baldwins and others from Southern Madison County. Lacking jobs, Madison County lost many of its brightest and best. Andrew Jack Gahagan, another son of George W.R. Gahagan, and uncle of Amos Stackhouse's good friend, Ben Wade Gahagan, had been home from the Civil War only a few months before he moved to Tennessee. He later wrote in a letter that, after helping put in the spring crop back at home, he could see no way to support himself on the Laurel farm: "In less than a week I was on a job at $125 per month."[49] Remaining in Chattanooga for the rest of his life, Jack became a successful, civic-minded businessman and an asset to his adopted city. Fortunately, Amos Stackhouse would return home to Madison County at every opportunity, keeping his mountain allegiance strong.

As families continued to move away, the termination of Runion bandmill became more than a rumor. "Everybody knew it was closing beforehand," recalled Anna Stackhouse Meek, many years later. Nealie Price also remembered, "The closing was gradual – in the Spring of 1925." He stayed on for two or three months to help get out the remaining lumber, "a million feet already cut and ready to ship," said Price.[50] One blacksmith, one loaderman and a few other personnel also stayed. The draining of the mill pond exposed the many "deadheads" – logs, which for some reason had not floated, but sunk to the bottom.

These last few months were recalled, too, by Carrie Landers Johnson, whose father was retained by Griffith after the mill closed. Her family lived in one of the few executive's houses, painted white-"the best house up there," stated Carrie.[51] It had running water and an inside toilet, albeit, "old and beat-up, and so was the kitchen sink, but they worked!" When the commissary closed, Carrie and her brother, Fred, were sometimes sent to Marshall on the train to buy groceries, "because Mama kept boarders." Carrie also had fond memories of walks to the Stackhouse store, where young Gilbert Stackhouse sometimes worked, and where the large glass showcase at the front of the store displayed bright-colored hard candies, chewing gum, cigars and snuff. On the floor nearby, in wooden kegs and barrels, were peanuts, crackers, sugar, flour and lard, sold by the pound, placed in a brown paper sack, and tied with a string, even the lard. "Those bags – saturated by the time we reached home – made the best fire starters," said Carrie. In the back of the store was the chopping block for the pork middlings that produced the sliced "streaked meat," or bacon, as well as the chunks of snow white salted "fat back" used to boil in vegetables for seasoning. Cut from a thick section of tree trunk (likely maple), the chopping block, about thirty inches across and very smooth, would be covered between uses with a white cloth.

Carrie missed, however, even more than the commissary, the Runion mill whistle, especially in the mornings, when it blew longer than it did at noon and at quitting time. The village now was quiet and lonely – feeling. "After the depot closed, too, there was only a handful of families left at Runion," Carrie remembered. Her father, Buck Landers, helped remove machinery and steel and "clean up the place." The bandsaw was sold to someone who set it up in Cleveland, South Carolina, and one of the old train engines was left sitting near the commissary for twenty years.[52]

Appearing in the *News-Record* during June and July, 1925, was the following item:

> Madison County Railway Company gives notice that June 8, 1925, it filed with ICC at Washington, D.C., its application for certificate that present and future public convenience and necessity permit the abandonment of the railroad which extends from a connection with the Southern Railway at or near the station of Runion, to Belva, a distance of 7 miles, all in Madison County, North Carolina.[53]

Stackhouse General Store scale used to weigh sugar, lard, nails, bacon and many other itmes.
Photo by John Newman.

As an old man, Nealie Price remembered that the Runion mill closing "depressed the people," who had practically no other choice of employment near their homes, "It had been there a long time and made jobs for a lot of people," said Price. "Elihu Helton, a foreman, was the last to leave," he added.[54] Gilbert Stackhouse also recalled the shut-down in later years, saying, "It would surprise you how quick the people got out of there when the mill closed down."[55]

In the Spring of 1926, another *News-Record* NOTICE from the Secretary of State carried the final detail – certification of dissolution of Griffith Lumber Company at Runion Station, Stackhouse Post Office, by unanimous vote of the stockholders, filed April 13, 1926.[56]

A few Runion workers went to Biltmore Lumber to work for Ernest Stackhouse, while others went to Carolina Wood Products at Woodfin, and a few went to the blanket factory at Swannanoa.[57] Bill and John Craigmile moved back to their home in Hot Springs to take odd jobs, while Chappell Norton ended up at Black Mountain working for Morgan Manufacturing Company. "He also brought several Waldroup boys with him from Runion," recalled his daughter, Jean, many years later.[58]

Writer Ronald Eller, in 1948, stated that after the Great War, the northern timber companies increasingly abandoned their southern mountain operations and turned to the unexploited woods in Oregon and Washington.[59] However, there were still a few bandsaw mills in western North Carolina. Blackwood Lumber Company, having built its mill, railroad, and village in Jackson County, began cutting by 1922. Likewise, in Graham County the Bemis Hardwood Lumber Company was organizing to begin sawing in 1927, and would operate, continuously, longer than any other North Carolina sawmill.[60] W.M. Ritter Company had operations in more than one county and was constantly buying up boundaries such as the 15,000 acres in Macon County on the Nantahala River, to be described in 1927 by an *Asheville Citizen* reporter:

> Macon County is considered fortunate in the big payroll the mill will furnish. But the county will lose natural beauty when this

region – the last big stand of virgin timber in the county – has been cut over. It will take decades of patient effort... to restore it.[61]

Eller also lamented over damage done to the Appalachians by the Shay locomotives, cableway skidders, logslides, river flumes and splash dams which destroyed stream beds and reproductive capacities of the land: "Great woods fires became almost a yearly phenomenon in the Blue Ridge, as lightning or sparks from machinery ignited sawdust and slash piles left by the loggers."[62]

In Madison County, back in 1912, much foresight had been shown by the respected Presbyterian missionary, Dr. W.E. Finley, who visited Runion as editor of the *News-Record*, writing a warning to Madison County residents two months later. Finley had talked to a man (likely Anson Betts) who said it would take ten years to cut off the timber which his company owned, "But when that is done what are the people of the county going to do?" wrote Finley. "We must do something if we are going to keep our people here."[63]

Now, with Runion's closing a decade after the barytes shut-down, Stackhouse reverses seemed to be the pattern. Not only were its hillsides bare of timber and scarred with ore dumps, adits and tram tracks, its hustle and bustle of boom days had all but ceased. Post-war continuity was giving way to change upon change within the Stackhouse family and community.

ENDNOTES FOR CHAPTER TWENTY

[1] *News-Record*, Marshall, N.C., January 17, 1919, p.3.
[2] Ibid., August 27, 1920, p.1.
[3] Madison County Board of Education Minutes, September 8, 1919.
[4] Madison County Death Register, p.49.
[5] Meek, Anna. Interview, August, 2001.
[6] *News-Record*, November 12, 1920.
[7] Cole, Carthene Stackhouse, letters to author, 1992.
[8] Ibid.
[9] Mizelle and Gwan. "History of Tobacco Control Progress," *Southern Extension Marketing Publication*, Raleigh: N.C. Agricultural Extension Service, September, 1979, p.3.
[10] Franklin, Phillip. Interview, October, 1999.
[11] Ibid
[12] Izlar, Sydney O. Interview, 2001.
[13] *News-Record*, May 7, 1920.
[14] U.S. Census Records, 1920.
    Betts, Horace. Interview, 1999.
[15] *News-Record*, May 7, 1920.
[16] Madison County Register of Deeds, Book 41, p.29.
[17] Ibid, Book 41, p.6.
[18] Izlar, Interview, 2000.
[19] *News-Record*, July 16, 1920.
[20] Madison County Book of Corporations, p.151.
[21] Madison County Register of Deeds, Book 41, p.417.
[22] Ibid., Book 44, p.211; Book 45, p.84.
[23] Madison County Book of Corporations, p.183.

[24] Price, Nealie. Interview, December, 1997.
U.S. Census Records, 1920.

[25] Waldrop, John Herbert. Interview, 1998.

[26] Fowler, Randy. Interview, November, 1998.

[27] Treadway, Kenneth. Interview, November, 1998.

[28] U.S. Census Records, 1920.

[29] Johnson, Carrie Landers. Interview, September, 1999.

[30] Ibid.

[31] *News-Record*, July 3, 1923.

[32] Author's private papers.

[33] Ibid.

[34] Meek, Anna Stackhouse. Interview, 1997.

[35] Cole. Interview, 1992.

[36] Aumiller, Nancy Stackhouse. Interview, 1997.

[37] Private papers.

[38] Ibid.

[39] *News-Record*, August 7, 21, 25, 1925.
Gennett, Andrew Jr. Interview, 1999.

[40] *News-Record*, February 10, 1922, p.1.

[41] Private papers.

[42] Meek, Anna Stackhouse. Interview, 2002.
News-Record, December 19, 1924.

[43] *News-Record*, February 2, 1923.

[44] Waldrop. Interview, 1998.

[45] *News-Record*, October 9, 1925.

[46] Ibid., January 2, 1925.

[47] Ibid., February 6, 1925.

[48] Ibid., November 20, 1925.

[49] Ibid., August 5, 1927.

[50] Price, Nealie. Interview, December, 1997.

[51] Johnson, Carrie Landers. Interview, September, 1999.

[52] Dockery, Clyde. Interview, 1999.

[53] *News-Record*, June 26, 1925.

[54] Price. Interview, December, 1997.

[55] Wolcott, Mary Ellen. "Stackhouse and Runion Community," *Asheville Citizen-Times*,
September 24, 1978, Sect. C., p.1.

[56] *News-Record*, April 20, 1926.

[57] Meek. Interview, 1999.

[58] Bailey, Jean Norton. Interview, August, 1999.

[59] Eller, Ronald D. *Miners, Millhands and Mountaineers*, Knoxville: U.T. Press, 1982, p.110.

[60] *Asheville Citizen-Times*, "Lumber Company Gets New Life," July 13, 1990.

[61] Ibid., June 20, 1927, p.12.

[62] Eller, p.110.

[63] *News-Record*, September 6, 1912.

Chapter Twenty-One

Even more noticeable at Stackhouse than the absence of industry was the regrettable loss of one of its oldest landmarks. In late February, 1925, about 4:30 one morning, the old frame house with wood-shingle roof, built nearly fifty years earlier by Amos' father, caught fire and burned to the ground. Anna Stackhouse Meek recounted later that she was not at home, but her parents told her about it.[1] Charles Dilworth and Clara and young Dilworth were in bed on the sleeping porch, which had a stove for winter. A noise wakened Clara and she "punched" her husband who listened, but heard nothing. As he turned over to go back to sleep, facing the window, he saw flames outside. Apparently, the fire had started over the kitchen.

All escaped safely, including Clara's two sisters, Margaret and Lucy, who were visiting at the time. Frank Hunycutt, living in one of Amos' rental houses, had started out to milk the cows when he saw flames and ran to help. Buck Landers, up at Runion, did the same, "jumping into his old Dodge car," as his daughter, Carrie, remembered much later.[2] Other neighbors came, forming a bucket brigade from the stand-pipe spigot used for washing in back of the house. Very little could be saved, except a few things from the first floor – the dining room table and chairs, three pieces of living room furniture, and a bookcase from the library. "One man dragged the piano out to the porch and broke one of its legs," recalled Anna Meek. When daylight came, there remained only three tall chimneys where the home of Charles Dilworth had stood. Clara's sisters went to Runion to stay with their brothers, George and Robert Phipps, while she and Dilworth moved into the three side rooms of the Stackhouse general store where Amos and Anna had started out half a century earlier.

Charles Dilworth Stackhouse crossing foot bridge over Woolsey branch at Stackhouse, c. 1923. Courtesy, Harvey Stackhouse.

The next afternoon, Charles Dilworth made his usual Friday automobile trip to Woodfin, to pick up his daughters, Anna and Helen, who were staying with their Grandmother Phipps to attend school – the five-month Stackhouse school having closed for the year in January. "That year when the hat was passed to the community, only eleven dollars was collected, and Daddy gave ten of that, but the teacher would not stay for that amount," said Anna Meek. Clara Stackhouse had arranged with her parents in Buncombe County that they should keep the girls during the school week, but they spent the weekends at home. "Daddy always stopped at Weaver College to pick up Gilbert,

This view of Stackhouse was marred in 1925 when the old first home (lower right foreground) burned. On hillside above is the long narrow ten-pin alley building; in center is home of Amos, Jr.; while lower left foreground shows Stackhouse general store with our buildings.

too, for the weekend," said Anna. Thus, Charles Dilworth had to break the horrible news to his nephew and to his daughters, within minutes of each other, that their beloved childhood home was gone, with practically all the girls' belongings. Gilbert had spent nearly as much time at his grandparents' house as he had at his own, next door. Although he could barely remember his Grandfather Amos, he had many fond memories of his Grandmother Anna and her companion, Teeny Thomas, and Christmases spent there. The old Stackhouse home had also held the last vestiges of that early Quaker influence.

In fact, Gilbert's dutiful, eighty-year-old uncle, Ellison, who had lived in the house himself for a brief time, and had visited his father and step-mother there many times, wrote a letter of concern to his nieces, Charles Dilworth's young daughters. From his new home in Salem, New Jersey, Ellison asked: "Have you room enough to live in the rooms at the end of the store?" Ellison told the girls a few things about Salem and his own children, using a steady, clear hand, before closing, "With love to you all."[3] This letter, no doubt, was one of the last written by Ellison, beloved first-born of the founder of Stackhouse, North Carolina. On May 29, 1925, a remorseful note in the small handbook of Amos, the lumber grader at Columbia, South Carolina, stated:

> "Brother Ellison died today... I am awful sorry to hear it. He was always good to me. I ought to have written him more often, but can't undo it now."[4]

Ellison Stackhouse at his home in Pennsylvania, c. 1920.

From Columbia, Amos sent a telegram to Laura Stackhouse extending his "heartfelt sympathy and regrets." Ellison was laid to rest in Stackhouse Burial Ground at Cardington, Pennsylvania, where his son, Ellison Dilworth, had been buried nineteen years earlier, to the day.[5]

Another Stackhouse loss came when Charles Dilworth, faced with the dwindling number of customers, and the need to rebuild his home, decided four months after the fire to move his family to Woodfin where he could get steady work at the Carolina Wood Products factory. He was likely encouraged by Clara since her brother, Frank, and her father already worked there. The Stackhouses rented a house recently vacated by Clara's parents when they moved into a larger one nearby – the whole situation not only pleasant for Clara, but also allowing school continuity for the children.[6]

Although born in Warm Springs, Charles Dilworth had no memory of any home but Stackhouse, with its unending hillsides, creeks and springs, its lovely vistas of the willful French Broad, and its friendly trainmen chugging by, practically within reach. How he would miss it all! Nevertheless, he became one more Madison Countian to leave the open farmstead for the confines of a factory, further depleting the community of prominent leadership. Besides serving as assistant postmaster and school committeeman, Charles Dilworth had maintained the one remaining point of commerce between Barnard and Hot Springs. "After we moved to Woodfin, Daddy tried renting out the store to first one, then another," said Anna Meek, "but they didn't last."[7]

The first one of these was Mr. Pinckney McDevitt, a school teacher who agreed to teach the Stackhouse school term while his wife ran the store and post office. Beginning in August, 1925, the McDevitts and their four children lived in the brick annex behind Hester's home. Much later, Edwin McDevitt recalled that he had been five at the time, "and we thought the Stackhouses were rich, in their big house."[8] His sister, Viola, remembered, however, the number of empty houses in the Stackhouse and Runion communities. "It seemed so desolate to me," she related, although the Runion depot, at least, had not yet closed. "They called it a flag station," stated Viola, "and we took my brother to Asheville once on the train to see a doctor, because he was very sick." Daily their mother prepared the outgoing mail sack and hung it up on the metal arm in front of Stackhouse store where the train man could grab it going by without the train's ever slowing. "But the incoming mail was just thrown off the train to land where it fell – on your head, if you happened in the way," Viola chuckled.[9]

Meanwhile, in Buncombe County, young Anna Stackhouse was trying to adjust to her new surroundings, although she missed her childhood home in Madison County and would carry fond memories throughout her life. "In the summer we always had cousins to visit, a week at a time," she reminisced in her old age. They played in the ice-cold creek or in the damp sand of the river's bank, molding "frog houses" over their hands. They loved to roll down the steep hill of the large lawn, and play on the swing that hung from the tall oak tree. "We always had a play house, too," she added. On rainy days they were allowed to play upstairs in the broad hallway, pushing each other up and down in the old wooden wheel chair which had belonged to her grandfather, Amos. "Daddy didn't mind how much noise we made," stated Anna.

Another treat was in following the unmistakable aroma of fresh-baked sugar cookies wafting up the hill from her uncle's house. "Aunt Hester made the best cookies, and we could smell them up at our house, so we'd go hang around until she gave us some," laughed Anna. Only one each, however, but they were large. Whenever they were in Hester's home, they were cautioned to "not touch anything." "Usually, though, we were just in the kitchen," remembered Anna.[10]

In the summers, ice cream came to Runion on Saturday afternoons by train from Newport and it was sold at the small "concession stand or shack" beside the depot. Everybody who could come up with a nickel met that train. "We used to try to carry some in the little cardboard boxes to the folks at home, but it melted before we could get there," Anna recalled.

During the school year, playmates for Anna and Helen came from the neighborhood and sometimes from Runion, where one of the company foremen – Will Parsons – had daughters their ages. (The Parsons lived in the big green house with the fancy fireplaces and living room balconies.) On Sundays the community children assembled at the Stackhouse school where "Mama and Uncle Amos conducted a Sunday School for us," said Anna. If there happened to be a preacher holding worship service at the Runion church, the Stackhouses walked up there on Sunday. When the Stackhouse school closed for the year, the Runion school would often begin its session, so that Anna and Helen attended both.[11]

After walking from either Stackhouse or Runion school to the store and post office where their mother worked, Anna and Helen were eager to get into the store's cracker barrel and round wooden cheese box for a snack. On nice days there would be a loafer or two on the store's porch, watching the trains pass and discussing any bit of news that had been brought by the upcountry mail carriers. Anna and Helen shared their day's events with Clara, perhaps reading for her from their upcoming lessons before heading up the steep hill to home where their Aunt Lucy minded baby Dilworth.

Another special memory was the occasional family trip to Asheville on the Carolina Special with its extra-plush upholstery, its Pullman and dining cars, and its interesting-looking travelers from faraway cities. "The Special didn't stop at Stackhouse or Runion," said Anna, "but we would ride #101, a local, at 7:20 in the morning to Hot Springs, eat breakfast at the café there, catch the Special to Asheville at nine, and come back home on #11 about four o'clock in the afternoon."[12]

Holidays, naturally, formed particularly fond reminiscences for Anna, who dressed up in homemade costumes with her sister for Halloween house-to-house "trick-or-treating." At Easter time her mother made their dresses, then boiled wheat and other natural materials to color their Easter eggs. "We had such a nice big yard to hide eggs in," said Anna. The Christmas tradition was her favorite, of course. The week before, there would be a program at the Runion church, since it was a little larger than the Stackhouse church. "The two churches went in together, but Miss Ola Boyd [a Dorland-Bell graduate], the Stackhouse teacher, was usually in charge," Anna explained. A play having many parts, learned and practiced for weeks; scripture reading and sermonette; and singing of Christmas hymns completed the program portion preceding the gifts presentation from the tree. The tree was always huge, with a small toy under it for each child and a brown paper "bag of treat," containing an orange or apple, nuts and candy for each person attending, regardless of age. The program was never advertised except through the children, but "Everybody came, no matter how far they had to walk or how bad the weather," concluded Anna.[13] This was the only observance of Christmas many of the area families could hope for.

Fortunately, at Anna's home there was always a Christmas tree decorated with tinsel, colored glass balls and other trinkets from the store. They hung their stockings on Christmas Eve at bedtime in great anticipation. Just before the children came into the living room on Christmas morning, Charles and Clara lit the many little candles in their tin holders attached to the tree limbs. "They blew them out after a short while, though," Anna reminisced. Although bringing a fairyland magic to the Stackhouse parlor, the beautiful flickerings posed a hazard as they burned closer to the conifer needles.

Anna and her sister usually received dolls, "made of china," and story books and puzzles. "One year little Dilworth got a tricycle," she said. Then, as in years past, when her grandmother was alive, the family gathered at the older Stackhouse home for the traditional dinner of turkey and dressing. "Mama always made pumpkin pies at Christmas, and Aunt Hester brought homemade rolls," Anna recalled. Occasionally some of Clara's relatives came, in addition to "Uncle Amos' family." "We had a large dining table and would move another table in to seat more," she added.

Even after Anna and her family moved to Buncombe County, Amos' family sometimes came for Christmas dinner. It was never held at Hester's house, but perhaps it was difficult for Charles' family to travel with children at Christmas time. The children did, however, accompany him back to Stackhouse sometimes on Sunday, when he not only visited his brother, but also checked on his farm and rentals. "At times we spent the night and stayed at Uncle Amos' house, but at others, we ate dinner and visited in the home of Sam Capps, a neighbor down there who looked after Daddy's place," stated Anna.

Quite often, though, Charles Dilworth came alone, staying at Amos' house.[14] He would tell Amos, no doubt, about his new job and the people who worked there. Named Asheville's largest industrial plant, Carolina Wood Products at Woodfin was also the state's largest manufacturer of bedroom and dining room furniture, ranking "about fifth in the whole world," according to the *Asheville-Citizen*.[15] Four hundred employees processed 7,500,000 feet of lumber annually. From kiln drying to cutting and building the "cases," to matching and gluing the veneer, to staining, rubbing and varnishing – usually with hand-sanding of each piece between steps – these four hundred workers did it all. Within two years after Charles Dilworth moved his family to Woodfin, the plant would add upholstering and two hundred employees. Soon Charles Dilworth was discussing with Amos property sites and house plans for his family of three growing children and three adults (Clara's widowed sister, Lucy Boydston, having come to live with them).

Additionally, Ernest Stackhouse had also settled in Buncombe County, on one of two Biltmore Village lots on All Souls' Crescent (bought in 1924 by his father-in-law, Hiram Vandervort).[16] Ernest built a brick house within walking distance of Biltmore Lumber Company (site of present-day Interiors Market Place), where Ernest and Hiram worked. Also in the same year, Ernest's brother-in-law, Ellsworth Vandervort, had purchased a lot in Biltmore Forest, a few miles from his parents. Finally, in August, 1925, Amos and Hester decided to buy a lot in Biltmore Forest at the corner of Hendersonville Road and Busbee, where they, too, planned to build a home.[17]

Biltmore Forest, lying against the side of George Vanderbilt's estate, set numerous restrictions into all its deeds, including Amos and Hester's. The property must be used solely for single-home residential purposes, be kept in good condition, and maintain general harmony with surrounding property. Owners could not permit any unsanitary, offensive or unsightly condition to develop, nor allow any nuisance to exist. The house itself must cost no less than $10,000, while the plans for any stable, garage or other detached structure should adhere to prescribed restrictions and meet the approval of the seller. Nor could the land or house be sold by the buyer to any person having any degree of Negro blood, or bad character.[18] To afford this house, of

A Sunday visit at Stackhouse, 1923. Left to right: Amos Stackhouse, "June" Stackhouse, Hester Stackhouse, Ernest Stackhouse, Hiram Vandervort, Carthene Stackhouse & Mrs. Vandervort.

course, Amos had to sell his home at Stackhouse. His reason for buying the lot, he stated, was that "We might as well move to Buncombe County with the rest of the family."[19]

Meanwhile, on Sunday, August 9th, Amos wrote in his notebook that he had been to see Hezekiah Davis of Doe Branch, "about his taking the post office – will let me know later." Davis must have declined, but the McDevitts were persuaded and the Inspector in Charge of post offices granted Amos a thirty-day annual leave of absence on September 4, 1925.[20] Perhaps he and Hester used it as a vacation, visiting the Stackhouse relatives up North.

As Hester and Amos contemplated moving to Biltmore, they must surely have considered the emotional pain of leaving their beloved home and heritage in Madison County, their relatives and friends, the graves of parents and infant son, even the landmark bearing their name; but, finally, they put their house on the market.

It is not known whether there were responding offers, but it was still unsold on June 1st, 1926, when Gilbert graduated from Weaver College's "Bookkeeping Course of Southwestern Publishing Company in Cincinnati." Forty-six others finished in the popular Business Class with Gilbert.[21] Rather than remain in Buncombe County where jobs were certainly more plentiful than in Madison, Gilbert Stackhouse returned home, taking whatever employment he could find. A good mechanic, he worked for an old family friend, Ben Wade Gahagan, a commercial contractor, and, at times, for Ben Wade's son, B.W., who operated a garage. Despite his new business certificate, Gilbert did not mind getting dirty when necessary. He was right at home working with boilers, pipes, machines and construction, having learned about them through his years helping Amos in Stackhouse, as well as in his job at Weaver College. "He could do anything at all with his hands, and fix anything that was broken," his daughter, Nancy, recalled later.[22]

One job he had was repairing and maintaining the boilers and machines of Buquo Lime Plant at Hot Springs: a messy, dirty, but satisfying job. In later years Gilbert enjoyed telling a story on himself about the time that his

1926 graduating Business Class at Weaver College. Gilbert Stackhouse, back row at right end.

automobile would not start at the end of the day, so he had to ride the train back to Stackhouse. His uncle, Will Reames (married to Hester's sister, Mae), happened to be the conductor, but Gilbert was so blackened with coal and oil that Will did not know him, and motioned him on to the colored car. When Gilbert teased, "Uncle Will, you would not make me ride with the Negroes, would you?" Will Reames recognized his nephew and laughed with Gilbert.[23] In the fall of 1926, Gilbert helped B.W. Gahagan remove the last of the equipment from Runion bandmill and store it at Amos' lumber yard near the Stackhouse rail siding. (Apparently Amos had made a deal with the Betts family to help them sell the salvage.) It was slow work because of frequent breakdowns along the river road. Back when automobiles and trucks had first come into serious use at Runion, a better road was needed from Stackhouse to Runion depot, prompting the building of a raised plank platform over the existing road between railroad and river. "It was like a bridge," recalled Juanita Stackhouse many years later, "because the dirt road along the river stayed muddy and washed out every time the river rose."[24] However, the decade or more of weather had taken its toll. As Gilbert drove across the old boards they began to break under the weight of the cargo, requiring delays for repairs.[25] When the task was finally finished, Amos Stackhouse became the agent, during the next two decades, for trading and selling LRLC residue for its owners.

The steel tracks of LRLC's railroad up Laurel River had also been removed and convict labor gangs brought from Ivy River to build #208, a new highway on the bed of the former Runion train route, connecting to Greeneville, Tennessee. "The grade will be about two percent," stated the *News-Record*, "instead of crossing over some of the high mountains which the present route crosses."[26]

This road, paralleling and even cutting through a portion of the former LRLC logging tracts, could have been a boon to E.W. Grove, but, before it was completed, he died in January 1927. Many of his projects in Buncombe County would be continued by his executors, but the Grove interests in Hot Springs and Laurel, for the most part, stopped growing with his death. In December 1928, Edwin W. Grove, Jr., and Edgar Betts sold 1,675 acres known as "the half-mile strip" to the United States government, to become part of Pisgah National Forest (begun in 1911 as part of the government's new conservation plan).[27] Evidently, Grove had not paid Betts fully for the land, since both men signed as owners.

Edgar's brother, Anson, had also become involved with another Madison County business – barytes mining on highway #209, just south of Hot Springs, although no records show the full extent of his participation. Herbert Waldrup recalled in a 1996 interview that "Betts was grinding rock above Hot Springs in the twenties," while Floyd Waldrop (born in 1918) said that when he was small, his father had worked at the Bluff mine, and "Anson Betts was the supervisor."[28] The *News-Record* of February 10, 1922, stated: "A barytes grinding and mining operation was situated on Spring Creek a few miles upstream from Lance dam and saw mill." Anson was mining the old Noah Waldroup workings at Bluff, hauling the ore to the Hot Springs mill by wagon, since the road was too rough for automobiles. While this deposit did not yield large amounts of ore for Betts, it had been one of the largest in earlier years, when the Warm Springs mill was operating. It was this Bluff deposit, no doubt, that offered the first reported barite in North Carolina by discoverer William Maclure in 1918.[29]

The North Carolina Geological and Economic Survey listed two barytes producers from Madison County in 1925 – Ben W. Gahagan at Stackhouse and Charles B. Mashburn at Hot Springs. Since Mashburn lived at Marshall, it is possible that the Hot Springs reference meant he was a partner with Betts in the Bluff mine and the processing mill on Spring Creek. John Harrison, the Doe Branch miner, also probably worked closely with Betts, as he did with Henry Moore over in Sweetwater and Del Rio, Tennessee, and with Tom Frisbee, a Hot Springs merchant who mined barytes at times. (In 1920 Anson Betts had bought the mineral rights to a hundred-acre tract "on the waters of Doe Branch and the French Broad River, opposite Sandy Bottom,"[30] from John Harrison, this being a portion of the entire barite zone labeled by geologists the "Hot Springs area.") Unfortunately, John Harrison was found dead in his bed of an apparent heart attack on March 20, 1926, at age sixty-four, ending a long life of prospecting and mining development.[31] Few men would amass the amount of information about Madison County minerals and mining that Harrison had. Although probably coincidental, according to an article in 1933 by Jasper L. Stuckey, prominent North Carolina geologist, "barite production in the state practically ceased in 1926."[32]

An earlier Geological Survey paper, summarizing the barite activity for the years 1918 through 1923, gave only two producers for the whole state in 1923, both at Stackhouse: "B.W. Gahagan, post office, Stackhouse, and Rollins Chemical Corporation, post office, New York City."[33] During 1921, 1922 and 1923, Col. James J. Riley, owner and president of Rollins Chemical Corporation, hoped, no doubt, to find another mother lode as had Henry Moore, but after tunneling in from King Creek to the old Klondyke, he soon gave up his lease on Amos' and Charles Dilworth's property. Nor did he try to extract ore from Betts' Sandy Bottom mines, some of which had been worked out in 1916, others having caved in years before. Riley mined on Mashburn and Gahagan lands at only one level, two hundred feet on the downslope, then out one hundred feet in one direction and four hundred feet in another, never deep enough to hit groundwater. On mining plats, his workings were labeled "the Riley mine."[34]

Anson Betts did not receive the returns from his barite mining that he had hoped for, prompting him to offer, in 1923, his Sandy Bottom property either for lease or sale, albeit unsuccessfully. However, while searching, apparently, for a way to separate lead from barite ore, he received a patent on April 14, 1925, for his "Betts process – an alternate separation of bismuth involving electrolytic refining of lead bullion," according to the Encyclopedia Britannica. Although he did not live in Madison County, Anson Betts would maintain an interest in the barite of the "Hot Springs area" and continue to have a presence in the Stackhouse community for many years.

The post-war continuity of life at Stackhouse was broken in other aspects as the "roarin' twenties" began to close. On May 14, 1926, the *News-Record* carried a notice that Amos Stackhouse, Jr., was ordered to appear in Superior court at the Marshall courthouse.[35] According to the item, Amos' son, June, had borrowed money from Jack Rice of Laurel and was unable to pay it back. The outcome is only conjecture, but since June had few possessions, except perhaps an automobile, Amos and Hester likely assumed his debt.

Not only had June's farming profits dropped with tobacco prices, but the tan bark market for leather producing had diminished because of the chestnut blight, the popularity of the automobile, and the introduction of synthetic fabrics.[36] Having exhausted his business ideas for Stackhouse, and having fallen into debt, June became yet another Stackhouse to leave home in search of employment. By December, 1926, he had entered the United States Coast Guard at Hampton, Virginia, no doubt recalling his childhood visit to the Jamestown Exposition ships at the same site.[37] His parents would, as during World War I, receive a military allotment from June's paycheck.

He faithfully wrote his mother nearly every weekend, feeling, as during the war, the military man's loneliness, and urging his family members to write to him. Hester, in turn, sent him news from home and sometimes shared letters from Ernest's family. She and Amos relinquished, finally, their dream of having the generations continue at Stackhouse under a successive "Amos." Moreover, June Stackhouse would subsequently be home only for brief visits, spending the majority of his remaining years in

FOR REPRESENTATIVE

TO THE REPUBLICAN VOTERS
OF MADISON COUNTY.

A member of the General Assembly from a county is one of the most important officers a county can have, and this year it will be more important than ever that Madison County send a strong man to the Legislature, one who knows the needs of the county, and has had experience, and is in harmony with the best and most progressive people of the county.

The State of North Carolina is spending great sums of money in the building of roads and highways, and the only way we can get our share of the highway developments and other things is to send a good man to The General Assembly, and one who will work in harmony with the people of his county.

We feel that Honorable John A. Hendricks is the man we need as he is a public spirited man and is willing to sacrifice his time for the people of the county.

We, the undersigned, feel that it will be to the best interest of Madison County to nominate Honorable John A. Hendricks for this office, and we hereby respectfully present his name as a candidate for the office of Representative in the General Assembly, subject to the approval of the voters of the county.

FRANK RANDALL,	G. B. ROBERTS,
M. B. WORLEY,	J. F. BLACK,
G. A. PLEMMONS,	ELBERT BARRETT,
W. E. KING,	J. P. EDWARDS,
FRANK ROBERTS,	E. E. TWEED,
S. B. ROBERTS,	A. W. WHITEHURST,
JETER RAMSEY,	O. W. DEAVER
A. GUNTER,	T. A. HIGGINS,
Big Laurel, N. C.	R. F. D., Mars Hill, N. C.
G. E. FARMER,	W. R. BARRETT,
Little Pine, N. C.	Mars Hill, N. C.
G. L. McKINNEY,	O. V. ENGLISH,
Walnut, N. C.	Faust, N. C.
REV. P. T. McFEE,	SIM CHANDLEY,
Hot Springs, N. C.	Mars Hill, N. C.
	W. C. ENGLISH,
AMOS STACKHOUSE,	Mars Hill, N. C.
JOHN JOHNSON,	AMOS STACKHOUSE, Jr.,
ELMER TREADWAY,	ROBERT NORTON,
MRS. A. STACKHOUSE.	M. H. BECK,
	MRS. M. H. BECK

Coincidentally, the May 14, 1926, *News-Record* also carried June Stackhouse's name, along with his parents' in an endorsement for a political candidate.

military service. One particular letter to Hester in 1927 was a request for a loan of $60 for "Chief's" clothes, "as I've passed the examinations and have been notified to that effect, so I will get first vacancy." June also told her, "Capt. Wilson is very good to me and said he could arrange for me to spend from Nov. 28th to Dec. 22nd in the Winton factory at Cleveland, Ohio." June thought this experience – at a cost of $200 – would be valuable to his career and worthwhile financially in the long run. "Do you think you could do without the allotment for Oct. & Nov. for me to do this?" he asked. "Write me what you think, at once, so he can make the arrangements for me," concluded June. His new rank would be "Chief Motor Machinist Mate," and would lead to the position of instructor in mathematics – his field of excellence from school days.[38]

Coast Gaurd instructor June Stackhouse, 1930s. One of June's pupils was the show business personality Arthur Godfrey. Courtesy, Clara S. Radin.

Another new title for June Stackhouse – that of husband – came from his meeting Ann Hoffman, Hampton native and sister of one of his Coast Guard mates. Four years younger than he, Ann married June at Norfolk on October 6, 1928.

In the meantime, June's home place at Stackhouse had almost been sold to a group of developers from Miami, Florida. Negotiations began in late 1926 through a proposal, likely composed and typed by Gilbert, since he had finished business college a few months earlier. Because of Amos' absence, Hester and Gilbert were handling the deal, corresponding about details with both Amos in South Carolina and the men in Florida.

The extant unsigned carbon copy of the proposal referred to a recent visit to Stackhouse by "Mr. Chambers of Miami." This document described the entire holdings of both Amos and Charles Dilworth, reserving, however, twenty-five of Amos' original 350 acres from his father, saying, "I have often heard my father remark that he would like to come back and spend a while each summer 'mid old scenes.'"[39] One particular section about Amos' farm follows

> The railroad side track I was telling you about is on this property... and the barytes mill building too, but about ten feet of the upper end which is on the Ellison Stackhouse tract... All of my father's interest in the water rights in the river is included, which is a one-half interest in about 4000 horse power. There being also about two dozen fine apple trees bearing every year, four

creeks, eighteen springs… about 200,000 feet of pine and oak timber, about 4000 cords of firewood, ten tenant houses, a school within five minutes walk, postoffice at the edge of the lawn. His sale price for the above property, including the residence… is $52,000, terms, cash balance 1, 2, and 3 years. (Residence site also includes a large brick building behind, chicken yards, orchard and garden.)

Room by room he listed the large sizes, grand materials and other special features of Hester's house, excepting the kitchen range – Majestic Brand – as well as all other household furnishings. Separate pages of the real estate offer outlined two more Stackhouse properties which were owned jointly by Amos and Charles Dilworth: the 56-acre Klondyke mine tract and the 65-acre Ellison Stackhouse tract. Ellison's former homestead contained his house (six rooms, bath and two porches) with gravity water lines and two smaller residences, plus heavily-bearing apple orchard, at a price of $6000. "This would make an excellent town site, as the land is rolling and the view unexcelled in every direction," stated Gilbert. About the Anna Myers Stackhouse property owned by Amos and Charles, he declared:

This 56-acre tract had the famous Klondyke barytes mine that contains several thousand tons of ore… there being one stump of ore 16'3" thick, 40' high and 100' long and contains about 200 car loads of ore. With very little repair on the roads these mines can be reached by truck as they are about a mile from the railroad. There is plenty timber on this property for all mining purposes. Our price on this tract in $10,000, terms same as other.

Moreover, Gilbert set forth that the 350 acres belonging to his uncle Charles Dilworth Stackhouse were for sale, and, if a dam were built thereon, would give a 20-acre lake site right on the road and not over three minutes' walk from the remaining Stackhouse residence. "If you are interested, let me know at once, as several other parties are talking to my uncle about it now," he pointed out. In conclusion, Gilbert noted that there were no debts, mortgages or other encumbrances against any of the different tracts listed.[40]

Unfortunately, that statement did not hold true for long, a result of Charles Dilworth's purchasing a lot on Dorchester Avenue in West Asheville in January, 1926, for $1175.[41] His job was steady at Carolina Wood Products where business had rapidly increased, but it was not adequate to pay for a new home as well as day-to-day living expenses. He was forced to borrow nearly $6000, securing the loan with 250 acres at Stackhouse which included the store, post office and burned house site.[42]

He hired his brother to build his house, although it is not clear whether Amos received permission from his employer, Taylor, to miss work, or whether there was a lull in his grading business, actually putting Amos out of work. For whatever reason, there were obvious advantages for Charles in dealing with his brother. He could trust Amos to cut no corners; Amos could get lumber at a savings through Biltmore Lumber Company; and, Charles could save labor costs by helping Amos during after-hours from his own job at Carolina Wood Products. "Uncle Amos stayed with us at Woodfin while he was building our house," remembered Anna Stackhouse Meek years later.[43]

After having lived in West Asheville only a short time, however, Charles Dilworth and Clara were required to turn house and lot over to the bank and move back to Woodfin – a devastating blow, marking the second loss of their home in as many years. Furthermore, according to family members, Charles suffered losses from stock investments, a sign of the period leading to the historic market failure. In fact, on September 23, 1929, the Madison County superior court ordered the rest of Charles Dilworth's property to be sold at public auction to satisfy his indebtedness.[44] This meant that he would lose ownership in the 56-acre Klondyke tract and in the 65-acre Ellison Stackhouse tract, leaving Amos in partnership with someone other than a Stackhouse descendent, a possibility that had worried his parents back in 1904 as Charles prepared to go out West. From the auction block, at the low sum of $400, Citizen Bank of Marshall bought half interest in these two important pieces of Stackhouse property.[45] (The store building and surrounding 250 acres were already under lien to the Bank of French Broad for Charles' previous notes.)

Perhaps Amos had attended the auction but could not raise the Citizen Bank's final bid. He now had annual property tax to pay on his new Biltmore Forest lot in addition to the over 300 acres and the buildings at Stackhouse; moreover, the Miami group had declined his sales proposal. If Amos and Charles Dilworth were having financial troubles, it would be only one month until the rest of the nation joined them, the "crash of '29" plunging all into a black abyss of painful poverty, and bringing even greater change to Stackhouse, North Carolina.

ENDNOTES FOR CHAPTER TWENTY-ONE

[1] Meek, Anna Stackhouse. Interview, 1999.
[2] Johnson, Carrie Landers. Interview, September, 1999.
[3] Author's private papers.
[4] Ibid.
[5] Swayne, Norman Walton. *Byberry Waltons, An Account of Four English Brothers.* Decorah, Iowa: Anundsen Publishing Co., 1989, reprint, p.489.
[6] Meek, Anna Stackhouse. Interview, 1999.
[7] Ibid.
[8] McDevitt, Edwin. Interview, May, 2002.
[9] Ramsey, Viola McDevitt. Interview, May, 2002.
[10] Meek, Interview, 2002.
[11] Ibid., 1999.
[12] Ibid., 2001.
[13] Ibid.
[14] Ibid.
[15] Cope, James. "Factory Equipped to Produce $3,000,000 Worth of Furniture Annually." *Asheville Citizen*, January 6, 1924.
[16] Buncombe County Register of Deeds, Book 280, p.305; Bk. 283, p.263.
[17] Ibid., Book 312, p.121.
[18] Ibid.
[19] Aumiller, Nancy Stackhouse. Interview, April, 1998.
[20] Private papers.
[21] *The Mountaineer for 1926*, Weaverville, N.C.: Senior Class of Weaver College, 1926, p.55.
[22] Aumiller, Nancy Stackhouse. Interview, April, 1998.
[23] Ibid., February, 2002.
[24] Stackhouse, Juanita C. Interview, 1999.

[25] Ibid.
[26] *News-Record*, Marshall, N.C., January 8, 1926.
[27] Madison County Register of Deeds, Book 54, p.199.
[28] Waldrop, Floyd. Interview, 2002.
[29] Stuckey, Jasper L. *North Carolina, Its Geology and Mineral Resources*, Raleigh: N.C. Dept. of Conservation & Development, 1965, p.365.
[30] Madison County Register of Deeds, Book 39, p.563.
[31] Madison County Death Register, No. 111.
[32] Stuckey, Jasper L. and Harry T. Davis. *Barite Deposits in North Carolina.* New York: American Institute of Mining and Metallurgical Engineering, February, 1933, p.1.
[33] Mineral Industry of North Carolina from 1918 to 1923. Raleigh: N.C. Geological & Economic Survey, 1925, p.43.
[34] Ibid., p.42.
[35] *News-Record*, May 14, 1926, p.8.
[36] Eller, Ronald. *Miners, Millhands and Mountaineers.* Knoxville: U.T. Press, 1982, p.122.
[37] Interview, Clara Hester Stackhouse Radin, 1998.
[38] Private papers.
[39] Ibid.
[40] Ibid.
[41] Buncombe County Register of Deeds, Book 329, p.245.
[42] Ibid., Book 386, p.242.
[43] Meek, Interview, 2002.
[44] Madison County Register of Deeds, Book 54, p.91.
[45] Ibid.

Amos "June" Stackhouse Jr., U.S. Coast Guard.

Chapter Twenty-Two

The beginning of 1930 in western North Carolina held nothing of the promise of the previous decade. In fact, not since Civil War days had the mountaineers felt as down-trodden. For those who had never known anything but poverty, it was not only more of the same, but a deeper misery, touching even their few well-off neighbors.

As a result of the 1929 stock market crash, five of Asheville's nine banks closed their doors, including Central Bank and Trust which held eight million dollars in city and county funds on deposit. Many factories and businesses ceased operations throughout western North Carolina. Impoverishment, personal tragedies and suicides by prominent men followed, throwing suspicion on the death of Madison Countian Bessie Rumbough Safford – daughter of the late James H. Rumbough of Hot Springs and former daughter-in-law of President Andrew Johnson, as well as long time friend of the Stackhouse family. According to newspapers, on January 9, 1930, ten weeks after the crash, Mrs. Safford was visiting friends in Tallahassee, Florida, when she was asphyxiated in the bathtub as she prepared to attend a party.[1] She was unfamiliar with the gas heater, explained her family, and probably lighted it improperly, causing a malfunction. Confusing the issue, the year before, she had made a will giving all her Hot Springs resort properties, her home (with a life estate), and other real property to the Jesuit Order of the Catholic Church.[2] Loss of this important tourist attraction would have further impact upon Madison County's economy. The poor around Hot Springs would also feel the loss, especially now, of the charity bestowed by Safford. At Christmas she had always ordered her cook to bake dozens of cookies and cakes for distribution to needy families and those in jail. "She brought us her canned blackberry juice when we all had dysentery – a really good woman," recalled Ora H. Burgin, one of ten children, many years later.[3]

In September, 1932, another prominent citizen, Thomas Frisbee, was killed at his Hot Springs home, "When a shotgun accidentally discharged as he prepared to go to Marshall," stated the *Asheville Citizen*. The word about town was "suicide."[4] Not quite two years later, Jean Garrett Ellerson, Dorland-Bell School librarian, and former Runion school teacher, shot herself at her Hot Springs home. She was the daughter of the Stackhouses' former Warm Springs neighbor, Thomas Garrett, and great granddaughter of Warm Springs founder, William Neilson. She was also the widow of William Ellerson, agent and close friend of Edwin W. Grove.[5]

Moreover, as the automobile plants shut down in Michigan, many Madison Countians who had worked there returned home to their farms, only to find that crop prices had dropped so low that some lost their farms altogether. Hobos filled empty cars on freight trains while other transients walked the highway, stopping at kitchen doors to offer wood chopping or garden work in exchange for a meal.[6]

The Presbyterian Board of National Missions in New York was forced to close the Laurel Hospital at White Rock in 1932, leaving the Laurel country, where some dangerous logging still took place, with no emergency medical service.[7] This hospital – the long-awaited dream of Frances Goodrich, fulfilled in 1919 – was Madison County's only such facility, and had a staff of ten. Its closing surely grieved the employees, the community, and the seventy-six-year-old Goodrich, who had tirelessly raised funds from her Northern acquaintances such as Francis R. Bellamy, Christian socialist and author of our "Pledge of Allegiance to the Flag." About 1920 the New-York-born minister and writer had visited the Laurel community, getting off the train at Stackhouse or Runion before continuing on horseback to White Rock. He afterwards wrote:

> I rode up a narrow trail in the North Carolina mountains some twenty miles from the nearest railroad. The road had been dwindling as it took its way over ridge after ridge, followed by stream after stream, crossed bridge after bridge, and climbed steadily toward the land of the sky. About us for hours had been only the precipitous landscape of the mountains; rocky creeks and steep hills, soft, weatherbeaten log cabins set along water courses that scarred the wooded slopes, a changing view of forest and sky.*

> And then abruptly we rounded a shoulder of the hills and stretched out before us, shimmering in the late afternoon sunlight, lay an open valley in whose center stood a large modern building. Beyond, as behind, stretches a wilderness. But in the valley stood the surprising building, accompanied by a couple of modern houses and an up-to-date white schoolhouse with a steeple.

> I stared. 'Who ever dragged all this material up here and built this place? And why,' I inquired. 'That's Laurel Hospital,' said my guide.[8]

Commenting in 1931 on Bellamy's lovely prose, another mission worker wrote:

> Mr. Bellamy took this trip over a decade ago. Now a modern automobile road takes the visitor up the mountains. The surrounding 'wilderness' is much the same. Considerable lumber has been cut from these mountains and no reforestation has been done. A beautiful new steam-heated, stone high school building has been built which will accommodate two hundred and fifty students.[9]

While the new school was a mark of pride for the Laurelites, there were half a dozen others in the county, but no other hospital. (In Hot Springs Dr. David Kimberly could keep two or three patients in his small facility.) The hospital's closing, besides the functional loss, brought a lowering of morale to add to the rest of the region's woes during this time.

Furthermore, Carolina Wood Products at Woodfin, where several former Runion employees worked, closed, as did Biltmore Lumber Company, leaving Charles Dilworth and Ernest Stackhouse without jobs.[10] (Years later, Charles Dilworth's son, Dilworth, would recall how, as a youngster, he had received toys one Christmas, and the next, a set of long underwear – the blow was so sudden.) Madison County banks, too, failed, except one – Citizen's in Marshall, with a branch at Hot Springs.[11]

*Those of us with roots deep in Madison County's fastness often forget the picturesqueness of our southern Appalachians until reminded by a silver-tongued Northerner.

One of Marshall's newspapers, the *Madison County Times*, went under in 1934, and was acquired by the *News-Record*, which, by eliminating competition, managed to stay afloat.

The response of Western North Carolina to the Great Depression was as varied as the classes of its inhabitants. George Vanderbilt's family, no less, began selling tickets to visitors in March, 1930, allowing tours of the famous castle and grounds. Not only did it defray the tremendous upkeep expense, but it promoted the tourist trade for a desperate Buncombe County and would slowly radiate to adjoining counties. About the only industry still operating – albeit on a reduced scale – was tourism; the beautiful Blue Ridge had not lost its appeal.[12]

Taking advantage of tobacco's importance as a commodity, even to a depressed nation, Asheville established the Burley Tobacco Market in late 1930, which would aid western North Carolina farmers for years to come. Fost. A. Sondley had written earlier in his 1930 history of Buncombe County:

> Madison County now has the largest tobacco crop of any in Western North Carolina. With 32,357 acres under cultivation, 1,791,000 pounds were produced last year, bringing a return of $340,351, but almost all of this tobacco was sold on the Tennessee market.[13]

Sondley thought that a Burley market in Asheville would be well supported by the western counties.

In these depression days, the average mountaineers relied on methods of survival employed by their grandparents in early times. They kept bees and sold honey; they tediously picked huckleberries, dewberries, blackberries, muscadines and other wild fruits; they gathered, dried, hulled, and cracked out the meats of black walnuts and hazel nuts; they harvested ginseng, solomon's seal, and other medicinal herbs; they picked fresh greens of branch lettuce, watercress, and poke weed in the spring time, switching to galax leaves, holly berries and mistletoe in the fall – peddling all on foot. At holiday time, it was not unusual, when answering a knock on the kitchen door, to hear the plea, "Christmas cheer?" accompanied by a basketful of natural reds and greens. For those who lived along the main roads, a display of their wares – apples, cherries, plums, pears, pumpkins, green beans, tomatoes and others – resulted in sales to passing tourists, while the farmers' wives proffered handmade quilts, crocheted bedspreads, hooked rugs, chair mats and loom-woven handbags with a varnished slice of black walnut shell for a button closer.

Martha Davis Treadway, who lived on Mill Ridge above Runion, could recall years afterwards that her father sold honey and garden produce down in Hot Springs, walking the several miles of mountain trail down and up again. She remembered that her family sometimes ate opossums that her father killed, and "They were pretty good meat, after we boiled them first, then baked them with sweet potatoes around them."[14]

Gilbert Stackhouse, too, sometimes hunted squirrels or rabbits, which were cooked much as chicken, with gravy and hot biscuits. He secured a trot line at each side of the river, catching many fish at a time. He made a large vegetable garden, planting enough for his family's needs, plus some to share with those who had none, "So no one has to steal," he always said.[15]

Stokely's Cannery at Newport would also buy vegetables from the larger-scale farmers who could raise sufficient quantities. "We sold cabbage to them for six dollars a ton," recalled Reeves Church of Hot Springs, who, as a boy, had helped his father, Dennis, a farmer and merchant.[16]

In some respects the mountain people fared better than their city counterparts because many had a garden plot, cow, pigs, mule and chickens, plus access to streams for fishing, and woods for hunting and trapping. "We always had something to eat, but there was absolutely no money for anything," Reeves Church recalled.[17]

For a few in western North Carolina, who had extra wooded property, the federal government offered a market. An amendment to the Weeks Law in 1924 had authorized buying land for the purpose of producing timber. "Unlimited New Deal funds and distressed landowners made possible the acquisition of lands at very low prices in practically all forested sections of the region," stated Percy J. Paxton, a later Forest Service historian.[18] Unable to turn down the cash, Monroe Sawyer of nearby Mill Ridge, for example, sold thirty-eight acres to Pisgah National Forest for $258.[19] Likewise, the Nantahala National Forest gained 13,055 acres in Graham County from the Gennett Lumber Co. family (who logged on Laurel, and who would soon have business with Gilbert). This virgin land brought the Gennetts $28 per acre, rather than the three or four dollars per acre being paid for some other lands.[20] In a 2003 interview, Andrew Gennett, Jr., explained about his father's need to sell the valuable tracts: "In the thirties, lumber was worth nothing."[21] (While most of Gennett's untouched pristine acres would be logged, the area around Little Santeetlah Creek was spared for the awe-inspiring Joyce Kilmer Memorial Forest.)

In Hot Springs the Rumbough heirs received $18 per acre from Pisgah National Forest for over thirty-six valuable acres (some having improvements) within city limits at the southwestern edge of town, further restricting the hamlet's growth.[22]

There were those, of course, who had never owned land, or had lost their land and home to creditors, and who had no means to buy seeds or fertilizer or tools, who owned no draft animals, cow, or pigs. The only way for these people to live was to bind themselves to a better-off farmer who could allow them to occupy a crude house on his place and to sharecrop. By planting, hoeing, and harvesting a crop for the owner, the workers received a portion of the product, giving them corn or potatoes to eat, but rarely any cash.

"It was awful," recalled long-time Madison County resident Lora Thomas, whose father had died in 1930. "You couldn't get a job nowhere; it was just 'over the washboard,'" she added.[23] This phrase referred to doing laundry for those more fortunate who could pay a few cents for this heavy task of carrying and heating water, then rubbing the soiled garments, towels and bed linens over a wooden washboard, using harsh lye soap, bluing, and starch, before wringing, wringing, wringing the pieces in one's hands to extract as much water as possible in order to hang them to dry. If the clothesline happened to break or an extra strong wind blew the sheets off into the dirt, the task had to be done over. Wash day could not be scheduled or controlled since it was totally dependent upon good weather. However, it was one way to earn a bit of money or to receive milk, produce and other items as pay.

One source of help for some poor mountain families came from the North through local missionaries. The Presbyterians distributed freight barrels of good used clothing as well as Christmas toys for the communities' children. The Roman Catholics did the same. School teachers tried to keep a few garments in their supply closets at the back of the classrooms for pupils who came to school from the worst of circumstances-ill-clad, cold, hungry and often needing medical treatment. Sometimes a teacher shared her own meager lunch in private with a destitute child. Store merchants across western North Carolina aided starving families as much as possible by extending credit, while druggists often released medicines in life or death situations, even though they suspected they might never get their money. A Jackson County historian quoted in an interview of a former merchant fifty years later: "Many a time I let a person have a sack of flour, knowing full well I would never be paid, but a family had to be fed."[24]

In addition, even those flour sacks, when emptied, were used to make shirts and dresses, towels and sheets by those who could not buy cloth. Hand-me-down clothing, no matter how ill-fitting, was an accepted fact in families at all levels during the depression. If shoes could be had, they usually covered bare feet; only a few people had socks. From May to November, children wore no shoes at all, and some adults went barefoot, too, especially at home. Nothing was discarded which someone didn't come along to claim. People who raised their own hogs often said, "We used every part of the swine but the squeal." Even from the inedible parts lard was rendered and soap was made.

Around Stackhouse, a few people who had no heat in their homes made stoves out of discarded metal barrels set upon old bricks. At Runion, the twenty-year-old row houses began to disappear as materials were taken for fuel.[25] Customary to looking to the family on the hill for livelihood, several neighbors and friends borrowed money from Amos, who signed notes that soon proved worthless. Finally, Amos, too, worn down by the hard times, had little to offer except the few jobs on the farm that paid five cents an hour for a ten-hour day. He despaired to watch his community suffer, feeling helpless, but responsible, nevertheless.

Anson Betts, also having no money to rent a house, or else having leased his home to others for the cash, moved his family to Runion into one of the few remaining officials' houses. Perhaps he worked for his brother as caretaker of the place, farming the ten or twelve acres which had always been cultivated apart from the bandmill location.

Ernest Stackhouse, furthermore, moved his family back to Stackhouse, living in the brick annex two-room apartment in back of Amos' home. His parents-in-law, Mr. and Mrs. Vandervort, who lived with them, rented their Biltmore Forest home to summer tourists, using the money to live on at Stackhouse.[26] Here, Ernest knew he could at least feed his own while he rode out the bad times, as long as his father held onto his land.

Apparently, afraid of losing her home when Amos' French Broad Bank went under, Hester Stackhouse, a Citizen's Bank patron, paid Amos $1905 to have their home, plus two and an eighth acres, deeded to her,[27] as well as 120 acres of the land Amos' parents had sold him in 1900, for which Hester paid $740. How she had amassed her savings is not clear. Perhaps she had deposited some of June's military allotment, or Amos' tenant house rents, or money she made as a seamstress before marriage; she had always been industrious and thrifty. One particular sum had come in May 1929 from the sale of her inherited interest in her parents' Walnut home, to her brothers, Lloyd and Frank, for which she received $150.[28] (Rachel Gilbert Honeycutt, Hester's mother, had died three months before.)

Meanwhile, Amos' brother, Charles Dilworth, in Woodfin, performed odd jobs such as mowing yards, and his wife, Clara, took in boarders to make ends meet.[29] He continued to visit his brother on Sundays whenever he could afford to.

With fewer citizens able to pay taxes, the counties and towns of North Carolina could not maintain their roads. Therefore, in 1931, the state assumed control of the entire highway system, initiating improvements to Number 20 from Hot Springs to Marshall which would include a hard tar surface for the first time. Since gasoline and automobile taxes had declined less than others, the road system fared better than most state services.[30] Gilbert Stackhouse, knowledgeable mechanic, received a job operating a steam shovel to dig river sand used in the road work. Thus he would remember this period with more fondness than the average man because it gave him the wherewithal to take a wife – Katherine Juanita Caldwell, or "Nita," from Mecklenburg County.

In 1929, as a senior at the Asheville Normal College, Nita had traveled with the school's Glee Club to the Walnut Presbyterian Church to present a

In Sunday suit, Gilbert Stackhouse poses on the steam shovel he operated during the work week.

Asheville Normal School's Glee Club in 1929. Juanita Caldwell (Stackhouse), first at left, back row.

program. In her part as the reader, she was noticed by some of the community leaders who needed a seventh grade teacher for the Walnut public school. On Monday, after the Glee Club's Friday return to Asheville, Nita was asked to take the teaching position upon graduation, which she accepted at once, glad to have a job.[31] (Many of her Asheville Normal classmates had already been forced to leave school, because their fathers had become unemployed.) Nita rented a room in Walnut's one hotel, the former dormitory of Bell Institute. It had been sold in 1919 by the Presbyterian Board of National Missions to Samuel R. Freeborn, a Walnut merchant who opened the large building as Hotel Switzerland. On January 1, 1926, Freeborn sold the hotel to Mrs. Frances Locke and son, Edwin, from Florida, who were the proprietors in 1929.[32]

Three other teachers lived there, one of whom (Dorothy Roberts, a Dorland-Bell graduate) was a Madison County native and acquainted with Gilbert Stackhouse. On a warm evening, as Nita Caldwell and the three other teachers sat on the tall flight of entry steps, Gilbert came to meet the hotel manager, a Mr. Sugart, who was interested in barite mining. Dorothy introduced Gilbert to Nita, and in a few days he was back, inviting the girls to ride to Hot Springs in his Ford automobile. "That was the beginning of our courtship," Nita related many years afterwards.[33]

Hotel Switzerland, Walnut, N.C. Front steps at left where Gilbert and Juanita Stackhouse first met in 1929.

Coming from the more affluent Piedmont section of the state, with its educational advantages, Nita had also graduated from a good lower school in 1925 – Albemarle Normal and Industrial Institute. The additional four years of college at Asheville Normal gave her superior preparedness compared to some of the local mountain teachers. Her 1929 Walnut School class of fifty-one seventh grade pupils particularly liked her progressive approach and her methods of adding interest to the curriculum. She taught the students songs and helped them produce skits and plays, and arranged field trips to enhance the study courses. By personality, Nita was jolly, energetic and enthusiastic. Carrie Landers Johnson, whose family had moved from Runion when the bandmill closed, to Hickory Flats, near Walnut, happened to be in that class

Team Captain Juanita Caldwell holds basketball at front.

taught by Nita. Carrie recalled years later, "We really liked Miss Caldwell; she was a good teacher."[34]

Unfortunately, despite her qualifications, Nita was not rehired at the end of the school year, a Walnut girl having graduated from the Normal in May, eligible for the position. Returning to Charlotte, however, Nita Caldwell took with her the affection of Gilbert Stackhouse. He first wrote her letters, then began driving to see her every other weekend, gradually gaining, also, the

Walnut School's 7th grade, 1930. Juanita Caldwell (Stackhouse), teacher, standing at left. A few pupils have been identified; 2. Carrie Landers 3. Aubrey Reeves 4. June Gahagan 5. James Plemmons 6. Kathleen Ramsey 7. Leila Law 8. Ted Davis 9. Jim Crane 10. Vonda Lee Reeves.

friendship and respect of her father, James Querry Caldwell, produce farmer and dairyman. Cattle-raising, crop-growing, milk and butter were certainly topics familiar to Gilbert, allowing him to establish an easy rapport with James, who had three other daughters besides Nita, as well as two sons. James made a sufficient living to send all his children through high school, but since Nita had aspired to further education, he told her she would have to do extra work – that of milking two of his dozen dairy cows. No matter how tired or busy, she had to be in the barn at 4 a.m. and 4 p.m., seven days a week. "If I had a Saturday or Sunday afternoon date, he would bring me home and come back later, after the milking," recalled Nita.[35]

Gilbert's parents had met Nita the Spring before, while she was teaching at Walnut, when Gilbert drove her to Stackhouse one Sunday afternoon. Out in the yard, where he sat talking with Ernest, Amos observed Nita, and told Gilbert the next day with a wink, "If I were thirty years younger, I'd give you a race, Son." Although she did not voice it, Hester, too, likely approved of Nita, who had come from a Christian home, was educated and mature – actually two years older than Gilbert – and closer to Hester's expectations of a suitable daughter-in-law than some of the local girls Gilbert had courted. Finally, Gilbert asked for Nita's hand, and they married on July 17, 1931, at the manse of the Sugar Creek Presbyterian Church in the company of her immediate family and friends. Because of hard times, Gilbert could not afford more than a simple honeymoon, which was an auto trip back to Stackhouse, stopping along the way to spend the night and arriving at Amos' and Hester's two days later.[36]

Newlyweds Gilbert and Juanita Stackhouse, 1931.

Nita was not a city dweller – her rural home had been five miles from Charlotte Square – but she had been used to having her siblings and lots of other young people at her home. In the remote Stackhouse community, she felt that she was "stuck back in the sticks," but as long as Gilbert was there, she could make herself content, even happy, as it would turn out.

Thus, through Gilbert's marriage and Ernest's return home, instead of an empty nest, Amos and Hester found their family expanding once again. June and his wife, Ann, also came for a week or more every year except 1931, when Hester went to New London, Connecticut, to see them in August. June had asked her to help out after the birth of his first child, a daughter named Clara Hester for her two grandmothers – Clara Hoffman and Hester Stackhouse.

Probably while she was gone, Gilbert discussed with his father the possibility of converting the small upstairs room, used as a bedroom by Gilbert before he married, into a kitchen. (It had been Amos' office when the house was first built.) Gilbert drafted a rough "blueprint" and they soon carried out the plan, also changing a small adjoining room into a dining room. These were located at the top of the stairs, beside the bathroom and across the hallway from their bedroom. Even though Nita and Hester got along well, the new arrangement gave the young married couple some sorely needed privacy away from Hester's dominance.

"That first year was the hardest to make ends meet," Nita Stackhouse remembered of her Depression marriage. Even though her mother-in-law's cellar shelves held many jars of food – each bearing a string-tied label showing canning date and contents – none were offered to Nita and Gilbert. Hester was not a cruel person, but she felt, possibly, that she needed to save for yet worse times, or else, it did not answer her perception of propriety, for which she was an absolute stickler. After all, she was trying to do her share by selling milk, butter and eggs, by making over her old dresses and hats, turning Amos' shirt collars, and by being as careful as she knew how. Hester also used cotton feed sacks for everyday sheets, towels, and table covers, extending the life of her "real" linens. Perhaps she thought that Nita and Gilbert were being too extravagant for the times, in some way.

However, a bit of fortune came Nita's way a year later when she was appointed to teach at the one-room Stackhouse school. Working alone, Nita served as teacher and principal for the year 1932-33, having not just one class, but a few students in each of seven grades. Besides the native neighborhood pupils, she taught the children of Anson Betts, who lived at Runion. Once

Stackhouse School report card, 1933. Juanita Stackhouse, teacher and principal. Courtesy Randall Fowler.

more, even though she was capable, trained and well-liked, county politics prevented her being hired for the next year. When the officials told her what she must do to keep her job – vote for their party and make donations to it – Gilbert would not allow her to continue. No matter how precious a job in hard times, the requirements were against his principles.[37]

Gilbert took Nita to visit her family as often as the expense could be met. "It cost only five dollars to go to Charlotte and back, but there was just no money," recalled Nita in 1999. At least once, though, when they managed to make the trip, Nita's father gave them a young Jersey bull for breeding. Gilbert built a wooden cage to fit into the rumble seat of his Ford roadster, and the calf rode to the mountains and eventually improved milk production on the Stackhouse farm, giving Hester more for selling or bartering.

Gilbert's brother, Ernest, resumed his old Stackhouse life of farming plus grading lumber whenever the opportunity arrived. He and Gilbert raised tobacco together, which usually provided a little profit, except for one year when the entire harvest was stolen after it had been handed, ready to take to market the next morning. The brothers had bought their seed and fertilizer on credit, to be paid when the crop sold, but had not counted on the desperation of their fellow man.

Having little or no cash, Gilbert Stackhouse found himself in the same predicament as his grandfather's early customers who bartered their crop harvests or their labor for current needs. He would feel the scars of the depression as long as he lived, resolving never to buy anything again "on time." Even after his work became plentiful, he saved up to make a purchase, large or small, but he never forgot the privilege extended to him in those bleak days. When he was old and unable to drive himself, he bade his daughter to buy gasoline from a neighbor's nearby filling station, albeit higher-priced than in town, saying, "You never know when you might need credit."[38]

Another Depression event to affect Gilbert's entire family, his community, and eventually his county, was the purchase from the Bank of French Broad in Marshall of the 250 Stackhouse acres lost by Charles Dilworth in 1929. Ellsworth Vandervort, brother-in-law of Ernest, paid two thousand dollars for this valuable property on October 26, 1931.[39] It is not known how Ellsworth retained his money when others lost everything, but he was employed by Grant chain store company in Houston, Texas, at the time, and had also invested in the Buncombe County real estate boom of the twenties.

Details of the verbal agreement between Ellsworth Vandervort and Ernest Stackhouse do not exist, but Ernest went to work on the property with some kind of assurance that he would be a part owner of his grandfather's homestead, perhaps when his financial situation improved. Down near the railroad, in an old house, he installed a grist mill, operated by a gasoline engine. "And Walter Treadway ran it for him," recalled Clyde Dockery, former Runion resident.[40] Since people around Stackhouse were often reduced to bartering, Ernest received, in one instance, a treasured "cap and ball" long rifle as pay for grinding two bushels of corn; at another time, for grinding one-and-a-half bushels, he took a target rifle – "An awkward thing, about sixty inches long," recalled his son-in-law, Jack Cole, many years later.[41] In yet another situation, Ernest ground ten bushels for half the meal in payment, a more common transaction and one which contributed to the supply of corn meal for Ernest's family.

Next, Ernest made plans to build a home for himself and the Vandervorts on the site of his grandparents' house which had burned down in 1925, but he needed a way to reach the project with modern vehicles. Enlisting Gilbert's help (and, possibly, the motorized equipment of neighbor B.W. Gahagan) Ernest built a new access from the Stackhouse Road up the steep mountain to the back side of his grandfather's old home, using dynamite where boulders refused to budge. It was also necessary to construct a sturdy wooden bridge across Woolsey Branch at the entrance, the entire project opening fresh possibilities for both Stackhouse households. The new road actually connected with the old wagon driveway leading into Amos' buggy house at the brick annex, enabling both Gilbert and Ernest to bring their vehicles nearer to their doorways, after years of climbing the long way from the lumber yard parking space at the railroad. Hester did not like this arrangement at all, still holding sacred her hard-won landscape of flower beds and back entrance lined with crepe-myrtle, even though her immediate yard was not affected.[42]

The Stackhouse Post Office sign was attached to the porch of Amos' brick annex building where his general store was also newly located in the 1930s.

Gilbert and Ernest tore down the old Stackhouse general store building, moved Amos' post office up to one end of the brick annex behind his home, then used the large hand-hewn beams, sills and joists in framing the new cabin. Thin wooden shipping crates from the old store provided a smooth ceiling material, while the salvaged wide floor boards of heart pine would prove their beauty and endurance for years to come.[43] A poignant reminder of the razed building's legacy was an old stage coach ticket discovered between the floor and walls, surely dropped over fifty years before by their grandfather Amos – before the railroad, before electricity, before the automobile. The store and its side rooms had seen much history pass. Besides having been home to Amos and Charles Dilworth, then again to Charles and his children, it had been the community nucleus since the 1870's. All that remained now of its importance was the mechanical arm at the railroad, where Amos would continue to hang the outgoing canvas mailbag, once he hurried down the steep hill, usually running late from the new post office location. Truly, Stackhouse, North Carolina, had lost another landmark.

The new structure, with its historic components, was built in the round-log pioneer style that had again become popular throughout the mountains.

Train passenger waiting shed built by Southern Railway after Stackhouse store moved. Juanita Stackhouse (second from left) with visiting relatives, 1940.

Log Cabin built by Ernest & Gilbert Stackhouse, c. 1933.

For those who had little money, but owned timber and a few tools, it was a means to new construction, which otherwise would have been unattainable during the depression. The pine logs, eight to twelve inches in diameter, were dragged up the fresh-built road behind Ernest's Chevrolet sedan, then peeled of their bark by hand and stacked to dry. When enough logs had accumulated, they were measured and notched at each end by a double-edged axe which had been shaped at the forge to make a saddle-cut for receiving the next member. Since the logs tapered, each one was stacked in the opposite direction of the log before, so that the finished wall would be level to support the roof. "They drove big nails partway into the top of each log to hold the chinking," related Jack Cole years later.[44] (Chinking was the name given to the mortar used to seal the cracks between the logs.) The finished product was durable and handsome as the smooth surface of the logs turned dark with age and the mortar grew whiter with curing. (This type of construction

243

Log cabin's porch overlooking creek.

became particularly popular for the individual cabins of tourist courts being built along the mountain highways.)

With no electricity, Ruth and Ernest relied upon kerosene lamps for lighting, and a wooden icebox for cooling their milk and butter. Indoor plumbing, fieldstone fireplace and small, upright, cylindrical kerosene heaters, completed the comfortable home – more spacious than the two rooms of Amos' annex, but a far cry from Biltmore Forest. The cabin would be home to Ernest, Ruth, her parents and Carthene for a decade or longer, except that Carthene and her Vandervort grandparents lived in their Biltmore house during school terms so that Carthene could attend Biltmore High School. (She had gone to St. Genevieve's private elementary school.)

Furthermore, Ernest razed the dilapidated old gazebo out on "the point," clearing his view of the river. At another place on the farm – near the Stackhouse Road – Ernest built, also with Gilbert's help, a rental house using lumber salvaged from the rest of the store building, the garden house, and, perhaps, Amos' old buggy house which had stood behind the store.[45]

Around this same time, faced with expensive repairs, Amos Stackhouse made changes to his own home's exterior by removing the upstairs front porch railing with its fancy newels, plus the door leading to it, and installing a window in the door's opening. The unprotected door had often allowed rain to blow in, and the banisters, in addition to being difficult and costly to paint, were rotting from years of weather exposure. Even though the alterations destroyed some of the structure's original Victorian charm, it made the upkeep more affordable for Amos. Primarily, the Depression called for pragmatism. Fortunately, there was benefit to community residents as they were hired to help with all these projects.

Ernest Stackhouse, incidentally, was also fortunate to receive work from his uncle's brother-in-law, Dennis Church of Hot Springs. (Dennis' sister, Mamie, had married Hester's brother, Lloyd Honeycutt.) In 1932 Dennis purchased five hundred acres of timberland from Edwin Grove's estate, which had been part of the Laurel River Logging Company's holding, and had been leased in 1923 by Gennett Lumber Company. Ernest began cruising timber and grading lumber for Church, a job that would last for several years.[46]

From his several occupations – farming, grist milling, timber cruising and landlording – Ernest evidently was able to make a modest living, because he decided to build a pond for swimming and boating just below the log cabin. Using chestnut timbers, dirt and stone, he dammed up Woolsey Branch, leaving a gate to be raised during rainy seasons.[47] Upon two close-growing trees left standing in the lake's center, he fastened a crude ladder and wooden platform for diving. Sometime later, however, at the dam crosswalk, he constructed a standard wooden tower with springboard, plus a long flight of wooden steps having pine pole banisters up to the cabin. Shower heads installed under the high porch finished off the affordable recreational center for Ernest's teenage daughter, as well as the rest of the family, and even the neighbors.

Hester's nephew, Charles Edwin Mashburn, and his friends came from Marshall to swim, as did young Dilworth Stackhouse and his friends from Asheville. Clyde Dockery, who lived at Runion, was another to enjoy the pool, recalling decades later, "I used to swim there a lot – it was open to the community." The large pool, eighteen feet deep at the diving board, was cold

Left – Carthene Stackhouse paddles her dog across their lake built on Woolsey Branch, c. 1939.
Right – First diving board at lake built by Ernest Stackhouse, c. 1938

and refreshing, its source high on the mountain. "On Saturdays and Sundays it looked like half of Asheville was down there," remembered Clyde. Nita Stackhouse, in her old age, also reminisced: "We had such good times there."[48]

June Stackhouse, as well, would send his small family home to stay with Amos and Hester while he went to work in South America. Details are not known about his tour of duty with the Peruvian navy, but it could have been connected to his work in the United States Coast Guard. Ann, his wife, and his young daughter, Clara Hester, slept on a daybed in Hester's library during their visit of a few months. (Hester always wanted the upstairs guestroom kept properly ready for "real" company.) Following his job in Peru, June Stackhouse took a job in Groton, Connecticut, as engineer and machinist for Electric Boat Company, but "When work became slack in 1937, I was loaned to Thermoid Rubber Company at Cranston, New Jersey," stated June, years later.[49] On September 26, 1935, a second child had been born to Ann and June – a son, named Amos Stackhouse III, called "Sonny" to avoid confusion. How thrilling for Amos to see this old, old name continued, even to his grandchildren's own time.

Moreover, Amos could boast another grandchild, born only six days before Sonny, to Gilbert and Nita, who named this daughter Laura Lexine after Nita's mother. (The name was later changed to "Lexyne" in an attempt to correct its mispronunciation.) Nita had gone to her Charlotte home for the confinement, staying about three months in all. While she was away, Gilbert, his father and Lloyd H. Honeycutt extended Nita's upstairs kitchen to include a den. Having several windows, it was a cheerful cozy room, catching the morning sun and giving the young family a complete apartment.

Although June Stackhouse changed jobs frequently during the Depression, and moved almost every year, he continued to bring his family to Stackhouse every summer for a week or two. His daughter, Clara Hester, stated years later, "Those were happy times, and there were lots of other people around." Ruth's brother, Ellsworth, his wife Beulah, and Ruth's parents visited Ruth, Carthene and Ernest at the log cabin, while Nita's sisters came from Charlotte to visit. Clara Hester also remembered that oil lamps were

Left – Steps leading from lake to cabin in 1939.
Right – New diving board at Stackhouse lake, 1940. L to R: Ruth Stackhouse, Carthene Stackhouse, Mr. and Mrs. Vandervort

used in the absence of electricity, but they still had ice cream, cranked by hand, and made from the rich cream of Hester's cows. Other fond memories included the sound of the French Broad through the open windows, Hester's churning butter on the back porch, the floating island pudding for dinner and the homemade jams on hot biscuits for breakfast. "I spent hours banging on the piano in the parlor, but otherwise, we did not sit in there; my father said it was for the preacher's visits," Clara chuckled.[50]

Lexine and Sonny grew, becoming same-age playmates during these visits. One time they managed to cut the legs from Amos' sawhorse with a child's carpenter set he had given Lexine the Christmas before. In July of 1939 the two cousins were baptized at the Methodist Church by Rev. M.T. Smathers. (This was somewhat late for infant baptism, but better than never, thought Hester.)

Thus, the Depression at Stackhouse, besides its economic woes, also made families closer to each other and more interdependent. In addition, for a few community residents, the various repairs and construction projects generated some employment. "The only jobs around there were those working for the Stackhouses; you had to leave there to live," stated Jean Norton Bailey, daughter of Chappell Norton.[51]

During the 1930s, Amos Stackhouse worked – as did his sons – at a variety of jobs to eke out a living. He continued to grade lumber in South Carolina for a short time; he rented the shipping yard at his railroad siding to men fortunate enough to sell lumber; he operated the Cold Springs service station, located on the Marshall highway near the home of his friend Ben Wade Gahagan; and he leased Sherman Ramsey's store in the Walnut village from 1933 through 1935, and possibly longer, hiring an assistant, Mr. Chandler, who had a large family and was out of work. Amos dug from his desk a partly-filled notebook with his name and an old address on the cover, crossed out "Putnam," added "Walnut Store," and used the remaining clean pages to keep charge accounts for his family members and a few others.

Amos Stackhouse in front of Cold Springs service station he operated on highway near Walnut. Attached building at right was a cafe likely managed by unidentified woman at right.

There were only two items purchased, usually: lamp oil and corn for the chickens and mules. In January, 1935, to make a little money and to cut down on his feed bill, Amos killed a calf named Sonnie Boy, listing the buyers' names and amounts paid:

Ernest M. Stackhouse		$2.10
E. Gilbert Stackhouse	stew (4 ½ lbs.)	.45
" " "	roast	.81
Kuykendall	stew	.35
Alice Honeycutt	stew	.78
Luther Williams	stew – .35 steak – .60	.95
B.W. Gahagan	steak	.50
Emmie Dockery	stew beef	.55
E. Davis	stew beef	.45
Amos, Jr.	roast or steak	.40
W. Reams	beef	.80

Jobie Dockery received fifty cents worth of the beef for his help in slaughtering. At ten cents a pound, the beef sale came to $8.14. Once in a while, in addition to the usual lamp oil and corn, there would be charged "flour and coffee," while on November 18, 1934, Gilbert made an unusual charge, sweet potatoes for sixty-two cents, no doubt for their Thanksgiving dinner.[52] The tradition of turkey on Stackhouse tables, no matter how long-standing, would be missing during holidays of the 1930s, but at least there was food,

Finally, the economy reached a turning point in Western North Carolina, as it did across America, when President Franklin Roosevelt's New Deal programs began to live up to their intentions of providing economic relief as well as social reform. The Tennessee Valley Authority (TVA), the Works Progress Administration (WPA), the Civilian Conservation Corps (CCC), and other agencies would bring lasting improvements to Madison County in the form of forestry projects, school houses, roads, bridges, recreational facilities, and hiking trails, plus classes for adults in sewing, mathematics, reading, and craft making, to name only a few. At the Hot Springs school, for instance, a small lunchroom and community center combination was constructed on the public school ground, in the style of the Stackhouse log cabin.

Hot Springs was also one of the towns to receive a CCC forestry unit, organized in 1933 at Fort Bragg with four commissioned officers and two hundred men, their camp built upon the upper lawn of the former hotel grounds, a natural location, since the Great War German detainees had been housed there. The CCC camp offered jobs, uniforms, meals, barracks, health care, education, job training and discipline to young men between the ages of 18 and 25 lacking other means of bettering their lives. Pay was thirty dollars a month, but twenty-five of that was sent back home to the enrollee's family. Two young neighbors of the Stackhouses – Hubert Treadway and George Dockery – joined the Corps at Hot Springs and participated in the building of the road to neighboring Mill Ridge – one that could carry a Hot Springs School bus, saving students the trouble of the long steep walk to and from Stackhouse school.[53]

Government lending programs allowed many banks and some factories to reopen, while a large number of needy families received supplemental food commodities, or "relief," as it would be called. Powdered milk, flour, nuts, dried beans, prunes, bacon, grapefruit and other items made up the dole, and provoked comments such as, "You could tell who was on the dole by the grapefruit rinds slung down the hillside behind their houses." Many threw the grapefruits away uneaten, the sour taste of the exotic fruit having never been cultivated by many mountaineers. Since these programs came through government agents, politics played its part. "A Republican could get no relief or job on WPA unless he wanted to be a Democrat," declared a Jackson County resident many years later.[54] Valerie Guthrie of Walnut also recalled, "Lots of families went over [changed political parties], but we did not."[55]

The New Deal program, TVA, brought several benefits to Madison County from its Knoxville district office. One was the 1934 placing of river gauges on the French Broad and the training of volunteers who read them daily, reporting the water depth to the Knoxville office and receiving a monthly stipend. In the case of heavy rains, the monitors checked the gauges and reported more often, even hourly, at critical stages, providing flood warning to the public in hopes of averting another 1916-type disaster. A wire-weight measuring gauge was mounted on the Hot Springs bridge, while a different device – a cylinder graph recording gauge – was installed in a tall concrete structure on the old Buncombe Turnpike road bed near Peter's Rock.[56] Downstream a hundred yards below the site of the old Stackhouse store, also on the former Turnpike, a two-seated wooden funicular-like carrier ran across the stream on a steel cable so that water samples could be taken.

Another good thing to come to Madison County from the Depression was the 1934 hiring by TVA in Knoxville of Benton MacKaye, whose sobriquet was "Father of the Appalachian Trail."[57] By 1930 there were already forty miles of the famous hiking path completed along the North Carolina-Tennessee line by way of the center of Hot Springs and northern Madison County.[58] MacKaye would push for the Trail's completion until 1937 when his dream was finally fulfilled. The Maine-to-Georgia corridor would bring a myriad of visitors to Madison County, a few of whom would choose to stay, raise families and develop businesses. Even the community of Stackhouse would benefit significantly in years to come.

Furthermore affecting Stackhouse through the TVA was the 1935 U.S. Geological Survey employee's examination and evaluation of the barite mines belonging to Amos, Ellsworth Vandervort, Edwin Mashburn, Ben Wade Gahagan and Anson Betts. TVA engineer Charles E. Hunter, working from his Asheville office, redrew a map (of the Klondyke mine tunnels) which had been made in 1910 by a draftsman named Dudley Chipley. In February, 1936, Hunter mailed his report to his Knoxville superior, Major Edwin Eckel, Chief Geologist of the TVA: "There now exists below the old workings a reserve of good barite, the amount being unknown." Although the underground work was in such condition that he and his aide, Philip W. Mattocks, could not gain entry to the old workings, Amos Stackhouse gave them a history of the operations from their beginnings. This TVA documentation, filed and protected for public availability, would prove valuable to the future of Stackhouse and Madison County. (Many years later, Mark Carter of the N.C. Geological Survey in Asheville described the maps as "pretty awesome.")[59]

Moreover, the Depression brought educational improvement to Madison and other counties when the state took over the public school system. In 1933 Governor Ehringhaus, faced with closing the schools because there was no operational money nor promise of funds to come, placed an unpopular three percent sales tax on everything sold in the state except bread, flour and

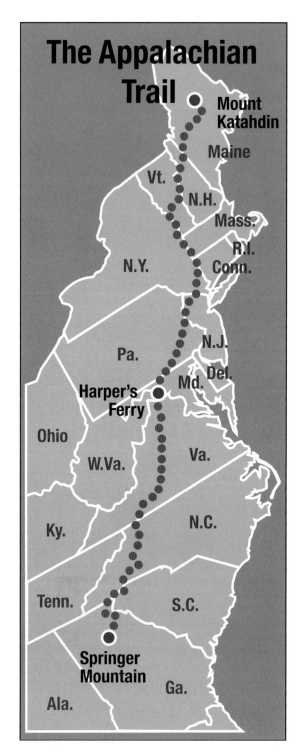

Appalachian Trail (AT). From Georgia to Maine, this is the most famous footpath in the United States. AT mileage in North Carolina is 305 miles. Popular access points are in Hot Springs, off Lake Fontana and at the Nantahala Outdoor Center. (*Asheville Citizen*)

meat. This measure enabled the schools to stay open, the teachers to be paid (albeit, not always monthly), and the school term to be extended from six to eight months.[60] Later in the decade, during Governor Clyde Hoey's term, North Carolina furnished free books to its school children in the first seven grades, an act intended to increase attendance, since children often dropped out because they could not afford books.[61]

Although improved, the schools offered no frills, and few, if any, extracurricular activities, as recalled by Eleanore Brown, a classmate of Carthene Stackhouse at Biltmore from 1933 through 1937:

> About the time we entered high school, the music and art programs were eliminated, as well as most sports. We had a basketball team and a football team coached by our algebra teacher, but there was no money for long bus trips so we played teams in Asheville and Buncombe County, only. We had no Senior Prom, no year book. There was a cafeteria in the building, but meals were no longer served and we had to furnish our own lunches. The principal of the school was our physics teacher and he sometimes asked me to get my father to explain a problem or find the answer to one.[62]

Still, Carthene enjoyed her school years and her friends, and following graduation, went to her father's alma mater, Weaver College, which was on a new campus and under a new name. Faced with hard times, as were all churches in 1934, the Western North Carolina Conference of the Methodist Church decided to merge its Weaver College, Brevard Institute and Rutherford Institute into one strong coeducational junior college in Transylvania County, named Brevard Junior College.[63] Regrettably, Carthene was not allowed to finish, either from lack of money or because her mother wanted to have her at home, as Ruth had stayed with her own mother before her.

In the meantime, Carthene's uncle, Ellsworth, of Dallas, Texas, added to his holdings at Stackhouse in June, 1935, through two documents. One was an agreement to perpetual water rights from the land of Amos and Hester for Ernest's new cabin. Vandervort received permission to construct a pipeline from his boundary at the edge of Woolsey Branch, over Amos' property, and crossing the Stackhouse Road to Amos' spring high above. "The pipe line is to supply water for property to any extent that will not diminish supply of the party of the second part [Amos]," stated the document.[64]

Carthene Stackhouse, at right and Elsie Cooper, graduates of Biltmore High School, 1937. Courtesy Eleanor Brown.

More significant to the Stackhouse community, however, was the deeding to Ellsworth by Edgar Betts of the one hundred acres purchased in 1885 by Amos' father for Amos and Charles Dilworth, but more recently owned by Laurel River Logging Company. Yes, the productive old "Laurel farm," as old Amos called it, later known as Putnam and Runion, with its arable fields, scenic Big Laurel Creek, railway access, band mill foundations, concrete stronghouse, and four remaining buildings – school house, plus three dwellings – would now lie fallow as far as the community benefit was concerned. Beyond the two or three families who would sharecrop there, Runion's hope of generating jobs was lost forever. Vandervort paid only two thousand dollars for little Runion mountain and its 100 acres, yet another sacrificial lamb upon the Depression altar.[65]

Though the New Deal had lessened hard times statewide, Madison County's economic misery had only grown ordinary. At Stackhouse, the worst of the Depression was over, but it would be some time before anything closely resembling prosperity would come along. In fact, the losses sustained would have long-term impact, changing the Stackhouse family's plane of living for generations to come, and challenging its matriarch, Hester, to present a close-mouthed, head-high façade. There would be no more Philadelphia vacations, no hats and gloves from Wanamakers, nor expensive accessories for her sacred Queen Anne house. Nevertheless, Hester, Amos and their progeny would call upon their German and Scot-Irish stoicism, plus their Quaker faith and resiliency, to accept the new order of things, having no idea of the conflicts waiting ahead.

Juanita Caldwell Stackhouse's alma mater, Asheville Normal School, Asheville, N.C.

[1] *Greeneville Democrat*, Greeneville, Tenn., January 10, 1930.
News-Record, Marshall, N.C., March 28, 1930.

[2] Madison County Deeds Registry, Book 40, p.178.

[3] Burgin, Ora Henderson. Interview, 1990.

[4] *Asheville Citizen*, September 14, 1932.

[5] Painter, Jacqueline. *The Season of Dorland-Bell*, p.228.

[6] Dotterer, Elizabeth Baker. Interview, 1989.
Burgin, Kenneth S. Interview, 1969.

[7] Underwood, Jinsie. *This is Madison County*. American Revolution Bicentennial
Committee of Madison County, 1974, p.43.

[8] "Snapshots," pamphlet by Board of National Missions of Presbyterian Church in the
U.S.A., N.Y., 1931.

[9] Ibid.

[10] Meek, Anna Stackhouse. Interview, 2002.

[11] Painter, Jacqueline. *The Season of Dorland-Bell*. Appalachian Consortium Press, Boone,
N.C., 1996, p.175.

[12] *Biltmore House and Gardens*, booklet by The Biltmore Estate, Asheville, 1980, p.2.

[13] Sondley, F.A. *A History of Buncombe County*. Asheville, N.C.: The Advocate Printing
Co., 1930, p.732.

[14] Treadway, Martha Davis. Interview, 1990.

[15] Stackhouse, Nita. Interview, 2000.

[16] Church, Reeves. Interview, 2002.

[17] Ibid.

[18] Paxton, Percy J. "Notes on the National Forests and Purchase Units of Region Eight," U.S.
Forest Service, Atlanta, GA., June 1, 1955, 2nd printing, p.3.

[19] Madison County Deeds Registry, Book 64, p. 389.

[20] Graham County Deeds Registry, Book 41, p. 148.

[21] Gennett to author, January, 2003.

[22] Madison County Deeds Registry, Book 64, pps. 288-291.

[23] Thomas, Lora. Interview, 2002.

[24] Coward, J. Kent. *History of Jackson County*. Sylva, N.C.: Jackson County Historical
Association, 1987, p.452.

[25] Aumiller, Nancy Stackhouse. Interview, 1997.

[26] Ibid.

[27] Madison County Deed Registry, Bk. 55, p.133, 134.

[28] Ibid., Bk. 51, p.520.

[29] Meek, Anna Stackhouse. Interview, 2000.

[30] Lefler, Hugh T. *North Carolina History, Geography & Government*. Yonkers-on-Hudson, New
York: Work Book Company, 1959, p.437.

[31] Stackhouse, Nita. Interview, 2001.

[32] Marshall *News-Record*, January 1, 1926, p.1.

[33] Stackhouse, Nita. Interview, 2001.

[34] Johnson, Carrie Landers. Interview, 1999.

[35] Stackhouse, Nita. Interview, 2002.

[36] Ibid.

[37] Ibid.

[38] Ibid.

[39] Madison County Deeds Registry, Bk. 56, p.63.

[40] Dockery, Clyde. Interview, 2000.
[41] Cole, Jack. Interview, 1999.
[42] Aumiller, Nancy Stackhouse. Interview, 2002.
[43] Ibid.
[44] Cole, 1999.
[45] Aumiller, 2002.
[46] Church, 2002.
Madison Co. Deeds, Bk. 44, p.421; Bk. 56, p.341.
[47] Cole, 1999.
[48] Dockery, 2000.
Stackhouse, Nita, 2001.
[49] Ibid.
[50] Radin, Clara S., letter to author, 1998.
[51] Bailey, Jean Norton. Interview, 1999.
[52] Author's private papers.
[53] Dockery, Clyde. Interview, 2001.
[54] Coward, p.453.
[55] Guthrie, Valerie. Interview, 2002.
[56] "Floods on French Broad River & Spring Creek," TVA Report, Knoxville: TVA Division of Water Control Planning, 1960, p.17.
[57] Bennett, Anne. "Making the World More Habitable," Appalachian Trail News: publisher unknown, Nov., 1985, p.14.
[58] *Madison County Times*, Marshall, N.C., Aug. 20, 1930, p.10.
[59] Carter, Mark. Interview, Asheville, 2001.
[50] Lefler, p.438.
[51] Ibid., p.441.
[52] Brown, Eleanore, letter to author, 2002.
[53] Pickens, Nell. *Dry Ridge: Some of Its History*. 2nd ed., Weaverville, N.C.: Friends of Weaverville Library, 1996, p.47.
[54] Madison County Deeds Registry, Bk. 60, p.265.
[55] Ibid., Bk. 58, p.494.

Chapter Twenty-Three

During the latter 1930s, Amos Stackhouse's journal pages reflected slightly improved economic conditions. Timber cutting for Anson Betts (living in Massachusetts), probably on his Sandy Bottom acres joining Stackhouse land, created some jobs. As supervisor, Amos received forty cents an hour for keeping the weekly payroll, grading the lumber, paying the men and shipping the carloads from his Southern Railway siding. At other times, he only watched the loading by car number, the customer furnishing his own handlers; National Casket Company of Asheville was one of these. Five or six employees from Stackhouse received fifteen cents an hour for their work of cutting, hauling, stacking and loading onto the rail cars.[1]

Moreover, in his journal, Amos made his income and expense declarations for tax year 1937 as follows:

Employed self		100.00	
Rents		677.00	
Barytes Royalty		100.00	
From Store		322.66	
	Total	1199.66	Gross income
Deductions			
French Broad Bank note	450.00		
M.E. Church	35.00		
Sunday School		2.00	
medical expense		10.00	
Citizens Bank note		150.00	
Travel expense		5.00	
		652.00	
Standard deductions		1000.00	
		1652.00	Expenses and deductions

Although unclear, Amos apparently did not need to pay tax that year because his deductions and expenses were higher than his gross income.

Since there was a "royalty" listed, someone had evidently been successful in finding more of the barite ore, but records are not extant. Amos also received $150 annual rent from L. Bledsoe Lumber Company in Greensboro for the old barytes mill buildings where the Laurel River Logging Company's bandmill machinery had been stored following the closing of Runion. In 1936, for instance, Amos sold chains, sprockets, bearings, pulleys, wheels, pipe and blowers for Bledsoe.[2]

Furthermore, Amos' journal indicated better times for the Stackhouse community as more varied items were charged. Besides the basic kerosene, flour, salt and lard, there would be matches, sausage, thread, coffee, tobacco, and, occasionally, candy, chewing gum or peanut butter. The price of a pair of overalls was 75 cents, while five cents would buy a cake of soap, a box of razor blades, or a large bar of candy. The stylish cigarette-smoking habit had replaced tobacco chewing for the younger men at Stackhouse, so they bought bright red tins of Prince Albert tobacco for 25 cents, along with little packets of OCB papers at five cents, and rolled their own, never purchasing the expensive manufactured ones.[3]

Jim Treadway, who lived on Mill Ridge, not far above Stackhouse, also kept good records of his Depression expenditures and receipts in a small notebook, writing a clear steady hand. He usually walked to Hot Springs to make any purchase or to sell his produce of honey and eggs. In 1936 he paid 17 cents for a pound of lard; 20 cents for a gallon of lamp oil; 35 cents for five pounds of sugar; and $1.10 for 100 pounds of flour. In 1937, Jim sold 117 dozens eggs for $24.65, but in 1938, he received only $23.74 from 136 dozens sold, reflecting the ever volatile farming market. Jim's "spring honey" had brought him $16.62 in 1938, at fifteen cents a pound. He was even able to afford a few Christmas purchases by December 22: candy, 30 cents; oranges, 30 cents; 1 pair stockings, 20 cents; and one rubber ball, 5 cents.[4]

Likewise, in 1938, Amos' store charges by his own family members showed no extravagance, but after their daily necessities and canning supplies, they bought Post Toasties, vanilla flavoring, and tea leaves, plus cold tablets, Vaseline, chest-rub ointment and cough syrup. From time to time, a five-cent charge would be listed as "candy by C. [Carthene]."

Unlike his father's larger store stock of everything from corsets, indigo and china to gunpowder, pianos and horse shoe iron, all purchased on trips to New York and Philadelphia, Amos' smaller merchandise amounts came by train from Taylor Grocery Company in nearby Newport, Tennessee, and Sprinkle Shelton Company and Rector Hardware at Marshall. Amos also carried a few clothing items such as work shirts, socks and overalls, plus plow points and singletrees for the farmers. Occasionally he ordered from the catalog of McClung in Knoxville, whose peddlers had sold to his father in Warm Springs sixty-five years earlier.[5]

Having some impact upon Amos' store trade would be the 1938 Agricultural Adjustment Act, which based the tobacco marketing quotas on acreage instead of previously-grown poundage. This meant that a farmer's allotted amount of tobacco to be grown was assigned to the land itself; a farmer could grow tobacco only by owning or renting land that had a quota. The allotment now stayed with the farm no matter how many times it changed hands. By limiting the tobacco supply, the market price was increased, giving support through artificially-raised sales income, rather than through direct government hand out. This same act, albeit much amended, would continue to benefit Madison County and the Stackhouse family as long as they held their land. The families living in the several tenant houses located on Amos' farm and Ellsworth Vandervort's farm (formerly owned by Charles Dilworth) raised the burley crops each year, receiving a percentage after the harvest and sale were completed. Thus they were able to pay their charge accounts at Amos' store. Amos and Ellsworth, of course, netted their owners' shares, respectively.

Gilbert Stackhouse frequently paid portions of his grocery bill by hauling hay, pulp wood, tobacco and other items for Amos. He also continued to work for their neighbor on Walnut Creek, Ben Wade Gahagan, building sawmills and other commercial buildings. On Sunday afternoons, the family outings for Gilbert, Nita and Lexine included the stop at Gahagan's home on the new highway 25/70 near Walnut, where the wives visited while the men discussed the upcoming week's work.[6] They traveled to jobs in Kentucky, Tennessee and Georgia, at times. Once when Ben Wade was too busy to take a contract, and about to turn it down, he said to Gilbert, "How about taking this job on your own; you can handle it." From then on, Gilbert worked independently, providing his own crew and equipment, and eventually becoming state-licensed.

International Paper Company mill built in Kentucky by Gilbert Stackhouse.

This decision seemed providential, when, within a short time – March 12, 1938 – Ben Wade Gahagan suffered internal injuries in a fall from his horse. He was taken to Takoma Hospital in Greeneville, Tennessee, where he died four days later.[7] Gilbert, Amos and the whole Stackhouse family would mourn the loss of their longtime friend and neighbor.

A year later, another time of grieving befell the Stackhouses, especially Amos, who wrote with slow careful script in his journal: "April 28th, 1939 – My brother Charlie died this morning at 5:25 o'clock at his home, 71 Brownwood Ave., West Asheville, N.C., age 62 years." Charles Dilworth had been Amos' childhood playmate, young adult business partner, close friend and only sibling. He would miss him tremendously. "We all loved to have Charlie come down to visit," remembered Gilbert's wife, Nita, many years later.[8] The funeral was at the Walnut Methodist Church where Charles Dilworth had attended when he lived in Madison County; burial was in the adjoining cemetery. Although shocked, the Stackhouse family had known that Charles Dilworth's health was deteriorating from injuries received about ten years before when a car had run over him, fracturing his skull and rendering him unconscious for three weeks. "He was never really well after the accident," stated his daughter, Anna Meek, "And he was in bed the last month before he died."[9]

Charles Dilworth had been called back to his job at the reopened Woodfin Manufacturing Company, once the initial critical period of the

257

Depression passed, enabling him to rent the house on Brownwood Avenue in West Asheville. Later, when he became too ill to work, Clara found a job at a local dry cleaning plant, leaving her daughters and her sister, Lucy Boydston, to care for him during the day. She would continue to work there, helping her son Dilworth to get a job at the same place.[10]

For the rest of the summer after Charles Dilworth's death, Amos Stackhouse, along with the rest of the nation, nervously followed news about Europe's current scourge, Adolf Hitler. Back on March 17, 1936, the Knoxville News-Sentinel's headlines had stated: "Last Shreds of Treaties Flung Aside by Hitler; Flouting of Locarno Pact Stuns Europe." From the Rhineland takeover, the German dictator had moved to Austria and Czechoslovakia, until finally, on September 1, 1939, he attacked Poland, provoking France and Great Britain to declare war on Germany two days later.[11] Subsequently, in June 1940, France fell, causing the United States to begin looking at its own defense. No American, however, wanted to even consider conflict so soon after the immense toll of the Great War. Amos Stackhouse and other "oldsters" shook their heads in disbelief at hearing, after twenty-two years, the same old names repeated: Liege, the Ardennes, Cracow, Antwerp, Compiegne.

Nevertheless, America began enlarging its army, navy and air force in fear that a German victory would endanger the United States. In September, the Selective Service System required all males between the ages of twenty-one and thirty-six to register for the draft.[12] Quite a few young men from Madison County enlisted, as well as Amos' nephew, twenty-year-old Dilworth, from West Asheville. Operating the dry-cleaning machine where his mother worked, Dilworth could see little promise in a still-depressed western North Carolina. Eventually, he was sent to the Army induction center at Charlotte before ending up at Fort Bragg.[13]

Thirty-four-year-old Gilbert Stackhouse registered, of course, but was classified "4F," unsuitable, because of his blindness in one eye. Meanwhile, Gilbert's work had also taken him away from home to Booneville, Kentucky, where Nita and four-year-old Lexine lived with him in a boarding house. Little Lexine had been chosen mascot for the Walnut High School's 1940 senior class by Elizabeth Gahagan, daughter of the late Ben Wade Gahagan. Also in the class was Harold Reeves, son of Amos Stackhouse Reeves, whose father Malley had been

Charles Dilworth Stackhouse, Jr., 1939, at Fort Bragg, N.C. Courtesy, Larry Stackhouse.

customer and friend of Gilbert's grandfather before the turn of the century.[14]

During the spring and summer of this new decade, Amos Stackhouse farmed as usual, his sons Ernest and Gilbert doing the same on their days between jobs. Unfortunately, on August 30, 1940, the French Broad rose out of its banks and flooded some of their crops, especially Ernest's sweet potatoes, which subsequently rotted in the ground. Moreover, at his cabin, Woolsey Branch exceeded its banks and washed out the timber dam holding Ernest's lake – another substantial loss.[15]

At Hot Springs the river's crest measured 16.1 feet, only five feet below the 1916 Great Flood stage of 22 feet.[16] "Rain-Swollen Streams Leave Trail of Death and Destruction in WNC," filled the top of page one in the *Asheville Citizen* the next day. As usual, the town of Marshall was hard hit and left with no electricity, telephone, water supply, railway or bus service. Its depot building was lifted off the foundation and set down again, at a tilt. Trains were suspended between Knoxville and Asheville, and, "U.S. Highway 25-70 closed because of high water at Marshall," stated the Citizen.[17] Fifteen feet of water covered the Hot Springs bath house, while the CCC buildings, also, stood deep in the swollen river.

The old Mountain Park Hotel swimming pool was again filled with rocks, sand and debris after having just been dug out by the CCC camp boys, who had looked forward to swimming there. It had been flooded in August, 1928 (17 ft.), and in January, 1936 (14 ft.), but not cleaned out until right before this 1940 inundation.[18] At Belva, up on Laurel, the bridge was swept away, but the Laurel River bridge on Highway 25-70 held, despite much damage.[19] Ruin to roads, crops, and private and public property set back Madison County's efforts to rise from the Great Depression and concluded a decade of weather adversities.

Four years earlier, right after the spring plowing, a record-breaking blizzard had hit western North Carolina, dumping twelve to twenty inches of snow, stranding motorists, bringing down electric and telephone lines, and causing widespread deaths and accidents. Wind-driven drifts were so deep that when Gilbert Stackhouse stretched out his arm at the shoulder, it rested on the crusty white surface. Amos asked Gilbert to do his feeding and milking for him, considering it too dangerous for an old man to be out.[20]

However, more serious problems for farmers had been caused by the absence of moisture beginning in 1932 and worsening periodically throughout the decade. At Hot Springs in 1935, the Dorland-Bell School's headmistress wrote some New York friends: "So serious is our situation that we are having to boil all our drinking water, the laundry works spasmodically, and baths are very much of a luxury."[21] At other times the school had to resort to its old outdoor "johns" when water was too low to flush indoor toilets. During these summers, Gilbert Stackhouse drove the livestock down to the river, albeit low, for drinking.

By the end of 1940, the weather had improved but the international predicament was worse. Back in September, Japan had joined Germany and Italy in a pact of AXIS support, should the United States enter the conflict. On January 6, 1941, President Roosevelt asked Congress to legislate his Lend-Lease program which would remove the nation from neutrality by extending aid to Great Britain, China and Soviet Russia in the form of supplies and arms.[22] American war vessels were ordered to patrol waters between Iceland and the United States, and America's merchant ships were armed to sail the seas.

Graduating class of Walnut High School, May 7, 1940.
Mascot Lexine Stackhouse, front right.

1. Delmer Payne, 2. Warren Massey, 3. Leonard Baker, 4. Clyde Worley, 5. Clara McDevitt, 6. Fred Randall, 7. Ralph Cantrell, 8. Harold Reeves, 9. Virginia McClure (Sponsor), 10. Viola Caldwell, 11. Christine Massey, 12. Geneva Price, 13. Joy Lunsford, 14. Peggy Ramsey, 15. Pansy Ramsey, 16. Kathleen Capps, 17. Anna Belle Cantrell, 18. Charles Wright (Sponsor), 19. Marie Meadows, 20. Evelyn McDevitt, 21. Frances Cantrell, 22. Cordelia Barnett, 23. Marie Worley, 24. Elizabeth Gahagan, 25. Ruth Goforth, 26. Katie Goforth, 27. Venita Roberts, 28. Wayne Faulkner, 29. Matilda Ramsey, 30. Gerald Payne (Mascot), 31. Lexine Stackhouse (Mascot)

260

In 1941 most American citizens were so concerned with bringing food to the table, they had nothing much but sympathy for the oppressed countries abroad. A few, the isolationists, didn't want any part of it, while the interventionists urged joining the conflict. Still other Americans were definitely against German atrocities, but not enough to send their boys back to Europe. Protestors visited the White House to petition against Roosevelt's Lend-Lease Act, as the President steadfastly built up the defenses of the United States.[23] He was accused by some of "preaching fear," but he could see where things were headed.

In Asheville, on August 2, 1941, women rushed to department stores to buy the last hose, following the government freeze the day before on all stocks of raw silk. Asheville Hosiery Company prepared to close its plant, as did Grey Hosiery Mills in Hendersonville. The same day, the *Asheville Citizen* announced that filling stations in all Atlantic states would begin "blackouts" of gasoline sales from 7 p.m. until 7 a.m. "If this does not save enough gasoline, we… must devise additional measures," stated Petroleum Coordinator, Mr. Ickes. Many motorists carried along reserve cans of gas for weekend travel emergencies during the dusk-to-dawn hours.[24]

Meanwhile, the Stackhouses, along with their fellow citizens, went about their daily lives hoping routine would override apprehension. Cruising timber and inspecting lumber through the week, Ernest cared for the cabin and farm on weekends. At the parking area above his cabin, he excavated for a garage, planning a small overhead apartment for "the Vans," as Ruth's parents, Mr. and Mrs. Vandervort, were called by the family. A tenant, Jack Reed, who lived on the farm and was an accomplished rock mason, built the field stone foundation walls, snug against the bank in back and around the front to complete the two-car garage. (In a few years Reed would also build the well-known Rock Café beside the courthouse in Marshall.)[25] Atop the garage, Ernest constructed the apartment framework, a little at a time, but the project would be left for years, at the dried-in stage, waiting to be finished.

At summer's-end – September 20, 1941 – little Lexine Stackhouse turned school age, preventing her and Nita from traveling with Gilbert to his long distance contracts. Gilbert's uncle, Frank Hunycutt, working with him, was picked up on Sunday evenings returned on Fridays, prompting Nita to stay with Frank's wife, Alice, in Walnut so that Lexine could attend the first grade at the Walnut School. Gilbert always took workers from around home to help on his jobs. He knew their methods, could trust them, and he communicated well with those he had known for years – a far better arrangement than hiring strangers.[26] In addition, this fulfilled the time-honored Stackhouse family tradition of providing work for those around who needed it.

It was in November, 1941, that Amos Stackhouse began a new page in his store journal, headed, "Sawmill Plant, Amos and E. Gilbert Stackhouse – $\frac{1}{2}$ each." Sitting on higher ground that Amos' father's mill, which had been located between river and railroad (and had been destroyed by the 1916 flood), this new building rested at one end on the old piers of the former barite crusher, then ran along the foot of the mountain toward Woolsey Branch and the county road.[27] From the old barytes plant, Amos also salvaged some of the large framing timbers, with the help of Troy and Jobie Dockery, brothers, who were also glad to get work.

Almost ten million people in America remained unemployed, and the Depression, though waning, was still felt in Madison County, causing Amos

Sunday visit with relatives at Stackhouse, c.1940. L to R: Frank Reams (son of Mae), Mae Reams (Hester's sister), Alice Gahagan Hunycutt, Frank Hunycutt (Alice's husband), Hester Stackhouse (sister to Mae and Frank Hunycutt), Amos Stackhouse (Hester's husband) and Gilbert Stackhouse (son of Amos and Hester). Lexine Stackhouse (daughter of Gilbert) in front.

to hope there would be profit in the sawing of logs again. Though most of the Stackhouse trees had been cut in the past, there was still some standing timber, albeit on mortgaged land. Amos wrote in his journal that he "Went to Marshall to see bank about cutting timber; said it was okay." In a later entry, he noted that he had logged 5527 feet "from my individual tract," which was land in his name only, and not shared. Working on his mill nearly every day, between mail trains, Amos had no idea that the Great Depression was about to come to an abrupt end.

On December 7, 1941, the United States was plunged into the world conflict when Japan killed hundreds of Americans and wounded thousands more in the surprise bombings of Pearl Harbor, Guam, Wake, Midway and Hong Kong. The Great War – waged to "end all wars" – would ironically become one of a pair. The government's New Deal changed to a full-scale economy involving massive spending in the war effort. Practically any man – and many women – could get a job. The draft age dropped from 21 to 18 and rose from 36 to 45, drawing from nearly every household in the nation. Out of North Carolina, some 362,000 young people (over 7000 were women) would enter the armed services and would participate in every battle of significance.[28]

Numbering among these were Stackhouse's relatives, friends and neighbors; for instance, Amos' nephew, Dilworth, already enlisted; Nita's brother, Robert Caldwell from Charlotte; Hester's nephews, Charles Edwin Mashburn, from Marshall, and Frank Hunycutt, Jr., from Walnut; Lloyd Hunycutt's nephew by marriage, Reeves Church, from Hot Springs; Malley Reeves' sons, Aubrey, whom Nita had taught in 7th grade, and Harold, whose graduation mascot had been Lexine Stackhouse; the late Ben Wade Gahagan's son, B.W., Jr.; Jack Reed's nephew, Jack Dockery; and Aaron Treadway's son, Hubert, from Runion. Former Laurel River Logging Company commissary manager, Bewley Tweed, now living in Hot Springs, also sent his son, J.B., while three grandsons of another Stackhouse friend, the late James H. Rumbough, went into service, as well as six Hot Springs grandsons of the late miner, John Harrison. At least two Madison Countians had been at the Pearl Harbor invasion, both, fortunately, surviving – Jay Nix from Paint Rock and Kenneth Gowan from Spring Creek.[29]

June Stackhouse, too, responded at once to the Pearl Harbor attack by moving to Newport News, Virginia, where he went to work December 21, 1941, as Assistant Principal Inspector in the shipyard under U.S. Navy supervision. Since August, 1939, June had operated his own business, buying and selling steel in Uncasville, Connecticut. Two years before that, June was employed as an experimental engineer for Thermoid Rubber Company in Cranton, New Jersey.[30]

The December, 1941, move back to Virginia brought June near his wife's family, the Hoffmans, at Hampton. Soon his brother, Ernest, had joined him, also working for the government (in the Corps of Engineers), inspecting the building of crates for shipping instruments, the building of barracks and other structures, and drawing wages far above what he had made in western North Carolina. Here, Carthene Stackhouse and Anna Hoffman Stackhouse's sister became friends, leading to Carthene's meeting another friend of the Hoffmans', Jack Cole, to whom she would become engaged.[31]

On New Year's Day, 1942, the seriousness of the war was reflected by Carthene's grandfather down in Stackhouse as he wrote in his journal: "The President set aside today for special prayer for the world's peace… and, while working in the mill Gilbert and I are building, I said a silent prayer that there would be some way for peace in the world." At another time – February 15th – Amos wrote, "Just heard Churchill say Singapore had been taken by the Japs, and looks bad for us." Amos listened to his large battery-operated radio every day (even though the reception was often static-ridden) for war news from his favorite analyst, Columbia Broadcasting System's H.V. Kaltenborn, who always spoke without script.[32]

Amos' journal of February 28th dealt with home matters which reflected the war: "Ernest, Ruth, Mr. and Mrs. Vandervort left for Newton, Alabama – Ernest working there." (Carthene, perhaps not surprisingly, did not accompany her parents, but went back to Hampton, Virginia, seeking a job and living with June's sister-in-law.)[33] Ernest had been assigned to Dale County, Alabama, where the new military installation of Fort Rucker would be raised out of farming fields. The nearest lodging he could find was in the small town of Newton, several miles southeast of the military base. Communities surrounding the site resorted to renting every empty house, apartment, and spare bedroom to the approximately 1500 workers flowing into the area.[34]

There was much lumber and building for Ernest to inspect as the J.A. Jones Construction Company of Charlotte began its 120-day contract to complete 1500 buildings, serving 30,000 men. According to a 1987 historian, "There were no masonry buildings, but neither were there any tents or tar-paper shacks; the buildings were of good wood frame construction, painted white, and the post had a clean, military look almost from the start."[35] Fort Rucker would develop into one of the nation's most vital air-support command bases.

741004 DA

WAR RATION BOOK TWO

IDENTIFICATION

Gilbert Stackhouse
(Name of person to whom book is issued)

OFFICE
OF
PRICE ADM.
R-123

_____
(Street number or rural route)

Stackhouse _____ N. C. _____ 31 _____
(City or post office) _____ (State) ____ (Age) ___ (Sex)

ISSUED BY LOCAL BOARD No. 45-12 ___ Mad _____
_____ (County) _____ (State)

_____
(Street address of local board) _____ (City)

By ___ Mrs. Naomi _____
(Signature of issuing officer)

SIGNATURE ___ Gilbert Stac
(To be signed by the person to whom this book is issued. If such person is unable to sign because of age or incapacity, another may sign in his behalf)

WARNING

1 This book is the property of the United States Government. It is unlawful to sell or give it to any other person, or to use it, or permit anyone else to use it, except to obtain rationed goods for the person to whom it was issued.

2 This book must be returned to the War Price and Rationing Board which issued it, if the person to whom it was issued is inducted into the armed services of the United States, or leaves the country for more than 30 days, or dies. The address of the Board appears above.

3 A person who finds a lost War Ration Book must return it to the War Price and Rationing Board which issued it.

4 PERSONS WHO VIOLATE RATIONING REGULATIONS ARE SUBJECT TO $10,000 FINE OR IMPRISONMENT, OR BOTH.

OPA Form No. R-121 _____ 16—30853-1

Q 8						
Q 5						
Q 2	R 2	S 2	T 2	2	2	2
Q 1	R 1	S 1	T 1	E 1	F 1	M 1
Z 8	Y 8	X 8	W 8	V 8	U 8	

INSTRUCTIONS

1 This book is valuable. Do not lose it.

2 Each stamp authorizes you to purchase rationed goods in the quantities and at the times designated by the Office of Price Administration. Without the stamps you will be unable to purchase those goods.

3 Detailed instructions concerning the use of the book and the stamps will be issued from time to time. Watch for those instructions so that you will know how to use your book and stamps.

4 Do not tear out stamps except at the time of purchase and in the presence of the storekeeper, his employee, or a person authorized by him to make delivery.

5 Do not throw this book away when all of the stamps have been used, or when the time for their use has expired. You may be required to present this book when you apply for subsequent books.

Rationing is a vital part of your country's war effort. This book is your Government's guarantee of your fair share of goods made scarce by war, to which the stamps contained herein will be assigned as the need arises.

Any attempt to violate the rules is an effort to deny someone his share and will create hardship and discontent.

Such action, like treason, helps the enemy.

Give your whole support to rationing and thereby conserve our vital goods. Be guided by the rule:

"*If you don't need it, DON'T BUY IT.*"

☆ U. S. GOVERNMENT PRINTING OFFICE 1942   16—30853-1

One of the ration books and stamps issued to Gilbert Stackhouse during World War II.

The national crisis brought other immediate changes to the Stackhouse family and community, similar to the ones of the Great War, but more restrictive. Amos received letters from the newly-created Office of Price Administration (OPA) at Raleigh concerning inflation price controls and the rationing of scarce goods.[36] In addition to ceilings on both prices and wages, rents were frozen. The American manufacturing of many ordinary items was being done now solely for the armed services, while some foreign exports had been unavailable since the outset, such as quality silk hosiery from Japan. Cadillac automobile factories built no cars, but tanks instead; Pontiac built torpedoes and automatic field guns; Packard turned out engines for airplanes, and Henry Kaiser became a genius at ship production. Civilians must wait "for the duration" (a phrase to be applied constantly) to purchase vehicles and most other manufactured items, since practically all raw materials were channeled into war use.

The Stackhouse family and other Madison Countians also lived with controls over their daily consumption, as each household in America, according to its number of inhabitants, was issued booklets of ration stamps and tokens for buying any of twenty essential items from sugar to shoes to gasoline. A driver received fuel amounts based on his vehicle's classification – pleasure, work, emergency, etc. Even though it carried more workers and was more comfortable for long trips, Gilbert Stackhouse parked his automobile and drove to jobs in Kentucky, Georgia and other places in his old farm truck which qualified for more gasoline.[37] A plumber could buy fuel for his blow torch, and Amos could run his sawmill engine for the purpose of cutting lumber, another premium commodity. Mileage records, "including furlough gasoline for servicemen," had to be kept and presented to the county rationing board before obtaining gasoline stamps. "When the gasoline is granted, the amount and reason are noted on the back of form which then accounts for every gallon of gasoline issued the car," stated one *Asheville Citizen* article.[38] Moreover, fuel for homes was regulated by the government: maximum temperature permitted, 65 degrees – lower at night and when absent from home.

The government's instatement of a thirty-five mile-per-hour speed limit, as well as the banning of pleasure driving, ensured the conservation of both gasoline and rubber tires. Only tires with absolutely no tread, nor any recap possibility, could be replaced with new ones. The OPA actually appointed tire inspectors for each section of Madison County.[39] Interestingly enough, golf balls could not be manufactured for civilian use, because they contained rubber, but a substitute, balata gum rubber, could be used to "retread" old balls, by permission of the War Production Board's rubber requirements committee.[40]

Other shortages of critical materials provoked posters and radio pleas to save scrap iron; it was said, "The iron in one old shovel could be used to make four hand grenades." At Runion the former Laurel River Logging Company's old steam engine, nicknamed "Anson" (for Anson Betts), sitting idle for nearly twenty years, was sold to dealers who dismantled it and carried it to Asheville.[41] Schools conducted drives for metals, newspapers and tin cans. At Hot Springs High School, for instance, the student body collected over 100,000 pounds of scrap iron, and, to further demonstrate its patriotism, erected a wooden flagpole over fifty feet high in the school yard. Additionally, higher-grade pupils placed boxes in the classrooms for depositing notebook paper which had writing on only one side, to be distributed to elementary pupils who would use the clean side.[42] (North Carolina's public schools later won national recognition for their wartime activities.)

America's housewives were told to separate garbage, because one pound of saved fat "contained enough glycerin to make one pound of black powder." Women's magazines offered recipes using honey or molasses as substitutes for processed sugar. Hard rock crystal candy could still be purchased at some stores instead of chocolate; Postum and chicory bean products, instead of coffee; and toys were manufactured of cardboard and wood, instead of metal, lead or rubber, and many reflected a military theme. Crude model soldiers were produced from wood or from a mixture of flour and borax. (By mid-1942, the government had stopped the production of balloons, skates, wagons and bicycles.)

Even basic foodstuffs went to the military, creating shortages and raising the farming occupation to essential status, as stated in the slogan: "Food will win the war and write the peace." (For instance, Asheville bakeries sometimes had to close from lack of flour.) The economic depression and harsh weather conditions had left many farmers with no energy or enthusiasm, but with the wartime demands for crops and the improved weather of the forties, a promise of profit and appreciation spread over the agricultural community. Many Americans joined the effort, although on a much smaller scale, by planting Victory gardens in their backyards, flower beds, rooftops, and parking lots, provoking the claim that these off-plots produced at least a third of all the vegetables eaten in the United States during the year of 1943.[43] Since Daylight Savings Time was considered more productive (the hours of work corresponding to the hours of daylight), it was ordered by the government that it should run year-round, "for the duration," and it was called *Eastern War Time* for the entirety of the Eastern Standard belt.

In addition to the extra work and deprivation caused by government demands, a five percent Victory tax was imposed on personal income taxes, and the lending of citizens' money was urged to defray the tremendous war cost. Through buying bonds and saving stamps, in denominations beginning at ten cents, then collecting the stamps into a booklet which, when filled, could be exchanged at the post office for a War Bond, civilians made another substantial contribution. The program, however, further burdened school teachers and postmasters already laden with drives and solicitations. No one complained for long, however, so strong was the desire to shorten the war. Madison County's school superintendent sent each school a spirited directive, including the following:

> "Our America is at War!... Our Government will need more money than we can ever imagine to defeat the 'Beast'... I hope every child in your school can buy Defense Stamps regularly."[44]

Young Lexine Stackhouse took butter and egg sales money, given her by her mother, to Amos' post office to purchase a bond for $18.75, which would pay $25 if redeemed ten years later.[45]

School students were inspired to join the Junior Red Cross units where a variety of service activities and educational programs enlisted their participation. One Madison County student, Nancy Lippard, recalled being taught by the Red Cross nurse to knit sweaters, scarves and socks for the soldiers from government-furnished "olive-drab" yarn.[46] School newspapers explained Air Raid Alarm procedures for school children and for parents in their homes. Night guards were posted at the French Broad River bridge in Hot Springs on Highway 25-70, a strategic route between Asheville and Knoxville. While it may sound farfetched today that the enemy could penetrate as deeply as western North Carolina, it was a quiet fact that the FBI had apprehended saboteurs who came ashore from U-boats at Long Island, New York, and Jacksonville, Florida.[1] These Germans carried orders, and were specifically trained, to destroy plants manufacturing aluminum airplane products in New York, Illinois, and Tennessee – at Alcoa, about seventy miles from Madison County.[47] (Volunteer plane spotters manned the Mt. Mitchell tower twenty-four hours a day, and, in North Carolina flat lands, vulnerable water towers were painted black.)

U.S. Army convoys regularly traveled down 25-70 through Hot Springs, their drab canvas-covered trucks with hard narrow benches carrying naïve young draftees on training maneuvers. Lonely and far from home, the boys often tossed out small pieces of gravel wrapped with paper scraps containing their names and addresses. Mail was one small thing they had to look forward to. At the Southern Railway station in Asheville, a comfortable lounge was furnished with a desk and letter-writing materials for servicemen waiting for trains. (Sewing of the room's curtains and organizing of the project was done by the Current Literature Club, including member Frances L. Goodrich, beloved missionary from Laurel.)[48]

Mail was also important to the civilians at home yearning to hear how their servicemen fared, even though their letters' content had prescribed limitations. Americans were cautioned to use care when composing letters: avoid news of family problems, deaths or serious illnesses; write about cheerful morale-boosting subjects; and refrain from any mention of military data. Any hint of a soldier's whereabouts or activities would be censored. (Ordinary conversation, too, could be harmful, according to posted war department slogans: "Loose Talk Costs Lives" and "A Slip of the Lip May Sink a Ship.")

As in the previous war, the government had power to censor all communications from foreign countries, plus domestic mail involving prisoners of war or troops at points of embarkation, headed overseas. Each letter was opened, examined, re-sealed with a numbered closure indicating that it had been censored. To reduce the tremendous bulk of wartime mail, the postal department designed V-mail – a process of microfilming letters which had been written on a standard form 8½" by 11", folded along prescribed lines into an envelope 5½" x 4½", to or from servicemen. Thus hundreds of letters on one reel traveled to their destinations where they were printed out in readable size, then forwarded to addressees. The photostat, size 4¼" x 5¼", arrived in a War Department envelope, size 4¼" x 3¼". Sometimes portions of a letter were not readable when the handwriting was too light for the camera to capture, but otherwise, it was an efficient method, speeding up mail delivery to those on the front lines. These V-mails were postage paid for military personnel and cost only three cents – regular domestic rate – for civilians.

[1] Recent records show similar landings actually on the North Carolina Outer Banks. http://www.insiders.com/outerbanks/main-history3.htm.

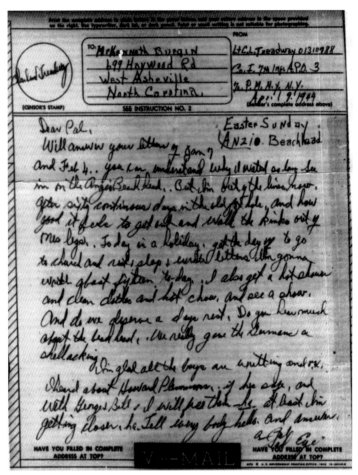

V-mail envelope and letter from Charles Treadway whose father was born on Doe Branch, written to Kenneth Burgin of Hot Springs, Madison County, 1944.

Newspapers and radio stations were also governed by a Code of Wartime Practices, to guide appropriate programming and to prevent any dangerous leaks of information. Following these rules, the *Asheville Citizen* and the Marshall *News-Record* carried regular features about Madison County servicemen and women who were home on furlough, or new draftees, or those receiving military promotions and awards, as well as reports of the dead and missing. Movie theaters presented war events each week on a "Newsreel" feature which showed before previews and main picture films, drawing movie goers who hoped to catch a glimpse of a loved one or learn of his company's activities.[49]

While there were some deferment classifications, the majority of America's young men, regardless of social standing, entered military life, including movie stars, baseball professionals, clergymen, doctors, lawyers and congressional members. Dr. David Kimberly, whose son David, III, was in the Navy, left his Hot Springs practice to serve on the military Board of Medical Review in Maryland.[50] Another from Hot Springs entered the Chaplain's Service of the Army – U.A. Brogden, pastor of the Presbyterian Churches at

Hot Springs, Walnut and White Rock, whose son Douglas was also a soldier. Many veterans of the Great War signed up and were accepted into non-combat jobs suited to their ages and experience. One of the Stackhouses' distant cousins in Philadelphia, forty-three-year-old Richardson Dilworth, who had received a Purple Heart in 1918 for an arm shattered at Soissons, left a successful trial-lawyer practice in 1942 for active duty in the Marine Intelligence Corps.[51]

A former classmate of Ernest and June Stackhouse at Weaver College and at Trinity (Duke), Edwin Burge of Asheville, had served as a cadet pilot from 1917-1919, but re-entered the Air Force in 1942 as an instructor.[52] June Stackhouse, too, left the East to work for the U.S. Army Transport Corps at Fort Mason near San Francisco. Here, due to his Coat Guard experience, he supervised engineering training of 1500 sailors who would operate small craft such as tugs and vessels up to 175 feet long.[53]

Besides the taking of its native sons, the war impacted western North Carolina in other ways, such as the closing of hotels and tourist attractions. Biltmore House, either voluntarily or by government order, did not allow public tours, except by servicemen at no admission charge. The National Gallery of Art stored 125 of its best paintings and 25 sculptures in the mansion for safe-keeping until the war was over.[54] As during the Great War, Asheville's Highland Hospital – formerly Kenilworth Inn (where typhoid-infected German internees from Hot Springs had been kept in 1918) – and the new and unfinished Sand Hill High School in west Asheville, were taken over for military hospital use. The government facility at Oteen, even with the new Moore General annex, had filled to capacity with wounded servicemen from abroad.[55]

Government orders also closed four hotels in the area to house AXIS diplomats and consular officials with their families and staff, awaiting repatriation. The situation at Grove Park Inn, for example, was similar to the one at Hot Springs during the Great War, in that an agreement between hotel owner and the government guaranteed the enemy nationals room and board while the Inn received payment from U.S.-controlled bank accounts. Local men guarded the nineteen-acre site with guns and extra lights, allowing the prisoners use of the grounds and most facilities. On April 3rd, 1942, without public announcement, two trains quietly pulled into the Asheville depot carrying 242 Italian, Hungarian and Bulgarian diplomats who were accustomed to luxury accommodations, according to observers. After a month, the first group of detainees were slipped out and replaced by 63 Japanese and 155 Germans, none of whom were diplomats. By mid-June, these had also been transferred from the Inn, freeing its use as a rehabilitation center for the U.S. Navy Department.[56] In October, 1942, the government further exercised wartime controls by bringing to Montreat (a Presbyterian Church college on the outskirts of east Asheville) 136 Japanese women and children; 126 German men, women and children; one U.S. State Department agent; and 25 guards. They took over the school's hotel facility, Assembly Inn, and the parking grounds for seven months.[57]

Had Madison County's only luxury hotel not burned in 1920, it too would likely have housed enemy aliens again as it had in 1917.[2] The hotel's

2 Painter, Jacqueline. *The German Invasion of Western North Carolina.* Johnson City, Tennessee: Overmountain Press, 1997, p.25.

replacement building, however, contained only fifty rooms and had just changed to a hotel in late 1940 when the Catholic Society sold it to three Marshall bankers. The upper lawn portion of the spa's 100 acres, under government lease since 1933, was being vacated by the Civilian Conservation Corps, which terminated nationwide in July, 1942, offering trained men ready for the military. (It was later said by some that the three million CCC boys won the war of the forties.[58]) During its nine years in Hot Springs, the CCC camp had become an integral part of Madison County's culture, and it would be sorely missed.

The world conflict brought another closing of magnitude to Hot Springs and Madison County. As Walnut community's Bell Institute had been moved to Hot Springs during the Great War, the Dorland-Bell School was moved to Swannanoa – six miles east of Asheville – in the summer of 1942.[59] On April 30th, the *Asheville Citizen* had announced that the Presbyterian Board of National Missions in New York would consolidate the Asheville Farm School for boys and the Dorland School for girls into a co-educational institution named Warren H. Wilson Vocational Junior College. The merger called for additional buildings, but construction had to be postponed for lack of materials. Other shortages in general – including heating fuel, gasoline and food – coupled with the drafting of students and faculty, made the merger more pragmatic and, even patriotic, some would say. Compared to the loss of the CCC camp, Dorland-Bell's leaving was an immeasurable loss to Madison County. (Likewise, in 1944 the Asheville Normal Teachers College – a presence in western North Carolina since 1892, and alma mater of Nita Stackhouse – succumbed to several years of financial problems, only emphasized by war conditions.)

Although far from western North Carolina, a different threat hovered close to the continental United States in the Japanese occupation of the Aleutian Islands, Attu and Kiska, on June 7, 1942.[60] However, two days earlier, the battle at Midway Island in the Pacific had been won, thwarting Japan's effort to command this base, from which they could have shaken up the American people. Suffering far fewer losses than their enemy, the U.S. Navy nevertheless lost one of its largest carriers, the *Yorktown*, from which Thomas Goode of Hot Springs was a fortunate survivor.[61] While the battle at Midway was a critical turning point for the Allies, their ships in the Atlantic were being sunk by the Germans at an appalling rate. Amos Stackhouse made concerned observations in his journal: "War is serious now," and "Almost every person is sad over war reverses, but are looking forward to some victory."[62]

On the other hand, reason for family celebration was presented when Nita Stackhouse gave birth in Charlotte to a second daughter, named Nancy Catherine. Six-year-old Lexine had suddenly lost her place as "family pet" in exchange for the position of "elder, responsible one." These girls would prove to be the blessing Hester Stackhouse had yearned for in her child-bearing years. Another happy event took place a month later – June 14, 1942 – when Amos and Hester's first granddaughter, Carthene, married John "Jack" Wesley Cole in Hampton, Virginia, where the couple lived for the duration.[63]

All through the winter and spring before, Amos' farm, store and postal routine had kept him busy, but he and Gilbert finally finished their saw mill, working around rain, snow, cold temperatures and illnesses: Gilbert's pleurisy,

AMOS STACKHOUSE

DEALER IN

GROCERIES AND GENERAL MERCHANDISE

HAY, GRAIN AND LUMBER

STACKHOUSE, N. C.

Business letterhead used by Amos in the 1930s and 1940s. Plain style for austere times.

Nita's pregnancy, and little Lexine's long critical bout with pneumonia. One of the mill's last needs had been water to cool the motor. Amos wrote in his journal, "Gilbert and Troy Dockery put in pipe from branch to gas engine." The first lumber was sawed on April 16, 1942.[64]

In April, Amos had written of a different challenge. "Fire set out by local train Number 11 – had to rake around upper chicken yard and up the hill. Riley, Lee and Harley helped me, since Gilbert gone to Charlotte." Three days later, a fresh outbreak occurred: "Woods on Walnut knob all afire. Burnt our garden fence, also chicken yard fence post, a row of sage in garden, and an apple tree. Smoked the house at least 3 shades darker." He noted the next week that woods were burning across the river in the Doe Branch section. Eventually, the spring rains began, eliminating the danger for the season, at least.[65] (Forest fires had threatened Amos' father, too, from his earliest days at Stackhouse, prompting him to keep the woods cleared for a considerable distance around his homestead.)

Other scattered entries in Amos' journal revealed his varied, if mundane, daily activities, even as war raged overseas:

"Commenced preparing for planting garden and farm work."

"After milking and feeding, worked in saw mill, post office, and continued planting garden and fields."

"Loaded car of locust – about $14^{3}/_{4}$ cords."

"Gilbert got two pigs for William to fatten on the halves – little red fellows."

"My mule is sick today."

"Made a plow beam, hoed in garden, worked on wagon harness, walked over to Ellison tract to check freeze damage to timber."

"Planted five bushels potatoes today – will finish tomorrow."

"Had Manly Ray haul us three sled loads of firewood."

"Planted tobacco, watermelons and muskmelons."

"Set out 178 tomato plants, 3000 sweet potato plants."

"Went to Hot Springs to vote."

"Graded car of white pine at Marshall."[66]

One not-so-common item in Amos' journal declared: "A Mr. Ray Stackhouse and wife from Chicago dropped in for an hour or so – bought 2 post cards and addressed them." No doubt, the visitor, like so many other Stackhouses around the country, wanted to see the one place in America named for his family, and to get copies of the postmark by mailing postcards to himself. This type of interest would continue through years to come.

271

July 1, 1942, Amos wrote about seeing his latest granddaughter for the first time: "Mrs. Caldwell came up from Charlotte with new baby girl named Nancy C." For nearly six weeks since his wife's delivery, Gilbert had been making frequent trips to Charlotte, but now Nita was considered to be beyond some of the common dangers associated with childbirth, such as "milk leg (phlebitis)," and was able to travel. Mrs. Caldwell stayed at Stackhouse with Nita and Gilbert until August 17th, helping with young Lexine, with the washing, ironing, churning, canning and other tasks of the rural housewife.[67]

Home canning sugar registration, which allowed one pound per person per annum, had been done by Amos on June 8th at the Walnut High School for his whole family. Taken seriously by the OPA, sugar consumption regulations appeared in the Marshall *News-Record*:

> "In no event shall the individual or family unit be permitted more sugar than is necessary to can the quantity of fruit which the Board deems to be reasonable, giving due consideration to the period within which the fruit will be consumed, the past practice of the family unit, the prevailing home canning practice in the locality among individuals and families in circumstances similar to those of the applicant, the number of fruit previously canned at home remaining in the possession of the family applying."[68]

At the end of the busy summer, Lexine began second grade at the Stackhouse school, a short way up the mountain, where her mother had taught in 1933. Ever since, Mrs. Jessie Laws (who walked to and from her Walnut home each day by the old Hopewell Road) had been teaching in the one-room school, which served not only Stackhouse community but also several outlying settlements. The Treadway children walked from Runion, and others came from Sandy Bottom, Big Pine and Walnut Gap. It took two coal stoves to heat the large building, two outdoor privies in back for the boys and the girls, and drinking water carried each morning from the nearby spring. Pupils brought their own tin cups to be filled at the common dipper resting in the bucket.[69] This would be the last of the eight-month school years for Lexine and other North Carolina school children, the State Assembly making provision for each term to be nine months.

Eventually, the long first year of the war neared end, its deprivations and anxieties becoming almost ordinary. As America and the other Allies fought desperately in the skies, on the seas, and across the land of four continents, more than one hundred army, navy, marine and coast guard stations were established in North Carolina, with western North Carolina's young men continuing to fill the ranks.[70] Approaching Christmas, Amos Stackhouse kept to himself the deepest fears and apprehensions he felt for his family and community, all the time praying for an end to the slaughter – indeed, for "Peace on earth, good will to men."

[1] Author's private papers.
[2] Ibid.
[3] Ibid.
[4] Treadway, Martha. Interview, Powell, Tenn., 1990.
[5] Private papers.
[6] Stackhouse, Nita. Interview, 2000.
[7] Baker, Elizabeth Gahagan. Interview, 2002.
   Asheville Citizen, March 19, 1938.
   Tennessee State Library, Department of Vital Records.
[8] Stackhouse, Nita. Interview, 2002.
[9] Meek, Anna. Interview, 2000.
   Asheville Citizen, May 1, 1939.
[10] Meek, Anna. Interview, 2000.
[11] Sulzberger, C.L. *The American Heritage Picture History of W.W.II.* New York, N.Y.: Bonanza Books, 1966, p.58.
[12] Harris, Mark J., Franklin D. Mitchell, Steven J. Schechter, *The Homefront.* New York, N.Y.: G.P. Putnams's Sons, 1984, p.46.
[13] Meek, Anna. Interview, 2003.
   Stackhouse, Larry B. Interview, 2003.
[14] Stackhouse, Nita. Interview, 2003.
[15] Cole, Jack. Interview, 2000.
[16] "Floods on French Broad River and Spring Creek, Vicinity of Hot Springs, N.C." Tennessee Valley Report. Knoxville: TVA Division of Water Control Planning, 1960, p.19.
[17] *Asheville Citizen*, August 31, 1940.
[18] TVA report, p.19.
[19] *Asheville Citizen*, August 31, 1940.
[20] Aumiller, Nancy S. Interview, 2002.
[21] Painter, Jacqueline. *The Season of Dorland-Bell.* Appalachian Consortium Press, Boone, N.C.: 1996, p.227.
[22] Lefler, Hugh T. *North Carolina History, Geography & Government.* Yonkers-on-Hudson, New York: World Book Company, 1959, p.443.
[23] Sullivan, Robert, ed. *Pearl Harbor.* New York: Life/Time, Inc., 2001, pp.33-37.
[24] *Asheville Citizen-Times*, August 3, 1941.
[25] Aumiller, Nancy S. Interview, 2002.
[26] Ibid.
[27] Dockery, Clyde. Interview, 2003.
[28] Lefler, p.445.
[29] Goode, John. Interview, Hot Springs, N.C. 1995.
   Gowan, Perry. Interview, Hot Springs, N.C., 1995.
[30] Radin, Clara Hester Stackhouse. Interview, California, 2000.
[31] Cole, Jack. Interview, 2000.
   Aumiller, Nancy S. Interview, 2000.
[32] Norris, Lexyne Stackhouse. Interview, 2000.
[33] Stackhouse, Nita. Interview, 1999.
[34] McGee, Val L. *The Origins of Fort Rucker.* Ozark, Alabama: Dale County Historical Society, Inc., 1987, p.116.
[35] Ibid.
[36] Private papers.

37 Stackhouse, Nita. Interview, 2000.
38 *Asheville Citizen*, May 1, 1945.
39 Marshall *News-Record*, February 11, 1943.
40 *Asheville Citizen*, May 1, 1945.
41 Hull, Edna Betts. Interview, 1998.
   Dockery, Interview.
42 Lippard, Nancy T. Interview, 2003.
43 Harris, p.64.
44 *The Panorama*, Hot Springs High School paper, January, 1942.
45 Norris, Interview.
46 Lippard, Interview.
47 Carr, Charles C. *Alcoa: An American Enterprise*. New York: Rinehart & Company, 1952, p.256.
48 *Asheville Citizen*, May 19, 1942.
49 Private papers.
   Graham, Richard B., "Mail Censorship, World War II, and V-Mail," Linn's Stamp News. State College, Pennsylvania: American Philatelic Society, 1988, pps. 10, 22.
50 Kimberly, David III. Interview, 2003.
51 McKelvey, Gerald, "Dilworth Dead at 75," *Philadelphia Inquirer*. January 24, 1974. (Courtesy, Free Library of Philadelphia.)
52 Burge, Hal. Interview, Asheville, February, 2002.
   Asheville Citizen, October 15, 1968.
53 Radin, 2003.
54 *Charlotte Observer*, September 7, 1957. (Courtesy, Pack Library, Asheville, N.C.)
55 Johnson, Bruce E. *Built For the Ages: A History of Grove Park Inn*. Asheville, N.C.: Grove Park Inn and Country Club, 1991, p.58.
56 Ibid., p.56.
57 Anderson, Robert C., D.D., *The Story of Montreat From Its Beginning*. Published by author, 1949, pp. 116-119.
58 Jolley, Harley E., "Hard Times and Happy Days," *Tar Heel Junior Historian*, Vol. 23, Number 2 (Winter, 1984), p.21.
   Cohen, Stan, *The Tree Army: A Pictorial History of the Civilian Conservation Corps*, 1933'1942.
59 *Asheville Times*, Aug, 26, 1942.
60 Sulzberger, p.330.
61 Goode, John. Interview, 1995.
62 Private papers.
63 Aumiller.
64 Private papers.
65 Ibid.
66 Ibid.
67 Ibid.
68 Marshall *News-Record*, June 4, 1942.
69 Norris, 1999.
70 Lefler, p.444.

Chapter Twenty-Four

With the passing of the first long year of war, many Americans wore popular lapel pins that helped keep the focus: *Remember Pearl Harbor.* It now appeared that this conflict, unlike its predecessor, would be a long one for the U.S. The answer given to all queries beginning with, "How long?" was "For the duration." Deprivations and anxieties were almost ordinary: Meatless Tuesdays, Wheatless Thursdays, Gasless Sundays and other sacrifices. When members of the Stackhouse family needed to ride the train to Marshall or Asheville, they often found all seats filled and more soldiers sleeping in the aisle floors, their heads on their duffle bags or on pillows rented from the conductor. The depots were always crowded, as were street cars, stores, eating counters and practically every other public place. Shortages and rationing continued, requiring patching and mending of many everyday articles. Stores sold cellophane repair packages of shoe heels and half soles made of leather or rubber substitute compositions, as well as packets of thin metal disks with short bolts and washers for plugging holes in worn-thin cooking utensils.

However, most rural western North Carolinians fared better than some in other parts of the country since they raised their own hogs, chickens and vegetables (they kept cattle but rarely ate beef), and did not have to rely, solely, on ration books. Nor did they buy the butter substitute, oleomargarine, sold in white, lard-like bricks, with small paper packets of yellow coloring to be mixed in by messy hand kneading. Mountaineers grew the grain for the wheat flour and corn meal used to make their daily bread; their draft animals consumed no gasoline.

Despite these advantages, the new year of 1943 presented an unhappy milestone to Amos Stackhouse, personally. On February second he wrote, "I am 70 years old today – must retire as postmaster, Feb. 28, 1943."[1] He had held the title for nearly fifty years, but unlike his father, he had no child waiting to be sworn in. His three sons had been forced to leave the county to find gainful employment, as had so many others. A partially-satisfying solution came when his wife was sworn in as "acting postmaster," allowing him to continue working up the mails, the stamp orders and everything else except the signing of official reports. On March 1, 1943, Amos wrote in his journal with some wistfulness: "Hester A. Stackhouse, my beloved wife, is postmaster today."[2] (She would serve in the "acting" capacity until April 15th when the postal inspector from Raleigh came to appoint her "postmaster," officially.)

Amos' low spirit likely lifted a bit, later in the month, at the prospect of joining other Madison Countians in Marshall to pay tribute to their native son, Major Edward Franklin Rector. The distinguished flying ace was on furlough after a year and a half of dangerous combat as a fighter pilot – first, in the famed American Volunteer Group of "Flying Tigers," then, as commander of the 23rd Fighter Group.[3] His first mission had been to help the Chinese protect the Burma Road against Japanese invasion. The title of "ace" was bestowed on a pilot who destroyed five enemy planes in the air; Rector downed six and a half, the half resulting from a "shared downing." Twice, the ace had been shot down, but managed to escape without serious injury.[4] He had grown up near Marshall, his farmer father, George Rector, working a side job of deputy sheriff during the prohibition years. Two of Edward's ten siblings were also in the service, one having served in the Great War. The town of Marshall was mentioned in the March 8, 1942 issue of *Life* magazine, profiling Edward and several other Flying Tigers in a long illustrated article. When Amos attended the Rector parade and celebration, the Moore-General Hospital band from Oteen played, banners flew, and dignitaries spoke to the attending crowd. Asheville newspapers and radio stations covered the event, including the writing of a song by Mrs. G.W. Corbett of Hot Springs.[5]

Another western North Carolina native, pilot Robert Morgan of Asheville, would also be pictured in *Life* magazine six months later with Margaret Polk, the girl for whom his famous B-17 plane was named, the *Memphis Belle*. The first American bomber to fly twenty-five raids over occupied France and Germany, the *Belle* and Morgan had just returned when *Life's* camera caught him.[6] Robert's father, David, had been manager of Carolina Wood Products at Woodfin before Charles Dilworth, Amos' brother, began working there, but Morgan moved out to Black Mountain to develop a new business called Dimension Manufacturing Company. Instead of producing complete articles, the plant cut lumber to the dimensions required by furniture factories – a modern concept based on Henry Ford's mass production principle.[7] The company soon became Morgan Manufacturing Company and employed a number of former Laurel River Logging Company workers, including Chappell Norton and Herbert Waldrop. Robert Morgan, like Edward Rector, would be lauded by his western North Carolina neighbors.

Almost weekly, other young men from Madison County came of draft age and entered the armed forces, frequently, more than one from the same family. Two sons of Danny Gillespie from Bluff received their calls at the same time, while five sons and three sons-in-law of Mrs. Bessie Norton of Hot Springs were already serving. Another son of Malley Reeves at Walnut, and namesake of Amos Stackhouse – Amos Kenneth Reeves – entered the Navy, to bring his family's total to three sons in the war.[8] Although not drafted, some of its young women also joined, for instance, Mildred Hardin, a Mars Hill teacher, and Jo Lunsford, daughter of Madison County's well-known balladeer, Bascomb Lamar Lunsford.[9]

Quite a few women joined the ranks of Civil Service in Washington, D.C., or took assembly-line defense jobs, or worked at Maryland and Virginia shipyards in order to release more men for combat. Actually, there were so many Madison County people in Baltimore that the *News-Record* carried a short item each week called "Baltimore News."[10] The families who had moved North in the 1920s and returned home during Depression lay-offs were also back in Michigan and Indiana working in converted-to-defense automobile factories.

Jobs were becoming plentiful in North Carolina, too (at least in the Piedmont and Coastal sections), with construction going on at the several military bases, especially Fort Bragg – enlarged for a maximum load of nearly 100,000 men. Textile mills worked overtime, sending (more than any other state) sheets, blankets, clothing, tents, bandages, parachutes and tire cords to the Quartermaster Corps. The Ethyl-Dow plant at Kure Beach manufactured all tetra-ethyl lead used in the war, while the mountain mines supplied more than fifty percent of all mica used. North Carolina sawmills put on extra shifts of men to rank fourth in lumber production for the armed forces.[11] At Hot Springs a small dogwood saw mill opened to furnish material for wooden shuttles, vital to the constant operation of the state's textile mills.

Men who were too old for the draft, or exempt, found jobs at the construction of TVA's Fontana dam in western North Carolina and at Douglas dam in eastern Tennessee. (A bus, nicknamed the Blue Goose, was actually sent to Jackson County to pick up workers each morning, at the same time returning those from the night shift.) These dams helped fill the tremendous wartime need for electric power.

Because of a similar need for minerals, the U.S. Bureau of Mines sent agents to Stackhouse and Sandy Bottom to search for barite ore. While Amos was glad to show them around, he felt disappointment when their operation with diamond drills was not productive.[12] He could have used the royalty to help pay his bank notes. According to Anson Betts (who continued to have faith that large amounts of good ore awaited the correct approach), the government engineers' plan had been fraught with errors and misconceptions.

Yet another wartime necessity brought more government money to western North Carolina in July, 1944, when Asheville's four largest hotels became distribution centers for army combatants arriving from overseas in need of rehabilitation before re-assignment – the same use that Hot Springs' Mountain Park Hotel had served during the Great War. Three months before, much publicity had surrounded the Grove Park Inn when Manuel Quezon, the exiled Philippine president, established his government's headquarters in a cottage on the grounds. Even earlier that year, after fleeing Europe, the famous Hungarian composer, Bela Bartok, stayed at the Grove Park for a time. His work while there – *Concerto No. 3 for Piano and Orchestra* – is often called "a monument to the birds of western North Carolina."[13]

Other Europeans, having escaped Hitler's persecutions, came to western North Carolina by way of the American Friends Service Committee. As Amos Stackhouse's ancestors had helped runaway slaves a century earlier, their Quaker descendents now saved refugees from Nazi ovens and prisons in 1939 and 1940. Before the United States entered the war, the Friends found sponsors such as Dorland-Bell School in Hot Springs, where Marianne Regensberger, a German student, lived for a time.[14] At Swannanoa the Asheville Farm School agreed to accept a German Christian Jew, Hans Forell, opening the door for more foreign students needing refuge.[15] The Friends sent talented teachers, poets, artists, scientists, philosophers and musicians to Black Mountain College. Because of North Carolina's large active Quaker community concerned with human rights, an influx of academic refugees received asylum at the University of North Carolina, Duke, North Carolina Central and others. These scholars greatly enriched North Carolina's intellectual environment and "contributed to the story of cultural transformation which took place in the United States through the teaching of refugees from Hitler's Germany," stated author Mary Emma Harris in her article, "Black Mountain College & Its Cosmopolitan Faculty."[16]

A Japanese-American, Kuni Hirokawa, enrolled at Warren Wilson College in Swannanoa, following his release from an alien internment camp in Arizona. Writing for the college newspaper, he described his family's evacuation from their California home just after Pearl Harbor; the sorrows of losing their home, belongings and business; their detention conditions (far cruder and more crowded than those of the WWI Germans in Hot Springs); and finally the United States government's permission, in January, 1944, to leave the camp and try to start a new life. Oddly enough, Kuni brought no bitterness to western North Carolina, stating in his essay: "The evacuation may have been a test from God as to whether we had a strong Christian character and a purpose in life to live for Him and not for the worldly things that we had left behind."[17]

The war was also responsible for another wedding in the Stackhouse family in June, 1943, as Anna, daughter of Charles Dilworth, married Milton Meek. The red-haired Irishman from Oklahoma had met Anna in West Asheville when his buddy, Dilworth, brought him from Fort Bragg to visit the Stackhouse family.[18] Unfortunately, Milton had been sent to the Philippines, where he "was all shot up by the Japanese," given a Purple Heart, and discharged with disability, said family members. He and Anna would live near Asheville for the rest of their long married life.[19]

Anna Stackhouse Meek, June, 1943.

Nita Stackhouse's brother, Robert Caldwell, became a war casualty, too, when he contracted tuberculosis and was sent to the veteran's hospital near Black Mountain for treatment. His wife often stayed at Stackhouse with Nita so that she could handily visit the sanitarium by train.[20] Like many other things, available hotel rooms and tourist cabins in the vicinity were at a premium or unattainable.

Few families even had spare rooms anymore, with the acute housing shortages. While Madison County men served in the armed forces, their wives and children often moved back to their parents' homes to keep from being alone, and also because they could not find quarters new the military bases. The wife of Frank Hunycutt, Jr., was one of these, living at Walnut with Frank and Alice. By combining households, food, and fuel, ration stamps could be stretched. Churches, too, saved coal by closing off rooms or by holding Sunday School classes and other meetings in members' homes. In Hot Springs the Presbyterian and Methodist churches sometimes held joint worship services so that only one furnace needed to be fired.

Amos and Gilbert found markets for any lumber they could manufacture at their small mill. Haywood County's paper mill needed pulp wood now more than ever. Morgan Dimension Lumber Plant in Black Mountain advertised in the *News-Record* for "Green or dry 4-quarter maple, birch, beech, basswood, ash and oak – highest cash paid."[21] For local people, Amos and Gilbert also cut small "house patterns" – the complete list of lumber pieces needed to frame a house.

Besides the home front struggle caused by shortages and restrictions, Madison County battled a poliomyelitis outbreak during the summer of 1943, prompting Hester Stackhouse's nephew, Dr. W.A. Sams of Marshall, to declare a county-wide quarantine for children under sixteen years old.[22] Public gatherings were banned, and swimming pools – thought to be a disease spreader – closed, but still the epidemic raged as doctors watched helplessly. Some children died, others clung to life in iron lungs, while a number suffered paralysis or lifetime crippling.[23] In Hot Springs one of John Harrison's granddaughters was paralyzed and did not walk for a year.[24] Finally, as the summer waned, so did the contagion, but only until the returning hot weather of subsequent summers. Hearing about the symptoms of sore throat, headache and high fever reminded the Stackhouse family of the influenza pandemic during the Great War years.

For once, Nita Stackhouse could appreciate the isolation of her mountain life, which now protected her young daughters, even though they had their share of normal childhood diseases and injuries that year. Both girls suffered whooping-cough, the killer of Amos and Hester's baby, Edmond, many years before. Crawling infant, Nancy, pulled up to the wood stove, requiring her hands to be lifted away by her mother, their flesh having stuck to the hot metal. In both cases, the Stackhouse cousin, Dr. Sams, came to their home to treat the children. At another time, when Gilbert was working out of the county, Nancy was so ill that Nita sent their mule with a neighbor, Lee Daniels, to Walnut to telephone Dr. Sams.[25] No one at Stackhouse owned an automobile except Gilbert.

Isolated though it might be, Stackhouse, North Carolina, received some war news by battery-operated radio, prompting Amos to write on Tuesday, June 6, 1944: "Our forces overseas left England at 3:15 o'clock and arrived in France about 4 to 6 o'clock, gaining beach heads to liberate Hitler's Europe."[26] He referred, of course, to "Operation Overlord," considered the greatest invasion the world has ever seen, and later called "D-Day," a military milestone marking the beginning of the end of the war. The *Asheville Times* newspaper published an EXTRA edition that day, announcing, "Complete Coverage with maps, news and pictures." WWNC radio station furnished "unsurpassed coverage" of the invasion, interrupting its regular schedule of programs at frequent intervals and operating additional hours, "as long as invasion news of intense interest continues to pour in," stated the *Times*.[27] Amos could not know that Dilworth Stackhouse, son of his beloved brother Charles, had been among the 23,000 men landing on that far away French shore. From Utah Beach, with the 9th Army, Dilworth luckily survived to fight many more times in the coming months, one particularly difficult and dangerous one being the Battle of the Bulge in December.[28] (Paul Dockery from Stackhouse was not as lucky, perishing December 18, 1944, third day of the month-long onslaught.)[29] Dilworth was promoted to First Sergeant in a light artillery platoon, trekking through France, Luxembourg, Holland, Austria and Germany, where he was sent into the Harz Mountains to bring in prisoners. Finally, on May 8, 1945, Allied Victory in Europe was official, effecting V-E Day celebrations practically worldwide.

Appreciation was warmly shown American soldiers by the liberated Europeans, as attested to by Alonzo Norton, son of Bessie Bullman Norton who lived in Hot Springs and had relatives at Stackhouse: "I have been kissed

Charles Dilworth Stackhouse, Jr. in Hurtgen Forest, Germany, 1944.
Courtesy, Harvey Stackhouse.

by almost every man, woman and child in France, Belgium and Holland...
people with tears in their eyes, shaking your hand and telling you how long
they have waited for you and how badly they have been treated," he wrote.[30]
Allied rejoicing, however, held certain reservations, since Japan and her
suicide bombers yet posed a grave threat to world peace.

During subsequent months, naval and air units attacked in the Pacific,
much as ground forces and planes had stormed the Atlantic shore at
Normandy. John Goode of Hot Springs (whose great grandfather had driven
the mail stage through Warm Springs, regularly stopping at Amos and Anna's
first store), participated in the invasion of Luzon and the battle of Leyte Gulf
– later called the greatest naval engagement in history.[31] Also of Hot Springs,
Perry Gowan was present at the Philippines invasion and the attack on New
Guinea, surviving both.[32] As American casualties mounted, however, men on
the home front who were age thirty-six or less and who had only slight
disabilities or other deferments, found their selective service classifications
changing from 4F to 3A and even 1A, ready to be drafted.

Finally, on August 6, 1945, a world-changing event occurred, having been
contributed to, oddly enough, by Perry Gowan's and John Goode's fellow
Madison Countians back home. When the Fontana Dam had been completed
in January, a secondary purpose was fulfilled – furnishing vast amounts of

electricity to the unrevealed project where hundreds of western North Carolinians had joined eastern Tennesseans for employment, with no idea what they were making at these jobs. Lance Holland describes it in his book, *Fontana: A Pocket History of Appalachia*, "Just west of Knoxville, a city for 75,000 people was built surrounded by a high fence; armed guards… patrolled the perimeter… The secret city was Oak Ridge."[33] Material produced there became part of the atomic bomb used on August 6th, bringing Japan, at last, to surrender, and the horrors of conflict to an end. The average American did not comprehend the bomb's potential consequences, only its immediate war-ending power, which brought jubilation nationwide.

The announcement on August 14, 1945, that Japan had accepted the Allied surrender terms in full, created instant celebrating in Asheville. "There were 10,000 people in the streets, singing, dancing, kissing and generally whooping it up," wrote Bob Terrell, an *Asheville Citizen* reporter.[34] Two uniformed sailors sat atop the Vance Monument, no one seeming to know how they had scaled the smooth granite obelisk, seventy-five feet tall. "Waynesville went wild; Canton flocked singing into the street, Franklin's fire siren sounded continually for nearly two hours, and Marshall went into a series of impromptu parades," stated the next day's *Asheville Times*.[35] Many western North Carolinians met at their churches for prayers of thanksgiving, an atmosphere of relief permeating hillside and hollow.

Within months, most Madison County wives and mothers enjoyed happy reunions with their servicemen, but other families awaited the long military process of returning loves ones' remains for home burial. The war had claimed a number of the local boys, including Beverly Izlar, great grandson of the late J.H. Rumbough, Stackhouse family friend from Hot Springs. One of John Harrison's grandsons, Bill Harrison, all but starved to death as a prisoner of war, while another one, Charles Treadway, wrote to a friend that after over

Sons of Bessie Bullman Norton, WWII. L to R: Arbuary, Alonzo, Solomon, Stanley, Johnny. On porch, Mrs. Norton and her daughter Adelia.

sixty days in a foxhole without a warm meal, he was then hospitalized, only to be returned to the front before combat ceased.[36] Miraculously, Bessie Bullman Norton's five sons and three sons-in-law had lived through it all, as did Amos Stackhouse's nephew, Dilworth.

On his way overseas in 1944, aboard the troop ship *Marine Wolf*, Dilworth Stackhouse had been miserably seasick for the entire voyage. When the time came for him to return home, he said he'd rather stay in Europe than ride a ship. Fortunately, "His berth was on some luxury liner like the Queen Elizabeth, and he did not get sick," related his son Larry Stackhouse over fifty years later. Dilworth, native of Stackhouse, North Carolina, gave the community its own hero, as he returned to western North Carolina, wearing the Silver Star, awarded "for gallantry in action… performed with marked distinction."[37]

Other Madison County soldiers and sailors – most having entered service as boys – came back as men, feeling old, and bearing their own medals and citations. Practically to the man, their fathers had fought in the Great War, their great grandfathers in the Civil War and their great, great, great grandfathers, in the Revolution. Patriots all, this generation, too, was reticent about its horrible experiences, hoping only to forget and begin anew.

One, nevertheless, would not be as reluctant to share his memories: Major Edward Franklin Rector, called "one of North Carolina's most glamourous war heroes."[38] His *Flying Tigers'* participation would be documented through books, magazines, oil paintings, moving pictures, radio broadcasts, television interviews and speaking engagements.[39] Major Robert Morgan, the much-decorated pilot of the flying fortress, *Memphis Belle*, enjoyed similar acclaim in his native Buncombe County.[40]

The Stackhouse family's distant cousin, Richardson Dilworth, having been in combat at Guadalcanal and the Russell Island landings, returned in glory, too, with a Silver Star added to his Great War honors. This two-war Marine, standing, at least partly, on his military records, proceeded to place the name of Dilworth solidly in Philadelphia politics as city treasurer, district attorney, mayor, and school board president. He brought sweeping reform to a city of long-standing corruption, prompting a terminal at International Airport and a public plaza to be named for him. Described as an awesome presence, a quintessential urban leader, a man of action, but also a voracious reader of Kipling and Dickens, Richardson Dilworth was curiously called "the last of the bare-knuckled aristocrats."[41] These comments would have both pleased and embarrassed his and Amos' Quaker ancestors.

Sharing not only name, but also military honor with Richardson, Dilworth Stackhouse in Asheville likewise settled into civilian life upon his return from war, finding employment at the American Enka Company, a rayon mill with over 3000 employees. Before long, he went to work for better wages as a driver at the Silverfleet trucking company in Biltmore, a move destined to provide a lifetime career. He also took a wife in Buncombe County, Virginia Anderson, adopting her young son, Larry, as his own.[42]

Out in California, June Stackhouse had added another limb to the family tree when his wife, Anna, gave birth to their second son, William Hunter Stackhouse (called Bill) in April, 1944. June had changed jobs again, moving from Sausalito to San Francisco where he was superintendent and consulting engineer for H.W. Parsons Ship Repair Company. June developed three chemical cleaning methods for tanks, evaporators and boilers that were patented under H.W. Parsons' company. Parsons paid June $10,000 for the rights, plus 25% of the gross profit on sales. The product was marketed as "Thermasol (Stackhouse process).*" Despite the distance from California, June continued to bring his family for summer visits to his parents' home in western North Carolina – now catching its breath from the frenzied wartime pace.[43]

Amos "June" Stackhouse in center holding son William Hunter. In back, L to R: Clara Hester, daughter; Amos "Sonny" Stackhouse, III, son; Ann Hoffman Stackhouse, wife. c. 1945.

Suddenly there was no need to save newspapers and scrap iron, although shortages would continue until manufacturing and foreign trade caught up. At Stackhouse a large pile of tin cans in the parking yard near Ernest's cabin served as a reminder of the lean times, as they began to rust away. During the last months of the war, "Word had come that the cans, if collected, would be picked up by someone from Marshall for the war effort," recalled Lexyne Stackhouse Norris many years later, "but no one ever came."[44]

In November, 1945, a memorandum came to Amos from the Office of Price Administration in Charlotte, addressed to "All Retailers and

* By coincidence and unknown to June, his cousin, Asa Matlack Stackhouse, of Moorestown, New Jersey, received a patent the same year for an improved sewage treatment method.

Wholesalers." The State's Food Rationing Officer, J.M. Robinson, declared that "registration files were being transferred from Local Boards to the District Office in Charlotte," preparing for an end to government controls and rationing.[45]

Manufacturers, too, were making the welcome transition from military goods to their pre-war production. The Nash-Kelvinator corporation began building automobiles and refrigerators again, instead of airplane engines and propellers, but the changeover would not take place overnight. Civilians had to wait months until their kitchen appliances, cars, sewing machines and other products arrived at the retail stores. To purchase a refrigerator, for instance, the customer had, first, to place his name on the merchant's waiting list. Even then, with materials still scarce, the long-awaited items were plain unadorned versions of the fancy chrome and brass-decorated pre-war merchandise.

Besides pulling North Carolina out of the depression, the wartime economic improvement brought the fist state appropriations for art and music, funding the North Carolina Symphony Orchestra and the State Art Society. Salaries of teachers and other state employees increased, the compulsory school attendance age rose from fourteen to sixteen, a ninth month was added to the school year, as well as a twelfth grade to the school program.[46] Madison County's teachers naturally benefited, but its farmers – the work force majority – suffered from having to keep their sons and daughters in school longer, when they needed them in the fields or at a job, bringing home wages. Madison farms had already lost young people who never returned from city defense work, cajoled by their taste of the world beyond Appalachia. Younger siblings and even a few parents, lured by the promise of steady work and easy urban living, sometimes joined their city-dwelling family members.

While large portions of the United States and eastern North Carolina had been aided by the industrial explosion, Madison County, in general, and Stackhouse, in particular, were little touched by this type of progress. "There were people still living in log cabins at Stackhouse in the late 1940's," recalled Nancy Stackhouse Aumiller over fifty years later.[47] The mountain economy had been stimulated, but no factories provided jobs in Madison County, requiring many veterans to leave their homes and roots. A few did stay to work the family farms or use the GI Bill to attend local colleges.

Ernest Stackhouse moved his family to Charlotte where he worked as an engineer for J.A. Jones Construction Company with whom he had been associated at Fort Rucker. His daughter, Carthene, and her husband, Jack Cole, came there to live with them, as well as Ruth's parents, Mr. and Mrs. Vandervort. The arrangement might have seemed odd to most people, but it was traditional in Ruth's family, no matter how small the living quarters, and no matter that each family could afford independent homes. They now used their Stackhouse log cabin for vacations and occasional weekends.

When first returning from his wartime job, Ernest had learned that more of this Uncle Charlie's former property had been bought from Citizens Bank in Marshall on March 1, 1945. Anson Betts paid $1000 for one-half interest in two Stackhouse tracts once owned jointly by Amos and his late brother Charles.[48] The first contained sixty-five acres, being the farmstead owned by Ellison Stackhouse when he had lived there during the late 1880's. The second was the fifty-six-acre Klondyke tract which Amos' and Charles' father had bought from Gahagan in 1883.

It saddened Amos that he could not buy back Charles' part of this land which had been in the Stackhouse family for over sixty years, but he, too, still owed Great Depression notes at Citizens Bank. (Amos was able to repay some of these in October, 1944, when he and Hester sold their lot on Busbee Place, Biltmore Forest, owned since 1925.)[49] Although the economy had improved, western North Carolina's wages continued low, Amos himself paying twenty cents an hour to the local men he employed around the farm. In fact, a few days before the bank sale, Amos had offered his part of the Klondyke to a barite prospector from New York, Edgar Wagner. Back on February 28, 1944, Amos and Hester signed a lease agreement with Wagner, allowing mining on the fifty-six acre tract, "about a hundred feet below the Thomas Clingman vein."[50] Wagner would pay fifty cents a long ton for ore, in addition to one hundred dollars at signing. One year later, Amos extended the lease for another year, further granting a year's option "to purchase outright the lands and minerals for the sum of $4250, payable in cash."[51] Either the ore played out or Wagner could not raise the money, because the sale was never consummated.

Fortunately, once again, timber cutting on Laurel, in conjunction with the rail siding rental at Stackhouse, brought income to Amos and his neighbors. Coming from East Tennessee, lumberman Cal Garland set up a small saw mill on Spillcorn Creek to serve the timbering in remote hollows throughout the Laurel Country.[52] "Logs were brought to the mills by chaining several onto a drag sled pulled by mules or tractor along the rocky muddy trails," remembered Gene Cantrell, former Garland employee and Walnut native. The lumber produced was then hauled to the Stackhouse wood yard at the railroad where Amos graded and loaded it onto rail cars, recording the workers' names and the amounts paid to them, beginning June, 1944.[53] Clyde Dockery recalled years later, "I used to help Amos load lumber for Cal Garland in the forties." Clyde's father, Troy, as well as Robert Daniels, Moss Helton, Dolman Sawyer, Charlie Helton and Horace Helton made up Amos' regular crew, with Elmore Helton, Lee Daniels and Jim Treadway also working at times.[54]

Garland paid Amos $30 a week for the rail siding rent and for grading and loading the shipments which often went to Broyhill Furniture Company or Heilman Lumber Company or Tennessee Eastman Corporation. Providing the only employment at Stackhouse (save the occasional freight car to be loaded by Amos for other lumber shipments), the budding Garland Lumber Company grew each year, opening another operation at Barnard, then a large one at Hot Springs.[55] Amos and Cal Garland became good friends and co-workers. "Mr. Garland ate dinner with us many, many times," remembered Nita Stackhouse decades later.

Regretfully, these pleasant occasions would be nearing an end when Amos was diagnosed in 1946 with leukemia, a disease having no known cure.[56] His illness, coupled with the changing times, would require considerable adjustments by the Stackhouse family and the dwindling Stackhouse community.

[1] Author's private papers.

[2] Ibid.

[3] *Raleigh News & Observer*, May 13, 2001.
Marshall *News-Record*, Feb. 11, 1943.

[4] Rector, N. Jack. Interview, January, 2003.

[5] Marshall *News-Record*, Feb. 11, 1943.

[6] *Asheville Times*, Aug. 11, 1943.

[7] Morgan, Robert. *The Man Who Flew the Memphis Belle: Memoir of a WWII Bomber Pilot.* New York, N.Y.: Dutton of Penguin Putnam, 2001.

[8] *Asheville Citizen*, May 1, 1945.
Watkins, Adelia Norton. Interview, 2002.
Plemmons, Ernestine Reeves. Interview, 2002.

[9] Marshall *News-Record*, Feb. 11, 1943.
Asheville Citizen, Nov. 11, 1995.

[10] Marshall *News-Record*, Feb. 11, 1943.

[11] Lefler, Hugh T. North Carolina History, Geography & Government. Yonkers-on-Hudson, New York: Worldbook Company, 1959, p.446.

[12] Hunter, Charles E., Office Memorandum to H.S. Rankin, U.S. Regional Products Research Division, Dec. 11, 1944. Courtesy of U.S. Geological Survey, Asheville, N.C.

[13] "Hotel History," undated advertising pamphlet, Grove Park Inn, Asheville, N.C.

[14] Painter, Jacqueline. *The Season of Dorland-Bell.* Appalachian Consortium Press, Boone, N.C., 1996, p.223.

[15] Jensen, Henry W. *A History of Warren Wilson College.* Asheville, N.C.: published by Warren Wilson College, 1974, p.61.

[16] Landsberger, Henry A. *They Fled Hitler's Germany and Found Refuge in North Carolina,* Chapel Hill, N.C.: Academic Affairs Library Center for the Study of the American South, 1996, pps. 115-128.

[17] *The Owl & Spade, Vol. XX,* No.4, Swannanoa, N.C., January, 1944, page 3.

[18] Meek, Anna Stackhouse. Interview, 2002.

[19] Stackhouse, Larry. Interview, Jan., 2003.

[20] Stackhouse, Nita. Interview, 2001.

[21] Marshall *News-Record*, Feb. 11, 1943.

[22] Stackhouse, Nita. Interview, 2001.

[23] Thomas, Doris Harrison. Interview, 2003.

[24] Ibid.

[25] Aumiller, Nancy Stackhouse. Interview, 2003.

[26] Private papers

[27] *Asheville Times*, June 6, 1944.

[28] Stackhouse, Harvey. Interview, 2002.
Stackhouse, Larry. Interview, 2002.

[29] Reed, Kenneth. Interview, 2003.

[30] Watkins, Adelia Norton. Interview, 2002.

[31] Goode, John. Interview.
Costello, John. *The Pacific War.* New York: Atlantic Communications, Inc., 1982.

[32] Gowan, Perry. Interview, 1995.

[33] Holland, Lance. *Fontana: A Pocket History of Appalachia.* Robbinsville, N.C.: Appalachian History Series, 2001, p.136.

[34] *Asheville Citizen-Times*, Feb. 4, 2001.

35 "WNC Area Launches Celebration," *Asheville Times*, August 15, 1945, p.1.
36 Private papers.
37 Stackhouse, Larry. Interview.
38 Price, Jay. "Madison County 'Flying Tiger,'" Raleigh *News & Observer*. May 13, 2001.
39 Rector, N. Jack. Interview, 2003.
   Bergin, Bob. "Flying Tiger Ace," *Military History*, Feb., 2001.
40 *Asheville Times*, August 11, 1943.
   Asheville Citizen, December 12, 1966; July 22, 1989.
41 Weigley, Russel F. *Philadephia, a 300-Year History*, New York: W.W. Norton Company, 1982, pps. 651-657.
   Binzen, Peter. "Glory Days," *Philadelphia Inquirer*, Dec. 17, 1989.
   McKelvey, Gerald. "Dilworth Dead at 75," *Philadelphia Inquirer*, January 24, 1974.
   (Courtesy, Free Library of Philadephia.)
42 Stackhouse, Harvey. Interview.
43 Radin, Clara Hester Stackhouse. Interview, 2001.
44 Norris, Lexyne Stackhouse. Interview, 2000.
45 Private papers.
46 Lefler, p.446.
47 Aumiller, Nancy Stackhouse. Interview, 2002.
48 Madison County Deed Registry, Book 72, p.135; Bk.54, p.91.
49 Buncombe County Deed Registry, Book 569, p.13.
50 Madison County Deed Registry, Book 70, p.637.
51 Madison County Deed Registry, Book 72, p.127.
52 Cantrell, Dr. Gene. Interview, 1998.
   Wright, Jane Garland. Interview, 1998.
   Asheville Citizen, October 23, 1963.
53 Private papers.
54 Ibid.
55 *Asheville Citizen*, October 23, 1963.
56 Aumiller, Nancy Stackhouse. Interview.

Chapter Twenty-Five

In the meantime, Stackhouse, North Carolina, continued to bask in the warmth of world peace, however brief it might be, and to agree, for the most part, with journalists who repeatedly wrote, "It was a war worth winning." (It would be some time before these writers began referring to it as "World War II," and to the Great War as "World War I.") But, moving onward to post-war changes, Stackhouse residents also understood Colonel Edward Rector (former Flying Tiger), who stated: "It was the beginning of a whole new phase of history."[1]

One change significant to Stackhouse was the 1946 closing of its school in order to consolidate with Walnut. Instead of one room and one teacher for all, the Walnut union (grades 1-12) school had separate class rooms and teachers for each grade – a big adjustment for Lexine Stackhouse and her neighbors. It was about this time, incidentally, that Nita Stackhouse decided to change the spelling of her elder daughter's name to "Lexyne," because new acquaintances often pronounced it, "LexEEN." "It didn't make much difference – people still mispronounce it," admitted Lexyne, in later life.[2]

When the new school year opened, there being no county bus available due to war shortages, the ten or twelve Stackhouse students were packed into a taxicab and driven to Walnut at the school board's expense. Soon afterwards, a pick-up truck's bed was fitted with a chicken-wire covered frame and roof, to haul the youngsters. They were not as crowded as in the taxi, but rain and wind blew through the wire where they sat exposed on wooden benches. "Eventually, they acquired a real bus for us," recalled Lexyne, who had begun sixth grade that year. The substantial Stackhouse school building on the hillside across from Amos' home had served the community since 1905, its closing bringing one more identity loss to the area. "Several other one-room schools, if not all, in the county, were closed at the same time," Lexyne added.[3] (Her sister, Nancy, entered first grade at Walnut the next year.)

The new phase of history for Amos Stackhouse, unfortunately, was not filled with progress or promise, but he made the best of it. Despite his cancer, Amos graded lumber and supervised the freight-car loading at his rail siding, milked his cows, looked after his cattle, his crops, his general store and post office. He began to depend on Gilbert for help with a few things, and he rested a bit more, his customers knowing to come knock at his kitchen door, just down from the annex, when they needed their mail, or a stamp, or jug of lamp oil.

Next door to the store, in the old buggy room of the annex, Amos kept two large barrels for the kerosene, but when Gregory Oil Company from Marshall sent their delivery truck, the driver could not make it up the narrow steep driveway. The oil had to be pumped into five-gallon buckets and hand-carried up the hill from the front-yard entrance, almost at the railroad.[4] Kerosene was a vital commodity to Stackhouse families, none of whom had electric lights.

Another necessity was milk for the children and for making bread. Amos walked down the long hillside and across the creek to his barn twice daily to milk his cows and feed them. Because of his habit of being late for everything, dark would usually overtake him in the late afternoon, requiring him to carry a lantern, as well as the milk bucket. Many times the cow would have lain down in the barn yard manure and Amos would take her to the creek and wash her udder before milking. Then he had the slow climb back home with the bucketful of milk, which Hester strained through a cloth and poured into gallon jars for drinking or churning into buttermilk and butter. To keep the sweet milk cold, it was carried outside to the door in the kitchen porch floor, and down the steps to the cellar. ("Aunt Ruth had an ice box at the cabin, but we did not," recalled Nancy Stackhouse Aumiller, years later.)[5] The tenant farmers often bought milk and butter from Hester, sometimes paying with labor about the farm. Helen Treadway Higgins, daughter of Walter Treadway at Runion, related in a future interview, "We used to get milk and butter from Hester Stackhouse, and I worked for her for ten cents an hour, sometimes." Helen helped in the garden and yard, pulling honeysuckle vines out of the shrubbery, for instance.[6]

As the poverty in Madison County hung on, different ploys were used to make ends meet. Helen's brother Jimmie Treadway remembered how, in the late 1940s, they picked bucketsful of wild strawberries, blackberries and huckleberries, carrying them the four miles to Hot Springs where they received ten cents per gallon. His father farmed Ellsworth Vandervort's Runion acres on halves, packing produce in wooden crates which they carried the two miles from Runion mountain to the Stackhouse siding. Here the local train to Asheville would pick it up for market. In the raising of the most profitable crop, tobacco, Vandervort bought the seed, fertilizer and any other supplies, while the tenant farmers did the work in exchange for house rent, plus two-thirds of sale receipts.[7] (Tobacco was said to be the thirteen-months-a-year crop and was labor intensive.)

These tenants, as well as those living in Amos' rental houses, would be hired to work at Stackhouse more and more as Amos' leukemia worsened. He made weekly trips, now, by train to Dr. Sams' Marshall office for liver shots, afterwards riding the Greyhound bus to Walnut school where he continued home on Lexyne's school bus. However, according to Lexyne, he got off the bus at the second stop on Walnut Gap road, as the sharp curves began, and walked the rest of the way home. Amos had always become mildly car sick, but the treatments increased his nausea. As the days went by, it took him longer and longer to walk home, until one day, Hester sent Lexyne back up the steep road to find him and help him down. "It took us the rest of the afternoon, he had to rest so many times," said Lexyne. Nearing the house, at last, they were met by Hester with a chair and a glass of water, telling Amos to sit awhile before coming on.[8]

Little Nancy Stackhouse so enjoyed Amos' playing checkers with her, she would beg him for a game, but as the summer of 1948 wore on, he just shook his head, saying, "Sweetheart, I'd love to play with you, but I just can't." She often accompanied her parents to Greeneville, Tennessee, where they took Amos to see Dr. Leroy Coolidge at Takoma Hospital. Though he was a Seventh-day Adventist, Coolidge was well liked and respected by Madison Countians of all ages who frequented his hospital and sanitarium. Once, when Nancy's mother had tried everything to get her to eat, Nita asked Dr. Coolidge to examine the child. He found that she was severely anemic and prescribed iron pills and cod liver oil, which brought her back to good health after a time.[9]

Takoma Hospital was approximately 30 miles from Stackhouse by way of Highway 208, built along the old Laurel River Logging Company railroad bed. Established in 1926, about the same time as the highway, Takoma Hospital and Sanitarium expanded in 1928 through donations by Harvey Reaves, entrepreneur and graduate of Dorland Institute in Hot Springs. As a young man, Harvey had walked from Greeneville to Hot Springs, enrolling with sixty-five cents in his pocket, and a small white flour sack holding his clothes slung over his shoulder. He knew that he could work his way at Dorland, once he got there. After graduation in 1903, he went from job to job, each one paying a bit more than the last, until his wages reached one dollar a day at a South Carolina cotton mill. Saving $80, Harvey came back to Tennessee, invested in a flour mill and began teaching school at thirty dollars a month. He continued to change jobs and invest profitably, on his way

Nancy Stackhouse, age 3.

to becoming a popular philanthropist, affecting quality health care for both eastern Tennessee and western North Carolina, and the Stackhouse family, in particular.[10] (As part owner of fifteen tobacco warehouses, Reaves further benefited Amos Stackhouse and other Madison County farmers, who usually marketed their cash crop in Greeneville.)

At Takoma, Gilbert Stackhouse gave his father blood, time and again, throughout the leukemia's worsening. Amos also consulted his father's 1872 medical text, *The Household Physician*, its "plain language" recipes, for once, not helping him. A wooden box of bucchu leaves, two-thirds full, remained on his office shelf, long after he became too weak to use it. "The bucchu grows at the Cape of Good Hope," stated the book, "and its leaves are stimulant, diuretic, antispasmodic and tonic."[11]

Amos kept a record of expenses incurred by his illness, in the beginning, showing that during a nine-month period of 1947, he paid Dr. Sams $112; Takoma Hospital, $97; and Roberts' Pharmacy in Marshall, $36.[12] (These were the days when a prescription was rarely over fifty cents, a visit to a doctor's office was two dollars and out-patient hospital treatment, three or four dollars.) The majority of mountaineers used home remedies when sick, never went to a hospital, and, when absolutely necessary, called a doctor to their bedsides, paying him with farm produce.

Incidentally, over fifty years later, Amos' granddaughter, Nancy, would recall the mullein tea and sassafras tea often made by Hester and given to Nancy and Lexyne when they were sick. For croup, a large scrap of cotton flannel was spread with mustard plaster, warmed at the stove, and placed upon the ill one's chest. For Nancy's frequent bouts with bronchitis, Hester dosed her with a spoonful of brown sugar and liquor (from the medicinal bottle). "It burned and tasted awful," stated Nancy, "but it usually worked."[13]

Last postmark from Stackhouse Post Office. Courtesy Carthene Cole.

According to Amos' 1948 ledger, he continued working for Cal Garland, grading and shipping lumber until at least May.[14] His post office work, however, came to an end on July 31, when he sadly stamped the last postmark as a souvenir for the family. The government had ordered the closing of the Stackhouse post office, changing the service to Marshall. Galvanized steel mail boxes atop locust posts would be erected up and down the roadways so that a carrier in an automobile could bring their mail to addresses of "Marshall RFD." This applied to all the Laurel country, too, which for years was served by a rider on horseback, carrying the mail sacks from Stackhouse. The families of Jim Treadway, James Clark and others living on Mill Ridge, just north of Runion, would walk the four miles to Hot Springs post office to get their mail.[15]

After making an inventory of stamps and supplies, Amos presented the final postmaster records to Hester for signing, then mailed all to Washington, D.C. The required thirty-days' review and recording period resulted in the official closing date of August 31, 1948, for the post office at Stackhouse, North Carolina, marking the end of an era for both the Stackhouse family and its namesake community.[16] (Early the next year, Hester received a Civil Service certificate, acknowledging her five years of service with a small monthly annuity payment.)

For the first time in Amos' memory, the mail trains threw out no mail sacks in the Stackhouse yard, leaving him to wait for his mail to be processed and delivered by others to the new rural mailbox standing a few yards away from the railroad arm where he and his father had hung the canvas bags, daily, for so long. Stamps were obtained by leaving three pennies in the box, for which the mail man would place a stamp on the letter. Sometimes Amos' mail could not be delivered to his new box, when the Walnut Gap road was snow or ice covered, or deeply rutted in mud from extensive rains. In these instances, the new mailman left their mail at Cook's little store near the Walnut Gap turn off. Anyone from Stackhouse community who happened to stop there picked up all the mail and brought it down the mountain to the respective addresses.[17]

It was probably fitting that the post office closing had come at this time, since Amos' illness was terminal and Hester's time was taken with her expanded household responsibilities. She closed the store, too, shortly thereafter, ending yet another Stackhouse tradition – older, even, than the post office. There had been a Stackhouse general store on the French Broad River since 1871 – two of them, in fact, for a brief period. Stackhouse community was growing less and less sufficient unto itself, the changes casting a ghostly profile over the old landmarks.

That summer of 1948, Amos' granddaughters endured, once again, a quarantine of every child under sixteen, to prevent infantile paralysis. In July and August, the state of North Carolina reported 2,516 cases, 173 of which were in Buncombe County. Those who could afford it packed their children off to northern states where the epidemic was milder. "An Army plane arrived with 900 pounds of canvas to make tent flies for the tents which had been set up as emergency rooms at the Asheville Orthopedic Home," stated the *Asheville Citizen-Times*.[19] Visiting cousins, going to church services and to Marshall on Saturday for the week's groceries, supplies, and, perhaps, a movie, were usually the only trips away from home for farm families. With the quarantine in place, Nancy and Lexyne had not even these. "Daddy felt so sorry for us that he took us on an outing to Mount Mitchell one weekend," recalled Nancy Aumiller.[20] Madison County schools extended the summer vacation for weeks until the weather cooled and the contagion waned. (The next year a Madison County Health Department opened with Dr. W.A. Sams, Hester's nephew, in charge, and Elizabeth Gahagan Baker, Stackhouse family friend, as County Nurse, but it would be seven years before a vaccine arrived for the crippling disease.)[21]

By summer's end, when Nancy and Lexyne were settled into their delayed school, Amos was spending more and more time sitting on his front porch, weakly waving to the passing mail trains and gazing upon his lovely old French Broad River, lifetime friend. He had been born at her side, grown up there, and remained there, catering to her whims and fancies, enjoying her providence. Amos also spent his days, in part, at his life-long hobby of reading – poetry by Thomas Hood, newspapers and magazines such as the *Farm Journal*, subscribed to at twenty-five cents per year.[22] Part of his time was given to reflection upon his seventy-five years. They had been good rewarding ones, producing deep love and pride in his three sons, his six grandchildren, the home he had built, and the community created by his father and further nurtured by himself. He had always striven for its improvement and best interests, leaving it better, he hoped, for his efforts. Amos had many friends throughout the county – no small accomplishment for a second generation Yankee and Quaker. His father's gentle ways and friendly personality had first gained acceptance by the clannish Madison Countians, finding, as the Laurel missionary, Frances Goodrich, had said: "Trust is given slowly in the mountains, but it is given fully."[23]

Finally, on September 19, 1948, Dr. Coolidge hospitalized Amos at Greeneville, where he remained to the end, dying on October eleventh.[23] His daughters-in-law, Ruth and Nita, had rented a motel room near the hospital, taking turns sitting by his bed and serving as family advocates when Hester was not there. At the point of death, Ruth Vandervort Stackhouse was present, albeit unknown to Amos, who was likely comatose. Next day, the *Asheville Citizen* carried an article, headed, "Stackhouse Rites Set For Wednesday."[24] There was a similar write-up on the front page of the Marshall News-Record, both papers referring to Amos as "prominent citizen." His funeral was held at the Walnut Methodist Church, with burial in the cemetery adjoining, just yards away from his brother, Charles Dilworth.

Amos Stackhouse had been a hard worker, but he was never rushed or impatient, and was always courteous. His daughter-in-law, Nita, recalled that "He was the slowest man you ever saw; slow talking, slow moving and always late for meals."[25] He was also considered "the sweetest, kindest man you ever met," by granddaughter Nancy. His wife Hester was a difficult, hard-to-please woman, but, "Oh, how he loved her," added Nancy.[26]

As Amos had taken the Stackhouse torch when his father died, so Ellison Gilbert, nearly forty years later, shouldered responsibilities of family and community when his Papa died (even if the community was a shadow of its former self). Though he was not the eldest and did not carry the name, "Amos," he was the only son living at Stackhouse. His duties were already many and varied, and had increased during Amos' illness. Besides his commercial contracting work, which took him away from home five days a week, he served as Sunday School superintendent at Walnut, caretaker for his mother, the family home and several rental houses, as well as manager of the large Stackhouse farm crops, cattle, fences and out buildings. In addition to his own tobacco allotment, which required weekly attention at the least, he helped Hester make arrangements for hers. With his father gone, Gilbert had to plan his construction jobs around the farming schedule. Even the Saturday grocery-buying or visits to doctors, dentists and oculists for his mother and his family fell to Gilbert. "Whenever we started to the store, if any neighbors were walking up the mountain to catch the bus for Marshall, Daddy would pick them up and help bring back their groceries, too," said Nancy Aumiller.[27]

According to his family, Gilbert worked all the time, practically never taking a weekday off. Once, Gilbert did take his wife and daughters to Myrtle Beach, South Carolina, for a week – their first and only family vacation. However, he also took them with him to his jobs when there was a place for them to stay. During the winter of 1946, while he was working in Mineral Bluff, Georgia, for W.M. Ritter Company, Nita and the girls lived with him in his boarding house room. Lexyne attended school there for a few months, finding the books, methods and system "so diffcrent from North Carolina's that I had to start over when we came back to Stackhouse," she said. Gilbert never again took his family with him during a school term. But, in August, 1947, he took them along to the North Carolina Department of Construction Standards in Raleigh, where he took the test for his commercial building license. (Prior to this time, licensing enforcement did not affect many small-time builders.) "It took hours," recalled Lexyne Stackhouse Norris.[28] To while away the waiting, Nita took Nancy and Lexyne to a moving picture show, "The Yearling." Returning home, the family stopped in Charlotte to spend

L to R: Lexyne, Nancy, Nita and Gilbert Stackhouse at Myrtle Beach, S.C. in the 1950s.

the night with Nita's family – always a treat for the girls. Several of Nita's siblings lived on the large Caldwell farm, providing her daughters with plenty of playmate cousins. "There was one my age and one Lexyne's age," Nancy remembered.

Another time, Gilbert took his family to Oklahoma where there was a certain engine or machine part for sale. In addition to his contract jobs, Gilbert, a skilled mechanic, built and rebuilt saw mills for small operators, gaining the reputation of knowing where mills and parts were located throughout the southeast. He had a blacksmith shop where he fabricated or repaired parts that were broken in the moving of the mills. Gilbert even sold his own sawmill, but kept his old gasoline engine (likely the one he and Amos operated in the 1940s). He then rebuilt his mill and sold it again, several times.[29]

According to Nancy, people contacted him frequently in search of a particular type of mill or a special chain or carriage, for instance. On one occasion, when Gilbert was transporting a huge boiler through Knoxville, he was stopped because his load was over-sized by city ordinance. He found Frank Reams, Hester's nephew, a Knoxville policeman, who managed to get a permit to move it at night.[30]

In 1946 and 1947, Gilbert built the plant of English Lumber Company on

Sweeten Creek Road in Biltmore for Clarence English, who had known the Stackhouse family since his young days of employment at Laurel River Logging Company in Runion. Some of Gilbert's crew came from Flag Pond, Tennessee, a community joining Madison County's Laurel country. Clarence English, Jr., called "Bud," was fourteen that summer and worked with the crew as a laborer, setting steel and carrying lumber, nails or bricks. The large job included a house for planers and other machines, a boiler and extra-tall smokestack, the dry kilns, office building and railroad siding. "We bought rough lumber from lots of small mills and produced wood that was sized and planed, ready for furniture factories or retailers," said Bud in a 1999 interview.[31] (A few years later, the flooding Swannanoa River caused wash outs at the siding and Gilbert was called back to shore it up.)

During the English factory project, Gilbert and his family lived with Dr. Sams' sister, Mrs. Grace English, up on the Asheville highway near Brush Creek, but on the Walnut school bus route for Lexyne. It saved Gilbert quite a bit of travel times, which meant money saved on the job. They rented an apartment within Mrs. English's large home. Her husband, Guy, a third cousin to Clarence, had died three years earlier and was remembered as having been Madison County sheriff for over ten years. "We took our cow with us when we lived at Mrs. English's," related Nancy Aumiller, later.[32]

The English Lumber project was typical of numerous other jobs completed by Gilbert. "He would go in, prepare the site, if needed, construct all the buildings, set the machinery, build trestle and rail sidings and erect smoke stacks, often climbing them himself, when he could not get his men to do it," said Nancy. "He always painted the buildings dark green," she added. A few other projects recalled by Nancy were a sawmill in Kentucky for International Coal and Lumber Company; a chair factory in Greeneville, Tennessee; a saw mill in Georgia for Gennett Lumber Company; a Magnavox plant in West Virginia; and a small saw mill for a man on Spring Creek in Madison County. For Banks Lumber Company at Burnsville, Gilbert built a diesel-powered mill, then rebuilt it after it later burned. (It was the only time he used the diesel-engine correspondence course he had taken from Muncie, Indiana.)[33] In Jackson County, Gilbert installed a planing mill and boiler at Hennessee Lumber Company. "He always took workers from home, leaving one behind at a lot of jobs," recalled Nancy Aumiller. For instance, Clyde Dockery became a fifteen-year employee of the Boling Chair Company of Siler City after he had helped Gilbert build their lumber plant at Azalea, near Asheville.[34] Known for its bentwood furniture, Boling Chair's increasing requirements for Appalachian hardwoods led to the development of the Azalea plant, to provide dimension stock from high quality mountain-grown trees.[35] Gilbert's Madison County crew members sometimes became acquainted with his employers, who, in turn, saw their potential and invited them to stay on as workers at the completed plant. Gilbert bore them no ill will, fully understanding the lure of a steady job, which usually did not depend upon the whims of nature as did the construction business, but it meant that he often had to spend more time on weekends filling crew vacancies.

Six months after her husband's death, Hester Stackhouse, unable to pay the taxes or look after Amos' half interest in the 56-acre Klondyke tract or the 65-acre "Ellison" tract, deeded these to her sons, Gilbert and Ernest, releasing her dower rights to the properties.[36] Hester also deeded a portion of

A typical mill under construction by Gilbert Stackhouse.

Amos' original farm to Ernest and a portion to Gilbert. (They probably paid her some amount for these tracts in order for her to pay taxes or bank notes.) With June living far away, unable to take part in the care of his parents and homeplace, he asked for only one acre of his father's land, "In case I might want a vacation place, someday," he told them.[37] Thus, a Memorandum of

Agreement was registered at the courthouse, ensuring that June Stackhouse would receive a deed for one acre from lands belonging to one of his brothers. The reason for delay is not clear. Perhaps a surveyor was not available, or Gilbert and Ernest wanted to wait until June could come and select his own acre.

June Stackhouse, though across country, still seemed to be his mother's best-loved son, according to her praising description of his successful career. In fact, she held up for comparison to Gilbert, both Ernest and June, as being university-educated, with well-paying jobs, fine homes and automobiles. "Daddy always drove a Ford, and Uncle Ernest, a Buick," explained Nancy Aumiller.[38] Consequently, Gilbert was made to feel unfavored to the degree that he began to build a house in Charlotte, so that he and Nita would have a home after Hester's death. He was positive his mother would never leave the Stackhouse home to him.

The large Caldwell dairy farm in Mecklenburg had been divided in 1946 among Nita and her siblings, so she urged Gilbert to move there. Gilbert took a small crew from Stackhouse, including Jack Reed, who would do all the masonry for the brick-veneer, one-story house with large garage in the "daylight" basement. But first they built a two-room shack at the edge of the yard for the men to live in during construction of the new dwelling; Gilbert called it "my hotel." One of Nita's sisters who lived next door cooked their meals. In the evenings, Gilbert and his Stackhouse helpers often visited Ernest, who lived hardly a mile away. After the house was put "in the dry," they returned home to Gilbert's other work, leaving the new structure to stand for years, ready for rough-wiring, heating and plumbing.[39]

House built near Charlotte in the 1950s by Gilbert Stackhouse for his intended home.

Meanwhile, on a saw mill Gilbert had built for himself, probably using parts from the mill he and Amos had assembled during the war, Gilbert cut

297

"acid wood" logs (pulp wood necessary to paper manufacturing) which were shipped in five-foot lengths to the large paper mill in Haywood County. Some hardwood trees on the Stackhouse farm were also cut and sold to Cal Garland. "Daddy would order a freight car to be brought to the siding, then he'd haul the logs on his old International truck to the saw mill and fill the car," recalled Nancy Aumiller.[40] Since most of these trees came from his mother's land, the profit was shared with her, giving her some income, too. (In this manner he had cut large hemlocks to make framing for his Charlotte house.) Jimmie Treadway, who lived at Runion, and was one of Gilbert's workers, at times, remembered years later, "We cut some trees that were three feet through, using a crosscut saw, hauling seven or eight logs at a time and four men on that old truck of his."[41]

Tree cutting was also taking place throughout the community, albeit limited to swaths forty feet wide, as needed for Rural Electrification Authority's (REA) clearing of rights-of-way to prepare for bringing electric power lines into Stackhouse. Because of the rough steep terrain and the few houses, Stackhouse and other communities had been passed over in the 1920s by Carolina Power and Light Company, who served Hot Springs and a few other spots of Madison. In 1939, under the North Carolina Rural Electrification Authority, the French Broad Electric Membership had been formed in Madison County, but the ensuing war years prevented installation to all parts of the county, as planned.[42] Now it was Stackhouse community's turn. Gilbert was not a "joiner," but he gladly paid his dues and became involved in this organization. (A slight advantage to belonging to the co-operative was the annual distribution of dividends, though these were admittedly small, initially.) Gilbert hired an electrician to install a meter base and any other items required to update the original wiring in Hester's house and the brick annex building behind. He likely took care of similar details at his brother's cabin, next door, too.

Finally, on September 19, 1949, a Wiring Inspection Record was completed, bringing the Electric Connect Order in Hester's name three days later. At long last the lights came back on in the great old landmark after thirty-three years. It was marvelous to Lexyne, who had "wished many times, as I read by flashlight, that I could reach up and turn on those light bulbs."[43] The family had been spoiled when they lived at Mrs. English's apartment, which, located along the highway, had full electric service. Gilbert had bought them an electric toaster and radio, but neither could be used when they returned home. Of course, the REA hook-up was a wonder-filled event for the whole community. Clyde Dockery remembered years later how exciting it was to have lights in his home where he and his father, Troy, had wired their own house.[44] Since the Stackhouse store could no longer provide lamp oil, the electricity arrival was timely. Kerosene lamps, nevertheless, would continue to be needed for the frequent power outages and for carrying about the farms and roads at night.

Even with the long-awaited power service, Stackhouse remained far from twentieth-century modern. Electricity was a luxury, not a necessity. Most mountain families had lights only – no labor-saving appliances and gadgets. They could barely buy bulbs and pay the monthly fee, which, incidentally, was determined unlike it is today. Instead of a power company employee traveling to each home each month, the French Broad Electric Membership company mailed cards for members to return. "It was MY job to read the meter," said Lexyne Norris, who had been in high school at that time. She wrote the reading on the postcard and mailed it back to Marshall for billing.[45]

Although the Stackhouses had no refrigerator, they still had a variety of desserts with rich whipped cream from their cow. The butter kept nicely in Hester's cool cellar and the milk was always right for drinking. Each day after dinner – the noon meal – the bowls of food were left on the table until supper time, a thin cloth made from flour sacks covering all, to keep out flies, cats and the like. Nevertheless, before long, from Jonas Chandler's hardware store in Marshall, Gilbert brought them a Frigidaire brand refrigerator, which was set in the annex building because there was not room in Nita's small kitchen. Later, Hester began to share the convenience by keeping her milk there, too. Even though they had to go outside to get to it, it was handier than the cellar. Nita already had a kerosene-fueled cook stove for use in summer, but, eventually, she received an electric range, also. They still had no central heating or hot water heater in the old house. For bathing, they filled large canning vessels with water and boiled it on the wood stove. "By the time it was poured into the large porcelain bath tub, it was just right for a bath," remembered Nancy Aumiller.[46] During coldest weather, they used a baby bath tub that they could stand in beside the stove. Another winter inconvenience was Hester's habit of turning off the bathroom water to prevent frozen and possibly burst pipes, thus requiring the family to use slop jars. After use, the enameled tin buckets were carried to the bathroom, emptied into the toilet and flushed with another bucket of water brought from the kitchen. (Luckily Nita's upstairs kitchen had been added after the original plumbing, placing it on a separate line which could be kept warm with the wood stove.)

Moreover, Hester Stackhouse continued to perform her weekly ironing task as she always had. After building up the fire in the kitchen stove, she placed two or three flat irons on its surface, laid her smooth worn ironing board to rest along the tops of two chair backs close by, and waited for the heavy irons to heat. "She would pick up an iron, spit on her finger tip and touch it to the bottom of the iron," recalled Nancy Aumiller.[47] If it sizzled, it was ready to use. When the iron cooled, it was placed back on the stove and a second hot one was put to use, alternating irons every few minutes until the chore was finished.

Nor would Hester change her wash day routine of using the slate tubs, wooden scrub board, and hand-wringing at the annex laundry room. However, a few years after power came to Stackhouse, Gilbert did buy Nita an electric washing machine, which Hester would suffer to be used in cleaning her largest sheets, as she grew older. The new washer still required some effort, there being little about it that was automatic. On legs with rollers, it had one large round tub with an agitator rising on a center stem and a wringer device fastened to the side of the tub. Often the washed items were too thick for the wringer, stalling the apparatus until a lever bracket could be used to open the rollers. A re-distribution of the fabric, a clamping of the bracket back into position, and a starting of the motor, again, enabled the wash day to proceed. When not in use, Nita's washing machine was kept in the room next to the kitchen, and pulled, on wash day, across the floor to the kitchen sink where the washer's tub could be drained through a rubber hose. As with the bathing, the washing procedure began with the large vessels of water, carried to the stove for heating, then poured into the washing machine for the first load of white clothes and linens. Colored pieces came second because they frequently left dyes in the wash water. After all was washed, and wrung on the wringer, the tub was filled again with rinse water, and the process repeated. It was still easier than the pre-electricity wash day, agreed Lexyne, who remembered how her mother would waken her early on Monday mornings, saying, "I'm going to milk now; you get up and start the wash water."[48]

While the Stackhouse residents enjoyed their good fortune, it would be yet some time before the completed power installation reached their distant neighbors at Spring Creek, Meadow Fork, Big Pine and others. Still and all – like the changes brought by the death of Amos, the closings of the school, post office and store – electricity's advent would irrevocably alter the Stackhouse community as it was further swept along in Colonel Rector's "whole new phase of history."

Unlike her daughter Lexyne, Nita Stackhouse had been privileged in 1917 to ride this schoolbus – Mecklenburg County's first.

[1] Bergin, Bob. "Flying Tiger Ace," *Military History*, February, 2001, p.80.
[2] Norris, Lexyne Stackhouse. Interviews, 2001, 2003.
[3] Ibid, 2000.
[4] Aumiller, Nancy Stackhouse. Interview, 2003.
[5] Ibid.
[6] Higgins, Helen Treadway. Interview, 2000.
[7] Treadway, Jimmie. Interview, 1999.
[8] Norris, 2003.
[9] Aumiller, 2003.
[10] *Greeneville Sun*, July 19, 1980.
    Knoxville *News-Sentinel*, Dec. 3, 1940.
    Moore, Martha Reaves, letter to author, Sept. 12, 1993.
[11] Norris, Ronald. Interview, 1999.
    Warren, Ira. *The Household Physician*, Boston, Ira Bradley Co., 1872, p.298.
[12] Author's private papers.
[13] Aumiller, 2005.
[14] Private papers.
[15] Treadway, Martha Davis. Interview, 1991.
    Treadway, Marie Clark. Interview, 1999.
[16] Stroupe, Vernon, letter to author, Nov. 19, 1998.
[17] Aumiller, 2003.
[18] *Asheville Citizen-Times*, Aug. 9, 1987, p. 1C.
[19] Aumiller, 2003.
[20] Baker, Elizabeth Gahagan. Interview, 2003.
[21] Private papers.
[22] Goodrich, Frances L. *Thirty Years of Trail Making*, n.d., Presbyterian Mission Board, New York, (c.1925), p.5.
[23] Tennessee Vital Records, Death Register, p.21774.
[24] *Asheville Citizen*, Oct. 12, 1948, p.8.
[25] Stackhouse, Nita. Interview, 2000.
[26] Aumiller, 2001.
[27] Ibid.
[28] Norris, L., 2003.
[29] Aumiller, 2000.
[30] Ibid.
[31] English, Bud. Interview, 1999.
[32] Aumiller, 2000.
[33] Ibid.
[34] Dockery, Clyde. Interview, 2000.
[35] Harden, John. *Boling, the Story of a Company and of a Family*, Siler City, N.C., Boling Company, 1980, p.4.
[36] Madison County Deed Registry, Book 77, p.521.
[37] Ibid., Book 77, p.534; Book 76, p.549; Book 83, p.418.
[38] Aumiller, 2002.

Chapter Twenty-Six

Early in the next decade, history's new phase began to resemble the old, as America's young men were again sent into combat. After World War II, Korea had been partitioned between Soviet and American occupation forces at the 38th Parallel, with a communist government in the North and an anti-communist government in the South. Hostile from the beginning, North Korean forces invaded the South on June 25, 1950, provoking President Truman, the next day, to pledge defense of the South. Journalist John Keegan, many years later, quoted General Douglas MacArthur as saying, "With no submission to Congress… and without even consulting the field commander involved, the Executive Branch agreed to enter the Korean War." Keegan, himself, continued:

> "The course of the Korean War was to be painful and ultimately indecisive militarily. In world affairs, however, its effect was to prove conclusive. Thereafter, both Stalin and Mao Tse-Tung knew they challenged the free world at their peril."[1]

At Stackhouse, Gilbert was able to follow the action on his radio, thanks to French Broad Electric. He had particular interest in the war because of his neighbors, Clyde Dockery, Hubert Treadway and Charlie Helton, who had been drafted. Jack Reed's son, Kenneth, was also in Korea, where he guarded a harbor from aboard a navy ship. Kenneth represented four generations of one Madison County family to serve this nation in war time. A few months before the end of the three-year war, another family friend, Joseph (Mac) Reeves, son of Amos Stackhouse Reeves, entered the military and was sent to Korea.[2] Fortunately, all five boys returned unharmed.

Just six weeks after the armistice, however, Gilbert's brother, June, found himself in the Pacific as assistant superintendent for a power distillation firm on the Marshall Islands.[3] These islands, captured from Japan in 1944, had been designated as testing grounds for atomic weapons, the native inhabitants having been relocated. June supervised over sixty men in the maintenance and operation of five power plants and four distillation plants at Bikini and Eniwetok atolls. According to his son, Amos III – "Sonny" – June also constructed bridges, water and sewer systems, roads and various types of buildings. "The idea was to quantify effects of the blast on various municipal systems," stated Sonny many years later.[4]

In 1954 June received a certificate for his participation in Operation *Castle*, a hydrogen bomb testing conducted by the Army, Navy, Air Force and Atomic Energy Commission. (This was the first United States test of an H-bomb fueled with lithium deuteride.) "He observed the blast through dark glasses, aboard a ship about fifty miles from ground zero," said Sonny. The Bravo, one of the *Castle* test series, was at fifteen megatons, the largest-yield thermonuclear device the United States ever tested. "I was on a ship that was thirty miles away," stated one observer, "and we had this horrible white stuff raining on us… It was a huge fireball, a much more awesome sight than a puny little atomic bomb."[5] Japanese fishing boats, as well as Japanese islands, were heavily exposed to Bravo fallout, the United States suffering high costs in damages and diplomacy. (Decades afterwards, when *Castle's* documents became declassified, June's relatives were curious about a possible connection to his later cancer.)

Although Hester was not privy to June's work details, she worried about his safety, as she had during World Wars I and II. She kept up with the news of the Cold War, a growing menace since the 1945 armistice. Fearful that tensions would provoke a nuclear attack, Hester would fill gallon jugs with water and carry them down to the cellar. "She was always afraid of the coming of the Germans or the Cubans or the Russians," recalled her granddaughter, Nancy, years later.[6]

Actually, several months of unemployment following the Pacific H-bomb tests allowed June time to come to Stackhouse. During one of those summer visits from California, June's wife, Ann, declared that the name Stackhouse should be changed to "Workhouse," because Nita and Hester were always picking, peeling, shelling or canning.[7] While everyone agreed that fresh fruit and vegetables, picked at their peak of flavor, were rewards of rural living, they forgot that this factor could not be scheduled around company visits, sickness or any other obligations. If the produce had matured, the harvest could not be put off or the work avoided.

When the work was more than Hester could manage alone, she hired Evelyn Helton, a tenant's wife, who probably took no cash but let it apply to her rent. Nita Stackhouse, however, had only her young daughters to help when Gilbert was away. "About four in the afternoon, we'd take our buckets and baskets on our little red wagon, down to the garden – a good half mile away," recalled Nancy Stackhouse Aumiller.[8] After picking all the ready vegetables, they loaded the small wagon, which held two filled bushel baskets side by side, and another, half full, balanced on top. Nancy pulled, and Lexyne pushed, down the dusty, bumpy road from the large garden, then up the steep driveway home, while Nita carried buckets-full. Later that evening, or early the next day, all began stringing, breaking, and washing the green beans to prepare for canning in Nita's double-decker, fourteen-quart pressure canner. First the jars had to be carried up from the cellar to the third-story apartment kitchen, then scrubbed, sterilized, filled, cooked, cooled, tested, labeled and carried back down the two flights to the cellar, a few quarts at a time. The same or similar procedures were followed for greens, peas, beets, pickles, kraut, corn, tomatoes, okra and other vegetables, interspersed with the fruits – cherries, strawberries, raspberries, blackberries, grapes and apples, to name a few.

Food preservation was one of several farm topics addressed by the state-sponsored Home Demonstration Club of Walnut, which Nita Stackhouse had joined in the early 1930s, when a member with a car offered to take her to the meetings. Once a year she took her turn as hostess, having the club meeting at Stackhouse (a pleasure she would enjoy far into her old age). At times, Nita served as president of the local group and of the county council, learning better and safer homemaking practices introduced by the Extension Agent assigned to Madison County. The club members performed community services such as helping with the bloodmobile unit, the tuberculosis X-ray unit, and clinics on avoiding typhoid and improving nutrition. One of their hardest-sought accomplishments, and one having lasting impact on the county, was the establishment in 1955 of a public library, albeit only a used bookmobile purchased from the eastern part of the state.[9] Through the club's continued support, this seed grew into a large modern library facility on land given, incidentally, by Hester's great niece and nephew. Nita was enthusiastically involved in all these efforts, playing the lead once in a pageant presented by Home Demonstration Clubs in Raleigh during Farm and Home Week. "The pageant was televised and a moving picture made of it," stated the Marshall *News-Record*.[10]

Gilbert, too, became involved with state and federal agricultural programs, having been selected with forty-one other Madison Countians to take part in TVA's Test Demonstration Farmers Association, which would "set the pace" for improvements in agriculture. "Seven states and 125 counties belonged," related former Madison County farm agent Harry Silver, years later.[11] At first, the agent met with the farmer to identify his resources and sketch a rough map for discussion. Then soil samples were taken and a plan developed to establish goals for increasing the farm's yield and reducing erosion. Upon authorized requisitions, TVA furnished fertilizer and some seeds, but the farmer was required to pay the freight and handling charges, and to keep complete record books. These projects would prove beneficial to the county (where a majority depended on agriculture for a living) and would, in time, become recommended practices for all North Carolina farmers.

Along with their parents, Lexyne and Nancy Stackhouse joined the agricultural programs for their age groups, mainly the 4-H Club at Walnut School, which was also supervised by the Home Demonstration Agent. Of the two girls, Nancy was the more enthusiastic member, preferring the outdoors and farm work to inside activities. One year she was delegated to present a program at Fontana and other dams in appreciation of TVA's contributions to agriculture. "The whole family were outstanding in farm work," commented Harry Silver.[12]

Nevertheless, inherent to farm life was also a lot of hard labor, requiring even young children's help in planting, weeding, hoeing, harvesting and preserving the produce, pulling and tying fodder for winter feed, carrying heavy swill buckets to the hog pen (always built at a distance from the house), and shucking mounds of corn to prepare for grinding into cattle feed. "We had a huge corn crib, and it was not very cold there in the barn out of the wind," Nancy recalled.[13] She did not, however, like having to kill the ever-present field mice as she worked. Nancy and her mother also had to help with the tobacco harvest, occasionally, if Gilbert was working away from home and bad weather threatened.

Another cool weather responsibility of Nancy's was to carry out ashes from both downstairs and upstairs stoves, returning with the coal scuttle full of coal – sometimes, more than once a day – and to clean the coal bin as needed. Every day after school Nancy also took the two mules down to the creek for water, and when school was out, she went twice a day. Nita watered them on school-day mornings, in addition to her milking and feeding chores. (Gilbert never owned a tractor, mechanic though he was, preferring his mules, Jim and Kate.) All the morning jobs fell to Nita when the girls were in school and Gilbert was away at work.[14]

Nor was any farm complete without its chicken house and fenced lot. As a small child, Nancy's job had been to feed the chickens and gather the eggs. After a few years, she became responsible for the newly-hatched chickens, called "little biddies" in the mountains. They came in April by mail order, in batches of twenty-five, packed in cardboard cartons punched with quarter-size air holes. Kept out in the old buggy room of the annex in a cage, the biddies' first few days were critical to survival, requiring Nancy to hang a light bulb over the cage's edge on cool nights, with a quilt to cover all. Daily she carried their special feed to the cage, changed the soiled newspapers lining the floor, filled their water jar apparatus and picked out the inevitable few that, despite the particular care, had died.

The biddies' cage had been manufactured by Gilbert after baby Nancy burned her hands on the living room stove. Built on a metal frame three feet tall, and covered with chicken wire, the cage blocked the stove from the infant, but allowed heat to come through – Gilbert's own design. Later, with the ends wired together, it made a good cage for the hatchlings. Soon the downy yellow balls took on gangly shapes, their wings developing traces of the rich auburn color of their variety – Rhode Island Reds. When they had grown enough protective feathers and could fly over the cage walls, they were moved to the chicken yard up on the hill. Even then, the bolder ones sometimes needed their wings scissor-clipped to prevent their flying over the fence.

Preparing chicken for Sunday dinner was a tedious job that usually fell to Nita, the daughters only watching. First, catching the selected bird, without being flogged and pecked, was no easy task. Next came the wringing of the neck until the head hung limp, but sometimes, Nita grasped the chicken's feet in one hand, laid the fowl on the chopping block, and with axe in the other hand, chopped off its head. The decapitated carcass reflexively jumped across the ground in every direction, blood spurting, for several minutes, before lying still – quite a scary sight for a child. Then Nita dunked the chicken into a large pot of boiling water to make the feathers easier to pluck. When all were removed except the small ones, Nita took a long twist of flaming newspaper and quickly singed away downy pin feathers while she turned the chicken with one hand. Removing the insides and the feet, Nita was ready to cut the dressed chicken into parts for frying. Hens were often baked, their undeveloped marble-size eggs a treat in the giblet gravy, while roosters were usually boiled whole for chicken and dumplings or chicken salad. As with everything else at Stackhouse, little was unused – the liver, heart, kidneys and gizzard were considered delicacies for which family members vied.

Another food procuring ritual at Stackhouse was the annual hog killing, parts of which the girls were not allowed to watch. Having fed the pigs daily, and having carried bedding of fresh weeds in summer and dry leaves in winter, and having sometimes given them names, Lexyne and Nancy would have been upset to witness the shooting, the squealing, the sharpening of the large knives, and the head removal. "By the time I got there, the carcass had already been hung by its four feet, slit down the center, and the entrails removed," remembered Nancy.[15] A large fire served to keep the November chill off the workers, and to heat the barrels full of water needed for scraping the hair from the hide. Several of Gilbert's neighbors and employees would help with the slaughter and the lifting of the three-to-four-hundred-pound hog, in return for Gilbert's help with their own, or for part pay and part fresh pork. After the twenty-four-hour cooling period, "to remove the animal heat," the carcass would be cut into hams, shoulders, side meat, fat back, loin roasts, chops, back bones and ribs – some to be eaten fresh, some to be canned, and still more to be salted or sugar-cured.

Then the work began in the kitchen for Nita and the girls. A hand-turned grinder extruded the sausage, which was seasoned, shaped into balls, browned, and canned in quart jars, ready for winter breakfasts or suppers. Likewise, Nita ground the liver, added seasonings and cooked it in a loaf pan, to be sliced for liver mush. A similar, though gelatinous, product used other parts of pork, made into "souse meat," to be sliced for frying or sandwiches. Nancy could recall that her mother rendered the hog fat into lard only once, as she had during the Depression years before Nancy's birth.[16] Hardly a meal would be cooked by Nita Stackhouse, or by Hester, that a pork product was not used, either as the main dish or for seasoning.

Somehow, in addition to all the food provision, Nita managed to make clothing for her daughters and herself. She sewed wool suits, sometimes using the fur collars from her own sisters' passed-on clothes as trim. She made other hand-me-downs from relatives into stylish dresses, skirts, blouses, shorts and slacks for the girls at little cost. "We had beautiful clothes," Nancy declared, years later.[17] As with food, nothing was wasted, and much was recycled. Nita made sure her daughters learned this, as well as the other homemaking and social arts, the work and study ethics, and the church leadership skills that she had been taught at the Asheville Normal School.

Thus, Lexyne, the elder, received lessons in Nita's kitchen from an early age, learning to cook, clean and more. One of her jobs was to fluff up the feather ticks when she made the beds. "Every so often, they had to be hung outside on the line for sunning," stated Lexyne in 2004.[18] (These were replaced with mattresses, later.) She began to iron the "rough" pieces, which included sheets, pillowcases, aprons, handkerchiefs, tablecloths and the like. (By this time, Nita had an electric iron.) Next, Lexyne learned to "sprinkle down" the stiffly-started items, roll them, and leave them long enough to become damp through – requiring more judgment and skill. Starched fabric scorched easily; a moment of miscalculation with a hot iron could leave a permanent brown stain or a hole in a good garment. Finally, she was allowed to iron the best shirts and dresses with their detailed collars, cuffs, pleats and ruffles.

In fact, as a young teenager Lexyne became responsible for all the family's ironing, and, when school was not in session, she did the house cleaning, freeing her mother to care for the many other chores. Lexyne was also called upon to churn when Nita needed to make butter and buttermilk. An avid reader, Lexyne always grabbed her book to help pass the time during this boring job. The tall wooden churn's dasher handle had to be lifted up and down in constant motion to turn the rich cream into butter. Perched on a stool, with book in one hand, she would have to release the dasher to turn pages, provoking Nita to chide, "Lexyne, you can't stop the churning until it is finished!"[19]

Nancy, too, had to perform some inside chores, especially after Lexyne left for college. Partly because she had a knack for satisfying the "impossible to please" Hester, it was Nancy's job on Saturday mornings to help her grandmother do sweeping, dusting and other weekly cleaning. However, in spring and fall, major tasks were undertaken from attic to cellar, every inch of which Hester cleaned and organized. First thing in warm weather, the heating stoves, pipes and floor pads were disassembled and carried the two flights to the attic (only to be brought down for re-assembly in the autumn). Next, the heavy wool oriental rugs and runners were carried outside to the sunshine for a hearty beating. Hester even had a child-sized wire rug beater made for Nancy when she was young.[20] The feather ticks and pillows, too, were spread outside on chairs or sturdy shrubs for sunning before replacing them on the beds.[21]

While the rugs sunned, the hardwood floors were cleaned and waxed, the windows and screens scrubbed, and the curtains washed, starched and ironed. Any sheer or lace curtains had to be dried on "curtain stretchers" – wooden A-shaped frames with small brads driven through from the back side at half-inch intervals. Painstakingly, each wet curtain panel was pulled tight and fastened at the very edge over the nail points, one at a time, up and down and across the width, the four sides stretched taut to dry in the sun. Occasionally, blood drops had to be rinsed out of the curtain because of finger pricks from the sharp tips. When finished, the curtains were smooth, wrinkle-free, and ready to hang back on the windows, their original size having been preserved by the blocking. Eventually, some of the house's curtains were replaced with modern fabrics and the outmoded stretchers were placed in storage.

Moreover, in Hester's later years, the work was further lessened when she bought linoleum facsimiles of oriental scatter rugs and stored her wool ones until company was expected. Every Saturday the new thin "rugs" were taken up, washed, and carefully stacked to dry in a way that protected the brittle, easily-broken corners – irksome, but better than rug beating.

Hester called upon Lexyne and Nancy, annually, to help her pack and mail evergreen cuttings to a nursery, one of the ways she made a little money. "Her English boxwood garden was about half an acre," recalled Nancy, "and had been there for years."[22] After Hester clipped mature branches at certain lengths, she placed them in large cardboard cartons, each layer turned in opposite directions until the boxes were filled. Then the girls carried the cartons and a dollar bill downhill to the mailbox for the mailman to take to the Marshall post office. Next day, he would leave Hester's change and receipt in her mailbox.

When Nancy had her preference, however, she chose working outdoors with her father. As a teenager, Nancy helped Gilbert re-roof Hester's barn and two rental houses, Hester paying Gilbert one dollar an hour, and Nancy, fifty cents. One summer Nancy and Gilbert painted the exterior of the Walnut Methodist Church. On the farm, they built fences, Gilbert needing Nancy to help line up the posts. "We fenced and fenced, always following the deeds," said Nancy.[23]

Moving the cattle from one pasture to another was a different challenge. "Oh my, we chased cows all over that mountain," Nancy later remembered. It would have been simple if Hester had been willing to sell Gilbert a small tract of land connected to his. For some reason, she refused, but Gilbert asked Nita's brother-in-law from Charlotte to buy it for him, and Hester did not know of the subterfuge for several years.[24] The cattle moving became a simple matter of opening a gate, leading one of the old cows through and watching the younger ones follow.

Gilbert also taught Nancy to drive at age twelve so that she could move his old dump truck around the farm when he needed help, particularly at haying time. As Gilbert walked through the field pitching hay up into the truck, Nancy drove – starting and stopping every few yards until the truck bed was full. After unloading at the barn, they returned to the field until all the hay was stored for winter. The old Ford had no license tag, no insurance and no ignition key. To start it, Nancy twisted wires together. (It would be another decade before she received a driver's license.)

On some autumn Sunday afternoons, Gilbert and Nancy gathered black walnuts, the soft green stain-filled hulls to be stomped away by Nancy, after which the nuts were placed in the barn to dry. On subsequent Sundays, Gilbert and Nancy cracked them open with a hammer, picking out the deep-seated nutmeats. It was a tiresome task, but necessary if they were to have nuts for the winter fruitcakes, pies and cookies. And during the cracking sessions, the walnuts made great snacking.

Fortunately, life on the farm was not all drudgery. To balance the chores, the Stackhouse girls had time for hopscotch, jump rope, catching lightning bugs, and other childhood activities. Gilbert cleared out the old buggy room in the brick annex for roller skating on its large wooden floor. "But there were uneven places, and when you hit one, down you went," reminisced Lexyne in later years.[25] Gilbert also mounted a basketball goal in the yard – not "regulation," but great fun. Additionally, the steep roads at Stackhouse furnished thrilling bicycle rides. "You could gain enough speed going down one hill to get you more than halfway up the next, without much pedaling," said Lexyne. Some of these same inclines provided good sledding when it snowed. Gilbert's old wooden sled served his daughters well, once they waxed the rusty steel runners. Lexyne and Nancy built snowmen and ate Nita's snow cream, made by briskly stirring sugar, vanilla and rich cow's milk into a bowlful of snow.

Sled used by two generations at Stackhouse. Photo by author.

In summer the girls played in the delightfully cold creeks and branches. They used a cloth sack from Nita's kitchen to seine for minnows to use as bait for river fishing. Once, Nancy discovered a large mud turtle at the lower end of their yard. She covered it with a number-3 galvanized wash tub overnight until she could get help in carrying it home. When she checked it next morning, the turtle was gone and so was Nita's big wash tub.[26]

Another summertime treat was the week or two spent in Charlotte with Nita's sisters, all the cousins and Ernest's family. Nancy usually spent a night or two with Ruth and Carthene at Ernest's, enjoying the attention lavished on the youngest child in the family. "It was fun to play with their pet squirrel and to watch their trained dog do tricks," Nancy later related.[27] For these visits, Gilbert drove his wife and daughters down to Charlotte on a weekend and returned the next weekend to bring them home. Some years, however, he was working so far away that he met them in Asheville at the bus station for the trip back to Stackhouse. (Nita received discount tickets from her brother-in-law, a Greyhound driver.)

When Gilbert was occupied with his full work schedule, Nita stayed busy with hers. Unlike her mother-in-law, Nita enjoyed community activities and socializing, She was also vitally interested in her daughters' education, which led her to join the Parent Teachers Association (PTA). Nita proved to be one of its most zealous members, serving as the organization's president three times during her daughters' years at Walnut School. Not allowing her lack of transportation to be an excuse, Nita rode the school bus whenever there were meetings or fund-raising projects. Nancy, even before she was school age, accompanied her mother and was permitted to sit in the first grade class while her mother was busy. Occasionally, Nita rode the train to Marshall, taking the Greyhound back to Walnut, located two miles from the railroad.

The county schools always needed things over and above the basics provided by the state. PTA mothers held bake sales and suppers and sold concessions at high school basketball games to make money. They gathered costumes for plays, cupcakes for class parties and clothing for the most indigent children. Sometimes they were needed to chaperone students, as when Nita rode a bus to Silver Springs, Florida, on Lexyne's senior-class trip. During Nita's three terms of office, Walnut PTA installed the school's first lunchroom, and bought its first cook range. They provided the heavy stage

Walnut High School seniors and chaperones at Silver Springs, Florida, 1953. 1. J.C. Worley, 2. Christine Boone, 3. Beatrice Robert, 4. Margaret D. Smith, 5. Jimmy Davis, 6. Lexyne Stackhouse, 7.Loraine Freeman, 8. Sally Ann Treadway, 9. Billy Allen, 10. Cline Allen, 11. Billy Guthrie, 12. Billy Beck, 13. Frank Johnston, 14. Nita Stackhouse, 15. Nina Sue Buckner, 16. Juanita Allen, 17. Sue Barnette, 18. Florine Faulkner, 19. Epps McClure, 20. Mrs Louie Zimmerman, 21. Ernestine Reeves, 22. Mrs. Ogle, 23. Muriel Smeltzer, 24. Mrs. Marie Eads, 25. Billy Payne, 26. Jeter Lewis, 27. George McDowell.

curtains in the auditorium, the sewing machines for Home Economic classes, and many other items to help the school reach standards set by the Southern Accreditation Association for Schools and Colleges.[28]

Since there was no regular Sunday School at the Walnut Methodist Church, Nita took her family to the Walnut Presbyterian Church. There she began her Sunday School teaching career, which would continue for fifty years. Gilbert served as Sunday School superintendent and the girls participated fully in the church's programs on weekends when Gilbert was home to drive them. At age eleven, each girl united with the church – Nancy, by baptism, and Lexyne, by reaffirmation of her faith, since she had been baptized as an infant. When Nancy was in fifth grade, the pastor's wife, Mrs. Ashe, held a weekly Bible Club at the manse, next door to Walnut school. With the Stackhouse bus route being second "run," Nancy received permission to attend the meeting until her bus arrived. Although Mrs. Ashe gave Nancy the next week's Bible readings and some cookies to take with her, Nancy always missed the games and refreshments that the others enjoyed following the Bible study. Nevertheless, Nancy treasured, for the rest of her life, the Bible passages she committed to memory in that little club.[29]

Despite the fact that Nita had grown up in the Presbyterian Church and Gilbert in the Methodist Church, they attended the denomination which happened to be meeting on Sunday, or sometimes, the one that needed them most. The four small churches in Walnut could not always afford full-time ministers, and often each held only one worship service a month. At these times, the Stackhouse family, as well as others in the community, made their worship weekly and regular by attending each of the four in turn – Methodist, Presbyterian, Freewill Baptist and Missionary Baptist. "Wherever they went, Daddy was always Sunday School superintendent, and Mother always taught Sunday School," recalled Nancy.[30]

As a teenager, Nancy attended the Walnut Methodist Church at the time when the new pastor, who served both Marshall and Walnut, began boosting the congregations to record-breaking attendance. The Reverend Barefoot was the "ball-of-fire" minister every church dreams of having.[1] He and his wife drove all the way to Stackhouse to pick up Nancy for Sunday afternoon youth group meetings. In summer, someone also provided transportation for a week of Daily Vacation Bible School, picking up Nancy as well as a few other children of the Stackhouse community, at Nita's urging. Years later, Pauline Gosnell Fowler, whose father was a sharecropper, thanked Nita Stackhouse for being kind and caring to her as a child. "I loved to go to their house, partly because Nancy was the one with the sled and the skates and the bicycle," chuckled Pauline.[31]

For several summers, Nancy and Lexyne even received piano lessons from Dr. W.J. Cunningham at the Marshall Presbyterian Church. He had actually taught at the Asheville Normal College when Nita was a student. After he retired, Nancy took lessons from the Methodist Pastor's wife in Marshall. Nancy was more interested in piano than Lexyne, whose passion lay in reading. In summer she read the books in Hester's library, including *Gone With the Wind*, the Gene Stratton Porter books and many others. When they were finished, Nita ordered boxes of books from the state library – Lexyne's favorites among these being the Nancy Drew series, the Pollyanna books and

[1] Unfortunately, Rev. Barefoot's career was cut short when he was killed in a tragic accident.

Anne of Green Gables. The library shipments came to Nita with return postage paid, a state service.[32] (Lexyne was already in college when the Madison County Public Library began.)

Some summers, the girls attended a week or so of camp – Lexyne at the Presbyterian Church camp, held at Tusculum College in Greeneville, Tennessee, and Nancy in 4-H camps, and once at a special leadership camp. Quite often, the church contributed to the camp fee for its youth, but 4-H members were required to raise their own registration fees of eighteen dollars each. Besides saving her weekly allowance of twenty-five cents from her father, she made and sold handcrafts such as rick-rack earrings, round paper-filter dolls and clown yo-yos, to name a few.

During the girls' growing-up years, Nita entertained at their home, frequently inviting the Sunday School classes, Home Demonstration Club, church youth groups, school classmates, and once holding a yard picnic for the congregations of all four churches of Walnut. Tables were set out in the grass and the "covered dishes" spread upon them, Nita and Gilbert furnishing the lemonade and coffee. If it rained, they moved everything under the broad shed of the annex building. On Lexyne's sixteenth birthday, her whole school class came for a cookout. Another time, Lexyne was allowed to invite the girls of her class, since there were only six or seven, to a slumber party. "We stayed up all night," remembered Lexyne, when older, but the family were not disturbed, since the party was in the annex. Even after Lexyne went up-county to college, she was encouraged to bring friends home with her. One time Gilbert placed piles of hay in the bed of his pickup truck to haul a group from Mars Hill to Stackhouse for a cookout. When the young people came, Gilbert always bought frankfurters and buns for hot dogs, while Nita prepared the rest of the meal. Gilbert also built them a brick roasting pit with a chimney pipe to take away the smoke.[33]

Contrarily, the more intimate family outings on summer Sunday afternoons counted among Nancy Stackhouse's best memories. Nita would prepare fried chicken, potato salad, deviled eggs, and other picnic fare for trips with the family of Nancy's classmate, Aileen, who lived up on the Barnard road. They often went to shady, cool Paint Creek or Silvermine Creek, both government-owned picnic sites at Hot Springs. While the fathers discussed farming, the mothers talked about PTA and Home Demonstration Club activities, and the girls had their common interests, like the basketball team, on which both played. In fact, this family made it possible for Nancy to play basketball by inviting her to spend the night with them so that she would have transportation to the night games and to those away from Walnut.[34]

Although Lexyne had not had transportation for participation in basketball, she took part in nearly every other activity offered at the small mountain school. She was a class officer, Beta Club president, salutatorian of her senior class, Glee Club member, and served on the staffs of the school newspaper and year book. Nancy, too, did most of these and was president of her class, as well as its valedictorian. Nita also urged both daughters to enter the county declamation contests every year because that had been her own forte at the Asheville Normal. Lexyne memorized easily and enjoyed the challenge, but Nancy found it boring, and tried – futilely – to dissuade her mother. In later life, however, Nancy was quick to admit that the public speaking experience helped her in her various jobs and responsibilities.

Nita's talent for working with children and her hospitality were both remembered by Dilworth Stackhouse in Asheville during the summer of 1959, when he sent his two sons, Charles Dilworth III (Charlie) and Harvey, to Stackhouse for refuge from possible violence connected to the Teamster Organization unrest. Dilworth, a driver for Silverfleet Motor Express, was an officer in his local union, which was meeting opposition and hostility in its attempt to organize Overnite Trucking employees.[35]

Dilworth's sons enjoyed the several days on their late great-grandfather's farm, having been warned by their father, however, to watch out for mine holes scattered over the property there, and, "Under no circumstances were we to enter one, because many dropped straight down for great distances," recalled Charlie Stackhouse.[36] And, as Nancy could attest, an innocent mine explorer could even run into moonshine stills operating in some of the abandoned tunnels. Besides exploring, the boys went with Gilbert and Nita to church and to the new drive-in movie theater on the Marshall highway, and they played with a neighbor boy named Raeford Helton. Gilbert, too, enjoyed having the boys at Stackhouse – their father, Dilworth, being the only person he ever really visited, except Gilbert's uncle and aunt at Walnut, Frank and Alice Hunycutt.

While at Stackhouse, young Charlie and Harvey likely told their cousins about a lighter side to Dilworth's trucking occupation. Three years earlier, when the Hollywood producer of *The Swan* came to Biltmore Estate, he called the local Teamsters for a member who knew the area well, was reliable and trustworthy, to be Grace Kelly's driver during her stay in Asheville. What better choice than Asheville-born, war-decorated Dilworth Stackhouse? His employer gave him a six-month leave of absence, and the movie company paid him fifty dollars a week.

Dilworth's first duty was to meet Miss Kelly at the airport in Greenville, South Carolina, an hour or so from Asheville. As they climbed the twisting mountain road on the hot afternoon, they passed a sign advertising cold beer, produce and souvenirs. Miss Kelly said, "Stack, I surely would like a cold beer," so he pulled over when they reached the road-side stand. He was amused to see the entourage of cars behind him also pulling over. "When all were refreshing, Miss Kelly offered Dad a beer, too, and he said, 'Thanks, but I'd better not – I'm driving,'" recalled Dilworth's oldest son, Larry, decades later.[37] For the rest of the filming period, Dilworth picked up Grace Kelly each morning at her Asheville hotel and took her to Biltmore Estate. He was able to get autographs from Miss Kelly, Louis Jordan, Alec Guiness and other stars for his son Charlie, who was in fourth grade at the time.

That same summer of 1956, Dilworth and his family were invited to Stackhouse for the social event of Nita and Gilbert's twenty-fifth wedding anniversary, hosted by Nita's three sisters from Charlotte. A large number of neighbors and friends came to celebrate, bringing silver-trimmed candy dishes, pewter vases and other appropriate gifts. Lexyne and Nancy had formal dresses and corsages, while Nita wore a lace gown of her own making. The spaciousness of the Stackhouse home and farm lent itself well to entertaining, except for vehicle accommodations. Situated on the hillside, there was a dearth of parking spaces, forcing guests to leave their automobiles down at the railroad and be shuttled to the gala in groups. Gilbert helped with this aspect, although not a socializer himself. He also permitted the boutonniere and other frivolity, enjoying his wife's pleasure. It made him happy to see her having a good time.

Gilbert had weightier subjects on his mind, however, his responsibilities continuing to grow since his father's death. When the county closed the Stackhouse school, there was the problem of the abandoned building surrounded by Stackhouse land, prompting Gilbert to try to buy it back. After months of legal fees and negotiations, he finally received the property deed, giving him freedom to use the land and building as part of the farm.[38]

Moreover, Gilbert and his brothers had inherited an unresolved lawsuit filed by Amos on August 6, 1948, against Anson Betts over some unpaid taxes (according to the family's memories) on the two tracts of land in which Betts and Amos each owned half interest – namely, the 56-acre Klondyke property and the 65-acre "Ellison Stackhouse" farm. No doubt the issue had been shelved because of Amos'

Nita and Gilbert Stackhouse celebrate their Silver wedding anniversary, 1956.

illness and death, then reopened after probate period. At least twice – in November, 1949, and in April, 1950 – the case was heard in court, with witnesses coming from Stackhouse, Marshall and Hot Springs. Ernest and Gilbert, too, had to leave their jobs to appear whenever Charles Mashburn, their attorney, called them. Details of the suit are sketchy, but the court ordered the land to be advertised and sold at public auction by the county commissioners. Consequently, instead of two tracts having half owners, each party received one whole-tract deed – Anson Betts paying $1010 for the Klondyke and Gilbert paying $1600 for Ellison's former farm.[39] As a result of the final accounting from Mashburn's office, he paid for court costs, deeds, witness expenses, advertising and commissioners' fees out of the sales receipts, then disbursed the balance of $360.53 to each of the three Stackhouse brothers and $562.93 to Betts.

Another Stackhouse lawsuit, troubling to Gilbert and friction-causing, was brought in 1950 by Ellsworth Vandervort against Hester and Ernest over the deed Hester had made to Ernest the year before for twenty acres and the log cabin. Although Gilbert's property was not involved, he would have been called as a witness, since he had helped Ernest build the cabin. Evidently, Ernest thought there was an oral agreement that he and Ruth would be owners, or at least co-owners, of the cabin, since he had built it and provided a home for Ruth and Ellsworth's parents. However, with no written proof, the court ruled that any claim made by Ernest and Ruth to the cabin or its land be relinquished and Ellsworth be acknowledged as sole owner.[40] Ruth

Vandervort Stackhouse never again spoke to her brother, Ellsworth, and she always felt that Gilbert had sided with him.

Gilbert had also inherited the maintenance of the family's water supply, which served all the houses on Stackhouse land, plus the Vandervort cabin. From the bold spring up on the mountain, the long lines of water pipe sometimes rusted, cracked or stopped up, requiring repairs by Gilbert. Nor were there any other municipal services available, such as fire protection. Gilbert, like his father and grandfather before him, developed the independence and resourcefulness needed for country living.

For instance, a particularly frightening incident occurred one Sunday afternoon in 1952 about the time that Gilbert was ready to leave for Kentucky, where he would be working the next week. Sparks from a passing train had set the woods afire near the railroad and burned up the mountainside, heading directly toward the Stackhouse home. When Gilbert smelled the smoke, he jumped into action, grabbing tools and telling Lexyne to "Go get the men," meaning his tenant neighbors who worked with him. She was breathless from running when she finally got to the nearest house, but luckily the workers happened to be gathered there, and responded quickly. "Daddy ordered us not to let Granny Hester know how bad the situation was, and somehow she stayed inside with no suspicions," said Nancy much later.[41]

Gilbert and the men set backfires along the perimeter of the yard and dug ditches. They wet down the porches and all else they could reach with the garden hose, carried buckets full of water to other areas, and laid wet quilts on the roof of the annex. Hearing the fire's terrible roar, young Nancy could only guess about its rapid spread; she was not allowed to go behind the house which had already blackened from the smoke. Suddenly, a large blazing limb fell across the driveway near the log cabin, starting a different area burning, and placing the fire beyond any hopes of containment by Gilbert and his few men. Fortunately, a U.S. Forest Service crew arrived, having spotted the smoke from the Rich Mountain fire tower. Although gardens and much vegetation were destroyed, the buildings were saved. Gilbert's grandfather, Amos, had kept the closeby mountains clear of trees to prevent such danger, but Amos II and Charles Dilworth had not been as diligent.[42]

That same spring, Southern Railway Company announced their elimination on March 5, 1952, of its last two steam-hauled passenger trains running between Asheville and Knoxville. "The two trains were losing money," stated the *Asheville Citizen*, but they would be sorely missed by many people.[43] Number 11 and Number 12 had been serving Stackhouse for over half a century, providing convenient daylight travel to Marshall, Asheville and Newport, the most frequented business places for Madison Countians.

Prior to the discontinuance, public hearings were held in Tennessee and in North Carolina, receiving protests in both states from local farmers, who would bear the greatest loss. At Stackhouse, while the stoppage meant fewer forest fires, it also meant reduced public transportation for its residents. Accustomed to campaigning for community needs, Nita Stackhouse accompanied her mother-in-law (by train, or course) to the North Carolina Commerce Commission in Asheville where the women explained their community's plight, no doubt reminding them of the railway siding belonging to the family, but used often by Southern. The commissioners promised the women that the fast-moving Carolina Special – Numbers 27 and 28 – would stop to pick up Stackhouse passengers when properly flagged. From then on, whenever Hester Stackhouse needed to ride the train, the engineer stopped, backed up or pulled forward, if needed, to align the passenger car door with her position by the tracks. A step stool would be placed on the ground so that Hester, who was always in hat and white gloves, could reach the train steps.[44]

Lexyne Stackhouse Norris remembered that when she bought her ticket to ride #27 home from Blanton's Business College in Asheville, she was always told by the agent, "Let me run tell the engineer he has to stop at Stackhouse."[45] Shortly later, Southern Railway System boasted that it was the first major railroad in America to become one hundred percent dieselized, having "pulled the fire" on its last steam locomotive June 17, 1953.[46] The end of these steam engines showed pride and progress for the nation, but one less service for the Stackhouse community.

Also having an impact upon the community – though more positive – were the leases between Ellsworth Vandervort and Cal Garland, bringing lumbering to the area again. Garland was allowed five years to cut any timber measuring twelve inches or more in diameter, and to set up a saw mill in the Runion bottomland between river and railroad. Garland also leased two hundred acres from Asley Sawyer on Doe Branch, and brought the logs across

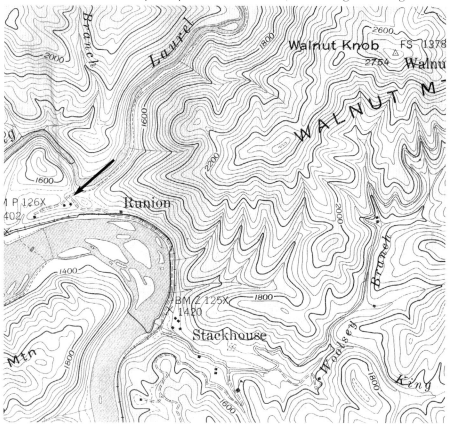

1940 map showing Runion hill and the three remaining houses of LRLC's lumber town. Flagged symbol of Stackhouse school marked near Woolsey Branch at lower right. Map by U.S. Geological Survey & TVA.

the French Broad to the mill by way of steel cables.[47] It was good to have local industry again, even small. On summer weekends the neighborhood boys hand-walked the cable to the center for a thrilling jump into the water. Unfortunately, before the five years ended, Garland had leased a larger saw mill in Hot Springs (formerly Heilman's operation) from Craig Rudisill, who now owned the famous mineral springs and surrounding acreage. Garland would close his small mill and build his Hot Springs operation into a million-dollar business, employing seventy men and boosting Madison County's economy, but never returning to Runion.[48]

In fact, the Runion buildings belonging to Vandervort were deteriorating, with only two houses being habitable. The large two-story green-painted house was being used as a tobacco barn when it caught fire, burning an entire tobacco crop, as well as a farm tractor parked in it. Paul Norton, whose father, John, owned the tractor, said that his family thought the fire had begun near the railroad and spread up to the Runion house.[49] Although steam engines were obsolete, sparks could still be generated, at times, by the passing diesel engines, or by a carelessly tossed engineer's cigarette, or by fusees, which were thrown from the engines as warning signals to following trains.

Fewer and fewer traces remained of the once-populated Laurel River Logging Company's mill village. Even the dam built on the Big Laurel just above the former commissary had been dynamited around 1950 by wildlife officer Raymond E. Ramsey, who wanted to open the creek so that fish could get through. "It was a log dam – hemlock – about thirty or forty feet long, by six or eight feet high, and no one used it anymore," stated Ramsey in a 1999 interview. He added that he and his helpers killed eight copperhead snakes "along there."[50]

Runion's owner, Ellsworth Vandervort, had also bought and sold property again at Biltmore, turning a profit on each. After his father's death in 1948, he bought his mother's one-third share of Lot Two and their home on All Souls Crescent, as well as the third inherited by Ruth Stackhouse, his sister, selling all to a motel. Ellsworth sold two other Biltmore Village lots to Gulf Oil Company for a gas station.[51] These profits likely provided him the means to acquire even more land near Stackhouse, some of it joining Stackhouse family properties. From Leslie Gahagan and the Citizens Bank he purchased two acres along the Big Laurel, joining Runion; and from Carolina Power and Light Company, he received four tracts, including the Mountain Island, plus 100 acres opposite the Stackhouse home across the French Broad.

Carolina Power and Light Company deeds stipulated that the land would revert to the power company if and when a hydro-electric power dam was built on the French Broad. Before the war ended, TVA and the power company had made plans for another dam on the French Broad at Stackhouse. The engineers told Amos that water level would reach the bottom of the front steps leading to his home. Fortunately, it never happened, and Carolina Power sold the land it had bought up along the river, but did not give up its right to a dam, should another need arise.[52] Ellsworth Vandervort's real aggregate in the 1950s stood at 1,452 acres, with a few exceptions, making him the largest landowner in the Stackhouse area, virtually surrounding the home of Hester and Gilbert, and holding the community's future in his hands.

[1] Keegan, John. "The Gentle Giant." *Modern Maturity*, Dec., 1991, p.49.
[2] Plemmons, Ernestine Reeves. Interview, 2004.
[3] Author's private papers.
[4] Stackhouse, Amos "Sonny." Letter to author, November, 1999.
[5] Rhodes, Richard. *Dark Sun, The Making of the Hydrogen Bomb*. New York: Simon and Schuster, 1995, pps. 541, 542.
[6] Aumiller, Nancy Stackhouse. Interview, 2004.
[7] Norris, Lexyne Stackhouse. Interview, 2004.
[8] Aumiller, Nancy Stackhouse. Interview, 2003.
[9] Stackhouse, Nita. Interview.
    Coxe, Ann Fuller F. Interview.
[10] Marshall *News-Record*, June 3, 1954.
[11] Silver, Harry. Interview, July, 1999.
[12] Ibid.
[13] Aumiller, Interview, 2003.
[14] Ibid.
[15] Ibid.
[16] Ibid.
[17] Ibid.
[18] Norris, Interview, 2004.
[19] Ibid.
[20] Aumiller, Interview, 2002.
[21] Ibid, 2004.
[22] Ibid.
[23] Ibid.
[24] Madison County Deed Registry, Book 84, p.166. Aumiller, Interview, 2004.
[25] Norris, Interview, 2004.
[26] Aumiller, Interview, 1998.
[27] Ibid.
[28] Stackhouse, Nita. Interview, 2001.
[29] Aumiller, Interview, 1998.
[30] Ibid.
[31] Fowler, Pauline Gosnell. Interview, 2000.
[32] Aumiller, Interview, 2000.
[33] Ibid.
[34] Ibid.
[35] Stackhouse, Charlie. Interview, January, 2003.
[36] Ibid.
[37] Stackhouse, Larry. Interview, January, 2003.
[38] Madison County Deed Registry, Book 78, p.212.
[39] Private papers.
    Mashburn, C.E. Letter, May, 1951.
[40] Madison County Court Records, Judgment Docket "U," p.172.
[41] Aumiller, Interview, 2003.
[42] Ibid.
[43] *Asheville Citizen*, March 2, 1952, Section B, p.1.
[44] Aumiller, Interview, 2000.
[45] Norris, Interview, 2000.

46 Southern Railway System advertisement, Washington, D.C., no date.

47 Madison County Deed Registry, Book 81, p.618.
    Treadway, Marie Clark. Interview, August, 1999.

48 *Asheville Citizen*, October 23, 1963.

49 Norton, Paul. Interview, 2004.

50 Ramsey, Raymond. Interview, June 30, 1999.

51 Buncombe County Deed Registry, Bk. 725, p.568; Bk. 785, p.305.

52 Madison County Deed Registry, Bk. 77, p.195.

Laurel River Trail following former logging railroad bed to Runion. Photos by author.

Chapter Twenty-Seven

Right away Ellsworth Vandervort became involved in another deal which had lucrative possibilities for him and the Stackhouse family, plus Charles Mashburn, Anson Betts and Hobart Bullman – all owners of old barite mines. They signed leases with Joseph Choquette of Atlanta, who promised to pay twenty-five cents per short ton for clays, bentonite, kaolin and other lesser minerals; fifty cents per short ton for all barite, talc, mica and all other minerals, except oil and gas; and one dollar a ton for chemical-grade barite, plus a minimum royalty of $350 per year.[1]

Strangely enough, after that initial signing, Choquette's name disappeared from the records. Unless he happened to have been an agent of Milwhite – a Texas corporation who sold industrial minerals, mainly to oil drillers – it is not clear why. Only a few months later, Madison County surveyor Ben Frisby completed a plat showing all the same lands and ore locations mentioned in the Choquette leases.[2] Nor were there any new leases signed over to Milwhite by the Stackhouse family, which indicated that there had been previous permission.

Enhancement of the barytes interest might have come from a report issued by the U.S. Dept. of the Interior in 1949, titled *Investigation of the Del Rio and Stackhouse Barite Deposit, Cocke County, Tennessee, and Madison County, North Carolina*. It's author, Laurence A. Dahners, declared that "the Hot Springs overthrust [which includes Stackhouse] is one of the major faults of the Appalachians." He also reported that there was a limited labor force, but enough men to run a small mining operation could likely be found on the adjoining farms. Dahners stated that small supplies were available in nearby towns, but "major supplies must come from Knoxville or Asheville." He described the mountain climate "as being pleasantly warm in summer, with frequent thundershowers and occasional cold spells of short term in winter."

Through the years the Stackhouses had granted numerous leases, received a few royalties, and watched prospectors come and go. Much of this Gilbert Stackhouse had witnessed first hand, but the rest he had absorbed from the accounts of his parents and grandparents, not to mention extant documents. Not only was Gilbert familiar with every foot of the Stackhouse land and quite a lot of the bordering properties, he was a commercial builder and knew the local labor potential, so he hired on as foreman for Milwhite. Although he did not make as much money as he did on his contracting, he was tired of working away from home all week, the constant figuring and bidding of jobs, and the waiting to learn if he might be awarded the contracts, sometimes without courtesy of a refusal notification.[3]

This mining job also held other advantages for Gilbert. For example, the day before his daughter Lexyne's wedding in 1958, Gilbert was able to take her to Asheville for a beauty-parlor appointment, though he did have to rush back to give the workers their paychecks before the end of the day.[4] As he hired and paid Madison County men, it was soul-satisfying to Gilbert that, once again, the Stackhouses could provide jobs at home for their neighbors.

Stackhouse community did begin to experience some of the hustle and bustle of extra people and delivery vehicles, freight trains hooking and unhooking cars at the Stackhouse siding, and dust and noise from the blasting for roadways. "We had a better road to the mines than the state road coming from Walnut Gap to Stackhouse," recalled former employee Robert Daniels, decades later.[5] Much of the road surface was topped with barite gravel, hard and enduring.

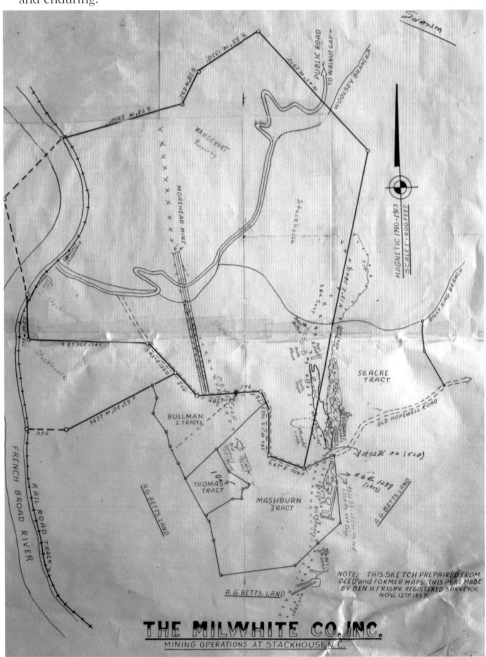

In addition to engaging Ben Frisby to make the map of the mine locations, Milwhite constructed the necessary buildings, opened up tunnels and strung electric lights throughout. "The tunnels were warm in the winter and cool in the summer – a nice place to work," said Daniels. While a crusher was being completed, the raw ore was hauled by dump trucks down to the rail siding for shipment to refineries. "We produced about a car a day," remembered Daniels.[6]

Gilbert Stackhouse was so busy, he taught his younger daughter to keep the time book for his weekly payroll – a big help to him, and a good opportunity for Nancy to earn a few dollars each week.[7] Alas, sometime during 1959, just as the operation gained rhythm and the crusher was nearly finished, Gilbert learned of its closing. "One Monday Gilbert told us that Friday would be our last paycheck, but he did not have a reason for the shutdown," stated Robert Daniels.[8] It had taken two years to bring the project this far; no one at Stackhouse could understand why their work had been in vain. Fortunately, Gilbert had paid the annual fees to keep his contractor's license valid. He threw his hat back into that ring, and left home for employment, taking a few neighbors with him, but not nearly as many as the mine had employed.

Within months, however, a fresh approach was taken by geologist Fritz Van Nest on barite reconnaissance for Bar-Tex Corporation of St. Louis, Missouri, and Houston, Texas – another oil-drilling-related firm needing to increase its mining reserves. Beginning in July, 1960, he obtained new leases from the Stackhouses, Mashburns, Betts and the others who had signed with Milwhite in 1957.[9] Van Nest drew his own map of the lease plates, and began an exploration program which he described in a 25-page report to Bar-Tex.[10] On August 5, 1960, he negotiated another lease between Ellsworth Vandervort and Albert Bailenson, president of Bar-Tex, allowing the firm to mine the old Morehead vein, which was formerly owned by the "first" Amos and then by Charles Dilworth.[11] This gave Bar-Tex a total of 720 acres for prospecting. Van Nest wrote of the Morehead that: "The vein consists, presently, of two tunnels (levels) and a 42-foot vertical shaft... length of vein and faulted zone unknown."[12]

On Hobart Bullman's 55-acre tract, a bulldozer, constructing an access road, uncovered a 30-inch-wide vein of extremely hard barite "with a 4.39 specific gravity," stated the geologist. Of the former mother lode, Klondyke, now on Betts' land, Van Nest wrote that the shafts had caved in but would be opened up in the immediate future for development preparations and inspection. "The mine is on Betts' 56-acre lease, while the dump portion is claimed by Gilbert Stackhouse," Van Nest observed.[13] "The Vandervort property contains no dumps of recoverable barite... but is a prime location for proper underground operations," he continued.[14] Van Nest defined the word "dump" to mean residuals concentrated in a convenient location to mining activities, usually at the mouth of a mine. Dumps also revealed the types of rock to be encountered underground, types of mineralized barite and gangue minerals, plus other important milling data. Van Nest also described his methods of measuring the area and depth of each dump, the gravities and barite percentages, and the resulting dump volumes of estimated derived tonnage. He wrote that:

> "The representative samples, over 1800 pounds in total, were analyzed by the North Carolina State Mineral Research Laboratory in Asheville, N.C... Split samples were sent to Bar-Tex, in St. Louis, for cross-checking... More than a month was

devoted to sample preparation and analyzation and the summation of the data obtained proved satisfactory for drilling fluid requirements... It is stated again that laboratory findings, though only under pilot conditions, revealed that commercial grade barite specifications can be met under two methods of gravity separation."[15]

Key to Van Nest's whole project, just as before, was Gilbert Stackhouse's provision of his family's old maps and mine histories, his intimate knowledge of the land, and his advice; except, this time he was not employed by the mining company. "Mr. Van Nest was always at our house, it seemed, and he ate with us a lot," related Nancy Stackhouse Aumiller.[16] Based on information from Gilbert and others in the area, plus Van Nest's own research, he reported to Bar-Tex his deductions as to why the area had "quit producing chemical-grade barite." He thought there had been a lack of basic capital and proper management; high overhead, poor quality control and slow production; the neglect of essential mining practices to prevent dangerous mining and milling conditions; poor haul-road conditions; the Carolina Barytes fire in 1912; discovery by state mine inspectors of pillar robbing; several blasting accidents producing costly law suits; unionization of contract haulers without agreement, so that stock piles were not moved to mill; water problems in the mines and poor pumping equipment to remove seepage. "All of these problems occurred in 1916 when the mines closed, stated Van Nest.[17]

He felt that a modern operation could overcome any of the named former obstacles. His report, based on his numerous tests and calculations, concluded: "Within the Stackhouse area, which includes the Spring Creek and Doe Branch sections... the prospects and holdings of this company are favorable for an extended mining operation."[18] He added that the plant already under construction was designed to produce 100 to 150 tons per day of barite ore. Fritz Van Nest's report was proficient, pragmatic and confident, redolent of success.

On October 7, 1960, Hester, Gilbert and Ernest signed an additional twenty-year agreement with Bar-Tex, allowing the building of an earthen dam on Billy King Branch, the water to cover 3.95 acres of land.[19] Three lakes resulted, to be used in the mining process for settling ponds, washing ore, and the like. Down the mountain at the railroad siding, Bar-Tex built a tall hopper with an access road above it, where the trucks from the mines could dump the processed ore. A chute at the hopper's bottom emptied into the freight cars for shipping. "There is no reason whatsoever that this endeavor will not be successful," Van Nest summarized.

Nevertheless, two years afterward, Bar-Tex executed a chattel mortgage, covering its Stackhouse operation, to Sam Bailenson for securing certain indebtedness. Later, Bar-Tex defaulted, and Bailenson received the leases, plus a long list of equipment, including dump trucks, conveyors, pumps, motors, pulley assemblies, ore screens, crusher, jig, bucket elevator, welder, compressor, hand primer, washer, storage trailer, road grader, and office furnishings, stove and refrigerator, to name a few.[20] Apparently, the mining stopped until July 19, 1965, when Bailenson transferred what he had received from Bar-Tex to Fluid Pump & Power Company, also from Texas.[21] Van Nest continued to be the field geologist at Stackhouse, employed by the new owner.

Curiously enough, three months later, Ellsworth Vandervort transferred the mineral lease with Bar-Tex to Jim W. Gray, of Tampa Florida, this being the same lease assigned by Sam Bailenson to Fluid Pump & Power Company in July.[22] Ellsworth did, however, reserve one-half interest in all rents and royalties derived from the leases during his lifetime and his wife's. On the same day of the transfer, October 25, 1965, Ellsworth Vandervort also sold his entire Stackhouse holdings of over a thousand acres to Gray at the price of $100,000.[23] This included the log cabin, within a hundred yards of Hester's home, the Runion Mountain and village ruins, the Mountain Island, and several other tracts acquired from Carolina Power & Light Company. Vandervort set terms of payment at $26,500 down, with the rest financed at $5^{1}/_{2}$ % over five years. The contract reservations granted Ellsworth reasonable time "to harvest and remove his crops" for the year, and to use the log cabin for one year (until September, 1966). Vandervort also reserved, until January 1967, the use of the tenant dwelling occupied by the sharecropper Herman Gosnell, "and the four acres of garden and pasture with it, free of rent."[24]

Afterwards, Ellsworth and wife, Beulah, rented a small house in the vicinity for a while, then moved into a garage apartment on highway 25/70 near Walnut, belonging to Elizabeth Gahagan Baker, longtime friend of the Stackhouse family.[25] The Vandervorts enjoyed the convenience of having a ready vacation place after their long drives from Texas, instead of having to clean out the water spring, mow grass and do the chores of opening a seasonal home. Even though they had sold all of their western North Carolina holdings, they loved the area, and continued coming there. "They spent their summers here for many years," recalled Mrs. Baker in a 2004 interview.

When it came time to empty the Stackhouse log cabin, following the sale, some of the furniture belonging to Ellsworth's sister, Ruth, and her husband Ernest, by pre-arrangement, was given to Lexyne Stackhouse ("the pet of the Stackhouse thirties' crowd," as a toddler), who used it with fond memories for many years. She even passed certain pieces along to her own daughter.[26]

Ellsworth Vandervort had tried to sell his Stackhouse property prior to 1965. His wife told her landlady, Mrs. Baker, about one incident when some out-of-state investors came to check its suitability for a theme park, centered on the flat, arable section of Runion Mountain. They had a morning appointment, but their enthusiasm kept them looking "all afternoon and overnight," stated Mrs. Baker years later. Despite the good impression made by the mountains, the railroad, the rivers and creeks, according to Mrs. Vandervort, the theme park was built in Atlanta, as a result of the industrial incentives offered by the city politicians.[27]

The Bakers and the Stackhouses could only heave a sigh of relief, just as they had over a decade earlier when the new highway, I-40, was being planned through western North Carolina. Somewhat paralleling the serpentine highway 25/70, the survey crossed the French Broad at Stackhouse where the old barytes mill dam had been.[28] Once again, through the interests of politicians, the new Interstate and its accompanying economy went through a different county, by-passing Madison completely. Much as they wanted to help their community, the Stackhouses and their neighbors were glad that they were not left at the bottom of a tall embankment, open to the noise, traffic view and pollution – night and day – of a busy thoroughfare.

Less invasive was a plan by the new owner, James Gray, to make his investment profitable. He heard that Hollywood's MGM studio planned to make a movie from Catherine Marshall's book *Christy*. He contacted them and they sent a filming crew twice, but an internal conflict with the magnate Edgar Bronfman not only resulted in Bronfman's leaving MGM, but also in the studio's dropping the picture. "It would have been such a good setting for that story," remarked James Gray in a later interview.[29] After holding the Stackhouse property a few more months, Gray joined several other men to form Mountain Island Development Corporation. On July 5, 1966, he deeded the 1400 acres to the new group, most of whom had never laid eyes on the land or Madison County.[30]

With some apprehension, the Stackhouse family and community awaited its fate, held by total strangers who had little affinity for the Southern Appalachians. Damage to its near-pristine loveliness and seclusion had been close at least three times already. How much longer could this prime chunk of real estate escape development?

In the meantime, the barite mining by Fluid Pump & Power Company (up on the mountain, quite a way from Hester's home) had been on-going under Fritz Van Nest's direction. His foreman in charge was Albert Haney from Hot Springs, who in turn hired others from the area – James Whitson, Manly Ray, Clifford Green, Jr., Roger Gosnell, Douglas Norton, and two of the Gahagan family, Steve and B.W., to name a few. In all, there were twenty-five to thirty men employed there, some driving the distance from Paint Rock (below Hot Springs) to Stackhouse every morning, glad to get the work.[31]

James Whitson recalled, many years later, that they did not work in the tunnels, but bulldozed through the old dumps, then graded and "grassed down," to leave no raw surfaces or stripped areas. Clifford Green, Jr., recalled that he helped build a small office building with a drafting table and a diesel-oil-fueled salamander stove for heating. One day the salamander was accidentally tipped over, burning the structure to the ground. "We built it right back," said Green.[32]

A worse tragedy occurred on February 9, 1967, in the death of Manly Ray, as he was welding atop an eight-foot steel scaffold. It was a cold winter morning with wet snow on the ground. The electric welder he was using had been known to "short-out," leading his family and friends to suspect that he had died of electrocution. The coroner in Marshall, nevertheless, reported the cause of death as heart attack.[33] Manly Ray had been friend and employee of Gilbert Stackhouse when both worked for Milwhite. "He had been to our home several times," remember Nancy Aumiller, later, "and Daddy was fond of him."[34]

Another expensive misfortune for Fluid Pump & Power was the loss of a large piece of earth-moving equipment as it was being delivered on a trailer down Stackhouse Road from the highway. "In one of the tight curves, the trailer turned over and the machine went down the embankment," related James Gray, years later. "They had to bring in a second one, because there appeared no way to retrieve the lost one," he added. Even with the thorough research and planning, these costly and disruptive events threatened to thwart the operation.

Eventually, though, after two years of preparation, the barytes mill was running smoothly, the ore reclaimed from the dumps, separated and crushed

Old Mine adit at Stackhouse, N.C.

to market needs, then trucked to the freight siding for shipping. "We hauled several loads of stone to the railroad – maybe twenty cars," Clifford Green recalled. But, incredibly, like a recurring nightmare, the project failed again. Steve Gahagan stated decades afterward, "One Friday, with no warning, we received our paychecks and were told the operation was closing right then."[35] None of the Fluid Pump & Power crew had seen it coming.

However, as soon as Gilbert Stackhouse heard the news, he went to the county sheriff's office to attach a lien against some of the buildings. "They owed everybody," Nancy Aumiller recalled, "and the mill never reopened."[36] In shock and dismay, the Stackhouse community watched their expectations carried away with each piece of equipment. Gilbert moved his two buildings on his farm sled down the mountain a mile or so to his land, where he combined the two mill structures into a "cute little rental house on one of the lakes," Nancy recounted. "Daddy owned lots of block and tackle, and he knew how to move just about anything," she concluded.[37]

Close as he was to Fritz Van Nest, Gilbert was never told the true reason for the debacle. He guessed that Fritz failed to show profit quickly enough to prove the worth of the operation, or perhaps the company needed a tax write-off, or maybe a more economical source of barite suddenly turned up for Fluid Pump & Power Company. The concrete ramps and foundations, the three broad lakes, and the white rock roads joined the other Stackhouse relics to inspire ghostly legends.

Periodically thereafter, new inquiries came, geologists poked through the dumps, and prospectors darkened the adits, but none ever developed as much promise as had the "Van Nest" decade. Although Van Nest's professional report had several references to drillings, it was said in geological circles that he had sampled only the ore dumps which had been exposed to years of rain, wind and sun, resulting in a concentrated reading. (Nevertheless, Anson Betts, up in Massachusetts, continued to believe in the Stackhouse lode and tried to interest investors for years thereafter.)[38]

When the last equipment had been taken away, the crushing and hauling dust finally settled, and the noise faded to melancholy quiet, the Stackhouse community tightened its belt and became resigned to even more shrinkage of its population. Sadly watching neighbors leave, the Stackhouse family felt responsible, but had no means to create jobs, as it done in years past. Hester, Gilbert and Nita, however, were no strangers to adversity or disappointment. By their optimistic natures and strong faiths, they knew they would survive and somehow keep the community's identity intact.

Concrete foundations left from last mining venture at Stackhouse, N.C.

ENDNOTES FOR CHAPTER TWENTY-SEVEN

1. Madison County Register of Deeds, Bk. 88, pps. 413, 416, 422, 487.
2. Author's private papers.
3. Norris, Lexyne. Interview, 2003.
   Norton, J.D. Interview, 2004.
4. Ibid.
5. Ibid.
   Daniels, Robert. Interview, 2003.
6. Ibid.
7. Aumiller, Nancy Stackhouse. Interview, 2001.
8. Daniels, Robert. Interview, 2003.
9. Madison County Deeds Register, Bk. 90, pps. 457, 462, 471.
10. Mashburn family papers, 2002.
11. Madison County Deeds Register, Bk. 90, p.500.
12. Mashburn family papers, 2002.
13. Ibid.
14. Ibid.
15. Ibid.
16. Aumiller, Interview, 2003.
17. Mashburn family papers.
18. Ibid.
19. Madison County Deeds Register, Bk. 90, p. 530.
20. Ibid., Bk. 92, p.226.
21. Ibid., Bk. 97, p. 123.
22. Ibid., p.161.
23. Ibid., p.150, 165.
24. Ibid., p.151.
25. Baker, Elizabeth Gahagan. Interview, 2004.
    Williams, Robbie. Interview, 2004.
26. Norris, Interview, 2004.
27. Baker, Interview, 2004.
28. Aumiller, Interview, 2004.
29. Gray, James W., Jr. Interview, 2004.
30. Madison County Deeds Register, Bk. 97, p.298.
31. Gahagan, Steve. Interview, 2004.
    Green, Clifford. Interview, 2004.
    Whitson, James. Interview, 2004.
32. Green, Interview, 2004.
33. Ray, Maxine. Interview, 2004.
34. Aumiller, Interview.
35. Gahagan, Interview, 2004.
36. Aumiller, Interview, 2004.
37. Ibid.
38. Hull, Edna Betts. Interview, 2000.

Chapter Twenty-Eight

In addition to the differences in the Stackhouse community, the fifties and sixties wrought changes within the Stackhouse family. Gilbert's daughter Lexyne, upon her 1953 graduation from Walnut High School, entered Madison County's only college – Mars Hill, affiliated with the Baptist Church and said to be the oldest in western North Carolina. Oddly enough, about a year (or probably earlier) before Mars Hill's founding, another Madison County college, Transmontane (Methodist-sponsored, and later called Madison Academy) was begun at Little Sandy Mush by the uncles of Malley Reeves, old friend of Amos Stackhouse and grandfather of Ernestine Reeves, Lexyne's good friend and classmate. Both Transmontane and Mars Hill were state-chartered by the 1859 Legislature, but Transmontane appears to have closed during the Civil War.[1] It had offered a one-third discount to young men preparing for the ministry and to preachers' children "of every denomination."[2]

Lexyne finished Mars Hill in 1955 and Blanton's Business College in Asheville a year later, accepting a job at Blanton's as typing teacher. "Mr. Blanton had promised me a raise, so after a while, I reminded him, and he raised my pay from $45 a week to $50," said Lexyne some forty years later.[3] At Blanton's, Lexyne also met her future husband, Bobby Norris, a student from Macon County who had returned from the Army, taking advantage of the veterans' education bill.

Bobby and Lexyne married June 7, 1958, in the Walnut Methodist Church, with a cake cutting and rehearsal the night before at the Walnut Presbyterian Church fellowship hall. Ernest Stackhouse's wife Ruth and his daughter Carthene made the tiered wedding cake, bringing it all the way from Charlotte. Gilbert gave away the bride, and Nancy attended as Maid of Honor. Afterwards, Lexyne moved to Henderson County, where Bobby worked for Cranston Print Works and attended night classes at Asheville-Biltmore College.[4] Hence, ten years following Amos' death, the household at Stackhouse was reduced by one more.

In 1960, Nancy, too, finished Walnut High and began Mars Hill College, leaving Nita to despair over her empty nest. She wrote to Nancy, visited her at times, and sent her home-cooked breakfasts on Monday mornings by Gilbert as he went to work in Burnsville. Still, Nita missed Nancy terribly. To assuage her loneliness, Gilbert bought Nita a television set, installing the antenna, necessarily, high on the mountainside, where lightning, wind and snow played havoc. The reception was faulty, frequently failed, and was difficult to repair, but when working, did fill some of the void for Nita.[5]

Near the end of Nancy's second year at Mars Hill, the Baptist State Convention approved the addition of a junior and a senior year, placing her in a quandary. To become the teacher of her aspirations, she needed the two more years, but Gilbert told her that he could pay for three years, only, since Lexyne had received merely three. He would, however, allow Nancy to raise the fourth year's money on his tobacco allotment, by growing a crop – the surest way to obtaining cash in Madison County.

For the three years' fees, Gilbert had already sold their uncompleted house and sixteen acres in Charlotte in 1961. Unfortunately, the sale money was being paid in annual installments and was not readily available.[6] Nita regretted the sale, but Gilbert actually felt relieved. "He would have been miserable living out of the mountains," stated Nancy much later. Nevertheless, Gilbert was still faced with the probability of Hester's leaving the home to one of his brothers, so he made an agreement with a friend for an option on a piece of land up on the Marshall highway. "He and Mother planned to use the Charlotte payments to put a mobile home on the lot, if the time came," Nancy added.[7]

Meanwhile, Nancy spent her Saturdays and vacation days setting tobacco plants, hoeing, suckering, spraying and performing all the other back-breaking tasks involved in growing tobacco. "After school began, Mother and two tenant wives did the handing, and Daddy put it into the barn and sold it for me after it cured," recalled Nancy.

During the summer, at times, she did have a helper – her boyfriend, Dave Aumiller, Seattle native and student from Bob Jones University, a Christian school in Greenville, South Carolina. Dave had been called to Madison County in 1961 to assist Rev. Charles Heirer, pastor of the Presbyterian parish. In July, 1963, Heirer moved away and Dave was left with the care of seven churches, so he did not return to South Carolina, but took classes at Mars Hill, instead. Besides his courtship with Nancy Stackhouse, he had also formed relationships with some of the hardened mountain boys, leading them to change, and he did not want to abandon them. In November, Marshall Presbyterian Church voted to withdraw from the Madison County Larger Parish, leaving Dave with the remaining six scattered churches to serve.

Nancy helped him with his work load, traveling from community to community. They held worship services at three different churches each Sunday, alternating Sundays with the other three. Hot Springs, White Rock

WALNUT PRESBYTERIAN CHURCH

September 29, 1963

"O come, let us sing unto the Lord: let us make a joyful noise to the rock of our salvation. Let us come before his presence with thanksgiving, and make a joyful noise unto him with psalms."   Ps. 94:1&2

*Doxology...........................
*Call to worship.....................
*Invocation.........................
*Lord's Prayer......................
*Apostles' Creed....................
   I believe in God the Father Almighty, Maker of heaven and earth; and in Jesus Christ His only Son our Lord; who was conceived by the Holy Ghost, born of the Virgin Mary, suffered under Pontius Pilate, was crucified, dead, and buried; He descended into Hell; the third day He rose again from the dead; He ascended into heaven, and sitteth on the right hand of God the Father Almighty; from thence He shall come to judge the quick and the dead.

   I believe in the Holy Ghost; the holy Christian Church; the communion of saints; the forgiveness of sins; the resurrection of the body; and the life everlasting. Amen.

* congregation stands

(Cont'd)

Hymn.........................#334
         "Jesus Saves"
Special music.....................
Scripture lesson..................
Pastoral prayer...................
Announcements.....................
Offertory prayer..................
Offertory.........................
Hymn..............................#278
         "Glory to His Name"
Special music.....................
Sermon............................
         Dave Aumiller
Prayer of committment.............
*Hymn.............................#152
         "Use Me Today"
*Benediction......................

ANNOUNCEMENTS:
   Tonight: At 6:00 o'clock this evening will be the regular meeting
   YOUTH RALLY   of the youth at the church.
   SATURDAY NITE
   OCTOBER 5   At 7:00 o'clock this evening will be the regular fifth Sunday choir practice. All are invited.

   Wednesday night at 7:00 p.m., at the Missionary Baptist Church, prayer will be conducted.

   Next Sunday at 2:00 p.m. there will be a session meeting here at the church. All session members are urged to be here at that time.

Typical church bulletin prepared weekly by Nancy Stackhouse and Dave Aumiller.

and Walnut had simple bulletins for Sunday morning services, which Dave typed and Nancy cranked out by hand on an old mimeograph machine. In a few of the congregations, the parishioners wore coats and ties, hats and gloves, while at the remote places, they came in clean overalls and cotton dresses.

Many of the people in these "distant parts" had had few advantages, making Dave's role more that of missionary than of pastor. Nonetheless, he had experience in mission work from his high school days, when, as a Christian-school student, he and his classmates sailed up from Seattle to conduct roving Bible camps for the youth of Alaskan villages during the summers, while the adults went ashore for evangelistic meetings with the older Indians.[8] Thus, Dave understood isolation, poverty, dialects and clannishness. In Madison County's Laurel region, Nancy, as a native from the nearby Stackhouse community, helped to soften the distrust and coldness sometimes reserved for outlanders with odd names.

Consequently, it did not take long for Dave to win the Laurelites' hearts. Dave and Nancy organized youth groups at each church, providing enthusiasm and giving attention to some who had never traveled from their own "holler," even to the county seat of Marshall. Years afterward, it was not unusual for Dave Aumiller to be approached on the street or at a service by a person with out-stretched hand, saying, "Preacher, I accepted the Lord when I was in your youth group, and I want to thank you."[9]

In addition to Sunday worship, youth groups, visiting the sick, and serving quarterly communion to the shut-in members, Dave and Nancy conducted Daily Vacation Bible Schools at each church during the summers. There was no operating money, leaving Nancy to cut pictures from magazines, borrow supplies, and devise crafts at low cost. Dave's father in Seattle, also a pastor, sent a donation for a few purchases, but mostly, they managed on their zeal and faith. Dave had a second-hand Volkswagen station wagon which they filled with children they picked up along the narrow crooked roads, driving through creeks, at times, to some of the churches deep in the Madison fastness. One had wooden shutters with no glass in the windows, and its benches were short, straight and handmade. There was no piano, only an ancient pump organ, which Nancy played as Dave sang. "Once Dave called on me to sing a duet with him, which was all but impossible – having to keep the pumping going with my feet, read the notes for my fingers, and sing the words between the clefs," remembered Nancy years later, with a chuckle.[10]

"Forty or fifty would show up for Bible School, so we divided them by grades – third grade and down were mine; fourth and up were Dave's," Nancy said. At one community, a boy brought in a young rattlesnake, causing the pupils to scream, climb upon the benches, run out the door or jump through the window openings. Another time, a fight erupted between two boys about ten years old, because one had grabbed a plug of tobacco from the other's hip pocket and taken a chew. "That was the most ferocious fight I ever witnessed," explained Nancy, shaking her head.[11]

Undaunted, evidently, by the preview of the years ahead, Nancy Stackhouse became engaged to the preacher, David Lee Aumiller. On May 30, 1964, she received one of the first baccalaureate degrees awarded at Mars Hill College, followed by her wedding a week later. Again, Ruth and Carthene from Charlotte helped with the details of a shoestring-budget affair.

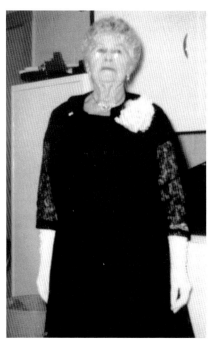

Hester Stackhouse in church kitchen after granddaughter Nancy's wedding, June, 1964.

"There was this wonderful woman in Marshall who made the attendants' dresses for $2.50 each," recalled Nancy. The ceremony was in the newly-built Walnut Presbyterian Church – one of Dave's charges – while the cake-cutting reception was held the night before at the Stackhouse home. "Grannie Hester had a conniption when Aunt Ruth moved the dining table from the center of the room to the bay window to make space for a reception line," Nancy added.[12]

The Stackhouse home and brick annex building overflowed with Ernest's family, Nita's family from Charlotte, and Dave's mother from Seattle, who had come for graduation and stayed for the wedding. Nevertheless, Gilbert chose the morning of the wedding to hook up an electric water heater which he had purchased earlier but not had time to install. "He never took a day off," stated Nancy, "but he had to be home for the wedding, so he grabbed the chance."[13] There was no space in Nita's small kitchen, and Hester would not allow it anywhere else in the house, leaving Gilbert to place it out in the annex bathroom, twenty feet away, hand-ditching the pipe deep underground to prevent freezing. In the afternoon, before her five o'clock wedding, Nancy turned on the bathtub faucet and luxuriated in a stream of hot water that had required no heating and carrying from the kitchen's wood stove.

Gilbert's procrastination had not come altogether from lack of time. Many other Madison Countians heated their water on a wood stove in the same fashion, and still others heated theirs in a galvanized iron tank connected to the kitchen range, also requiring a hot fire for a period of time – restricting summer baths to mealtimes when a fire was in the stove. By doing this, they kept their "light bills" as low as possible each month. An electric water heater used the expensive 220 volts, making it a high monthly cost, not just a one-time purchase price for the appliance itself. Gilbert had been reluctant to incur the added liability. Years later, Nancy Stackhouse Aumiller was shocked to learn that her friends and schoolmates had thought she was rich because "we lived in the 'big mansion,' but almost the opposite was true – we lived frugally and counted every penny."[14] Hence, for Nancy on her wedding day, the automatic stream of hot water made a memorable gift.

What's more, she would be able to enjoy it further, when, after a short honeymoon trip to the Shenandoah Valley, the newlyweds moved into the Stackhouse annex apartment supplied by the same water heater. When Nancy got a job in the fall, teaching mathematics at Enka High School, however, she and Dave moved to Buncombe County, leaving the Stackhouse household short yet another member. Nita hardly had time to mourn this loss, because her mother-in-law suddenly needed extra care.

Hester's heart had begun to fail, prohibiting her from making a garden, canning, and climbing the stairs to her bedroom. To keep from disturbing the house furnishings, she slept in the library on the hard, horse-hair-stuffed studio couch whose wooden arms folded down to make a small bed. Somehow, without her knowing, Gilbert was able to crawl under the house and connect water and sewer pipes to the floor of the pantry, just off Hester's kitchen. Then, over her protests, he installed a toilet so that she would not have to go outdoors and down the steps each morning to empty her slop jar into the annex bathroom. It proved to be even more helpful as Hester's condition worsened. Finally, she suffered a heart attack requiring hospitalization at Takoma in Greeneville, Tennessee. Afterwards, she was sent to Brentwood nursing home in Asheville, but she refused to stay. "She was a large woman; it took three people to lift her," recalled her daughter-in-law, Nita, decades later.[15] Hester was also a strong-willed, independent woman, used to getting her own way.

From Brentwood, Hester was taken to the sanitarium section of Takoma, where she knew Dr. Leroy Coolidge would be available almost daily, and she felt familiar with the facility from having attended her husband there. Hester's postmistress retirement benefits paid half her medical bills, the other half coming from her hard-earned savings, rentals, royalties and small pension. She tolerated the Seventh-day Adventists and gave no trouble to the caretakers. To Gilbert and Nita, however, she continued to make demands and accusations about Gilbert's handling of her rentals and tobacco sales. She thought he sometimes held back a portion when he paid her. Gilbert and his family visited at least once a week, as Gilbert's work permitted, but she complained to the staff that he rarely came to see her. She also told the nurses that Nita and Gilbert were selling her furnishings and ruining her house. She was so convincing that one nurse made a trip to Stackhouse to check on the situation, but there was no one at home. Gilbert and Nita were on their way to Takoma. At nearly every visit, Hester made requests for some item she needed from her home – hairpins or stockings, for instance. Perfectionist that she was, she could tell Nita its exact location – which room, which bureau, which drawer and which side of the drawer.[16]

After twenty-two months at Takoma, on October 29, 1966, Hester's heart gave up its struggle, diminishing the Stackhouse population by one more. Dr. Coolidge signed her death certificate, as he had signed Amos' eighteen years earlier.[17] Two of Hester's former pastors, along with a younger Methodist minister – Joseph MacDonald "Mac" Reeves, son of Amos Stackhouse Reeves – conducted her funeral in the Walnut Methodist Church. From among Gilbert's many friends, the pallbearers were chosen to carry Hester's casket to the church yard where it rested beside Amos' under the double, previously-set, granite monument.

Hester had never had time for friendships. "She worked all the time," said Nancy Aumiller, "and I was probably her best friend." Occasionally, however, even Nancy had walked out on Hester's criticisms of Nita and Gilbert. "But I always went back," she admitted.[18] Hester had been a woman more respected than loved, except by her husband. He loved her to his death, despite her nagging and her straight-laced idiosyncrasies.

The rest of the Stackhouse family members had not attended the funeral because of the distance – June, serving as Director of Engineering at the U.S.

Tombstone for Amos and Hester Stackhouse at Walnut Methodist Church cemetery. Photo by author.

Naval Station on Midway Island; his wife and children in California. June's daughter, Clara Hester, had become a Certified Public Accountant and part-time instructor at Cabrillo College, and she and her husband, John Radin, had two daughters, Cathryn and Susan.[19]

Dilworth Stackhouse, nephew of Amos and Hester, was in Indiana, just across the line from Louisville, Kentucky.[20] He had been transferred in 1961 when Mason-Dixon bought Dilworth's employer, Silverfleet, requiring Dilworth to sell his Richmond Hill Park home in Asheville.[21] His four grown children – Larry, Harvey, Virginia and Charles Dilworth, III (Charlie) – were scattered, Charlie and Harvey serving in the Vietnam War. This was another United States involvement intended to create conditions for an independent democratic government in a foreign country. Fortunately not among the 57,605 U.S. servicemen who died there, Charlie came home after four years at Shaw Air Force Base repairing electronic systems on bombers, and Harvey, after a year as jet engine crew chief during the Tet Offensive in Vietnam.

U.S. Naval Academy graduate and distant cousin from Ohio, Charles David Stackhouse, receiving ribbon in 1966. He would be held for six years as a prisoner of war in North Viet Nam. Courtesy Harvey Stackhouse.

Some of the Pennsylvania Stackhouses might have attended Hester's funeral had they been notified, but Ellison's daughter, Laura, the last to visit Stackhouse, had died in 1953, leaving no children.[22] Hester, alone, had maintained the link with the Northern relatives, whom she saw as educated, well-to-do and sophisticated, while acknowledging but a few of her Honeycutt and Gilbert relatives, apparently embarrassed by them. "There's no telling how many cousins we have that Grannie never mentioned," Nancy Aumiller declared years later.[23] "If she considered them 'common,' she would not foster relationships," explained Nancy. Hester did her best to behave as she thought a lady should, back straight and head high. When she had been able to make the Saturday trips to Marshall, she wore a pair of white gloves until she reached town, whereupon these were exchanged in her purse for a fresh, snow-white, better pair, before she got off the train or out of the automobile. Hester's aristocratic sense of propriety had been almost unnatural – even snobbish – to her mountain upbringing, as she strove to rise above her childhood poverty. Whatever her motives, neither Hester's family nor her community would ever be quite the same. An era had ended with the death of this proud matriarch.

Some days later, Hester again shocked her family through her will reading in Charles Mashburn's office. The 1961 document's first two pages listed possessions and property left to the older sons, June and Ernest, but it was "Item Four" that caused jaws to drop.[24] To her youngest son, Gilbert, Hester bequeathed "my home and home tract of land which covers almost three acres, which I purchased from C.D. Stackhouse…"

Even though Hester left Ernest 120 acres of Stackhouse land, his wife, Ruth, was so upset that she never again set foot in Stackhouse, nor did she allow her husband to, except to pick up the possessions his mother had left him, such as Haviland china, sterling hollow ware, inlaid mahogany chair, costume jewelry, pictures, books, cut glass, "one-third of my linens," and much more, including the precious "walnut work box made of the door jambs of the Stackhouse mansion in Philadelphia." Ernest also inherited another Quaker heirloom: "the sampler made by Aunt Sarah Ellison in 1800."[25]

These "linens," to be divided among the three sons, were stacks of store-bought sheets, likely birthday, Christmas or Mothers' Day gifts, plus pillowcases and furniture scarves edged with her hand-tatted laces, along with handmade cotton quilts pieced together through long winter afternoons when she could not work outdoors. Hester's own bed was always made with sheets sewn from flour sacks in the Depression days. She saved her new linens for company or for more hard times.

To her son June, Hester also willed a combination of valuable and sentimental items, including sterling silverware, pictures, books, embroidered cushions, her personal Bible, set of leather-bound encyclopedia, suitcases, "his father's gold watch and chain," and, again, "one-third of all my linens." Hester further wrote in June's paragraph of her will, "We have heretofore given to my son, Amos Stackhouse . . . more than our other sons and for that reason, I do not devise him real estate other than that set forth in Item Five."[26]

Item Five bequeathed Hester's land "known as lumberyard bottom and private railroad siding," to her three sons, jointly. "If, upon my death, I own war bonds, cash or savings account, I want all divided equally between my three sons, share and share alike," the will concluded. Unfortunately, since the drafting of Hester's last testament in March, 1961, much of her modest nest egg had gone to pay Takoma Sanitarium, but at least she had not been forced to sell her home, any land, or other possessions.

In fact, had it not been for Hester's scrimping and tenacious protection of her precious home, it could have been greatly altered or lost in the lean days, as was much of the other Stackhouse real estate. During her eighty-eight years, she preserved her farmstead through the coming into western North Carolina of the train, highways, the elevator, the flush toilet, electric lights, the telephone, the automobile, airplane and television, adopting only the few of these amenities which were built into, or did not threaten, her house as it stood. She also, without choice, met the demands and challenges of the Spanish-American War, two World Wars, the Korean and Vietnam conflicts, the Cold War, the Great Depression, food rationing, integration, epidemics, floods, fires, droughts, the loss of one child to whooping cough, and the blinding of another's eye. Hopefully, never again would so much be asked of Stackhouse women.

About a week after the funeral, a letter of sympathy came to Nita and Gilbert from June's daughter, Clara Hester Radin, in California, stating, in part:

> It is a blessing that Grandma has gone to her heavenly place. I know it was a terrible drain on you to visit her and care for her all these years…The old house will never be the same, again, as I know you will distribute the furnishings and rearrange things to your preference; this is as it should be. I will always remember the house as it was during my childhood. She was a tough 'old girl,' but I'm sure she could not have carried on so successfully without a will of iron.[27]

It comforted Nita and Gilbert to know that June's daughter had understood and sympathized with their situation. She was correct, of course, that the house would not be the same again. Beyond the fact that many of the furnishings, books, and other accessories left the premises as stipulated in the will, there were other measures needed to keep the sixty-two-year-old structure from deteriorating and to bring it up to date for present-day livability. "When Grannie died, the house needed a lot of work," recalled Nancy Aumiller, thirty years later.[28] In fact, it took all Gilbert's cash inheritance and more to replace the roof, repair gutters and fascia, paint the entire outside and most of the inside. (A shingle roof had already been installed on Hester's greenhouse where snow had caved in the glass one.)

One of Gilbert's bad memories was that of his aging parents' climbing the stairs on bitter cold nights, in each hand a kerosene lamp, its glass chimney leaning dangerously. They were carrying these to the bathroom where they would place them as near the pipes as possible in hopes of preventing frozen water. Gilbert always feared they would catch the house afire. He allayed those fears by changing waterlines from exterior to interior walls, as he repaired and remodeled for his and Nita's moving downstairs to live. A friend who was an electrician helped Gilbert update the wiring in all the second floor and parts of the first floor.

Another aspect of this renovation involved tearing out the small marble sink on the original dining room wall (which backed to the kitchen porch), neatly plastering and painting over the holes. He also completed the downstairs bathroom he had begun in Hester's pantry, and knocked out a wall to enlarge the kitchen for Nita's use. By sealing off the original cellar door in the kitchen porch floor, and adding a new exterior door to the cellar at ground level, he was able to extend Hester's small kitchen the length of the porch. He had found several large salvage windows, either free or at low cost, which, when mulled together, created a light, airy kitchen-den combination.

One more alteration moved the dining room back to its original location, eliminating the library, and turning the former dining room into a bedroom; it connected conveniently to the kitchen, the new bathroom, and the foyer stairwell. As Clara Hester had predicted, the house was not the same as it had been during her grandmother's day, but it was more functional for Gilbert's family, who would use and enjoy every inch of space. Nor would the upstairs guest room ever be locked again. Social being that Nita was, she would often fill the house with guests, relatives, grandchildren, and at times even a few strangers in need of lodging.

Gilbert did not restrict his remodeling to the interior. Outside he made changes of which Hester would not have approved. He cut a row each of blue spruce and crepe myrtle trees along the back driveway, took out part of the masonry wall at the annex, and built an access to the kitchen yard for his automobile. At the front of the house, he widened the old carriage driveway to accommodate modern vehicles. He also removed two of his mother's favorites, a cucumber tree and a chinaberry tree, whose habits of dropping fruit and seed pods had always irritated him.[29]

Gilbert saw even more work the farmstead needed, contributing to his decision to retire at age sixty-two. He had experienced some dizziness in climbing the tall smoke stacks, and he had developed a hernia.[30] His jobs away from home also left Nita alone in the big house, with no close neighbors, except when the log cabin owners happened to be visiting from Florida. Even though his financial position was far from desirable, he preferred to stay in Stackhouse and attempt to augment his social security with rental and farming income, depending heavily upon his mainstay crop, tobacco. However, he paid the annual state fee to renew his contractor's license for at least four more years, in case he needed to go back to building commercially.[31]

Meanwhile, Gilbert moved his work shop from a small building downhill, near the lumberyard, up to the annex buggy room, a much handier location, and one that had been forbidden by Hester. He had inherited his mother's penchant for neatness and organization, building compartments for nuts and bolts, screws and nails, then labeling each one as to size. "I've never known a man who was as neat and orderly," stated a Stackhouse neighbor, Jenny Koranek, years later.[32] "However, before reaching down into the bins, he would always shine a flashlight to check for snakes," his daughter Nancy added. (Copperheads and rattlesnakes were not uncommon around the Stackhouse home.)[33]

Next, using block and tackle, he lifted the old log barn, in which he kept his horses, onto sled runners, and pulled it to a more convenient location, closer to the creek. The farmer's sled, used since pioneer days, was a versatile mountain vehicle, capable of traversing rough, steep and wooded terrain. It could be made at little cost from material at hand, and customized for particular tasks – wide or narrow, high off the ground or low, with or without upright sides. Although nearly obsolete, it was still found in the late 1960s on a few Madison County farms. Gilbert always made his sled runners from sourwood trees which grew with the natural upward bend that was necessary. After the runners became worn, Gilbert "half-soled" them by attaching oak strips to the bottoms, beveling them at the end to ensure the smooth original contour.[34]

When he had settled the log barn onto its new foundation, he built himself a large new barn for the cattle he planned to raise. He did all the work alone, except for handling the extra large timbers he had salvaged when the old Laurel River bridge on U.S. highway 25/70 was torn out in 1959 by the Highway Department.[35] He had been saving them, along with other used lumber, for his retirement. This structure was Gilbert's dream barn, designed to his own needs. Less than a quarter mile from his home, up on the next mountainside, it was handy, but down wind. The first floor had two animal stalls, a screened fertilizer-and-feed room, and a large room open at one end, so that the cattle could be easily loaded onto a truck. He had also brought Hester's slate laundry tub from the annex, and it made a nice feed trough. The upper story was reserved for hay. After it was cut in the field, loaded by pitch fork onto the sled and pulled to the barn, the loose hay was pitched from the sled up to the large opening in the barn loft, where a second person, (when available) pushed it to the back of the barn to make room for the next load.[36] Gilbert never felt that he could afford a bailing machine, preferring to "make do" with the time-honored method of his forefathers.

Gilbert mowing with mules Jim and Kate.

After Nancy moved away, it was difficult for Gilbert to find help at haying time, the young men having been forced to leave Stackhouse in order to find work. Only two or three houses were even occupied, now, and these by the elderly or women. When Gilbert's hay crops were ready to harvest, he sometimes had to hire females, like Hobart Bullman's granddaughters – Pamela and Sheila Robinson. "We helped take the hay from the fields, toss it onto the sled, and then, from the sled up into the barn," recalled Pamela, years later.[37]

These girls were also special friends of the Stackhouses. Missing their own daughters, and still possessing the desire to help and guide youngsters, Gilbert and Nita had taken Pamela and Sheila under their wings when they were eight or ten years old. Since Gilbert owned the only automobile on Stackhouse Road, "They picked us up every Sunday morning for Sunday School and church until we were grown, greatly influencing my life," stated Pamela in an interview, decades later.[38] Nita always stressed the importance of education and encouraged the girls to finish high school. Consequently, Sheila completed a cosmetology course to give her a beautician's career, while Pamela worked her way through Mars Hill College to a degree in accounting. Later still, she earned her realtor's license. "I loved Mr. and Mrs. Stackhouse as my own parents," Pamela concluded. Nita had always been fond of people, especially children and they, in return, usually responded.

Nita and Gilbert also urged other children within the Methodist Church area to attend her Sunday School class, eager to contribute to their character building and welfare. Lawrence "Lonnie" Ramsey, who lived across the road from the Walnut Methodist Church, remembered what a wonderful teacher Nita had been to him and his several siblings. In 2004, he still owned one of the silver dollars she passed out at Christmas to each child in her class. Each one's birthday was further marked with a small toy or trinket from Nita, and the class was transported to the Stackhouse home for Easter egg hunts every year. When Lonnie was about twelve, his father died, and "Mr. Stackhouse would take me aside whenever he saw me to give me attention; we just talked about anything at hand," Lonnie recalled. "Those two people – Gilbert and Nita – taught me about giving," he added, "and I've never forgotten them."[39]

What's more, if their neighbors were ill, Nita and Gilbert took them food or drove them to the hospital. They continued to feel responsible for the community's well being even though the Stackhouse family no longer owned all the land or furnished all the jobs. During the remodeling of his home, Gilbert discovered his father's business ledgers from the depression years. The records showed several store charge accounts and notes owed to his father, Amos, but never paid. As he burned the papers, he told Nita, "My brothers would like to get hold of these, but it would cause more hard feelings than it would be worth, and I'm the one who has to live here."[40] Knowing that he could not prosecute old family friends and employees without damaging relationships, he passed up the opportunity to collect the long overdue money.

He did help raise Ernest's tobacco crops, sending him his share of the profit after the autumn harvests and auction sales. Although Gilbert would never again see his brother's face at Stackhouse, they kept in touch by mail and sometimes visited in Charlotte when Nita went to see her sisters.

Toward the end of the 1960s, Westco Telephone Company, which served most of the rural counties of western North Carolina, finally extended telephone service down to Stackhouse. Gilbert had made numerous requests before, but had been told that he would have to furnish and set all the poles within the two-and-a-half miles from Walnut Gap – a prohibitive cost for Gilbert. Now that Westco had completed the service (albeit a four-party line), Gilbert did not worry as much about Nita whenever he had to leave her alone, and he could also talk to his brother, Ernest, in Charlotte, as well as to other relatives and to his children when they called. Gilbert and Nita did not make toll calls on a whim; there had to be a reason and need, as with other expenditures at the Stackhouse home. Even though much of the United States had considered telephones a necessity for over half a century, they were just another late-arriving luxury to Stackhouse and other parts of Madison County.

One more change at Stackhouse, affecting both family and community, had occurred within two years of Hester's death. As with the passing of the matriarch, this death marked the end of a part of Stackhouse culture. Southern Railway Company, who once offered six passenger trains a day to Madison Countians, withdrew its last one, the Carolina Special, on December 5, 1968, prompting the *Asheville Citizen* to state, "There were more crew members than passengers that final trip."[41] Thus, another facility – one which might have drawn people to Stackhouse – had ceased operation.

Subsequently, Southern Railway began razing its depot buildings between Knoxville and Asheville, as well as the small three-sided passenger-waiting shelters. Gilbert Stackhouse received permission to take down the one at Stackhouse, using the materials in a small rental house he built on the mountainside. While this simple train-stop structure, with its single bench along the inside walls, had held no personnel, office or flag pole, it carried the sign STACKHOUSE, recognizing the community's location, and placing it on the map, so to speak. Since the closing of Stackhouse store and post office, the little waiting room had been the only public place where residents could gather.

Nevertheless, a last vestige of identity was salvaged by Gilbert when he decided to hang the twelve-inch by sixty-inch green metal sign, with its white-lettered name – STACKHOUSE – on the fascia board above the front steps to his home.[42] It fit well and could be easily read by passers-by on river and railroad, a faint reminder of by-gone days.

Oddly enough, unbeknownst to Gilbert, and far beyond the 19th century

Stackhouse home with former railroad sign.

rail-travel phenomena so important to Stackhouse, North Carolina, the Stackhouse name was now involved in the advanced travel of aerospace. NASA's Apollo Mission spacecrafts each carried an Apollo Lunar Surface Experiments Package (ALSEP), which used a self-contained power supply and communications equipment to collect and transmit scientific and engineering data to Earth for extended periods following the astronauts' departure. Responsible for verifying that the equipment would "shake hands" with the Central Station when deployed on the moon was Amos "Sonny" Stackhouse, Jr., June's son who was an electrical engineer working for Bendix Corporation in Ann Arbor, Michigan.[43] How proud Hester would have been to know that her county of Madison and her family of Stackhouse had played this small but vital role in these important national ventures. However, after years of working on classified projects for other employers, Sonny was not accustomed to discussing his work.*

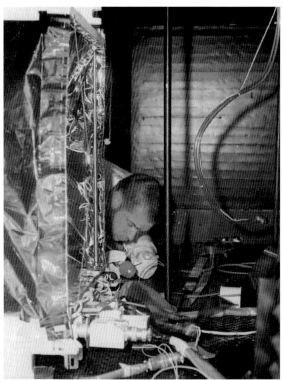

Amos "Sonny" Stackhouse, III, works on Apollo Mission spacecraft parts. Courtesy Amos Stackhouse.

On the other hand, Sonny's avocations were something Gilbert knew about and fully related to – a twelve-acre farm and half-interest in a horse-feed mill on the outskirts of Ann Arbor. Sonny's three children rode and cared for horses, and he and his son harvested five acres of hay filling their own stacuse every season, much as each generation of Amoses had done for decades.[44] On Sonny's visits to see Gilbert and Nita, they all met on the age-old grounds of Stackhouse tradition – progress and technology aside.

At last, Gilbert and Nita had settled into the sunset years of their lives, their family and career responsibilities completed. They were free now to enjoy their grandchildren, produced by Lexyne in 1960 and 1964, respectively – Ronald Caldwell Norris and Grace Deidre Norris – and by Nancy, in 1965, 1972 and 1974 – Randall Stackhouse Aumiller, Brent Edward Aumiller and Catherine Jeanine Aumiller. Despite the changes and diminutions in the Stackhouse home, the future would see its rooms once more occupied, and its grounds once again a place of adventure for children.

* In 2006 Sonny's Heat Flow Experiment remains on the moon with spent hardware from other Apollo missions.

[1] Melton, Larry. *History of the Sandy Charge*, undated ms., p.27.
Reeves, Venita Price. *Little Sandy Methodist Church History*, undated, private ms., p.2.
Wellman, Manly Wade. *The Kingdom of Madison*. Chapel Hill: UNC Press, 1973, p.70.

[2] Reeves, p.4.

[3] Norris, Lexyne Stackhouse. Interview, 2004.

[4] Ibid.

[5] Aumiller, Nancy Stackhouse. Interview, 2004.

[6] Author's private papers.

[7] Aumiller, Interview.

[8] Ibid, 2004.

[9] Ibid.

[10] Ibid.

[11] Ibid.

[12] Aumiller, 2003.

[13] Ibid.

[14] Ibid.

[15] Stackhouse, Nita C. Interview, 2000.

[16] Ibid.

[17] Tennessee Dept. of Vital Records, 2003.

[18] Aumiller, 2004.

[19] Private papers.

[20] Stackhouse, Charles Dilworth III. Interview, 2003.

[21] Buncombe County Register of Deeds, Bk. 856, p.176.

[22] Swayne, Norman Walton. *Byberry Waltons, An Account of Four Brothers*. Decorah, Iowa: Amundsen Pub. Co., 1989, reprint, p.489.

[23] Aumiller, 2002.

[24] Private papers.

[25] Ibid.

[26] Ibid.

[27] Ibid.

[28] Aumiller, 2000.

[29] Ibid.

[30] Ibid.

[31] Records secretary, telephone interview, N.C. Department of Construction Standards, Raleigh, 2003.

[32] Koranek, Jenny. Interview, 2004.

[33] Aumiller, 2004.

[34] Ibid.

[35] Bullman, Emmitt. Interview, 2004.

[36] Aumiller, Interview, 2004.

[37] Allison, Pamela Robinson. Interview, 2004.

[38] Ibid.

[39] Ramsey, Lonnie. Interview, 2004.

[40] Aumiller, 2000.

[41] "Last Train to Oakdale," *Asheville Citizen*, Dec. 6, 1968, Section Two, p.1.

[42] Aumiller, 2003.

[43] Stackhouse, Amos, Jr. Interviews and letters to author, 2005.

[44] Ibid.

Chapter Twenty-Nine

Gilbert's retirement years continued to bring change to the Stackhouse family and community – losses, gains, good times and bad. One rewarding incident was the receipt of a Century Farm certificate and plaque from the governor and the agricultural commissioner of North Carolina, honoring Gilbert's farm, which had remained in his family "for one hundred years or more, lending to the rich heritage of this great state."[1] Over a decade later, the state Department of Agriculture published a large book containing brief histories and photographs of each Century Farm, Gilbert's being one of four listed from Madison County.[2]

Throughout the 1970s, more recognition of Stackhouse appeared in several other books, magazines, and newspaper articles. Gilbert granted interviews to Manly Wade Wellman for *The Kingdom of Madison*,[3] and to Mary Ann Wolcott for an extensive article in the *Asheville Citizen*.[4] He guided college students to the Runion ruins and to the barytes sites, providing information for their history projects and essays. Even Gilbert's granddaughter, Grace Norris, joined the act with a high school history paper titled, "Stackhouse, N.C."[5] Gilbert usually received the writers on his broad porch, and he became angry when photographs of his home's interior were published. Although he was proud of his heritage, and not selfish with its information, he did reserve his right to privacy. The old house, though notable, was above all his home.

A few journalists wrote about Stackhouse without permission or first-hand knowledge; they made photographs from the Stackhouse yard, and did not notify Gilbert where or when the articles might appear.[6] Through these reporters, and even those to whom Gilbert granted interviews, errata occurred, due to interviewers' misinterpretations of Gilbert's words, or from transcription shortcuts forced by deadlines, or from shallow research, or simple typographical mistakes. However, they each gave the ghost community deserved acknowledgement, and prevented its identity from being lost in time.

Michael Southern, archivist in the Asheville office of the North Carolina Department of Cultural Resources, visited Gilbert and Nita as part of a survey of Madison County buildings eligible for the National Register of Historic Properties. Gilbert declined the honor, being concerned that he might be obligated to tourists, or more journalists. The following letter, in part, came from Southern to Gilbert in October, 1979:

> We have... no intention of trying to force you into something... you have no interest in. My concern is simply to see that all historic properties in western North Carolina that appear to be eligible receive due consideration, and I believe you deserve recognition for your good work in keeping the place in such fine condition. I hope you will give the matter some thought. I am certain that National Register listing would be much to your advantage and will not obligate you in any way.[7]

Nevertheless, Gilbert was not persuaded, nor did he reply.

Gilbert received a different type of letter as a result of the *Asheville Citizen* article by Wolcott. It came from Richard Gilbert Stackhouse in Ontario, Canada, who had been sent a copy "over a circuitous route, because of the circumstances of our similar names," he wrote.[8] Although unheard of by Gilbert heretofore, this probable cousin stated that he was hoping to visit Stackhouse, North Carolina, someday, now that he knew where it was.

Stackhouse would be further recognized through industry started at Hot Springs in 1973 – whitewater rafting on the French Broad.[9] Smoky Mountain River Expeditions sold rafting and kayaking trips from Barnard – 4¹/₂ miles above Stackhouse – to Hot Springs, where the take-out point was at the foot of Lovers Leap Mountain on the old Turnpike, the road often traveled by Gilbert's grandfather, Amos.[10] The recreational novelty proved popular with tourists, many of whom were surprised to see the large Victorian home rising suddenly from its small cleared knoll. Reading the STACKHOUSE sign across its front, they asked questions of their guide such as: "Is it a school, or a hotel?" and "How long has it been there?" He explained as well as he could, using his scant knowledge of Stackhouse history. The river guides were well-versed, however, in their warnings about "Rebar Rapids," or "Steel Rod Rapids," the names given the steel reinforcing bars, standing dangerously in the water where the old barytes dam had washed out in 1916.[11]

A second company, Carolina Wilderness, began operations next door to Smoky Mountain at Hot Springs in 1980, but the summer was dry, leaving the French Broad too shallow for rafting between Stackhouse and Mountain Island. Rather than refunding customers' reservation fees, which could have bankrupted the business, one of Carolina Wilderness' guides, Glenn Goodrich, offered a half-day trip from Barnard to Stackhouse. "It was a brilliant idea," said Glenn's coworker, Mike Tousey, years later.[12] Soon, there were other rafting companies "putting in" at Barnard and "taking out" at Stackhouse, while still offering the full-day trip to Hot Springs when the river depth permitted.

These companies thought the sandy area in front of Gilbert's home, between railroad and river, to be public property, judging perhaps from a few western North Carolina families who continued to fish and camp there, as they had since Amos' day. Because the strip, once owned by Gilbert's uncle, was now owned by the absentee Florida corporation, he had no say in the matter. On the other hand, he did have the right to object to a second Goodrich scheme: tours of the historic Stackhouse home, as part of a "rafting package." An angry, emphatic "No" was the answer from Nita and Gilbert.[13]

Nevertheless, the new industry was sustained by way of Stackhouse, and a different culture was introduced to Madison County. The long-haired, grass-smoking tent dwellers inundating Hot Springs and the other French Broad communities were often college students, teachers, engineers or other educated young people in search of a low-cost, fun vacation spent in the water and out of doors. After work hours, they played by riding the Big Laurel Creek from the mill wheel bridge on 25/70 downstream to Runion, where it joined the French Broad – the Laurel having more challenging rapids than the river. "But only during high waters," added Mike Tousey in the 2004 interview.[14] Called "river rats" by the Hot Springs natives, some of these bearded, tanned outlanders nonetheless fell in love with Madison County, homesteaded and made positive, valuable contributions to its society.

Still, at Stackhouse, the feeling was not mutual, at least in the early years.

Besides their cultural differences, the whitewater operators' buses, vans and trailers often blocked the narrow winding Stackhouse road, causing inconvenience and danger to the residents. Additionally, the noisy groups of tourists, removing their bright blue rafts from the water and flashy orange life jackets from their persons – occasionally even stripping – spoiled the pristine view usually seen from Gilbert's front porch and windows.[15]

Buses meet rafters at Stackhouse Boat Launch. Photo by author.

He and Nita would adjust and accept with time, especially in the future when their grandson actually became a river guide himself. As the whitewater companies grew to five in number, Barnard river bank was turned into a park with six launching ramps. The number of annual tour-rafters would grow to 40,000 by 2002, in addition to many private rafters and canoeists.[16] The Stackhouse community was back "on the map," at least in recreational circles.

Stackhouse played a small part in sorely-needed service industry for Madison County. The Hot Springs Health Program began in 1971 with one doctor and two nurses, who received limited support from non-governmental sources, but were basically volunteers.[17] They saw the tremendous need in Madison County, where one doctor – located in Mars Hill – had attempted to serve its entire populace of 16,003. Beginning the next year, the Hot Springs Health Program gained support from the Appalachian Regional Commission, from community donations, and fees from patients, based on their ability to pay. In 1973, Nurse Practitioner Kathy Johnson joined the program, but could not find a place to live. Someone on the board of directors asked Gilbert and Nita to rent their annex apartment, beginning a long-term relationship between the health program and the Stackhouse family.[18]

As the Hot Springs Health Program grew, its use of nurse practitioners and its community-based ownership provided the state a model for all North Carolina rural health facilities. In fact, the expanding Madison County program would eventually employ over a hundred persons at its medical centers in Mars Hill, Laurel, Marshall and Barnardsville (Buncombe County), besides the original Hot Springs site. By 1986 it was self-supporting, and in 2002, the Marshall center moved into a modern new building donated, in great part, by the children of Hester Stackhouse's grand-nephew, Charles Edwin Mashburn, and his wife Mattee, for whom it was named.[19]

Back in 1975, when Kathy Johnson left the health program, her replacement – Ginny Koranek – also needed the Stackhouse apartment, moving in right away. Kathy had told Ginny about her landlords, how she respected and loved them and their beautiful spot on the French Broad. "Nita and Gilbert were wonderful," Kathy reminisced years later.[20] Not surprisingly, Ginny's experience at Stackhouse was practically the same as Kathy's. The new nurse practitioner became like a daughter to Nita and Gilbert. "They took good care of me," Ginny said in a 2004 interview. On icy mornings Gilbert got out early to put chains on her automobile tires; he reminded her to get more firewood when he saw her supply running low; and he shared his garden produce in summer. Nita took her blackberry picking and gave her much advice about mountain living. On her days off, Ginny often walked with Gilbert to the barn to feed the mules, listening to his fascinating storytelling, and learning about the Stackhouse past. Although of Polish descent, Ginny had grown up on a Texas farm, giving her rapport with the Stackhouses. "Gilbert was such a fine man, and I loved him dearly," she added.[21]

When Ginny's fiancé moved from Atlanta, Gilbert fixed up the old Stackhouse school-building rental for him, while he sized him up. A typical seventies youth, Danny Wyatt had long hair and a full beard and mustache, not unlike some of the "river rats," a style hardly approved by the

Danny Wyatt (c. 1977) on porch of his rented home, the former Stackhouse school building. Besides school and tenant house, it also served the broader Stackhouse Church of God congregation as a church at times.

Stackhouses. "Nevertheless, Nita and Gilbert accepted him," recalled Ginny, years later, "and they never pried or preached."[22]

The fact that Danny and Ginny were hard workers went a long way toward Gilbert's acceptance; he could not help but admire that characteristic, no matter the form. He abhorred slothfulness, and since Ginny and Danny exhibited the opposite, his tolerance soon turned to fondness. Until Danny became established in Madison County with a regular job, Gilbert was glad to give him work around the farm "Gilbert taught me how to harness the mule, and how to plough with him," Danny recalled many years later.[23] Danny also helped Gilbert do painting, plumbing, roofing, fencing, planting and harvesting, to name only a few of the jobs. He had grown up in an Atlanta suburb, knowing little about rural living, but he was a former camp counselor, and loved the outdoors.

According to Danny, Gilbert also taught him how to cut hay with the horse-drawn mowing machine, how to store the hay, how to feed it to the cattle, how to pasture the cattle, how to herd them and how to load them for market. Danny learned the mountain customs of burning off the garden in the spring, of making a wooden frame for sowing seeds saved from the previous year's crops, then covering it with white tobacco cloth until germination and first leaves. Gilbert showed him how to dig post holes with a wooden-handled posthole digger, how to string fence wire, pulling it straight and taut before sinking the staples with a hammer. "For digging the rocks out of the post holes, he said we needed a digging rod, so he showed me how to make one in his blacksmith shop," Danny added.[24] Gilbert rummaged in his Depression-days stockpile to find an old car axle, then heated the ends (while Danny turned the blowing apparatus) and shaped them with the hammer to make the needed tool.

What's more, Gilbert had a pipe threader in his shop from pre-plastic days. As he pulled out lengths of long-saved galvanized pipe, he instructed Danny in threading the ends, coupling it, adding tees, ells or wyes to take it from the house lines to the bold spring on the mountain. Danny was exposed to different forms of manual labor and farming practices, as well as tools and methods considered obsolete by much of the United States. (When he, himself, had aged, he would look back in appreciation to his unique education at the feet of a master teacher and good friend.)

During the winter of 1977, the temperature dropped to eighteen below zero, freezing water lines and making mountain roads treacherous for weeks. Danny and Ginny could walk to Gilbert and Nita's house in the long winter evenings, where they allayed cabin fever by playing setback – a nineteenth century derivation of All Fours, the old English card game which had been the favorite of American card players from the 1700s through the Civil War, until the rise of poker.[25] Madison County was likely one of the last places to hold on to Setback, and only through its traditionalists like Gilbert. Neither Ginny nor Danny had ever played the game, but they learned quickly, Gilbert taking Ginny as partner, and Nita pairing with Danny. "We usually won," Danny said with a chuckle, as he told about Nita's enthusiastic competitiveness.[26] She was a passionate player, kindling laughter and fun in the foursome. She also served ice cream or some other dessert after the game. The simple social broke the monotony of the long harsh winter and bridged a gap of age and culture.

The next May, amid blossoming shrubs and fragrant perennials, Danny and Ginny were married in the Stackhouse side yard. Using her own fresh flowers and greenery, Nita made a bridal bouquet for Ginny and a boutonniere for Danny. She also prepared a wedding breakfast, opening her house to the couple's friends, and her guest rooms to Ginny's family from Texas. "Gilbert and Nita were the warmest, most open-minded people I've ever known," declared Danny years later.[27]

In need of a home, the newlyweds – after much thought and trepidation – approached Gilbert about buying a piece of his land for homesteading. Knowing how Gilbert loved his farm, they did not want to jeopardize their friendship, but he surprised them. Without hesitation, he agreed to discuss the matter. Nita and Gilbert needed neighbors in their twilight years, and Ginny and Danny had proved to be good ones. Consequently, they walked over the farm, talked, looked, surveyed and negotiated. Finally, in the early spring of 1979, the deed for the tenant house, where Troy Dockery had lived, plus twenty-three acres, was signed and registered.[28]

Actually, this was not the first land Gilbert had parted with since his mother's death. In February, 1972, Ernest sold the sixty-seven acres he and Gilbert owned jointly to Edward and Gladys Molter of Fort Lauderdale, Florida.[29] Four months later, Gilbert was again persuaded to sell a tract of his and Nita's land to David Henderson, the son of Dr. Henderson, a former Walnut physician, who had treated Gilbert in the past.[30] David, too, lived in Florida, but came to Stackhouse on vacations. Both the Molter and Henderson deeds were held in trust for a number of years, payments coming to the Stackhouses by installments.[31] (When the Hendersons' note was paid, they bought twenty-two more acres of Stackhouse land which Ernest had been given by his mother in the 1950s.[32]) Using the sale proceeds, Gilbert built a new road from the railroad bottom strip up the mountain to access the Henderson land and other sections, replacing the old road that led through his pasture land.[33]

Other significant real estate transactions the next year included a deed to Gilbert from June Stackhouse for his third interest in the lumberyard bottom and railroad siding which Hester had bequeathed her three sons.[34] Two more deeds were made by Gilbert at his lawyer's advice, to prevent future legal confusion. First, Gilbert granted to "Nita and Gilbert Stackhouse," all property he had received in his own name by purchase or by inheritance, thus ensuring Nita's right of joint ownership.[35] Next, a deed from Gilbert and Nita to his brother, June, clearly described a tract – one and a quarter acres – to fulfill the Memorandum of Agreement made as part of his father's estate settlement in 1953.[36] The following year, June Stackhouse, in turn, deeded the tract to his son, Amos Stackhouse III, called by the family "Sonny."[37] In 1978 Ernest sold David Henderson an additional eighty-six acres, the last of his singly-owned property at his birthplace.[38] In a clean-up deed to Gilbert on August 14, 1978, Ernest also relinquished his third ownership in the lumberyard and rail siding strip along the river where his grandfather's sawmill had stood. "It is the intent of this deed of conveyance to convey all of my right, title, and Interest in, and to, the Stackhouse lands in No. 6 Township, remaining unsold, whether herein particularly described or not," stated the document.[39] Gilbert and Nita were now the sole owners of Stackhouse property in the Stackhouse name, except for the small parcel belonging to Sonny, who lived up North.

Further changing the Stackhouse community had been the 1973 purchase of Robert Bullman's farmstead by Wallace and Betty Bearse from Michigan, after the aging Bullman moved to Walnut. A Madison County native, Betty was the daughter of the late Coleman Caldwell, who had been a friend of Gilbert's from Marshall. Betty and her husband, both school teachers, wanted their children to have the experience of country life, so they remodeled the Bullman home and spent their summers there. "The Stackhouses were wonderful neighbors, and Gilbert looked after our place when we were away," said Betty, years later.[40] Nita occasionally invited the Bearses to supper, and at other times she and Gilbert ate with Wallace, Betty and their children. "Gilbert was a great storyteller; he could make any story funny," she added. The Bearses particularly enjoyed sitting on the Stackhouse front porch, absorbing the beauty of the river-scape.

Yet another 1972 real estate transfer to impact the Stackhouse community was the dissolution of Mountain Island Development

L: One of three remaining houses at Runion in 1978.
R: Chimney remnant from large two-story dwelling at
    Runion. Photos by Dan Slagle.

L: Former LRLC superintendent's home, one of few standing structures at Runion.
Photo by Dan Slagle.
R: Runion school/church building, the bell having been sold.

Corporation, and delivery of a deed from the stockholders to the broker, Carl Helton, who held a $213,000 note on the lands formerly owned by Ellsworth Vandervort.[41] On February 1, 1973, Helton sold the 1,452 acres to Reuben Schneider, also of Florida, but kept the log cabin with one and an eighth acres, next door to Gilbert, for his own.[42] Schneider, in turn, deeded the large tract to Walnut Gap Estates, a new Limited Partnership of thirteen partners besides Schneider, the General Partner, all of whom lived in Florida, except one New Yorker.[43] From 1973 to 1978 the log cabin at Stackhouse changed hands three times before Arlen Myers from Florida bought it.[44]

Despite the steady real estate activity during the seventies, the only neighbors to come immediately to Stackhouse were the Wyatts, year round, and the Myers and Bearses, in summertime. Neither Walnut Gap Estates nor the Molters improved their properties, and the Hendersons merely used theirs for a week or two each year. The Hendersons would eventually sell a few parcels to others, but the Stackhouse community's population remained mostly static.

Its character, however, was changing, there being left only one of the old mountain residents, Troy Dockery, with his wife, Emma. Even before Danny Wyatt bought his plat, Troy had moved to a different Stackhouse rental house, down the mountain toward the railroad and river, near the old barytes mill. His children were grown, but often came to visit, considering Stackhouse their home. The new landowners in Stackhouse, except for Betty Caldwell Bearse, had little understanding of traditional Madison County culture. Nevertheless, the community needed inhabitants to sustain itself.

Fortunately, this need was on its way to being met, albeit in a small way, in 1982, when Ginny Koranek brought two of her coworkers in the Hot Springs Health Program who were desperate for a house. She showed them the log cabin built by Ernest and Gilbert in the Depression's bleak days. Because Arlen Myers had died in Florida after a long illness, the dwelling had not been lived in or maintained for some time. The roof leaked, the sill logs had rotted, much of the chinking mortar had fallen out, and mold covered all surfaces. It needed a tremendous amount of work, but it had over an acre of land, with spectacular views of creek, river and mountains, as well as good neighbors in Gilbert and Nita. "Plus, it was the best shelter we'd found on the AT," joked one of the doctors, who had realized the area's critical medical needs when hiking the Appalachian Trail through Hot Springs with an injured trekker.[45] Therefore, after negotiating with Myrtle Myers, Arlen's widow in Florida, they became the owners of the cabin, and the Stackhouse community received a permanent, contributing family. (In the near future it would seem providential that the doctors had found their way into Stackhouse at this particular time.)

Since Gilbert had been one of the log cabin's builders, and had a lifetime of experience in the field, he could advise the doctors about ways to repair supporting timbers without their having to move out of the house. "After thinking about it for a bit, Gilbert could come up with an easy and inexpensive way to solve most any problem," recalled one of the doctors later.[46]

Gilbert also had tools and equipment to lend – his faithful heavy-duty house jacks; block and tackle; old, but reliable, air compressor; and his well-used concrete mixer. As they worked, Gilbert told them stories about

Stackhouse and about the origins of some of the cabin materials – ceiling boards from shipping crates, stamped on the back with manufacturers' names; the hundred-year-old hemlock joists; and heart pine flooring – all from the Stackhouse general store, built about 1878.[47]

Though their house was partly open to the elements that first winter, the doctors survived with a wood stove and electric blanket. Eventually, the holes and gaps were filled; the logs cleaned of dirt and mildew, then sanded and sealed; the floor leveled and refinished; wiring and plumbing updated; kitchen modernized; and the fifty-year-old cabin was rehabilitated into a handsome, comfortable home.[48]

The Stackhouse family were pleased at the transformation of the former eyesore, and, consequently, with their new neighbors (a surprising benefit of the Depression's national forest and Appalachian Trail development). Since the homes were within a stone's throw of each other and shared the driveway as well as water system, a different outcome might have been disastrous to the Stackhouse family's quality of life. But the new cabin owners, with their slightly newfangled values and viewpoints, melded into the old neighborhood, bringing enhancement and fresh interest. Both doctors, man and wife, had come from urban Kentucky, but their parents had lived in rural places, which inspired the couple to feel fondness and respect for the country and simpler times.[49] Exhibiting that virtue hallowed by the Stackhouse family – sober hard work – the young doctors soon won the approval, and eventually, love, of Nita and Gilbert.

In spite of the many community changes, Gilbert's retirement years moved smoothly and in ordinary fashion. He began preparing his fields for access by a tractor, which he would hire, at last, to plough and harrow. He removed the tongue from his hay rake, adapted it for machine use, then sold his last mule, reducing the work demands upon his aging body. To make his wife's work easier, also, he bought electric kitchen appliances, even an electric churn and a mangle (a machine for pressing fabrics by means of heated rollers).[50]

Now Gilbert and Nita were able to devote more time to family and to their church and civic activities. Gilbert worked with the Walnut community group cleaning up the overgrown Methodist Church cemetery where his parents and his Uncle Charlie were buried. Some old graves still had fencing used to keep out cattle and wild animals in the old days. Gilbert and the other volunteers removed the fences to allow lawnmower access; cut down trees, briars and vines; leveled and aligned leaning tombstones; and finally raked and sowed grass. The once-neglected site became a source of community pride, spurring organization and fund-collecting for its perpetuity.[51]

Unfortunately, the French Broad and its tributaries flooded in November, 1977, and Gilbert was forced to turn his attention back to Stackhouse. When Woolsey Creek threatened to take Gilbert's old log barn, he wrapped it with a cable, hooking it around a tree on the other side of the road. The tree held, but the barn was undermined and required a new foundation.[52] In addition, the road from Runion to Stackhouse washed out, though Stackhouse community suffered little damage compared to the rest of Madison and surrounding counties.[53]

Across the mountains, eleven people were killed; 165 homes were destroyed, and 486 severely damaged; roads and bridges were ripped apart;

and some train tracks, washed out. The French Broad deposited many inches of mud in Marshall's main street, but in Hot Springs, a grocery store was demolished and several other businesses damaged. The disaster brought Governor Hunt from Raleigh, news reporters, and television cameras to Hot Springs. Headlines stated: "Worst Flood in 61 Years Hits Mountain Area," referring, of course, to the Great Flood of 1916, which Gilbert well remembered.[54] As in his grandfather's time, the French Broad had ongoing influence on Gilbert's family and community.

While Gilbert repaired and farmed and made improvements to the grounds, Nita pursued her hobby of sewing. Although she had an assortment of electrical appliances, she still used her faithful old treadle sewing machine to make sure her granddaughters had stylish and appropriate clothes. Relatives sent Nita remnants from their own sewing, which were often enough to make garments for young Grace and Jeanine. Adding hand-worked edgings or fabric scraps from her own collection, she was able to design fashionable garments at little or no cost, as she had for her own daughters.[55]

Nita also joined the Walnut community ladies for regular quilt-making sessions at the Freewill Baptist Church, where she taught Sunday School on alternate Sundays. After a quarter-century of Sunday School teaching, she was on her way to setting a lifetime record. Gilbert, too, still superintended Sunday School, as he had done for many years.[56]

Another favorite activity for Nita was her long-time participation in the Home Demonstration Club, which provided social outlets combined with service projects, such as the Open House Tour fund raiser they sponsored one summer. Nita enlisted Lexyne from Arden to help her clean and polish the house the week before. On tour day, she directed Lexyne, who was dressed in costume to complement the 75-year-old house, to serve coffee and doughnuts from the front porch. Nita had found a long white petticoat of Hester's which buttoned at the waist, and ended with wide tiers of eyelet ruffles at the hem. Lexyne wore her own white blouse, added an old-fashioned apron from Nita, and topped all with a white embroidered dustcap, also Hester's. About a hundred ticket-holders attended, and Nita took them through the house in small groups. Many thought Lexyne was the Stackhouse maid.[57]

Additional retirement pleasures came to both Nita and Gilbert through trips to Arden, two or three times a month, to visit Lexyne and her family, and to Tennessee two or three times a year to visit Nancy. Occasionally, Lexyne and Nita traveled to Nancy's house, though Gilbert preferred staying behind to care for the farm and his dog, Spot. Lexyne's son, Ronnie, often chose to remain with Gilbert, whom he adored.

Having Ronnie and other family members come to Stackhouse was particularly satisfying to Gilbert, as well as to Nita. Every holiday and vacation, Nancy and her family visited the farm, staying a week or more in summer. When Lexyne was called back to her former insurance job to fill in temporarily, she took her pre-school daughter, Grace, to stay at Stackhouse. Grace loved being at her grandparents', too, especially when she got to play in the extra-large old clawfoot bathtub. "We always went to church on Sundays," Grace added.[58] Standing beside her grandmother for the hymns, she would never forget how Nita, who did not have a beautiful voice, nevertheless sang all the hymns with gusto, just as she approached everything in life.

Grace's brother Ronnie found the Stackhouse farmstead to be a city child's paradise, further enriched by his grandfather's stories about each upturned relic or moss-covered foundation. "He was still farming the old-timey way in the 1970's, so I learned how to 'Gee' and 'Haw,' among other things," Ronnie reminisced thirty years afterwards.[59] In Gilbert's blacksmith shop, the large anvil sat on a log stump near the hand-cranked drill press. Ronnie helped by turning the blower handle, but it was also fitted with a counterweight, enabling Gilbert to operate it with one hand when no helper was there. Some days Ronnie's grandparents took him on picnics with fishing at the barytes lakes or the Big Laurel at Runion. They caught brim and bass on long poles cut from strong river cane, just as Ronnie's ancestors had used through the ages. Ronnie, Gilbert and Nita often hiked the old stagecoach road, passing the green tobacco fields of the tenants. "Each little house in the community had its spring, and each spring had its tin cup; I always stopped at each one and drank from the tin cup," Ronnie added nostalgically.

Other Stackhouse visitors were Patty and Freda, daughters of Nita's sister, Nancy Lee. The two nieces had come from Charlotte to Stackhouse in their childhoods with their Grandmother Caldwell and had continued the tradition as grownups whenever possible. Gilbert's brother, June, also came to visit, once a year, sometimes stopping to see Nancy in Tennessee on the way. Often he also visited Lexyne in Arden to take advantage of the Veteran's health facility at nearby Oteen.[60]

Calling at Gilbert's home, periodically, from Massachusetts, was Anson G. Betts, former Runion resident, and current Stackhouse landowner, who came to check on his property adjoining Gilbert. "He was very old and walked with two canes," stated Nita Stackhouse in later years.[61] When he died in 1976, it was said that Betts had reached the age of one hundred. He no doubt still carried his strong belief in the barite potential at Stackhouse, which he had failed to sell during several attempts. He did realize some success, however, with his laboratory experiments as a chemist. Two patents were granted him in 1970 and two more in 1972 for his treatments of phosphate rock with acids; the separation of fluorine and phosphorous; and the recovery of sulphur dioxide gas steams.[62] (Though posthumously, Betts would have ongoing impact upon the Stackhouse community through the six hundred acres inherited from him by his children.)

There were other deaths of former Stackhouse residents to bring sorrow to Nita and Gilbert: Ann Hoffman Stackhouse, June's wife, in 1976 at Watsonville, California; Ruth Vandervort Stackhouse, Ernest's wife, in 1978 at Charlotte; and Gilbert's friend and neighbor, Troy Dockery, in 1980, whose widow Emma, lived still in Gilbert's tenant house – the last of the old-time families in the Stackhouse community.[63] Then, a year later, June Stackhouse, Gilbert's oldest brother, died in New London, Connecticut, from cancer. His corpse was cremated and sent to California to rest beside his wife's.[64]

Strangely enough, the sad news of June's death had arrived at Stackhouse just six days after the particularly happy occasion of Nita and Gilbert's Golden Wedding Anniversary celebration on July 17, 1981. Lexyne and Nancy mailed over fifty invitations, plus a notice to the county paper for local friends. "We put up four extra beds in the annex," Nancy recalled later.[65] She and her two younger children spent six weeks at Stackhouse, planning the affair, cleaning the house and the annex from top to bottom, preparing the yard, shopping and cooking food ahead. They made corsages for the party principals, and bouquets for the house. "It was lots of fun," added Nancy. Dilworth came from Indiana, Sonny from Michigan, and all of Nita's family from Charlotte. Many Madison County friends also attended. Nancy stayed a week afterwards to clean up and put things back in place. As she was leaving to return to Tennessee, Gilbert took her hand and asked, with tears in his eyes, "Aren't you ever going to move back home?"[66]

Gilbert and Nita Stackhouse celebrated their Golden Wedding anniversary, 1981.

In retrospect, Nancy would see that Gilbert had had a premonition, because within two Christmases, she found herself planning that very move. While she and her family were spending the holidays of 1982 at Stackhouse, Dave accompanied Gilbert on a drive to a Marshall hardware store ("Daddy always had a list of things for Dave to help with, when we came home," Nancy said laughingly.)[67] After the men returned, Dave took Nancy aside, explaining that they needed to move back to Stackhouse as soon as they could. Gilbert, with the razor-

Stackhouse extended family gather for Gilbert and Nita's anniversary.
1. James Caldwell, 2. Brent Aumiller, 3. Robin Caldwell, 4. Heather Kreider, 5. Tracy Mills, 6. Jeremy Caldwell, 7. Jeanine Aumiller, 8. K.C. Wooldridge, 9. Laura Wooldridge, 10. Carol Brown, 11. Grace Norris, 12. Grace Norris, 13. Freda Conrad, 14. Terry Kreider, 15. Doris Brown, 16. Lexyne Stackhouse Norris, 17. Bobby H. Norris, 18. Ronald C. Norris, 19. Libby McDaniel, 20. Amy Brown, 21. Julia Lynn Mc Daniel, 22. Bobby Caldwell, 23. Beverly Caldwell, 24. Juanita Caldwell Stackhouse, 25. Jimmy McDaniel, 26. Dave Aumiller, 27. Nancy Stackhouse Aumiller, 28. Randall Stackhouse Aumiller, 29. Jimmy Caldwell, 30. Gilbert Stackhouse, 31. Dorothy Caldwell, 32. Robert C. Caldwell.

sharp mind, the quick, dry wit, the analytical perception, incredibly, had exhibited serious signs of dementia. Nancy found it hard to believe that her physically, mentally and emotionally strong father, upon whom everybody depended, was now, himself, dependent.

At Memphis, Dave was serving as assistant pastor and administrator of Macon Road Baptist Church and School. He had also just been ordained into full ministry, with a promising future ahead. Nevertheless, he presented his notice of resignation, to be effective June 1, 1983.

All along, Dave's typical ecclesiastical career had required frequent moving. Before Memphis, he and Nancy lived at Redbank, Tennessee, near Chattanooga, where they had started a Christian school for fifty children from kindergarten through sixth grade, called Independent Baptist Church and School. Its membership grew quickly to one hundred. Their previous job had been at Chattanooga, in answer to what Dave felt to be a direct call from God to be house parents at Orange Groves private home for twenty-eight high-functioning developmentally delayed people ages sixteen to forty-eight. Dave was also faced with remodeling and repairing the 1910 building in which they were housed. To Chattanooga, he had come from Temple Baptist Church on Patton Avenue in Asheville, where he had been youth leader and assistant pastor. Prior to Temple, Dave and Nancy had been houseparents to a cottage of eighteen boys at Eliada Home in West Asheville, where Dave had also been activities director and physical education teacher to the overall body of one hundred, ages two through eighteen. Nancy and Dave both worked the fields and gardens at Eliada, teaching the youth how to plant, grow, harvest and can vegetables, as well as how to study the Bible and lead devotional programs. "You name it and we did it," said Nancy about their varied Eliada duties, which called upon her skills learned on the Stackhouse farm, in 4-H Club, in Sunday School and from her Grannie Hester.[68]

Nonetheless, in January, 1983, when Dave tendered his resignation at Memphis, he had no idea how he would make a living in the Stackhouse community, from whence most people had gone to find jobs. However, he answered the call to help Gilbert and Nita, just as he had his other demands of faith. When summer came, the Aumillers bade goodbye to their Tennessee friends, packed their belongings and crossed the state to Madison County. Unloading their boxes and furnishings into the Stackhouse annex, they spent the weekend with Gilbert and Nita, repacked their suitcases and set out for Ketchican, Alaska. It was the fiftieth anniversary for Dave's parents this summer, and they expected him to attend the event with his family.

Dave had bought a used Toyota pickup truck from a man who had rigged it as a camper, and somehow, there were places, albeit tight ones, for each of the three children, Dave and Nancy, and their camping gear, saving the cost of motel rooms and restaurants.[69]

Instead of the traditional golden anniversary celebration with tea, cake and gold-trimmed trinkets, Dave's sister, Lorraine, who lived in Seattle, had rented a houseboat for a family fishing and sighteeing trip to Alaska. She rounded up winter boots, gloves and snowshoes for the younger children, fishing gear and other necessities for all. They sailed around Ketchican Island, catching enough halibut and salmon to fill seventy tin cans which they canned in government-operated cabins on the mainland that were outfitted for the purpose, cans furnished. In addition to the salt water fishing, digging for clams was a new experience for the Aumiller children, as were the sightings of porpoises, sharks and killer whales. Inland, they saw bears, birds and other wildlife, known only from books or movies by most North Carolina mountaineers.[70]

For the trip home, the little Toyota was hard pressed to carry the cases of tinned fish, along with its original cargo, but it met the challenge. Dave took the Canadian route, stopping at Glacier National Park, then dipping down into Montana and other Western states, camping each night on the way, and offering the children an educational excursion they would always remember. Indeed, it was a vacation of a lifetime for all, accomplished the Stackhouse way – on a shoestring budget. It would also be the last carefree time they would have together, for responsibilities of a size they could not imagine awaited them at home in Stackhouse.

ENDNOTES FOR CHAPTER TWENTY-NINE

[1] Author's private papers.

[2] *North Carolina Century Farms*, ed. Jearlean Woody and Deborah Ellison. Raleigh: Dept. of Agriculture of N.C. 1989, p.149.

[3] Wellman, Manly Wade. *The Kingdom of Madison*. Chapel Hill: UNC Press. 197, p.210. [This source contains factual errors.]

[4] Wolcott, Mary Ellen. *Asheville Citizen-Times*. Sept. 24, 1978, p.1-C.

[5] Private papers.

[6] Aumiller, Nancy Stackhouse. Interview, 1998.

[7] Private papers.

[8] Ibid.

[9] Crosby, Wayne. Interview, 2004.
Tousey, Mike. Interview, 2004.
Goodrich, Glenn. Interview, 2004.

[10] Ibid.

[11] Ibid.

[12] Tousey, Mike. Interview, 2004.

[13] Aumiller, Interview, 2004.

[14] Tousey, Interview, 2004.

[15] Aumiller, Interview, 2004.

[16] Goodrich, Interview, 2004.

[17] Plemmons, Jerry. Interview, 2004.
Flynn, Michael. *Asheville Citizen-Times*. "Hot Springs, the Model in Rural Health Care." August 10, 2004, p.H8.

[18] Johnson, Kathy. Interview, 2004.

[19] Plemmons, Jerry. Interview, 2004.

[20] Johnson, Kathy. Interview, 2004.

[21] Koranek, Ginny. Interview, 2004.

[22] Ibid.

[23] Wyatt, Danny. Interview, 2004.

[24] Ibid.

[25] *According to Hoyle*, ed. Richard L. Frey. New York: Ballantine Books, 1996, pps. 59, 61.

[26] Wyatt, Interview, 2004.

[27] Ibid.

[28] Madison County Deeds Registry, Book 132, p.578.

[29] Madison County Deeds Registry, Book 109, p.33.

[30] Private papers.

[31] Ibid.

[32] Madison County Deeds Registry, Book 131, p.126.

[33] Aumiller, Interview.

[34] Madison County Deeds Registry, Book 115, p.263.

[35] Madison County Deeds Registry, Book 115, p.413.

[36] Madison County Deeds Registry, Book 115, p. 521; Book 83, p.418.

[37] Madison County Deeds Registry, Book 117, p. 488.

[38] Madison County Deeds Registry, Book 131, p. 126.

[39] Madison County Deeds Registry, Book 131, p. 128.

[40] Bearse, Betty Caldwell. Interview, 2004.

[41] Madison County Deeds Registry, Bk. 112, p. 525.

[42] Madison County Deeds Registry, Bk. 112, p. 533.

[43] Madison County Deeds Registry, Bk. 115, p. 511; p. 490.

[44] Madison County Deeds Registry, Bk. 130, p. 501; Bk. 131, p. 125; Bk. 123, p. 598; Bk. 132, p. 183.

[45] Private papers.

[46] Ibid.

[47] Ibid.

[48] Ibid.

[49] Ibid.

[50] Norris, Lexyne Stackhouse. Interview, 2003.
Aumiller, Nancy S. Interview, 2003.

[51] Plemmons, Ernestine Reeves. Interview, 2004.

[52] Aumiller, Interview, 2004.

[53] Wyatt, Interview, 2004.

[54] *Asheville Citizen-Times*, "Pictorial Review," Nov. 29, 1977, pps. 1-8.

[55] Aumiller, Interview, 2004.

[56] Ibid.

[57] Norris, Lexyne S. Interview, 2004.

[58] Lenox, Grace Norris. Interview, 2004.

[59] Norris, Ronnie. Interview, 2004.

[60] Aumiller, Interview, 2004.

[61] Stackhouse, Nita. Interview, 2000.

[62] Carrie A. Green, Specialist, U.S. Patent Office, D.C., letter to author, August 23, 1999.

[63] Radin, Clara Stackhouse, letter to author, 1998.
Cole, Carthene Stackhouse, letter to author, 1999.
Norton, Gertrude Dockery, interview, 2003.

[64] Connecticut Dept. of Health Services; Radin, 1999, letter to author.

[65] Aumiller, Interviews, 2004, 2000.

[66] Ibid.

[67] Ibid.

[68] Ibid.

[69] Ibid.

[70] Ibid.

Chapter Thirty

Returning to Stackhouse from their cross-country trip, the Aumiller family were met at the door with Nita's announcement that the Freewill Baptist Church of Walnut needed a pastor; Dave was to preach for them that very Sunday. It was not a large city charge, but it answered part of Dave's prayer about employment. He still had to search for supplemental income to support his growing children. Randy, at age seventeen, was enrolling at Tennessee Temple University; Brent, age eleven, and Jeanine, age nine, would be attending Walnut Elementary, where their mother had gone to school.

For the next few years, Dave took whatever odd jobs he could find: school bus driver, general store clerk, fuel truck driver, and, in 1991, he became a pharmacy technician with the Hot Springs Health Program, where he remained for at least a decade. Meanwhile, after two years as minister in Walnut, he was called to the Red Hill Freewill Baptist Church on Brush Creek, still in Madison County, pastoring there for eight or nine years. He and Nancy next started two consecutive Bible Study churches at communities in the northern part of the county near Ivy River, finally taking a full-time charge in 2000 at Weaverville, called Maranatha Baptist Church.[1]

When Nancy first brought her family home to live in 1983, Nita made it clear that they were to have dinner with her every Sunday after church, a tradition they would honor from then on. Also, as soon as Nancy came home, Gilbert stopped driving, apparently unable to trust his memory any longer. "He made sure that I understood all the property boundaries, the bank accounts and other family business, too," stated Nancy twenty years later. Gilbert was able, however, to help Dave cut a door opening upstairs between the living room and large bedroom (once Hester's bedroom), increasing the apartment's convenience by giving a more direct route to the kitchen and to the bathroom, without having to go through the small bedroom off the stair landing.

Through this room, Nancy and Lexyne had walked to get to their own bedroom, and to the bathroom, when they were growing up. It was here they often found Gilbert on his knees by the bed, conducting his nightly prayers, a habit that inspired and nurtured them as they grew. Likewise, his early morning ritual of going to the kitchen for daily Bible reading before Nita began breakfast provided a guideline that no amount of preaching could have accomplished. Sadly, these practices were fading by degrees, as Gilbert's memory waned.

Nancy and Dave took over the farming and the care of the dozen or more cattle Gilbert kept. They continued his method of renting the tobacco allotment to families who were able to handle the labor-intensive crop, and who paid Gilbert and Nita the meager, but usual, ten cents per pound of profit. Young Brent Aumiller, after a childhood spent in town, was now called upon to do farm chores – in winter and in summer, in bad weather and in good. For instance, on bitter cold mornings, he must break up the ice in the creek, so that the cattle could drink, and make sure they had feed when the pastures were frozen and dormant.

The Aumiller family also cultivated a large vegetable garden, as well as

357

fields of hay and corn for the cattle, taking a portion of the corn to a place in Tennessee where it was ground – ear, leaves and stalk – then mixed with molasses into "sweet feed." "The cattle loved it," stated Nancy years later.[2] At haying time, if the children were in school, Dave drove the farm truck and Nancy rode the hayrake behind.

Once, soon after they returned to Stackhouse, Nancy and Dave were planting corn in the small field below the house, near the railroad. Dave was mixing fertilizer in the laid-off rows and Nancy was dropping the seeds. Hoping to involve Gilbert, who had walked down with them, Nancy said, "Daddy, you can cover the seeds, if you like." Gilbert replied, "Honey, I don't know how."[3] Skills which had been second nature all his life, and which he had taught to Nancy, Danny Wyatt, Ronnie Norris, and others, now eluded Gilbert.

The winter before, Gilbert had become confused by the Setback games with neighbors Ginny and Danny. "He began to make some really stupid plays – totally unlike Gilbert – and it embarrassed him so much that he would not play again," said Ginny Koranek in a 2004 interview.[4] Gilbert even began wearing his cap backwards, as he used to do when plowing beneath the hot sun, the turned bill protecting the back of his neck. Once he went with Nita and Nancy to a birthday celebration for the next-door neighbors' daughter, where he wore two caps – one turned over his eyes, the other turned over his nape.

These symptoms, plus the slack, expressionless facial muscles, led one of the neighbor doctors, an internist, to diagnose Gilbert's affliction as Parkinson's Disease, which slows the thought processes and leads to dementia. Gilbert also lost his ability to wiggle his ears, a trick he had learned in his childhood, and one he used to amuse visiting children. His hands developed the classic Parkinson's tremor and his gait suffered, causing him to shuffle when he walked. It prevented his going downhill without assistance, but he could manage uphill climbs with a cane.

Gilbert soon began to have spells of confusion at night, even becoming violent on two occasions. By morning, he was docile and apologetic, but he had to be watched constantly, because he often wandered away from the house and could not find his way home. At these times, Nancy's children, Brent and Jeanine, tracked him down, or Nita telephoned the Bearse's and other neighbors, who quickly took up the search. Sometimes he went down to the home of his old neighbor, Troy Dockery, and sat on the porch, while Troy's widow called Nita to let her know Gilbert's whereabouts. At other times, if Nancy or Dave caught up with him near the house, they could simply lead him around to the kitchen door, and say, "Well, here we are back home; let's go inside," and Gilbert would enter agreeably.[5] Occasionally, he got away to the mountainous part of the farm, and when Nancy found him, he refused to get into the car, forcing her to get help.

Once, when Gilbert was out prowling around, he fell off a bank and skinned his hands and arms badly. One of the doctor neighbors found him, took him home with him, stopped the bleeding, and cleaned and bandaged the abrasions. At another time, Gilbert became agitated, wanting to leave the house, telling Dave that he must hurry to the barn because the mules had climbed into the barn loft and must be brought down. Dave replied, "Don't you worry, if those mules are smart enough to climb that ladder, they'll be smart enough to get down by themselves," soothing Gilbert's anxieties, surprisingly.[6]

Eventually, though, as his health worsened, Gilbert did not venture out alone. His young neighbor, Danny Wyatt, observed that Gilbert seemed to give up when his little dog, Spot, died. Every morning for years, Gilbert had gone outside to the wood shed where he fed his cherished pet, sat down on a wooden box, and, after Spot had eaten, petted him and talked to him. Spot was injured in a fight one day, and did not respond to the usual home treatments. Gilbert was so worried that he asked Danny to take Spot to a veterinarian. However, Spot did not recover and "Gilbert went downhill from then," commented Danny, years later.[7]

Gilbert Stackhouse and his faithful Spot.

Gilbert's poor health even prevented his attending the funeral and burial of his brother, Ernest, at Charlotte in January, 1984. Dave stayed with Gilbert, while Lexyne, Nancy and Nita made the trip. Ernest's daughter, Carthene, who had no children, now had only her husband, Jack Cole, since both her parents and grandparents were dead. Ernest had not been well for several years, suffering from lung cancer, perhaps related to his smoking habit.

Back in the 1950s, Gilbert had given up his own habit of smoking, astounding his family. "He had a persistent cough," recalled Nancy, later, "and it worried him." One day he laid his cigarette pack on the piano and it laid there untouched for a week before Gilbert asked, "Well, isn't anyone going to say anything about my smoking?" "We had all been too afraid to mention it, we were so shocked; we had no idea what was going on," Nancy related.[8] Of course, they were delighted that he had taken this step to better his health. Gilbert was now the last of Amos Stackhouse's sons, and sadly, despite his not smoking, his prognosis was not good.

In addition to the mental problems, physical infirmities affected Gilbert.

He had frequent eye infections, perhaps another side effect of the disease. When Nancy applied the prescribed ointments, she was apprehensive that she might break his glass eye, so she persuaded him to get a plastic one. These prostheses needed changing more often than they did before his illness. Sometimes she had to take her father to Knoxville, Tennessee, for the fittings; at others, the company representative came to Asheville, shortening the trip for Nancy and Gilbert.

Pneumonia was another complication of Parkinson's, giving Gilbert several close calls. At these times, the doctor and nurse neighbors associated with Hot Springs Health Program were an absolute godsend, according to Nancy. She remembered one long episode, in particular, when Ginny Koranek stayed all night, pounding on Gilbert's back periodically until she was satisfied that the infection had broken up, and he was out of danger.[9]

Around 1986, Gilbert's hip failed from osteoarthritis. "The joint seemed eaten away, and his leg atrophied," Nancy explained. For awhile he could stand on one leg, enabling Nancy to get him out of bed by herself, with the aid of a lift apparatus having a canvas seat. Dave asked a friend – a Gideon, who worked at Mills Manufacturing Company in Weaverville – to make a harness rig which would go around Gilbert's waist and over his shoulder, then under his arm, so that he could still stand on his good leg. With the harness fastened to the hydraulic lift, Nancy could get Gilbert out of bed to bathe him.

After one hospital stay in the beginning of his illness, Gilbert had begged Nancy not to send him back. Though the effort was great, she and the family continued to care for him at home, knowing that he would not last long in a nursing home. They installed a simple intercom system so that Nita could summon them instantly from downstairs. They removed the sofa from Nita's kitchen/den (a room kept warm by an oil-burning heater), and installed a hospital bed in its place.

Gilbert eventually became so weak that it took two persons to lift him. As it happened, Nancy's son, Randy, was working night shifts at his Marshall job, and living at home in the annex apartment. When he arrived from work each morning, before going to bed, he helped Nancy lift Gilbert out of bed and into a wheel chair, so that she could change the bed and clean and dress Gilbert for the day. When he developed a bed sore on his hip, the Hot Springs Health Program sent a nurse to attend him two or three times a week. After a time, his skin began rubbing off when he was being turned in bed. He would plead with Nancy not to touch him, the pain was so great. "We used very soft synthetic lambs wool to handle him and move him," recalled Nancy.[10]

Throughout these trying months, the doctors next door and the nurse practitioner up the road were invaluable; they checked Gilbert's heart and blood pressure, answered questions, prescribed medicines, offered helpful suggestions, and arranged through the Hot Springs Health Program for services, such as a man to stay with Gilbert one day a week. This freed Nancy to take her mother to appointments, and to get groceries and any other necessities. Practitioner Ginny Koranek stayed with Gilbert one Sunday morning a month, and Lexyne came from Arden one Sunday a month, so that Nita could attend church.

The two neighbor toddlers – one belonging to Ginny and Danny, the other to the doctors – were daily visitors at the Stackhouse home, and they often played at Gilbert's bed when he felt well enough to be amused. If they did not come by for awhile, he asked for them. They provided a bright spot in his bleak days.

As time passed, however, he recognized fewer people, even his family. Nonetheless, occasionally he would have unexplained moments of awareness, thrilling his loved ones. Lexyne's daughter, Grace, after several empty visits had caused her to think she'd lost him, happened to be there on one of these clear days. She asked him to tell her the old stories again, since they gave her a precious sense of fulfillment. "He had never really talked to us a lot, but he told us tales; he was a wonderful story teller," reminisced Grace in later years.[6] For about three years, Gilbert Stackhouse remained bedridden, most often understanding little of what was going on about him. Normally, he would have shown high interest in the fact that a distant cousin, George Herbert Walker Bush, was elected to the presidency. Gilbert's great, great grandfather, Amos Stackhouse, was also Bush's great, great, great, great grandfather.[12]

Nor was Gilbert aware that Nancy had sold his cherished cattle. Not only had the bottom dropped out of the beef market, but the animals required too much work and expense. "We had to buy a lot of feed, besides raising the corn and hay; and we had no modern equipment," Nancy explained.[13] Gilbert's cattle had been a favorite retirement occupation, but now they meant nothing to his diseased mind.

His caretaking consumed an increasing amount of his family's time. "It was hard on Brent and Jeanine, because I could not attend their school functions and ball games – all the things we had done for Randy, the first child," stated Nancy.[14] She tried to maintain some normalcy in their lives, despite the confinement. In October, 1989, even though Gilbert's condition had progressed to critical, she strove for a traditional wedding for Randy Aumiller and his bride, Lynn Metcalf, a Madison County girl. Nancy had been able to arrange for the man who usually stayed with Gilbert once a week to come that Saturday, so that all the family could attend the wedding at Red Hill Freewill Baptist Church, where Dave was pastor. Dave performed the ceremony, and his father, Rev. Clarence Aumiller, also participated. The mild October day was bright blue and calm, as guests crossed the lawn to the reception hall next door. For the absence of rain or cold wind, Nancy was grateful.

She was also grateful that the ceremony had not been interrupted by a summons to her father's bedside, which she had expected. Gilbert lasted through, but his caretaking was growing more intense by the hour. Nancy was exhausted and at wit's end when Nita's niece, Patty Winter, called from Florida, asking if she might be of any help. "It was the answer to a prayer," Nancy admitted later.[15] Patty took care of Gilbert's night needs, permitting Nancy to get some rest.

By November fifth, Patty had stayed about three weeks, and was preparing to go home the next day. Gathered in Nita's dining room for Sunday dinner were Dave, Nancy, Brent, Jeanine, Nita, Patty, and Dave's parents, who had stayed to visit after the wedding. (Lexyne had been coming from Arden every day, but was not there on that Sunday.) As they left the table and began the clean-up, Nita fed Gilbert while Nancy washed dishes. Having had trouble swallowing for some time, Gilbert was reduced to eating meals of almost liquid form, such as Jell-O mixed with the protein supplement

Ensure. Nevertheless, Gilbert began to choke. Nancy yelled for Dave, who jumped onto the bed and performed the Heimlich maneuver. Although Gilbert vomited, he could not regain his breath. Nancy called the doctors from next door, but the internist, too, failed to resuscitate his old friend, and sadly filled out the death certificate. His wife, the pediatrician, took Nita away to the dining room; Patty took Dave's mother upstairs, while Nancy called her sister and the funeral home. Next, Dave shaved Gilbert and Nancy made all other preparations for her father's departure of his earthly home. Ellison Gilbert Dilworth Stackhouse had died on the other side of the wall of the same room in which he had been born eighty-three years earlier, cared for and surrounded by those who loved him.[16]

Curiously enough, just the day before, he had had a short lucid period when he called Lexyne, "Sisser," the childhood name Nancy had used when she was learning to say Sister. He had also told Nita the he loved her "more than ever." These endearing utterances helped them through the next days of mourning, visitations and funeral rites.[17]

Dilworth came alone from Indiana, having been recently widowed himself. Sonny came from Michigan, serving as his Aunt Nita's escort for the funeral at the Walnut Methodist Church, where Gilbert, his father and his grandfather had worshipped, and where Sonny had been christened. Dave Aumiller officiated, as well as the Methodist minister from Asheville; granddaughters of Malley Reeves – Ernestine and Dorothy – sang duets. For November, the day was warm, but more typical cold wind began just after the burial in the Stackhouse section of the church cemetery. As at the October wedding, the Stackhouses considered the good weather a special blessing.

In time, a granite double tombstone was erected at Gilbert's grave, bearing both his and Nita's names – her death date left blank, naturally. Gilbert's engraved birth and death dates reflected the fact that he had died within six months of his eighty-fourth birthday. His brother, Ernest, coincidentally, had died twenty-three days short of his eighty-fourth birthday, and their brother June had died eight months past his eighty-fourth birthday.[18]

After Gilbert's death and burial, for awhile, at least, it seemed the life had gone from the Stackhouse farmstead. "Mother had always made Daddy the focus of the household; everything revolved around him," stated Nancy.[19] When he worked away from home, Nita saw that the girls wrote him on Monday or Tuesday, then on Thursday they began preparing for his Friday homecoming. Nita worshipped Gilbert, and he, her. While holding Nita's hand in his 1978 response to a journalist's question about his job travels, Gilbert answered, "I always came back home because my sweetheart was here."[20] The couple had always sat close in Sunday morning worship services, Gilbert's arm around Nita's shoulder. During the time that Nurse Practitioner Kathy Johnson lived in the annex apartment, she used to tease Nita and Gilbert, calling them lovebirds. "Through the kitchen windows at night, we sometimes saw Nita sitting on Gilbert's lap," laughed Kathy.[21]

Besides losing her beloved husband, Nita Stackhouse suffered the deaths of two siblings during 1989 – her brother, Robert, and her sister, Nancy Lee – leaving Nita the remaining one of the six Caldwell children. It had been a difficult year for her, and she was grateful to have Nancy, Dave and the grandchildren in the house. Without them, the loneliness would have been unbearable. She knew that, as they had been there for Gilbert in his days of need, they would be there for her.

Not only was Gilbert missed at home, but a void was left in his community of friends. The Methodist Church members, where he had been Sunday School superintendent for thirty years, felt the loss, as did neighbor Betty Bearse, who said, "It isn't the same without Gilbert; he protected our little community."[22] His authoritative presence was both feared and respected, according to Betty. Even fifteen years later, Ginny Koranek stated, "I loved him dearly, and I miss him to this day."[23] Danny Wyatt, too, missed his old friend, but a cherished tree provided some remembrance. Once when Danny admired a large Norway spruce growing on Stackhouse property, Gilbert found a seedling under the tree and gave it to Danny, instructing him how to plant and care for it. "It's now forty feet tall and just beautiful," related Danny in 2004.[24]

Second only to his integrity, Gilbert's witty storytelling about childhood pranks and funny situations in the old days of Stackhouse would be most remembered by his friends and loved ones. His favorite poem had been "Sleepin' at the Foot O' the Bed," by Luther Patrick. "He would read it, and laugh and laugh," chuckled Nancy Aumiller in later years.[25] Patrick, who died in 1947, had been a Southern radio personality, a member of Congress, and a poet, often called the "poor man's Will Rogers." Since Gilbert had been his family's youngest child, whose opportunities were, perhaps, thwarted by the failed barytes operation, ensuing family indebtedness, and World War I, he no doubt related to the "feller at the foot o' the bed." The following excerpts come from the first and last stanzas of the poem:

> Did ye ever sleep at the foot o' the bed,
> When the weather was whizzin' cold…
> An' give your good warm feathers up
> To Aunt Lizzie and Uncle Fred…
> I've done it , an' I've done it many uv a time
> In this land o' the brave an' the free.
> An' in this all-fired battle uv life
> It's done left its mark upon me,
> Fer I'm allus a-strugglin' around at the foot
> Instead of forgin' ahead,
> An' I don't think it's caused by a doggone thing
> But sleepin' at the foot o' the bed;
> I've lost all my claim on fortune and fame,
> A-sleepin' at the foot o' the bed.[26]

Gilbert's grandson, Ronnie Norris, would always remember his grandfather as a strong man, but gentle at heart. Ronnie's grieving had begun, however, months before, when Gilbert's dementia showed to be irreversible. "It was very sad; I realized I'd lost him long before his death."[27] Gilbert's granddaughter, Jeanine Aumiller, missed his wisdom, complete honesty and dry wit. She would be reminded routinely of Gilbert's presence about the farm, but his legacy was more than tangible. As Grace Norris reflected later, Gilbert had influenced her sense of humor, her appreciation of history, her love of the outdoors, and her habits of Bible reading and church attendance.

She also recalled that her grandfather and her grandmother had not lavished gifts on their grandchildren, but what Gilbert did give was usually lovingly handcrafted. Once, Gilbert made her a doll's table and chairs. "He was a very smart man," Grace concluded.[28]

From his seventeenth-century Yorkshire ancestors – Thomas and John Stackhouse, who came to America in search of equality and freedom of worship – Gilbert's grandfather Amos had passed on the traits of charity, sobriety, industry and thrift. As his distant Canadian cousin had deduced long ago about the Stackhouse family, there likewise prevailed "a religious feeling" and a bent for teaching among Amos' descendents.[29] Gilbert had carried the Stackhouse torch high and well, holding onto his family's heritage and beliefs, and exhibiting good stewardship. His death, like his mother's 20 years earlier, marked the end of an era in his part of Madison County. And, though Gilbert was the last male at Stackhouse to bear the ancient surname, his spirit and influence would be manifest through coming generations. Similarly, the settlement of Stackhouse, despite its ghostly reminders of depleted resources, continues to have economic impact upon Madison County
– *even to our own times.*

Nita and Gilbert Stackhouse, 1980's, at home.

ENDNOTES FOR CHAPTER THIRTY

[1] Aumiller, Nancy Stackhouse. Interview, 2005.

[2] Ibid.

[3] Ibid.

[4] Koranek, Ginny. Interview, 2004.

[5] Aumiller, Interview, 2004.

[6] Ibid.

[7] Wyatt, Danny. Interview, 2004.

[8] Aumiller, Interview, 2005.

[9] Ibid.

[10] Ibid.

[11] Lenox, Grace Norris. Interview, 2004.

[12] Roberts, Gary Boyd. *Ancestors of American Presidents*. Santa Clarita, California: Carl Boyer, in cooperation with the New England Genealogical Society, Boson, Mass., 1989.Stackhouse, Eugene. Private records, 2002.

[13] Aumiller, Interview, 2004.

[14] Ibid.

[15] Ibid.

[16] Ibid.

[17] Ibid.

[18] Connecticut Dept of Health Services.
Mecklenburg County Vital Records.

[19] Aumiller, Interview, 2005.

[20] Wolcott, Mary Ellen. *Asheville Citizen-Times*. Sept. 24, 1978, p.1-C.

[21] Johnson, Kathy. Interview, 2004.

[22] Bearse, Betty Caldwell. Interview, 2004.

[23] Koranek, Interview, 2004.

[24] Wyatt, Interview, 2004.

[25] Aumiller, Interview, 2004.

[26] Patrick, Luther. *"Sleepin' at the Foot O' the Bed,"* A Book of Historical Poems, ed. Wm. R. Bowlin, Chicago: A. Whitman & Co., 1939, pps. 26, 77.

[27] Norris, Ronnie. Interview, 2004.

[28] Lenox, Interview, 2004.

[29] Author's private papers.

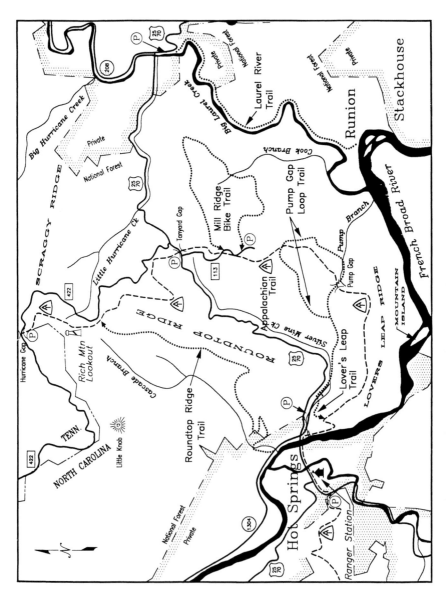

U.S. Forest Service Hiking Map showing Laurel River Trail to Runion along old LRLC railroad bed. October, 1997.

EPILOGUE

The spring after Gilbert died, Nita's nieces, Patty and Freda, having lost their own mother, Nancy Lee, the year before, persuaded Nita to visit them in Florida. She stayed a month or more, accompanying them on a cruise to Nassau, her first time out of the United States, and her first time on the ocean. Although in mourning, Nita was good company and enthusiastic about her new experiences. (On subsequent spring visits, the nieces took her to visit relatives in Colorado – Nita's first airplane flight – and they also encouraged her to get her ears pierced for earrings, another first for Nita.) Not having their own mother to pamper, the nieces lavished attention upon Nita, who loved them in return as daughters.[1]

While Nita's spirit gained strength and healing from the vacations, the memory of Gilbert's passing would be freshened as she was notified of other Stackhouse deaths. Carthene Stackhouse Cole died at Charlotte in April, 1991.[2] Within a month, word came of Dilworth Stackhouse's death at his home in Jeffersonville, Indiana.[3] Additionally, when Dave Aumiller's mother was dying of cancer in 1990, he had brought her to Stackhouse where he and Nancy could care for her in their home during her last months.

Dave's mother had had her heart set upon a damask-covered casket like the one in which her own mother was buried, but none could be found, leading Dave to build one by hand. After Dave's sister, Lorraine, purchased the cloth, Dave glued it to the wooden rounded-top coffin, the lining of which was padded white satin. He added mahogany molding, piano hinge and brass handles. "It was beautiful," said Nancy Aumiller afterwards. "But," she added, "as people heard about it, they came to the funeral home to see the unusual homemade casket, and out private plans went out the window."[4]

Only two years later, Dave's father, who had insisted on staying in his own home, died alone in Seattle. Death further took Gilbert's good friend, cousin and attorney, Charles Edwin Mashburn, in February, 1997, leaving a void in the family and the community. On April 4, 2003, Larry Stackhouse, adopted son of Dilworth, also died, followed in four weeks by the death of Milton Meek, husband of Dilworth's sister, Anna Stackhouse Meek.[5]

Fortunately, these sad times were interspersed with happy ones, as Nita watched her grandchildren mature, finish school and take their places in the world. Lexyne's son, Ronnie, became a pharmacist, with successive promotions taking him to Nashville, Tennessee. His sister, Grace, received a Director of Religious Education degree from Pfeiffer College, and married a Duke Divinity School graduate, John Patrick Lenox. She teaches school and serves in the demanding roles of mother and pastor's wife.[6] Nancy's son, Randall, took a managerial position with a Madison County manufacturing company, while his brother, Brent, joined the Navy – yet another Stackhouse to serve his country in time of conflict.

Brent was assigned to a ship in the Persian Gulf during the Clinton administration. Although it was considered a war zone, its threat came mostly from indiscriminate contact with small fast boats, and from commercial ships carrying contraband. Brent's ship and others in the fleet, as part of their patrol watch, monitored the Oil for Food program and launched aircraft whenever points of treaty were violated. At times they were in danger of bombings. When going ashore, they were ordered to wear civilian clothes, to have no visible insignia, and to keep a low profile.

A few years after returning home, Brent joined a Navy buddy at Snyder Driving School in Ohio – the state, oddly enough, where his great, great grandfather, Amos, had lived before coming to Madison County. Brent married Bernadette Curtiss, who home-schools their children through their church's network. Moreover, after driving his tractor-trailer rig all week, Brent drives his church's bus on Sundays, from early to late.[7]

Jeanine Aumiller, Nancy's daughter, finished at her father's alma mater, Bob Jones University, with a Master's degree in Public Rhetoric and English. She joined their faculty, teaching in the speech department and coaching the debate team.[8]

During Jeanine's college years, Nita had continued making clothes for her, even when her arthritic knee could no longer operate her treadle sewing machine. She then made garments completely by hand, using needle, thimble and thread. Nita was gradually forced to give up more activities as her body aged to ninety, then to ninety-five, her mind and spirit remaining sharp, however. She charmed friends and strangers alike, albeit from the background, as she watched and directed Nancy in the duties of Stackhouse chatelaine.

Besides hosting the Madison County annual meeting of Nita's Home Demonstration Club, Nancy fed and housed visiting ministers, friends of her children, relatives and stranded victims of car wrecks or other troubles. In fact, throughout Dave's ministry, she and Dave had opened their home to several foster children and individuals in need of shelter or a meal. "We always had some food and a bed, even if only a mattress on the floor," Nancy explained.[9]

Still, back in 1989 when Nita Caldwell Stackhouse was widowed, she had stepped into the role of Stackhouse matriarch, as Hester Honeycutt had done in 1948, and Anna Myers had in 1909. Nita embraced changes to preserve and protect the Stackhouse community, and resisted offers she felt to be harmful. She turned down those seeking parts of her land for golf courses, subdivisions or other development, preferring to retain the old farmstead for her family and to follow her husband's stewardship. Unfortunately, she had no control over the largest landowner affecting Stackhouse – Walnut Gap Estates.

This corporation had hired Dave Aumiller to watch over their property by checking fences and signs of poachers. They paid him fifty dollars a month and furnished a small motor boat for crossing the river to the southern portion. Once, the stockholders made plans to develop the Stackhouse acres by dotting the mountainside with A-frame vacation homes. Dave drove them around and humored them, knowing that the precipitous terrain all but kept fire fighters from walking over it during forest fires. After receiving bids of a million dollars to build roads into the proposed area, the Florida men gave up the idea.[10]

Around 1988, Charles Edwin Mashburn, who was attorney for Walnut Gap Estates, had told Dave to expect surveyors; negotiations were afoot to sell the property. In May, 1989, a letter went from Mashburn to the stockholders, Russell Seal and Irving Rosen of Miami (named grantors), and to realtors Dabney Manning and Edwin Poss of Clayton, Georgia (named grantees), outlining Mashburn's progress in achieving title insurance. "While the surveyor is finishing… I will proceed with the extensive documentation of the title matters, which involves… some eight tracts of land," stated Mashburn. "Despite discrepancies and disputes, it appears we can now proceed… to complete the transaction," he ended.[11]

And yet, it was not until 1991 that Manning and Poss received the Madison County tracts as part of their quest to obtain 659 acres on Scaly Mountain in Macon County owned by the U.S. Forest Service. The Forest Service had said it would swap the Macon land, if the realtors would buy the Madison acres for Pisgah National Forest, plus a tract in Jackson on the Blue Ridge Parkway, for Nantahala National Forest. Finally, in August, 1991, the exchange having great impact upon the Stackhouse community was made between Manning and Poss and the United States of America, wherein the Georgia men received their Macon County tract, and the Forest Service received its Jackson County land, plus $5,500 equalization cash and the 1,249 acres formerly owned by Ellsworth Vandervort, including the Stackhouse and Runion communities.[12] This meant that Stackhouse would retain its pristine nature on three sides, at least, with no highways, dams, chalets, golf courses or other developments – a great relief to Nita, her family and her neighbors.

The Forest Service would, however, continue to sell permits to the rafting communities for use of the river bank "take out" area in front of Nita's house, saving the Madison County rafting industry, an important part of Madison's economy. Not only would Stackhouse Boat Launch be featured on recreational maps, but "Stackhouse Shrimp Cocktail" would be a menu choice at Paddler's Pub and Grill (a Hot Springs restaurant), both listings preserving the Stackhouse identity.[13]

The Forest Service has also developed the Laurel River Trail for public use – three-and-a-half miles down the old Laurel River Logging Company Railway bed, along Big Laurel Creek to Runion, with a sign and parking lot at the Laurel River bridge on Highway 25-70. According to forester Paul Bradley, Runion Mountain is managed on a custodial basis, protecting the historic remnants and openings, as well as the Runion identity. In a 1999 interview, Bradley stated that the Runion site's largest value to Pisgah National Forest is its historical significance to the region.[14]

The badly overgrown fields, where the Stackhouses, Treadways, and Dockery's formerly planted tobacco and corn, were cleared by Forest Service workers and re-sown with a mixture of rye, clover and fescue seeds, providing wildlife habitats while retaining much of the land's early years' appearance. "We had to use a chain saw on a lot of it, it was so large," stated Arthur Frisbee, a Forest Service employee.[15] They also "scraped a little off the top of the old railroad bed with a dozer," according to Frisbee, preserving the site so that hikers can follow the path of the steam-pulled logging trains which had been so meaningful to impoverished Madison County.

Another government project to affect Stackhouse came through the North Carolina Division of Highways in April, 1998, when Nita signed a right-of-way agreement giving the state permission to take twenty-two-and-a-half feet on each side of the road's center line through her property, for the widening of secondary road #1319, Stackhouse Road.[16] One day, however, as Nancy Aumiller drove home, she found workers preparing to blast apart the monolith called Barbershop Rock by the community. "Daddy always told us that there used to be a barber shop built atop that rock," Nancy explained later.[17] She told the workers they could have all the space they needed on the other side of the road if they would leave the historic rock. By her persuasion the landmark was saved, but in time it will be subject to splitting, as rain collects and freezes in the holes drilled before Nancy arrived.

The old Morehead mine adit, however, which had been highly visible in the dirt-bank edge of Stackhouse Road, was obliterated during the straightening and widening project. It had marked the place of the first ore brought from Stackhouse property, mined by the noted James Turner Morehead, and before that, by the eminent Thomas Lanier Clingman.

Otherwise, the roar of chain saws, the jolts of explosives, the banging of dump trucks, the thick dust on dry days, the slick mud on wet days, and the inconvenient periods of waiting in their vehicles – were all suffered in silence, usually, by the Stackhouse family, so glad were they to have a paved, two-lane road, where rafting buses and delivery trucks and other travelers could pass without danger. In fact, during Nita's sixty-nine years at Stackhouse, she had already endured the rebuilding of the road three times, each an improvement over its predecessor.[18]

At last, one day in 2000, when the road crew had all but finished, Nita, Nancy and Dave showed their appreciation by inviting them to noon-day dinner. Nancy was actually recovering from a broken leg, but Dave took the day off and helped with chicken-frying and carrying food down the stairs from their second-floor kitchen. A few other Stackhouse residents brought dishes of food or donated money to buy the ham and chicken. "There must have been twenty or more workers, and they really enjoyed it," said Nancy.[19]

Through subsequent years, Nita has been periodically approached by developers who need other parts of her land for their projects, but all in all, the changing of boundaries in the Stackhouse community remains infrequent. Occasionally, there is turnover, as in 2000, when a young couple bought thirty-one acres formerly owned by Gilbert and Ernest Stackhouse. While building their home, they camped on the property, causing concern to Nancy Aumiller when the night temperatures dropped low. She persuaded them to stay in Nita's annex apartment until their house was finished, saying that mountain winters were too cold for tent living.[20] Ultimately, the couple's new home resulted in an innovative design of unusual recycled materials, of which Gilbert would have heartily approved.

Carrying deeper impact to the community, however, was change on property joining Nita's – the large tract purchased in 1914 by Anson Betts from the Candler family. In 2000, Betts' children sold 534.08 acres to River Club Investors, owned by Agee and Fisher of Atlanta, who also bought, at the same time, 200 adjoining acres from Ralph Gahagan, cousin of Elizabeth Gahagan Baker of Walnut.[21] The Gahagan tract ran from Highway 25-70 at Walnut to the Sandy Bottom road south of Stackhouse, and joined the Betts tract that ran all the way to the French Broad at Sandy Bottom. Fisher and Agee built roads, subdividing the nearly 750 acres into home sites, and reserving 400 of the more precipitous for hiking trails and nature enjoyment by a gated community of affluent vacation-home owners.

The Atlanta partners (one of whom was Jack Fisher, Madison County native and entrepreneur) had previously acquired 1200 acres across the river in the Little Pine community, developing it under the name of Preserve at Little Pine, but conserving large easements with each of its even higher-priced home sites.[22] While these gated communities would never likely cause disturbances – visible or audible – to Stackhouse, they brought decided cultural change to the area, since practically no Madison Countians could afford to live there. Hopefully, for local people, there would at least be employment opportunities or other economic benefits in exchange.

Although the former Klondyke mine was not included in the Betts-to-Fisher transaction, there would not likely be a barytes revival at Stackhouse. Gilbert had told an *Asheville Citizen-Times* reporter in 1978, "Every few years the mines open again; it's been that way as long as I can remember."[23] However, since then, no one has shown commercial interest in the barite. Occasionally, a geologist will poke around the adits and dumps for evidence of a profitable venture, but mostly the mine visitors are members of the North Carolina Geological Survey's Asheville branch, who are updating the Hot Springs and Spring Creek quadrangle maps.

These will show the old Stackhouse mines through the confirmation of previous maps. No new research has been done, but the new maps will be the first detailed geologic maps on record of the Spring Creek quadrangle to cover the Stackhouse mines, according to Carl Merchant, Senior Geologist in charge of the Asheville office. "There will also be an accompanying mineral resource summary booklet in which Stackhouse mines will be discussed as part of the overview," stated Merchant in a 2004 interview.[24] He also predicts it will be published by 2006, as a part of the complete commodities documentation for state records – valuable in case there is ever a need for the minerals, or if the world market becomes equalized. Now, the United States finds it cheaper to import most of its metallic ores, rather than mine them at home.[25]

There have been other changes and modifications at Stackhouse since Gilbert's death. When it became increasingly difficult to find someone willing to paint the three-story structure for an affordable amount, Nita made the decision to cover her house's poplar clapboard with vinyl siding. The new cream-colored facsimile appears no different from the original wood siding, to the uninformed eye. When she could no longer climb steps, Dave Aumiller built a wooden ramp and railing from the ground to her kitchen door, enabling Nita to walk outdoors without assistance.

Additionally, Gilbert's large dream-barn accidentally burned, as did the old Stackhouse school building. The last original tenant house, which had been at Stackhouse since the turn of the previous century, at least, was intentionally burned by Dave Aumiller, with Nita's permission, after it became dilapidated and unsafe. It had been a dwelling during the Stackhouse early years, then Gilbert's workshop until he retired and turned it back into a rental home.

In 2004, Nita gained further peace of mind when she approved Dave's use of a bulldozer to clear the fields at the side and back of her home on the north side, and to reseed with grass. These fields, which had been used for pasture in Gilbert's day, but contained orchard, boxwood and vegetable gardens during Hester's years, had become thickly overgrown, posing a wildfire hazard.

"People don't realize how quickly a forest fire can whip through the tree tops, before you can even call for help," said Nancy Aumiller, at the time.[26] Expansive forest fires had come threateningly close to Stackhouse in recent years, bringing helicopters to carry water from the French Broad in front of

Nita's house to the fire scene. One time, the Forest Service dipped into Nita's lake up at the old barytes operation. Still another large wild fire at Hot Springs in 2002 filled all the Stackhouse valley with thick acrid smoke, forcing Nita to stay indoors for its duration.

Representing more change, these same helicopters are used to spot and report forest fires in Madison County and Pisgah National Forest. Their presence, coupled with the fact that nearly every household now has a telephone to report fire sightings, has rendered the old fire watch towers obsolete. However, during high-danger fire seasons, Rich Mountain tower, overlooking Hot Springs, is still manned for its communications value between land crews and helicopters, and will be maintained, according to forester Paul Bradley in Burnsville.[27] Meanwhile, the other towers slowly rot to the ground, marking yet another change in Madison County culture.

The Forest Service also uses helicopters in Madison County to reseed large areas eroded by landslides from rain storms and flash floods, especially in the Laurel area. The method is quicker and more efficient than using hand crews on the ground.

Occasionally, helicopters hover around Stackhouse, too, for the filming of movies and TV commercials, according to Nancy Aumiller.[28] She has even observed food-services vans meeting with film crews in the rafters' parking lot on the river in front of Nita's house. The picturesque junction of river, railroad and lush green forest also presents allure to aerial photographers in some of the helicopters. Norfolk-Southern Railway actually used this composition, which included the Stackhouse home, on the cover of its large 1991 company calendar.

The loud vibrating choppers that "shake the entire house," as Nancy Aumiller says, have even modernized the age-old timber industry in Madison County. For instance, on January 14, 2004, the flying machines removed large log piles, of seven to eight thousand pounds at a time, from the Mars Hill watershed. The log piles were attached to choker cables and dropped at the landing zone miles away.[29] The logs are unhooked by three men, and the 'copter leaves to bring another load only minutes later. Although the noise is loud, scarring and erosion of the land is greatly reduced – much different from the methods available to the first Amos of Stackhouse, as he cleared his farm; or to the loggers at Putnam and Runion; or to the second Amos, as he fed his sawmill; or to June Stackhouse in his telephone pole operation; or even to Gilbert, as he pulled "acid wood" from the mountainside by mule and sled.

Two helicopters served more dramatically at Stackhouse one cold January night in 1998, when, working through wind and lightning, their military crews used night-vision goggles and infrared spotlight to rescue an overturned rafter clinging to a tree and suffering from hypothermia. The water's speed, estimated at thirty to forty miles per hour, was deemed too dangerous for boat rescue. "Nothing but rafting pros were in that river, and they said, there's no way," stated Madison County Fire Marshal Eddie Fox to an *Asheville Citizen-Times* reporter.[30]

One of the "pros," incidentally, was Brent Aumiller, the grandson of Gilbert Stackhouse, chosen by his former employer, Ron West of the French Broad Rafting Company. Despite the water's roughness, two rafters had roped themselves to the raft and put in at Barnard, upriver from Stackhouse. One man had been able to get loose underwater and grab the tree. When a passing trainman reported the troubled watercraft, Ron West called Brent to assist in the search. The crew spotted the raft and life jacket, but still could not have reached them until the river subsided. Thus the helicopters were requested. West's crew had also found the man's drowned partner lodged in a tree on an underwater island at Stackhouse, but the river was too dangerous to retrieve the body. The next day, bringing out the corpse was especially sad for Brent, who had graduated from Marshall High School with the victim.[31]

Another change at Stackhouse came with Nita's decision in 1999 to drop her farm's tobacco quota, which had been in place since its 1938 inception. This termination left the Stackhouse community with no tobacco production at all.[32] It had become more difficult each year to find lessees, making Nita's nominal profit hardly worthwhile.

Tobacco raising – the century-old way of life in Madison County, and the core of its economy – is still changing rapidly, county-wide. Lawsuits and other pressures on the tobacco products manufacturers have resulted in low prices paid to the farmers, leaving them in a predicament. For the majority of Madison County's farmers, the only way they have had to raise a sum of money to pay a child's college tuition or a hospital bill, or to buy a tractor replacement, has been a tobacco crop. It has been for the country dweller what the insurance policy, the bank loan, or the income tax refund has been for city dwellers – all of which financial sources are taken for granted by those in urban areas when dealing with their emergencies. Nevertheless, many of these Madison County natives are forced to plant crops that bring smaller returns than tobacco, but that carry some state funding, available only to burley growers.

The Asheville Burley Tobacco Marketing Center – serving all of western North Carolina, and North Carolina's last remaining burley auction – closed its normal season in January, 2005, maybe forever, some said.[33] In October, 2004, the federal government had passed a ten-billion-dollar tobacco program buyout, offering to the farmers sales contracts with the tobacco companies rather than open-floor auction, which had been used for years. The new system eliminates quotas restrictions dictating how many pounds the farmer may grow and where it may be grown, but gives no guaranteed bottom price, and will likely lower the usual price paid by forty to sixty cents. Madison County burley growers – North Carolina's top producers for a century – will not give up their traditional ways quickly, but some signs of diversification can already be found through the production of Christmas trees, vegetables, livestock, and greenhouse crops.[34]

Another Madison County and Stackhouse tradition, all but lost in October, 2000, was the century-old *News-Record*, bought by the Madison County *Sentinel*, but continuing under the name *News-Record* and *Sentinel*. Even though the name "*News-Record*" appears in thin one-fourth-inch type, while "*Sentinel*" stands one and one-eighth inches tall in bold thick letters, the historic newspaper title still appears on the front page of each issue. Nita Stackhouse looks forward to her weekly copy with great anticipation, as she did the *News-Record* for so many years.

Further change for the Stackhouse family comes through a large modern supermarket near Marshall, which has replaced many small general stores in Madison County, there being better roads and numerous families owning automobiles. However, one store remains at Walnut, where there used to be four, but, "It has about anything you might need," says Nancy Aumiller.[35]

Nor is there a school left at Walnut; it was taken by consolidation, and its old brick building fell to arson, leaving little public activity in the once-bustling community. Even the Walnut Methodist Church, supported for well over a century by the Stackhouse family, finally closed its doors in 2002. The building, on its historic site of Madison County's first courthouse, was sold by the Methodist Conference to a private party.[36]

Still, the Stackhouse family take pleasure in the few things that haven't changed around them. The French Broad is still queen of the valley, luring those who can respect her frequent whims, her risings and fallings, her gifts and demands. Nancy frequently feeds the geese who live along the river in summer, remembering that her grandmother, Anna, had raised geese for the making of feather ticks (mattresses) and pillows. "But they would stay only awhile, then take off to the river; she had trouble keeping them," said Nancy.[37] There are also wood ducks on the island, and a pair of blue herons living nearby year round. With the presence of Pisgah National Forest and civic cleanup efforts of the French Broad, a variety of wildlife is coming back to Stackhouse, making the area increasingly resemble the pristine setting found by the first Amos.

Although not as pleasant, another constant is the "queen's" flooding. In September, 2004, her wrath reached a ferocity akin to that of 1916 and 1940, but did little damage at Stackhouse. In front of Nita's home, the parking lot for the rafting companies was covered, despite their attempts to build the area above flood stage with tons of gravel. Marshall was again hit hard, however, as well as Hot Springs. Fortunately, no lives were lost, nor were any railroad tracks dislodged.[38]

Furthermore, Southern Railway Company (now Norfolk-Southern) trains continue to pass daily with freight cars, and to use Amos' siding for the occasional repairs of engines and cars. Once or twice a year, circus trains, with "Barnum & Bailey" painted on the sides in bright colors, go past Stackhouse, as they have since the 1880s.[39]

The early Stackhouse friends, the Gahagans, also remain steadfast at Walnut, living on land of their pioneer ancestor, George Robert Washington Gahagan, who represented Madison County in the state legislature from 1865 to 1871, and was a customer at Amos Stackhouse's Warm Springs store. Gahagan's great grandson, James L. "Jim" Baker, Jr., was elected in 2002 to his second eight-year term as Senior Resident Superior Court Judge of the 24th Judicial District, which includes Madison County.[40] Jim Baker is the son of Elizabeth Gahagan Baker, and the grandson of Ben Wade Gahagan, Gilbert's close friend and work associate. Jim continues to live in Madison County, within a few miles of his parents, who occupy the Gahagan land that has been in their family for a century-and-a-half, and the home often visited by Gilbert Stackhouse in his young years.

As Nancy Stackhouse Aumiller reflects on her own community's population of different values, carrying traditions and unusual names, she recalls that she is a product of one discontented Yankee and his teenaged bride with their oddly-used pronouns, who were, nonetheless, kindly accepted and allowed to gain a foothold in the mountain fastness. Also captivated by the ancient French Broad, they plowed her banks to plant seeds of faith and works, as in the words of Laurel missionary Frances Goodrich,

374

"Conserving the old in what measure it is good and helpful, that the old landmarks may not be swept away, and that the elements of independence and thrift and steadfastness in the time now passing, may be carried on into the coming days.[41]"

Though the Stackhouse family are now the only pioneer representatives left in the Stackhouse community, others return regularly to visit – the Bullmans, Dockerys, Gosnells, Nortons, Ramseys, Reeds, Thomases, and Treadways, to name a few. They bring their children and grandchildren, pointing out old home sites and landmarks; they meet annually to maintain and decorate the cemeteries, share picnic lunches, reminisce, sing, preach and pray together; they tell all the stories handed down from their grandparents about boom days at Stackhouse, Runion and Sandy Bottom, about their hard times and their happy times. In this way, their traditions and their values connect the generations.

Besides these visits by former neighbors, Nita Stackhouse looks forward to visits from her great grandchildren, who, incidentally, call their grandfather (Dave Aumiller) "Papa," as Gilbert called his father years ago. Two of the youngsters are biracial, adopted by Randall Stackhouse Aumiller – a reflection, perhaps, of his Pennsylvania ancestors who struggled for the equality of all men and women.[42] It could also test the courage of the entire Stackhouse family in Madison County, where the African-American population is .08 percent of the whole.[43]

Nevertheless, courage is part of their Christian armor. Nita's children and grandchildren are active in their respective churches – worshipping, teaching and leading. In his 2003 Christmas letter to family and friends, Dave Aumiller wrote from his Stackhouse home: "We are blessed to have all three of our children busily serving the Lord Jesus Christ!"[44]

Other visitors to Stackhouse, always anticipated with pleasure, are Clara Hester and Amos III (Sonny), children of June Stackhouse, as well as the children of Dilworth, who drop in annually, and Anna Meek, sister of Dilworth. Nita's nieces, Patty and Freda, come from Florida regularly, as do Lexyne and her husband, often keeping Nita company while Nancy takes a break from her duties as caregiver, Sunday School teacher, pianist, Bible Study leader, hospital and nursing home visitor, counselor, cook and organizer of suppers and workday meals for workers in the construction of their church building at Weaverville. In 2004, she accompanied Dave on a mission trip to the Philippine Islands, evangelizing and carrying funds to help churches in dire need.[45]

Also, in 2004, just before the mission trip, Nancy and Lexyne celebrated their mother's 100th birthday by inviting friends and family from far and wide. About 200 people attended on the cold November weekend, while others paid tribute through cards, gifts and telephone calls. A few friends opened a teachers' grant for local schools through the Madison County Education Foundation, to honor Nita's years of teaching and educational support in Madison County. Even at age one hundred, she stays informed through television and reading; keeps her jolly disposition; and maintains her matriarchal position at Stackhouse. Danny Wyatt, her neighbor, who was out of town on Nita's birthday, wrote her the following:

Nita,

> Thanks for your wonderful friendship and gifts over the years:
> > great lunches while I worked with Gilbert.
> > greater stories of Runion and environs,
> > greatest wedding ever, on your lawn and in your castle.
> Thanks for training us in the fine art of "Setback," for making that special Christmas candy, and always greeting us with a smile and "Come in!"
> You've provided Ginny and me with a home away from home for years, finally offering us the best homestead in the state.
> > Happy 100th Birthday to the most
> > phenomenal woman we know!
>
> > Love always, Danny and Ginny.[46]

Although Nita is no longer able to can beans, or make jam, jelly and applesauce, as each fruit ripens on the farm, Nancy continues the traditions. One recent dry summer, when there were practically no blackberries or raspberries to be had, Nancy and Dave picked the tiny wild elderberries and made jelly from their juice – a time-consuming, tedious job, but rendering delicious results. Further maintaining the Stackhouse tradition, she and Dave plant a vegetable garden each year (albeit smaller than former ones), canning and freezing the surplus for winter. Late in the summer, sometimes, after their own garden has finished, the Aumillers and Nita are treated to a gift of fresh sweet corn for their supper from the patch of Danny Wyatt, who remembers how Gilbert provided seeds and helped him with his first garden at Stackhouse.[47]

The Hot Springs Health Program, responsible for bringing Nita's special neighbors to Stackhouse over twenty years ago, continues strong. It requires its physicians to take 150 hours per year of study and seminars on new techniques and medicines – a constant benefit to Nita, as well as to her family and community.[48]

Thus, since the first Amos Stackhouse ended his peregrinations in 1879, and even since Gilbert's death in 1989, much has changed at Stackhouse, North Carolina, but much remains the same. Jeanine Aumiller, Amos' great, great granddaughter, wrote the following in a school paper, one hundred ten years after he came there:

> The place is still occupied by my family... There is still an incomparably beautiful view from the porch of Nita Stackhouse's home. Although most of the historic landmarks that identified Stackhouse as a thriving community at the turn of the last century have disappeared, its secluded beauty remains unchanged, and memories of its frontier days linger on in our minds.[49]

Yes, even to our own times.

[1] Aumiller, Nancy Stackhouse. Interview, 2004.
[2] Mecklenburg County Department of Health & Vital Records.
[3] *Asheville Citizen*, May 6, 1991.
[4] Aumiller, 2004.
[5] *Asheville Citizen-Times*, May 2, 2003.
[6] Norris, Lexyne Stackhouse. Interview, 2004.
[7] Aumiller, Interview, 2004.
   Madison County Register of Deeds, Bk. 266, p.66.
[8] Aumiller, Interview, 2005.
[9] Ibid., 2004.
[10] Ibid., 2005.
[11] Poss, Edwin C. Interview, 2005.
   Poss, private papers.
[12] Madison County Register of Deeds, Bk. 194, pps. 376, 394.
   Jackson County Register of Deeds, Bk. 498, p. 176.
   Macon County Register of Deeds, Bk. F19, p. 961.
[13] *Carolina Connections, Your Guide to National Forests in North Carolina*, Issue 6, 1998.
[14] Bradley, Paul. Interview, 1999.
[15] Frisbee, Arthur. Interview, 1999.
[16] Madison County Register of Deeds, B. 254, p. 651.
[17] Aumiller, Interview, 2005.
[18] Stackhouse, Nita. Interview, 1999.
[19] Aumiller, Interview, 2000.
[20] Ibid., 2004.
[21] Gahagan, Ralph. Interview, 2005.
[22] Fisher, Jack. Interview, 2005.
[23] Wolcott, Mary Ellen, *Asheville Citizen-Times*. Sept. 24, 1978, p.1-C.
[24] Merchant, Carl. Interview, 2005.
[25] Ibid.
[26] Aumiller, Interview, 2005.
[27] Bradley, Interview, 2005.
[28] Aumiller, Interview, 1999.
[29] *Asheville Citizen-Times*, January 15, 2004, p.C1.
[30] Ibid., January 10, 1998, p.1.
[31] Aumiller, Interview, 2004.
[32] Zink, Charles E. Executive Director, Madison County Farm Service Agency. Letter to author, May 29, 2002.
[33] *Asheville Citizen-Times*, January 27, 2005, p.1; November 17, 2002, p.D1; December 29, 2002, p.C2; January 16, 2003, p.B1.
[34] Aumiller, Interview, 2005.
   Asheville Citizen-Times, January 27, 2005, p.1; December 29, 2002, p.C2; June 15, 2003, p.2.
[35] Aumiller, Interview, 2005.
[36] Plemmons, Ernestine Reeves. Interview, 2005.
[37] Aumiller, Interview, 2003.
[38] Ibid.
   News Record & Sentinel, September 22, 2004.
   Asheville Citizen-Times, September 9, 2004, p.A9.
   Ibid., September 17, 2004, p.A1.
[39] Aumiller, Interview, 2004.
[40] Baker, Elizabeth Gahagan. Interview, 2005.
[41] Goodrich, Frances L., "Old Ways and New in the Carolina Mountains," *Southern Workman*, Hampton, Virginia: April, 1900, p.211.

[42] Trueblood, D. Elton, *The People Called Quakers*. New York: Harper & Row, 1966, pp. 2-4.
Weigley, Russell, F., *Philadelphia, A 300-Year History*. New York: W.W. Norton & Co., 1982, p.388.

[43] U.S. Census, 2000.

[44] Aumiller, Rev. David. Letter to author, December, 2003.

[45] Aumiller, Nancy. Interview, 2004.

[46] Wyatt, Danny. Letter to Nita Stackhouse, November, 2004.

[47] Aumiller, Nancy S. Interview, 2004.
Wyatt, Danny. Interview, 2004.

[48] Aumiller, Nancy. Interview, 2005.

[49] Aumiller, Jeanine. Essay, March 18, 1988, Marshall Elementary School.

Current view of private Stackhouse, North Carolina, home, as seen from public road.
Visitors are asked to honor the distance.

STACKHOUSE COAT OF ARMS

This coat of arms was painted by Thomas Chalkley Matlack, an artist and authority on heraldry. The head of our family in Tasmania, Australia, has a copy of the original grant of these Arms and the edict of the Emperor Maximillian granting these arms follows:

1518

These underwritten Arms an Ensigne viz: A shield whose area of white or silver colour, A barn open on all sides, the roof covered with red tiling, under which a handful of wheat of a yellow colour having on each side a cross after the manor of St. Andrews of Saffron or gold colour and beside above one of the same colour consequently in such sort as they appear, better designed by the skill of the painter.

We of our clemency confer and grant, decreeing and enacting by this our Caesarian edict. 1518 A.D.

In his book *Stackhouse, An Original Pennsylvania Family*, Eugene Stackhouse further states that the College of Arms in London, England, reported in 1983: "Arms were in unofficial use in the mid 17th century by a family named Stackhouse in Yorkshire. These arms were granted by Maximillian, Holy Emperor, to Christopher Stackhouse on 11 December 1518. These arms were not granted by the King of Arms of England, thus, they have no validity in English law. (The name Stackhouse seems to have come from a stack-house or shed for the stacking of grain.)"

In July, 2006, Harvey Stackhouse (great grandson of the founder of Stackhouse, N.C.) visited Stackhouse, England which has dwindled in size much as its local counterpart. Harvey took pictures and researched Stackhouse history, his pilgrimage providing another similarity between Stackhouse, England, and Stackhouse, America. In an undated booklet titled *Stackhouse*, Dr. T. Ian Roberts' admonishment applies to both communities:

> Though the residents of Stackhouse, England, have been most cooperative in helping towards the production of this booklet, it must be remembered that much of Stackhouse is private property, and that there is no public right-of-way through the grounds and yards of the houses there. It is hoped that visitors will remember this, and respect the privacy of this quiet hamlet.

Harvey W. Stackhouse on the road to Stackhouse in North Yorkshire, England, 2006. Photo by Lynette Stackhouse.

One of several original outbuildings on Stackhouse farm, England, facing east. Photo by Lynette Stackhouse, 2006.

Harvey W. Stackhouse greets John Helliwell, current owner of Stackhouse farm and home (built c. 1840) in England – the same house photographed by Wm. Romig Stackhouse, Harvey's cousin, around 1900, and pictured in chapter one. Photo by Lynette Stackhouse.

NORFOLK SOUTHERN   Thoroughbred freight train rolls along the French Broad River between Marshall and Hot Springs, N.C.   1991

Stackhouse home, Stackhouse, N.C., as shown on Norfolk-Southern Railway calendar for 1991.

Historic Morehead mine adit in bank of Stackhouse Road was destroyed by road widening in 2000. Photo by author.

Above: Juanita Caldwell Stackhouse celebrates her 100th birthday at her home.

Above: Current view from Stackhouse front porch. Tree-covered Runion Mountain and farm, center background. Photo by author.

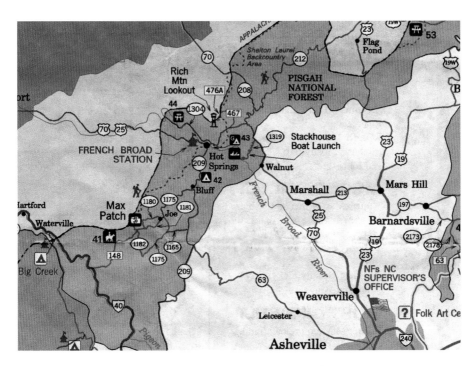

U.S. Forest Service map showing Stackhouse Boat Launch, *Carolina Connections*, Issue 6, 1998.

Brent Aumiller, front left, and three other French Broad Rafting Co. guides search for drowned rafter in the dangerous current of the French Broad River at Stackhouse, January, 1998. Ewart Ball, III, *Asheville Citizen Times*.

After thirty years, mining building foundations on this remote Stackhouse mountain are almost obscured by vegetation. Photo by author, 1998.

Below and Right: These three private lakes at Stackhouse, NC, were built for use in barytes operations in the 1960s. Photo by author, 1998.

At least three-quarters of a century later, in 1997, these original foundations of the former Laurel River Logging Company operations were visible at Runion. Photos by author and John Newman.

Remaining at Runion is this strong house which was located in the commissary of LRLC.
Photo by author, Nov., 1997.

Tall chimney from one of three LRLC homes remaining at Runion when it burned in the 1960s. The 1997 closeup shows amount of deterioration to chimney face compared to the 1977 photo in chapter 29.
Photos by John Newman.

Bloomy rind *Stackhouse:* loaf shaped with a white rind, a thin layer of our own applewood ash down the center and a dusting of ash under the rind. It has a mushroomy flavor with a hint of fresh milk. *Named number one goat cheese in the south by Southern Foodways Alliance.*

Naming one of her cheeses "Stackhouse" was Madison County's Spinning Spider Creamery owner Chris Owens' way of honoring the Stackhouse community.
Couresy Chris Owens.

Walnut Methodist Cemetery graves of Amos Stackhouse, Jr., and his son, Gilbert. Both men were dedicated members of this church located on the site of the first Madison County Court convenings. Photo by author, 1999.

Dilworth Stackhouse family, 1977.
Standing, L to R: Larry, Charles Dilworth III and Harvey.
Seated, L to R: Charles Dilworth, Jr., Virginia and Eileen.
Courtesy, Harvey Stackhouse.

1. Jimmy Curtiss
2. Bethany Lenox
3. Breanna Aumiller
4. Ronald Norris
5. Becca Lenox
6. Nita Stackhouse
7. Greg Curtiss
8. Jeanine Aumiller
9. Dallas Aumiller
10. Bernadette Aumiller
11. Nancy Stackhouse Aumiller
12. Lexyne Stackhouse Norris
13. Grace Norris Lenox
14. Brandon Aumiller
15. Lynn Aumiller
16. Randy Aumiller
17. Patrick Lenox
18. David Aumiller
19. Brent Aumiller

Nita Stackhouse and her offspring, Christmas, 2000. Courtesy Lexyne Norris.

Nancy Stackhouse Aumiller and her family, 1979. Seated, L to R: Dave, Nancy and Brent Aumiller. Standing L to R: Randall and Jeanine Aumiller.

In Back, L to R: Bobby Norris, Lexyne Stackhouse Norris, Ronnie Norris.
In front : Grace Norris.

Ninety-three year old Stackhouse home shows few changes in autumn, 1997.

Stackhouse rail siding in 1999 looking north. Old barytes plant foundation in foreground. Woolsey Branch bridge between white posts in background. Photos by author.

Post card of Mars Hill College, *alma mater* of Stackhouse daughters Lexyne and Nancy. Courtesy Talitha Price.

Juanita Caldwell (Stackhouse) graduated from this Asheville Normal School, Asheville, N.C., where Memorial Mission Hospital now stands.

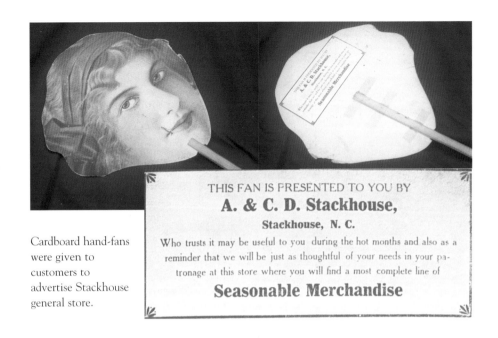

THIS FAN IS PRESENTED TO YOU BY
A. & C. D. Stackhouse,
Stackhouse, N. C.

Who trusts it may be useful to you during the hot months and also as a reminder that we will be just as thoughtful of your needs in your patronage at this store where you will find a most complete line of

Seasonable Merchandise

Cardboard hand-fans were given to customers to advertise Stackhouse general store.

Amos "Sonny" Stackhouse sets up Heat Flow Experiment for integration test with central station in thermal-vacuum chamber of Apollo Mission spacecraft, Ann Arbor, Michigan, 1971. The reflective gold foil was used to control the extreme sun temperatures of outer space.

Thomas Stackhouse (arrived America, 1682)
       b. Yorkshire, England, about 1661
       d. 1744, Bucks Co., Pa
       m. Grace Heaton

Robert Stackhouse
       b. 1692, Bucks Co., Pa
       d. 1788 (age 96)
       m. Margaret Stone

James Stackhouse (arrived America, 1682)
       b. 1757, Philadelphia
       d. 1759, Philadelphia
       m. Martha Hastings (1706-1722)

Amos Stackhouse
       b. 1757, Philadelphia
       d. 1825, Philadelphia
       m. 1779, Mary Powell (1763-1841)
                  see Chart A

Powell Stackhouse
       b. 1785, Mt. Holly, NJ
       d. 1863, Philadelphia
       m. Edith Dilworth (1787-1865)
                  see Chart B

Amos Stackhouse
       b. 1819, Philadelphia
       d.1863, Stackhouse, NC
       m. 1st Rebecca Shaw
          2nd Anna Williamson
          3rd Anna Myers

Chart A

Children (13) of Amos Stackhouse and Mary Powell married 1-14-1779

Susanna	Esther	Amos	Mary
Hastings	Martha	Robert	John
Martha*	James	Robert*	
Powell	Samuel		

*Parents often named a baby after its deceased sibling.

Chart B

Children (11) of Powell Stackhouse and Edith Dilworth married 1-31-1809

Sarah, m. Franklin Townsend 1st; Abram Vandervoort 2nd.
Charles Dilworth (named for Edith's father), m. Alice Meredith
Emlen, m. Catherine Meredith
Joseph, m. Sarah Shaw
Susan, m. Dan Morrell
Anna D. (did not marry)
Powell, Jr., m. Emily Townsend
Amos, m. Rebecca Shaw 1st.
(Three other children died young)

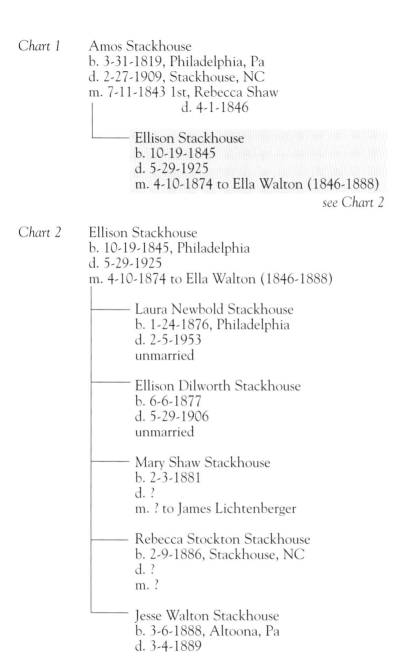

Chart 1   Amos Stackhouse
b. 3-31-1819, Philadelphia, Pa
d. 2-27-1909, Stackhouse, NC
m. 7-11-1843 1st, Rebecca Shaw
                d. 4-1-1846

         Ellison Stackhouse
         b. 10-19-1845
         d. 5-29-1925
         m. 4-10-1874 to Ella Walton (1846-1888)
see Chart 2

Chart 2   Ellison Stackhouse
b. 10-19-1845, Philadelphia
d. 5-29-1925
m. 4-10-1874 to Ella Walton (1846-1888)

         Laura Newbold Stackhouse
         b. 1-24-1876, Philadelphia
         d. 2-5-1953
         unmarried

         Ellison Dilworth Stackhouse
         b. 6-6-1877
         d. 5-29-1906
         unmarried

         Mary Shaw Stackhouse
         b. 2-3-1881
         d. ?
         m. ? to James Lichtenberger

         Rebecca Stockton Stackhouse
         b. 2-9-1886, Stackhouse, NC
         d. ?
         m. ?

         Jesse Walton Stackhouse
         b. 3-6-1888, Altoona, Pa
         d. 3-4-1889

Chart 3

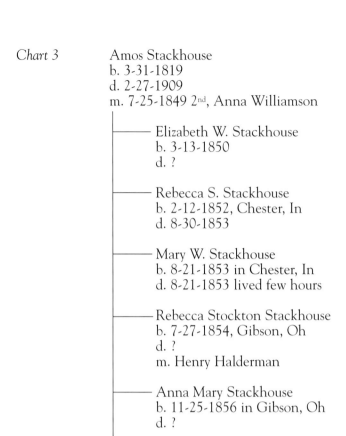

Amos Stackhouse
b. 3-31-1819
d. 2-27-1909
m. 7-25-1849 2nd, Anna Williamson

Elizabeth W. Stackhouse
b. 3-13-1850
d. ?

Rebecca S. Stackhouse
b. 2-12-1852, Chester, In
d. 8-30-1853

Mary W. Stackhouse
b. 8-21-1853 in Chester, In
d. 8-21-1853 lived few hours

Rebecca Stockton Stackhouse
b. 7-27-1854, Gibson, Oh
d. ?
m. Henry Halderman

Anna Mary Stackhouse
b. 11-25-1856 in Gibson, Oh
d. ?

m. Thomas W. Stackhouse
b. 5-18-1858, Philadelphia
d. ?
m. ?

Chart 4   Amos Stackhouse
b. 3-31-1819, Philadelphia
d. 2-27-1909, Stackhouse, NC
m. 2-2-1871, Anna Myers (1851-1916) in Jacksonville, Fl

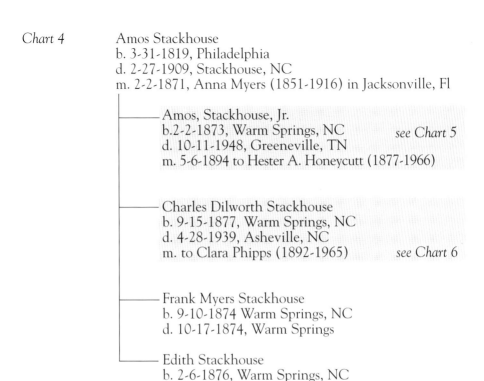

Amos, Stackhouse, Jr.
b.2-2-1873, Warm Springs, NC   *see Chart 5*
d. 10-11-1948, Greeneville, TN
m. 5-6-1894 to Hester A. Honeycutt (1877-1966)

Charles Dilworth Stackhouse
b. 9-15-1877, Warm Springs, NC
d. 4-28-1939, Asheville, NC
m. to Clara Phipps (1892-1965)   *see Chart 6*

Frank Myers Stackhouse
b. 9-10-1874 Warm Springs, NC
d. 10-17-1874, Warm Springs

Edith Stackhouse
b. 2-6-1876, Warm Springs, NC
d. 2-21-1876 Warm Springs

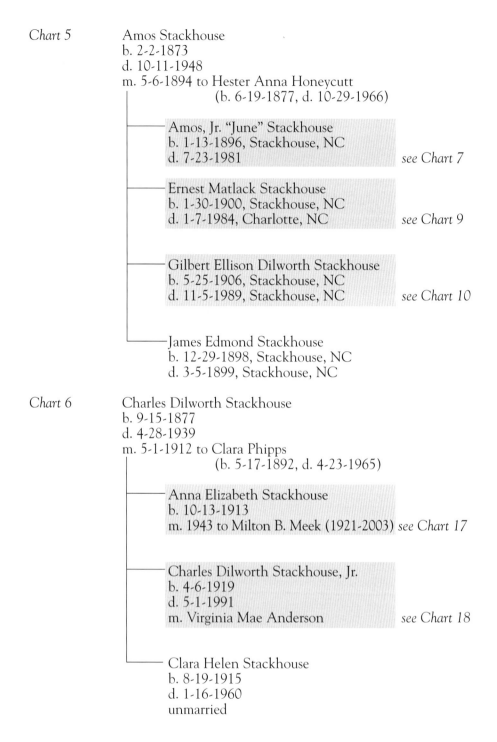

Chart 5   Amos Stackhouse
b. 2-2-1873
d. 10-11-1948
m. 5-6-1894 to Hester Anna Honeycutt
     (b. 6-19-1877, d. 10-29-1966)

  Amos, Jr. "June" Stackhouse
  b. 1-13-1896, Stackhouse, NC
  d. 7-23-1981   *see Chart 7*

  Ernest Matlack Stackhouse
  b. 1-30-1900, Stackhouse, NC
  d. 1-7-1984, Charlotte, NC *see Chart 9*

  Gilbert Ellison Dilworth Stackhouse
  b. 5-25-1906, Stackhouse, NC
  d. 11-5-1989, Stackhouse, NC *see Chart 10*

  James Edmond Stackhouse
  b. 12-29-1898, Stackhouse, NC
  d. 3-5-1899, Stackhouse, NC

Chart 6   Charles Dilworth Stackhouse
b. 9-15-1877
d. 4-28-1939
m. 5-1-1912 to Clara Phipps
     (b. 5-17-1892, d. 4-23-1965)

  Anna Elizabeth Stackhouse
  b. 10-13-1913
  m. 1943 to Milton B. Meek (1921-2003) *see Chart 17*

  Charles Dilworth Stackhouse, Jr.
  b. 4-6-1919
  d. 5-1-1991
  m. Virginia Mae Anderson *see Chart 18*

  Clara Helen Stackhouse
  b. 8-19-1915
  d. 1-16-1960
  unmarried

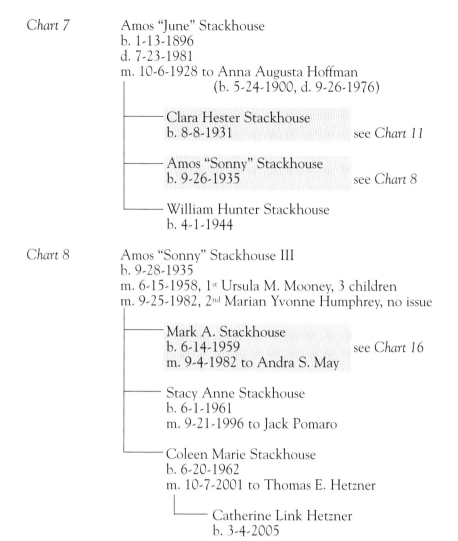

Chart 7   Amos "June" Stackhouse
b. 1-13-1896
d. 7-23-1981
m. 10-6-1928 to Anna Augusta Hoffman
        (b. 5-24-1900, d. 9-26-1976)

        Clara Hester Stackhouse
        b. 8-8-1931   see *Chart 11*

        Amos "Sonny" Stackhouse
        b. 9-26-1935   see *Chart 8*

        William Hunter Stackhouse
        b. 4-1-1944

Chart 8   Amos "Sonny" Stackhouse III
b. 9-28-1935
m. 6-15-1958, 1ˢᵗ Ursula M. Mooney, 3 children
m. 9-25-1982, 2ⁿᵈ Marian Yvonne Humphrey, no issue

        Mark A. Stackhouse
        b. 6-14-1959   see *Chart 16*
        m. 9-4-1982 to Andra S. May

        Stacy Anne Stackhouse
        b. 6-1-1961
        m. 9-21-1996 to Jack Pomaro

        Coleen Marie Stackhouse
        b. 6-20-1962
        m. 10-7-2001 to Thomas E. Hetzner

                Catherine Link Hetzner
                b. 3-4-2005

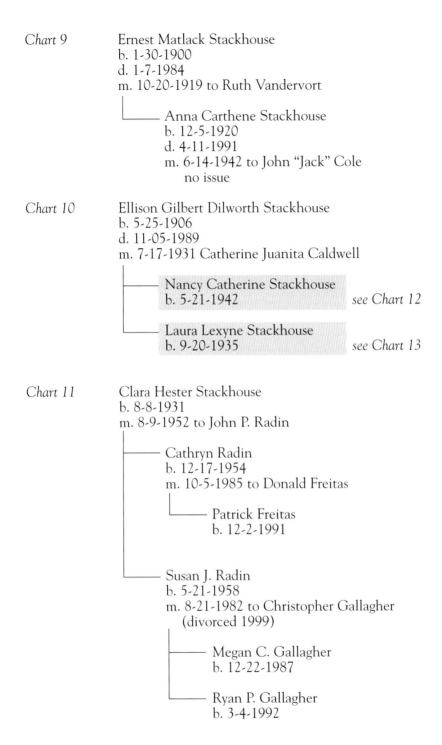

Chart 9   Ernest Matlack Stackhouse
                 b. 1-30-1900
                 d. 1-7-1984
                 m. 10-20-1919 to Ruth Vandervort

                 └─── Anna Carthene Stackhouse
                        b. 12-5-1920
                        d. 4-11-1991
                        m. 6-14-1942 to John "Jack" Cole
                          no issue

Chart 10   Ellison Gilbert Dilworth Stackhouse
                 b. 5-25-1906
                 d. 11-05-1989
                 m. 7-17-1931 Catherine Juanita Caldwell

                 ├─── Nancy Catherine Stackhouse
                 │   b. 5-21-1942   *see Chart 12*

                 └─── Laura Lexyne Stackhouse
                        b. 9-20-1935   *see Chart 13*

Chart 11   Clara Hester Stackhouse
                 b. 8-8-1931
                 m. 8-9-1952 to John P. Radin

                 ├─── Cathryn Radin
                 │   b. 12-17-1954
                 │   m. 10-5-1985 to Donald Freitas
                 │
                 │   └─── Patrick Freitas
                 │   b. 12-2-1991
                 │
                 └─── Susan J. Radin
                        b. 5-21-1958
                        m. 8-21-1982 to Christopher Gallagher
                          (divorced 1999)

                        ├─── Megan C. Gallagher
                        │   b. 12-22-1987
                        │
                        └─── Ryan P. Gallagher
                               b. 3-4-1992

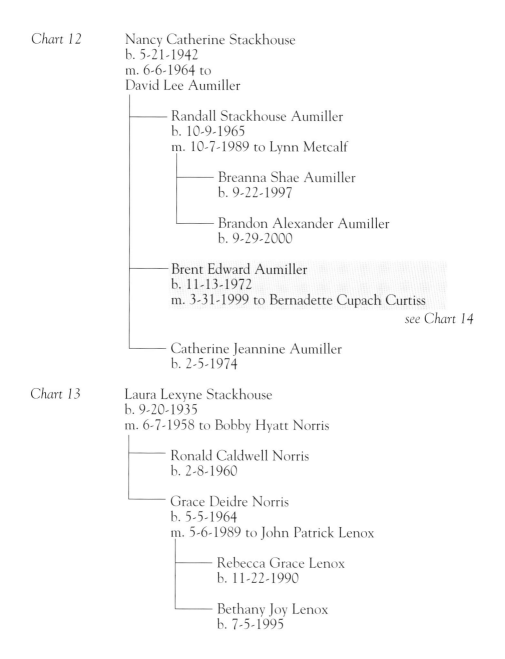

Chart 12   Nancy Catherine Stackhouse
b. 5-21-1942
m. 6-6-1964 to
David Lee Aumiller

      Randall Stackhouse Aumiller
      b. 10-9-1965
      m. 10-7-1989 to Lynn Metcalf

            Breanna Shae Aumiller
            b. 9-22-1997

            Brandon Alexander Aumiller
            b. 9-29-2000

      Brent Edward Aumiller
      b. 11-13-1972
      m. 3-31-1999 to Bernadette Cupach Curtiss

                                        see Chart 14

      Catherine Jeannine Aumiller
      b. 2-5-1974

Chart 13   Laura Lexyne Stackhouse
b. 9-20-1935
m. 6-7-1958 to Bobby Hyatt Norris

      Ronald Caldwell Norris
      b. 2-8-1960

      Grace Deidre Norris
      b. 5-5-1964
      m. 5-6-1989 to John Patrick Lenox

            Rebecca Grace Lenox
            b. 11-22-1990

            Bethany Joy Lenox
            b. 7-5-1995

Chart 14   Brent Edward Aumiller
                  b. 11-13-1972
                  m. 3-31-1999 to Bernadette Cupach Curtiss

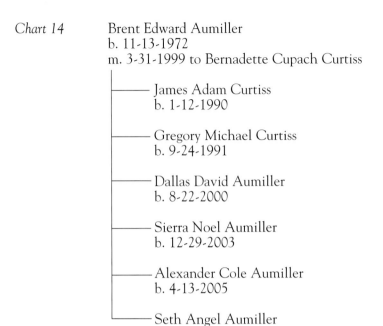

James Adam Curtiss
b. 1-12-1990

Gregory Michael Curtiss
b. 9-24-1991

Dallas David Aumiller
b. 8-22-2000

Sierra Noel Aumiller
b. 12-29-2003

Alexander Cole Aumiller
b. 4-13-2005

Seth Angel Aumiller
b. 5-4-2006

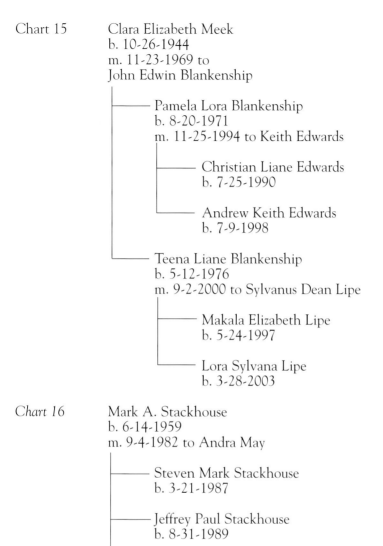

Chart 15   Clara Elizabeth Meek
b. 10-26-1944
m. 11-23-1969 to
John Edwin Blankenship

                Pamela Lora Blankenship
                b. 8-20-1971
                m. 11-25-1994 to Keith Edwards

                        Christian Liane Edwards
                        b. 7-25-1990

                        Andrew Keith Edwards
                        b. 7-9-1998

                Teena Liane Blankenship
                b. 5-12-1976
                m. 9-2-2000 to Sylvanus Dean Lipe

                        Makala Elizabeth Lipe
                        b. 5-24-1997

                        Lora Sylvana Lipe
                        b. 3-28-2003

Chart 16   Mark A. Stackhouse
b. 6-14-1959
m. 9-4-1982 to Andra May

                Steven Mark Stackhouse
                b. 3-21-1987

                Jeffrey Paul Stackhouse
                b. 8-31-1989

                Lisa Ann Stackhouse
                b. 2-9-1993

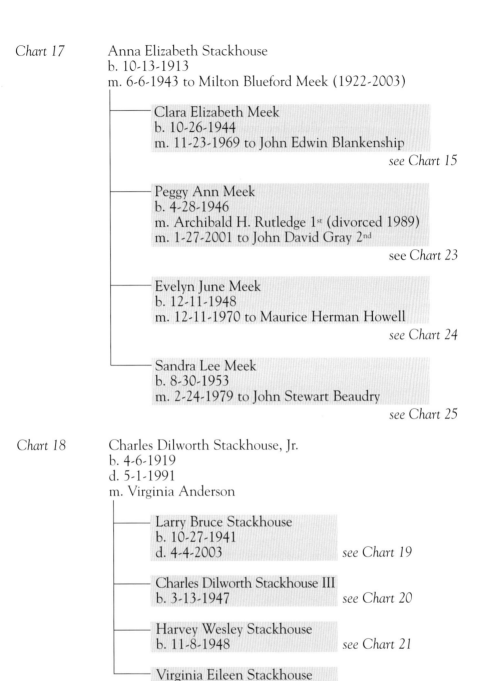

Chart 17   Anna Elizabeth Stackhouse
b. 10-13-1913
m. 6-6-1943 to Milton Blueford Meek (1922-2003)

Clara Elizabeth Meek
b. 10-26-1944
m. 11-23-1969 to John Edwin Blankenship

see Chart 15

Peggy Ann Meek
b. 4-28-1946
m. Archibald H. Rutledge 1st (divorced 1989)
m. 1-27-2001 to John David Gray 2nd

see Chart 23

Evelyn June Meek
b. 12-11-1948
m. 12-11-1970 to Maurice Herman Howell

see Chart 24

Sandra Lee Meek
b. 8-30-1953
m. 2-24-1979 to John Stewart Beaudry

see Chart 25

Chart 18   Charles Dilworth Stackhouse, Jr.
b. 4-6-1919
d. 5-1-1991
m. Virginia Anderson

Larry Bruce Stackhouse
b. 10-27-1941
d. 4-4-2003   *see Chart 19*

Charles Dilworth Stackhouse III
b. 3-13-1947   *see Chart 20*

Harvey Wesley Stackhouse
b. 11-8-1948   *see Chart 21*

Virginia Eileen Stackhouse
b. 6-19-1951   *see Chart 22*

Chart 19   Larry Bruce Stackhouse
               b. 10-27-1941
               d. 4-4-2003
               m. 1-14-1960 to Brenda Marion Bridges

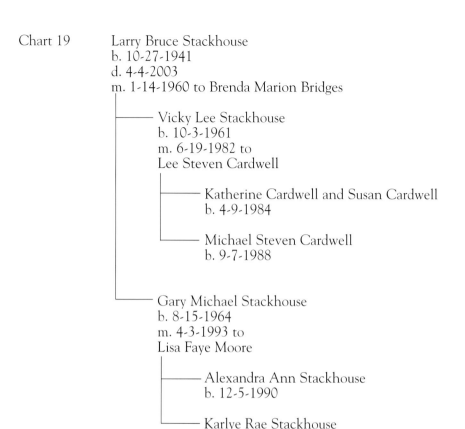

                  Vicky Lee Stackhouse
                  b. 10-3-1961
                  m. 6-19-1982 to
                  Lee Steven Cardwell

                        Katherine Cardwell and Susan Cardwell
                        b. 4-9-1984

                        Michael Steven Cardwell
                        b. 9-7-1988

                  Gary Michael Stackhouse
                  b. 8-15-1964
                  m. 4-3-1993 to
                  Lisa Faye Moore

                        Alexandra Ann Stackhouse
                        b. 12-5-1990

                        Karlye Rae Stackhouse
                        b. 12-22-1994

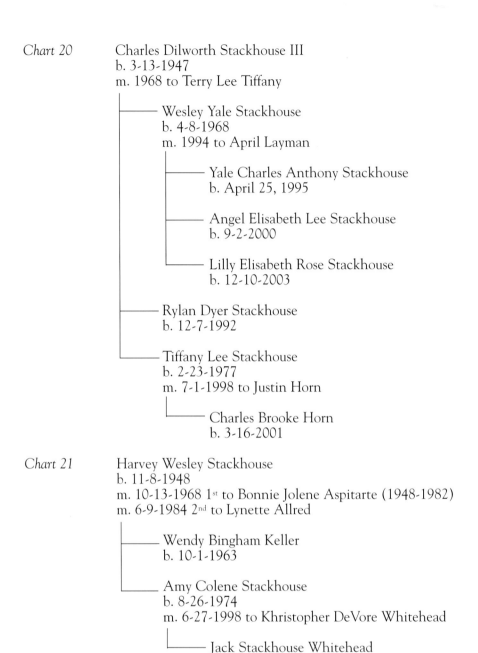

Chart 20   Charles Dilworth Stackhouse III
b. 3-13-1947
m. 1968 to Terry Lee Tiffany

———— Wesley Yale Stackhouse
b. 4-8-1968
m. 1994 to April Layman

———— Yale Charles Anthony Stackhouse
b. April 25, 1995

———— Angel Elisabeth Lee Stackhouse
b. 9-2-2000

———— Lilly Elisabeth Rose Stackhouse
b. 12-10-2003

———— Rylan Dyer Stackhouse
b. 12-7-1992

———— Tiffany Lee Stackhouse
b. 2-23-1977
m. 7-1-1998 to Justin Horn

———— Charles Brooke Horn
b. 3-16-2001

Chart 21   Harvey Wesley Stackhouse
b. 11-8-1948
m. 10-13-1968 1st to Bonnie Jolene Aspitarte (1948-1982)
m. 6-9-1984 2nd to Lynette Allred

———— Wendy Bingham Keller
b. 10-1-1963

———— Amy Colene Stackhouse
b. 8-26-1974
m. 6-27-1998 to Khristopher DeVore Whitehead

———— Jack Stackhouse Whitehead
b. 6-2-2004

Chart 22   Virginia Eileen Stackhouse
b. 6-19-1951
m. Kelly Harrod (1st)
m. Wayne Gentry (2nd)
m. 1987 to Robert Dean Peck (3rd)

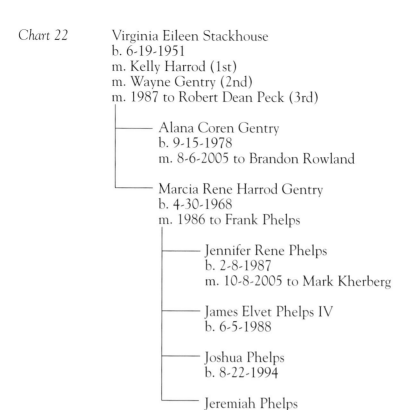

———— Alana Coren Gentry
b. 9-15-1978
m. 8-6-2005 to Brandon Rowland

———— Marcia Rene Harrod Gentry
b. 4-30-1968
m. 1986 to Frank Phelps

———— Jennifer Rene Phelps
b. 2-8-1987
m. 10-8-2005 to Mark Kherberg

———— James Elvet Phelps IV
b. 6-5-1988

———— Joshua Phelps
b. 8-22-1994

———— Jeremiah Phelps
b. 1-24-1998

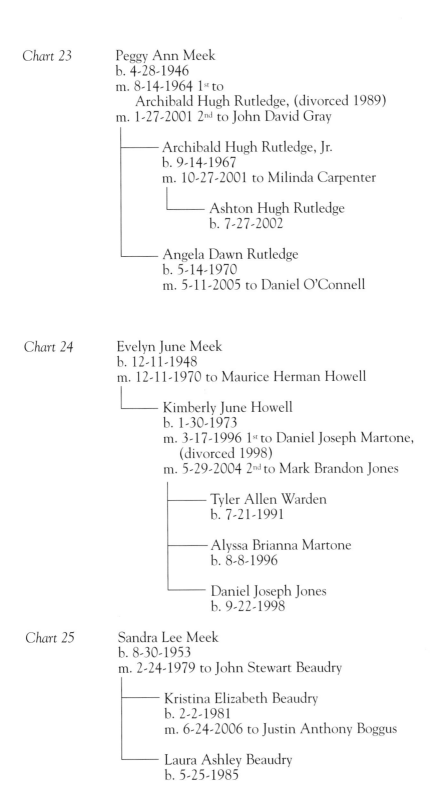

Chart 23   Peggy Ann Meek
b. 4-28-1946
m. 8-14-1964 1st to
   Archibald Hugh Rutledge, (divorced 1989)
m. 1-27-2001 2nd to John David Gray

──────── Archibald Hugh Rutledge, Jr.
b. 9-14-1967
m. 10-27-2001 to Milinda Carpenter

└──── Ashton Hugh Rutledge
b. 7-27-2002

└──── Angela Dawn Rutledge
b. 5-14-1970
m. 5-11-2005 to Daniel O'Connell

Chart 24   Evelyn June Meek
b. 12-11-1948
m. 12-11-1970 to Maurice Herman Howell

└──── Kimberly June Howell
b. 1-30-1973
m. 3-17-1996 1st to Daniel Joseph Martone,
   (divorced 1998)
m. 5-29-2004 2nd to Mark Brandon Jones

──────── Tyler Allen Warden
b. 7-21-1991

──────── Alyssa Brianna Martone
b. 8-8-1996

└──── Daniel Joseph Jones
b. 9-22-1998

Chart 25   Sandra Lee Meek
b. 8-30-1953
m. 2-24-1979 to John Stewart Beaudry

──────── Kristina Elizabeth Beaudry
b. 2-2-1981
m. 6-24-2006 to Justin Anthony Boggus

└──── Laura Ashley Beaudry
b. 5-25-1985

INDEX

The index attempts to include the most significant references and does not include every name or subject mentioned.